Midland Railway
NORTH OF LEEDS
The Leeds–Settle–Carlisle Line
and its Branches

Sir James Allport.

Midland Railway
NORTH OF LEEDS

The Leeds–Settle–Carlisle Line
and its Branches

Peter E. Baughan

DAVID & CHARLES
NEWTON ABBOT LONDON NORTH POMFRET (Vt)

In memory of E.B.B.

British Library Cataloguing in Publication Data

Baughan, Peter E.
  Midland Railway north of Leeds: the Leeds–
  Settle–Carlisle line and its branches. –
  2nd ed.
  1. Settle & Carlisle Railway – History
  2. British Rail, London Midland Region –
  History
  I. Title   II. Baughan, Peter E. North of
  Leeds
  385′.09427   HE3020.S4
  ISBN 0–7153–8852–8

First published 1966 under the title *North of Leeds*
by Roundhouse Books. This second edition published by
David & Charles Publishers plc, 1987.

© Peter E. Baughan, 1966, 1987

Printed in Great Britain
by Redwood Burn Ltd, Trowbridge, Wiltshire
for David & Charles Publishers plc
Brunel House, Newton Abbot, Devon

Published in the United States of America
by David & Charles Inc
North Pomfret, Vermont 05053, USA

Contents

List of Illustrations

MAPS

Author's Preface

When Michael Higson asked me to write a history of the Settle and Carlisle line it did not then seem that there was much need to chronicle the earlier days of the Midland Railway Company who built it. The fallacy of this reasoning became apparent as soon as the question arose as to why the Settle and Carlisle line was made. To see it in perspective the formative years of the Midland had to be discussed; they provide abundant evidence of the Midland's aspirations to reach Scotland. I make no apology, therefore, for returning to square one. In so doing, the history of the other Midland lines north of Leeds, out to Lancaster, Morecambe, and Heysham, inevitably became linked into the tale.

The story is one of a great beginning which to some extent fizzled out in later years. Primarily the Settle and Carlisle line was built with one purpose; to gain separate access to Scotland and, in so doing, to challenge the monopoly of the London & North Western Railway. Almost as soon as the line was open through to Carlisle the Midland was faced with a dilemma; whether to run non-stop through some of its most lucrative territory, between London and the West Riding of Yorkshire and thus attempt to better the West Coast route timings to Scotland, or to attempt a profitable competition by calling at all the major stations and offering a superior standard in both comfort and punctuality.

It took the latter choice for some twenty years. In the interim the West Coast route looked to its laurels and offered improvements in coaching stock and timekeeping which forced the Midland in the 1890s to promote an expensive cut-off route through Bradford. Once again the old problem arose; this time how to placate Leeds, one of the largest cities in the Scotch trains' itinerary, but one which had already been occasionally sacrificed in the name of speed. As it turned out, economic difficulties made the Bradford venture impossible. With the benefit of hindsight it does now seem that the Midland Railway Company, formed by an amalgamation of three independent concerns in the heart of England, was in truth blind to its one inherent weakness; its geographic position and the early lack of far-sighted planning – unlike the East and West Coast routes – made it virtually impossible for the company ever truly to compete. As the years rolled by, and its two main rivals gathered power to themselves, the Midland made a very gallant effort to keep pace with their far easier strides to the north. That it had some of the best of British rolling stock is undeniable. But even with this and a sound policy of locomotive design, its record of punctuality fell badly during the early years of the Twentieth

Century. A complete reorganisation, and an overhaul of the timetable, did little to help. It became a race between the erratic working of the trains and the introduction of more advanced safety precautions and signalling before a point was reached where a serious accident would occur. The results were the Hawes Junction and Ais Gill disasters, two of the most terrible tragedies in the history of railway accidents.

There are, for those interested in the timetable history, many passing references to trains and services which can, however, be conveniently skipped without affecting the general story. In telling of these long-gone services and their trains I have had of necessity to draw heavily on contemporary surveys and accounts. Out of the welter of railway periodicals and journals of the time there emerge many extracts by those great recorders of the past such as Charles Rous-Marten, R. E. Charlewood, and others. I have thought it best to quote them word for word as something of the flavour of the times is bound up with their descriptions.

As to the locomotive side of the story, I have had no thought of attempting a detailed study. Indeed, this side of the picture offers little which is fresh; much has been taken direct from the works of the late E. L. Ahrons and I have only included the locomotive history in outline, where it may supplement the main thread of the narrative. Similarly, regarding the rolling stock, there is abundant material of an excellent nature already in print. I have, therefore, thought it best to confine this aspect of the work merely to presenting extracts and material from the minute books of the companies concerned.

To those readers who are already acquainted to some extent with the history of the Settle and Carlisle line, the absence of any mention of the engineer Sharland may come as a surprise. In truth, however, all known references to him appear to have originated from Frederick Williams's book on the history of the Midland Railway Company, published in the 1870s. There is no mention of Sharland in the minutes of the Midland Railway; the Secretary of the Institution of Civil Engineers has no record of him as being at any time a member of the Institution; and the City Librarian at Carlisle cannot trace any note of him. However, in the minutes of the Maryport & Carlisle Railway Company for 1865 there is the following, dated June 12 : 'Resolved, that Mr. C. S. Sharland, Assistant in the Engineer's Office, be allowed pay at the rate of 20s. per week'. This was not a large salary for the times, and as it is known that he was young at the time of the construction of the Settle line, and that he died shortly after, it would seem likely that his connection with the route has been magnified out of all proportion. Williams was in all probability merely writing about a man who was one of a number of surveyors in a junior position but who, because he was very tall, came from Tasmania, got snowed up in the hills, and then went away and died at Torquay, provided some good copy. He has become posthumously a somewhat legendary figure.

My apologies to those readers from north of the Border for the recurrent use of the term 'Scotch'; this is to conform with all early references.

Considerable assistance was given to me in compiling this work, particularly by Mr E. Atkinson, Archivist to the BRB in London and Messrs Fawkes and Whatson on his staff, Mr W. F. Beatty, Chief Civil Engineer, London Midland Region who, through his General Assistant Mr J. S. Shaw, permitted me to draw on the Parliamentary and civil engineering records at Euston, staff of the House of Lords Records Office and the British Museum Newspaper Library at Colindale. Mr James Taylor of Settle, Mr William Sharpe of Ribblehead, Mr J. D. Graham of Dent and Mr D. Wood of Garsdale, respectively station masters at those places, gave of their private time to answer questions. Mr Tot Lord of Settle Museum loaned material to me, Mr Kenneth Smith, City Librarian of Carlisle, supplied press cuttings respecting the opening of the Settle line and its early rolling stock, and the Secretary of the Institution of Civil Engineers searched the Institution's Library for references to the engineer Sharland and advised on material concerning the construction of the Settle and Carlisle line. Individual friends who have encouraged and assisted are numerous. Particularly I would mention Mr F. J. Harrison of Rayleigh, Mr J. D. Stanbra of Leeds and Mr B. Thomas of Stevenage. Most of all my thanks are due to Anne, my wife, for her continual help and encouragement in preparing the manuscript and acting as secretary and critic.

Pinner, October 1963 – June 1965

In preparing the second edition I have been fortunate in friends who have given help. David Tee, to whom I and others defer in matters Midland 'Ancient & Modern' offered penetrating observations on the original and new text and freely made available his collection of photographs; Martin Bairstow, well-known for his knowledgeable writing on West Riding transportation, made valuable suggestions. Roy Anderson and Gregory Fox and I have trod the same path before now; our works complement each other, and I acknowledge much friendly help and an introduction to Martin Welch and his photographs. Having admired Dr Bill Sharman's work for some time I am pleased to be able to include some of the photographs he very generously sent to me. My good friend Terence Barry has for many years supported my railway interest with a constant supply of information and practical help and advice. I thank my publishers, David & Charles, and especially Geoffrey Kichenside, for their enthusiasm and for permission to use photographs from the Locomotive & General Railway Photographs collection. And as before, most fortunately of all, I can only repeat my gratitude for continued all-round support from my wife Anne, who shared with me two recent very crowded journeys of inquiry on ordinary weekday trains over this supposedly failing and redundant railway.

Burgess Hill, May 1986   P.E.B.

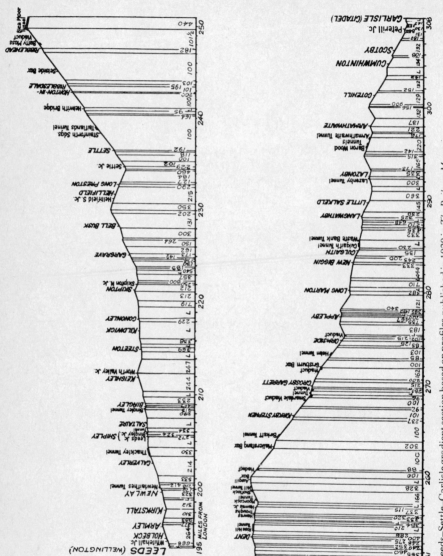

Leeds–Settle–Carlisle gradient section based on profiles published in 1929 in *The Railway Magazine*.

I

Introductory

The Long Drag

The Leeds-Settle-Carlisle line of the former Midland Railway Company was constructed in stages between 1844 and 1876 not as one route but as a series of individual railways in a manner which can only be described as fortuitous. The Settle-Carlisle portion—known to countless enginemen as 'The Long Drag'—was conceived in pique, nearly abandoned through blackmail, and finally built with great difficulty through some of the most mountainous terrain south of the Border. This book attempts to describe the route and how and why it came to be made. At the close of its separate existence the Midland was perhaps the best of the old railway companies. Its tentacles reached furthest of all others; the service it gave was superlative; and the rolling stock was legendary for its comfort. Of all its many lines, that which took it north from Leeds over the Pennines to Carlisle was by far the most dramatic achievement. Its history is one of great endeavour. Its making made the Midland.

Undoubtedly the best way to see the Leeds-Settle-Carlisle line is to take the only remaining named train—the 'Thames-Clyde Express'—on the down trip, which leaves Leeds for the Settle road in mid afternoon and arrives at Carlisle in time for tea. (The 'Waverley' still runs, but only during the summer season.) Leeds, of course, is not a through station; it was at one time the terminus of two railways which joined together before entering the town. This means that passenger trains on the through run from London to the north have, if calling at the station —and all do nowadays—to leave in the reverse direction to that from which they arrived, retracing their path for a short way, back on to the main line. It also means, in effect, that passengers who religiously reserve seats from London 'facing the engine', find at Leeds that they are destined to travel the remaining 113 miles, over by far the most scenic part of the route, with the uncomfortable feeling that the system has got the better of them.

After leaving Leeds City station the train passes over the junctions at Holbeck, then under the old Great Northern line from Leeds Central station to Doncaster, with its barely visible remains of Holbeck High and Low Level stations, and takes the rising gradient of 1 in 264 over the first mile towards Armley (Canal Road) station. Immediately after passing Holbeck the spur to the high level line can be seen curving away in a reverse direction to the right, and a ¼ mile further on the Harrogate line of the former North Eastern Railway also bears away to the right. The Midland

15

line falls, about here, for $1\frac{1}{4}$ miles at a gradient of 1 in 310. After passing through the long island platforms of the station at Armley, and the rock cutting that precedes it, the line passes over the Leeds & Liverpool Canal before coming to the Kirkstall flyover where the up and down slow lines, on the right, pass over the fast road and return to the same level on the left. The seemingly superfluous set of double track which leaves the main line to the right immediately after the flyover and continues as far as Kirkstall station is the original Leeds & Bradford line. As will be seen later, the Leeds & Bradford main line was extensively doubled and modernised at the turn of the century to allow fast running; the flyover permits the northbound trains to cross the slow lines at speed so as to take the curve at Shipley, to the right of the Leeds & Bradford line proper. By now the water meadows of the River Aire have come into view. From here to Skipton the line takes a mainly west-north-west direction, following the course of the River Aire through the lower reaches of the dale which bears its name. Immediately after passing the station the ruins of Kirkstall Abbey can be seen to the right of the line which curves to the left, on an upward gradient which from here over the next 6 miles or so towards Shipley is mostly between 1 in 214 and 330. After passing Kirkstall Forge, with the remains of the old station to the left, a short distance further on brings the line to Newlay & Horsforth station, $4\frac{3}{4}$ miles from Leeds, after which comes a deep rock cutting where many years back there was a short tunnel. The next station is Calverley & Rodley $1\frac{1}{4}$ miles beyond Newlay & Horsforth. The railway here takes a gentle curve to the left with a series of junctions for the Guiseley and Ilkley line which leaves, climbing at 1 in 60, away into the wooded country to the right. A short distance beyond the junctions comes Apperley Bridge & Rawdon station, $7\frac{3}{4}$ miles from Leeds, and shortly afterwards the train passes over Apperley viaduct before entering the Thackley tunnels (1,496 yards in length). Immediately after passing through the tunnels there is a short level stretch. To the right of the train the Baildon line can be seen coming in to join the main line just east of Shipley station while to the left the weed-grown single line branch of the old Great Northern Railway from Laisterdyke drops down to run parallel to the Leeds & Bradford Railway just before it curves away to terminate in its own small station. Those familiar with the works of the late E. L. Ahrons will recall his account of a fine runaway down this slope in 1883 which ended with the engine anxiously overhanging the road beyond the G.N.R. station. In 1916 a repeat performance took place with similar results.

Almost immediately after the junction with the Baildon line the train leaves the Leeds & Bradford and passes on to that company's extension line to Skipton and Colne. In so doing the train takes a sharp curve to the right and the Midland Railway's station at Shipley can be seen on the left with the triangular junctions to the Bradford line.

The next 15 miles or so to Skipton take the railway through the calm, flat, open strip of the floodplain of the Aire. Away to the right between Shipley and Steeton is Rombalds Moor, reaching a height of 1,323 feet—a puny foretaste of what is to come. To the left is Keighley Moor, stretching over many miles of high ground to Burnley.

For the most part the gradients of the line through Airedale are undulating and, though there is a regular climb as far as Keighley at gradients between 1 in 223 and 1 in 244, the distance of 9 miles from there to Skipton hardly adds a foot of altitude. Shortly after leaving Shipley the small station of Saltaire is passed and a further $2\frac{1}{2}$ miles brings the line through a short tunnel (151 yards) to Bingley. Just under 3 miles further on the long-abandoned station of Thwaites is passed— just grass banks now—before Keighley station is reached. Here there is a junction with the Keighley & Worth Valley line. There was once a branch of the ubiquitous Great Northern Railway into Keighley, and this also climbed out parallel to, but at a higher level than, the K.W.V. Whilst the latter gropes its way up to Oxenhope, passing through the Bronte's Haworth on its way, the old G.N.R. line rambled south through Culling-worth and Thornton to join others more fortunate than itself at Bradford. Between Keighley and Skipton there are three stations; Steeton & Silsden, Kildwick & Crosshills, and Cononley. About $\frac{1}{2}$ mile beyond Keighley the line descends for $1\frac{1}{2}$ miles on a gradient of 1 in 247 following which comes a level mile before the last $6\frac{1}{4}$ miles to Skipton, all on a moderately easy upward gradient. Just before entering on to the approach curve to Skipton station, the line passes under the Skipton and Ilkley branch of the former Midland Railway, which has made its way around the northern slopes of Skipton Moor out of Wharfedale. On the approach curve to Skipton station, and to the right of the train, may be seen the substantial stone buildings of the former station, replaced by the present structure in the 1870s.

The town of Skipton is situated near the head of Airedale, with Wharfedale away to the right, and Ribblesdale yet to come. These three dales cover roughly the area known as the Craven district of Yorkshire, through which the train will be passing for the next 40 miles or so. The town may be said to be the capital of the Craven district. Sheltered by the heights of Skipton Moor its origins are remote in the past; a Roman road between Ilkley and Elslack passes through, and the castle site dates back to near the time of the Norman Conquest.

On leaving Skipton station a short down grade of 1 in 212 is taken, and $\frac{1}{2}$ mile out the original Leeds & Bradford Extension Railway to Colne can be seen leaving the main line which bears to the right, with a fairly severe slack to any fast running. The train is now on the metals of the old North Western Railway and for some four miles there follow gradients of as much as 1 in 130 to the next station at Gargrave from where there is a climb at a ruling gradient of 1 in 131 through the closed station of Bell Busk to the summit of the North Western line about $1\frac{1}{2}$ miles south of Hellifield. Gargrave is a small place and is said once to have boasted seven churches. All were destroyed except one which happened to be dedicated to St. Andrew. It seems hardly necessary to say who destroyed the others. Bell Busk station, closed on May 4, 1959, and now in a ruined condition, was once the alighting point for tourists who, met by pony and trap, were taken 6 miles up the little road to the right of the station to Malham and Gordale. There, earnest Victorians and Edwardians, in frock coats or Norfolk jackets, doing the tour of Craven, saw the white limestone of Malham Cove, a natural rock formation some 280 feet high with, above it, Malham Tarn. Occasionally in the past the tarn has overflowed down the rock face with dramatic results.

From the summit there is a short descent, on gradients of 1 in 350 and 215 over the last 1½ miles to Hellifield, but before arriving at the station there can be seen, coming in from the left up lower Ribblesdale, the former Lancashire & Yorkshire Railway's Blackburn, Clitheroe and Hellifield branch. Hellifield was at one time quite an important exchange station for Lancashire traffic. There were high and low level sidings and the two signal boxes totalled 112 levers. Now the sidings are mostly derelict, and the engine sheds, once so busy, have been made weathertight for their new duty of housing an exalted and ossified collection of veteran locomotives in the keeping of the Railway Board's Curator of Historical Relics. From Hellifield the main line takes a down grade, mainly of 1 in 215 and 1 in 184, for some 6 miles ending with a level stretch at Settle Junction where the North Western Railway diverges to the left towards its twenty-six mile journey to Lancaster, and the Settle and Carlisle line commences its climb into upper Ribblesdale. There could be only one route from here to Carlisle. Nearly every history so far written on the Settle and Carlisle line has a passage somewhere to the effect that for many years engineers had considered it impossible for there to be any railway to Carlisle other than round by the west coast of Westmorland and Cumberland. When, in the 1840s, the Lancaster & Carlisle Railway was made over Shap Fell this was considered to be the ultimate in railway civil engineering. The very nature of the ground by any other route was thought to be prohibitive, entailing vast engineering works of a magnitude so far unattempted. There is, however, a chain of valleys, stretching roughly north-south and cutting through the Pennines, which indicated a possible route where a line might be made. The first of these valleys, which starts at Settle, is that carved by the River Ribble between the masses of Ingleborough and Pen-y-ghent, but at the far end of the valley towers Whernside and the lower but no less formidable Blea Moor. Once past this barrier a way was open through to the Vale of Eden on the far side.

The complete un-English bleakness of this area must be seen to be understood. It is elemental; trees, such as they are, and there are but few, cling to the crags in twisted shapes, poor stunted apologies, bent double by the wind. There is no cultivation, just moorland and rock outcrops and waterfalls. The alien magnificence of this fierce, lonely country defies description. I have travelled it on the railway with mist and fog for company on a November afternoon, and found Whernside looming its great back out of the cloud layer at what seemed from the train to be an impossibly high angle, shaping to bury the railway in its mass. That same journey, however, produced one of the most spectacular sunsets, seen over the other side of the high land, as the train coasted through the Vale of Eden down to Carlisle with dusk fast approaching. The first stopping train out of Carlisle on the next morning, hauled by a 'Jubilee' class locomotive and with as mixed an assortment of coaching stock as one could wish for, through sheets of near horizontal rain, produced sights and sounds along the line probably unobtainable on any other English railway. The vast viaducts, seeming to hover in mist and rain gave glimpses of great rivers surging beneath where but a few hours before had been little becks. Waterfalls innumerable cascaded from black rock and bounced away down the moors, their spray sheeting into atoms in the wind. Hooded figures on the stations, stumbling and cursing at the wind and rain, loaded up the few parcels, and Carlisle people with town shoes soggy after but a few steps, catapulted themselves from the train to the nearest waiting shelter. It was this weather, and worse, that the engineers and navvies who built the line had to contend with. That and snow. Reality, and a lessening of the rain, came on Hellifield platform where the train terminated and a prosaic diesel from Morecambe took the passengers on to the south. The raw energy of a steam engine battling with the full power of whatever the elements have to offer on this high, bleak line, is something to be experienced and not talked of, for it cannot be savoured other than at first hand.

It has been said that the engineer who made the line compared it to a whale 'lying on its belly, with its nose at Settle and its tail at Carlisle. A steep ascent carries us up, a long incline carries us down.' The climb starts almost immediately after Settle Junction. The junction itself, once the site of an interchange station between the North Western Railway and the Settle and Carlisle line, is 425 feet above sea level and about 234 miles from St. Pancras. The mile posts along the Settle and Carlisle line show the through St. Pancras distances but for the sake of clarity, and since the Settle line is our subject, the mileages used henceforth in this chapter in describing the route are mostly given as starting from the junction, and I have called them points as opposed to posts. It is hoped that should the reader wish to follow the text with a map, this arrangement may be of more use.*

On approaching Settle station, about 2 miles from the junction, and on the initial ruling gradient of 1 in 100, the goods yard and shed are seen on the right. The main station buildings are on the down side of the line and are built in Bradford stone in a style freely called

* To convert the local mileage to the through St. Pancras mileage, add 234¼ miles to the local figure.

'Gothic' but more properly *à la* Midland Railway. The gardens at Settle are a joy to see. They have been built up from nothing since late 1959 when the present station master, Mr. James M. Taylor, came from the neighbouring station to the north, Horton-in-Ribblesdale, where he had just won the 1959 shield and premier award in the Carlisle district of British Railways for the best kept station and garden. In 1961 Settle station was entered for the competition and won the district award as it has done in 1962, 1963 and 1964. In fact Mr. Taylor says that since 1953, when the present competition was started, his stations of first Horton and then Settle, have won the top award each year. A unique feature is that Settle station has found itself successively in the districts of Leeds, Manchester North, Carlisle and now Barrow, winning each district award. In a recent BBC interview Mr. Taylor said that he was allowed 15s. a year towards seeds, and since he has won the shield many times, ploughing back the £10 award which goes with it, his garden is understandably well supplied. Besides the five thousand or more plants on the station, Mr. Taylor has added a colourful painted sign on the down platform which—under the heraldic arms of the town and the West Riding—states that the local population is 2,300 and the altitude 510 feet.

Settle is a market town; it has a tourist appeal due to the proximity of the best of the Yorkshire dales. Through the town runs the A65 road, connecting the West Riding and the Lake District. All around are limestone outcrops, and the area abounds in caves and potholes. Away to the right of the station towers Great Scar, 1,815 feet, with the 300 feet crags of Castlebergh coming down almost to the side of the railway and making an ideal backcloth to Settle church, just north of the station. Inside the church can be seen a marble plaque which commemorates the navvies who died or were killed—there is a difference—whilst the line was being made in the 1870s. The church is not old; for many years the town came within the parish of Giggleswick.

On leaving Settle station the train passes over the first two of the many viaducts—Marshland (four arches) and Settle (six arches)—small affairs both. Just north of Settle, to the right of the line, lies the village of Langcliffe, reputedly a mile to the south of its original site which was obliterated in a Scotch raid in 1318. Originally a larger village than nowadays, it contracted in size during the mid 1850s when the cotton mill on which its inhabitants depended for work failed. At about the 3 mile point the line passes through a rock cutting, runs parallel with Ribble Bank Road and then on to an embankment before coming to the remains of the Craven Lime Company's sidings, now abandoned, on the right of the line near Stainforth at Winskill Scar. Curving to the left, Stainforth tunnel (120 yards)—also known as Taitlands tunnel—is approached through a rock cutting. The tunnel carries the Stainforth to Langcliffe road over the railway just south of Great Stainforth and Little Stainforth, once one village and joined by a pack-horse bridge over the Ribble and a bridge over the railway beyond the tunnel. Still following the river, and with the high masses of Moughton Fell on the left and Fountains Fell on the right bunching closer in, the railway climbs over Little viaduct and Sheriff Brow viaduct (each of three arches), both of which span the river which is now parallel with the railway on the left—though lost to sight for a moment in a rock cutting. The line continues through Helwith Bridge and on to the 6 mile point where the river passes beneath the railway under Ribble Bridge (five arches). Running on embankment now, the Ribblesdale Lime Company's sidings are shortly afterwards seen running off to the left, and then the line curves gently round to the right climbing steadily and still on embankment past the 7 mile point, with Crag Hill Farm and Garth House Barn on the right. Approaching Horton-in-Ribblesdale station, just short of 8 miles from Settle Junction, the line curves to the left and enters a deep cutting, partly of rock, and passes Horton Lime Works on the left immediately before coming in sight of the station, somewhat smaller than that at Settle. Between Settle and Horton the B6479 road runs parallel with the railway, first on one side and then on the other. The coming of the railway froze the road system in these parts so that it has never really advanced into the twentieth century. Indeed there are really no roads worth the modern name between Settle and Kirkby Stephen and at the latter place it is the A66 to Penrith which is joined, not one direct to Carlisle down the Eden Valley. If the railway should ever be closed then, though the two biggest towns of Appleby and Kirkby Stephen—both of which apparently attract sufficient traffic to stop important trains—are on the main road, the country to north and south of them between Settle and Carlisle will be devoid of a through route.

Horton station is some way from the town, down in the dip to the right and another centre for those who wish to stay a few days to explore Ribblesdale. The lime sidings at Horton date back almost to the beginnings of the Settle and Carlisle line, for it was in 1887 that John Delaney came from Norfolk to quarry limestone. Of late the company he formed has joined with others to become the property of Settle Limes Limited—now part of Imperial Chemical Industries—and whose works are now some of the most up-to-date of their kind. Lime traffic from Horton by rail has been immense. As we have seen, Horton-in-Ribblesdale station had a reputation for its gardens. Now it has a forlorn appearance with only the flaking paint of an informative coloured sign, like that of Settle, to remind passengers of its past colourful appearance. There are other 'Delaney's Sidings' by the way; one is on the Grassington branch and another on the main line about a mile south of Gargrave. The lie-by sidings at the latter are on an awkward gradient so that northbound freight trains backed in when the rails are wet have a struggle to get out again.

North of Horton station the line runs practically straight for the next two miles or so. Away to the left, and ahead of the train, lies the great mass of Ingleborough, rising to 2,373 feet, whilst to the right and only just over two miles away is the peak of Pen-y-ghent, with its mists and ravens. Still climbing, the line passes through Selside, curving to the right on a high embankment through the village. Not far away are many potholes including the fearful 300 feet deep chasm of Helln Pot. The signal box at Selside was manned—if that is the right expression—by women throughout the Second World War. Selside itself lodged many of the navvies who built the line hereabouts. At the side of the road stands Stone House, a relic of a navvy settlement, its name marking it out as having been superior to the rude hutments in which most of the men lived. From Selside the railway runs almost straight for the next mile as it approaches Ribblehead station, the last mile being on a gentle left curve and passing the disused Salt Lake Quarry on the left, with its attendant cottages on the other side of the line. During the building of the line a navvy settlement known as 'Salt Lake City' was sited near the old quarry.

Ribblehead station, which is at a distance of some 12½ miles from Settle Junction, and stands at a height of 1,025 feet, takes all the winds and weather that this altitude brings. In 1938 its unique position prompted the authorities to make it an official meteorological reporting point. In so doing it replaced an existing railway anemometer at Crosby Garrett, further down the line. The present station master, Mr. William L. Sharpe, has the added responsibility of telephoning hourly meteorological reports, between 08.00 and 21.00 hours, to the Air Ministry Weather Station at Dishforth. The station has some complicated equipment to enable him to do this; in the goods yard, on the down side, there is a rain gauge, which is inspected morning and night, changed each day at 9.00 hours and the rainfall graph is reported weekly. The average yearly fall is 70 inches. In 1954, when the gauge was first installed, it recorded 109½ inches, 5 of these falling in one December day. Wind velocity, cloud formation and height, and depth of snow in centimetres, are all communicated to Dishforth, the first two hourly. For many years the station booking hall was a focal point for the scattered local community. Up until February of 1956 the Reverend Croft of Ingleton held monthly Evening Service there at 7.30 p.m. on Sundays, the small congregation being accompanied by an old organ, played by Mrs. Whinray, also of Ingleton.

Immediately after the station the railway passes over Low Sleight Road—the old Ingleton to Hawes coach route over the moors—and as the train curves round to the right on a lofty embankment towards Blea Moor, with Whernside thrusting its 2,419 feet towards the clouds—and it is often obscured by them—the line approaches the most dramatic engineering work on the route; Ribblehead viaduct, of twenty-four arches, just 13 miles from Settle Junction. Seen from the inside of the curve it is magnificent. Below, adjoining the Ingleton to Hawes road, and under and alongside the viaduct, there is a pitted barren stretch of open moorland where nothing grows save rough grass and nothing lives save a few wild creatures. It is hereabouts that some of the enginemen swear they have seen wild cats—perhaps long-lost descendants of those on the navvy camp for here, during more than seven years, and nearly a century ago, there lived many of the men who built the viaduct and tunnelled under Blea Moor, in the most atrocious weather conditions. There have been many descriptions of the wild navvy armies, drawn from all parts of the British Isles and herded together in hutments, with their outlandish and garish clothes, rough, brutal code of life, and incredible endurance. Tales of the terror they spread into the nearby villages, of the lawless hard-drinking era that once was, have been recounted many times. Only their ghosts remain, conjured sometimes out of the swirling mists which come down from Whernside. Of the raucous nights, of the carousing and wild fights, when anything went as battles bloody raged over the encampment—nothing is now left save the overgrown vestiges of the roadways on Batty Moss where once their huts stood. When the line is quiet and there are no sounds from the railway passing above this silent sombre monument to the Victorian engineers and men who built it, only the curlew's cry is to be heard, high above the moor. As the train crosses over this place, now so utterly lonely, it seems as if the air hangs heavy with history.

There is a 75 m.p.h. speed limit over the viaduct. Mr. Sharpe says that though there is no maximum wind velocity laid down to prohibit trains from passing over the viaduct he has known wind speeds of 70 to 80 knots substantially hold them up, instancing a case some ten years ago when a banking engine had to be employed at the rear of a goods train to push it through. In November 1961 the anemometer recorded a speed of 92 m.p.h. Ribblehead is, perhaps, one of the most isolated of stations; Ingleton is the nearest town, 10 miles away and, after that, Hawes some 14 miles distant.

No sooner over the viaduct than the approach to Blea Moor tunnel comes into sight as, with the embankment giving way to level ground, the railway cottages—some still occupied—and signal box of Blea Moor are passed just before the 14 mile point. Now the line enters the heavy approach cutting to the tunnel, passing over Little Dale Beck, and just after—through a short tunnel—under Force Gill which joins the beck a few yards further on. The heavy stone portal of the tunnel lies beyond. The approach from Ribblehead has been made at a climb of 1 in 100 but about 365 yards inside the tunnel this changes to a level stretch for some 40 yards, with a following down grade of 1 in 440. The first 400 yards or so within the tunnel is on curve; otherwise the remaining length is straight. Blea Moor rises to 1,753 feet in height; the tunnel bores through its shoulder for a length of 2,629 yards. It was a devil to build and, so we are told, a devil to drive through on the footplate, for the enginemen always seem glad to be out of it. A long dead dank smell of ageless rock and years of stale engine smoke greets the trains. Windows are hurriedly shut tight while for some two minutes the vapours somehow find their way into the carriages.

On emerging from the tunnel the line takes a left curve, crossing two bridges in quick succession, and a culvert sandwiched between carrying Long Gill under the railway, before coming to the 16½ miles point and the Dent Head viaduct of ten arches and 596 feet in length. 100 feet below is Fell End Gill, with the Dent to Hawes road curving round into Dentdale. Another ½ mile and the first of the snow fences, protecting the line from drifts in winter, can be seen up on the high ground to the right. Arten Gill viaduct comes next (eleven arches), 645 feet long, and crossed on a curve at the 17½ mile point. It spans the Dent-Hawes road which has twisted round to cut under the line again, Arten Gill 117 feet below, and some old quarry workings. After a short level stretch over the viaduct the line is again climbing, at 1 in 248, and passes through a cutting with double-banked rows of snow fences before coming to Dent station, 18¾ miles from Settle Junction. Dent Head viaduct stands on' the birthplace of its neighbour at Arten Gill, for that at Dent Head has its piers in the quarry from which the stones for the latter were taken. The local blue limestone, known as Dent marble, was worked for many years at Nixon's marble quarries nearby to provide the heavy marble objects beloved by the Victorians; some of it went into the building of Manchester Town Hall. It was sent from Dent station to monumental masons in London; it may be found in many far-flung places, but in the end the demand for it dropped and the trade died out, Italian marble coming into the country and taking its place. Dent station waiting room has a fine example of a mantle worked out of the marble. Lea Yeat, to the left of Dent station and ¼ mile away, is another of the now small settlements which mushroomed into bigger status during the building of the line. Cowgill church, not far away, had its graveyard extended, at the expense of the railway company, during construction of the line to take the numerous dead from the smallpox epidemics which plagued the navvy population. The station, at an altitude of 1,150 feet, is the highest main line station in England, and the difference of some 725 feet in altitude between Settle Junction and Dent means that the railway has climbed, with some dips in between, at an average of 38 feet each mile since leaving the North Western line.

Away to the left is Dentdale where the River Dee stumbles its way over a marble rock bed. The town of Dent is some 5 miles down the dale from the station, which, unlike the three preceeding layouts has its main buildings on the left of the line, together with a small goods yard. Once the centre of the knitting industry and a flourishing town, Dent became impoverished and depopulated with the industrial revolution. The coming of the railway, however, at almost the eleventh hour, meant that at least some of the small yeoman farmers who eked out a subsistence with both their land and the knitting industry, were able to transfer their employment part-time to the railway, becoming platelayers and gangers on the line, leaving the farms in their wives' names. This, of course, was necessary then as the railway company would not have taken on a man with two jobs, but those days are long since gone. Talk of the snow fences shows that this particular stretch of the line is very prone to deep drifts in winter. Indeed it is so exposed that the station master's house had double glazing in the windows for many years. Mr. J. D. Graham, the station master, remarks that this was removed in the early years of the war and has not been replaced. As to the snow fences they are now in a rather dilapidated condition and are not to be renewed, probably because the clearing methods are much improved. The huts in the station yard are used in severe weather as a canteen for the snow clearing crews who man the ploughs, and a cook with the food comes to Dent on the first snow plough out of Skipton—previously Hellifield—when bad weather is forecast. Apparently in the extreme bad weather of 1963, says Mr. Graham, the snow clearing gangs had a mess coach on the ballast train and if required to work long, food was brought out to them, on a special train, from the refreshment rooms at Preston.

Beyond Dent station, on the left, Monkey Beck passes under the line and immediately afterwards there is a four-arched bridge over the railway carrying the Dent to Kirkby Stephen road. From here the line continues on for another ¾ mile, on a down grade of 1 in 286, passing more derelict snow screens, before coming to Rise Hill tunnel (1,213 yards). The engineers planning the line had, of course, an eye to the conditions likely to affect the locomotives. At Blea Moor tunnel they had endeavoured substantially to ease the gradient. Through Rise Hill tunnel the line is on the level. Above the tunnel, with its two air shafts, are the forgotten remains of the earthworks on which once stood the machinery and pumps necessary to bore through Rise Hill. The tunnel takes a curve to the right about 300 yards from its northern outlet and just before emerging into the daylight the gradient drops to 1 in 355 for a short space until, now in the open, the line crosses Assey Gill where the gradient levels out. Shortly after comes an upward climb of 1 in 333 and the railway passes through rock cuttings and to an embankment where are the highest water troughs in the British Isles. A short distance further on is the water tank for the troughs and after passing High Scale Farm, the train reaches Garsdale station, 22 miles from Settle Junction Approaching the station, there is a large tank for watering the engines, the water coming from a reservoir on the fell out beyond the station to the right of the line.

Garsdale station has seen several changes of name and for some time it was known as Hawes Junction & Garsdale, for here, immediately after leaving the station, the abandoned branch line to Hawes leaves to the right to curve round into Wensleydale. Built by the Midland Railway to join the Hawes and Leyburn branch of the North Eastern Railway at the time of the construction of the Settle and Carlisle line, the branch was closed to all traffic on March 16, 1959; the rails were lifted some time back and at the time of writing there is a scheme to use it as a public footpath. It had but three heavy works; Moss Dale Head tunnel and

Moss Dale Gill viaduct, bracketting the $2\frac{1}{2}$ miles post, and Appersett viaduct, just before the $4\frac{3}{4}$ mile post. Garsdale station takes its water from the same fell as the locomotives, and there are drinking fountains dated 1873 on the up island platform and 1888 on the down, though these dates do not necessarily have any meaning as the station was opened in the late 1870s. Most of the sidings have been removed as has the goods shed and the stockaded turntable, the latter being the subject of much pen and ink work in the past in describing the reason for its existence. Briefly this was that years ago an engine, standing on the turntable, was caught by a freak wind and twirled round and round until in exasperation, and some considerable time later, someone had the presence of mind to throw some ballast into the pit to stop it. The winds at this spot, at one time the highest L.M.S.R. junction in England, often reach a velocity of 100 miles an hour. In 1937 the then station master, Mr. J. F. Ferguson, told how he had been called out one night and had been unable to walk against the wind.* The present station master, Mr. D. Wood, relates that until the station was partly rebuilt in 1957 there was for some time a library of about 200 books, presented by an unknown lady who had the idea when waiting hours for a connecting train. (Another version is that the books were given by two old ladies living in Garsdale who thought the station staff needed some comfort against their loneliness.) Like Ribblehead, Garsdale station had its own church services, held in the down waiting room, where every fourth Sunday the Vicar of Garsdale used to arrive with an altar cloth and portable organ—the lectern being kept at the station.* Hawes Junction, once so named, was very busy at times of seasonal heavy traffic, and underneath the water tank to the south of the station there is a large room which, once a repair shop, now does duty as a meeting place for the local railway welfare institute. It has seen parties and other social occasions, which no doubt the directors of the old Midland Railway would have been surprised to see. Understandably, however, television has almost ended what was once quite a usual event.

There is a distance of some 10 miles from Garsdale to the next station at Kirkby Stephen. From the Hawes branch junction the line again begins to climb on a left curve on the final leg to the summit at Ais Gill. Within the first mile it crosses Moorcock viaduct of twelve arches, spanning Dandry Mire and once known by that name, just after the 257 mile post. Beyond the viaduct and still curving to the left, comes Moorcock tunnel (98 yards) and then immediately before the $257\frac{3}{4}$ mile post Lund's viaduct of five arches, spanning another site of one of the many quarries from which stone was taken to make the line. To the left lies Baugh Fell, rising to 2,216 feet, whilst to the right are the foothills of Great Shunner Fell, out-topping Baugh Fell by 124 feet. The line now curves round to the right and, under a mile from Lund's viaduct, comes Shotlock Hill tunnel (106 yards), at the $258\frac{1}{2}$ mile post, with

* 'On Time—The Journal of the L.M.S. Operating Department', October, 1937.

the Hawes to Kirkby Stephen road by the side of the line on the right, coming down to pass under the railway at Shaw Paddock. From Moorcock the line has climbed at a gradient of 1 in 166 up to Shotlock Hill tunnel and then at 1 in 328 to the beginning of the short left curve on the approach to the summit at Ais Gill Moor. The track runs almost on the level past Ais Gill signal box and the refuge siding for banking engines, before passing the summit signs—two vitreous enamel notices, erected in 1954—proclaiming the fact that the line has reached 1,169 feet above sea level. The sign comes just before a mile post denoting 259¾ miles from St. Pancras. As to the banking engines—these are now virtually things of the past. Mr. Wood at Garsdale says that the last time he remembered one being used was during the winter of 1963. The refuge sidings are now disused but Ais Gill box remains open.

This area is known as Mallerstang Common—or Mallerstang Forest—where before the Conquest, border warfare was so terrible and of such destruction that it is said the Conqueror thought it not worth surveying. To the left Baugh Fell has given way to Wild Boar Fell—legend has it that the last wild boar was killed there—and just beyond Ais Gill the railway crosses the county boundary between Yorkshire and Westmorland. The line now encounters the first of the down grades on the long run to Carlisle—1 in 100—past Hellgill Force on the right, and the embryo River Eden and Smithy Gill waterfall. A long curve to the right brings the Hawes to Kirkby Stephen road back again and as the line approaches the 260¾ mile post, crosses Ais Gill viaduct of four arches spanning the gill in a ravine below, and enters upon the straight run of 6 miles to Kirkby Stephen, the down gradient stays nearly steady at 1 in 100. During the next 3 miles the railway passes over and under a series of small bridges, past Mallerstang signal box and disused lie-bye sidings due for lifting – and on to the great Intake embankment just beyond the 263¾ mile post. Originally the engineers intended to have a viaduct here but so poor was the ground that the embankment took its place, earth being tipped for a year during construction before solid bottom was found. After the embankment there comes a short rock cutting on the approach to Birkett tunnel (424 yards), immediately north of the 264¼ mile post, and boring through the Pennine Fault, with Birkett Common to the right. Before coming to the cutting, and about 3 miles from Ais Gill, there can be seen ½ mile away to the right and standing on a knoll the remains of Pendragon Castle, supposedly founded by Uter Pendragon who, according to Williams, was murdered there by the poisoned waters of a nearby spring. For some time Sir Hugh Morville, one of the murderers of Thomas à Becket, lived at the castle. All this area of North Yorkshire and Westmorland suffered from border warfare for many years—even farm houses were fortified to keep out marauders. The gloomy history is most fitting to its surroundings.

Beyond the tunnel the line runs on a fairly easy straight stretch along Keld Brow and on to the sweeping curve of the approach to Kirkby

Stephen. Here the River Eden has joined the line to the right and the beginnings of the Eden Valley come into view. From the gaunt, bleak, windswept uplands with their treeless vastness, the terrain through which the railway passes begins to assume a kinder face. At Kirkby Stephen the station buildings are very similar in accommodation to those at Settle. Rows of railway cottages, with the station master's house at the end on the right, adjoin the road under the railway at the end of the station, just before the 266½ mile post. The town is some 2 miles north of the station. The 3 miles to the next station sees the line rounding Smardale and biting into its flanks with a rock cutting ¾ mile before coming to Smardale viaduct at the 34 mile point. Here a closed single track line passes under the railway. It runs from Tebay—away to the left—to Darlington, and ceased operating in January, 1962. At one time there was considerable iron ore traffic from the Durham area through to the west coast. As will be seen this apparently insignificant line was well in the running many years back for a scheme to permit of through traffic from Euston to the east coast. At Kirkby Stephen it meets the Eden Valley Railway—a line which to some extent duplicates the Settle and Carlisle railway for the next few miles before swinging away at Appleby to make a connection with the Euston-Carlisle main line south of Penrith.

Smardale viaduct, which comes immediately before the 268¾ mile post, is the highest on the old Midland Railway system. It has 12 arches and was constructed from some 60,000 tons of grey limestone to span by a length of 700 feet Smardale Beck, 130 feet below. A ¼ mile further on is Crosby Garrett tunnel (181 yards), closely followed by Crosby Garrett viaduct of six arches, and some 50 feet above the village. A short distance beyond, at the 269¾ mile post, is the closed station of Crosby Garrett, situated in cutting and with an overbridge dividing the site of the station buildings from the major part of the platforms. Except for the down side building much has been demolished and the platforms cut back. The goods yard, with its shed and cattle dock, were on the north side of the station. From Kirkby Stephen the gradient has been all downhill, except for a short level stretch over Crosby Garrett viaduct. Two miles beyond Crosby Garrett the railway crosses Griseburn viaduct of seven arches followed closely by High Griseburn quarry and the now disused ballast sidings. At the 38½ mile point the railway enters Helm tunnel (571 yards) before running on embankment towards Ormside station—a small derelict building on the left side of the line beyond the 40 mile point.

From Ormside station there is a short level stretch over the 90 ft. high Ormside viaduct of ten arches, with the River Eden curving away to the left under the train to follow the line into Carlisle. After the viaduct the railway begins to climb at 1 in 183 towards Appleby and to the right, as the train approaches the curve into Appleby West station, the Eden Valley Railway can be seen. This too is now closed between Appleby and Penrith and in effect the line between Appleby and Kirkby Stephen, which parallels the Settle and Carlisle line, is all that is left of the two once thriving branches of the old North Eastern Railway. There is a spur from the Settle line to the Eden Valley Railway at Appleby, seen curving round to the right at the north end of the station and a glimpse of the old Eden Valley station can be caught at this point too. The main station buildings at Appleby West are on the left hand side. There is a footbridge connecting the two platforms—the first station footbridge met with so far on the route, 42½ miles from Settle Junction. Immediately south of the station the 'Express Dairy' Company have a rail depot for milk from the Eden Valley with a large advertisement which proclaims 'MILK FOR LONDON'. Appleby itself once housed some eleven thousand people. The town was granted a charter by Henry I on the same day as that received by the City of York and must have been, at that time, quite an important place. Border warfare and the plague reduced it almost to ruins and in 1388 it was burnt down completely. Now it is but a quiet and pleasant shadow of its former self, with a population of about 1,700. It is, of course, the county town of Westmorland, and its former greatness at the head of the Vale of Eden is symbolised by the castle keep, the remains of a fortification constructed on a site which held military value from times before the conquest.

Almost immediately after leaving Appleby a last glimpse of the Eden Valley line can be seen passing under the railway on its way to Penrith. From here to Carlisle the Settle line is fairly easy going. The heavy works are behind and no doubt the Vale of Eden provided a welcome respite to the Victorian engineers. With the valley broadening out, away to the right can be seen the high lands of Warcop Fell, Hilton Fell, Dufton Fell, and Cross Fell. These last three cover an area known generally as the Millburn Forest and the highest point of Cross Fell is only 70 feet short of the 3,000 mark. The run down from Appleby to the next station at Long Marton—a distance of 3 miles—includes Long Marton viaduct of five arches, passing 60 ft. above Trout Beck, and just preceding the station which is one of the smaller variety having its buildings on the up side of the line. The goods yard is now closed and the track lifted but the shed is used by Lunesdale Farmers Ltd.

From Long Marton there follows a relatively straight stretch of another 3 miles to the next station at New Biggin, similar in size to Long Marton. Only 1½ miles further on is Culgaith station, the shortest distance between stations for the whole line between Leeds and Carlisle. It makes up for this, however, by including within this length New Biggin viaduct of four arches which crosses Crowdundle Beck and Kirkandrews Wood before it joins the Eden. The beck also acts as the county boundary between Westmorland and Cumberland and the remainder of the journey is within the latter county. From Appleby the line has been on a ruling down gradient of 1 in 121. A short way beyond Culgaith station, which has on its platform the 284¾ mile post, the railway threads two tunnels, Culgaith (661 yards), and Waste Bank (164 yards), both on the level, with Hag Wood, Wastebanks Wood, and the River Eden close to the line on the left. On emerging from the first of the tunnels, the River Eamont, which has journeyed down from Ullswater, can be seen joining the Eden. A further 2½ miles brings the line, with a short up grade of 1 in 275 and 1 in 354, to Langwathby station, 53½ miles from Settle Junction, with its buildings on the left of the line and the Alston-Langwathby road passing under the railway beyond. To the right the heights of Cross Fell have given way to the lesser eminences of Alston Moor and Gilderdale Forest. A short distance beyond the station the down grade recommences and about a mile after passing through Langwathby comes Little Salkeld viaduct, of seven arches, crossing Briggle Beck and with the Langwathby corn mill below on the left. A few yards further on is Little Salkeld station, like Culgaith only 1½ miles beyond its predecessor. But these are timetable distances; the official station centre to station centre gives the shortest length to Culgaith which beats its rival by 132 feet.

With the Eden on the left and the high ground on the right the railway now approaches Long Meg plaster sidings and then crosses the river for the last time by Long Meg (sometimes known as Eden Lacy) viaduct of seven arches, built in the local Lazonby sandstone, and coming immediately after the 291 mile post. Here the scenery becomes at times quite beautiful as the river, with larch and pine plantations for company, winds its course beside the railway. Frederick Williams, in his monumental history of the Midland Railway, written while the line was under construction, remarked that 'the scenery at this point is such that the traveller will often wish he were able to stop the train every few minutes to enjoy it.' It was this green agricultural countryside that proved such a mixed blessing to the engineers of the railway, for though contours and weather conditions were far and away easier than the preceding lengths of the line, there was an annual dearth of construction workers at harvest time, the men taking the opportunity to play truant from the works to get the hay in.

About ½ mile beyond Long Meg Sidings the line runs on the level for ¾ mile before commencing a series of undulating gradients, both up and down, which last for the next eight miles or so. Over a mile beyond Long Meg viaduct the closed Lazonby ballast sidings come into view to the right of the line which immediately afterwards passes through Lazonby tunnel (99 yards), before coming to Lazonby & Kirkoswald station, just south of the 292¾ mile post. The next 5½ miles are perhaps the most scenic in the Eden Valley. To the right the river winds in long sweeps through heavily wooded slopes. For the most part the railway is on embankment for some two miles, and Sampsons Cave Plantations with coniferous trees on both sides of the line, lend to the view. Some 2½ miles from Lazonby the railway enters a cutting and approaches the last tunnels on the route—a group of three, Baron Wood No. 1 (207 yards), Baron Wood No. 2 (251 yards), and Armathwaite (325 yards), there being about one mile of rock cutting separating the last two. The line curves to the right on leaving the last tunnel, and ½ mile further on passes over Armathwaite viaduct, of nine arches, and 80 feet high, just beyond the 297¼ mile post, before coming to Armathwaite station a mile further on and 5½ miles from Lazonby.

The remaining 10 miles to Carlisle are mostly on a continuous down gradient and include three stations now closed to passenger traffic. Between Armathwaite station and the next at Cotehill there is a distance of some 3 miles during which the line crosses Dry Beck viaduct of seven arches, with high embankments preceding and following it, curves round to the left through a heavy rock cutting and then reverses the curve at the 300 mile post from St. Pancras and runs on to the quarter-mile long Eden Brow embankment—another of the works which gave considerable trouble—with the River Eden below on the right beyond Eden Brow Wood. It is at this point, the 300 mile post, and ½ mile beyond Low House crossing, that the final uninterrupted down grade commences, mostly at 1 in 129 to 134. After the embankment comes High Stand Gill viaduct of four arches, at the 301 mile post, followed by Cotehill station where a siding on the left once served Knothill Plaster and Cement Works. Now demolished, the small Cotehill station had a 250 yard approach from the Armathwaite-Carlisle road. A further 1½ miles brings the railway to Howe & Co's Sidings, reversible working loop, and box on the down side, serving plaster works, and another mile to the station at Cumwhinton. There follows an extremely short stretch to the last intermediate station on the line—that at Scotby which if not now closed would, with Cumwhinton, beat Culgaith for the shortest distance between stations. Here the country on either side of the line is almost level, being part of the plain of the estuary of the Eden into the Solway Firth. The last 1¼ miles of the Settle and Carlisle line brings the former North Eastern Railway's Newcastle & Carlisle line into view, coming in on the right, and with ever increasing building and urban development apparent on both sides the two lines join at Petteril Junction, 307 miles from St. Pancras. Trains making their way into Carlisle Citadel station do so from here mainly on the metals of the older railway. Before joining the Newcastle & Carlisle, however, the site of the former Midland Railway engine shed at Durran Hill is seen to the left. Closed in 1936, and later reopened, finally closed in 1959 and demolished in 1964, it is a far cry from the days when the shining red engines of the Midland coaled and watered here before taking trains through the magnificent scenery of the Settle line. The shed was of the roundhouse type. It had an interior 55 ft. turntable and could house two dozen engines. Outside was another turntable of 60 ft., together with repair shops. Beyond the sheds lay the Midland goods station and tranship shed, with sorting and carriage sidings. Shortly after passing Durran Hill the line takes a sharp right turn, away from the Newcastle & Carlisle Railway, to bring it to the junction with the Lancaster & Carlisle line of the former London & North Western Railway—the old rival of the Midland for the London-Carlisle traffic—just south of Carlisle station.

II

Springboard

The Formation of the Midland Railway

When the Midland Railway Company came into being there was no indication that one day it would stake out a claim to Scottish traffic. It was a provincial railway formed in 1844 by a fusion of three existing companies—the Midland Counties, the North Midland, and the Birmingham & Derby Junction. The first—a railway promoted by Derbyshire and Nottinghamshire coal owners, and with its shareholders' list including the Prime Minister, Lord Melbourne, with £5,000 worth of shares, and John Ellis of the Leicester & Swannington Railway with £500, was authorised by an Act of Parliament of June 21, 1836 to make a railway from Derby to Long Eaton—now known as Trent—where it was to divide into lines north and south; one to Nottingham, and the other via Leicester to Rugby where it connected with the already opened London & Birmingham Railway. At one time it was proposed that as the London & Birmingham had by-passed Northampton, the Midland Counties should extend to that town, but the idea came too late for the Parliamentary session of 1836 and was dropped. The M.C.R. Bill had originally contained provision for a line up the Erewash Valley from Trent to Pinxton but the opposition of the canal interests and the proposed North Midland Railway, which would have thus found some 20 miles of its own line rendered virtually useless, secured the removal of this part of the scheme.

The North Midland Railway was authorised by Act of July 4, 1836 to construct a railway from the Midland Counties at Derby to run north via Ambergate, Chesterfield, Rotherham, and Normanton, to Leeds. As has been seen, from the start there was a veiled hostility between the company and the Midland Counties; for the rejection of the latter's Erewash Valley line removed the core of the coal owners' project. Having slapped the M.C.R. face in the north, the N.M.R. stamped on its feet in the south by backing the last of the triumvirate—the Birmingham & Derby Railway—a line enthusiastically supported by Sir Robert Peel and designed mainly to give the North Midland separate access on to the London & Birmingham.

The Birmingham & Derby was planned to leave the first two lines by a junction at Derby and then to run south through Burton-on-Trent and Tamworth to Whitacre, where it was to fork, one line going to Stechford and the other to Hampton-in-Arden, at which places both were to join the London & Birmingham Railway. The Hampton-Whitacre link was to be the N.M.R.s required short cut, being specifically made

32

to permit the Derby-London traffic to reach the south independent of the Midland Counties Railway. Even this latter short line had been the subject of controversy between the Birmingham & Derby, and the Midland Counties. The latter had undertaken to drop its Pinxton branch if the B.D.R. did likewise with the Whitacre-Hampton line—known as the Stonebridge branch. At the very last minute, despite the agreement between the two companies, the M.C.R. included the Pinxton line in its Bill too late to allow the B.D.R. to get its Stonebridge line included in the advertisements required by Parliament to be published in all the local newspapers of the districts through which the line should run. The difficulty was surmounted by the quick promotion of a small and nominally independent company—the Stonebridge Junction Railway—which required advertising in only one Birmingham newspaper. When the two Bills got to Parliament they united, the B.D.R. company adding 'Junction' to its title. Royal Assent was obtained on May 19, 1836.

These three projected main lines dominated a potentially lucrative area of the industrial midlands and despite the fact that the committee of the House of Commons, which examined the Bills of the Birmingham & Derby Junction, and the Midland Counties, was assured by the former that it was not competing with the latter, it soon became apparent that the question of who was to take the North Midland traffic on to the London and Birmingham would be the subject of contention. By March of 1838 the M.C.R. had won the first round. Arguing that its route would, overall, be shorter than that comprising the B.D.J., the company talked the N.M.R. into a seven year agreement for exchange of traffic at Derby. In the same year the three companies agreed that there should be a joint station for the town.

The B.D.J., 48½ miles in length on completion in 1842, and costing £1,173,000, was surveyed by George Stephenson, and opened from Derby to Hampton—38¾ miles—on August 12, 1839, providing the first through rail link from Euston to Derby—some 141 miles. The M.C.R., 48 miles long between Derby and Rugby, and 57 miles overall including the Nottingham line, costing £1,725,000, and surveyed by Charles Vignoles, was not far behind. The sixteen mile main line from Derby to Nottingham came into use (as a single track) on June 4, 1839, this being followed by Trent to Leicester, and Leicester to Rugby, on May 5, and July 1, 1840, respectively, thus cutting the B.D.J.'s lead for London traffic to a head start of just under a year. Thereafter the locomotives of each company were to outdo each other for the traffic between London and the north in one of the first classic rate wars to an extent which threatened the solvency of each. Not unnaturally the agreement between the N.M.R. and the M.C.R. had outraged the B.D.J. which until then had had fond expectations of most of the traffic. Work on the Hampton link had been pushed ahead with ruthless determination, while the Whitacre-Stechford line took very much of a back seat; it was not opened until nearly three years later.

The North Midland Railway was an altogether worthier affair. Costing £3,344,700, its route, again by Stephenson—though Vignoles, his assistant on the Liverpool & Manchester Railway, had tendered a rival plan and was called to give evidence in the Commons' committee—took it through terrain demanding far heavier engineering works than either of the other two companies. Just under 73 miles long, it by-passed Sheffield which was joined to the main line by the Sheffield & Rotherham Railway, a little over 5¼ miles in length, authorised on the same day as the N.M.R. The S.R.R. was opened first of any of the lines so far discussed, as far as Masborough on the N.M.R. on October 31, 1839, and was to be amalgamated with the Midland in 1845, the latter company having worked the line from October, 1844. The North Midland started operating from Derby to the junction with the S.R.R. on May 11, 1840 and was completed through to Leeds by the end of June, 1840, Robert Stephenson driving the first train. By November 1840 the service consisted of seven trains daily each way, except on Sundays when there were five. The company then had some fifty locomotives. Frederick Williams, in his book *The Midland Railway* (written in 1878), has a pleasing anecdote about one of the chief opposing landowners on the line—a naturalist of considerable eminence, who was held in some awe by Frederick Swanwick, the resident engineer, due to his known past ill-temper over the Barnsley Canal which had previously almost invaded his bird sanctuary. An irascible man—'he had odd and energetic modes of expressing his wrath'—he nevertheless happily failed to live up to expectations as far as Swanwick was concerned. To the relief of all, after being asked whether he would at least be neutral to the line, he replied that he would provided that the company would promise that when their line was made it would 'ruin those infernal canals'.

The North Midland joined the York & North Midland Railway (opened on the same day as the N.M.R.) at Normanton, giving the company access to York and making possible passenger and freight communication from the metropolis to that city. It is at this point that George Hudson appears unobtrusively on the scene. In the committee report of the House of Commons of May, 1836, on the proposed York & North Midland Railway he makes his first bow with by far the largest number of shares in the company, two hundred, totalling £10,000. A friend of George Stephenson since the early 1830s, Hudson early became enamoured of the idea of profiting by railway speculation. He inherited the sum of £30,000 and threw himself into their promotion. So persuasive was he that Stephenson was inveigled to put money into the Y.N.M. and though the railway was hardly one productive of big returns Hudson kept everybody happy by ensuring that at least the dividends were acceptable. His manipulative skill stood him in good stead; when the North Midland found itself in trouble, it was Hudson who was called in to clear up the mess. Its dividends were 3½ per cent. in 1841, just over 2½ per cent. in 1842 and 3½ per cent. in 1843. Shareholders increasingly criticised the company's board for extravagance and by the summer of 1842 affairs had reached a point where the Liverpool party among the proprietors demanded a committee of inquiry. In the spring of that year George Carr Glyn had resigned from the office of chairman and had been succeeded by William Leaper Newton. (Glyn was at the same time chairman of the London & Birmingham.) The committee was naturally headed by Newton but the most influential member was Hudson, who as chairman of the seemingly successful Y.N.M., was asked for his views on the shortcomings of the N.M.R. The committee reported by the middle of September and suggested some far-reaching reforms, with cuts in wages, salaries and dividends. This occasioned some resentment in various quarters, noticeably among the enginemen who came out on strike. Dismissals resulted—these included some of the officers of the company —and the locomotive department was re-organised by Thomas Cabrey of the Y.N.M., one of Hudson's officers and a living example in the art of infiltration. Cabrey was a Stephenson protege; he and his brother Henry, and their father Joseph, had all been at Killingworth with George Stephenson when the latter started his climb to the top of the new science of railway engineering.

Despite the committee's recommendations, however, not all its ideas were put into effect, Newton declaring that some of the proposed measures, which entailed operating economies, would create a danger to the public. This prophecy was only too soon borne out. Lack of switchmen, watchmen, and trained locomotive men, resulted in several bad accidents. Many of the good enginemen left, to be replaced by rejects and misfits from other companies. Passengers, frequently delayed for exasperating reasons, or arriving in hair-raising manner before time, complained violently. Dark hints were heard as they climbed shakily from their open wagons after some particularly bad journey of bringing back the 'horse coach', and there was much partisan ink spilt on the subject in the railway and other press.

Nevertheless, Hudson had made his mark and before long he was on the North Midland board. His diagnosis and treatment had put the company's finances back on a sound footing but his arrival on the stage as a sort of Yorkshire Solomon was to precipitate a chain of events which was to lead to his gaining absolute control of the Midland group of lines and promoting their expansion. It was in 1842 that Hudson tried to persuade Sir Robert Peel to support him in an attempt to extend the line, via the Y.N.M.R., to Scotland. 'I was then, however, politely bowed to the door.' He then offered to obtain pledges from the two companies for repayment of the £2 million he wanted. 'Sir Robert gave me one of his peculiar shrugs of his shoulders—so much as to say that he could not hear anything more on the subject.' This piece of information was vouchsafed to the Midland's meeting in October of 1846. It was one of the many near misses during the Hudson era which might have completely altered Midland history. During the time that Hudson had been putting the North Midland house in order the Birmingham & Derby Junction and the Midland Counties had been running each other into the ground and the continuing deterioration of their finances was soon to prompt Hudson to suggest this as one reason for their amalgamation with the North Midland.

The locomotives of the two companies differed somewhat. In early 1842 the passenger engines of the B.D.J., facing a ruling gradient of 1 in 339, were all of the 2-2-2 classification, having 5 ft. 6 in. driving wheels and 3 ft. 6 in. carrying wheels. It appears from Francis Whishaw, writing in 1840, that none were numbered; all were named. Engines *Tame, Blythe,* and *Anker* were made by R. & W. Hawthorn; *Barton, Tamworth,* and *Hampton* by Mather Dixon & Co.; *Derby, Birmingham,* and *Burton* by Tayleur & Co.; and *Derwent, Dove,* and *Trent* by Sharp Roberts & Co. Two others, the only ones of the 0-4-2 type, and used for goods workings at that time, were *Kingsbury,* and *Willington,* supplied by Thompson & Cole. The company's locomotives were shedded at Birmingham, Derby, or Hampton. A peculiarity was their gauge—4 ft. 9 in. In 1841 the company took on Matthew Kirtley—then 28 years of age—as its locomotive superintendent, promoted from locomotive foreman at Hampton where he had been in charge of four engines. The Midland Counties, with a ruling gradient of 1 in 330, favoured four-wheeled engines, mostly with 5 ft. 6 in. driving wheels and 4 ft. carrying. According to Board of Trade returns, in October 1841 the company had 37 locomotives in the working stock, of which 29 were passenger, 6 were goods, and 2 were for ballast trains. 35 of this total were four-wheeled. Turning to Whishaw again, in 1839 none of the M.C.R. engines were numbered but some were named. Those that were bore agreeably apt names for the prevailing temper between the company and its rival. *Hawk, Vulture,* and *Eagle* were made by Stark & Fulton; *Sun* and *Tiger* were Bury engines. Three others at that time, by Nasmyth & Co., were not distinguished by number or name. Various other similar types by different makers eventually brought the company's complement to some 50 engines. E. L. Ahrons, in his book *The British Steam Railway Locomotive, From 1825 to 1925,* records that in 1841 one of the company's early locomotives, *The Bee,* was fitted up with perhaps the first successful arrangement for consuming its own smoke. The North Midland mainly operated six-wheeled locomotives, on a line having a ruling gradient of 1 in 264. They were mostly supplied by the firms of R. & W. Hawthorn, Tayleur & Co., Mather Dixon & Co., and Robert Stephenson & Co. In 1839 Whishaw spoke of there being some 50 engines, costing each about £1,150 to £1,600. They were not numbered or named and were at that time all of the 2-2-2 arrangement. The first three makers invariably supplied the locomotives with 5 ft. 6 in. or 6 ft. driving wheels, and 3 ft. 6 in. or 4 ft. carrying. Stephenson's went up to 6 ft. on the driving and 5 ft. 6 in. on the carrying. At a slightly later date the latter firm began producing goods engines of the 0-4-2 type—this classification having found its way on to the Leicester & Swannington as early as 1833. The 1841 Board of Trade returns gave the total stock number of North Midland engines as having fallen to 40, 10 of which were of the 0-4-2 type. By 1842 Stephenson's 'long-boilered' engines were in use on the N.M.R., one of which, No. 71, employed the first use of link motion. At this time W. P. Marshall, one of Robert Stephenson's assistants, who had joined the N.M.R. in 1840 as locomotive superintendent, left the company. His successor was the energetic Mr. Cabrey. All this, however, is anticipating somewhat and cannot be other than of a general nature. Anyone who has attempted to sort out the locomotive history of the three pre-Midland companies will have found that all is not as meets the eye and conflicting evidence is common.

In 1839 the competition between the B.D.J. and the M.C.R. was about to start. For some time the Government had been concerned about the rapid and seemingly increasing amount of railway growth, and a series of Parliamentary committees were set up to examine qualified witnesses on all aspects of railway finance and working. The Second Report from the Select Committee on Railways, which gathered evidence between April and August, 1839, brought to light some interesting facts regarding the Midland companies.

Captain Constantine Richard Moorsom, R.N., secretary to the London & Birmingham Railway, was examined in June. He told the committee that the locomotives of the B.D.J. were to run through to Birmingham from Hampton—some 9 miles over the L.B.R. As to southbound traffic no decision had at that time been reached but he thought that the L.B.R.'s engines would take over in that case. A month later the L.B.R. had changed its mind. Its engineer, Robert Stephenson, told the committee that the company had decided to allow through running of carriages of both the Midland Counties from Rugby, and the B.D.J. from Hampton, but through locomotive workings were definitely ruled out. B.D.J. trains would be arranged to meet the L.B.R.'s Birmingham to London trains at Hampton where through carriages to the south would be attached. The Birmingham coaches were to be taken on by a L.B.R. engine stationed at Hampton for that purpose. Stephenson admitted that the L.B.R. changed its mind as to through Birmingham workings only because there was even at that time severe congestion at the Birmingham Curzon Street station. Edward Bury of the L.B.R., giving evidence, said that he had happened to be in the office of Joseph Baxendale (who happily combined his position of superintendent of the L.B.R. with that of chairman of the South Eastern Railway) when the latter, in conference with officers of the B.D.J., had decided on the new arrangements. Next year the B.D.J., dropping altogether the idea of using the L.B.R. route to Birmingham, took powers by the Birmingham & Derby Junction Railway (Alteration) Act, 1840, to abandon the Whitacre-Stechford line and replace it with a line $2\frac{1}{2}$ miles longer and running down the Tame Valley to the company's own terminus at Lawley Street, Birmingham, near where it was also able to make a connection with the Birmingham & Gloucester Railway. This direct Whitacre-Birmingham line was opened on February 9, 1842, from which day the Hampton-Birmingham traffic of the company ceased, saving it the expense of tolls over the L.B.R. To increase the traffic Stephenson had suggested that three additional stations should be made on the new line and these were quickly opened at Castle Bromwich, Water Orton, and Forge Mills (renamed Coleshill on July 9, 1923). At Birmingham the company constructed a wagon lift at its sidings so that B.D.J. traffic could be hoisted up to make connection with the Birmingham & Gloucester Railway—a line which comes into the story a little later. The 'lift sidings' at Lawley Street were opened at the same time as the Whitacre-Birmingham line. To complete the story of the Midland's access into Birmingham, by the Midland Railway Birmingham Extension Act of 1846 the company was authorised to make the connecting link from Saltley to Derby Junction on the London & Birmingham and this was opened at the beginning of 1851. This line, according to the half-yearly report, was completed by November 1, 1850, but owing to an accident to the viaduct was not opened until some weeks later.

Competition between the B.D.J. and the Midland Counties was acknowledged by the boards of the two companies to be wasteful almost from the first and, despite the initial dog fights, with B.D.J. fares from Derby to Hampton reduced to 1s. 6d., an uneasy truce was called in 1840. Traffic was hardly sufficient to warrant two different train services from the Midland towns to the south. In 1842 the B.D.J. broke the truce, and fares for London passengers over its line were reduced to 1s. The Midland Counties retaliated with special inducements to travellers from Nottingham and Derby to Birmingham to go via Rugby. The shareholders of each company were, of course, hardly delighted at the way their elected representatives were running things. The Midland Counties had a minor palace revolution on its hands by November of 1842 with shareholders demanding and getting a committee of investigation to look into all aspects of the company's business. It transpired at the time that John Fox Bell, the company's secretary, had sensed which way the wind was blowing and had beforehand privately voted himself a salary cut of £200.

In 1842 the Board of Trade issued a report on the railways of the kingdom in which there was much information on the train services and traffic then existing. In the matter of third class passengers all companies had been required to complete a questionaire. The North Midland reply showed that there were four third class trains daily each way. The coaches had spring buffers, were open with sides 2 ft. 8 in. high, had no partitions, and held about 40 people by means of seats all round the carriage and a double back-to-back seat running down the centre. The Midland Counties provided a similar number of third class trains and again the carriages were open. At first sight their sides of 3 ft. 9 in. height above the floor were a distinct improvement on the N.M.R. lot, until it was realised that there were no seats, and passengers—about 60 when full—were expected to stand all the way between places only on the M.C.R., gripping rails which quartered the interior of the carriage at a height of 3 ft. 8 in. above the floor. Where M.C.R. trains connected with those of the other companies, however, seats were provided. The B.D.J., on the other hand, appeared to provide the best accommodation. Its services for third class passengers were as inadequate as the others but it provided spring-buffered carriages with sides 3 ft. 6 in. high. Seating was on the N.M.R. pattern but seems to have been more liberal as regards the size of each seat per passenger—35 persons per carriage.

The foregoing, bad though it was, seemed extravagant compared with what the London & Birmingham Railway offered at the time : one train each way, Sundays excepted, with a stop of no less than 110 minutes at Roade of all places, ostensibly 'to allow time for the day mail and other fast trains to pass, and for the passengers to refresh themselves'. The down train left Euston at 7 a.m. and reluctantly crawled into Birmingham at 3.15 p.m. The average speed was 22 miles per hour, and the carriages were open, with leather buffers stuffed with hair, sides 2 ft. 8 in. high, and three compartments each seating eight passengers. The company hurriedly added, as if appalled at having committed this to print, that it intended that the thirds would henceforth be 'assimilated in construction to those in which the second class passengers are now conveyed and shall also be fitted with spring buffers'. Note was also made of the shelter and refreshment facilities available to third class passengers at Roade.

More details of the competition between the B.D.J. and the M.C.R. came out in the *Fifth Report from the Select Committee on Railways,* published in May, 1844, just before the incorporation of the Midland. Samuel Laing, described as Law and Corresponding Clerk of the Railway Department of the Board of Trade, appeared before the committee for seven days of questioning and his testimony ran for 143 pages of the Report. In answer to a series of questions from Gladstone, President of the Board of Trade and chairman of the committee, he confirmed that the M.C.R. had an advantage of some 12 miles over the B.D.J. in the matter of the Derby to London traffic. According to Laing, if the London & Birmingham showed any partiality it was to the latter company, simply because its coaches produced more revenue from tolls than those of the former, in that they had to travel further over the L.B.R. line. Also the fares had been stabilised by an agreement between the two warring companies as soon as they had agreed to seek powers to amalgamate. Apparently the boards of both lines had foreseen trouble from the start. They had at first agreed that the traffic from the North Midland to the south should be divided between them at Derby, each train arriving from the north to be taken on by only one of the companies. This worked well for a time but eventually they quarrelled over the arriving trains at Derby and the agreement went by the board, fares reaching an absurd low. The reverse of competition is monopoly : John Swift of the Grand Junction Railway, giving evidence to the committee in March, 1844, pointed out that since the agreement to amalgamate the fares had risen above the average.

The committee's report resulted in Gladstone's Act of 1844 which, amongst other things, protected the third class passenger from some of the evils he had suffered at the hands of unscrupulous companies in the years before. It is of interest that a fair amount of additional evidence was forthcoming from Laing as to the treatment meted out to such passengers by the Midland Counties. Only two of the company's daily trains then carried third class passengers, there being two carriages attached each time for the purpose. The carriages were still open and, to the best of Laing's belief, uncovered.* None of the Midland Counties trains connected at Rugby with the L.B.R. trains, going either north or south; whereas third class passengers travelling south from Derby on the early morning train were eventually able to join the L.B.R. afternoon third class up train, the only one—and taking about 8½ hours from Birmingham to London, those taking the later train from Derby were obliged to stay at Rugby overnight or pay second class fares for the rest of the journey south. All this contrasted rather unfavourably with other lines; the L.B.R., though providing seemingly interminable journeys, had at least started to make available seats and tarpaulin covers in the winter. The Manchester & Leeds was cited as a line with bad accommodation, but though the third class carriages were uncovered and without seats, they were on nearly all its trains, which ran at ordinary speeds, at a fare of 1d. per mile. 'Ordinary speeds' were put by Laing at about 24 miles per hour so one can guess at the freezing eternity of a winter journey on the slower lines. A point in mitigation of the M.L.R. system was that in the main uncovered carriages were less of a horror than imagined, as the average journey by third class passenger was of short duration, ticket holders at that time being mostly confined to weavers and other workmen seeking employment and local markets for their wares, from town to town.

Besides being jolted almost silly whilst standing for long periods in open trucks with barely adequate springing, the passengers unfortunate enough to travel third class frequently suffered from burnt clothing and damaged eyesight from the sparks. The Poor Law Commissioners, questioned by Gladstone's Committee, made no bones of their abhorrence of third class travel; apparently paupers, who paid no fares, if offered any other mode of conveyance opted for the most part to travel by canal. This was not because the railways were still felt to be 'new-fangled'—they simply wished to avoid a more than unusually unpleasant experience. Of course, second class carriages were only a little better—they were

* Francis Whishaw, writing in 1840, said that some of the seconds were covered over for the night trains.

provided with roofs but had open sides instead of windows. The main concern of the railways seemed to be to make the second class so unbearable as to drive passengers into the first class.

The Birmingham & Derby Junction was a particularly bad offender. Daniel Plowman, assistant overseer of the poor of Lichfield, gave evidence before the committee. Talking of the B.D.J. incorporation Act he noted the clause which stated that it was unlawful for the company to receive tolls of more than 2d. per mile for travel in their carriages. He went on :

'Thus the public were to have the advantage of travelling rapidly from place to place for 2d. a mile; but observe how easily the good intentions of the Legislature have been evaded. The Acts omitted to describe minutely the carriages in which the public were to be carried for 2d. a mile. The public could not claim which of the carriages they would ride in; but all their right was, to be carried in some carriage at 2d. a mile.

'The directors proceed to carry the Act into effect, and they construct three different classes of carriages, the first, second, and third—All who ride in the first must pay 3d. a mile. It is the interest of the company to get all they can into the first class, and immediately ingenuity is set to work to see how this object can be effected. All attractive means are used to draw passengers into the first class, and all repulsive means to drive them out of the third and second.

'The first class have cushions, lounging boards, plate-glass windows, and all the appliances for ease and luxurious travelling. The second class carriages (made the Act of Parliament carriages), those carriages charged at 2d. a mile, the sum at which the public was to have the privilege of travelling (in), have, at first, doors and windows; it is not then positively unhealthy; it is not positively uncomfortable to travel in them; but there are no cushions, lounging boards, or other luxuries. The public prefer these at 2d. a mile, and do not resort to the first class in sufficient numbers. The second class windows are taken out; the internal partitions are removed, and a thorough draught is immediately the consequence; they are, according to the opinion of many, made actually injurious to health.'

A friend of Plowman, refusing to be driven into the first class, braved the second on a journey to London, and caught a violent cold. On being asked why he had not taken an extra cloak or mackintosh to tack over the end of the carriage, thus to minimise the howling gale which inevitably roared the length of the second class carriages, he replied that the company would undoubtedly have prosecuted him, under its bye-laws, if he had so much as stuck a pin into the carriage. Apparently the London & Birmingham were partly to blame :

'In answer to my enquiries as to the change from glazed and comfortable second class carriages to the decidedly uncomfortable, if not absolutely dangerous ones, I was informed that as the Birmingham and Derby company had to seek accommodation from the London and Birmingham company, on to whose line their carriages had to pass, a condition was imposed upon them as part of the arrangement that the Birmingham and Derby company should take out their glazed windows, and make their future second class carriages open. I can only suppose that the object of the London and Birmingham company was to prevent the Birmingham and Derby from taking the many passengers who would prefer a glazed second class to their open ones, or to drive them into the first as being more lucrative to the companies.'

The clause, in Plowman's view, merely meant 'that Her Majesty's subjects may, if they please, submit to being killed at 2d. a head per mile.' When the B.D.J. was opened receipts on the line averaged £95 per day. There were at that time three trains daily in each direction. By August, 1840, the average receipts had doubled; five trains were running to Derby and six in the opposite direction. Sundays saw two each way. During the first four months of operation 74 per cent. of the receipts went in operating expenses, including the tolls payable to the L.B.R. The almost immediate effect that the line had on the Midland Counties can be seen from the following fares charged by that company. At the time of its opening these were : first class at 3.096d. per mile and second class 1.935d. Within a month they had been reduced to first class 2.7d. and second class 1.547d. By November, 1840 the fares had reached the very low rate, on the Derby-Rugby line, of 1.193d. first class, and 1.673d. for the second class. During the year 1842, at the height of the competition between the B.D.J. and the Midland Counties, the latter's gross receipts amounted to over £135,000 just double those of the former. Comparison of receipts with the construction costs given earlier, show that the shareholders of the B.D.J. had the worst of it. An abstract from the Appendix to the Fifth Report, detailing the number of passengers carried, and the average fare charged by each of the companies for the half-year ending December, 1842, shows the parlous state of the B.D.J.:

Company	Number of Passengers			Average Fare per Mile		
	1st Class	2nd Class	3rd Class	1st Class d.	2nd Class d.	3rd Class d.
Birmingham & Derby	19,824	44,097	34,246	2.87	2.03	1.44
Midland Counties	44,626	119,282	97,247	3	2	1

The difference of 12 miles was enough. Statistics can be used too freely, however, and no account has been taken of other traffic. The relative position of the two companies is shown to be no less biased towards the Midland Counties in the total percentage expenditure to receipts—57 per cent. for the B.D.J., and 58 per cent. for the Midland Counties. Finally, the matter of dividends. Again, taking 1842, the figures given in the Fifth Report are : B.D.J. 2 per cent.; Midland Counties 3 per cent.; and North Midland 3.25 per cent. These contrasted badly with that shining Hudsonian example, the York & North Midland, still regularly paying its cooked-up 10 per cent.

Whilst the snapping and snarling went on in Derbyshire between the two companies, there was a threat building up which could adversely affect them both; the forces of the Great Western were on the move. One of these, the Bristol & Gloucester, was under construction. A connecting line, the standard gauge Birmingham & Gloucester—authorised on April 22, 1836, had been opened throughout by the end of 1840 to a terminus at Camp Hill in Birmingham. On August 17 of the following year an extension from Camp Hill to the L.B.R. was opened, and the first B.G.R. trains ran into the overcrowded Curzon Street station. The thought of a probable Great Western attack over the Bristol & Gloucester, a possible change of gauge on the Birmingham & Gloucester, and a logical follow-through into Birmingham, put the Midland companies into a fright. The Birmingham & Gloucester had already made overtures to the G.W.R. but had so far been unsuccessful. In the year of the Midland incorporation it was to retire baffled from talks with Paddington and let the working of its line to a Bristol contractor. Before this time the B.D.J. had at last had enough and was seriously considering a proposal made by the North Midland for amalgamation of the three companies. In September, 1843, Ellis of the Midland Counties swung that company over to accept the idea. Pulling strings in all directions was George Hudson, boosting the discussions with dire reminders of the common threat from Paddington. Tacit agreement having been reached the companies decided to go to Parliament in the next session and, as has been related, this had the effect of ending the rate war.

In the vacuum before the Midland's incorporation, more indications of the penurious circumstances in which the companies found themselves came to light. The *Railway Times* in January of 1844, seeking a weapon with which to attack General Pasley of the Board of Trade—an institution most unpopular in railway circles at that particular time—used the B.D.J. for copy with some quick results. The General had apparently been speaking his mind on things the paper claimed he knew little of, and it drew the attention of the B.O.T. to the dangerous state of Oakley station (later renamed as Croxall) where, after a recent extension of the platform so that it abutted on to the parapet of an underbridge, the B.D.J. had been so parsimonious as to neglect the provision of any additional fencing or adequate lighting. The result was that someone had got out of a train late at night, expecting to be met by his carriage and on hearing the driver call out to him had blundered about on the platform and ended up by taking the short, unorthodox, and painful route to the road below. He was now in hospital and—perhaps fortunately for the company—in what was described as a speechless condition. The paper thought General Pasley would be better employed looking into this sort of thing than spending his time meddling in matters he didn't really understand. Though the General had cleared up that little business by early February, the *Railway Times* came back again with complaints about the deplorable condition of the company's level-crossing gates. It cited cases of trains arriving at Burton station with woodwork festooned around the locomotive buffers. It is difficult to see just what this was meant to prove—after all no gate will stand being rammed in such manner—but it was one more excuse for getting at the B.O.T., and Joseph Peyton of the B.D.J. Complaints on staffing were also made; seemingly the North Midland could not afford to employ good porters—those that it did at Normanton were rude on principle to all passengers but especially to those arriving from the Manchester & Leeds line. Unattended single ladies were frequently put into a state of near hysteria at the thought of using the station. Nothing any of the three companies did was exempt from criticism; it was high time something was done about it.

Hudson thought so too. Behind the scenes he worked to arrange the amalgamation. By February of 1844 all had been agreed, and in the case of the North Midland that company had approved the formation of the Leeds & Bradford Railway which was, almost from the start of its existence, to launch the Midland on its first steps to Scotland. The L.B.R. idea had been taken up by a nominally independent company in deference to the B.D.J., and the Midland Counties, who did not as yet want to get involved if the amalgamation should not secure Parliamentary approval. The B.D.J. was particularly anxious to avoid tying itself up with the new ventures whilst still on its own as it was at last beginning to find its feet. The better its financial condition when the time for amalgamation came, the better the deal for is shareholders. With the fare struggle finished traffic was improving with receipts up and working expenses down. Most of the credit for this was due to economies introduced by James Allport and Matthew Kirtley in the traffic and locomotive departments respectively. In fact the B.D.J. could claim the distinction of having introduced to its successor two of the Midland's most successful officers. For though Allport left for a time, as will be seen, both he and Kirtley were to figure largely in the build-up of the Midland system. Their backgrounds were dissimilar. Allport, who joined the B.D.J. as an officer in 1839, had been schooled in Belgium and was the son of a Birmingham small-arms manufacturer who had done nicely out of Government contracts during the Napoleonic Wars. Kirtley, on the other hand, had come up from the ranks. He had started by being a fireman to his elder brother Thomas on the locomotives of the Grand Junction Railway's Warrington branch. After this he had gone to the Leeds & Selby Railway as a driver. There followed a move to Kensal Green and later to Watford in charge of the engine shed of the London & Birmingham Railway. After this had come the Hampton job. Both these officers were bitterly attacked by one of the many anonymous letter writers on railway matters in the 1840s. For some reason 'Veritas Vincit' harboured a bitterness against them which lasted over several years. The sort of thing Kirtley was up against is typified in an unpleasant letter of August 14, 1843, to the *Railway Record* in which a careful attempt was made to belittle his background. Not content with generalities there were some direct questions put, one of which was: 'How many hours each day since he came to Birmingham does he (Kirtley) owe the Company for the use of a lad from the shed to assist Mrs. Kirtley's servant in her kitchen, and run her messages?' Though this may raise a smile today it must have been a constant source of anxiety each week in the days immediately before and after the *Railway Record* came out. 'Veritas Vincit' was considerably put out when Kirtley landed the top Midland locomotive job in 1844; for some years he had canvassed for Joseph Kearsley, the locomotive superintendent of the M.C.R., an individual who in the eyes of 'Veritas Vincit' could do no wrong. On September 12, 1844, he wrote that 'the appointment of Mr. Kirtley has led to other evils, as a necessary consequence. Of course he would not select a person to be under him who possessed brighter talents than himself, and accordingly he appointed Mr. Marlow (who was under him on the Derby line) as his locomotive foreman. Now, Mr. Marlow is as unfitted for the situation as Mr. Kirtley is for his—.' And so it went on. Cabrey, who later went to the Brighton line, Joseph Peyton, and many others, were attacked too. It seems as if it was a necessary evil to be borne with as much fortitude as could be assumed. It was not unlike some savage initiation ceremony, carried out in public, which was attendant upon reaching a position of seniority.

In April, 1844, the shareholders of the three Midland companies formally approved their directors' decision to amalgamate, and the Midlands Railway company (the 's' was dropped soon after) came into being by an Act of May 10, 1844, with Derby as its natural headquarters. The new company's architect, Hudson, was it first chairman—in command of the then largest single railway in the country. The first general meeting, held at Derby on Tuesday, July 16, 1844, set the tone and pace of the company's policy and, what was more, indicated that the Midland was now a force to be reckoned with. From his position in the chair Hudson declared that the company was jumping straight in with plans for extensions into the counties of York, Lincoln, and Nottingham. In a tone of outraged sanctity he chided the London & Birmingham with the fact that its trains had kept Midland passengers waiting three hours at Rugby for a connection. This was not good enough—what was more he knew that this practice was only for the purpose of forcing them to travel first class. Shades of the Midland Counties! Hudson was pleased to learn that the London & Birmingham freely admitted its guilt and had promised to mend its ways. The extensions do not concern the Midland's move to the north, save that in Yorkshire—the Leeds & Bradford. Suffice it to say that the Swinton-Lincoln, and Nottingham-Lincoln schemes were for the purpose of meeting a projected branch of the Eastern Counties Railway at March (another Hudson line), thus cutting out the then current London & York scheme. So was the rivalry with the Great Northern Railway conceived early.

What of Hudson's own position at this time? In his forty-fifth year he had come to rule a huge railway empire. Though his star was in the ascendant he had but a few years of power to come. Yet in those years he dwarfed other railway figures and established the Midland, or so it seemed, as second only to the railways of the Liverpool party. In those years he fought off the Great Northern to protect the Midland—it was his eventual seeming capitulation to the former that hastened his downfall. Before this happened he had alienated for good the Manchester & Leeds, soon to become the Lancashire & Yorkshire, and thus, as will be related, had assured the Midland a line reaching as far north as Skipton.

When he eventually crashed the Midland tottered on the brink of disaster and remained for years a mediocrity of a line. Hudson was a forceful, capable, and ruthless businessman. His bent was money, not railways. If the cultivation of mushrooms had seemed a better proposition he would have taken it up. Railways happened to be handy at the time the money was available. Having got into them, however, he developed almost overnight a startling flair and knowledge. Besides the legacy of £30,000, he had previously amassed by his own efforts the then considerable sum of £10,000 in the business he had joined as an apprentice at the age of fifteen—the draper's shop of Messrs. Bell & Nicholson, in College Street, York. He had worked hard at his trade, married the sister of Richard Nicholson in 1821, and on the death of William Bell had been offered a partnership by his brother-in-law. The York Tory party elected him their leader in 1833, and in the same year he founded the York Banking company. Shortly afterwards it was to be his support and enthusiasm which brought the York & North Midland Railway into being. In the years 1835, 1836, and 1837, he was elected successively a member of the York City Council, Alderman, and Lord Mayor. His one main wish was to make York the railway centre of the north of England —with the companies running therefrom to London and Scotland to be under his control. At the time of the Midland incorporation he was half-way there, for the already promoted York to Berwick line was falling into his hands.

The year 1844 saw Hudson's most heady achievement yet—one which brought him the gratitude of all railway shareholders; this was his successful one-man attempt to win over Gladstone from the latter's policy of state ownership of the railways. At the end of the series of Parliamentary reports, the Government had decided to incorporate their recommendations in a Bill to be made law in 1844. Apart from the well-known 'Parliamentary train'—every railway company was to run at least one train per day each way over its lines, which would stop at all stations and carry third class passengers at 1d. per mile—the Bill also provided for the state to purchase any new railway made after the passing of the Act, after a period of fifteen years. Delegations from the railway interests —and these were powerful bodies—failed to move the Prime Minister, Sir Robert Peel, or the other members of the Government, from their decision to pass the Bill. On the Bill being successfully read for the second time the outlook for the railway promoters and investors was appalling. It was then that Hudson called privately on Gladstone. He put the railway case so well at that meeting that Gladstone agreed to amend the Bill to make state purchase of railways conditional on their having paid over 10 per cent. for three consecutive years, the period of time at which this could be done being extended from fifteen to twenty-one years. From the copious evidence collected about the travelling conditions of the third class passenger, it had seemed that the Select Committee had been most anxious to effect relief on their behalf, and

Hudson's agreement to the clause in the Bill for 'Parliamentary trains' no doubt contributed to Gladstone's softened attitude towards the future of the companies themselves. If one can believe Hudson's public utterances—and like most able politicians he said what he knew would please his audience—there were some rewards other than money. Speaking to the Midland shareholders in 1846 he said that he rejoiced at his connection with railways in that by the reduction in the carriage of coal, bringing it down at York from 16s. to 5s. a ton, great benefits had been bestowed upon the poor. If in making a profit, he could bring profit to others, he was not displeased.

In this, it must be said, enviable position of being absolute ruler of a great railway empire, it was an irony that Hudson was to interest himself, in the same year as his triumph with Gladstone, in the small company which was eventually to start the Midland on an independent journey to Scotland, long after the latter had split away from the York to Berwick tie-up, and many years after Hudson himself had disappeared from the scene. For the Leeds & Bradford Railway was to play a major role in Hudson's dethronement.

III

First step to Scotland

The Leeds and Bradford Railway

The Leeds & Bradford Railway had a pedigree somewhat better than any of the original companies which formed the Midland at its incorporation. One of the first schemes for a line between the two towns was projected in 1832 as part of a major link to connect Manchester with Leeds. Though nothing came of the idea, business interests in Bradford seized the opportunity in 1835 to approach the embrionic North Midland Railway for an extension to the town. The N.M.R. was at that time engaged in surveying its main line and, feeling sufficiently occupied not to be bothered with Bradford, its engineer, George Stephenson, advised the Bradford people to form their own company, intimating that he was prepared to act on their behalf in his professional capacity. By 1838 Leeds was of similar mind to Bradford and during the next summer Stephenson and Daniel Gooch, while working a few miles to the south on the surveys for the authorised Manchester & Leeds line, took the opportunity to examine the country between Leeds and Bradford. Plans were prepared for a line up the Aire Valley but the venture did not proceed as there was at the time a depression in railway property. The Bradford people entertained a hope that the Manchester & Leeds might extend a branch to their town but, when by 1843 it had become apparent that this was unlikely to happen, Stephenson was again approached. He put the idea to Hudson who raised it at the summer meeting of the N.M.R. As has been related, the N.M.R. decided to support the new company financially and otherwise, and it was with gratification that the two towns learned that the N.M.R. engineer, by this time Robert Stephenson, had been instructed to prepare a survey.

Pending the approval of Parliament the intending company formed a provisional committee, at the first meeting of which—on December 22, 1843—Hudson was elected chairman, and John Waddingham, of Leeds, deputy chairman. William Clarke was appointed secretary at £120 per annum, Robert Stephenson retained as principal engineer, with Francis Mortimer Young as his assistant, and S. D. Martin was employed at a rate of £25 per mile to survey the line. On December 30, the committee met and Hudson made the first of his several tactical mistakes, *vis-à-vis* the Leeds & Bradford, which were to go hard against him later on, for the distribution of the shares of the company which followed the meeting was grossly unfair. The lists had been heavily over-subscribed and many people were not included, or had only a few allotted to them. Hudson, on the other hand, took up his quota almost to the full—£30,000. Being in the public eye he was more liable to criticism than Waddingham who, in fact, had grabbed a further £10,000 worth. Questions were asked at the next meeting of the N.M.R. When the lists for applications for shares in the L.B.R. had been found to include the names of Hudson and Waddingham, that was considered fair enough, but the meeting found much fault with what had followed. Newton, the N.M.R. chairman, seems to have been remarkably philosophical about Hudson. Rather plaintively he announced at the meeting that he had not put in for any L.B.R. shares as he had known it would be useless anyway. Hudson talked his way out of trouble by saying that if he hadn't backed the L.B.R. so heavily it would have folded up. He also threatened to resign if there was any more questioning as to the ethics of what had occurred. Only threatened—the tone of the meeting suggested that someone might have taken him at his word if given the chance. Waddingham kept quiet.

During this time Stephenson had been busy with the survey, assisted by Young and Martin. He had before him the choice of two routes. One was the direct short line from Leeds to Bradford, passing through Stanningley on the way—through hilly country and following the 1832 proposal; the other was the Aire Valley route similar to that of 1839. The backers of the short line of 1832 had hoped that he would agree to their route and when it became known that the Aire Valley was to be the choice, they proceeded to mount a heavy attack against it in Parliament. The line as planned was to be some 14 miles in length starting from Wellington Street, Leeds and passing through the lower part of Airedale as far as the village of Shipley, where it turned abruptly south to terminate on the northern outskirts of Bradford. By January of 1844 Young was able to report to the provisional committee that the estimated cost of the line was £284,416. He was asked to estimate for a branch to the North Midland at Hunslet, and reported that the extension would cost £30,158. By June the Bill had reached the House of Lords. The estimate for the line had now reached £392,000. Merchants from Bradford told the Parliamentary committee that it cost as much to bring wool by wagon from Leeds to Bradford—say 10 miles—as it did to bring it from Hull to Leeds, a distance of some 58 miles, at a cost of 5d. a hundredweight in each case. Engineering evidence heard before the committee favoured the valley route more than the short line, but it was agreed that the latter could indeed be made to work successfully. The short line party tried to call evidence against the L.B.R. but as they had not deposited a Bill this was ruled inadmissable. The preamble of the L.B.R. Bill was found to be proved on June 6, 1844, and the defeated short line interests went over to the Manchester & Leeds. After several more attempts they finally got powers in 1852 for the Leeds Bradford & Halifax Junction line, which eventually became part of the Great Northern Railway in 1865.

The Leeds & Bradford Railway Act received the Royal Assent on July 4, 1844. The new company had a capital of £400,000 and powers to make, as well as the main line, a branch of 1 mile 15 chains in length to the N.M.R. south of that company's terminus at Hunslet Lane, and a connecting loop of 34 chains completing the triangular layout at the Holbeck, Water Lane, and Canal junctions at Leeds. The Act also provided for the company to lease or sell its line to the North Midland. Besides Hudson and Waddingham there were three other directors; George Goodman, William Murgatroyd and John Rand. It is of interest that they were also liberally provided for in the matter of shares. The average number alloted to individual proprietors was 12. The five directors of the company each averaged 450.

At the time of the Act the company had already negotiated with some of the principal landowners along the line. Indeed as early as March 1844 Young had had about a mile staked out at the Leeds end but had rather naturally found himself unable to proceed further at the time since the landowners were objecting to the Bill in any case. As soon as the Act had been obtained work started on the heaviest engineering obstacle on the line—that of Thackley tunnel. The passage of the Bill through Parliament had drawn promises from the company that it would extend the line on to Keighley, some $6\frac{1}{2}$ miles up Airedale. At this point a new concern, the Lancashire & Yorkshire Junction Railway, brought out a prospectus for a line to connect the intended Blackburn & Preston Railway with the L.B.R. at Shipley, by following roughly the route of the later East Lancashire line to Colne and then coming south through Airedale. The whole of the new line, surveyed by Charles Vignoles, was to be about 45 miles in length and would require a capital of £800,000. Needless to say this was seen as a threat to the L.B.R. and in July the company instructed Murgatroyd and Young to meet the provisional committee of the L.Y.J.R. to try to come to some arrangement. That month was a busy one. When it ended Martin had been told to get out a survey of the Shipley-Keighley extension; Young had completed staking out the main line from Leeds to Shipley; a Mr. Sharp had been engaged to plan the new station at Leeds; and Waddingham was in communication with the G.P.O. at Leeds to arrange an agreement for handling the mails at the station. The following month saw Thomas Gooch busy with two tasks; a new survey taking the extension on to Skipton, and preparation of a census of traffic likely to use the new line. Thomas Longridge Gooch was the elder brother of Daniel Gooch. Both had worked with Stephenson on the Manchester & Leeds and when, in 1837, Daniel had left to join the Great Western Railway, Thomas had joined the younger Stephenson's coterie.

Also in July, deputations from the Blackburn & Preston Railway, and from the town of Skipton, called on the board asking for an extension to be made through to Colne but were sent away disappointed, whereas one from Haworth got a promise that powers would be sought in the next session for a branch to that town. On August 28, Thompson & Forman's tender for 3,300 tons of rails was accepted, together with tenders from Losh, Wilson & Bell, and Kitson, Thompson & Hewitson, for the supply of chairs.

The passing of the L.B.R. Act of 1844 had had other strings attached besides the Aire Valley extension. The company had been authorised to go ahead with its own line only if it undertook to construct a railway to run south out of Bradford, from the terminus, to join the Manchester & Leeds Railway in the Calder Valley, passing through Halifax en route. This it now proposed to do by promoting a new company—the West Yorkshire Railway. In September 1844 the railway committee at Halifax approached the L.B.R. to find out if the company was indeed honouring its pledge and was told that the line was being surveyed by a Mr. Buck and that the Bill would be deposited in time for the session of 1845. By early November the West Yorkshire sub-committee of the L.B.R. had agreed as to the point of junction between the two railways at Bradford—somewhere near the proposed station at Dunkirk Street. There was to be considerable opposition, however. From the time of the opening of the North Midland Railway, the Manchester & Leeds had possessed running powers over that line into Leeds. Both railways had been planned by George Stephenson for the session of 1836; both were to follow identical routes from Normanton into Leeds. There was an argument of course, but the problem was successfully solved by permitting the N.M.R. to make the line, the M.L.R. to have rights of way thereover. In default of the N.M.R. carrying out the work, the M.L.R. was to be given the opportunity. No doubt grateful for small mercies, the N.M.R. did the job and dished the Lancastrians. From that time the M.L.R. had been on the prowl to get into the industrial West Riding in its own right. It was particularly anxious to get the wool traffic from Leeds to Bradford, and considered it its bounden duty to take it to Liverpool in conjunction with its colleagues further west, for shipment abroad, rather than let Mr. Hudson take it via Hull. In 1845, therefore, the M.L.R. was directly threatened by the proposed West Yorkshire scheme as to future West Riding traffic. Already edged out of Leeds, it saw itself within an ace of defeat. But, as has been seen, help was to hand. When the short line party threw in its lot with the M.L.R. its engineer, John Leather, who had previously been engaged in surveys for an independent line running south from Bradford via Halifax to the M.L.R. near Luddendenfoot, brought the plans with him. On joining these with the short line scheme, the M.L.R. was in a position to challenge effectively the West Yorkshire with an alternative line—the Leeds & West Riding Junction. Before continuing with the outcome of this struggle, an important development should be noted which was taking place to the north of the L.B.R. main line. For in September of 1844 that company's board had finally decided to extend its line through to Colne.

There were several reasons for this; the coming conflict with the M.L.R. for Lancashire traffic, the threat of the Lancashire & Yorkshire Junction and, finally, the ready made connection soon to exist at Colne, through to Lancashire, where the extension would join the terminus of the proposed East Lancashire Railway. This latter was an amalgama· tion of the Manchester Bury & Rossendale and the Blackburn & Preston companies, both authorised in 1844. In particular, it was the sudden possibility of the new through Lancashire route, via its extension line, that determined the L.B.R. to construct the additional $11\frac{1}{4}$ miles from Skipton to Colne, thus enabling it to rival the existing M.L.R. route. November of 1844 saw agreement with the Lancashire & Yorkshire Junction, for in face of the L.B.R.'s determination to reach Colne, the L.Y.J. agreed to accept £250 towards defrayment of expenses and then gracefully withdrew. Meanwhile another agreement had been made— this time with the provisional committee of the Leeds & Dewsbury—as to station accommodation, and the junction between it and the L.B.R., at Leeds. Similarly, the committee of the proposed Leeds & Thirsk line had also been approached in an effort to agree on a future junction at Leeds. The year ended with the payment of £2,000 to Stephenson for his services so far, and the sum of £25 to the Midland for the use of their offices at Hunslet for the board's meetings.

The year 1845 started well. In January the company let four contracts for making the main line. The Armley contract was let to James Crawshaw at £66,351; the Calverley to Tredwell's at £73,818; Thackley to Nowell & Hattersley at £68,000; and Shipley to James Bray at £34,329. The board had decided to complete the work by May 30, 1846, instead of the following September 30, as originally arranged, and to spur on the contractors additional payments of £1,000 and £2,000 were authorised to Tredwell's and Nowell & Hattersley respectively. In March William Clarke was replaced as secretary by William Edward Greenland, the latter being installed in an office in Park Row, Leeds, at a salary of £150 per annum. By April three of the contractors were in trouble with Hudson. Nowell & Hattersley had been using the truck system for their workmen and Hudson met Hattersley on Derby station, having called him there for a carpeting. As soon as the unfortunate man arrived he was told that truck payments must cease forthwith and, furthermore, that he must reside at Thackley to keep an eye on the works, with the progress of which Hudson was not impressed. Next it was the turn of Tredwell's and James Crawshaw. Doubtless impressed by the urgency of getting the works finished by May they had been carrying on Sunday working. A scandalised board ordered them to stop it forthwith. The works throughout were fairly heavy; deep rock cuttings at Armley and Horsforth, a ten-arch viaduct 40 feet high at Apperley —which was to give trouble later—and Thackley tunnel, $\frac{3}{4}$ mile in length, the greatest depth reached being 250 feet. In addition there were six large bridges over the River Aire, four over the Leeds & Liverpool Canal and many over and under roads. All were executed in plain style, doubtless due to the company's demand for a speedy completion.

Activity at Westminster over the extension line Bill had been in progress during the early part of the year. Thomas Gooch appeared before the Commons committee in May to give an un-opposed evidence on the engineering aspects and the Bill received the Royal Assent on June 30, 1845. In the indecent haste of the time the company omitted to say in its Act where the books of reference to the plans of the new line were to be deposited, and a further Act of August 4 in the same session was required to put matters right. The extension Act included powers to make the branch to Haworth. The following August 6 £500,000 of shares were created for the extension line and, just to even things up, £200 was voted by the half-yearly meeting to be put at the directors' disposal to promote the moral and religious welfare of the workers on the line. The further history of the extension line to Colne is told in the next chapter.

At the summer half-yearly meeting of 1845 the shareholders were congratulated by Hudson on the successful backing of the West York-shire scheme against the L.W.R.J. Though in the Parliamentary cam-paign the W.Y.R. had gone down, it had dragged the M.L.R.'s protégé with it. The meeting also learned that the directors were busy with a survey for a line to join the Leeds & Thirsk near Castley. Hudson let it be known that if such a new line—about 20 miles in length—was worth making he considered an established company more suited to do the job than a new one. This was a smack at a new company then preparing to go to Parliament in the next session—the Lancashire & Yorkshire (North Eastern)—which did in fact get powers in 1846, as the Wharfdale Railway (sic), for a Skipton-Castley line, only to peter out in the 1850s. The meeting went on to discuss the £200 voted for religious instruction. It seemed that the workmen had already been subject to interruptions from two 'visitors' who regularly perambulated the workings and had been recommended to Hudson by a Dr. Hook. Hudson must have con-sidered that concern over other people's moral welfare exonerated his own behaviour. It was at this time that he was buying privately many thousand tons of iron rails from Thompson & Forman. In 1845 the price was low; according to *Herepath's Journal* it was later to be artificially raised by bogus demand so that Hudson and the firm, which was in on the deal, could sell the rails jointly, under the firm's name but at the current price, to one of Hudson's own companies, with the result that both Hudson and the firm pocketed big fat cheques at the expense of the railway.

With the L.W.R.J. line a non-starter the Manchester & Leeds, deter-mined to get into Leeds and Bradford by a direct line, casually offered the Leeds & Bradford an amalgamation. This was to be the beginning of the big let-down for Hudson, for from here on he seemed to lose some of his judgement, and events took on a dizzy unreality which must have left the Midland board in Derby wondering what their chairman was doing—or more likely, whose side he was on—for Hudson appeared to agree to the proposition. This bewildering *rapprochement* led to the rival subsidiaries—the West Yorkshire and its sparring partner—pooling their resources to unite as the West Riding Union Railways, strongly backed by the M.L.R. and tacitly approved by the Leeds & Bradford. The new company was to go to Parliament in 1846. The L.B.R. offered the W.R.U. a junction at Bradford and to settle this point Stephenson met John Hawkshaw, the M.L.R. engineer. If their discussion bore any fruit it was doomed before it could be put into practice, for the amalgamation was to founder shortly afterwards.

Leaving the foreign policy and getting back to domestic matters, it had been decided in September to alter the proposed line into Wharfedale to serve Rawdon en route. October came and with it a salary rise for the secretary—£200 per annum, backdated to August 17, The town of Idle came into the board's discussions at this time when a deputation from the neighbourhood asked for a station on the main line. They were told that no decision could be made at that time but were offered a sop of £10, handed over to the Rev. E. M. Hall, for religious instruction of the workpeople on the line. The main line works had been advancing steadily; nearly half of the earthworks were completed, and over a third of Thackley tunnel. This augured well for the desired opening date of May, 1846. A deputation from a proposed railway company, with what must have been one of the longest sounding titles, arrived in front of the board on October 22. It came from the provisional committee of the Manchester Hebden Bridge & Keighley & Leeds & Carlisle Junction Railway. Both this and a similar party from a proposed Halifax & Keighley company wanted to know if the L.B.R. intended to oppose them. It did not, and in any event probably knew that such bubbles would burst of their own accord. As to the line into Wharfedale, the board decided to stop the survey at Addingham. At the other end of the line Young had already come to a tentative arrangement with the Leeds & Thirsk for a junction near Pool.

On November 20, 1845, representatives of the Leeds & Bradford, and the Manchester & Leeds, met in London to conclude an agreement as to the terms of the amalgamation. The capital of the L.B.R. was to be merged in the M.L.R.; the Midland was to be allowed to work its through trains into Bradford but not so as to take a profit from the L.B.R. line; and the station at Leeds was to be the joint property of the M.L.R., the Midland, and the York & North Midland companies. In early December the news of this agreement was worrying the East Lancashire Railway, which had got powers a few months before for the line to Colne, joining the L.B.R. extension. The East Lancashire was not on good terms with the M.L.R.—offering as it did the possible competitive line from Yorkshire into Lancashire—and the company had been anticipating L.B.R. traffic working over its extension line. Now, suddenly, it found that the arch enemy would shortly be banging on the back door. Not mincing its words the E.L.R. board chided the L.B.R. but received the reply that as it had not consulted the Leeds company about the Liverpool Ormskirk & Preston's incorporation it could expect similar treatment in return. The E.L.R. was not beaten yet, however. As will be seen it had already dreamed up an extension into Wharfedale, hoping thus to avoid the M.L.R. altogether.

The first public announcement of the intending amalgamation came out in the L.B.R.'s half-yearly meeting in December—an event which must have been awaited with some apprehension by the Midland board at Derby. At the meeting Hudson said that he considered it disastrous to continue with the Leeds & Bradford as a separate entity, up against bigger companies. To ally with the Midland would only alienate the M.L.R. and the only solution was to amalgamate with the latter. He said that the L.B.R. would be applying in the 1846 session for the junction line, and also for the extension lines to Yeadon, Guiseley, and Otley, and along the Wharfe Valley. What the Midland board thought of all this can only be guessed. Amalgamation of the L.B.R. with the M.L.R. was all the more heinous in that the latter was friendly with the London & York, a concern to be successful in the 1846 session as the Great Northern Railway, a potential rival, and the source of many a future Midland headache. On the same day as the agreement the L.B.R. decided to call on the £500,000 additional capital required for the Colne extension.

In February, 1846, the L.B.R. gave an order for rolling stock to W. Hamer, of Leicester. This was for four first class carriages at £350 each, two composites at £300 each, ten second class coaches, with brakes, at £280 each, twelve third class at £165 each, sixty low-sided goods wagons at £68 each, and four brake and parcel vans at £180 each. In February Stephenson's delivered some of the company's locomotives to Cabrey at York. Both Cabrey and the firm were asked to forward these, and any to follow, to the M.L.R. to whom they were to be let pending the opening of the L.B.R. The weather during the early part of the year was bad; January was very wet and the works were considerably delayed, especially those at Thackley tunnel and the Leeds and Bradford stations. In March fifty additional men were put on each of the Armley and Horsforth cuttings in an effort to keep to schedule. They apparently had little effect as in the following month Crawshaw was to be reprimanded for the slowness of the work. At about the same time two of the Stephenson engines were let to the M.L.R., and three to the Midland, at £7 each per week. In April Edmundson's ticket machines were ordered for the stations, together with another fifty wagons, at £76 each, from Smith & Dagley of Derby. By May the extensions into the Wharfe Valley had been dropped, the company deciding to restrict the Bills in the 1846 session to three; the junction line at Bradford, the amalgamation with the M.L.R., and an alteration of the levels at Bingley. The L.B.R. board now got down to the business of appointing staff. The wages offered were good for the times; porters got 17s. weekly, guards 21s. to 24s., and the station masters at Leeds and Bradford £100 per annum. (A list of the staff at the time the main line was opened will be found in Appendix I.) Also at this time signals were ordered from Stevens & Sons. On June 16 invitations were sent out to the special guests who were to attend the opening of the line. The list was voluminous and included the principal engineering staff and the contractors; all the directors of the M.R., Y.N.M.R., M.L.R., the acting West Riding Magistrates, the West Riding Union Railway committee, the Leeds Borough Magistrates, the directors of the North Western Railway, with which the company made a connection at Skipton, and the Leeds Town Council.

Before this event took place, however, the whole situation of the company had altered, for the amalgamation with the M.L.R. was off. In the original agreement the L.B.R. had supposed that when the time came its shareholders would be permitted to participate in future M.L.R. capital, and the Bill as drawn had read to that effect. The M.L.R., thinking no doubt that it had the L.B.R. in the bag, had since added a clause which expressly excluded this from happening, the effect being that the amalgamation would to all intents and purposes become a purchase. For five months the L.B.R. had tried to get the M.L.R. to see that this would not do, but the latter had let the matter stew. Houldsworth, the chairman of the M.L.R., had appointed a referee, Mr. Gill, to thrash the question out with Waddingham of the L.B.R., but to no effect. Two days before the Commons committee was to sit on the Bill Houldsworth suggested a conference. He had left it too late. Just beforehand the M.L.R. had asked the L.B.R. for an agreement to secure it a joint interest in the L.B.R. station at Leeds if the amalgamation Bill should not go through. This piece of cheek was refused point blank by the Leeds company, apparently causing considerable offence to the M.L.R. which replied that it might now have to throw in its lot with the rival Leeds Central Station project. An impasse having been reached, Waddingham wrote to Houldsworth on June 17 informing him that he had given instructions to withdraw the Bill. A letter from Houldsworth the next day accused the L.B.R. of a breach of faith and asked for an immediate meeting. It drew the following reply:

12 Abingdon Street,
18th June, 1846

Dear Sir,

I have just received your letter of this morning and have read it with feelings of astonishment—After telling me, yesterday, that to give way on the matter in dispute would break your Board;—after saying—in the presence of several gentlemen, in Mr. Darbyshire's room, that if a sixpence would turn the scale, it would not be given;—after Mr. Gill had told me, that the amalgamation was either 'off or on' unless I submitted etc;—I could not for a moment expect to be charged with breach of faith for not proposing a reference.

Had you proposed this at an earlier stage, instead of so peremptorily giving us the decision of your Board, we might, perhaps, have acceded to it; but now, we must respectfully decline the proposal.

I am, Dear Sir, &c.
John Waddingham

56

There was only one way out; on June 30, 1846, the company agreed to offer its line to the Midland Railway. To the Manchester company Hudson's name was now mud. It proceeded to do all it could to discredit the L.B.R. but the latter replied in July by arranging an exhibition of documents, proving the guilt of the M.L.R., at the temporary Wellington station at Leeds. The L.B.R., guided by Hudson, now approached the Midland to ask it to lease the line and Hudson rushed to Derby to take his place on the Midland board. This was ill advised, for at the Midland meeting of July 25, when he supported the lease proposal, he was roughly used. The fact he had played no small part in the amalgamation negotiations with the M.L.R., and was chairman of both the L.B.R., and the M.R., brought cries of 'You are buyer and seller too.' Losing his temper he shouted that the trouble makers were members of the Liverpool party—members of the same blood brotherhood as the M.L.R. He was undoubtedly correct in this assumption but the charge reduced the proceedings to a slanging match. With the meeting in an uproar it was John Ellis who steered it back to the lease. He used a potent argument—the threat of the Great Northern. If Derby did not want the L.B.R. perhaps Kings Cross would. The Great Northern had already tried to include in its authorising Act powers for a Doncaster-Leeds line but that portion of the Bill had failed to get approval. It would undoubtedly try again. The point went home. The shareholders voted to take a lease of the L.B.R., from August 26, 1846, the terms being 999 years at a rent of £90,000, this being 10 per cent. of the L.B.R.'s share capital. It meant in effect that the Midland would shortly be as far north as Skipton.

Meanwhile the main line had been opened in three stages. First came the contractor's opening on May 30, 1846. A special train left the temporary station at Leeds just before 1 p.m. Hauled by the engine *Linsay* and composed of about a dozen open carriages, and one closed for the ladies in the party, the train carried two musical bands aboard. On the front of the engine, which was laden with flowers, were two flags, one of which bore the inscription 'Who'd have thought it.' As this was a Hudson line and the amalgamation proposals with the M.L.R. were at the time in full swing, the Midland fraternity at the opening might have been forgiven for reading a double meaning into the legend. Though things started with a swing the proceedings in the open carriages at least were temporarily dampened by the considerable dripping of water from the roof of Thackley tunnel. Matters got worse at Bradford where the train, contrary to usual practice, was received in stony silence. These were times of severe distress in the manufacturing towns of the north and not even the arrival of the railway alleviated the gloom then prevalent in the town. The train returned to Leeds hauled by the engine *Stephenson*. It stopped at Apperley to inspect the viaduct, and presumably to dry out after the return through the tunnel. At Kirkstall Forge cannon fire hailed the travellers on their passing. Another train, filled

57

with the workmen on the line, and hauled by the *Malton* closely followed
the first throughout the journey. At Leeds the whole party trooped into
the 'White Horse,' for a dinner presided over by George Goodman, one
of the directors.

Following an inspection a few days before by Major-General Pasley
of the Board of Trade, the formal opening took place on Tuesday,
June 30. Trains arrived at Leeds from the Midland and the York &
North Midland lines and just after noon the guests left Leeds in a train
of some fifteen coaches. Shortly after another train left with all the
notables including the Lord Mayor of York, the Mayor of Leeds, the
board of the L.B.R., and, of course, George Hudson. The journey took
about 45 minutes and on arrival at Bradford where, in contrast to the
previous occasion, a general holiday had been declared, the whole party
detrained for a glorious binge in a specially erected pavilion facing the
station. At about 2.25 p.m. the train left for Leeds, arriving precisely at 3
p.m., where again the party betook itself of yet more eats and speeches, the
Music Hall being the venue for this occasion. Hudson's Leeds speech
is of some interest in that he remarked that whilst ordinary trains
rarely travelled above 35 miles per hour, speeds by some trains had now
reached 55 miles per hour. He quoted a cutting from the *Times* of
December 19, 1806, which he thought should be pasted up on all railway
stations. It went as follows :

'Awful Pace—The first division of the troops that are to proceed by Paddington
Canal for Liverpool, and thence by transports for Dublin, will leave Paddington
today, and will be followed by others tomorrow, and on Sunday. By this mode of
conveyance the men will be *only* seven days in reaching Liverpool, and with comparatively little fatigue, and it would take them above fourteen days to march that
distance. Relays of fresh horses for the canal boats have been ordered to be in
readiness at all the stations.'

He was, of course, giving the assembled company an early variation of
'You've never had it so good.'

On Wednesday, July 1, 1846 the line was opened for public traffic.
The first service—operated from 5 a.m. to 10 p.m. and with a journey
time of some 35 minutes—was run non-stop between the two towns as
there were no intermediate stations yet open. The company had recalled
its locomotives let out, and ordered two more from Stephenson's, the
board having agreed that it would be impossible to work the line with
less than six. It also ordered some more carriages. From the date of
public opening the Midland ceased using the Hunslet Lane terminus at
Leeds, taking the L.B.R. extension line from the N.M.R. into Wellington
station; Hunslet Lane was henceforth to be used for freight only. As
to goods traffic over the L.B.R., this started in September 1846.

The Midland had now arrived in Bradford and through services from
the town to Euston via the former N.M.R. and Midland Counties line
started at the same time. The L.B.R. had its first fatal accident barely
two months after the opening; John Johnstone, 33 years of age and an

employee of the company, was run over by the whole length of one of the morning trains from Leeds to Bradford near Kirkstall Forge. He was walking the line and took no notice of repeated whistles. People frequently behaved in a peculiar fashion in the early days of the railway age, running along the tops of the carriages, leaping off at speed to retrieve hats, and other similar stupidities, which can only be attributed to a lack of appreciation of the speeds ushered in by the new mode of travel. But poor Johnstone happened to be on a particularly bad acoustical stretch of the line : as the train curved through Kirkstall Forge and approached the bridge over the canal, the engine's whistles could easily have been swept away by the wind or muffled by the embankments. Another accident occurred 27 days later, this time near Kirkstall Abbey. The engine and tender of the 3 o'clock Leeds train jumped the rails approaching another bridge over the canal. Luckily the coupling between the tender and the carriages parted and though the driver and firemen were injured no passengers were hurt, though the carriages, which were quite crowded, suffered some damage. It is possible that this accident was in fact caused by faulty permanent way for on September 9 the board told Young to get all the men possible from the Armley, Calverley and Shipley contracts on to getting the way into a proper state of repair. The portion between Leeds and Thackley tunnel was entirely relaid at this time by David Duncan of Leeds. Duncan, by the way, was another contemporary of the Stephensons at Killingworth Colliery where he was employed as a boy; he was destined to become a permanent way engineer of some note. Each 15 ft. rail was supported on four intermediate chairs, and Duncan was ordered to supply an additional chair to each rail length and replace the existing joint sleepers with wider ones. In November a report was sent to Hudson that many of Thompson & Forman's rails were defective—this was to have unpleasant personal repercussions for him later when his deal with the firm leaked out : Waddingham had noted with surprise, in 1845, that Hudson had suddenly ordered 2,000 tons of rails additional to requirements but at that time nobody was asking questions. At the same time the remaining portion from Thackley to Shipley was relaid by George Lewin who also took over the Thackley-Leeds length from Duncan. Lewin continued the work until June 23, 1847, when James S. Taylor took over the maintenance of the whole of the permanent way. Lastly, Young and Taylor handed over all the works to the resident engineer, W. H. Barlow, in August of 1849, the whole of the L.B.R. and its extension by then being open. The cutting at Armley was also giving considerable trouble—so much so that from November 1846 the line was closed at this point. Crawshaw got into hot water for this, the company threatening action if the line was not quickly reopened. At the height of the trouble he had 347 men at work, night and day. On December 2, the board made a personal inspection and in desperation ordered Young to take charge. Under his supervision the line was re-opened early in the following

January. Though Crawshaw's work was finished his bill was not agreed by the company—the difference being some £23,000—and it took a touchy legal argument lasting until June 1848 before it was finally settled, more or less in Crawshaw's favour.

An extract from a letter from the company to the Board of Trade, giving details of its Parliamentary trains, and dated September 2, 1846, tells of the contemporary train services:

'—by the trains leaving Leeds—and Bradford at 5 a.m. and 10 p.m. on week-days, and at 7 a.m. and 8.30 p.m. on Sundays (being the first train each way every morning and the last train each way every night) passengers are booked at the charge of one penny per mile in Midland second class carriages. These trains run the whole distance between Leeds and Bradford (14 miles) in 45 minutes and call at all the road-side stations. They are fixed so as to correspond with the Parliamentary trains from Leeds to London. There are eighteen third class trains each way per day by which the fare is considerably less than a penny per mile. On Sundays the fare is the same but the third class trains are five each way.'

As has been seen, the intermediate stations were not in use at the time of the opening of the line, the first trains all running express. Within two months, however, temporary wooden platforms of the island type had been erected at Kirkstall, Newlay, Calverley, and Shipley. In December Brayshaw & Shaw's tender for a permanent station with outside platforms at Apperley Bridge was accepted—the price being £2,809. By February, 1847, the company was replacing the other stations with similar structures. The following July the board agreed, after a lengthy campaign by the local inhabitants, to provide a temporary passenger station at the west end of Thackley tunnel, to serve the town of Idle.

As to the termini, only that at Leeds concerns this story. For the opening there was only a single platform. As late as February of 1846 Young had reported to the L.B.R. board that work at Leeds had been held up because of difficulty in getting possession of the land. The wet weather in the early part of the year had not helped by hindering work on the river bridge forming part of the station. The following April land was still being purchased but by July construction had started. On February 17, 1847, W. C. Boothman was let the contract for the permanent passenger station at a price of £9,250, the work to incorporate the existing platform. At the same time the iron work at the station was let to the Ireland & Longdin Iron Foundry for £8,460. In both contracts the board reserved the right to extend the works and either to re-let them or compel the contractors to continue on the same terms. As planned at the time the passenger shed was to be 500 feet long and 180 feet wide, constructed on arches over the River Aire. A year later additional iron-work was let to Robert Croslands of Bradford at £3,000, and additional masonry to George Thompson at £13,300; some of the stone used, to be got from Armley Cutting. In June 1848 Boothman agreed to construct the booking offices for £5,500. With the station nearly complete the refreshment rooms were let in July 1849 to a Mr. Pollard at a rent of £1 per week 'provided he sells no excisable articles'. As to the engine shed, this was let to Woodhead & Co. of Leeds in October 1846 for £7,134 and was completed by February 1848 in which month the tender for offices to the shed, required by Kirtley, was let.

By the beginning of 1847 a regular pattern of train services, slightly different to that quoted above, was operating over the L.B.R. Both from Leeds and Bradford trains left hourly from 6 a.m. to 9.30 p.m. during the weekdays. On Sundays there were five trains each way : at 8.30 and 9.30 a.m., and 2, 6 and 8.30 p.m. stopping at all stations. The weekday trains, except those at 10 a.m. and 2 p.m., which were express, stopped at Kirkstall, Calverley, Apperley and Shipley. Newlay station was served by alternate stopping trains from 7 a.m. onwards. The daily Parliamentary trains were the first out of Bradford and the last out of Leeds.

At Leeds trains from the L.B.R. connected with the Midland service which consisted of ten trains daily, eight of which ran between Leeds and Euston. The fastest of these—first class only—ran non-stop between Rugby and Normanton, the down train leaving Euston at 9.25 a.m., Rugby at 11.45 a.m., Normanton at 2.50 p.m., and arriving at Leeds at 3.15 p.m. to catch the 4 p.m. stopping train to Bradford. The slowest Midland train was the Parliamentary which left Euston at 7 a.m., arriving at Rugby at 1.40 p.m., and then stopped at all stations to Leeds where it arrived at 9 p.m. The fastest up train—again first class only—left Leeds at 2.50 p.m., Normanton at 3.20 p.m., Rugby at 6.40 p.m., and arrived at Euston at 9.10 p.m. The up Parliamentary left Leeds at 6 a.m., arriving at London at 7 p.m. There was also an additional train from Derby and one from Rugby. As to the up trains the 10.20 a.m. from Leeds terminated at Derby, where it made connection at 1.40 p.m. with the 11 a.m. from Normanton. The 4 p.m. from Leeds stopped at all stations except Spondon and terminated at Rugby. Finally, on Sundays there were only four trains into and out of Leeds, one terminating at, and two starting from Rugby.

Though the Midland had now taken over the working of the L.B.R., the lease should be viewed against the prevailing background. As in most parts of the country, and perhaps more because of its potential, the West Riding and the country to the north was subjected to many freak railway schemes, none more than at the time of the 'Railway Mania' of 1846. Some of these made only brief appearances and, for want of backing and allies in the intense competition of the 1846 session, quickly succumbed. One such had the grand and impossible title of Huddersfield & East & West Coasts Railway—though it was to be only a short line. Others were entirely spurious. A letter to the *Railway Times* of April 4, 1846 from a correspondent who delighted in the name of 'Hawk-Eye' complained that he was being chased by the Leeds Huddersfield Sheffield & South Staffordshire Railway company for some money on shares he had applied for the previous September. At that time the company had informed him that as there was an unprecedented demand for stock the shares would only be allotted to local parties along the route. Three months had passed and now he had been offered the full allotment originally requested plus a call on the deposit. 'Hawk-Eye' himself must have smelled a rat and gone to ground after this as no more was heard of him. The following June, however, the company had the sauce to put an advert in the *Railway Times* to all reluctant subscribers threatening legal action if they didn't pay up. The paper pictured the company as being one man, waiting in vain every day for the postman to arrive with the amounts due. In desperation he drafts the advertisement, gives it to a solicitor, and gets it published. Hope rises—he spends the money in advance on a wild extravagant evening out on the town. And in the morning—still no postman.

Of the projected lines in the 1846 session some could have clipped the Midland's wings if they had ever really started moving. Though the company was not at that time interested in Scottish traffic as such, there were a number of proposals concerning lines to the north, or connecting lines in the district to others already pointing north. Most of these relied on reaching some point on the Lancaster & Carlisle line, from where easy access to Scotland seemed assured, at a price. These schemes must wait their turn until the story reaches the Midland interest in one of the most successful of them—the North Western Railway, but some of the more interesting of the West Riding ones, in L.B.R. territory, provide the reason for the Midland lease of the smaller company at what was generally agreed then to be an exorbitant figure.

First and foremost was the threat of the Great Northern. That company had got powers in 1846 but not before several rivals had been booted aside in the process, all of which would have made the Midland's London traffic look silly. One of these was the Great Leeds & London Direct Railway, an affair boasting an extremely 'top drawer' and lengthy provisional committee list including Lords Dunboyne and Chichester; five Baronets; Captain Polhill, the M.P. for Bedford; Major General Sir Robert Barton, director of the York & Lancaster Railway; and directors of various other lines including the Liverpool & Leeds Direct, the Leeds & Carlisle, the West Yorkshire, the Liverpool & Newcastle, etc. The line was to leave the M.L.R. and Y.N.M.R. near Wakefield and terminate by a junction with an intended branch of the Eastern Counties Railway at Bedford. Despite the fact that at one time it reported it had 60 surveyors working on each mile of the line—a phenomenal number— the company failed to deposit a bill for the session of 1846 and quietly disappeared. Throughout the story of the Midland's piecemeal progress from Leeds to Carlisle, however, there appears at various stages an opposition—an anti-establishment railway party—that was prepared to plan the most outrageous lines cutting through every existing railway interest. A whole group of them appear later in the country north of Skipton. They worried and exasperated existing companies for some years before finally becoming bankrupt of money and ideas. But a thread common to all runs through them—they were all quite powerful nonstarters. Most of them never got beyond the stage of provisional registration. One such was the Birmingham Carlisle Leeds & Newcastle-upon-Tyne Direct Railway which planned a line out of Leeds to the north. It was to connect at Wath with the Leeds & Thirsk, authorised in 1845 : at Richmond with the Leeds & Carlisle, and at Bishop Auckland with both the Bishop Auckland & Weardale, and the Newcastle Durham & Lancashire. There was also to be a branch from Wath direct to Burton Salmon, joining at its mid point, near Wetherby, the Y.N.M.R.'s Leeds and York, and Harrogate and Church Fenton lines. The Birmingham part merely came into the title by virtue of the running powers the new company was going to claim over the Midland.

The failure of the Great Northern Railway to get included in its Act powers for a Doncaster-Leeds line sparked off a series of ventures in the countryside between. The Midland, which had a rather round-about route, avoiding Wakefield, diligently opposed all comers in the area whilst promoting its own line in lieu. One of these concerns thrown out in the session of 1846 was the Doncaster Wakefield & Bradford Railway which sought powers to make a line from Doncaster to join the Midland at Oakenshaw. In 1846 the Leeds Dewsbury & Manchester Railway was busy promoting a line from Churwell to Wakefield, there to join the Manchester & Leeds, and several of the new proposals of the 1846 session ended by a junction with the L.D.M. line. Another scheme which lasted just over a year was the Bradford Wakefield & Midland Railway. From the M.R. at Oakenshaw, and the M.L.R. at Wakefield, it was to run along the Wrenthorpe Valley to Churwell where it was to join the L.D.M. From there it was to take off for Laisterdyke (then Leicester Dyke), under which it proposed burrowing for a distance of 2,350 yards, towards Bradford which it was to enter over the metals of the L.B.R., interfering with the Junction Line. The B.W.M. wound itself up in July 1846, just in time to make way for one of Hudson's own schemes—the Leeds Wakefield & Midland Junction. This had been an independent line which had failed to secure Parliamentary powers in July 1846. When the Great Northern had been thwarted in its 1846 attempt on Leeds it had seemed that the Midland's province was safe. The London company, however, saw an opportunity to get at least part way to Leeds over the line of the Wakefield Pontefract & Goole Railway's Askern and Methley branches, authorised the same session, which would take it from Doncaster via Knottingley to Methley on the North Midland. It only required the promotion of a short connecting line from there to Leeds to make a grand entry into the West Riding. Accordingly a Bill was deposited, closely followed by a re-hashed deposit from the Leeds Dewsbury & Manchester of its 1846 line plus an additional line from Lofthouse to Methley. By now Hudson was alarmed. In September 1846 the unsuccessful Leeds Wakefield & Midland put itself up for sale to the highest bidder and the following December Hudson offered to guarantee the company to the amount of £10,000 if it would make another attempt in the session of 1847. Its route was to be from Leeds to the W.P. & G. at Wakefield, and the company was to seek powers to lease or sell to the Midland. In return Hudson arranged that if successful the Midland would work the line at a minimum guaranteed 4 per cent. By May 1847 all was over. The three Bills had foundered, but not before the Commons committee had said that the G.N.R. line would have been best anyway; it had been thrown out on a technicality. That was enough for Hudson. The G.N.R. had by then arranged to run over the W.P. & G. (shortly to become part of the Lancashire & Yorkshire Railway). If the Great Northern went for powers again it would no doubt succeed and from the Midland's point of view it was best to have some control. In October 1847 Hudson agreed to give Kings Cross running powers over the Midland into Leeds. This was not to come about for another two years, and when it did it brought trouble. From then on the Great Northern was to be in the background as one of the opponents of the Midland in its attempts to get north of Leeds, appearing at the most odd places and times, well north of its usual habitat.

Returning to some of the smaller companies which were unsuccessful in the area perhaps one of the most unlucky was the Midland & Thirsk which put all its money into the Leeds & West Riding Banking company. Shortly afterwards, in 1846, the Bank was unable to meet its obligations, and the railway succumbed. Another company which saw itself as part of the main London to Carlisle line was the Huddersfield & Western Union. This proposed making a line from Huddersfield, on the Huddersfield & Sheffield Junction, to Keighley on the Leeds & Bradford Extension. From there its route to the north would be over the North Western Railway and the Lancaster & Carlisle. The company was provisionally registered in April 1845, prior to the amalgamation agreement between the Leeds & Bradford and the Manchester & Leeds. It never got off the ground. A railway backed by the Manchester & Leeds in 1845 was the Wakefield & Harrogate Junction. This was to run fom Wakefield, where it left the M.L.R., and proceed north via Stanley, Lofthouse, Rothwell Haigh, Temple Newsam, Seacroft and Thorner, and then between Bramham and Collingham, to Wetherby where it was to join the Y.N.M.R.'s Harrogate and Church Fenton line.

The 'Railway Mania' in the West Riding was a real 'free for all' with plots and counter plots flying thick and fast. Any of them might have come to fruition, but luckily for the Midland it was able to enter 1847 with the Leeds & Bradford secure in its hands. The climb-down over the Great Northern was yet to come. The main thing was that it had now reached Bradford, and the works on the extension to Skipton and Colne were going ahead. Though the company would not then have acknowledged such a proposition, it had, willy nilly, taken the first step on the road to Scotland.

IV

Approach to the Dales

The Leeds and Bradford Extension

After the passing of the Act in 1845 for the extension to Colne, the board of the Leeds & Bradford Railway immediately set about letting the first contract. The line was to be some 15¾ miles in length from Shipley to Skipton, and 11¼ from there on to Colne. Rather naturally the company decided to deal first with the southern end of the line, and the Bingley contract for the works between Shipley and Keighley was let on October 15, 1845 to Thompson's of Salter Hebble at £73,711; Thompson was told at the time of letting that the land would not be available until the following February. Gooch, busy in mid-February with preparations for the contract on the Colne line, had to remind the board that the lands on the Bingley contract were even then still not wholly in the company's possession, and pointed out that with summer coming Thompson should be under way. The land was not the only difficulty—the levels on the contract were considered to be bad, and it was not until the company obtained an Act on July 27, 1846, to alter them that work was able to start.

A few days later came the not unexpected decease of a small company which might have rendered a large part of the northern portion of the L.B.R. extension useless for through traffic to the East Lancashire Railway. It may be recalled that in December 1845 the East Lancashire had upbraided the L.B.R. over its proposed deal with the M.L.R. only to get a rude reply. The previous September it had allowed for such an occurrence by promoting the East Lancashire & Airedale Railway which planned a line from Colne to Steeton, on the L.B.R. Leather & Sons were the engineers and almost before the L.B.R. had got its breath the new company stated that after talks with the Leeds & Thirsk Railway it intended to press on to Wharfedale to join the line of the proposed Lancashire & Yorkshire (North Eastern) Railway. This latter company emerged from the battleground of the 1846 session with the new and incorrectly spelled title of 'Wharfdale' Railway with, as has already been recounted, plans for a line from Skipton to join the L.T.R. near Castley. The East Lancashire link line was not successful. As a proposed atmospheric railway it did not take to the air, meeting to evaporate itself on August 8, 1846.

The next month saw trouble on the Bingley contract. For some 350 yards of the line the ground was found to be swampy. The earthworks already made sunk into the ground leaving an artificial lake in their place.

For some time Thompson and the company feared that the route of the line would have to be deviated to the nearby hillside following the course of the Leeds & Liverpool Canal. The marshy ground, then known locally as 'Bingley Bog', extended to a depth of some 30 feet and, after attempting the use of brushwood hurdles, as had been successful on the Liverpool & Manchester Railway, Thompson finally solved the problem by making an embankment of some one million cubic yards of gravel, brought from the side cuttings along the line. The other works on the contract included the removal of 150,000 cubic yards of rock and earth near Shipley station, a cutting at Hirst Wood from which about 70,000 cubic yards were dug, and a tunnel at Bingley of 200 yards lengths, later shortened to 151 yards. On September 9 the Skipton contract, for works from Bingley to that town, was let to Tredwell's for £100,000. On the same day G. Boulton & Co. were let the Thornton contract for completing the line on to Colne at a price of £67,000.

The company's confident anticipation that the line would be open throughout to Colne by the end of 1847, had received a setback with the difficulties at Bingley and in November Thompson was offered £1,740 if he was able to complete his contract to time. Mid-way through the following month the contracts for building the stations at Bingley and Keighley were given to Sugden & Clarke, and Sudgen & Simpson, respectively, each at a cost of about £2,860. The same contractors were also given the job of constructing five level crossing cottages along the line. Until the stations were ready the company arranged to have temporary wooden structures erected in a similar manner to those about to be removed from the main line and in all probability these were, in fact, used for the purpose.

On February 9, 1847, Gooch reported to the board that though works on the extension line were well advanced they would not be ready for March 1, as had been hoped, because they had been delayed by heavy frosts. A good piece of news was that Bingley Bog had at last been conquered, though he thought that reduced speeds should be used over it until he was sure it was firm. Gooch went on to recommend that the board should advertise tenders for booking offices at Cross Hills, Skipton and Colne stations. He believed that the type of wooden station then being erected at Bingley and Keighley, would do very well for Steeton, Thornton and Foulridge—'as I think we shall find it desirable to try these points as stations before finally fixing them.' The contracts for stations at Skipton and Kildwick were let in May to Sugden, Simpson & Clarke, and Sugden, Simpson & Wade respectively, that at Skipton to cost £2,330.

By this time the line from Shipley to Keighley had been open nearly two months. An experimental trip was made on the afternoon of Monday, March 1, 1847. The train, of three carriages, drawn by the engine *Camilla*, had started from Leeds, and left Shipley at about 2.20 p.m. with a Bradford portion attached. The passengers included three of the directors, the engineers, and the contractor. As the *Camilla,* with two Union Jacks, and many olive branches, festooning the smoke box, entered the temporary station at Bingley—then near Park Road corner, not far from the present station—the people on the platform included a representative of the women navvies. To the cheers of the crowd one of the directors presented her with a coin. Some forty minutes after entering on the line the train reached the temporary station at Keighley —the other side of the road bridge to the present station. Here all the passengers alighted to inspect the permanent works under construction. After a dinner at the 'Devonshire Arms' with a dozen 36-gallon casks of ale, and bread and cheese, provided for the workmen outside by the contractor, the train returned to Leeds and Bradford.

On Saturday, March 13, Captain Simmons, of the Board of Trade,* accompanied by Murgatroyd and Thompson, as well as the engineers Gooch, Young and Grundy, inspected the line between Shipley and Keighley and pleased the company by announcing that he found the standard of construction highly satisfying. Three days later the line was opened for public use, and huge crowds from the surrounding districts poured into the valley for the occasion. The first service consisted of eight trains each way on weekdays, with three on Sundays.

During this time work was progressing between Keighley and Skipton. On Wednesday, September 1, the directors made the usual trial trip with a repeat performance of noisy and excited crowds and decorated stations, that at Skipton being some way south of the present one. Public traffic commenced exactly a week later. The company was, however, labouring under a difficulty—it was short of rails. On August 6, Young had reported that he was in urgent need of rails which in fact belonged to the company but were in the custody of the York & North Midland company. For some reason, despite frantic appeals from Waddingham, the Y.N.M. refused to part with them. One suspects that there was more to this than met the eye at the time—it is possible that Hudson's stockpile of Thompson & Forman's output had been exhausted. In any event the L.B.R. had to go without for the time being and the line to Skipton was opened as a single track. The board was more than usually concerned as this prevented it from taking freight and mineral traffic.

During September the company agreed with the East Lancashire Railway as to the details of the joint station at Colne. At the same time tenders were accepted from Sugden & Simpson, and Isaac Shaw, for the construction of stations at Cononley and Steeton respectively, at a price of about £900 each. On October 6 the Wharfdale Railway was slapped down for its presumption in asking for an agreement for its proposed junction with the L.B.R. at Skipton. It was told that as it hadn't even started thinking of any serious construction an agreement was quite premature. To mar the prevailing mood of optimism December brought a bad accident on the main line. On Monday, December 13, as the

* He rose to become Field Marshal Sir J. Lintorn A. Simmons.

67

2.00 p.m. Bradford to Leeds express was passing through Armley cutting, about a mile west of Leeds, one of the cranks on the engine snapped causing it to turn turtle and embed itself in the side of the cutting. The following coaches were strewn over the line and, though the driver and passengers escaped with slight injuries, the stoker—a married man named Charles Smith—was killed instantly. The year ended with Tredwell & Gow completing the double line of rails between Cononley and Skipton.

With the arrival of Midland trains in Skipton, doubts began to be entertained among the shareholders of the L.B.R. as to the good faith of both their own directors and those of the Midland company, regarding the opening of the remaining portion of the line on to Colne. By April, 1848, complaints were being voiced that the two were in league with each other—as indeed they were—to hold over the opening as long as possible. To be fair to the L.B.R. it should be said that the Y.N.M. was still obstinately holding some 1,000 tons of the company's rails. The main reason for the delay in completing to Colne, however, was tied up with the lease of the L.B.R. by which the Midland need not pay the 10 per cent. rent until the line was fully open. 'Engineer', writing in *Herepath's Journal* in late April, said that two years previously it had been anticipated that the 10 per cent. would shortly become payable. Since then the time for payment on the line had been put off till the opening to Colne. 'This opening, however, seems likely to be put off to the Grecian Kalends.' Indignation was whipped up by 'Scrutator', another anonymous L.B.R. shareholder, in the Journal's issue of May 20, where a letter he had written resulted in a meeting of the proprietors at the London Tavern the following August. One of the shareholders had walked the line to Colne just recently and he told the meeting that the works were ready for traffic but were being kept just short of final completion until the East Lancashire line was completely operative. That company would be taking traffic on to the Lancashire manufacturing areas, connecting with Liverpool and Manchester, but with the lease as an excuse for penny-pinching, the Midland saw no reason for opening the Colne line until the E.L.R. was ready.

During this time the East Lancashire had been steadily pushing ahead with its various lines. As well as tackling the L.B.R. over the amalgamation issue, it had also gone for the M.L.R. One outcome of the altercation with the latter company was the Clifton Junction affair, and the E.L.R. too found itself welcoming the coming of the L.B.R.'s extension to Colne so that it could be more than just verbally offensive to the Manchester company by challenging its traffic, albeit with a round-about route. During 1846, the post 'Mania' period brought with it a general lowering of the economy. Many companies were to wither away through lack of funds. Calls on shareholders were to be ignored. Labour was cheap due to unemployment; Leeds and Bradford in early 1847 were full of navvies thrown out of work by railway companies unable to continue construction. Whereas the L.B.R. had at least the backing of the Hudson camp, the E.L.R. was on its own and construction work was slow. On February 1, 1849 the long-awaited opening from Burnley to Colne took place. Previous openings of the company's eastern lines had been from Blackburn to Accrington on June 19, 1848, and Accrington to Burnley on the following September 18. It was not until the opening of the Liverpool Ormskirk & Preston line on April 2, 1849, however, that the through route from Leeds to Liverpool became a reality. Apparently the L.B.R. shareholders' meeting had some effect; after an inspection of the works by Captain Wynne of the Board of Trade, the opening of the Leeds company's line to Colne anticipated that of the E.L.R., services beginning on October 2, 1848. The previous August the two companies had agreed that each should work its own line to Colne and that the station should be provided with a small engine shed, capable of holding two locomotives. The Leeds company undertook to build this and a contract was let to W. Brayshaw at the end of the month at a price of just over £400. In October of 1849 the Midland traffic committee ordered that the passenger station at Shipley, on the main line and not now suitable for a junction, be transferred to serve its purpose at Elslack.

The details of the train services on the Colne line do not concern this story, but of the Midland's efforts at catering for the line as far as Skipton the following is of interest. *Bradshaw* of September, 1848, shows that seventeen trains on weekdays left Leeds for Bradford, seven of which either connected at Shipley, after a wait of some six minutes, with Bradford-Skipton trains, or ran straight through taking the Bradford trains on from Shipley. Arrival times at Skipton were 8.10 a.m. (a mail train running non-stop from Leeds to Apperley and taking 1 hr. 10 mins. for the journey), 10.50 a.m., 12.20 p.m., 2.20, 4.20, 6.20, and 9.50 p.m., this latter being the Parliamentary. Similarly there were seven return runs—all to Leeds, connecting at Shipley for Bradford. On Sundays there were three trains from Leeds to Skipton, leaving at 7.00 a.m., 1.00 p.m. and 7.00 p.m., and arriving at 8.00 a.m., 2.30 p.m., and 8.30 p.m. respectively. (In November of 1849 the Midland's traffic committee ordered that tickets were to be collected at Skipton before the trains entered the station.) By mid 1848 another station had been provided on the main line—at Armley. Both this and Idle had only an infrequent service. Of the three return runs, one terminated at Bradford —the 9.00 p.m., taking an hour for the journey.

On the Midland main line, the August 1848 timetable showed ten trains arriving daily into Leeds from Derby, at 5.20 and 9.30 a.m., 12.50, 3.15 (the express from Rugby at 11.55 a.m. and Derby at 1.10 p.m.), 3.50, 4.35, 6.50, 9.00 (Parliamentary), 9.15 and 11.20 p.m. Those leaving Leeds were the 12.45, 3.25, 6.30 (Parliamentary), 7.30 and 10.30 a.m., 12.15, 12.20, 4.00, 4.10, and 7.55 p.m. The 4.10 was the first class only express, stopping at Normanton and Masborough only and arriving at Derby at 6.15 p.m. From there it left 5 minutes later and, with a stop at Leicester, reached Rugby at 7.40 p.m. On Sundays there were four trains into and out of Leeds.

1848 was a bumper year for revolutions, with most of Europe engaged in casting off old forms of government, and in England Chartism caused much trouble. The distress of the workers in industries such as the railways, turned off for lack of work, was very real. Chartism appeared to offer a solution and for a time the country was threatened with insurrection. In April, Feargus O'Connor, the Chartist leader, put a monster petition, backed with spurious signatures, to Parliament, demanding universal suffrage. With troops called out to guard London and feelings running high the rest of the country was in a tumult. It has been said that, but for the railways, which permitted of speedy troop movement, the situation might have got out of hand. It happened that the West Riding was a particularly active Chartist area and the Leeds & Bradford Railway shared in the general melee. As an example of how the new line proved its worth, the happenings at Bingley are worth recording. Local trouble-makers had been active for only a short time when to their astonishment into the town by rail rolled a hundred Chelsea Pensioners. Together with some hastily sworn special constables, they were armed with a few extremely doubtful old matchlocks and posted at Park Road Bridge, near Crossflatts on the Keighley road, and at Cottingley Bridge, thus sealing off the main approaches to the town. The remainder lined the railway station platforms. There they stayed on duty, subject to a great deal of good humoured barracking. On Royal Oak Day matters came to a head with a riot and the troops were called out. On May 31, when the trouble had subsided somewhat, the ringleaders were arrested whilst at work in the mills and taken to the station where a special train, guarded by soldiers and amid considerable uproar, left for York Prison.

The last phase in the story of the Leeds & Bradford Railway comes with its acquisition by the Midland. But before then, in 1849, the company's circumstances had materially altered for George Hudson had been deposed. The year had started with a piece of usual Hudson generosity; the company's clerks and workmen all received free passes for Christmas. But the February half-yearly meeting gave the lie to any outward signs of prosperity. In a noisy and frenzied atmosphere, Hudson agreed that he owned some shares in the L.B.R. John Ellis was attacked for having personally gained from the take-over of the Leicester & Swannington—a company in which he had been interested from its beginnings. The Liverpool party amongst the shareholders tasted blood and wanted more. Accusation and counter accusation were bandied about, with Hudson in the chair powerless to stop it. When the voting for directors came up, Waddingham, one of the original L.B.R. men, found himself off the Midland board. Most of the shareholders were apparently bemused by the violent revelations being made, and as a drowning man clutching the proverbial straw they turned with relief to the closing speech, made with some difficulty by the High Sheriff of Derby. It was to his credit that he managed to put and have carried a vote of confidence in the chairman. Hudson's end was now only a matter of time, however, and a geometric progression of nasty facts started to come to light.

Since the formation of the Midland, Hudson had steadily consolidated his hold on the East Coast lines in an attempt to win traffic from those of the West Coast. Though he and Ellis had managed to bring the Bristol & Birmingham, the Sheffield & Rotherham and the Erewash Valley into the Midland orbit, he had unquestionably damaged his reputation with his volte face in the Leeds & Bradford affair and his capitulation to the G.N.R., whose trains were now happily running into Leeds. In 1848 he had been unsuccessful in applying to Parliament for a lease to the York Newcastle & Berwick of the Maryport & Carlisle, and Newcastle & Carlisle lines. In the south he had failed to stop the coming into being of the G.N.R. After taking over the Eastern Counties Railway in 1845, he had promoted a line north to Lincoln, there to meet a proposed Midland Swinton-Lincoln branch, with the object of frightening the London & York line out of business. His intended intimidation failed, however, as both Hudson lines were withdrawn after the London & York had shown no signs of flinching. In 1847, Hudson had again failed to challenge the G.N.R. with a Midland Leicester-Hitchin Bill to tie in with an Eastern Counties' promotion for an extension from Hertford to Hitchin. The latter Bill was thrown out, whilst the former was worse than useless as, though passed, Parliament insisted that it make physical connection with the G.N.R. It was not to be until 1857 that the Leicester-Hitchin line was revived, at a time when railway politics had undergone yet another upheaval. Perhaps Hudson might have staved off defeat altogether if the economy of the railway companies generally had been of a more healthy nature. After the 'Mania', however, company after company held meetings of inquiry into their finances. All new works were to be curtailed, services and dividends cut. It was to be the committees of inquiry set up to look into the running and finances of the Hudson companies that finally removed their chairman from the scene. Not so with the Midland. In that case it arose solely from Hudson's infatuation with the East Coast lines, at the expense of the Midland. He had already let the G.N.R. into Leeds; now he let it into York, by agreeing to construct a line between Burton Salmon and Knottingley over which the G.N.R. was to run from the L.Y.R.'s Askern branch on to the York & North Midland line. This would usher in a new north-south route which would benefit Hudson's companies north of York by providing a shorter journey from the city to London via the G.N.R. than was then available over the L.N.W.R., and so attract traffic. As part of the old London to York route, the Midland would be hard hit. The Liverpool party took the opportunity and struck hard. Towards the end of April, 1849, they prevailed upon the Midland board to call a special meeting for the purpose of forming a committee of inquiry. This time John Ellis was in the chair. To a crowded meeting he read a letter from Hudson in which the chairman of the company resigned his position. And in the next few sentences Ellis unknowingly spelt out the future of the Midland for the next ten years or so, advising friendship and alliance with the London & North Western Railway and war against the G.N.R.

Hudson was now gone—his resignation from the Midland board was but the prelude to a whirlwind series of resignations and dismissals lasting a month, which left him with no further say in railway matters, and everyone in his companies, from director to station clerk, looking over their shoulders. His final fall does not concern the Midland story further. Suffice it to say that he was in all respects a remarkable man who had brought the Midland, by dubious means, to a position of greatness in the railway scene. Deprived of its captain and with all its alliances suddenly dashed away in the storm of his downfall, it was to run before the gathering Great Northern wind towards the treacherous shelter of the still powerful L.N.W.R.

Let a leader in *Herepath's Journal* of Saturday, May 12, 1849, have the last say on Hudson and the Leeds & Bradford. It put the matter very clearly :

'People are now raking up all manner of things. We heard a gentleman the other day, describing, in humorous terms, the manner in which the Midland had become possessed of the Leeds and Bradford. He said, there were three gentlemen, Mr. Hudson, Mr. Waddingham, and Mr. Murgatroyd, who were, at the time, Directors both of the Midland and Leeds and Bradford. The two first held each 800 Leeds and Bradford, and 1000 extension shares, and the last about half the number. Being clever, smart men they cast about them, as men should to know how to make the most of their property. First, they called upon the Manchester and Leeds, and having described the desirableness of the line to them, as lying within almost their own breast, and giving a wink or two that the Midland eye was in that direction, they induced the Manchester and Leeds to bid a rent of 8 per cent for it. That offer, of course, they did not forget to tell to the Midland Board, adding no doubt, a few hints of the great value the line would be of to them. In fact, the Midland ought not to let it slip out of their hands. Whether it was they who replied to themselves, or the other members of the Board, deponent saith not, but some such reply as the following is said to have been made—"Well, gentlemen, if you think it desirable, we will have it. Offer 10 per cent for it." Of course, the three gentlemen approved of the offer, and as members of the Midland Board would do their best to secure the Midland so good a bargain. Having left the Midland board room, they of course became Leeds and Bradford Directors, and as such gravely considered the proposition, and asked themselves whether they should take 10 or 8 per cent. After, it is supposed, a long and disinterested debate, they determined to favour the Midland proposition and take the 10 per cent. Mr. Waddingham shortly after bought some land, and retired from the toils and tumults of the railway world, determined, like a wise man, to enjoy his "otium" digging "taties"; Mr. Hudson has become eminent for his misfortunes; and Mr. Murgatroyd, we believe, is still in the land of the living, gallantly fighting for the interests of others, regardless of his own.'

An over-simplification, but the mud stuck. Mr. Waddingham must soon have tired of his physical exercise as he turned up at the Leeds & Bradford meeting the following August where he managed to salvage his position on the L.B.R. board, even though it later transpired that he had made a personal profit out of the L.B.R. lease of no less than £62,500.

The surviving members of the Hudson group on the L.B.R. board now sat and waited for the purge to begin. The secretary, by then Samuel Gatcliffe, was to have left the company at about this time, just before the row blew up. He had been asked to leave by the board, but with too many secrets about for the finding it had changed its mind by September, and Murgatroyd hurriedly asked him to stay on. On October 30, 1849, John Rhodes of Leeds was elected a director in place of Hudson. Waddingham was elected as chairman, with Murgatroyd as his deputy. John Rand sat tight, waiting to retire in the normal course of events early the next year. On the same day as Rhodes's appointment there arrived from Derby, in awful majesty, Sir Isaac Morley, Joseph Paxton (later Sir Joseph), and William Beverley. They put aside Murgatroyd's wishes, and terminated Gatcliffe's appointment as secretary there and then. A new secretary, Mr. Best, was appointed in his place, with strict instructions not to let anyone see the company's books without the consent of the board. Gatcliffe was ordered to hand over everything, including the cupboards, and other furniture in his office, untouched. In fact a very precise inventory was made out. It is of interest that Best's salary was about a quarter of that of the outgoing secretary. With the doors bolted everyone sat down to look at the financial state of the L.B.R. Some unpleasant arithmetic followed. The company's liabilities were found to be £110,338 4s. 5d., its assets £261 10s. 2d. Sacrifices became the order of the day. The first—a human one—came in person at the command of one of the members present at the ceremony; Mr. G. H. F. Brown, the secretary's clerk, was called in and informed that his services had already been dispensed with. Feeling slightly better the board decided to see if the company's creditors would accept payment of their debts with Midland debenture stock. To the undoubted relief of both the Midland and the L.B.R. they agreed to do so.

At about this time the Midland shareholders were becoming increasingly concerned over the terms of the L.B.R. lease. They were paying 10 per cent., whether they liked it or not, for a line on which the traffic was steadily decreasing, when the Midland dividends were also falling alarmingly—that of the ordinary stock for 1850 was only £2 1s. od. per cent. Demands for an annullment of the lease began to be heard. Meanwhile, following Ellis's advice, the company had entered into a traffic arrangement with the L.N.W.R. In September, 1849, it divided its various departments into committees; finance, locomotive and carriage, permanent way and stations, traffic, etc. In the matter of expenses salaries were reduced; that of the secretary from £1,000 to £700 per annum, and other officers likewise. According to *Herepath's Journal*, it cut the pay of its lower employees to such an extent as to endanger the running of the line—poor quality switchmen and the like being all that were obtainable for the wages offered.

In the following February Waddingham had come up for re-election on the L.B.R. board and, probably to his own surprise, was successful. Rand quietly vacated his seat to be replaced by Henry William Ripley. In the same month Ellis and Beale of the Midland met the directors of the L.B.R. at Derby. They proposed that the Midland should purchase the line. This led to some disagreement as to whether even the lease was valid and for a time the proposal got no further. A good proportion of the Midland shareholders were all for ditching the L.B.R. completely, and the idea of a purchase did not appeal. To give point to the Midland case, the company withheld some of the rent due to the L.B.R. at the time, mainly because the latter company still had power to raise money by mortgage and was relying on the rent to get it out of trouble instead.

The success of the Great Northern in its attempt on York preyed on the mind of Captain Mark Huish, general manager of the L.N.W.R. Between 1849–1850 a series of secret treaties were concluded with various companies, all of which were aimed at full scale war with Kings Cross. The Midland, with John Ellis still in the chair, despite the attempt of the Liverpool faction to unseat him, toed the L.N.W.R. line, and on August 3, 1850 the Midland announced that on and after the 7st inst., the day appointed for the opening of the G.N.R. from London, the fares and rates of the L.N.W. and Midland companies from Leeds, Wakefield, Doncaster, Sheffield and York, etc., would be brought into line to match those of the G.N.R. At this time, too, the Midland made an attempt to arrange for the L.B.R., and the Bristol and Birmingham line to be worked by contract, but as the tenders were too high it was decided to continue with the existing arrangements. Towards the end of the year it was rumoured that the Great Northern was showing some indications of interest in lines to the north of the L.B.R. As will be seen, this was indeed so. In the intense competition of the period it was unthinkable from the point of view of the L.N.W.R. alliances that this should happen and by December the Midland had had any doubts as to the correctness of complete acquisition of the L.B.R. swept away. In any case repudiation of the lease, or hiving off of the Leeds company might well have caused investors to shy away from the Midland. Messrs Paget and Lewis of the Midland board attended a meeting of the L.B.R. on December 27, 1850, to urge its directors to submit a Bill to their shareholders for sale of the L.B.R. to the Midland—a Bill Derby was prepared to put to Parliament in any case in 1851. As some £95,000 of the rent was still outstanding the L.B.R. said it could not agree unless at least £20,000 was paid at once. This counter blackmail worked and at a special meeting of the L.B.R., held at the Court House, Leeds, on Tuesday, February 11, 1851, the company finally approved the sale to the Midland. On the following June 4, the Midland proprietors held a special meeting at which they gave their formal consent to the proposed purchase Bill.

At the Midland's half-yearly meeting, held in the same month, Ellis told the shareholders that passenger receipts were falling due to competition from the G.N.R. Some betterment was expected from the estimated increase of traffic likely from the Great Exhibition, and in consequence the company had decided to provide an additional thirty-five locomotives, a hundred enclosed third class carriages, and some two hundred wagons. By July the new carriages, more roomy than the old, were in service and attracting, for once, the praise of the railway press. This determination to get the traffic to the Great Exhibition in London was mirrored in many facets of the companys operations in 1851. As an example of the sort of thing the competition inspired it was recorded in July that the Midland employed a man with a band of music to walk the streets of York shouting to the world at large that the company could take people to London—490 miles, there and back—for five shillings. Despite this the traffic was poor; the Great Northern took most of it. In this profit-seeking atmosphere there were some bad accidents on the Midland during the latter part of the year—thirty-one, in which out of 3,310,791 passengers carried on the line 32 were killed or injured. Quite a few of the accidents were caused by collisions : on July 24 nine passengers were injured when the train in which they were travelling rammed a goods train at Newlay on the Leeds & Bradford; three were likewise injured at Normanton on September 7, and two on December 17 at Leeds Wellington when a mail train collided with a disabled engine. Accidents to the company's servants, and trespassers, were all too frequent. Platelayers appeared to be the most prone; it appears from the Board of Trade reports that in many cases they actually fell asleep on the line and were decapitated. In fact it happened with such regularity that one is tempted to wonder whether sheer exhaustion due to over-long working hours might have been responsible. Firemen fell from trains, an intoxicated man fell from a platform, and passengers still blithely leaped off fast trains—notably excursions—to rescue hats. Perhaps the most pathetic case occurred at Keighley on the Leeds & Bradford extension when on August 25 a lad who had come to collect some coal took shelter from heavy rain under—of all things—a wagon on a siding. A shunting engine came up and the wagon took off his leg. Surprisingly he survived but on the following day another boy trespassing under a train was killed. To complete the picture the Midland was blessed with the only conventional railway suicide of the year who aptly laid himself down on the line on September 13.

But enough of morbidity; the Midland Railway (Leeds and Bradford Railway) Act received the Royal Assent on July 24, 1851. It authorised the payment of £1,800,000 as a commuted sum of the yearly rent, the actual vesting of the L.B.R. in the Midland not to take place until the sum was paid. By August the money was on its way and the final meeting of the Leeds & Bradford Railway company took place on Friday, August 20, 1852.

It was perhaps understandable that 1852 should have shown what were the most promising traffic returns on the Leeds & Bradford so far. For the fifteen weeks ending on June 27 there had been, against the corresponding period in 1851, an increase of 6,525 first class passengers, and 16,316 others. Surprisingly enough these figures resulted in the number of first class trains being reduced from five to three and in the third class fare being raised from 9d. to 10d. Perhaps the Midland's fares policy as to season tickets had done something to better the returns. In 1850, at the time of the take-over discussions, season tickets were introduced on the L.B.R. between the two cities, for first class passengers only and issued half-yearly at an annual rate of £35, to come into operation on July 1. On August 20 first class seasons were introduced between any of the stations and on the same day the traffic committee in Derby ordered that the Leeds-Bradford traffic was to be worked independently of traffic over the extension line. On December 17 the annual rate of £35 was reduced to £30, to come into operation on January 1, 1851. February saw further discrimination as to the local traffic—passenger trains on the extension line were to be separate from those of the local service between Leeds and Bradford. On April 1 the Midland and the little North Western Railway—discussed in Chapter VI—agreed on the issue of return tickets, at one fare, to be available from Saturday through to Monday from stations on the L.B.R. to Morecambe Bay. Following this, on June 17 day returns were introduced at all stations on the L.B.R. and on December 16 a further reduction was made in the first class only seasons— yearly at £24, and half-yearly at £14. It was this steady reduction in fares that had probably built up the traffic. Now in 1852, as well as limiting the number of first class trains as mentioned above, the traffic committee suddenly put the Shipley-Bradford yearly season rate for first class passengers up to £10 8s. 0d. This undoubtedly compared badly with the £24 season for the full journey. There seems at this point to have been a determined attempt to turn the passengers over to the third class as being more profitable. At the time of the Shipley-Bradford fare-fixing the traffic committee ordered that season holders should not have the right to insist on a first class seat if the carriages were full; and this, after deliberately reducing the number of available seats.

The Midland was now, in its own right, as far north as Skipton. There it connected with the 'little' North Western—so called by the railway press from its inception to distinguish it from the London & North Western. The North Western Railway was destined, like the Leeds & Bradford, to be incorporated eventually into the Midland system, and so to form part of the route from Leeds to Carlisle. In 1851 it was the northern link between the Midland—still a fairly compact affair in the centre of England—and the lengthy and powerful West Coast route, an association of companies from Euston to the Scottish border. The portion of this attenuated line which the western extremity of the little North Western joined, belonged to the Lancaster & Carlisle Railway. It is this company, and its erratic alliances, that will be examined in the next chapter. For a short time the Lancaster & Carlisle was to be used by Midland passengers on their way to Scotland. For a while it was to consider joining the Midland camp, thus putting that company within reach of Scotland, and perhaps obviating the need for the later Settle to Carlisle line; its eventual fall to the L.N.W.R. was to make that latter magnificent stretch of railway essential to Midland survival. In looking at the early story of the Lancaster & Carlisle the stage will also be set for the part the little North Western was to play in forcing the Midland finally to cut away from the L.N.W.R.; for in 1851, with the L.B.R. in its hands, that company still had no thoughts of reaching the Border. It was indeed only starting to pass into the period of its close, smothering, and destructive alliance with Euston.

V

Everybody's Friend

The Lancaster and Carlisle Line

Four years before the incorporation of the Midland Railway, and about a decade previous to the completion of the East Coast route, the London & Birmingham Railway, and the Grand Junction Railway, had together virtually connected London with Scotland. That about half the journey time was taken up by a sea voyage did not then matter for, apart from a laborious overland journey by stage coach, there was no other opposition. The two companies operated their trains between London and Liverpool, connecting with steamer services from that town to Ardrossan. By 1841 the point of departure from England had been changed to Fleetwood, trains running from the North Union Railway to Preston, whence the Preston & Wyre Railway took them on to the new port which took its name from its founder, Sir Hesketh Fleetwood. Having established themselves long before the rival East Coast line, the West Coast companies determined to keep ahead. One of the most difficult pieces of any through route to Scotland, however, loomed ahead of them in the counties of Cumberland and Westmorland. The story of the route north of Lancaster, up to the time of the first appearance of the little North Western Railway—connecting the Leeds & Bradford with the north—is of interest in that it gives the background for much of what followed concerning the Midland's final drive for Carlisle.

In 1837 there had appeared the Grand Caledonian Junction Railway —a project to connect Lancaster with the west coast of Cumberland and Carlisle. George Stephenson, asked to report on its merits, thought it 'the most expeditious, certain and safe conveyance' obtainable through the countryside where it was to run. Next year John Urpeth Rastrick, engineer to the London & Brighton Railway, was also asked to comment on the line, and though by then another and better inland line was being planned at the behest of the Grand Junction, he came to the same conclusion as Stephenson. By this time the project was known as the West Cumberland Railway. It proposed to cross Morecambe Bay by an embankment of nearly eleven miles in length, with another of about $1\frac{3}{4}$ miles across Duddon Sands. From there it was to follow the coast of Cumberland as far as Maryport, there to join the Maryport & Carlisle Railway, which latter was not to be opened throughout until February of 1845. Though the engineers seemed to favour the line the possibility of the gigantic dyke across the bay so alarmed the Admiralty that the scheme never proceeded. Stephenson, of course, had been at one time engineer to the Grand Junction. By 1835, however, he had been succeeded by Joseph Locke, and the company, seeing the necessity for a more direct through rail link to Scotland, had asked Locke to survey such a route from Preston to Glasgow. This he had done, and in 1837 the West Coast route was further lengthened by the incorporation of the Lancaster & Preston Junction Railway, authorised to construct a line some 20½ miles in length connecting Lancaster with the North Union Railway then under construction. 'Connecting' is perhaps not quite the correct word for at its opening on June 26, 1840 there was no physical junction between the two. A point of interest is that the evidence for the Bill included a statement from Locke that he considered the extension of the railway northwards to Glasgow to be practicable, and that he had laid out the levels of the Lancaster & Preston line accordingly. The opening of the L.P.J. was to bring Lancaster within eleven hours of London.

Concurrent with Locke's survey for a continuation on to Glasgow, the Government was also showing considerable interest in the question. It appointed a Royal Commission to look into the whole business of rival routes between England, Ireland and Scotland and by December of 1841 support for the commissioners' report—that there was only room for one line between England and Scotland, and that Locke's route seemed the best—was being drummed up in Scottish towns. At that time the line was planned to run from Lancaster to Carlisle and thence by Lockerbie and Beattock through Clydesdale to Symington, from where lines were to diverge to Edinburgh and Glasgow. By January of 1842 the surveys were under way and in mid-month Locke returned from finishing the work in Scotland and started to inspect the ground about Lancaster. At that time the local landowners were up to their usual tricks of misleading the surveyors and generally being as obstructive as possible. This caused resentment among responsible business people in Lancaster—the recent opening of the railway between York and Darlington had taken two-thirds of the posting traffic away from the town. If the East Coast line was pushed on to Newcastle before the West Coast reached Carlisle, the remaining trade would suffer. On February 11 the *Carlisle Patriot* reported that the inhabitants of the Lune Valley were against the line. To surmount this opposition Locke had decided in 1838 on two surveys providing for alternative lines between Lancaster and Penrith. The Government commissioners had agreed by 1841 that the inland line could be taken through one or two routes and Locke hoped that by sending both schemes to Parliament a compromise could be reached. The westerly of the two lines proposed followed the present course of the Lancaster & Carlisle line as far as Tebay from where it deviated a little to the west of the Shap incline and made straight for Bampton. From that point it ran due north, skirting Lowther Park, to join the present route near Yanwath. The easterly line left Lancaster and ran north-east to Hornby from where it curved to the north passing through Kirkby Lonsdale and followed the River Lune to Low Gill. From there both east and west lines followed a similar route as far as Tebay. The easterly line then continued north through Orton to Sleagill from where it ran in a north-westerly direction through Clifton to rejoin the westerly line, again at Yanwath. The first of these lines owed a lot to George Larmer, an engineer who had come forward with his own suggestions for a route based on the commissioners' report. Larmer's original scheme had not included Kendal, but at the request of the town he had investigated the possibility of a route between it and the Lune Valley and had found that by taking a curve due east, about three miles north of the town, a connection could be made via Grayrigg, thus joining the northern portion of the Lune Valley line with the southern portion of the Kendal line. The amended route provided an answer to the objections coming from the Lune Valley and in March of 1842 the plans for the two lines went to Parliament under the title of 'Caledonian Railway, Section 1'. The second section of the railway, from Carlisle to Edinburgh and Glasgow, was to be deposited a month later. By April the Lune Valley line was shelved and all survey work concentrated on the Kendal route. Towards the end of the month 'C.E.', writing in the *Railway Times*, called for a single line of rails only. He cited the case of the London & Birmingham Railway which had asked Stephenson, at the time of its construction, for four tracks, only to be told that such expense was absurd. Stephenson considered at the time that if the L.B.R. had two lines they would still carry six times as much traffic as the company could expect.

In September 1842 Locke reported on the two rival routes. That via the Lune Valley would be some $1\frac{1}{4}$ miles shorter than via Kendal and would cost £36,400 less. Despite this, and the fact that from an engineering point of view the Lune line was better, Locke thought that the Kendal route was a sounder proposition—for the most part because of the industry and population in the town. As to the lines north of Tebay, the westerly one, called the 'Lowther', and the easterly, called the 'Orton', were still under discussion. A point in favour of the former was that it was about a mile shorter and cost £141,286 less. There was also heavy tunnelling of 2,640 yards involved, some 360 feet under Orton Scar.

By this time the threat of the East Coast route was beginning to become apparent and in early November a meeting was held in Birmingham of the interested parties in the West Coast route, including the London & Birmingham, and the Grand Junction. To meet the challenge they decided to limit the works on the Caledonian to the southern portion between Lancaster and Carlisle. The year ended with two meetings. The first was of the supporters of the Lune Valley line, hitherto dormant, at the 'Royal Hotel', Kirkby Lonsdale. It was presided over by the Vicar, the Rev. J. H. Fisher, and the main argument was that the Lune Valley line was shorter than that via Kendal. The second—far more important

—was of the Lancaster and Carlisle portion of the Caledonian scheme. It was held on Boxing Day at Carlisle. Colonel Graham was in the chair and he congratulated the meeting on the support the scheme was having from the southern companies. He introduced John Swift of Liverpool, law agent of the associated railways, and John Errington, their engineer. Swift told the meeting that Captain Huish of the Grand Junction had backed the idea from the start and that the companies proposed investing £½ m. if a similar amount could be raised in the locality of the line. It was suggested that £1 m. was ample for the whole scheme if there was a single line of rails where there was least traffic—between Kendal and Penrith. Swift also said that the companies had not yet decided between the Kendal or Lune routes. The matter of the Lowther or Orton lines had, however, been settled. The latter was so disadvantageous that despite the opposition of Lord Lonsdale to the Lowther line, in that it was undesirable to pass so close to Askham, they had decided to go ahead nevertheless. In fact his Lordship's support was obtained in the following February. At Kendal, four days before the Carlisle meeting, there had been an enthusiastic reception for Swift and Errington when they asked for support for the line. This took the form of local landowners agreeing to take the fair value for their land in shares in the company. Not to be outdone, Locke had promised his resignation if the contractors were not hired to his estimates. There was some disapproval. A shareholder from the Grand Junction wrote to the *Railway Times* that he thought the East Coast route too advanced to be overtaken. Another letter to the paper in February, 1843, gave some interesting figures on the population to be found in the areas through which the line was planned. Burton, on the Kendal Canal, 11 miles from Lancaster, with a population of 673 in 1831; Kendal, 22 miles from Lancaster, with 8,984 inhabitants in 1831; then Shap, a mere village 38 miles from Lancaster; Penrith, 48 miles from Lancaster, with the whole parish containing only 5,385 souls; and finally Carlisle, 66 miles, with 15,476 inhabitants. He considered that there were not nearly enough people to support the line and gave the comparison between Westmorland, then with a density of one person to eight acres, and Cumberland with one to five—the two most thinly populated counties in England—with the whole country, which averaged one for every two acres.

There appeared to be a general feeling about this time that the line was doomed to failure. In March 1843 the whole West Coast scheme was in abeyance because of apathy on the part of landowners on the route. The following May Hudson had another interview with Sir Robert Peel asking for government aid to complete the East Coast line to Scotland. By this time Newcastle had been reached and it was not lost upon the West Coast supporters that when the Government commissioners had reported on the East Coast line they had said that if it got that far on its own the Government ought to assist with the remainder. Hudson suggested to the Prime Minister that if the line was extended as far as

Berwick-on-Tweed the directors of the Edinburgh & Glasgow Railway would be prepared to carry it on to Edinburgh. By July the East Coast companies had decided to go ahead to Berwick and in November the church doors in the parishes through which the line would pass were filled with notices of its coming. This had the effect of finally removing any doubts among the West Coast parties. On Monday, November 6, 1843, a meeting at Kendal was told by the chairman of the provisional committee of the Caledonian Railway that it was seeking powers for a line from Lancaster to Carlisle in the next session.

By January, 1844 the line had more realistically taken the name of its route. By then out of the owners of the 70 miles length of line, those of 65 were in favour of the project—in fact over half the distance was already in the hands of the shareholders. February saw contracts let to Bagnell & Co. of Staffordshire for rails—the line was to be single throughout—and the following month contracts let to Mackenzie & Brassey, and J. Stephenson jointly for the construction of the line, all at tenders below Locke's estimate. The Lancaster & Carlisle Railway Act received the Royal Assent on June 6, 1844. It empowerd the company to raise capital of £900,000, some of which was to be provided by the associated companies to the south as follows : London & Birmingham £100,000; Grand Junction £250,000; North Union, and Lancaster & Preston Junction £65,000 each. This, of course, cut both ways—out of sixteen directors, eight were to be appointed from these companies, a situation which was to prove an embarrassment to the Lancaster & Carlisle in its later efforts to deal with the Midland lines. Though the line was to be single the works were to be made for double track and a provision in the Act made it possible for the Board of Trade to compel the laying of the second line at a later date if it thought fit. This was to cover the possibility of the passing of the Caledonian Railway Act in the next session of Parliament—as is well known, an eventuality which did occur. In fact the Lancaster & Carlisle board decided to go ahead with the double track in January 1845.

By August 1845 work had been in progress for about a year, nearly all the land purchased, and another Bill passed for a deviation of the line taking it west of Lancaster. Earlier in the year an agreement had been reached with the Grand Junction Railway for that company to work the Lancaster & Carlisle for a period of five years. It has until quite recently been accepted that this is in fact what happened but in an article in the December 1955 issue of the *Journal of the Stephenson Locomotive Society,* Mr. E. Craven produced evidence that besides the Grand Junction agreement, the Lancaster company actually purchased two engines for the coal trains from the firm of Jones & Potts, and that they were in use from the opening of the line.

The construction of the Lancaster & Carlisle Railway forms no part of this story. Its importance to the Midland's northerly march is that for a period, especially from its incorporation to the time it was taken over by the London & North Western Railway, the Lancaster & Carlisle possessed a commercial popularity among promoters of railways in the area. It became everybody's friend, providing a perfect ready-made north-south line for any new aspiring local railway to batten on to.

Irish and Scots navvies hewed and toiled along the route of the Lancaster & Carlisle and bloody were the many battles between them. It was only a century before that this part of England had reverberated to the noise of men marching and fighting, for the '45 Rebellion had retreated north along the Shap road which runs parallel to the railway. At Clifton, south of Penrith, had been fought one of the last battles on England soil —more of a skirmish really—with tired, bedraggled Highlanders keeping up a rearguard action, in frightful conditions, against the forward troops of 'Butcher' Cumberland.

The line was opened to passenger traffic as far as Oxenholme on September 23, 1846, and on to Carlisle by the following December 17. The first train of the Earl of Carlisle's coal ran through Penrith twelve days later, and goods traffic commenced a week after that. Mail trains started running on February 1, 1847. Such, in brief, was the coming of the Lancaster & Carlisle. Having arrived in the district it immediately attracted one of the first of the many schemes wishing to make a junction to the West Coast route. This was the North Western Railway, with whom the Lancaster & Carlisle was to have blow hot, blow cold, relations for some time until eventually far bigger events took the whole business of private and local railway politics out of the hands of both companies.

VI

North of Skipton

The little North Western

Towards the end of 1844, with the Leeds & Bradford planning its line
north to Skipton, and the Lancaster & Carlisle about to start construction, there existed a promising stretch of so far untapped country between
Skipton and Lancaster. Several projects came forward to take advantage
of the through traffic which must accrue to a line between the towns.
Only one was to succeed—the little North Western. In February, 1845,
the provisional committee issued its prospectus for a main line to connect
the West Riding with the West of Scotland. The committee list was
headed by Pudsey Dawson, of Hornby Castle, High Sheriff of the County
of Lancaster. With an intended capital of £1 m., the committee planned
a line from a junction with the Leeds & Bradford near Skipton to join
the Lancaster & Carlisle Railway some five miles south of Tebay station,
at Low Gill. There was to be a branch to Lancaster, leaving the main
line at Clapham, and two short connections to the L.C.R. at Sedgwick
and Milnthorpe. At the latter place the line was to make connection
with a proposed Ulverstone Furness & Lancaster & Carlisle Railway,
which in turn was to join an extension of the Furness Railway to Ulverston,
thus giving a through route from Barrow to Yorkshire.

The prospectus informed the public that the committee had engaged
the services of Charles Vignoles as engineer in chief, with John Watson
as acting engineer. It estimated that the cost per mile for double track
would be about £16,000. If constructed the saving of distance by the
North Western Railway between Leeds and Carlisle would be about
62 miles over all other projected lines. Two of these, which appeared at
the same time as the North Western, can be quickly disposed of at
this point. The Leeds & Lancaster Direct Railway, which proposed doing
just what its title suggested, appeared in mid 1845. Its provisional committee was composed, for the most part, of the same persons who
appeared in the guise of the Great Leeds & London Direct, and the Leeds
& Carlisle—a company to be met again later. As before, Lord Chichester
headed the list. The other company was that of the York & Lancaster
Railway. It appeared at about the same time as the Leeds & Lancaster
Direct and proposed a line, planned by its engineer, John Miller, to
run from York through Knaresborough, Harrogate, Long Preston, and
Settle, to Lancaster, completely countering both the North Western, and
the proposed Lancashire & Yorkshire (North Eastern). As to rival schemes
the U.F. & L. & C. itself comp eted with a proposed branch of the

84

Whitehaven & Furness Junction Railway from Ulverston to the L.C.R. at Carnforth. What fate had in store for these lines will shortly become apparent.

On February 25, 1845 the inhabitants of Settle met at the 'Golden Lion' to declare their support for the North Western. Having secured the approval of the local landowners, the committee now set about courting the Leeds & Bradford. This it did by the simple expedient of allotting 16,000 shares to the L.B.R. and installing all its directors on the committee—all that is except Hudson. The L.B.R. had wanted its engineer to plan the North Western but on the committee refusing, a compromise was reached whereby Gooch was to associate with Vignoles in preparing the scheme. A month later Stephenson replaced Gooch. The last task was to win the support of the Lancaster & Carlisle. This was not hard—North Western traffic would undoubtedly bring considerable revenue with it. There was, however, some argument with the L.C.R. as to the point of junction. The L.C.R. suggested in April that the North Western abandon the idea of branches to Tebay and Lancaster in favour of a new line from Wennington through Arkholme to join the L.C.R. at Hyning, about 9 miles north of Lancaster. As this would save a considerable mileage the North Western was tempted, but by July the committee had agreed that the original proposals should stand, all the lines to be included in the Bill for Parliament. As to the Tebay line, however, this was understood to be abandoned unless events justified construction, in which event the L.C.R. was to assist in the cost. At the same time the committee agreed to support two newcomers, the Clitheroe Junction, and the Liverpool Manchester & Great North of England Union. The latter concern will appear again later in different and less cumbersome guise. For the time being the North Western was sympathetic to its aims to make a line due north and promised its support in return for an undertaking that the company should construct a branch from its main line to the N.W.R. at Ingleton for Liverpool traffic. The N.W.R. was also considering a branch to join the L.C.R. at Carnforth where a connection would be made to the proposed Whitehaven & Furness Junction Railway. This branch the N.W.R. decided to shelve until the Whitehaven company had obtained permission from the Admiralty for a portion of its line to cross the Duddon Sands. The W.F.J. dithered about over requesting the necessary approval and to the relief of both the L.C.R. and the North Western, neither of whom desired a junction at Carnforth, the scheme did not proceed. Meanwhile another company, the Milnthorpe & Furness, in opposition to the Ulverstone Furness & Lancaster & Carlisle, approached the N.W.R. with an offer of shares in its undertaking. On the N.W.R. declining to participate, however, it disappeared as quickly as it had arrived. At the same time the N.W.R. withdrew its support from the Liverpool Manchester & Great North of England Union as that company had allied itself with another concern and its original intentions had undergone a change.

In January 1846 the York & Lancaster project was bought off with 3,500 N.W.R. shares and 3,500 Morecambe Bay & Harbour company shares, the latter concern to go to Parliament in the 1846 session and then to unite with the North Western. On April 9, 1846, the York and Lancaster met briefly to suspend operations and petition Parliament for release from its Bill. The preamble of the North Western Railway Bill was found to be proved in the House of Commons on April 29, 1846 save as to the line between Kirkby Lonsdale and Milnthorpe with its attendant Sedgwick branch. The rejection of the Milnthorpe line coincided with the decease of the U.F. & L. & C. At the same time the latter's opposition to the Whitehaven & Furness line bore fruit for that concern's scheme was also thrown out. This was viewed with some relief by the North Western, who had been bound by agreement, if the W.F.J. was successful, to construct the Carnforth branch, a proposal not at all to the liking of the Lancaster & Carlisle. So in the session of 1846, in one grand slam, all but the North Western had gone to the wall.

The North Western Railway Act received the Royal Assent on June 26, 1846 and gave the company powers to raise capital of £1,100,000 with loans of £366,000, and to construct the main line from Skipton to a junction with the L.C.R. at Low Gill—immediately north of the then site of the L.C.R. station, and the Lancaster branch leaving the main line at Clapham. The first directors, twelve in number, were Thomas Birkbeck, William Clayton, Edward Dodson Salisbury, Hugh Hornby of Liverpool, Henry Anthony Littledale, Messrs. Burrow, Dawson, Hinde, and Roughsedge of the Morecambe Bay & Harbour Railway, and the three L.B.R. directors, Murgatroyd, Rand and Waddingham.

On July 17 the board of the North Western Railway held its first meeting. Dawson was elected chairman, with Birkbeck as his deputy. Edmund Sharpe, also a director of the M.B.H.R., was appointed as secretary at £600 per annum, and William Whelon as book-keeper and chief clerk to Sharpe at £150 per annum. Eight days later came the first general meeting, held at the 'Kings Arms Hotel' at Lancaster. The shareholders were told that the directors had decided that the Clapham-Tebay line, or Orton branch as it was called, was to be made by the Lancaster & Carlisle. The Morecambe Bay & Harbour undertaking, then before Parliament, was in danger of having to withdraw through lack of funds. This company intended constructing, besides various harbour works, a railway to join the little North Western at St. George's Quay, Lancaster with a line from Poulton—the William Lands branch, which was to join the L.C.R. north of the town. On the advice of its engineer, the N.W.R. had decided to back the M.B.H. through Parliament in its own interests. The Morecambe Harbour & Railway Act—the title had been altered slightly—had received the Royal Assent on July 16, and the company was now ready to join the N.W.R.

On July 29 the board formally appointed Vignoles as consulting engineer at a yearly salary of £300, with Watson as acting and resident engineer at £700, on condition that the latter devoted all his time to the company. Watson was to stake out the line between Skipton and Lancaster immediately. Two months later the company advertised for 10,000 tons of rails and chairs and sent Hinde, Watson, and Sharpe to Dublin to attend a timber sale. One month after this it received a jolt when the L.C.R., with its own line nearly complete, decided to take a breather and declined to make the Orton branch. At the end of October a meeting of the shareholders voted to approve the sale, transfer, and construction of the M.H. & R. Mr. Hartley, the harbour engineer, was asked to state the nature of the approach to the proposed harbour from the sea. This he did by telling how he had come up the channel to the site of the dock in a steamer drawing ten feet, at dead low water of an ordinary spring tide, unassisted by a chart, without the slightest difficulty. Also agreed at the meeting were four deviations to the N.W.R.—one at the eastern terminus to join the L.B.R. and the Wharfedale line, a second at Casterton, a third from Sedbergh on the authorised Orton branch to a new junction with the L.C.R. near Dillicar Park, and a fourth at Bulk, just north of Lancaster. The meeting ended with the chairman informing the company that he hoped work would start in the following December, and that Lord Morpeth had consented to cut the first sod.

The ceremony took place on New Year's Eve, 1846, in a field at Cleatop, two miles from Settle, and near the conveniently adjacent main road—then known as the Keighley & Kendal turnpike. As promised, Lord Morpeth—one of the M.P.s for the West Riding of Yorkshire— officiated, dressed to the obvious amusement of the crowd, in navvy's attire. Hard frosts had made the ground almost unworkable and it was only after a considerable struggle that he managed to fill the mahogany barrow provided for the occasion. Not to be outdone the chairman followed suit, and after him came Vignoles, dressed as a lab- ourer. After much badinage from the assembled navvies a barrel of ale was broached and the usual toasts given. Other guests invited to the ceremony included Lord Wharncliffe, Lord Harewood, and the M.P.s for Bradford, Halifax, Lancaster, the northern division of Lancashire, and Westmorland. Also present were Edmund Denison of the Great Northern, and George Hudson. Like Hudson, a Yorkshireman, and with the Yorkshire trait of plain speaking, Denison equalled the 'Railway King' in stature, leading the G.N.R. in its battle against Hudson's domination of the railway scene with an obstinacy and tenacity which not only defeated the Midland group of companies but which was eventually to outwit even Captain Huish to whom the crown passed when Hudson fell. Denison was also possessed of one asset not common to many of the other great figures of these years : that of a basic honesty of purpose. He was for the Great Northern—not for himself. On that cold day at Cleatop in 1846, with the G.N.R. at last successful in gaining powers to make its railway, and with bitter conflicts to come, one wonders what, if anything, the two men had to say to one another.

January of 1847 saw the formation of two committees by the N.W.R. board—one to agree with the L.B.R. as to the junction and station arrangements at Skipton, and the other to superintend the arrangements necessary for the company to construct its own rolling stock. In the same month the tender of Millar & Nelson—contractors on the Chester & Holyhead Railway—for the construction of the Settle and Clapham contract, was accepted at a price of £57,267, and in February George Thornton took the Long Preston contract at £85,000. By the end of April it had been agreed that the L.B.R. should build the station at Skipton, and W. Fairbairn & Sons had successfully tendered to supply twenty locomotives at about £2,500 each, Vignoles having previously recommended the firm to the board, after telling the latter that this was the minimum number required to work some 62 miles of line. It had also been decided to write to the Bishops of Ripon and Chester for the appointment of two clergymen 'to undertake the pastoral care of the workmen on the line'. The other event during a very busy month was the resignation of Edmund Sharpe from the office of secretary so that he could take over the sole superintendence of the construction of the line from Wennington to Morecambe. His place was taken by Whelon, thus precipitating a brilliant career which was to end in the best traditions of Victorian high tragedy some years later. In July the Ingleton contract was let to Messrs. Coulthard & Allen for £108,600. A resolution of the board that month agreed that while the Skipton-Lancaster line should be constructed for double track, only a single line of rails would be laid.

This was in fact the beginning of hard times. Following the general economic difficulties facing many railway companies immediately after the 'Mania' of 1846, the North Western was forced to cut its expenditure. After a personal inspection of the works in November, the board suspended all operations on the Morecambe line and the William Lands branch, and reduced the works elsewhere. In the following month it decided that the Ingleton contract should cease north of the town, at least until the autumn of 1849. Indeed the company had decided to restrict all its efforts to the line between Skipton and Clapham. In February of 1848 Stephenson was asked to report on the whole of the proposed works and the value of continuing with each. The following month Watson was able to inform the directors that the Gargrave and Long Preston contracts were well under way with work on the Bell Busk viaduct in a forward state, the piers and abutments being by then above water level. Works on the Paley Green cutting were proceeding, the foundations of the Ingleton viaduct were ready, and the timber structures across the River Lune on the Ingleton contract were complete and had been tested.

Meanwhile, the board had changed its mind and decided to complete the Morecambe line. After an inspection earlier in the month by Captain

88

Wynne of the Board of Trade, the branch was opened to passenger traffic on Whit Monday, June 12, 1848. The first service consisted of eleven trains from Lancaster to Poulton, and twelve in the opposite direction. On Sundays there were four each way. On June 30, the Royal Assent was given to the company's Bill for the deviations of the main line, and the Lancaster branch. The board had by that time decided to abandon the William Lands branch but the Act specifically provided for it to be constructed—even laying down a time limit to expire by July 16, 1851. One suspects the hand of the Lancaster & Carlisle was behind this as the branch provided the only link between the L.C.R. and the opened portion of the N.W.R.; it also permitted the Lancaster company potential access to Morecambe harbour.

The following month a disgruntled Scarborough shareholder baulked at paying up on further calls on the capital. He argued that as the line was now ready between Skipton and Settle, the company should not fritter away any more of the shareholders' money on further works, but should apply for an extension of time, cease further construction, open to Settle, and sit back and see what traffic would materialise. The Midland, he said, was far more interested in getting to Lancaster than was apparent and, if pushed to it, might guarantee the remainder of the line. The half-yearly meeting of the company in August brought the news that Stephenson had issued his report—Gooch had done the groundwork—and had recommended immediate construction of the Lancaster branch as opposed to the main line to Orton, thus reducing the outlay of the company from £1,100,000 to £750,000. He urged that a single line of rails should be laid as soon as possible between Skipton and Lancaster, and that for the time being the Orton line should be shelved as it had far heavier works than the remainder of the railway. He also thought that a junction line should be laid in at Lancaster to the L.C.R., necessitating Parliamentary powers in the next session. His report in fact confirmed the directors' decision of the previous December.

On August 25 a deputation of Leeds shareholders—who required both calls on capital and further work to be stopped—was met by the directors and conducted over the line. Stephenson's report was read to them and, after looking at the books, they went away suitably mollified. Early next month there was swift agreement with the L.C.R. as to the junction line and a final decision was taken to abandon the William Lands branch thereby rendered superfluous. Powers for the construction and abandonment respectively were obtained in the company's Act of May 24, 1849. In order to shorten the walking distance between Settle and the railway station the Act also empowered the company to make a road from Duke Street to Beggar's Wife Bridge—about midway between the two—where it joined the existing road to the station. Also at about this time Coulthard & Allen switched their efforts from the works north of Ingleton to a contract on the Lancaster branch, between Clapham and the River Hindburn and, as Vignoles had left the country, the board decided to terminate his services and to give the job of consultant engineer to Gooch. It would seem from the minutes that he was offered the post of engineer-in-chief but refused to accept unless he could have Young of the Leeds & Bradford as his personal superintendent. This would have made Watson's position somewhat invidious and it appears, to its credit, that the N.W.R. board devised the consultantship as a compromise. The last quarter of the year brought more trouble from the shareholders. With Hudson almost on his final lap, and the financial condition of the company only kept from being too depressing by the glimmer of hope in the 5 per cent. return then coming from the Morecambe line, a letter from a proprietor of North Western stock, published in *Herepath's Journal* in September, aired some of the dark thoughts then prevalent. After apologising for his own absence at the forthcoming half-yearly meeting he exhorted the shareholders present to put four questions to the chairman. These followed the current witch-hunting pattern and included the chestnuts of how many shares Hudson and Waddingham held in the Leeds & Bradford, whether they held any North Western stock, and if not, when and to whom did they sell. It had the desired effect and started a rumble of discontent against the Midland which was to persist until that company finally took over.

All told 1849 was a happier year for the North Western than the preceding one. It did not start too well—bad weather brought all work on the line between Skipton and Ingleton to a close for a time, though in any event Thornton was considered by the board to be slacking in his efforts. The board had found on investigating the state of all the current works that the contract on the original main line to Orton was so far advanced south of Ingleton as to make it more beneficial to complete the section south of the town to Clapham at an additional cost of £37,000.

On April 5 Fairbairn called on the board. The locomotive contract of April 1847 had arranged for delivery in the Spring of 1849. At that time the line as planned was considerably longer and was to be of double track throughout; also locomotives were scarce. Fairbairn was now told that the company required no more than twelve engines—eight passenger and four goods. The reason lay in the general economies then being practised, and the intention of laying only single track throughout. At the same time the carriage accounts were looked at with a jaundiced eye and for a while the board seriously wondered at the propriety of constructing its own rolling stock. A slightly more hopeful outlook was reflected, however, in an order placed that month for some of Edmundson's ticket machines. About a week later it was decided that all the stations should be constructed 'in the most convenient manner of timber and plaster'. Meanwhile Fairbairn had decided rather magnanimously to release the company from part of its contract for locomotives for a sum of £3,200. The month ended with Thornton in full swing again on the works on the Skipton to Ingleton contract.

June saw an agreement with the Midland as to supply of rolling stock sufficient for the opening of a portion of the line that month—the service to consist of four daily passenger trains. If the Midland was unable to do the honours, the board decided to purchase the necessary stock. At the same time an order was placed for Brett & Little's telegraph apparatus for the whole of the line. The company still wanted complete annulment of Fairbairn's contract, and on June 7 his offer to accept £7,100 for engines already supplied was accepted. The intended opening in June was delayed by a series of offers and counter offers made between the N.W.R., the M.R., and the L.B.R. all of which ended in deadlock. Somewhat at a loss the company gratefully accepted an offer from the indefatigable Sharpe to work the line. The company's minutes indicate that he was to provide all the locomotives, rolling stock, and operating staff, to work a service between Skipton and Lancaster, at 11d. per mile run, the passenger trains to run at an average speed of 22 m.p.h. There were to be no fewer than four trains each way on weekdays, and Sharpe was to provide engines similar to those formally used on the London & Birmingham line—constructed by Edward Bury, with 13 in. cylinders for the goods types. As to the goods trains he was to provide all wagons and staff at 1s. per mile run, the trains to run at an average speed of 15 m.p.h. The company, however, undertook to supply all the heavy goods wagons itself. The contract was to remain in force for seven years from the date of opening the line throughout, but before this Sharpe was to work the Skipton-Ingleton line. The remaining staff—guards, porters, brakesmen, pointsmen, etc., the company would make available. To superintend all these arrangements, on July 5 the board appointed James Midglie as general traffic agent, at £100 per annum, and on the same day accepted Sharpe's terms. A week later the locomotive stock was almost reinforced by the purchase of an engine from the North Union Railway at £600, an agreement was reached with the L.B.R. as to the traffic arrangements at Skipton, and the first permanent servants of the company were appointed. (A list of their names appears in Appendix II.) Compared with the Leeds & Bradford personnel of 1846, porters appeared to be considered barely necessary.

Another week passed and the board, presumably having wondered just what it was buying in the locomotive world for £600, rescinded its resolution as to the N.U.R. engine. It was at the time busy casting about for something on six wheels which would impress Captain Laffan of the Board of Trade, due shortly to inspect the line, and it decided to try hiring an engine from the Lancaster & Preston Railway. If this failed it was to fall back on the Leeds & Bradford to see it over what might prove a trying time. Also realising that it was woefully short of carriages and other rolling stock, and with Sharpe to hand, it decided to let him the company's carriage works at Lancaster for a term of seven years—Sharpe to construct all rolling stock required by the company. Some of the articles he was to turn out were later to be reviewed in shocked terms by Gooch. With events catching up on it, the board saw Sharpe safely installed and immediately gave him an order for a hundred goods wagons, at £75 each, five carriage trucks at £85 each, twenty cattle wagons at £100 each, and two horse boxes at £120 each.

On Thursday, August 30, 1849, the company held its half-yearly meeting at Skipton. The report to the shareholders told them that on July 30 the 25 miles of line between Skipton and Ingleton had been opened for public traffic. It was hoped that Lancaster-Wennington, 12 miles or so, would be opened the following October, leaving the remaining intermediate portion, again some 12 miles, to be completed by the spring of the next year. The traffic on the Morecambe line was still on the increase, and to be more in the centre of things the company had decided to move its offices to Settle. As to the abandoned works north of Ingleton, these had cost about £18,500 so far. Though it was a matter for regret that the amount had been so large it was accepted with the philosophic view that if in the future the company wished to extend to the L.C.R., much of the work was already done. The recent rescission of Fairbairn's contract was explained as was the new arrangement for Sharpe to work the line. With a decrease in the size of the undertaking the board had also decided to cut its number to six. Sharpe, of course, accounts for one of the members who left; Roughsedge and Murgatroyd were the others. As to the latter, part of the reason for his resignation was that he had, to his own discomfort, found it impossible to act impartially during the recent abortive negotiations with the M.R. and L.B.R. as to the N.W.R.'s request for working arrangements. Whelon, still apparently the perfect secretary, was given a salary increase from £250 to £300 per annum as well as a cash bonus of £100 in recognition of his services to the company.

During this time the Bentham contract was still not completed and in August the board appointed one of its own number, Humphrey John Hare, of Bramhope Hall, to supervise the final stages. Hare looked into the matter and came up with some stringent things to say about all concerned—Watson and the contractor included. Apparently the contractor had been heavily misusing the rails and sleepers and had done considerable damage. There was also some questions of falsifying the returns on earthworks, with consequent over-payments. For this Hare blamed Watson and the sub-engineers, and ordered them to present themselves before the board to tender an explanation. Watson, who had worked hard for the company, took exception to this high-handed accusation and forbade the sub-engineers to attend. In a state of scandalised amazement the board decided to play it rough and Watson, seeing dismissal round the corner, finally appeared contrite and apologetic. Meanwhile the earthwork business had proved to be without doubt a mistake on the part of Hare, and though the other accusations against the contractor were justified, Watson was let off the hook and returned to the works with stinging ears.

92

In August Watson was told to prepare for doubling the line between Settle and Long Preston, and on November 17 the opening took place of the Lancaster-Wennington portion, agreement being reached as to the use of the L.C.R.'s Castle station a week later (see note to Appendix IV). The determination of the directors to go no further north than Ingleton was reflected in the following month by an order for two pairs of Webster's patent buffers for the branch terminus. In the same month Gooch was asked to report on whether there should be a double or single line between Skipton and Lancaster. On December 7 came one of the first recorded accidents on the line; the solicitor was asked by the board to 'take proceedings against the parties who took an engine from Ingleton along the line towards Settle yesterday by reason of which a collision took place near Paley Green between the said engine and the goods train going towards Ingleton causing considerable damage to property, and a detention of one hour to the Lancaster mail train.' Up to this time the terminus at Lancaster, since November 17, had been at Green Ayre, then called in the timetables Green Area. The N.W.R. board minutes for Wednesday, December 19, 1849 noted that on the previous Monday Captain Laffan of the Board of Trade had inspected the junction line to the Castle station and announced himself satisfied with the works. He also looked at the company's locomotives at Lancaster. The minutes then noted that North Western trains started using the Castle station the following day, December 18 (some authorities give this date as being December 12 and others as December 19). It was now hoped to have the entire line opened in the coming June.

As will be seen the locomotives and rolling stock used by the company at this time were a heterogeneous lot. Indeed Sharpe, tinkering away in shops at Lancaster, had produced such inordinately wide carriages that in early January of 1850 Watson had to do the double up and down the line checking all the clearances. The first month of the year was troublesome throughout. On Tuesday, January 22, the locomotive of the 5 p.m. train from Lancaster got off the rails at Caton—a circumstance that earned a rebuke for the Caton station master, William Sandham. Added to this, Brett & Little's telegraph was proving anything but satisfactory and was replaced shortly after. In February a meeting with the Midland at Derby produced an agreement for through working of carriages to Lancaster, and complete trains if necessary. Local traffic was looking up; from February 20, third class carriages were to be attached to the 8.30 and 10.30 a.m. trains from Wennington on Saturdays for the convenience of farmers attending market in Lancaster.

Meanwhile Gooch had produced his report, strongly recommending that a double line be laid as soon as possible to connect the two big systems of the Midland and the West Coast route. The board accepted his findings and, while giving orders for the work to be put in hand, offered Sharpe the contract for the additional locomotives which would be required. In March all the station platforms were ordered to be ashphalted and the station masters to be supplied with uniforms; also at this time John Harker was appointed as goods agent at Hawes. Two months later Watson was asked to estimate the size and costs of the down platforms which would be necessary when the doubling was complete. With the remaining portion between Wennington and Clapham nearly finished the N.W.R. came to an agreement in May with the Midland and the Lancaster & Carlisle as to through running of trains between Derby and Glasgow. At the same time the company turned down an offer from Sharpe to lease the line at £500 per week for a term of 7 years.

At the end of May the last link was inspected and on Saturday, June 1, 1850 the line was opened throughout for public traffic. Five trains ran each way daily and through workings were instituted from Leeds and Bradford to Lancaster and Kendal without change of carriage, though as to the Kendal coaches these were detached at Green Ayre, taken on to Lancaster Castle, and then worked to Kendal by the L.C.R. At the same time the private road coach service between Clapham and Bentham was discontinued, as was that from Ingleton to Milnthorpe. The following Thursday saw a celebration dinner at Morecambe given by North Western directors to their opposites on the boards of the Midland and the L.C.R. On October 2 return tickets made their first appearance on the North Western, and a month later the company made an offer to the G.P.O. to take the Yorkshire-Glasgow mails on any of its trains at £300 per annum. Incidentally, in the early years there was a passenger station at Claughton (pronounced Clafton), and at Low Bentham, 7 and 13 miles from Lancaster respectively. Both disappeared from the timetables in August, 1853. Later, another station appeared for a short time at Wray, about ¾ mile east of Hornby station. (As to Ingleton, see Appendix IV.)

1851 was to be the first of the critical years in the history of the Midland's northern advance, for during it the little North Western nearly fell into the hands of the Great Northern Railway. The year started with Gooch's report on the locomotives and rolling stock then operating the North Western's services. (A table, extracted from his report, will be found in Appendix III.) At that time the company owned eleven engines, five of them fairly new, and three of these being for goods workings. The passenger engines were of two types—there were two six-wheeled tanks and six four-wheeled tender engines. Though approving of the tank locomotives, Gooch thought the 0-4-0s unsuitable to passenger workings. There were thirteen carriages of the Sharpe speciality. All were considerably lower and wider than usual—indeed they were more akin to broad gauge stock. Apart from this they were much heavier than normal but had had no provision made for increased axle load. Gooch was insistent that this be put right, and also advocated sliding doors to the carriages to replace those opening outwards, which tended to sweep the platforms clear if opened too soon. Sharpe was duly informed of the report and told to carry out its recommendations. On February 27 the company held its half-yearly meeting at Leeds. The directors' report stated that during the previous Autumn two further portions of the second line had been opened, giving a route mileage of double track between Hellifield and Hornby of approximately 22 miles. Traffic, however, was poor though new arrangements with the Midland were expected to help.

On March 7, 1851, Lupton, the N.W.R. chairman, told the board that he had had several meetings with the chairman and solicitors of the Great Northern Railway with a view to arranging for the construction of the Ingleton-Orton line, and for the working thereover of G.N.R. and Midland traffic to Glasgow. The N.W.R. had then gone to the Midland with a proposal dreamed up by the G.N.R. that both it and the Midland should guarantee capital sufficient to make the line, the Midland to give powers to the N.W.R. to run into Leeds where it would receive Great Northern traffic. The Midland, as might be expected, did not like the idea at all. It pointed out in a hurt tone that it had, from the opening of the N.W.R., worked the Leeds & Bradford in connection with that company's services, and could see no reason why the North Western should require running powers into Leeds.

If the Midland would not bite the Lancaster & Carlisle might. It was engaged in one of its periodic estrangements with the L.N.W.R. and announced itself interested in the scheme. A year later, on March 5, 1852, dissatisfaction was to be voiced at the L.C.R. half-yearly meeting at the amount of power the L.N.W.R. seemed to have over its policies. To the astonishment of the shareholders, the following September, it was found that five of the directors of the L.C.R., nominated by Euston, did not even hold any shares in the company. As the Midland was at this time considering amalgamation with the L.N.W.R. it was obvious that the only acceptable alternative was an alliance with the Great Northern. For a while the Lancaster & Carlisle and the Great Northern both considered making the Orton line and, when nothing was decided, the matter was only left in abeyance. One thing was certain—the G.N.R. was determined to find a way to Scotland. The reasons were plain to see. In August of 1849 the Midland had made an agreement with the L.N.W.R. to the effect that the Edinburgh traffic by the York and Carlisle routes should be thrown into a common fund and divided in proportion to the earnings of the respective companies. A critical clause in the agreement was that which invited the companies north of the Midland to recognise in the alliance the existing routes only. The arrangement was to continue in force after the G.N.R. main line was opened. If the companies north of the Midland—and these were the East Coast lines—objected to the proposal for accepting the existing routes, the Midland was not to object to the traffic being sent by the Carlisle route. In any case the little North Western was unfortunate since it could not be included in either category. Though the terms had been settled in 1849 their implementation was held over pending a possible last-minute traffic agreement with the G.N.R., but at a meeting between the three companies at York in 1850, to divide the north-south traffic, the negotiations had broken down. Euston and Derby had thereupon concluded an agreement with the York Newcastle & Berwick Railway, thereby hoping to frustrate G.N.R. aspirations in the north.

The railway press had condemned this arrangement, and had pointed out that with money now cheap the G.N.R. might well join with the York & North Midland, with whom it had a working agreement, to promote a York-Carlisle line. A suitable route did exist, following closely the old coach road between the two cities. For the time being, however, the G.N.R. was content to try and seize advantages where it could do so without undue effort. At the end of 1850, with the immense traffic likely to arise from the Great Exhibition, an arrangement based on an award made by Gladstone, acting as arbitrator, was made between the eight companies likely to benefit, for the proportional pooling of traffic receipts. An agreement to this effect was signed by the participants in early 1851 and was known, reasonably enough, as the 'Octuple Treaty'. The signatories were the L.N.W.R., L.C.R., Caledonian, G.N.R., York Newcastle & Berwick, York & North Midland, North British, and Midland. The agreement was to run for five years. From the Great Northern point of view, joining in the Treaty was more in the nature of a holding operation to forestall severe competition. As regards the little North Western the Octuple agreement had one vast drawback; it only recognised existing routes and thus, even if the Orton line was made, it would not 'rank for grant'. By 1852, however, matters had reached a confusing position. On August 14, the L.N.W.R. made a proposal to the Midland for an amalgamation, and two days later Denison of the Great Northern approached the Midland with similar intent, citing as evidence for such a move the increasing number of station duplications in towns served by the two lines. It would seem that the complete uncertainty of just who was with or against who was probably the cause of the anticlimax to the Orton line proposal. As to the Midland *vis a vis* the L.N.W.R., in order to smooth the path of amalgamation, the former's chairman, Ellis, was persuaded by Glyn of the L.N.W.R. to partake of £2,000 worth of shares, thus giving him, it was hoped, more authority with his own shareholders. In fact it had the reverse effect. The 'United Board', as it was pleased to term itself, answered Denison's offer for amalgamation with a counter proposal—that the G.N.R. should promote a Bill for amalgamation with a joint L.N.W.R. and Midland concern. It must have known what Kings Cross's answer would be; the proposal had the effect of making the G.N.R. revert once more to its quest for its own line to the north. Denison was quite content to wait, and meanwhile enjoy syphoning off Midland traffic when and where he could. As to searching for a route, he did not have far to look. Seizing the chance to use existing concerns rather than trigger off a costly fight for a new line, the Great Northern cast its eye towards Westmorland, for the country beyond the little North Western was burdered with two abysmally impoverished schemes ripe for take-over. Their history is of interest as they were forerunners of the Settle and Carlisle line.

When in 1846 the Leeds & Bradford Railway had broken away from the Manchester & Leeds amalgamation proposals, the latter company had immediately taken what it hoped was its vengeance by allying itself with a new concern, the Liverpool Manchester & Newcastle-upon-Tyne Junction Railway. Roughly speaking, at that time the L.M.N.J.R. proposed constructing a line from Preston and another from a junction near the northern termination of the L.B.R. extension, to the Richmond branch of the Great North of England Railway, following a line similar to the later Settle-Carlisle line of the Midland as far as Kirkby Stephen. At its northern end it was to join with an amalgamation of several companies seeking to join the two north-south trunk lines between Darlington and Clifton. As will be seen this network nearly came to fruition, and would have effectively kept the Midland from making any physical connection with Carlisle.

Amalgamated with the L.M.N.J.R. was the Lancashire & North Yorkshire Railway which planned a line some $47\frac{1}{2}$ miles in length from Elslack, on the L.B.R. extension between Skipton and Colne, through Gargrave, Kettlewell, and Middleham, to Scorton. Itself an amalgamation of two schemes of June 1845 proposing lines through Wharfedale and Wensleydale, its route competed with that of the Liverpool company. On joining forces the main line of the L.N.Y.R., and the Hawes branch of the L.M.N.J.R., were adopted as the new combined system which took the name of the Liverpool concern. The composition of the provisional committees of the various schemes at this time gave a fairly reliable guide to their affiliations to the major companies. That of the L.N.Y.R. included directors of the Manchester & Leeds, the Wakefield Pontefract & Goole—closely tied to the M.L.R.—and the Great North of England. The engineers were John Hawkshaw and Alfred S. Jee. The L.M.N.J.R. was partly financed and led by the Manchester & Leeds—the chairman of the M.L.R. was one of the first directors of the new company.

To the north of the L.M.N.J.R. there was a welter of various schemes for the session of 1846, some of them quite impracticable. To list them all would be tedious—those which eventually proceeded will suffice. One such appeared in early 1845 with the conventionally cumbersome title of York & Carlisle & Durham Westmorland & Lancashire Junction Railway. To general relief it was soon shortened to that of York & Carlisle. Again, its provisional committee indicated its allegiance; besides the Member for Westmorland, the Hon. Col. Lowther and the mayors of Kendal and Carlisle, the directorate of the Lancaster & Carlisle and the Caledonian were well represented with, for good measure, Joseph Pease of the Stockton & Darlington Railway. J. M. Rendel was the engineer. He had planned a line leaving the Great North of England near Northallerton and passing along the Tees Valley, then following

the River Greta to Brough, through Kirkby Stephen, via the Eden Valley
to Appleby, and thence to join the Lancaster & Carlisle near Clifton. One
third of the capital was to be at the disposal of the L.C.R. board. The
hangers-on which the scheme attracted were many. Only one was dangerously near to competing with it—the Yorkshire & Glasgow Union.
Appearing at about the same time as the York & Carlisle, the line proposed by the Y.G.U.'s engineer, H. Fulton, was to join the Great North
of England at Thirsk with the L.C.R. at Clifton, passing through Bedale,
Leyburn, Askrigg, Hawes, Kirkby Stephen, Appleby, and thence by
Threlkeld and Keswick to join the Cockermouth & Workington Railway.
Though the western continuation of the railway between Clifton and
Cockermouth was to be made for single track only—the works, however,
were to be made for double—the main line was in fact to be a fully
fledged trunk line in opposition to the York & Carlisle. It was not in
such a favourable position as the York company though; a meeting in
June of 1845 of the company's supporters spent most of the time trying
to sell the idea to the L.C.R. but as has been seen the York & Carlisle was
already entrenched.

Another affair, the Leeds & Carlisle, made up the triumvirate which
was soon to join together to form the Northern Counties Union Railway.
The Leeds & Carlisle—its title when first mooted was Leeds & Carlisle
or Northern Trunk Railway of England—proposed a line from the Leeds
& Thirsk, to pass through Otley, Kirkby Stephen and Appleby, to join
the L.C.R. at Clifton near Penrith. There was also to be a branch from
Otley to Bradford. The works were estimated to cost about £2 m. In
May 1846 the Leeds & Carlisle and the York & Carlisle amalgamated
with the Yorkshire & Glasgow Union to form the Northern Counties
Union Railway. The new company was authorised by its Act of July
27, 1846, to construct the 69 mile Thirsk-Penrith line and the Wath
branch of 7 miles (together known as the 'Wensleydale Line' and being
made up of the original Leeds & Carlisle and Yorkshire & Glasgow Union
projects); and the Bishop Auckland-Tebay link of 50 miles (known as the
'Stainmore Line' and being the former York & Carlisle company).
Together with a short branch at Bishop Auckland which was to be
purchased from the Stockton & Darlington company, the total length
came to $126\frac{3}{4}$ miles.

The L.M.N.J.R., received the Royal Assent in the same year as the
N.C.U. and almost immediately quarrelling broke out between the various factions on both boards representing the former individual concerns
amalgamated in each; for to construct all the lines authorised was to
provide a railway network out of all proportion to the needs of the
district. The Liverpool company received powers in 1847 to abandon
part of its line where it duplicated that of the Northern Counties Union
between Aysgarth and the Richmond branch of the Great North of England company. This portion was henceforth to be the joint property
of both lines. In the same session the L.M.N.J.R. got powers to con-

struct a short connecting line from the Burnley branch of the Manchester & Leeds Railway to the East Lancashire Railway, thus permitting the M.L.R. through access to the north. Needless to say the East Lancashire fought the proposed branch tooth and nail.

The Northern Counties Union, meanwhile, had let the Wath and Tebay contracts, about 9 miles and 6½ miles respectively. While its prospects remained bright those of its neighbour to the south did not. The affairs of the Liverpool company ran in one year through about all the moods permissible to a railway board. To begin with the board itself was split into two factions—one representing the northern interests which resented the close tie-up with the M.L.R. as well as the fact that almost all the shares had been allotted to the supporters of that company; and the other which desired a union with the M.L.R. and feared a similar proposal from the northern directors in respect of the N.C.U. A tug of war resulted as to whether the offices should be in Manchester or Newcastle. Manchester won and the Newcastle party retired from the contest. A pending amalgamation Bill with the N.C.U. was also dropped. Capital was short and for a time it looked as if the company would abandon its project but by the end of 1847 it approached the Railway Commissioners for an extension of time. Next year a Bill for abandonment, deposited by a refractory group of shareholders, got as far as the Lords before being thrown out. In its place there arrived a two-year extension of time from the commissioners. By October, however, this meant nothing, for the original directors had been pushed out and their places taken by the dissolution clique.

A similar state of affairs existed on the N.C.U. That company was hindered all through its short career by a clause in its Act—the 'simultaneous clause' which required that both the Wensleydale and Stainmore lines should be constructed at the same time. This was the result of the fear of the original shareholders of the York & Carlisle that their piece of line would be jettisoned if the Liverpool company's line, which competed with it, was authorised. In the Acts of 1846 the latter had been precluded from constructing the offending part for a period of eighteen months to give the N.C.U. time to make its complete line, and to make sure that the York & Carlisle people were not quietly throttled the clause was inserted in the Act. Designed to keep tempers within the N.C.U. under control, it had the opposite effect and, after the patent failure of the Liverpool company to produce anything other than a picture of complete disorganisation, its *raison d'etre* had vanished. The plain fact was that the N.C.U. could probably have constructed some of one part of its line; with the clause it was unable to move. The small part which was started, at Wath in conjunction with the Leeds & Thirsk company, progressed no further than a few earthworks. The *Railway Chronicle* of November 21, 1846, noted in its gossip column :

'The Northern Counties Union,—having obtained an Act for the formation of two lines, which expressly provides that the two lines shall be proceeded with

99

simultaneously, lately decided to proceed with the line up Wensleydale and postpone the making of the other from Auckland to Tebay. The shareholders resident at Barnard Castle are very indignant and threaten law proceedings.'

Additional light was thrown on this in the issue of December 5:

'The York and Carlisle, it is said, have abandoned that portion of their line—from Bishop Auckland, in Durham, to Kirkby Stephen, in Westmorland, for the following reasons. The immense tunnel, of two miles in length, which would be required on Stainmore Fell, through a stratum of limestone rock, is looked upon as an insurmountable difficulty; and the undertaking, it is thought, would occasion the expenditure of so large an amount of capital as to place an adequate return out of the question. About two months ago a partial new survey was made, to ascertain whether the line could be carried from the south-eastern extremity of the proposed tunnel over the summit of Stainmore. It was supposed that by leaving the original line to the south-west, proceeding northward about 4½ miles, close by Brough to Hall Garth; and then turning again to the south-west, they might run into the original line near Smardale (where the Yorkshire and Glasgow line, adopted by the united companies, is crossed), and join the Lancaster and Carlisle near Orton. This, however, is likewise found to be impracticable, owing to the steepness of the gradients over Stainmore. The promoters, therefore, have no alternative but to desert the undertaking.'

The trouble was though, that the promoters could not 'desert the undertaking' just like that and in 1847 the N.C.U. directors sought to promote a Bill to repeal the simultaneous clause. By a large majority the 'shareholders' voted against—most of the votes being cast as blocks by the L.C.R. and L.N.W.R., both of which did not now want the company to succeed. For the time being, nothing more could be done. Meanwhile the L.M.N.J.R. had been wasting away. One of the last glimpses of the Liverpool line before it faded out in the 1850s had a certain humour, however. At the half-yearly meeting in February, 1849, the company, with £19,000 in hand was greatly amused to receive a demand from the Duke of Leeds for £10,000, a sum which had been agreed would be paid for passing through his lands. This was the usual extortion, but on the grand scale. His Grace, probably realising that the £19,000 was a fast dwindling amount, and hoping that the card he dealt would be an ace, made his play. Amidst much laughter the company faded into history. At its last meeting in April 1852 only five shareholders presented themselves. According to *Herepath's Journal* it was still being wound up in 1855.

For two years the Northern Counties Union slumbered. Then, early in 1851, the Great Northern Railway, and the Glasgow & South Western Railway, concluded a secret treaty with the N.C.U. to join in the making of the line; Sir William Cubitt was to be asked to resurvey the route and suggest improvements. The treaty needed the sanction of Parliament, however, and before the Bill had been lodged the G.S.W.R. backed out. No reason had been given as to the rejectment of what would have been independent access to the south for the Glasgow company, but as time went on it became clear that it had been threatened by the L.N.W.R. in some way. In fact such was the wish of the G.S.W.R. to have access to the south independent of and better than the L.C.R.—the Stainmore line gradients were not as bad as the L.C.R.'s over Shap—that in August of 1852 it was prepared to give £200,000 towards this end. The effect of the G.S.W.R.'s back-down, however, was to make the G.N.R. drop the idea of taking over the N.C.U. and revert to its interests in the little North Western. Isaac Burkhill, one of the directors of the G.N.R., had managed to infiltrate the N.W.R. board and immediately attempted to swing a number of the shareholders over to an alliance with Kings Cross. At the same time the G.N.R. backed yet another company—the Great Northern Doncaster Wakefield Leeds & Bradford Railway, with Cubitt as engineer. The line was to run from Doncaster to Wakefield, and then throw out branches to Leeds and Bradford with access to the L.B.R. at Shipley. It would have had the effect of giving the G.N.R. running powers over the Leeds Bradford & Halifax Junction. As will be seen the little North Western did not fall at this first attempt to the G.N.R. but it was a near thing for the Midland. There were to be several calls in later years, some very much closer, before the company finally passed into Derby's ownership.

To return for a moment to the domestic affairs of the little North Western, in 1851 Sharpe had still done nothing to alter the axles of the carriage stock. He was informed that as they were in a dangerous condition they would be withdrawn unless the work was immediately carried out. It was. At the same time the board told him that henceforth all the passenger trains must be worked by the six-wheeled engines. A month later he had put the carriages back into service with modified axles, and in September it was decided that express trains should be permitted to call at stations where no stops were shown in the timetable, for the purpose of picking up and setting down first class passengers only who were travelling a distance of not less than four miles. At this time Gooch offered some useful advice to the company. He told it that he considered the local traffic was such that the line could survive on this alone and he warned it not to make the line to Orton but to leave construction to the bigger companies. The board decided to play it safe and prepared a Bill for Parliament for an extension of time for making the line, and powers to sell or lease the whole railway to either the Midland, the G.N.R., or the L.C.R.

Much of the through Yorkshire-London traffic had been lost by the Midland on the opening of the G.N.R. 'Towns Line' and in November a movement was afoot among some of the North Western shareholders to reopen negotiations between the three companies, whereby the Midland would link the N.W.R. at Skipton with the G.N.R. at Leeds. It was even considered that if the Midland proved awkward the N.W.R. should promote a line to join the G.N.R., or alternatively the latter might construct an extension to the N.W.R. from the intended Leeds Bradford & Halifax Junction Railway near Stanningley, between Bradford and Leeds. One of the shareholders published a letter in *Herepath's Journal* to the effect that in its relations with the N.W.R., the Midland was more the serpent than the dove; new working treaties between that company and others, about to come into force, might well be harmful to the North Western. The North Western board, however, thought differently. On December 22, determined to arrest the drift towards the Great Northern, it delegated Messrs. Alcock, Lupton, and Kitson, to meet the Midland for the purpose of negotiating an agreement for the latter to work the line. It also gave notice to Sharpe that his contract was to cease on January 31, 1852.

By February, 1852, a draft agreement for the working of the North Western Railway by the Midland Railway company had been sent to Derby. Parliamentary sanction for just such an agreement had been got by the N.W.R. in its Act of 1849, at the time of the abortive negotiations with the Midland. On hearing of the agreement the same shareholders that had advocated alliance with the Great Northern, had formed a committee to put pressure on the directors and it was only after a careful study of the traffic likely to follow on working by the Midland, and lengthy explanations by the directors, that they agreed to withdraw their opposition. They succeeded in getting the terms altered, however; whereas the original agreement was to have been for a lease of twenty-one years, both the North Western and the Midland had perforce to shorten the period to fourteen, with powers to the North Western to amalgamate with the Midland after seven. Also the running costs payable by the N.W.R. under the terms of the amended agreement were reduced from 50 per cent. on £52,000 to 50 per cent. on £47,000, with $66\frac{2}{3}$ per cent. of any excess, the Midland to take upon itself all accidents and losses. The North Western was to renew any permanent way that required replacement, the Midland to find the labour. The agreement between the two companies came into force on May 1, the actual working to commence from June 1, 1852, and to be exactly as if the line was part of the Midland, thus virtually extending its system to Lancaster and Ingleton, the northernmost point yet reached. To put its own house in order, the North Western took powers by an Act of June 30 to dissolve the company and re-incorporate it under the same title. Also by this Act the company was enabled to start a steamer service between Morecambe and Barrow; an extension of time for 5 years was received for the construction of the Orton line; and powers to lease or sell the portion north from Uphall to the Lancaster & Carlisle were confirmed, as was the right to conclude traffic and working agreements.

As handed over the line was rather a hotchpotch. From a report on the state of the works, made in July, it appeared that the Morecambe branch, still a single line, was for the most part unfenced. There were stretches of single line between Lancaster Castle and Hornby, Bell Busk and Skipton, and on the Ingleton branch (a list of the openings of the line will be found in Appendix IV). The engineering works, though for the most part complete, were in a poor state with several earth slips along the line. The stations were in need of considerable overhaul and repainting—that at Ingleton was stated to be out of repair and not watertight. Fencing in many places was broken down, the electric telegraph was still out of order, the water supply at Lancaster and High Bentham was insufficient for the engines, and there were no spare permanent way materials. The locomotives and rolling stock handed over to the Midland, which were to be purchased from Sharpe, consisted of four goods engines, three tank engines, five four-wheeled passenger engines—still obviously in use despite Gooch's report—the thirteen large passenger carriages, two third class carriages, two old first class carriages, eight new coke wagons, two old vans, an old horsebox, eight old wagons, and one engine 'in course of alteration'. The Midland's official valuation for this motley little collection was summarised as :—

	£	s.	d.
Engines and Tenders	14,950	0	0
Carriages and Brake Vans	6,735	0	0
Wagons, Horse Boxes, Vans etc.	11,912	0	0
Machinery, Tools, etc.	830	19	7
Stores	2,843	13	1
Stores furniture, etc.	455	16	5
Horses, Harness, etc.	230	15	0
	£37,958	4	1

It is of interest that Sharpe, far from fading away in these circumstances, merely transferred his affections elsewhere after the Midland took over. Mr. E. Craven, in an article in the April, 1957, issue of the *Journal of the Stephenson Locomotive Society*, mentioned that when the Liverpool Crosby & Southport Railway decided to work its own line in 1854, in place of the L.Y.R., Mr. Sharpe was well to the fore with advice as to locomotive stock. Not unnaturally he leaned on his experience with the little North Western with the result that Fairbairn got some more business.

Finally, note can be taken at this point of a line so far not mentioned but which was to play a big part later on when the Settle and Carlisle was built. In the session of 1846, at the time of the little North Western's incorporation, a new venture was launched supported by the little North Western and with Vignoles and Watson as engineers, to connect railways at Blackburn with both the N.W.R. and the Leeds & Bradford Extension line. The Blackburn Clitheroe & North Western Junction Railway Act of July 27, 1846, authorised construction of railways from Daisyfield Junction through Chatburn to Long Preston on the N.W.R. and to Elslack, on the L.B.R. extension, where a junction would have been available to the Lancashire & North Yorkshire Railway, mentioned earlier. The branch was not built and the main line was only constructed as far as Chatburn, the extension to the little North Western not materialising until several years later. As originally authorised the line north of Chatburn was to run roughly in the same direction, but west of the present Chatburn-Hellifield line and was to make connection with the N.W.R. at a point immediately south of Long Preston Beck, near the present station of that name. The line was to have few earthworks and was planned for a ruling gradient of 1 in 132 north of Chatburn. There was to be a viaduct 220 yards long and 150 ft. high over the River Ribble. The gradient contrasted with the portion which was constructed south of Chatburn, and which includes a tunnel and a length of about 4½ miles at about 1 in 80 down to Whalley from the summit at Wilpshire. The second line was to leave the first near Rimington and was to run west-north-west some 9 miles or so on a ruling gradient of 1 in 105 to join the L.B.R. about ½ mile south of Elslack station. The estimated cost of the authorised lines was £600,000. At the Blackburn end the company was to make connection with the proposed East Lancashire Railway and the Act stipulated that if the E.L.R. had not been laid out and made ready for the junction within two years, the B.C. & N.W.J. was to be permitted to construct its line up to, and make connection with, the Blackburn Darwen & Bolton Railway to which its incorporation Act gave it powers to lease its line. By an Act of 1847, however, the B.C. & N.W.J. amalgamated with the B.D. & B.—a protégé of the L.Y.R.—to become the Bolton Blackburn Clitheroe & West Yorkshire Railway. Four years later the company changed its name to become the Blackburn Railway, and an extension of time was granted for construction of the 1846 lines to Long Preston and Elslack. In 1858 the Blackburn company vested jointly in the Lancashire & Yorkshire and East Lancashire companies. At the time of the take-over the Blackburn Railway consisted of a short terminal branch at Blackburn and the Daisyfield Junction-Chatburn line, divided by a short length of the E.L.R. As the Blackburn had been worked by the L.Y.R. from 1850 this short link caused considerable friction as the E.L.R. and the L.Y.R. were decidedly bad neighbours. The joint ownership eased matters, however, and in the following year trouble ceased entirely when the East Lancashire amalgamated with the L.Y.R. This, however, is far ahead of the story to date. If constructed the original B.C. & N.W.J. could have brought the L.Y.R., via the Lancashire & North Yorkshire, into the territory now occupied by the Settle and Carlisle. That this did not happen can be attributed both to the failure of the L. & N.Y. and its partners to agree on a construction policy, and to the poor finances of the post 'Mania' period.

VII

Independence

End of the Confederacy
1852 – 1857

No sooner had the Midland taken over the working of the little North Western than the latter's board began to realise the traffic was not dependent on the will of Derby but of Euston. Towards the end of 1852, with both the large companies considering amalgamation, the N.W.R. asked the Midland for an assessment of the future of the working agreement should the amalgamation proceed. As an indication of the prevailing mood of uncertainty, the Midland had not even officially informed the N.W.R. of the proposal.

With the situation in a state of flux the L.N.W.R., M.R. and G.N.R. met on May 5, 1853 at Manchester to try to iron out an equitable traffic policy, and it was decided that on and from May 23 a fares agreement between them would come into force between London and the midland towns. To counter the inherent threat in the proposed fusion of the L.N.W.R. and Midland, the little North Western had already suggested its own amalgamation with the latter but by April, 1853, however, the crisis for the N.W.R. board was temporarily averted, Parliament having reported against the L.N.W.R. and Midland amalgamation Bill and deferred it until the next session.

At this time there were some changes within the Midland hierarchy. Bell, the secretary, was made a director, his place being taken by Sanders, the traffic manager. Concurrently, James Allport was poached from the Manchester Sheffield & Lincolnshire Railway to be appointed as the Midland's general manager at a salary of £1,500 per annum. Allport had left the Midland at its formation in 1844, there being a superfluity of officers from the three constituent companies. Hudson had then found a place for his talents by appointing him to manage the Newcastle & Darlington Junction. He had joined the M.S.L.R. in 1850 as general manager.

In May 1853 a further agreement between the Midland and the L.N.W.R. as to equal division of the traffic between Leeds and Edinburgh, received the grudging approval of the little North Western. As to the progress of the North Western itself, the frequent exhortations from the Midland for doubling the line in the interests of safe operating were bearing fruit and by mid 1853 double line working was in operation between Skipton and Hornby. The traffic too was on the increase but a dispute in November between the York Newcastle & Berwick and the Midland over demurrage on the latter's wagons engaged on the iron ore traffic between Consett and Morecambe, whereby the wagons were held at Leeds for some time and were not available for the coal trade, showed the little North Western how dependent it had become on the Midland for its livelihood.

Mention of the state of the line between Hornby and Lancaster—still single—was made in the North Western board minutes of July 22, 1852. There was apparently a quarry—from which stone was obtained for the Morecambe harbour works—situated athwart the line about $\frac{1}{4}$ mile east of Halton station at Denny Beck. By the time the Midland took over the working of the line the quarry had been in use for a few years and the single track line of the N.W.R. still passed over the workings by means of a temporary wooden structure; it was evidently not regarded as being even of bridge status. On August 3, 1853 the N.W.R. board was insistent that a second line of rails should be laid from Denny Beck to Lancaster ' . . . for the sole use of the stone trains'. This order came immediately after instructions had been given for the doubling of the Morecambe branch. As will be seen in Appendix IV, neither of these widenings took place until 1889.

March of 1854 saw an anxious N.W.R. again seeking reassurance from the Midland over impending traffic arrangements between Derby and Euston. The Midland replied in April that the amalgamation idea between it and the L.N.W.R. had now been completely dropped but that in any event it would always protect the N.W.R. interests. Foiled as to amalgamation, however, it was at this juncture that the L.N.W.R. and the Midland concluded the private and illegal traffic arrangement based on a common purse, contrary to the prevailing anti-monopolistic policy of Parliament and aimed against the Great Northern. The Midland still regarded its hold over the N.W.R. as of little value. The overall annual profit from operations was diminutive—that very year was only to yield £1,000. The company showed scant respect to the requirements for strict time-keeping as to connections with the steamboat services at Morecambe. These had been taken over by the Midland in early 1853 and were to remain at Morecambe until August 31, 1867 when they were removed to Barrow-in-Furness. The general attitude of Derby annoyed the North Western board so much that it was in two minds whether to try once more to reach agreement with the G.N.R. and in October 1854, with time for the Orton branch fast running out, it determined to put a straight question to the Midland as to its intentions for completion of that line and operation of Scotch services thereover. With the North Western plainly unable to afford the cost of construction the Midland was once again faced with the possibility of G.N.R. and L.C.R. attempts to muscle in. This time the Caledonian too was interested. In mid October Alcock of the N.W.R. met Ellis at Normanton and was told that the Midland agreed that the line should go ahead but that the board required to know the part the Lancaster & Carlisle would play in it. If the L.C.R. was willing to share the risk, then the Midland would probably agree. But as to G.N.R. participation—that was completely ruled out. Alcock left the Midland to ponder the situation. The L.C.R. meanwhile had rejected the possibility of giving financial aid but asked in turn what the Midland intended. With both these companies eyeing each other in mutual suspicion, the N.W.R. turned in desperation to the Great Northern. That company intimated that if the Midland was not prepared to go ahead—and Alcock had given it a time limit for a definite reply—then the G.N.R. would complete the line and apply for powers to work over the Midland from Leeds so as to gain access to Scotland. December came and with it a letter from the Midland completely reversing what Ellis had told Alcock. Somehow Derby had got to hear of the hesitance shown by the L.C.R. as to providing any money, and was not now prepared to back the N.W.R. Once again the latter's board glimpsed the might of Euston behind this *volte face*. Despite Midland protestations that its alliance would not affect the little North Western it had now become apparent that indeed that was just what was happening. Left with no alternative, the North Western went back again to the G.N.R. Alcock and Hare met the Great Northern chairman in late December, and 1854 ended in a frustrated suspense, for the G.N.R. board was to give a verdict after its next directors' meeting early the following month. The N.W.R. was again doomed to disappointment, however, for Huish of the L.N.W.R., learning what was afoot, offered the G.N.R. a pooling arrangement which the latter was only too glad to accept, at the price of dropping the little North Western.

Meanwhile Hare, on behalf of a thoroughly alarmed N.W.R. board, made an appointment with the Midland for an inspection on January 2 at Derby of the new traffic agreement between that company and the L.N.W.R. When, accompanied by Whelon, he got to Derby, Allport refused him access to the document saying that it contained nothing in it affecting the interests of the N.W.R. but that there were things in the agreement which should be kept secret. Hare angrily returned to Lancaster where a letter was drafted to the Midland asking if the chairman of the little North Western might inspect the document on an assurance that the contents would not be disclosed. It was not until February 14 that Derby agreed. During all this activity the North Western shareholders were stalled in the company's half-yearly report for February with vague assurances of the Orton line's usefulness and the present inability of the company to complete it.

At this point the Lancaster & Carlisle comes back into the picture. It was again at loggerheads with the L.N.W.R., this time ostensibly over the Preston station enlargement Bill, the L.C.R. having run over the Lancaster & Preston Junction since the former's opening and taken over the smaller comany by an Act of August 1, 1849. Early in March of 1855 John Barker, a prominent shareholder in the L.C.R., together with seven fellow proprietors, approached the little North Western with a proposal for amalgamation and, after a favourable reception, he advised the L.C.R. board on March 28 that it should take advantage of the situation. He also suggested that if it did so it should have nothing to do with the L.N.W.R. solicitors, at that time acting on the L.C.R.'s behalf. The little North Western, nothing loth at this unofficial advance, and seeing renewed hope for the Orton line, had suggested that each company should construct half of the works, to meet at Uphall. In June the N.W.R. board, in an attempt to jolly things along, decided to go for powers to purchase the outstanding lands required for the Orton line, taking care to let the Midland know what it was doing. At the same time Smallman, the company's resident engineer, was to make a survey of a deviation which would be required on the Orton line and Peto, Brassey & Company were instructed to inspect the route north of Ingleton and then make an offer for its construction. The deviation was intended to alter the point of junction from Dillicar Park, where the line was intended to join the L.C.R., by means of a viaduct over the River Lune, 1,300 feet long and 150 feet high, at a place where the public could have no access to the junction, to a point near the L.C.R.'s Tebay station where the Lune could be crossed by a two-arched bridge only 44 feet in height. The report by the company's solicitor on the Midland and L.N.W.R. traffic agreement had convinced the board that it was definitely harmful to the N.W.R., despite Midland assurances to the contrary, and the company, thinking the L.C.R. was ready for talks, made an appointment for a delegation to meet the latter's board to discuss the deviations and the amalgamation.

The little North Western might have been excused for thinking that Barker's sudden and welcome appearance in March was a reflection of the current attitude of the L.C.R. But the Lancaster company still had its fifth column. Out of seventeen directors seven were nominated by the L.N.W.R. and two by the Lancaster & Preston Junction. The L.C.R. chairman, E. W. Hassel, found that any terms suggested by Barker were vetoed by his board. An influential section of the shareholders, however, were concerned at the way the L.C.R. was rapidly losing any independance it once had and Barker returned to the attack. After highlighting the L.N.W.R. strength on the board and its 'baneful' influence, he ended a letter to the directors as a whole, dated July 16, 1855, with 'whether conduct like this on the part of a board of directors towards its constituents is respectful or proper, I offer no further remark, but if you expect to drive us with such means from our purpose, you will find yourselves mistaken'.

Of course though, they were not mistaken. They had the L.N.W.R. behind them. And behind the L.N.W.R. was Captain Huish. At that time the Midland was much in tow with the L.N.W.R. and Huish had no wish to entangle himself in litigation with Derby over the little North Western at a time when both companies were unlawfully conspiring to keep traffic from their mutual *bête noire,* the upstart and dangerous Great Northern Railway. Added to this was the fact that the L.C.R. stood to gain far more from remaining within the provisions of the Octuple Treaty than it did from amalgamation with the little North Western. So Mr. Barker was defeated, the board giving legal gloss to the proceedings by obtaining the opinion of the Attorney General that in any event the whole idea of amalgamation with the little North Western was fraught with obstacles, not least being that the L.C.R. was lawfully incapable of completing the N.W.R.'s Orton line. A resulting committee of inquiry set up by the L.C.R. shareholders talked around the subject of the L.N.W.R. influence over their company but realised that for the time being the bread and butter could only come from Euston. To a small point, however, there had been a shake-up of the Lancaster's board with a slight decrease in the L.N.W.R.'s power as a result.

By September Hassel had publicly put it on record that he too was now against any tie-up with the little North Western, going so far as to say that he would quit the company as soon as any such move became policy. In fact Euston had decided, that month, to call a halt to the whole business and administer a sharp reminder to the L.C.R. by giving notice that it did not intend to renew the working agreement. It was this more than anything else which effectively stopped the amalgamation, for without the L.N.W.R.'s support the L.C.R. would have been out on a limb. With locomotives and rolling stock to be found for its own line now that the L.N.W.R. trains were to be withdrawn, and the enmity of the Midland which would be incurred by filching from it the N.W.R., coupled with the expenditure which would be necessary on the Orton line as part and parcel of an amalgamation, the Lancaster company dared not take the risk. In any case a good argument could be made from the accounts side—there really did not seem much point for the L.C.R., currently paying 7 per cent., to ally itself with the N.W.R., which barely managed 1 per cent.

Thus it was that when in early November of 1855 the North Western deputation knocked on the L.C.R. front door to talk terms as arranged, it was unfortunate but understandable that the latter company had made sure both to misunderstand the time fixed for the appointment and to have finished its board meeting so that the members had dispersed. No decision, the North Western was told, could be made at the present time; the N.W.R. would have to take its chance on whether to go ahead with the Orton line alone. Bewildered by events, Hare, who led the delegation, asked Hassel off the record what he thought. The answer was vague and discouraging. Lieutenant-Colonel Maclean, a director of the L.C.R. who happened still to be present, and who was obviously not a Euston man, told Hare that he could put his finger on several members of his board who were hostile to the little North Western. That, Hare must have thought, was that. For the N.W.R. had just about exhausted every possibility. Only the Great Northern continued to show interest. Still determined to break out from between the unspeakable L.N.W.R. and the insufferable Midland, the North Western board decided to make one last effort. In so doing it lit a fuse leading to one of the biggest bangs yet in railway politics.

As has been seen Euston and Derby were clearly quite closely tied together at this time. Though the Midland had all along been vaguely bothered on its dependence on the L.N.W.R. for London traffic—it still handed over all south-bound trains to the latter at Rugby and had for some time privately thought that Euston was having too big a share of the cake—its fears were now somewhat calmed by the slow palliative of constructing the Leicester-Hitchin line. This had been authorised in 1847, during a short courtship period with the G.N.R., but the powers were later dropped. In 1853 they had been revived and even if the line seemed to end most inopportunely in the heart of enemy territory at least it possessed the merit of pointing south. As it turned out it was to be a blessing in disguise far sooner than the Midland realised. The pact with the L.N.W.R., publicly announced by Ellis in 1849, had become popularly known as the 'Euston Square Confederacy'. Into this amalgam the Manchester Sheffield & Lincolnshire had been dragged at the end of that year, the Lancashire & Yorkshire (the old M.L.R. renamed) having been embroiled from the beginning. Euston and Derby had for some time been working the illegal common purse agreement, to the detriment of the G.N.R., and by 1856 Captain Huish could fairly think that he had Kings Cross at his mercy. A rate war was again in full spate between the two groups and Euston's absolute monopoly of West Coast north and south traffic was unchallenged within the Confederacy itself, though there were rumblings of discontent at the Euston 'diktat' amongst the members. It was at this point then that, far away and seemingly quiescent, the little North Western decided, after considerable heart-searching, that it had had enough and would come to Parliament with a Bill for the session of 1856 to get it out of trouble. Running powers were to be sought over the Leeds & Bradford lines from Skipton to Bradford and from Shipley to the Hunslet Lane and Central stations at Leeds, as well as over the Lancaster & Carlisle from the junction with the Orton line to Carlisle, and over the Caledonian Railway to a junction with the Glasgow & South Western Railway at Gretna. The new Glasgow-Leeds route thus created so munificently at the expense of others would be the shortest by some 60 miles. To be sure there would be no hindrance to traffic, existing agreements with the Midland and L.C.R. as to the rights into the stations at Skipton and Lancaster were to be confirmed, and powers sought to make the required deviation from Dillicar to Tebay. In addition, and with the view that if there was going to be a gamble it might as well be a big one, the company decided to attack the sacred cow of the Octuple Treaty, then about to come to the end of its five-year term and due for renewal. As has been seen, by confining its provisions to traffic over existing routes, it cut out the Orton line—the very necessary part of any independant North Western route. To put the record right the company told the Midland that its joining in any new arrangement similar to the Octuple Treaty was absolutely inimical to the interests of the North Western. Tying up all the loose ends, the N.W.R. board also sent a letter to the L.C.R. confirming that it had duly noted the statements made by Lieutenant-Colonel Maclean the previous month. With an air of panache the little North Western sat back to wait upon events. Behind it sat the Great Northern.

The background to the current unpleasantness between Kings Cross and the Confederacy contained the usual tale of accusations of aggression and bad faith made by each of the parties about the other, though this time perhaps the G.N.R. was in truth more to blame. It all started with an internal letter from Seymour Clarke, the general manager of the Great Northern, to Denison, his chairman. Dated July 18, 1855, it noted the impending termination of the Octuple Treaty and suggested that talks should be had with the other parties with a view to widening the scope of Gladstone's original award to include some towns and their traffic not so far dealt with under its provisions. Denison gave him the go-ahead and after a series of letters to Huish and Allport in August there were seven meetings spread over November and December, which Seymour Clarke attended with Huish, Allport, and Watkin, the latter gentleman being from the M.S.L.R. Seymour Clarke may have been an excellent general manager, but as a railway politician he was a babe in arms compared with his hard-bitten opposite numbers on the Confederate side. At the meetings they worked out a new draft agreement based on Gladstone's award that was calculated to give the G.N.R. a very poor deal. Out-manoeuvred and out-gunned, Seymour Clarke agreed the terms. If the Confederacy thought the G.N.R. was now at its mercy it had a rude shock for when the minutes of the meetings were put to the G.N.R. board on December 18, 1855, they were not accepted. After a horrified look at what Seymour Clarke had agreed, Denison repudiated the arrangements and asked for further talks. Meanwhile the same minutes had been solemnly approved by the Confederate boards and Clarke had the unfortunate task of having to write to Huish on December 19 asking for an armistice, knowing there was to be a declaration of war. Huish granted time until the end of January but the Confederate companies made it a condition precedent to further talks that the G.N.R. should agree to the minutes of the seven meetings. This, of course, Denison would not do. In vain he wrote to the L.N.W.R. chairman, Lord Chandos, to make a final appeal to reason '—ere it becomes too late; for if war be declared, no one can tell when, in our case as in others, peace may be restored'. He inferred that Seymour Clarke had not had authority from the G.N.R. board to negotiate a final settlement at the time of the meetings and that he thought the others had understood this.

Now it was Huish's turn to feel out-smarted and bad temper took over at Euston. The Confederate companies started running fast trains into G.N.R. territory causing the shares at Kings Cross to drop by some 3 per cent. Ridiculously low fares resulted from the ensuing rate war, with many people taking their first chance to travel to London from the midlands. It was perhaps galling to Euston to find that the public appeared to prefer the G.N.R. for their London jaunts, finding it for the most part more direct and with easily more courteous staff. When the G.N.R. complained of the warlike measures adopted by Euston, however, Ellis of the Midland, at that company's half-yearly meeting of February 20, 1856, publicly reminded Denison that according to the Railway Clearing House returns the G.N.R. had all along done better than the Midland out of Gladstone's award. The G.N.R. traffic from the towns jointly worked with the Midland was greater, even though the Midland had been there first. In the case of Peterborough, for instance, the G.N.R. had gone so far as to arrange with the Eastern Counties Railway to exclude the Midland from the north-south traffic as much as possible. Words alone, however, would not have done the trick. Percentages did. By the end of February 1856, and despite all that had gone before, Lord Chandos felt able to announce that all differences between the Confederacy and the G.N.R. were at an end. He may even have believed it. The G.N.R. played along by participating in a new 14-year arrangement —the 'English and Scotch Traffic Agreement', made by the L.N.W.R., L.C.R., Caledonian, G.N.R., North Eastern, North British, and Midland. In truth, however, it was merely waiting to see whether its quaint little ally up in the north was about to present it with the means of delivering a knock-out punch to Euston. That the means were to be entirely different to what was expected, but no less effective, nobody could have foreseen, least of all the little North Western.

Open hostilities between the N.W.R. and the forces of the Confederacy had started as soon as the former's Bill was deposited. The Lancaster & Carlisle kicked off by initiating proceedings in the Court of Chancery to stop the Bill. This procedure failed, however, and on January 24, 1856 Whelon reported to the N.W.R. board that the Bill was going ahead. On February 27 the company's shareholders met at Leeds for the half-yearly meeting. They learned of the L.C.R.'s failure to stop the Bill, of the new traffic agreement which must affect them adversely, of the perfidy of the Midland in yet again disregarding their interests, and of the progress of the Bill by which it was hoped they would be able to thumb their collective nose at all concerned. On the same day the company's Parliamentary committee told the board that the Bill had been successfully read for the second time in the Commons. By the end of June it was safely through the Commons committee, after nineteen days of argument. The committee had decided against the deviation but to the delight of the N.W.R. had agreed that the route via Ingleton would be the shortest to Scotland. Clauses were to be inserted in the Bill to compel companies taking north-south traffic to make reasonable arrangement to use it.

Defeated on this major point, the opponents of the Bill—the L.N.W.R., L.C.R., N.E.R., L.Y.R., and Midland—decided to oppose the third reading and to appeal against the running powers on standing orders. This gambit was successful, the Standing Orders Committee of the Commons striking out the clauses dealing with running powers on the contention that the powers sought did not come within the terms of the notices published. Though it killed the heart of the Bill and caused the N.W.R. immediately to withdraw the rest, it had been a very close thing. Withdrawn at the same time, and dependent upon the first, was another N.W.R. Bill to lease the whole of the railway to the L.C.R. or the Midland. It was supported by the former and opposed by the latter. The very nearness that the company had achieved to its goal determined it to try again at the next Parliamentary session. One thing the Bill did, however, was to split the Confederacy down the middle, for during the evidence on the traffic question raised by the running powers the joint purse agreement between the L.N.W.R. and the Midland had come out in the open. It had to be repudiated in public, and quickly, as it went against the terms of the existing traffic agreements. In so doing the Midland was shortly to find itself virtually freed from the L.N.W.R. The little North Western's half-yearly report for August of 1856 took note of this and was happy—the company had only entered into the 1852 working agreement with the Midland because the latter was progressing with the Leicester-Hitchin line and seemed, as an already adjoining neighbour, a better bet at the time than the Great Northern. The closer tie-up between Derby and Euston which had followed had sown doubts as to the correctness of this decision but now the N.W.R. was able to hope for better treatment, especially as its claim to be the shortest north-south route had been upheld in Parliament, even though defeated on a technicality. The report ended by thanking Edmund Denison for his efforts on the company's behalf during the recent conflict.

With the clear possibility that the N.W.R. would be successful next time, the L.C.R. approached the company in August to see whether some agreement could be reached to avoid another expensive Parliamentary contest. At a meeting held at Morecambe on August 28 the N.W.R. board informed its shareholders that it had retained Mr. Blyth, an Edinburgh engineer, to examine all the schemes so far prepared for the Orton line. It was hoped that a total stranger would pick out the best points of each and, after surveying the district, come up with a new line. In his report to the board the same month Blyth did just that. The new line he had planned would save some £60,000 to £70,000, routed along the Lune Valley to Tebay, instead of terminating at Dillicar. In essence it was a repeat with variations on the 1855 survey, but on September 18, when committees from the L.C.R. and N.W.R. met at Low Gill station to inspect the new point of junction, no decision was reached. Blyth reported later that he and Errington, the L.C.R.'s engineer, had discussed the matter privately but had also disagreed. He still thought his Tebay line the best whereas Errington wanted the junction to the L.C.R. to be at Scufton House, about ½ mile north of the site of the old Low Gill station, with steeper gradients.

To this latest proposal the N.W.R. replied that if it could agree to a junction at Scufton it would require the L.C.R. to reimbuse it for all the land not used but already purchased, as well as providing a banking engine for the line, a joint station at Scufton, and an agreement for exchange of traffic. To this rather lengthy reply the L.C.R. remained silent until November 18 when it is said that its policy had changed and it could not now agree to the N.W.R. proposals. This led the latter to retort that at least the L.C.R. might have suggested an alternative, seeing that it was the party which had asked to avoid renewal of the fight. Having made its point the N.W.R. board instructed its engineer and solicitor to prepare a Bill for the next session for a new line to Tebay and abandonment of the Dillicar Park line.

The N.W.R. might well have wondered at the changed attitude of the L.C.R. but on December 1 the awful truth was out. The latter had been successfully stonewalling in order to prepare its own Bill for a line from Ingleton to Scufton. The reason for this was not hard to find. If the L.N.W.R. was ceasing to work the L.C.R. then it behoved the latter to gain as much advantage as it could from an increased length of line, particularly as the Ingleton-Orton section was now officially recognised as the potential short Scotch route. In the opinion of Hassel, the Lune Valley needed a railway and it was best that the L.C.R. should go for powers both for profit and defence. In order to work its lines the company had contracted earlier in the year to purchase from the L.N.W.R. forty engines and tenders. It also placed orders for twenty new goods and five new passenger locomotives from Messrs. Rothwell & Company, and had let contracts for engine sheds and workshops at Carlisle. The L.N.W.R. would, however, still be providing the coaching stock. The existing L.N.W.R. working was to cease on July 31, 1857.

Before the year was out, 1856 was to provide for the Midland one further mild piece of excitement, created by the East Lancashire Railway. At that company's meeting at Bury in the previous February, the shareholders had learned that after some years of bad connections with the Midland at Colne, due it was said entirely to the fault of the Midland, an agreement had come into force whereby the E.L.R. was to work its trains through to Skipton. There was, therefore, no outstanding cause for bad feeling between the two companies. Nevertheless, what the E.L.R. tried next would, had it succeeded, have made life difficult for the Leeds & Bradford Extension.

The E.L.R. was currently engaged in a struggle with the Lancashire & Yorkshire Railway for the Southport traffic. In June of 1855 a legal case highlighted the competition when the E.L.R. prosecuted a Mr.

Bowes for avoidance of fare. Bowes had bought a 6d. ticket at Liverpool to travel to Southport—the ticket not being available for intermediate stations—but had got out at Ormskirk. There he was asked for an extra shilling, the full fare from Liverpool to Ormskirk being 1s. 6d. For though Southport was a good distance further on the company was rate cutting on the full distance to beat the L.Y.R. The court held that the E.L.R. was in the right; while not interfering with Bowes's liberty, it was merely a matter of convenience to the railway that he should be carried between Liverpool and Southport for 6d. The E.L.R. was generally jittery about money at this time. Redpath's frauds on the G.N.R. had just come to light and the E.L.R. had one of its own in September, though of a different nature. Ormskirk was again in the news when its station master, John Johnson, was found to have embezzled £29. He was arrested, put on bail, and absconded. The general manager, James Smithells, obviously thought that this was bad publicity for the company as he put out an advertisement that the E.L.R. held sufficient of Johnson's securities to cover the loss.

To return to the main theme; by 1856 the competition with the L.Y.R. led to a scheme for a new line from Bradford to Colne, 20 miles long and passing through Haworth and Thornton, to join the eastern extension of the company's system with the G.N.R. Adolphus Street terminus at Bradford bringing Colne, and thus the E.L.R., 15 miles nearer Bradford and 11 miles nearer Leeds. It would have been quite expensive —there were to be two tunnels, one of 2 miles and one of $1\frac{1}{2}$, boring through millstone grit and coal. As has been stated the line was not aimed directly against the Midland—it was essentially a furtherance of the conflict with the L.Y.R. In the end Derby did not have to worry; the line was stopped dead within the E.L.R. itself. The company voted for a Bill for the line at its meeting on November 12, 1856. Good local traffic was expected and all looked set fair for a grand entry into Bradford. During the meeting, however, there was considerable opposition from a Mr. J. E. Vance who said that the proposal was 'the maddest scheme in which sane men ever embarked their property'. Nobody listened. By December 6 Vance had filed a Bill in Chancery to stop the line and five days later an injunction against proceeding with it was granted and the Bill was withdrawn. It turned out, not very surprisingly, that Vance was a shareholder in the L.Y.R.

The other event in 1856, perhaps too small to excite much attention but significant if taking into account both the little North Western's hopes in the coming session, and the fact that the G.N.R. could have been involved, was reported in *Herepath's Journal* in mid October. Apparently a number of meetings of parties from Wharfedale, Bradford, and Leeds had been held recently to discuss the possibility of making a railway to leave the Leeds Bradford & Halifax Junction near Stanningley, in G.N.R. territory, to pass through Wharfedale and thence to Skipton, there to connect with the N.W.R. An intriguing item of intelligence but one which, again luckily for the Midland, led nowhere.

1857 started with a New Year pact between the L.C.R. and the N.W.R. that neither would attack the other's Bill at Standing Orders stage. It seemed that the lessons of last session had not been in vain. In the hope that its Bill was going to get Royal Assent the N.W.R gave its support to a proposed British & Irish Grand Junction Railway—a line from Castle Douglas to Portpatrick, north of the Border. Also backing this new venture were the G.N.R. and the G.S.W.R., on the same side as the N.W.R., and the Lancaster & Carlisle which proposed contributing £40,000 and two directors to the undertaking. The line, with the title changed to a more reasonable 'Portpatrick Railway' was successful, receiving the Royal Assent on August 10, 1857. It will be discussed later in another chapter for it was in time to form the main line of the Portpatrick & Wigtonshire Joint Railway, the most northerly outpost of the Midland, excluding the company's interest in the Forth Bridge Railway. By March the L.C.R. Bill had been read for the second time in the Commons and on June 19, after fifteen days of argument and after having examined both proposals, the Commons committee gave a decision in its favour, with the proviso that the Orton line should be looked upon as a through route with all the traffic implications which that entailed. The L.C.R. was to construct the line, purchasing the lands and the few barely commenced works from the little North Western. The L.C.R. agreed to this and two Acts set the record straight. The Lancaster & Carlisle & Ingleton Railway Act of August 25 authorised construction of the line from Scufton House on the L.C.R. to an end-on junction with the N.W.R. at the latter's Ingleton station, and a branch just over a mile in length from the new line to join the L.C.R. at Grayrigg. These, in effect, would give through running on to the L.C.R. in both directions. The works were estimated to cost some £300,000 and were to be completed within four years. The N.W.R. Act permitted the company to abandon its authorised line north of Ingleton and to lease or sell at some future date the whole railway to either the Midland or the L.C.R.

If the truth were known, it appeared that the little North Western was quite satisfied with the way things had gone. With the completion of the line, at someone else's expense, a line moreover running nearly 19 miles through a very sparsely populated area, the full benefits of the through traffic should shortly become apparent. As to the Lancaster & Carlisle, it was blossoming forth in all directions. Support for the Portpatrick Railway went hand in hand with backing for another new concern, the South Durham & Lancashire Union Railway, which would bring coal and iron from the east across country through Kirkby Stephen to join the L.C.R. at a point immediately north of Tebay station. When the Portpatrick line received the Royal Assent it was with satisfaction that the L.C.R. noted that any clauses which might have benefited the G.N.R. or the N.W.R. had been deleted and those permitting the L.C.R.

to subscribe allowed. When the S.D.L.U. was also successful the company guaranteed that it would assist by enlarging Tebay station. On August 1, 1857, with most of the new engines safely delivered, the L.C.R. started running its own line, after eleven years of L.N.W.R. domination. Promising to start construction of the Ingleton line soon, it was in a mood anxious to placate old enemies, hopeful to win new friends.

To the south the East Lancashire was beginning to be wooed to some purpose by the L.Y.R. for, finally realising that it had a prickly neighbour with some useful tricks up his sleeve, the latter company decided that amalgamation was preferable to war. To some extent this remarkable change of outlook can be traced directly to the Bradford-Colne proposal. It would appear that the E.L.R. was none too happy about the possibility of making the line. It is even probable that it secretly thanked Mr. Vance for stopping what was merely a piece of spite. It was a timely warning of what could happen when one side lost its judgement. In any event general approval for amalgamation had been reached as early as January of 1857. It was, of course, too late for a Bill that session. In 1858 a Bill for amalgamation went to Parliament only to be thrown out. The marriage was finally to take place in 1859.

As to the Midland in this year of 1857, momentous things were happening. When the common purse agreement with the L.N.W.R. bobbed to the surface during the previous May at the hearing of the little North Western Bill, one of the horrified spectators to this unpleasant sight was Mr. Isaac Burkhill of Leeds—the same Mr. Burkhill who had so very nearly appropriated the North Western from the Midland six years earlier. Now, as then, Burkhill was acting in the interests of the Great Northern. This time he was to attempt to prise the Midland away from the L.N.W.R. —to do anything in fact which would weaken the Euston Square Confederacy. This time he succeeded. More to the point, it was his initial action which was indirectly to push the Midland into active participation for Scotch traffic. In summarising the sequence of events which was to lead to the Midland breaking free from the L.N.W.R. the scene will be set for the future rivalry which was ultimately to lead to the construction of the Settle-Carlisle line.

At the Midland's half-yearly meeting in August, 1856, Ellis told the shareholders that in consequence of proceedings instituted against the L.N.W.R. by Burkhill, and by some of the Midland shareholders against their own company to break the common purse agreement, the directors had felt obliged to cancel it. He also said that there was trouble between Euston and the M.S.L.R. This was an understatement. When Derby had withdrawn from the agreement, Huish had been determined to keep the initiative. He approached Seymour Clarke at Kings Cross and, to the latter's amazement, offered a territorial agreement with the G.N.R., to the exclusion of his own allies. Though this was very tempting, Clarke wondered at the apparent change of heart. He realised that whilst an alliance with such a tricky partner as the L.N.W.R. might have some benefits, it would alienate the other members of the Confederacy against the G.N.R. for good. Far more capital could be gained by turning the tables on the L.N.W.R. and this he decided to do. News of the offer was leaked to the M.S.L.R. Furious at Euston's betrayal, that company swung over to the side of the G.N.R., incidentally bringing with it what the former had always desired, access to Manchester.

As to the Midland, now divorced from the L.N.W.R. and with a ready-made line to Hitchin, what better to complete Huish's humiliation than to offer Derby running powers over the G.N.R. into Kings Cross. To this the Midland agreed. The Leicester-Hitchin line, costing close on £1 m. and about 65 miles in length, was inspected by Colonel Yolland of the Board of Trade on April 29, 1857, the line having been opened for mineral traffic a fortnight earlier. On May 8 the first regular passenger train, of eighteen carriages, left Hitchin station at 7.33 a.m., passing Bedford at 8.15 and reaching Leicester at 8.50 a.m. Throughout the previous day, which was a public holiday along the route, six engines and a hundred carriages took part in the formal opening ceremonies which were carried out along the length of new railway and symbolised the new-found freedom of the Midland company.

About this time Allport left the Midland. Though the reasons were more likely to be found in the fact that he was unfortunately tarred with the Huish brush, the shareholders were informed that 'an offer of partnership—in a firm of high standing was unexpectedly made to him a short time ago'. He was, however, elected a director; the Midland board valued his experience and it would not be long before he returned to the company. September of 1858 saw the resignation of Captain Huish. His was a policy which could only succeed with success. The image of the company had undoubtedly become tarnished during the past few years. His going was nicely done. He had been with the L.N.W.R. for some eighteen years. He left with the signatures of five thousand workmen on the L.N.W.R. to a testimonial, and a donation of £500 towards a 'suitable work of art'. What this was one hesitates to imagine.

Leave-takings were the fashion at the time. Ellis, and Beale his deputy, left the Midland in 1857 but both were to return very soon, Ellis on a temporary basis, to take the chair at the end of January 1858, and Beale to succeed him a short while later. Ellis's successor and predecessor, all within one month, was George Byng Paget. For many years chairman of the Midland locomotive committee, Paget had hardly settled into Ellis's chair when he died on January 25 at Brighton, after an illness of only a few hours. Allport had meanwhile been replaced by W. L. Newcombe as general manager, and W. H. Barlow by John Sydney Crossley as engineer. Such was the new crew with which the Midland was to sail into the sixties. By the beginning of 1858 a spirit of rejuvenation had taken hold. The company's shares were now quoted higher than those of the L.N.W.R. The tone of the half-yearly meeting in January 1858 affords a picture of the scene, with £1,000 being voted so that Ellis should have his portrait painted for the boardroom before his final retirement in March. His last words as chairman to the shareholders included an exhortation to remain on good terms with the L.N.W.R. But unlike previous calls of this kind there was an afterthought—if the L.N.W.R. failed to preserve the peace, then the Midland could help themselves to the pickings. To a gale of laughter he epitomised the prevailing mood of the company—'I never felt half so independent as I do at this moment.'

VIII

Consolidation

1858 – 1864

Having got powers to make the remainder of the Orton line, the L.C.R. seemed at first to be more concerned in making it unworkable for fast through traffic. For the session of 1858 it deposited a Bill for a deviation in the authorised line whereby a curve of 10 chains radius —far too sharp for fast running—was to be installed where it joined the L.C.R. main line, altering the point of junction at Scufton to one immediately south of the old Low Gill station, at the same time as abandoning the short branch to Grayrigg. This the North Western determined to oppose. Its engineer, Smallman, had recently resigned to join the Bahia Railway and the engineering affairs of the company were now in the capable hands of the Midland. Generally the N.W.R. was in a carping mood during 1858, seeing all the world against it. An attempt was made to persuade the Midland to run through services to the Lakes over the line, but to no avail, and once more there were muttered comments of Midland unconcern with N.W.R. affairs. Matters were not helped when Derby informed the N.W.R. board that the sharp curve intended by the L.C.R. at Low Gill was only after all of the same radius as one on the main line at Derby. If the L.C.R. could be persuaded to stop all the trains at Low Gill, that was all the little North Western could reasonably hope for. The L.C.R. agreed to pay some £16,500 for the uncompleted work of the late Ingleton branch of the North Western, and started construction towards the end of the year, the deviation from Scufton to old Low Gill having been rejected by Parliament but the abandonment of the short branch sanctioned. At the L.C.R. half-yearly meeting in September, Errington reported that the line was completely staked out and four contracts let; stone for the Lune viaduct was already on the site.

Early in the year the little North Western learned of a recent new traffic agreement completed between the G.N.R. and the L.N.W.R. The company decided to round-robin all the parties to the English and Scotch Agreement to try to get an abandonment to the terms which still precluded its line being used for through north-south traffic. To this it received a reply from Seymour Clarke in April to the effect that the N.W.R. had been represented by the Midland at the time of the relevant discussions. He would probably have been surprised if he had known that the N.W.R. minute book answered this by virtually calling him a liar. By September, however, things were looking up. Midland trains from Kings Cross were beginning to percolate as far as the N.W.R. and through bookings from London to North Western stations had commenced by August. The L.C.R. was again bothering the company at this time by supporting a local scheme for a line similar to the William Lands branch, long-forgotten and unmourned, which would take the Durham traffic arriving at Tebay on to Morecambe from a point about three miles north of Lancaster. This branch, coupled with the South Durham line, would effectively drain off considerable coke and iron ore traffic. At the other end of the system, the N.W.R. board was interesting itself in yet another attempt for a line through Wharfedale, to the tune of £50,000, and to the annoyance of the Midland.

The Lancaster & Carlisle also had reason to feel put out. It had not gone unnoticed that advertisements were appearing in Lancaster extolling the virtue of travelling to London to arrive at Kings Cross instead of Euston. The company considered the N.W.R. hypocritical in bleating about its right to be considered the shortest route whilst attempting to take passengers from Lancaster to London by what was undeniably a very long way round, and told it so. In a pugnacious humour, the little North Western, which had been threatened with competition from the L.C.R. for Yorkshire traffic, told the latter that as it was merely a matter of through bookings between one Midland station and another, it was no business of the L.C.R. Furthermore, if the L.C.R. wanted trouble it could have it. One wonders what the Great Northern would have thought of Kings Cross being described as 'one Midland station'. In October the nominal promoter of the Hest Bank line, William Jackson, offered the N.W.R. a half-share in the scheme. He was laughed down aud told the idea was a waste of time and that it was hoped that he would not put the company to the expense of having to oppose him in Parliament. During October a series of blistering letters were exchanged between the Midland, the L.C.R., and the G.N.R. Their subject—the little North Western, once more vociferously in revolt over the traffic agreements in operation between the big companies and threatening to go to court to get the Engish and Scotch Agreement broken. It was becoming increasingly apparent that the N.W.R. had a nuisance value out of all proportion to its size. It had successfully rubbed all its neighbours up the wrong way for some time past and it was to the relief of all that towards the end of the year the Midland decided to lease it. On November 26 the Midland board issued a circular to the shareholders telling them of the proposed lease. As the friendship with the L.N.W.R. was at an end the Midland would have to fend for itself and in the directors' opinion the generally altered circumstances rendered it 'absolutely necessary that the Midland company should be made as independent and as strong as possible'. The circular went on to say that, bearing in mind the geographical position of the little North Western and the Scotch traffic situation, it had become most important to acquire absolute control over the N.W.R. instead of the limited power possessed under the existing working agreement. On November 12 Alcock, Hare, Hinde and Whelon had met Beale, the new chairman of the Midland, and two other members of the board, together with Newcombe, and had arranged to lease the line for 999 years from January 1, 1859, the lease to be complete so as to virtually vest the company in the Midland. On the following day the North Western board had met at 'Morley's Hotel', London, and decided to put the question to a full meeting of the company. On Wednesday, December 8, the meeting took place in, perhaps fortuitously, the Philosophical Hall, Leeds, and the lease was agreed. As it turned out, the company was to remain in being until 1871 when an outright sale ended what had been an unfortunate and chequered career. For all practical purposes though, the Midland Railway now extended to Lancaster, Morecambe, and Ingleton. It was not to be long before, with access to London finally secured by a direct line to St. Pancras, the authorities at Derby were to begin seriously concerning themselves with similar thoughts aimed at Carlisle. The revenue account for the last half-year of working before the lease took effect shows that £12,597 16s. od. was paid to the Midland for working the line, other expenses adding up to £1,415 15s. 7d., making a total of £14,013 11s. 7d. This was set against traffic receipts amounting to £25,489 10s. 1d. plus an additional amount of £1,730 1s. od. for other incidental monies received, making a grand total of receipts of £27,219 11s. 1d. It left a balance of £13,205 19s. 6d. in the N.W.R.'s favour.

Beale had taken over as chairman of the Midland in the previous March. Since the break-up of the Confederacy there was once more heavy competition between the L.N.W.R. on one side, and the G.N.R. and M.S.L.R. on the other. It was condemned by the *Times* in an article of March 8. Fares between London and Manchester had reached a new low of 5s. return, with an interval of seven days between journeys if required. It was a natural consequence to the new access to Manchester given by the M.S.L.R. to the G.N.R., and which infuriated Euston. The *Times* thought it furnished 'another evidence of that utter demoralisation of the classes having the control of the financial resources and general enterprises of the nation which has been exemplified during the past few years in every other channel of business'. The same policy of the stage coach proprietors of thirty years before, 'as ignorant as the animals they drove, is in 1858 the highest resort of boards of directors composed of noblemen, Members of Parliament, merchants, and bankers who profess to claim sway as the most exalted representatives of our commercial progress'. By July 1858 the agreement to run into Kings Cross had been sealed by the Midland board. At this time the board ordered that a sufficient number of second class carriages to accommodate passengers in competing districts were to be padded and provided with cushions. By August 4 a model padded carriage had been constructed and approved by the board, and Kirtley was ordered to alter the number considered necessary. Earlier in the year the board also ordered that all third and fourth class carriages were to be lit at night.

The year 1859 was to isolate the L.N.W.R. still further. Aggressive Bills aimed at the Midland and the L.Y.R. tended to throw the two latter companies together. In Yorkshire the L.Y.R. took action by promoting rival lines to those of the L.N.W.R.—Dewsbury to Thornhill, and Thornhill to Ossett and Wakefield—and though neither of the companies was successful, at least the status quo was preserved. The Midland, however, was to oppose the amalgamation Bill between the L.Y.R. and the East Lancashire mainly on the contention that the traffic from Colne would be adversely affected. An arrangement to ensure reciprocal rights between the E.L.R., L.Y.R., and Midland was made in July, however, as mentioned earlier, and stilled Derby's fears on this point. On August 13, 1859 the amalgamation Bill received the Royal Assent, a clause in the Act permitting the Midland to run over the former E.L.R. line of the L.Y.R. and thence into Manchester and Liverpool, and the L.Y.R. to run over the Midland into Leeds and Bradford.

By February 1859 the competition between Euston and the East Coast Allies had abated. Trade and traffic were better, and the Midland found itself in a position where, because there were so many new lines added to the system, a serious shortage of locomotives existed. One of the L.N.W.R. Bills which worried Derby at this time concerned the Wichnor-Burton line. An agreement with Euston was patched up—albeit unwillingly—and the Midland still seemed to hope for good relations with its erstwhile ally. By the end of the year agreement had been reached on the necessity for a Wharfedale line, and the Midland agreed to work it.

Though now part of the Midland Railway, the little North Western company was still nominally in existence; its presence was still felt. Early in 1859 the N.W.R. board noted that the L.C.R. was going for powers to make the Hest Bank line to Morecambe, with a pier extending into the bay, and a branch to the N.W.R. on the east side of the latter's Morecambe passenger station. Powers were also sought to use the whole of the N.W.R.'s harbour works and lines. The little North Western countered by depositing a similar Bill for effecting improvements at Morecambe—a $\frac{1}{2}$ mile line joining the L.C.R. with the Morecambe branch at Skerton. Another Parliamentary conflict seemed inevitable but by August the company had agreed with the Midland and the L.C.R. to let the latter's Hest Bank line pass, but with the harbour works and running powers deleted. In return, the N.W.R. dropped its counterproposal of harbour improvements and the connecting line, and the L.C.R. was permitted running powers into Morecambe over its new line. These ceased into the N.W.R. station on June 1, 1866. Despite the existing traffic agreements, the Midland was now finding that some of the little North Western's previous grumbles as to the lack of Scotch traffic were only too true and, in April, 1859, it protested strongly that the main carriers were not using the line as the shortest route. Its protest went in vain.

Towards the end of the year there was another of the critical moves in the game leading up to the eventual construction of the Settle-Carlisle line. The Lancaster & Carlisle was becoming increasingly worried, as was Euston, at the nearness of the Midland to the West Coast main line. In August the L.C.R. circularised its shareholders to ascertain support for a lease of the railway to the L.N.W.R. for a period of 1,000 years. *Herepath's Journal* expressed surprise at this and asked, 'If the Midland had not been so near the Lancaster and Carlisle line, should we ever have heard of the London & North Western leasing the Lancaster and Carlisle?' On September 10, the L.C.R. met and agreed to the lease, the guaranteed dividend to be not less than 8 per cent. per annum. One of the reasons why the L.C.R. forwent its independence was that it already envisaged heavy Parliamentary battles with the Midland in the not too distant future, if it was to stay free. It preferred the devil it knew. *Herepath's Journal*, which disapproved of the move, asked with heavy humour whether the lease was the right way round, pointing out that the L.N.W.R., a 4 per cent. line, proposed taking over the L.C.R., paying about 10 per cent. Meanwhile, the Ingleton works of the L.C.R. were progressing reasonably well, and on August 3, 1859 the Midland board instructed its engineer, Crossley, to lay down the second line of rails between Clapham and Ingleton, in readiness for the reopening of the line. The latter company also asked the Midland whether it would now join in a joint station at Ingleton—provision for which had been included in the Lancaster & Carlisle & Ingleton Act of 1857—and the Midland board sent Crossley to confer with the L.C.R. on this point, at the same time as asking the traffic committee for a survey of the traffic prospects of the N.W.R. and the surrounding district.

Before leaving 1859 note can be taken of a traffic agreement in November between the Midland and the Leeds Bradford & Halifax Junction—nominally still independent but with a pronounced G.N.R. flavour to it. It was agreed that certain economies could be made. Some trains were discontinued. Fares were raised on both lines : the third class Leeds-Bradford fare by either line, for instance, was raised from 10d. to 1s.

During 1860 there was a welcome lull in major events. It was perhaps more in the nature of an intermission. Construction of the L.C.R.'s Ingleton branch proceeded slowly and it was not expected to be opened until the following spring. The company received powers for its Hest Bank line on August 13.

The closer relationship between the Midland and the L.Y.R., brought about by the traffic agreement of 1859, gave weight to rumours current in December 1860 that the two companies wished to embarrass and annoy the Great Northern, which was then again applying for a direct Doncaster-Wakefield line at the expense of the L.Y.R.'s Askern branch (the G.N.R. Bill was rejected at committee stage); and also the L.N.W.R., in that traffic from the L.Y.R. from Manchester and Liverpool would be tended henceforth to be handed over to the Midland for destinations in Yorkshire where both it and the L.N.W.R. met. Euston also had cause for another complaint against Derby during the year; a Bill deposited by the L.N.W.R., M.S.L.R., and G.N.R., to clear up outstanding traffic problems, was negatived at the last moment by the Midland insisting, too late, to be included, together with the North Staffordshire Railway. The Midland was in fact attempting to get the whole of the London traffic of the North Staffordshire conveyed by the Midland and Great Northern routes. It was also quietly thinking of throwing over the G.N.R., and seeking separate access to London. As it turned out, the N.S.R. saw a chance to promote an extension from Sandbach towards Liverpool—justifying this to the Midland as a necessary move to get independent of the L.N.W.R. Such a proposition caused the Midland to drop the N.S.R. like a hot brick. In any event, there had been considerable friction for some time between Derby and Euston in the Buxton area, with the suspicion on the L.N.W.R. side that the Midland was in fact preparing to launch itself towards Manchester.

Throughout 1860, prospects for the Midland seemed rosy. With a steady increase in traffic, the dividend in January was a healthy 6 per cent. By June Midland stock was quoted at $117\frac{3}{4}$ and by July at 119. In August Allport returned, Newcombe relinquishing his position as general manager to become the London agent of the company. Though this was indeed a responsible post with the London Extension just round the corner it seems as if Allport's installation as general manager called for considerable sacrifice on Newcombe's part. The company entered into a programme of hotel provision at about this time, with the acquisition of premises at Derby and Normanton, and arrangements were made to build a new hotel at Sheffield. Another development was the taking-over of the Wharfedale's Bill, then in Parliament, for a line from Shipley to Otley and Ilkley, the first link in what was later to become a separate Midland access to the Scotch route, avoiding the majority of the Leeds & Bradford lines. On October 3, 1860 the board decided to make the line to Otley—commencing from the L.B.R. at Apperley Bridge and passing through Guiseley—the North Eastern Railway to construct a branch from Arthington on the old Leeds & Thirsk line to join it at Otley, with the portion between Otley and Ilkley to be a joint line made and operated by both companies. The Shipley-Guiseley link was to be constructed by the Midland at a later date. Powers for the Otley and Ilkley lines were obtained by both companies on July 11, 1861. 1860 was in all a relatively quiet year as regards the coming problems of Scotch traffic. Before we leave it, however, a glance at the timetable of the North Western Railway gives a picture of the services operating a short time before the opening of the L.C.R.'s Ingleton line, the coming into being of which was to spark off the competition between Euston and Derby for the Carlisle traffic.

The North Western Railway timetable for January-June 1860 shows four down trains on weekdays. The first in the morning was the 6.00 a.m. from Leeds, connecting with the 5.50 from Bradford at Shipley, and the 6.40 from Colne at Skipton, where it arrived at 7.15. It left Skipton 5 minutes later, to stop at all stations to Lancaster Castle. These were Gargrave, Bell Busk for Mallam (sic), Hellifield, Long Preston, Settle, Clapham, High Bentham, Wennington, Hornby for Kirkby Lonsdale, Caton, Halton, Lancaster Green Ayre, and Lancaster Castle. It arrived at the latter at 9.10 a.m. from where connections could be made to reach Carlisle by 1.15 p.m. Edinburgh by 8.00 p.m. and Glasgow by 8.20 p.m. The second train left Leeds at 10.20 a.m. and, calling at all stations, reached Morecambe at 1.45 p.m. A connection from Lancaster reached Carlisle at 5.00 p.m. The third train was a semi-fast; leaving Leeds at noon, it made connections at Lancaster with the 2.40 p.m.—a train to the north which reached Carlisle at 5.25 p.m., Edinburgh at 8.40 p.m. and Glasgow at 9.05 p.m. From Lancaster the semi-fast ran on to Morecambe, which it reached at 2.45 p.m. The last train in the day was the 5.40 p.m. out of Leeds, calling at all stations to Lancaster Green Ayre, with no connections to the north. On Sundays there were two down trains. The first was the 6.00 a.m. from Leeds, calling at all stations to Morecambe; there was a 'connecting' train to the north from Lancaster, which crawled into Carlisle at 9.15 p.m. The other train was the 4.00 p.m. from Leeds, calling at all stations to Lancaster Castle. All the down trains had Bradford portions, attached at Shipley. The up service was virtually similar to the down, with four weekday trains and two on Sundays. On the Lancaster-Morecambe run there were seven daily trains with no intermediate stops. The first was the 6.35 a.m. from Lancaster Green Ayre, then came the 9.10, 11.00, 1.35 p.m., 2.35, 4.15 and 5.45 p.m., all with 10 minutes journey times. On Sundays there were three trains. In the July-December timetable an additional train was run on the main line for the weekday service, and two on the Morecambe line. Fares from Skipton to Lancaster were 3s. 3d., third class, and 8s. 4d. first class. During the year a new station came into use on the Leeds & Bradford main line—Kirkstall Forge, opened in time for the commencement of the second timetable on July 1.

Early in 1861 the Midland concluded a new traffic agreement with the L.Y.R. as to interchange facilities, and declared a dividend of 6¾ per cent. Though a bright start, as the year developed there was a general trade depression and the receipts fell off. The board, however, did not let this stop it from giving consideration to shortening the main line route to the north by a Sheffield-Chesterfield link, and opinion hardened for an extension from Bedford to London, or at least a separate London station. In November the company decided to back a new undertaking, the Keighley & Worth Valley Railway. It agreed to work the new line for half of the receipts, the number of trains run to depend upon the traffic; the local company had suggested six or seven each way daily.

In August the company's way and works committee was instructed to build a new station at Ingleton for the opening of the line throughout to Scufton House where a new station, named Low Gill, replaced the old L.C.R. structure about a mile to the south. The second line of Midland rails had been completed by August 17 and the L.C.R. branch to Ingleton was opened for goods traffic on August 24, and for passengers on September 16. The L.N.W.R. service from Tebay to Ingleton was started by two slow trains which were of no use at all to the Midland as connections for Scotch traffic. It was not until the next year that the L.N.W.R. put on a reasonably fast train which afforded a through service from the Midland to Carlisle. The first timetable for the Ingleton-Tebay line, as it appeared in the official L.N.W.R. timetable for October, 1861, and with connections which markedly ignored the Midland line, appears in Appendix V. Clapham-Ingleton was reopened on October 1st.

The Ingleton branch leaves the Lancaster line at Clapham station and, after passing the signal box with its incongruous name of 'Clapham Junction', runs for the 4 miles to Ingleton over Newby Moor. There are rising gradients to a point about midway along the Midland portion of the line, where the summit is reached, the remaining 2 miles or so into Ingleton being on a down grade. Leaving the Midland station, the line passes on to a viaduct of nine arches, crossing over the River Greta, with the grey stone town of Ingleton immediately below, and the hump of Ingleborough in the distance beyond. A short way further on the line passes the site of the former Ingleton station of the L.N.W.R. From here the branch runs a further 2½ miles to the Yorkshire-Lancashire border, and then continues about 2 miles to the next station at Kirkby Lonsdale, situated on the A65 road where it crosses the old Roman road to Carlisle near the county boundary between Lancashire and Westmorland. Between Ingleton and Kirkby the line skirts the lower reaches of Leck Fell and after leaving Kirkby it continues almost due north for another 3¼ miles to Barbon station, deep in the Lune Valley, with Barbon High Fell to the right and the river and the first high outcrops of the east Westmorland Fells to the left. Passing through Middleton-on-Lune the line hugs the northern extent of Middleton Fell, curving slightly to the east before crossing the River Rawthey by a single span iron skew bridge. It then turns a quarter-circle to the west and arrives at Sedbergh, 18¼ miles from Clapham. Away to the right lies the Rawthey Valley, cutting between Baugh Fell and Ravenstonedale Common, and up which the A683 road climbs some 14 miles to Kirkby Stephen. For a short time before and after Sedbergh, the line is again in Yorkshire. It finally leaves the county when crossing the Lune viaduct, of one iron and six brick arches, about 1½ miles further on from Sedbergh. From there another 3½ miles, with the railway, climbing mostly at 1 in 100, the B6257 road, and the Lune, all bunched together in the valley, brings the branch to a sharp right-handed turn over Low Gill viaduct, of eleven arches and built on the curve, to join the Lancaster & Carlisle line at Low Gill station,

23 miles from Clapham. The station at Low Gill, now removed, was of a curious arrangement—there were separate platforms to the main line and the branch, the actual junction being a short distance beyond. The country through which the Ingleton branch passes is as beautiful as any in the district. The area has strong associations with the Bronte family. At Cowan Bridge, 2½ miles south-east of Kirkby Lonsdale and quite near to the railway, are the remains of one of the first Clergy Daughters' Schools in England. The two elder Bronte daughters were educated there and died of typhus contracted whilst at the school. Charlotte and Emily, luckier than their sisters, came afterwards safely through their schooling at Cowan Bridge during 1824–1825. Such was the impression made by the school on Charlotte Bronte that she used it for 'Lowood' in Jane Eyre. Likewise in the same novel 'Lowton' is based on Kirkby Lonsdale.

Returning to the events of 1861, the L.N.W.R. found the year both momentous and sad. The chairman, Admiral Moorsom, who had given evidence so many years ago at the time of the pre-Midland era to Gladstone's committees examining the state of the railway system, died after the effects of an operation rendered necessary in consequence of a wound received in the arm at the time of the seige of Copenhagen. His place was taken by Richard Moon, a stern disciplinarian and a power to be reckoned with. Under his leadership the L.N.W.R. was to develop mightily. The company had its eye well to the north in 1861, for it appeared to be contemplating an attempt to reach the east coast at Hartlepool. Early in 1861 the preamble had been proved of a Bill for a new company, the Newcastle Derwent & Weardale, which sought a direct route between Liverpool and the Tyne. The L.N.W.R. was only too pleased to assist and agreed to furnish a large proportion of the capital. It also, with the North British, was to provide two directors. The real intention of the scheme was to force the North Eastern's hand over traffic arrangements through Normanton. By August the N.D.W. Bill had been rejected in the Lords, and an agreement with the N.E.R. was concluded. Even more heartening was the opening for mineral traffic on July 4 of the South Durham & Lancashire Union, passenger traffic commencing on August 8 with a service of two trains a day. This was the line which had bothered the little North Western on account of the resultant loss of iron ore traffic over its lines. Apparently when the S.D.L.U. was opened its clean coke fired Stockton & Darlington engines contrasted strongly at Tebay with the dirty coal burning L.N.W.R. breed. Two of the passenger engines on the S.D.L.U. at this time were S. & D.R. locomotives Nos. 160 *Brougham* and 161 *Lowther*, both early 4-4-0s. The old Northern Counties Union line, incidentally, was in a state of torpidity by this time. The only reason it did not disappear altogether was that to do so would cost too much, the business of formally winding up being of enormous expense. In the previous year it had held its penultimate meeting at which the last dividend was made of a shilling per share. The final meeting was to take place on August 25, 1864, at which the company was informally dissolved.

With the current good relations between the Midland and the L.Y.R., the latter prepared a Bill for an extension of the Blackburn branch from Chatburn to Settle but though it got to Parliament in 1861, the company decided shortly afterwards to withdraw it. The L.Y.R. thought to try again in the next session but due to a severe trade depression in the Lancashire cotton areas and falling receipts caused by the interruption of trade consequent on the American Civil War, the Bill was again postponed. The idea was only temporarily shelved, however; it was to be brought out again later and was eventually to provide the Midland with a new direct route from Liverpool and Manchester to Carlisle. For the Midland, February of 1862 brought with it a dividend of 7 per cent. Despite the fact that trade was poor, traffic over the company's line was slightly increased over the previous year. This comfortable feeling was not to last, however, for trouble brewed up in July with the Great Northern again over the English and Scotch Agreement. The Midland was paying the G.N.R. £60,000 a year in tolls to get to London on a line which was very overcrowded, and it could not take any of the local traffic. In an attempt to entice the public on to its northern lines, the Midland started issuing cheap tourist tickets to Scotland and the Lakes from Kings Cross. Congestion on the G.N.R. main line, resulting from Midland traffic using it south of Hitchin, was already heavy enough with the burden of tourist trains, but the 1862 International Exhibition in London proved too much of a temptation for both companies and a fares scramble resulted. Low excursion rates fixed by Derby for journeys of 400 miles (London and back) at 15s. first class and 8s. second class, proved very damaging to the G.N.R. which in retaliation reduced coal rates from the South Yorkshire coal field, which both companies served, to 1s. 6d. a ton. The Midland, of course, was still bound to hand over a portion of the receipts for traffic which it alone carried. The treaty had, in the eyes of Derby, long outlived its usefulness. The company was no longer merely an adjunct of Euston. It was a fully fledged main line railway with access to London and a potential access to Scotland, neither of which could be used profitably in the present conditions. In 1862 the Midland was sending traffic to London via Rugby and over the L.N.W.R. and paying the latter to the tune of £193,000 to do it. For this privilege it had to put up with queues at Rugby some five miles long of Midland coal trains waiting to get on to the L.N.W.R. The resulting chaos and loss of good will were enormous. A feeling of similar frustration on this point also existed in the case of the Ingleton line. At the half-yearly meeting of the little North Western in February, 1862, the directors had complained that despite the fact that the line had been open to Low Gill for some time the requisite arrangements for through traffic had still not been made. It was generally thought that this was the fault of Derby; violent letters appeared in the railway press throughout the year castigating the Midland for its past and present treatment of the N.W.R.

In fact the company was doing the best it could. As to the complaints regarding the N.W.R., since the Midland had taken over in 1859 considerable additions had been made to the system, including enlargement of the harbour works at Morecambe, stations enlarged and sidings extended, the second line to Ingleton, and the erection of permanent station buildings at the end of the branch. The Midland had also strengthened some 49 miles of single line by the use of fish-plates, extra sleepers and fastenings. Where the Midland's own system was at fault in bottling up the traffic, and wherever expansion was justified and possible, the company made amends. In June 1862 powers were obtained for a line from the Rowsley and Buxton branch, opened that month, to join a new protegé of the M.S.L.R., the Marple New Mills & Hayfield Junction. This was soon to give the Midland access to Manchester and open the way to its later joining in the Cheshire Lines Committee, taking it on to Liverpool. The story of the negotiations leading up to the agreement with the M.S.L.R. does not concern us here; it was, however, a further slap in the face for Euston. On October 1 the Midland made an agreement with the Furness Railway for the joint construction of a line from Wennington on the little North Western to Carnforth, on the L.C.R., there to join the Furness main line and give access to the coast of West Cumberland. A month later it agreed with the North British Railway for interchange of traffic by the Carlisle route. It was indeed determined to break out. In November it sought true independence in the south by depositing a Bill for an extension of the main line from Bedford to London, only a few days after the architect of its freedom from the L.N.W.R., John Ellis, Quaker and Member of Parliament, died. It was to be the last major Midland construction Bill in the south, or indeed anywhere, before the Settle-Carlisle Bill of 1866, and for a few years it was to exercise a shadowy influence on the whole future of the northern line. During the year the Eden Valley line was opened—for minerals on April 8 and passengers on June 9, a new north junction being added in 1863 to give access to Penrith. Both the Eden Valley, and the S.D.L.U. were taken over by the Stockton & Darlington in June 1862, and a year later the S.D.R. was itself amalgamated into the North Eastern Railway.

There were some developments at Leeds during 1862-1863. The first was the opening of the Midland's Holbeck station in 1862 followed by the coming into use of the old 'Queen's Hotel' on January 10, 1863. This preceded the enlargement of the arrival side at Leeds Wellington station, ordered by the board in May. At the northern end of the system the N.W.R. board was still complaining at the lack of traffic over its line. During 1862 there had been a considerable falling off in coke and iron ore traffic due to the opening of the S.D.L.U. It was also a sore point that the Ingleton line diverted any of the Scotch traffic which once used the whole length of the N.W.R., despite the fact that the Midland had still not been able to secure any substantial new traffic over the route. In the south the G.N.R. was understandably worried over the London Extension Bill. It was rumoured in March that the directors at Kings Cross were endeavouring to lure the Midland away from the idea with the promise of perpetual running powers over the G.N.R. It was a forlorn hope; the Extension Bill, together with the Furness and Midland line to Carnforth, both received the Royal Assent on June 22, 1863, the former Bill authorising construction of a line about 50 miles in length, which necessitated the raising of £1,750,000 in new shares, and loans of £583,330. At the end of the year, with traffic over the Ingleton line no better, the Midland and L.N.W.R. started negotiations for an agreement on joint use of the Lancaster & Carlisle main line, and from this point events were to lead inexorably towards a head-on clash between the two big companies as to the Scotch traffic.

Throughout 1864 there was a marshalling of forces for the coming struggle, but before returning to the happenings in the north there were some minor events occurring at the Leeds & Bradford end of the line which can be disposed of. At Leeds the N.E.R. had a scheme for a line into the city from the east and proposed a new joint station on the site of Leeds Central. It was opposed by the other companies then in residence and the Midland offered them the use of Leeds Wellington. In July John Edward Smith, the Town Clerk of Leeds, wrote to Derby asking the Midland to cease promoting a general wrangle in the city and to join with the N.E.R. in its new venture. The Midland replied in a hurt tone that it was doing what it could to agree and was already in correspondence with the other railways at the station. By August the trouble was over; Derby had agreed with the N.E.R. and L.N.W.R. on plans for a new joint station to be built adjacent to its own. During October there were two schemes for lines to connect the L.Y.R. at Bradford with the Midland; the Bradford Junction & Thornton Valley, and the Bradford Junction & Thornton & Keighley. Both prospective companies applied to Derby for assistance but were turned down.

At the half-yearly meeting of the Lancaster & Carlisle, held on Tuesday, February 23, 1864, the company gave much time to discussing the pending arrangement between Euston and Derby whereby the Midland was to be granted full rights over the line into Carlisle. The meeting learned that for some time the Midland had been anxious to carry its traffic through to Scotland, and had meditated constructing a rival line to the L.C.R. The L.N.W.R., as lessees of the Lancaster company's line, were extremely anxious to prevent such a happening and, therefore, proposed to introduce a Bill to grant rights to the Midland over the L.C.R. for Scotch traffic. Hassel said that he was glad to see that the two companies were behaving sensibly. In the autumn of 1863 some of the L.C.R. directors had met Richard Moon and he had proposed that they should enter into a lease with both companies, whereby an annual dividend of 9½ per cent. to the L.C.R. would be guaranteed. The L.C.R., however, was determined to make as much of the situation as possible, and had stuck out for 10 per cent. In August, 1864, the L.N.W.R., in anticipation of the agreement with Derby, obtained powers during the duration of the L.C.R. lease to enter into agreements for the use by the Midland of the L.C.R., including the Lancaster & Preston Junction and the Kendal & Windermere lines. In November the Midland also deposited a Bill for similar powers to put the scheme into effect, and on December 7 the board approved the draft agreement.

During these moves the later allies of the Midland had been busy north of the Border. In August the *Kilmarnock Standard* spoke of a proposed new through line to Glasgow, being surveyed via Crofthead by the Glasgow & South Western Railway. It went on :

'It cannot be said that this project has been set on foot through any prospect of remunerative traffic along the line itself, and the intention is, therefore, simply to construct a feeder that shall make the trunk line more valuable to the company, and more advantageous to the public. Considering it altogether apart from the benefit it will confer on Kilmarnock and neighbourhood, and taking it in connection with the coming City of Glasgow Union Railway, its great importance becomes immediately apparent. If we put into the scale, likewise, the possibility of a special arrangement with the Midland company in England, the feasibility of the prospect is still more clearly demonstrated.'

This was at a time when negotiations between the G.S.W.R., and the Caledonian, very firmly on the side of Euston, had failed. The North British also saw glittering possibilities in an agreement between Derby and Euston. Despite the continuing obstruction to traffic at Ingleton, there was already some sparse passenger traffic over the route and through to Leeds which originated from N.B.R. stations. Beale of the Midland thought likewise that the truce between the companies at Ingleton, and a solid pact with the L.N.W.R., would draw both concerns closer together, though this time the Midland would be speaking from a position of strength, unlike the Confederacy days. The latter company decided to do all it could to shorten its own route south of Leeds at this time, in order to take full advantage of the Scotch traffic which would ensue from the entente, and promoted the Sheffield-Chesterfield cut-off, the Bill receiving the Royal Assent on July 25. In August Beale retired as chairman of the company, though remaining on the board. His going was due to bad health and he was advised not to be present at his last meeting in the chair. His place was taken by William Evans Hutchinson, the deputy chairman, like the late John Ellis, a Quaker. In October Hutchinson was elected to succeed Beale; William Philip Price, the M.P. for Gloucester, became his deputy. With this team the Midland approached what was to be its most decisive period, for before the new year had barely got into its stride, Euston and Derby were to be once more poles apart, and the necessity for an independent line to the Border had begun to assume paramount importance.

IX

The Settle and Carlisle Bill

1865 – 1866

1865, and what was to be an important year for the Midland, started with a major eruption of bad feeling against the L.N.W.R. On Wednesday February 1, Hutchinson reported to the board that, together with Price and Allport, he had had an interview with the directors of the L.N.W.R. as to the proposed lease of the L.C.R., and that the negotiations had failed. The summary of what had happened was contained in a long letter sent to the L.N.W.R. by Carter, the company's solicitor. Dated three days earlier, it sought to rationalise the points of difference between the two companies so as to forestall any future L.N.W.R. attempt to put the blame on the Midland.

The Midland had required that, on becoming joint lessees of the L.C.R. as a means of access to Scotland, it should have equal rights over the line with the L.N.W.R., including the power to regulate its own charges for traffic from the Midland system over the L.C.R. as it thought fit. Apparently the L.N.W.R. had seemed willing that the Midland should fix its own charges for through traffic to Scotland but had demanded that with regard to all traffic stopping at any of the stations on the L.C.R. the rates to be made by both companies should be such as only both could agree upon, or as should be fixed by an arbitrator between them. This, of course, was the usual and perfectly reasonable attitude to take; the company was after all protecting its local traffic. What was not reasonable, and proved the stumbling block, was that Euston insisted on including Carlisle in the category of a station on the L.C.R. Strictly speaking this was again a more or less correct attitude to take, but for the Midland it meant that it could not feel free to fix its charges on the Scotch traffic. Derby contended that as any trains north of the Border, originating from the Midland system, would only run with the agreement of the Scottish companies, and that, therefore, all Midland trains might very well have to stop at Carlisle anyway, the L.N.W.R. would be regulating the whole of the Midland's charges. To this Euston assured Derby that it only had in view the protection of its own terminating Carlisle traffic, and must insist on the extension of the restriction applied to the L.C.R. to include the Midland's Carlisle traffic. There was stalemate and the discussions broke down. Carter's letter concluded :

'This was the sole difference between the companies on which the negotiation went off; for, though some other points remained to be further discussed, there was no reason to apprehend any difficulty with regard to them.

'The traffic of Carlisle proper compared with the English and Scotch traffic, which was the main object of the agreement, is, as everyone knows, wholly insignificant in amount; and the difference between what either company might obtain with the restriction on the mode of charging or without it, from the traffic of Carlisle proper, must be a matter, comparatively speaking, of no consideration whatever.

'The Midland directors cannot, therefore, regard such a termination to their long continued and important discussions without the greatest pain and regret.

'I am instructed by them to forward this statement to you with a request that it may be laid before the London and North Western directors. etc. etc.'

One other reason for the termination of the negotiations, though not as important as the main issue, was that the L.N.W.R. in suggesting a joint lease, would have expected the Midland to bear half the rent—a proportion somewhat at variance with the amount of traffic each side would take over the line.

It was a particularly bad time for the L.N.W.R. to start trifling with the Midland. 1865 was the year of the second "Railway Mania'. Money was cheap and new schemes many and varied. In the area north of Skipton there were several new proposals for connecting lines to the north, in one of which the Midland was taking a decided interest. It left its complaint with the L.N.W.R. for just over a month and when there seemed to be no relaxation in Euston's grim determination to get the last ounce out of the Midland whenever it could, the latter's board set about looking for its own route to Carlisle.

Before continuing with events which followed the break-up between Euston and Derby, the little North Western again comes into the news. It very literally hit all the local headlines with one of the biggest and saddest railway scandals yet. Early in May the board learned that all was not as it should have been with the company's secretary and general manager. Major Hare, the deputy chairman, and William Douglas, a director, arrived in Lancaster on Saturday, May 13, to see Whelon. They taxed him specifically on the question of his having privately borrowed some money on some of the company's share certificates issued to a Mr. E. G. Paley. Whelon admitted that he had done so. Hare next asked Whelon whether he had deposited with the Lancaster Banking company some of the company's 'A' coupons valued at £2,400 and Whelon had again agreed that it was so. He further intimated that the coupons had been 'manufactured'. In reply to the question of how he had obtained the signature of the director on the spurious coupons, the secretary said that 'he had managed it'. All along Whelon maintained that he had not compromised the company in any way. Some of his friends had agreed to help him out of the difficulty and were prepared then and there to square the account by a payment of £8,000. Hare refused, not knowing just how much was involved, and informed Whelon's friends that no compromise could be reached. After telling Whelon informally that he was dismissed from the company, Hare left. Whelon then called in his clerk, Benjamin Gregson, and told him to alter several figures in the company's book, saying that there had been a mistake. While he was doing this Gregson saw Whelon tear several counterfoils from the books.

Luckily Gregson kept an account of all Whelon's doings at that time, and some of the more fantastic reasons advanced for them, and was later able to give Hare a fairly accurate picture of what happened.

That evening Hare and Douglas returned with a warrant for Whelon's arrest. When they and the police arrived at the secretary's house they found that he had gone. Hare thereupon promised payment of all expenses provided Whelon was caught. He need not have bothered; by the following morning everyone knew where Whelon was. Let an extract from the issue of the *Railway Times* for Saturday, May 20, 1865, take up the story :

'The whole of North Lancashire was startled on Monday by announcement of the suicide of Mr. William Whelon, a gentleman of high position, and carrying on business at Lancaster and Preston, through pecuniary difficulties and the fear of exposure. Mr. Whelon rose from an office-boy to be secretary of the little North Western; then he became a merchant and manufacturer; afterwards he was made town-councillor, mayor and magistrate of Lancaster. While mayor of Lancaster he was distinguished for his liberality and hospitality, and his wife, during his year of office, was presented with a silver cradle by the inhabitants. In addition to the above positions, he was chairman of the Lancaster Athenaeum Club and the Morecambe gasworks, vice-chairman and director of the new wagon company, a church-warden, a leading Conservative, and generally a man of high influence and position. On Friday he was at Preston on business, and returned home in the evening. On Saturday it was rumoured that he had forged and embezzled sums to a large amount, varying, according to report, from £6,000 to £20,000. On the evening of that day a warrant was issued for his apprehension on the charge of stealing scrip belonging to the company. The police went to his house but he was absent. A dead body was found in the water at Fleetwood on Sunday. The evidence at the enquiry showed that he had left home on Saturday evening in good health and spirits, that he walked along the coast towards Fleetwood, and that at mid-night he got a boat at Knott-end, opposite Fleetwood, and about ten miles from Lancaster, rowed out a short distance in it, took something to drink, and jumped off the boat into deep water, that his body was seen floating next morning off Fleetwood by a seaman, and was afterwards picked up and taken to one of the hotels. The jury recorded a verdict of "found drowned". The deceased was about forty-three years of age, and has left a widow and seven children.'

Their presence, the pleadings of Whelon's friends, the long and devoted service he had given the little North Western, and the offer to make restitution; all these must have made Hare's decision to publicise the scandal very difficult. He did it as firmly as he had once done to Watson, over the business of the contractors' accounts. Here was no clannish covering-up. Here was Victorian moral rectitude at its apogee. Leafing through the musty squeezed old print of a century ago one feels an underlying tone of grief for Whelon. He must, one feels, have been such an ordinarily pleasant man. Bigger operators, who drove their victims to despair in thousands, who floated companies and disappeared, or worse who having floated a company legally milked it in directors' expenses; these went free. Whelon did not. There must have been many in Lancaster that weekend who murmured to themselves 'there, but for the Grace of God . . .'

The Whelon affair led to some awkward times with some of the shareholders who suddenly found that they had nothing to do with the little North Western at all, the transactions having been false. The company had to break open the box in which the seal was kept, one of three keys necessary to open it having gone with its owner to the sea. By August the accountants had straightened out the mess and it was found that Whelon's defalcations were by no means as bad as had been thought. There the matter ended, the company appointing William Frankland Dean as the new secretary. From the previous May the offices of the N.W.R. had been moved to 22, Commercial Street, Leeds.

The schemes in preparation for the session of 1865 were many. Of those concerning the area north of Skipton, and north Yorkshire generally, one of the biggest was the Leeds North Yorkshire & Durham, a nominally independent company promoted or backed by the L.N.W.R. At a proposed cost of £2 m., the promoters intended to construct a new line from the L.N.W.R. terminus at Leeds Wellington, passing through Wetherby and then running across the Plain of York and over the North Yorkshire moors to make a connection with the West Hartlepool Harbour & Railway company. Radiating from it were branches in all directions intended to tap off traffic in the North Eastern's sphere of influence. Though not directly bearing on the Midland, it affected the later history of the Settle-Carlisle line in that the N.E.R., fearful of the L.N.Y.D., had quickly to promote competing lines to satisfy the districts intended to be served by the new railway. It was, therefore, to be in a friendly mood to the Midland later in the year when the latter company was shopping around for its Carlisle route. In the event the L.N.Y.D. was rejected on account of bad estimating and the N.E.R. managed to buy out some of the promoters shortly afterwards.

The importance of obtaining N.E.R. tolerance to Midland expansion was quickly seen when three schemes likely to affect the N.E.R. adversely were launched from the Midland Railway system in Craven during the session. One was the Skipton Wharfedale & Leyburn Junction, proposing to make a line some 31 miles in length from a junction with the little North Western at Gargrave station, then turning northwards through Kettlewell to join the Northallerton, Bedale and Leyburn branch of the N.E.R. near Spennithorne. This would have let the L.Y.R. and the Midland deep into N.E.R. territory. Another scheme was that of the East & West Yorkshire Union, incorporating a threat from the L.N.W.R. for a line some 60 miles in length commencing from a triangular junction with the Lancaster & Carlisle & Ingleton Railway near Sedbergh and then running through Garsdale and Wensleydale to Leyburn, with various branches to Wath and Melmerby, and what was more important, a branch from Hawes down Ribblesdale to Settle. At first the project was intended to continue from Wensleydale to join the Eden Valley line at Kirkby Stephen. On the N.E.R. seeing this as a threat to the South Durham & Lancashire Union, the idea was dropped and the L.N.W.R. approached. The third scheme, and the most dangerous from the N.E.R.'s point of view, was the North of England Union. The *Railway Times* of February 4, 1865, gave particulars :

'This project, which is now before the public, is one deserving of notice. A glance at "Bradshaw's Railway Map of England" will suffice to show that in the middle of Yorkshire there is a wide distance, between Leeds and Barnard Castle, which has no railways. Right through this district of some 1,200 square miles the North of England Union intend running their line. Such a route would open out a direct line for iron and coke of Durham straight to Lancashire. Amongst the provisional committee is Lord Wharncliffe, the Hon. W. E. Duncombe, M.P., W. J. S. Morritt, Sir W. R. G. Chaytor, Bart., Cleervaux Castle, Darlington, R. H. Allan, etc. Capital £900,000 in 90,000 £10 shares. The requisite Parliamentary deposit of 8% upon the estimated cost of the line has been made.'

The main line of the North of England Union was to leave the little North Western about 500 yards south of Giggleswick station and then follow roughly the same route as the present Settle and Carlisle line as far as Garsdale where it turned east into Wensleydale, eventually terminating in a junction with the Bedale and Leyburn branch of the N.E.R. at the west end of Leyburn station. From there lines were to connect with Darlington, the West Hartlepool Railway, and the Richmond branch. In the south there was to be a connecting line from Sedbergh on the Lancaster & Carlisle & Ingleton to the main line at Aysgarth, and another from the little North Western at Clapham to the main line at Horton-in-Ribblesdale. It was altogether a very ambitious scheme. Extensive running powers and working arrangements with the L.Y.R., Midland, L.N.W.R., N.E.R. and West Hartlepool Railway were to be sought. The engineers were John Hawkshaw and J. Brunlees.

The North Eastern was not slow to act. It succeeded in limiting the Skipton Wharfedale & Leyburn Junction to a line only as far north as Grassington, thereby cutting out the remainder of the route to Spennithorne. The small company obtained powers as the Skipton & Wharfedale and lingered on, hamstrung, for a short time. In the sessions of 1866 and 1867 it went for powers to extend its line but was finally abandoned in 1869. The East & West Yorkshire Union was likewise disarmed, though in this case the N.E.R. bought out the scheme and turned it into a merely local line—the Hawes & Melmerby Railway, shedding the remaining parts, the N.E.R. to contribute half the capital. The Hawes & Melmerby was eventually to be abandoned for a more direct line from Leyburn to make connection with the Hawes branch of the Midland Railway, authorised as part of the Settle and Carlisle line.

With respect to the North of England Union, however, it was a different story. With the termination of the agreement with the L.N.W.R., and with a current dividend standing at 7¾ per cent. the Midland was in no mood to trifle. *Herepath's Journal,* in June of 1865, pointed out that 'the Midland is now so good a property that calls on their new share issues are welcomed as benefits, for the terms of issue are liberal'. Determined to reach Carlisle, the company saw in the North of England Union the means of so doing. That company had gone to Parliament in late

1864 with a proposal for its line to run from Settle to Kirkby Stephen. This soon shrunk to a Settle-Hawes line and the Hawes-Leyburn link had been handed over to the N.E.R.—which now had the choice of two lines east of Hawes—in exchange for reciprocal running powers, the N.E.R. to Settle and the North of England Union to Leyburn. By an agreement of March 31, 1865, the Midland took over the N.E.U. and paid £7,257 towards its expenses and liabilities. After the Bill had passed through the Commons, and with the L.N.W.R. being difficult over the L.C.R. negotiations, the Midland directors on the N.E.U. board had examined their line closely and had found that whereas the latter showed gradients of 1 in 70 it would be possible, at a slightly increased expense, to construct the railway at a ruling gradient of 1 in 100, though if passed as it stood there would have to be some deviations. Despite the fact that the N.E.U. would probably have passed through the Lords, it was therefore agreed, with the blessing of the N.E.R., that there should be an arrangement with the N.E.U. whereby the company withdrew its Bill, turning the line over to the Midland which would promote a new railway from Settle to Carlisle in the next session. On June 29 a meeting of the N.E.U. formally suspended the Bill and on August 2, 1865, the Midland board ordered Crossley, its engineer, to prepare the necessary plans for the Settle-Carlisle line. It was not long before Euston knew what was happening; a special committee minute of the L.N.W.R., dated August 16, 1865, noted that 'the Midland officers were reported to be looking at the country with a view to a line of their own to Carlisle'.

By November the scheme was fully in the open, one of the first recorded public reactions being a petition from the inhabitants of Dent, away from the main line as planned, to have a branch railway to the town. Concentrating all its energies on the new line, Derby turned down proposals from various new schemes for assistance. All the resources of the company would be needed both to get the Bill safely through Parliament, and when through, to construct the works.

As to the situation locally at the time, the Otley and Ilkley lines had started working during the previous August. The little North Western was still haranguing whoever it could about the evils in the English and Scotch Traffic Agreement. The company pointed out that during the seventeen years it had been open, thirteen of them worked by the Midland, the average dividend had been only $1\frac{1}{4}$ per cent. per annum. Meanwhile Alcock had gone to France and resigned the chairmanship; his place was taken by Hare, with Isaac Burkhill as vice-chairman. True to type the company disagreed with the current Midland policy, and petitioned against the Settle-Carlisle line, presumably on the grounds that even less of its line would be used if the new route came into operation.

Before the year ends a glance at the timetable for the Leeds-Ingleton-Carlisle service is of interest. As will be seen, it verged on the fictional at times. This was to come out in the evidence on the Midland's Bill during its passage through Parliament. On weekdays the first train from

Leeds was the 5.35 a.m. which left Shipley at 6.07, having there collected the 5.55 Bradford portion. It arrived at Skipton at 6.50, stopped for 5 minutes and then ran on to Ingleton, from where the L.N.W.R. took it on at 8.50, calling at all stations to Tebay which was reached at 9.50. There, if they were lucky and arrived soon enough, the passengers could catch the 6.00 a.m. from Liverpool Lime Street which left Tebay at 10.35 a.m., stopping at all stations to Carlisle where it arrived at 12.10 p.m. Other trains from Leeds were the 9.20, which avoided Ingleton and went through to Lancaster making a connection to arrive at Carlisle at 4.40 p.m.; the 11.20 a.m. from Leeds arrived at Ingleton at 1.50 p.m., left with a L.N.W.R. engine at 1.58 and arrived at Tebay at 2.57, catching a train on to Carlisle 13 minutes later. The last train was the 4.10 p.m. from Leeds, arriving at Ingleton at 6.20. Leaving Ingleton at 6.33, it arrived at Tebay at 7.32 where connection was made with the 7.57 from Tebay to Carlisle, reached at 9.10 p.m. On Sundays there were no trains via Ingleton and only one through Lancaster. And this was meant to be the Midland's Scotch service.

Hardly had 1866 got into its stride than the Midland began to experience opposition from some of its shareholders to the Settle-Carlisle line. One gentleman, a Mr. Hadley of Birmingham, was shouted down in the half-yearly meeting in February. He refused to be quiet and after a long rambling speech criticising the company's spendthrift policy, it took a general vote to silence him. At a meeting at Derby on May 15 the shareholders voted to go ahead with the line. It was pointed out that the Scotch traffic generally amounted to over £1 m. a year, and the proportion allotted to the Midland by virtue of the English and Scotch Agreement was a trifling £30,000. One of the shareholders, Dr. O'Brien, opposed the Bill. He said the Scotch traffic did not in fact amount to more than £700,000 per annum and that the Bill would antagonise the L.N.W.R. Up jumped Hadley of Birmingham again with the view that as the estimated cost was given at £1,650,000 he thought he should point out that it was more likely that the line would incur an expenditure in the region of £3 m. Though nobody believed him at the time he was in fact to be proved correct, and if his views had been accepted it is very doubtful if the Bill would have gone ahead. As it was there was a necessity for a vote, the numbers for the Bill being 14,558, some by proxy, and the numbers against 484.

Five days earlier the committee of the House of Commons sat to hear the evidence on the Bill. Mr. Venables, Q.C., was counsel for the Midland; he started the batting by examining Lord Wharncliffe who, in the last session, had been the provisional chairman of the N.E.U. He briefly told of the way in which the Midland had taken over the scheme —much more evidence on this point was to be brought to light from his Lordship three years later when he was again before the committee, this time on the opposite side of the fence. Following Lord Wharncliffe came Christopher Other, a one-time director of the Yorkshire & Glasgow

Union, and the Northern Counties Union, proving by his presence the long unbroken pedigree of the Settle and Carlisle project. Venables, speaking on behalf of the Bill, added an extra £½ m. to the estimated Scotch traffic as given to the shareholders of the Midland later in the week. He outlined the reasons for the Bill. It transpired that the Midland had at one point considered adopting part of the Eden Valley line between Appleby and Kirkby Stephen but had dropped the idea for engineering reasons. Venables pointed out that the Midland already had rights into Carlisle and that when the recent Caledonian and Scottish Central amalgamation Bill was passed the Midland had successfully petitioned to secure running powers over the amalgamated company to Perth and Dundee. This session the Caledonian had a Bill before Parliament for amalgamation with the Scottish North Eastern which would take it to Aberdeen. The Midland was once more petitioning as it too was in effect at both Edinburgh and Glasgow, and it was more than likely to succeed again.

Evidence heard on May 11 from witnesses in support of the Bill highlighted the question of delays on the Ingleton line. Joseph Foster of Carlisle, employing some four thousand operatives in one of the city's largest cotton mills, told how bales sent to Leicester via Ingleton had taken nine days to arrive. All the influential people in Carlisle were behind the Midland's attempt to get a new line to the city. Messrs. Carr & Co. of Carlisle, the biscuit people, had been debarred from sending goods to Leicester and Burton and had found considerable delays in getting transit through to other midland towns. There were in fact so many people in Carlisle who wanted to tell of their troubles that not all could be called.

In fact the sudden interest in Carlisle was rather at variance with Carter's statement, in his letter from the Midland to the L.N.W.R. in January 1865, that 'the traffic of Carlisle proper . . . is . . . wholly insignificant in amount'. It seems that its value fluctuated depending upon who was being addressed and with what intent. There can be no doubt at this juncture, however, in May 1866, that nobody required assuring more of the need for the Settle-Carlisle line than a number of the Midland's own shareholders. It was indeed rather a case of the platform being against the floor, or at least a noisy minority of it. Hence the battery of evidence from the Border city.

William Johnstone, the general manager of the Glasgow & South Western Railway, said that it was very desirable that the Glasgow traffic should connect with the Midland. At the present time, doing so by Ingleton, there was considerable delay to traffic in either direction. He thought Carlisle amply sufficient to take the additional Midland traffic some of which in any event already arrived in the city, though drawn by L.N.W.R. engines. Thomas Kenworthy Rowbotham, the general manager of the North British Railway, expanded on the Carlisle-London traffic. He pointed out that ordinarily the L.N.W.R. had about 300 miles interest in it; when sent by Ingleton this shrunk to about 70 miles. At the present time the N.B.R. was stopped by the L.N.W.R. from receiving traffic from over its line destined for Edinburgh or the north; the matter was now being thrashed out in the Court of Chancery. Meanwhile the N.B.R. was actively sending its traffic over the Midland via Ingleton. The Midland and the N.B.R. had agreed to open their routes to each other in the public interest. He went on to say that since the coming into effect of the Octuple Treaty and its successor, the N.B.R. had opened a new line through the middle of Scotland by way of Hawick to Carlisle—the 'Waverley Route'—which constituted a third railway from the north to Carlisle. If the Midland and N.B.R. could only meet properly at Carlisle they could beat the Octuple Treaty, for at that moment some 30,000 to 40,000 tons of goods were exchanged annually with the Midland and all of it passed through Ingleton.

John Hawkshaw, engineer to the L.Y.R., was called to give evidence and agreed that any extra traffic carried to Carlisle would be insufficient to cause trouble in the Citadel station. Following him, James Allport added strength to Hawkshaw's argument when he told how the Midland, N.B.R. and G.S.W.R. had already provided their own separate goods station in the city. He thought the goods traffic was one of the main arguments for the Midland to have independent access. As to the passenger traffic, the Midland trains got as far as Ingleton and were then carried on by the L.N.W.R. to Tebay where one, or at the most two, coaches were carried on to Carlisle. Though some of the passengers were changed at Ingleton in the first instance, the bulk of them were turned out at Tebay. It is difficult to write of the evidence before the committee. So many complaints of bad time-keeping, of missed connections, of active hostility to Midland and N.B.R. traffic on the part of the L.N.W.R., that to put it all down would take far too long. Suffice it to say that throughout the examination of witnesses there were a whole series of sharp explosions of frustrated bad feeling against the L.N.W.R. which had been building up for some time. Taking the evidence at its face value it would lead to the supposition that the L.N.W.R. was a very bad railway; it manifestly was not. The Carlisle problem, however, was not calculated to show the company up in a good light.

After having passed safely through the Commons the Bill went to the Lords. There the previous evidence was elaborated. As to the Eden Valley Railway, it was learned that the original promoters, when handing over the line to the N.E.R., had obtained a promise that the transfer should not preclude construction of a line at some future date down the remainder of the valley to Carlisle. This had not materialised. The Settle-Carlisle line would now open out the valley and bring it into touch with the outside world. It would greatly assist in the handling of the Scotch cattle traffic. It seemed that feeling was so high as to the problems of the agricultural community that when it became known that the Midland Bill had passed safely through the Commons the inhabitants of Appleby got up a spontaneous demonstration of sheer pleasure which ended in a lengthy ringing of the church bells. The cattle from the Vale of Eden wintered in the Craven district, coming down from Westmorland through difficult country to do so and the evidence was overwhelming as to the necessity for a line to take the local traffic. Butter sold at Appleby on a Saturday for the Sheffield market arrived after butter bought at Shap, on the Lancaster & Carlisle, on the Monday.

Allport, reappearing for examination before the Lords committee, said that as to running over the L.N.W.R. the Midland had applied again and again for through carriages to Edinburgh but without success. Passengers booking on the Caledonian Railway at Glasgow for Derby were booked to travel via Crewe. He thought the C.R. would be far more likely to co-operate if the Midland was at Carlisle. Crossley appeared, and made the telling point that the gradients by the proposed new line would be far more favourable than those on the L.C.R.

The L.N.W.R. put its general manager, William Cawkwell, in the stand. He produced considerable invoice evidence to show that a great deal of the delay occurred to goods whilst in transit on the Midland part of the journey, and rather saucily gave as examples a three day journey from Sheffield to Leeds, wholly by Midland, and one of one day between Leeds and Carlisle via the L.N.W.R. He also corrected some of Allport's evidence as to the connecting services from the Ingleton branch —there were at least two L.N.W.R. trains which daily took on Midland coaches. When Venables came to cross-examine Cawkwell it came out that in nearly all the cases of the invoices which had been so blatantly produced—18 out of 26—a careful check on the dates thereon showed that a Sunday had intervened on the Midland portion, a day when freight traffic was traditionally almost nil.

Summing up the case for the Midland on Tuesday, June 26, Venables asked whether the Midland Railway company, collecting traffic from a million persons, should take that traffic along one of the best routes in England and be forced afterwards to discharge it through the neck of the bottle belonging to the L.N.W.R., or whether the company should have independent access to Scotland. He pointed out that from starting in the Commons with an announcement that it did not intend to oppose the line but merely objected to the interference at Carlisle, the L.N.W.R. had swung over to a position of outright hostility. The evidence had proved the company's actions to be wrong and it was now fearful of the Midland getting the powers it sought. The Lords' committee found the Bill's preamble proved on June 26 and by July 6 the Bill had passed on to the next stage.

The Midland Railway (Settle to Carlisle) Bill received the Royal Assent on July 16, 1866. It authorised the company to raise an additional share capital of £1,650,000 and loans of £550,000. The line was authorised in three parts. Railway No. 1—28 miles and 1 furlong in length—was to commence from a junction with the little North Western at Cleatop, south of Settle, and then run north on the present route as far as Garsdale where it turned into Wensleydale, there to make a junction with the authorised Hawes & Melmerby Railway at Hawes. The plan showed the roof of Blea Moor tunnel to be 492 feet below ground level at its deepest point. Railway No. 2—just over 20 miles and 5 furlongs long—was to leave the first at Garsdale and continue the line on to make a junction with the Eden Valley Railway at Appleby; finally Railway No. 3—just over $29\frac{1}{2}$ miles in length—was to leave the second at the north end of the present Appleby Midland station and run through the Vale of Eden to connect at Carlisle with the Newcastle & Carlisle Railway of the N.E.R. on the east side of the River Petteril. The Midland was to be given running powers over the N.E.R. into Carlisle Citadel station and over the Hawes & Melmerby into Leyburn. In return the N.E.R. and the Hawes & Melmerby were to be allowed powers over the whole of Railway No. 1. The line as authorised differed from the original deposited plan in that Railway No. 3 terminated at the east side of the River Petteril. It was originally intended to continue it alongside the Newcastle & Carlisle line beyond the London Road bridge after which it was to cross the N.C.R. on the level and then follow the inside of the latter's curve all the way into Carlisle Citadel station, though without making any junction with N.C.R. rails. There was also to be an additional line, Railway No. 5—just under $\frac{1}{2}$ mile in length—from No. 3 almost immediately after it had crossed the N.C.R. from where it was to curve round, run parallel to No. 3 on the east side of Lancaster Street, and finally cut back to rejoin No. 3 at the south-east end of the station. Early on in the proceedings the Midland had decided to remove the main public reason for the L.N.W.R.'s opposition—that new construction into Carlisle itself would disrupt traffic—by dropping from the Bill the lines west of Petteril. The N.E.R. had objected to the proposed crossing on the level, so this move effectively placated opposition from that quarter too. Indeed as early as February 7, 1866, the Midland board gave instruction that Thomas E. Harrison, engineer to the N.E.R., was to be consulted as to the mode of junction at the river bridge.

With the passing of the Bill the L.N.W.R. had, for the time being, suffered a setback. Perhaps shamed by some of the evidence as to its Ingleton line service, the company added just one train to the daily timetable, a summary of which can be found in Appendix VI, for the period October-December 1866.

On August 11 *Herepath's Journal* had a premonition of trouble to come. It thought that the Midland had as many irons in the fire, all at one time, as was possible. Traffic was increasing but the profits were being swallowed in extra working expenses. The dividend was good as compared with the early 1850s but the company was paying large sums out of revenue as interest on lines in course of construction, as well as meeting additional operating costs. The Journal thought the Settle and Carlisle line an unnecessary expense; the L.C.R. could have been used, 'but the older railway companies get, the more antagonistic they become'.

On August 14 the Midland shareholders attended the half-yearly meeting. They were told that the company had obtained the longest period allowed by law to make the line—5 years. Originally the Bill had had a period of 7 years inserted, and was passed as such by the Commons committee. The Speaker's Counsel had discovered, however, that there was a rule which forbade any period longer than 5 years and so an alteration was made. The company had been successful in obtaining clauses in the Caledonian and Scottish North Eastern amalgamation Bill whereby the Midland was fully recognised as one of the main routes between England and Scotland, and had also obtained running rights and full facilities for its traffic—facilities equal to other companies. This meant that the Midland could in theory get access over the Caledonian to Glasgow, Edinburgh, Perth, and as far north as Aberdeen, materially adding to the potential of the Settle and Carlisle line.

On September 5 Crossley was asked to stake out such portions of the route as he thought advisable before the onset of winter. He was also to report on the governing works and the probable amount of outlay which would be required from time to time. Before leaving the affairs of the Midland for 1866, however, the company suffered a setback in November when, after heavy storms had turned the River Aire into a fast and over-flowing torrent, Apperley viaduct fell, disorganising all traffic on the L.B.R. A report from Inspector E. Browne of the Midland's permanent way department, dated October 21, 1893, tells what happened :

'I have seen the late station master, Mr. T. Masters of Apperley and Rawdon, who was at that station when the accident took place, and he says it happened between 5.30 and 5.40 p.m. on November 16th 1866 after which for two days no trains ran further than Apperley station on the south side and Shipley on the north side, towards the gap, when on the 19th November, crossover roads had been put in on either side, and a temporary footbridge erected, and passenger trains ran to and from the point of obstruction on both sides, the passengers walking across the gap; this working continued until January 1st 1867 on which day the new viaduct was so far erected to enable the traffic to resume its ordinary working, and on the proper lines, Masters adding that no single line working was adopted.'

According to Williams an up goods helped to demolish the viaduct. The station staff attempted to stop it when it emerged from Thackley tunnel but though the driver and fireman shut off steam and leaped off, the locomotive plunged down to the river below pulling its train with it. It took three days to get the goods engine back on the line. This piece of drama was not all; during the same storm lightning flung coping stones from the east entrance to Thackley tunnel onto the line immediately after an express had entered. At the west end of the tunnel, meanwhile, a deluge of water poured along the line, released from a nearby reservoir by the owner so that it should not flood his property. When the water met the express in the tunnel it was already to a height of some 3 feet.

The storm which produced this excitement was apparently the worst known 'in the recollection of the "oldest inhabitant" of the district'.*

It was estimated that the viaduct would take all of six months to rebuild. Crossley outdid himself to get the line open again in five weeks.* A fortnight after the re-opening the directors noted in the board minutes that they felt it their duty to offer to their engineer 'their thanks for the extraordinary energy and talent he has manifested in the reconstruction of the Apperley viaduct'. With their gratitude went the not inconsiderable sum of three hundred guineas.

Before leaving 1866, there were some other developments which could have affected the Midland. With a view to shortening its connections by running straight through Bradford, the L.Y.R. had deposited a Bill for the previous session for a junction line through the town connecting its system with that of the Midland which, together with the Leeds Bradford & Halifax Junction, had been invited to participate. At an estimated cost of £260,000, the line would have been of considerable use to both the Midland and the L.Y.R. in later years after construction of the Settle-Carlisle line. At the time, however, the Midland had preferred to stall such an idea and the L.Y.R. had reluctantly withdrawn the Bill. Now in 1866 there came another proposal, this time by a nominally independent company—the Bradford & Colne Railway. It was true that a lot of mileage would be saved between the two towns if the weary ramble around by Skipton could be avoided. Once again, as in the 1850s, the scheme would have damaged the Midland's local traffic between Bradford, Leeds and Colne. The Bradford & Colne Bill proposed a line of just over 18 miles in length to leave the L.Y.R. by a double junction at Colne and then to run south to join the Midland at Shipley. The company obviously intended to put itself up for sale to the highest bidder after getting the necessary powers. In January of 1866 it approached the Midland, asking for a traffic agreement but not unnaturally the latter replied that such would be against its own interests. It seems that the L.Y.R. was only too keen to keep on the right side of Derby at this critical point in their relationship, and with the prospect of the Settle-Carlisle line in the offing it was not too happy about stirring up trouble by adopting the Bradford & Colne. The Bill did not proceed. To clear the area south of Skipton, there was also a Bill before Parliament in 1866 promoted by another new concern—the Skipton & Ilkley Railway, intending to join the Otley and Ilkley joint line with the Midland. The Bill was withdrawn, however; not for another 22 years was there to be a line open on that route.

The final scheme which made a brief appearance in the session of 1866, and which suffered a similar fate to the Skipton & Ilkley, was a line planned by the Sedbergh & Hawes Railway. As has been seen at the end of the last chapter, there was a natural route carved through the Pennines from Sedbergh up the Rawthey Valley to Kirkby Stephen.

* *The Midland Railway.* Frederick S. Williams. 1878.

There was also another access through Garsdale to Garsdale Head and thence into Wensleydale. In the previous session the East & West Yorkshire Union had attempted to get powers for a line through the dale; now the Sedbergh & Hawes did likewise, planning a railway 16½ miles long, almost exactly the same as the westerly portion of the E.W.Y.U. As in the case of the Bradford & Colne, the line was to be offered to the highest bidder once powers were got. With the passing of the Midland's Settle-Carlisle Bill its worth dropped, and as in the other cases the Bill was withdrawn by its promoters.

The Midland was now left with a clear field for the construction of the Settle and Carlisle line. Within three years the company was to be actively seeking Parliamentary approval for its abandonment; once again it was to be ranged alongside the L.N.W.R. against the latter's rivals. This bewildering turn of events, which was so to infuriate all the parties which had supported the Midland through the session of 1866, will be seen not to have been due to the Midland board but to conditions over which it had no control. For, as in the last railway boom of 1846, when a depression followed which almost spelt ruin to some of the most established companies, so twenty years later after the Parliamentary sessions of 1865 and 1866, when no less than a total of 804 Bills were lodged, the country was once again to suffer acute financial indigestion with consequences fatal to many of the new schemes.

X

Abandonment Foiled

1867 – 1869

When in mid 1866 the Midland received the necessary powers to construct the Settle-Carlisle line, the company started almost immediately to look around for firm allies to the north of Carlisle. The Glasgow & South Western had supported the Midland throughout the campaign and it seemed to Derby that this particular company had more in common with the Midland than the others operating into Carlisle from Scotland.

The G.S.W.R. had started its career as an amalgamation of two companies; the Glasgow Paisley Kilmarnock & Ayr, and the Glasgow Dumfries & Carlisle. It had been opened throughout from Cumnock to Gretna, whence it ran over the Caledonian to Carlisle, on October 28, 1850. By an Act of June 2, 1865, the Kilmarnock Direct Line had been authorised. This event occurred at a time when its two companion lines north of the Border, the Caledonian and the N.B.R., were linked to the West and East Coast routes respectively. The Midland might well have thought that the Glasgow company would provide the third route to the northern capital, unencumbered by ties with its rivals. On August 17, 1866, however, the Caledonian sought to queer the Midland pitch by seeking an amalgamation with the G.S.W.R.—in effect bringing the latter into the Euston camp. The Midland, seeing its access to Scotland threatened, and with a very expensive line to construct which if this happened would be practically useless, was quick to react. It countered the Caledonian move by offering the G.S.W.R. better terms and it was not long before agreement had been reached between the two concerns to unite. (The Kilmarnock Direct Line was, by the way, abandoned by the G.S.W.R. in 1869 in favour of a joint line with the Caledonian—the Crofthead and Kilmarnock—to which the N.B.R. was admitted.) Directors from the Midland and the G.S.W.R. each made careful inspection of the line of the other and the accounts of both were made available. The upshot of all these manoeuvres was that a Bill for amalgamation was prepared by the two companies and deposited at Westminster for the session of 1867. The amalgamated company was to take the name of 'Midland and Scottish Railway Company'.

It was not until the half-yearly meeting of February, 1867, that the Midland shareholders had a chance to say what they thought of all this, and it soon became apparent that the company was going to have a fight on its hands to get the Bill passed through its own internal

147

machine, let alone through Parliament. The meeting started badly for, to the mortification of those present, Hutchinson had the unenviable task of telling them that the dividend was lower than usual. He pointed out that the traffic had been affected by the fall of Apperley viaduct, which had incidentally been reconstructed out of revenue. This was not the whole story, however; traffic all over the system had been down in 1866 compared with other years, or at least it had not increased at the same rate as heretofore. One of the reasons for this were the severe floods of the previous autumn. Another was that a heavy landslip at Buxworth (then Bugsworth) on the Midland's Manchester line, shortly after traffic had started over it, had closed the line completely for some time. After the usual report on the state of the company, Hutchinson got to the amalgamation Bill. He thought the G.S.W.R. a well run company with useful connections—amalgamation would, he believed, be mutually beneficial.

What followed was meant to be a general discussion on the merits of the Bill. In fact it developed into a series of quick-fire attacks by shareholders against the board, with the directors doing all they could to justify their existence. One of the first speakers was the indefatigable Dr. O'Brien of Liverpool who declared that he would oppose to the uttermost any attempts to increase the financial burdens of the company. Speaking against the amalgamation, he thought the Midland should rest for a year, rather than attempt union with the G.S.W.R. He attacked the proposed Halifax and Huddersfield line—a joint venture to be attempted with the L.N.W.R. as a follow-up to the Midland's running powers from Penistone to Huddersfield, acquired in the previous session. Other shareholders took up the theme, citing gross overspending. Thomas Shepherd of London said that £650,000 had been spent on the new station and hotel at St. Pancras—and this was before the works had been started. He saw no necessity for such a big station. (St Pancras hotel was not opened until 1873.) Mr. Garnett of Leeds thought that traffic arrangements with the G.S.W.R. were all that were necessary, not an amalgamation. At this point the directors sprung a trap. It was triggered off by a Mr. Day, one of the shareholders, speaking in favour of the directors' decision and asking for a vote of confidence in it. By this time there were several votes to be taken including one on the amalgamation and the question of whether to proceed with the Settle-Carlisle line. As to the latter case, Hutchinson said that he considered it imperative that the work should go ahead quickly as the time factor had been reduced from seven to five years. On the amalgamation point he thought that if this were shelved until the Settle-Carlisle line was made, the Caledonian might well have stolen a march at Carlisle. Very quickly he then read through the various amendments to the report made by O'Brien, Shepherd, Garnett and others and said that as Mr. Day's had been put last, he would dispose of it by vote first.

This was too much for Dr. O'Brien. Struggling to his feet he shouted that this was unfair as it only echoed the directors' own resolution to their report. If carried it would automatically make the other votes unnecessary. By now there was a considerable amount of noise in the hall between the two factions. Notwithstanding Dr. O'Brien's argument, the chairman put Day's resolution and declared it carried. Complete uproar followed, with the movers of the other resolutions demanding a poll and declaring that the votes should have been taken in order. This Hutchinson agreed to do. The first taken was, of course, the original motion of the directors, approving the official report and proposed by Hutchinson at the beginning of the meeting. He declared it carried. This was the signal for a renewal of the shouting. The two resolutions already voted, and in agreement with the company's policy, effectively sandwiched those of the dissident parties. Garnett of Leeds stormed at the chairman's conduct, but Hutchinson blandly said that as the two carried resolutions virtually disposed of all the others, he saw no point in carrying on. The tactics so successfully adopted were to rebound on the board within a very short time.

The only people apparently in favour of the amalgamation were the shareholders of the little North Western; they confidently hoped that the deal would go through for if it did the small company saw a much improved prospect for the Scotch traffic. They still had reservations over the Settle-Carlisle line; if constructed it would once more diminish the length worked over the little North Western by Scotch trains, already substantially cut by the opening of the Ingleton route. With regard to the construction of the Settle line, on March 5 the board ordered that the North Construction committee was to be responsible henceforth. Crossley was to take steps to obtain tenders for certain shafts in Blea Moor tunnel which were to be commenced. On the amalgamation proposal, the shareholders of the G.S.W.R. gave their approval to the Bill at a meeting on March 13.

On May 11, 1867, G. N. Browne, the Midland's secretary, published a disclaimer in the railway press to a rumour that the Midland directors had been negotiating with the L.N.W.R. with a view to repeal the Settle-Carlisle Act; ' . . . these statements if uncontradicted being calculated to lead to misapprehension, I am instructed to say that no such negotiations have taken place'. Clearly something was in the wind, however. Over a fortnight later there was a shareholders' meeting at Derby—so crowded that it had to move to the Corn Exchange—to discuss the amalgamation Bill. Hutchinson again put forward all the arguments in its favour. Despite some strong opinions expressed on both sides, there was no uproar, no calls for dropping the idea; the meeting solemnly voted the Bill through. Far from being reassured, Hutchinson was now worried. The unexpected calm had a hint of hidden knowledge of bigger things afoot.

In fact the shareholders had formed a committee to approach the L.N.W.R. for a resumption of the talks which had broken down in

1866. It seems as if the Midland board got to hear of this rather quicker than was expected, for the next meeting to discuss the future of the Settle-Carlisle line and the amalgamation Bill was held very soon after the first, on June 4. Hutchinson was determined this time that as the shareholders obviously knew that their doings were revealed to the board, he would keep the floor as long as possible to delay discussion and a vote. His performance was impressive. In a long repetitive speech he outlined practically the whole history of the need for the Settle line and the amalgamation Bill. All aspects were minutely touched upon, and he spoke at length of the opposition and its stupidity. His delivery was interspersed by outbursts from O'Brien, Garnett, Shepherd, and the other main leaders of the retrenchment faction. Replying to their objections, he spun out the discussion until just after 5.15 p.m. when a vote was taken and passed that the meeting be adjourned until Thursday, June 13. This, of course, was not to the shareholders' liking but Carter, the company's solicitor, said the vote was binding. The adjournment, however, acted in the shareholders' favour rather more than in the directors', for by the time June 13 arrived, the former party had taken the initiative. When the meeting opened Hutchinson had to admit that the Manchester committee of the shareholders had entered into a treaty with the L.N.W.R. and had asked for terms by which the latter would now grant access to the Midland to get to Carlisle over the Ingleton line and the L.C.R. The committee had informed Carter of the position and he was now acting as a go-between for the shareholders and the Midland board. To a discord of derisive laughter from some of the shareholders, Hutchinson then read out the terms of the treaty. These included the reference of the whole problem of access to Carlisle to the President of the Board of Trade who was to ascertain the points of difference between Euston and Derby, and also what could be achieved by the abandonment of the Settle line.

Hutchinson appeared nettled but as will be seen both he and Allport had also taken advantage of the adjournment. Finished with reading the treaty, he said that it would be pointless to discuss the terms made by the L.N.W.R. to the committee as these were childish. The whole matter had nothing to do with the Board of Trade; it had already been discussed in Parliament at the time of the Settle and Carlisle Bill. His remark that the terms were 'childish' caused great anger; Rawson, of the Manchester committee, shouted that the terms had not yet been accepted. Rising to defend the board Carter pointed out that the terms, accepted as he thought, had been handed to him on a piece of paper by William Sale of Manchester, the solicitor acting on behalf of the committee. This drew an immediate reply from Sale who claimed that Carter had misunderstood him. At this point there was some side-changing. To the surprise of the abandonment party Garnett and Shepherd suddenly swung round to the side of the directors, the latter saying that certain votes he held by proxy could not now be used against the board. His action drew the remark from Rawson that this was the 'dirtiest trick' ever attempted. One must wonder at the temper displayed throughout these meetings. Perhaps it was lucky for all that they were enjoying the benefits conferred by living in the latter part of the nineteenth century. Otherwise it is most probable that a considerable number of the gentlemen involved might well have suddenly been called to higher business whilst looking down the wrong end of a duelling pistol. To return to the meeting; time was by now running out. A vote to adjourn was taken after a poll on the Bill, the results of which would have taken so long to count as to render the meeting almost a danger to life and limb if the participants had been forced to sit and look at each other during the process. No doubt it was considered wiser in any event to let the tense atmosphere ebb somewhat and it was agreed to continue the business at 11 a.m. the following morning. When the time came on the next day to announce the results of the poll taken the previous evening, Rawson, who was one of the scrutineers on behalf of the committee, claimed that his vote included 977 proxies. This was disputed but, even allowing his claim, there were 572 votes and 1,008 proxies for the company's policy against 34 votes and 994 proxies disapproving it. According to C. H. Jones and William J. Beale, the board's scrutineers, this meant that the necessary majority in favour had been obtained. In any case, Hutchinson said that even if the amalgamation Bill had failed to get approval, or was thrown out by Parliament, the Midland and G.S.W.R. boards were pledged to reintroduce it next year. The damage for this session had already been done, however. Less than a month after the two critical Midland meetings the Bill, after passing through the Commons, was rejected by the House of Lords on July 16. The reasons for this were various. The Bill was opposed by the L.N.W.R., C.R., and N.B.R. Euston alleged that the Midland was not in earnest in making the Settle and Carlisle line, and that there would, therefore, be a long gap between the two portions of the amalgamated system. Venables, the counsel for the Midland, stressed throughout the time the Bill was in the Commons that the company fully intended to make the line. In fact he thought that he had made the matter so plain that in his speech to the Lords committee he understated this aspect of the Midland's case. His reticence was seized upon by Mr. Hope-Scott, counsel for the L.N.W.R., who charged the Midland with a change of policy between the Commons and the Lords. There were other arguments. Hope-Scott alluded to the 1867 Reform Bill, then pending, which if passed would affect the composition of Parliament. He thought the amalgamation Bill should be postponed until after this event. Addressing the chairman of the committee he said, 'Perhaps, sir, by the time when this question ought properly to come before Parliament, your places may be filled by gentlemen whose seats depend considerably upon the votes of lodging enginemen and discompounded stokers, whose views of railway legislation may be entirely different from your own'. Edmund Beckett Denison, speaking on behalf of the North British, said the amalgamation was premature—the Settle and Carlisle line had not even been commenced. 'Every argument for this Bill,' he said, 'will be just as good when the Settle and Carlisle is within a few months of completion as it is now'. Despite the evidence given in support of the amalgamation it had become obvious, during the time the Bill was before Parliament, that the opposition of the Midland share-holders had become very active. It had, as will be seen, less to do with the amalgamation than with their determination to discontinue the Settle line. Such was the picture of falling confidence in the Midland directorate that the Lords committee thought it best that the Bill should not proceed.

In August the company held its half-yearly meeting. The directors' report stated that considerable progress had been made in staking out the Settle-Carlisle line. On August 6 the following contractors had been invited to tender for the works at and around Blea Moor : Messrs. Brassey; Thompson; Benton & Woodiwiss; Eckersley & Bayliss; Firbank; Ashwell; and Oliver. Meanwhile, the board had ordered that the remainder of the line should be laid out to Crossley's directions. His estimate for contract No. 2, including Blea Moor tunnel, was £238,516 0s. 7d. At the August meeting the proceedings developed into one long dog fight. Shepherd complained that he was being charged by Rawson with having taken a bribe from Allport to join the side of the directors. Allport would have none of this; taking Shepherd's part, he told the meeting that all that had happened was that Shepherd had been shown the paper with the L.N.W.R. terms on it at a meeting between Shepherd and the directors on the morning of June 13. Allport swore upon his honour that nothing else had occurred—they were only there for some ten minutes and were as incapable of doing anything so dishonest as were Mr. Rawson and his associates. To this Shepherd added the remark that as to Rawson's censures upon him, that gentleman was now known to have a large interest in the L.N.W.R. and only about £200 in the Midland whilst he, Shepherd, had some £22,000 invested in the latter. Immediately after this interesting piece of information there was a violent quarrel between Dr. O'Brien and Carter. In fact the whole meeting was in thoroughly bad taste, redolent more of the times of Hudson and Huish. One thing was apparent though, the Settle-Carlisle line was still to go ahead.

On October 1 the tenders for contract No. 2 were received. Only two seemed to interest the board, that from Oliver who tendered for £242,941 3s. 10d. and from Benton & Woodiwiss for £243,095 13s. 6d. By November 5 Oliver had withdrawn and Benton & Woodiwiss had reduced their tender to £241,865 19s. 10d. on condition that the firm could have first class passes on the Midland during the time of the works and for the period of the maintenance thereafter. This was a mistake, for the board immediately accepted the revised tender but refused the passes. During December various rumours and letters directed against the Midland board appeared in the railway press—mostly calling for an investigation into the affairs of the company. It seemed that there was to be no let-up in the attempts of the abandonment party, discreetly backed by the L.N.W.R., to get the Settle line stopped. By this time the after effects of the 1865 'Mania' were beginning to be felt throughout the country. Edward Baines of Leeds—Member of Parliament and later knighted—who was a member of the 'audit committee' of the shareholders set up to look into the Midland's affairs, wrote to the *Times* calling for a *rapprochment* with the L.N.W.R. and the jettisoning of an independent route to Scotland. On December 31 a worried board, seeing that the opposition was gathering strength from the general financial difficulties in the country, difficulties which in three weeks that autumn had caused Midland shares to fall from around 117 to par, called upon the contractors to wait. The operations on the line were not to proceed until the present period of financial uncertainty was over. At the same time the land purchases for the line were halted. (They had not really been started; the land purchase plans prepared by Henry C. Roper, engineering surveyor, of Dudley, were dated November, 1867.) The directors had in fact realised by October that to complete outstanding works some £5 m. new capital would be required and had advised the shareholders to this effect by a special circular on December 17.

During what must have been one of the stormiest years of the Midland's existence since its independence, the ordinary run of the mill events took their normal course. The main event in the Yorkshire area during 1867 was the opening of the Keighley & Worth Valley line, passenger traffic commencing on April 15, and goods on July 1, bringing a small amount of welcome extra traffic on to the Midland system. With a ruling gradient of 1 in 56—between Ingrow and Damens—and with several embankments which caused trouble by slipping, and a short tunnel at Ingrow, the single track line had taken some three years to construct since the cutting of the first sod by Isaac Holden, later Sir Isaac, on Shrove Tuesday, 1864. The working was commenced by Midland tank engines but the line was not officially handed over to the Midland until April, 1868, the contractors maintaining it in the interim. Further north, at Ingleton, various improvements to the layout were made during the year, with additional sidings and a new goods shed.

Another event during 1867 was the opening to goods traffic on April 10 of most of the 9½ mile long Furness and Midland joint line from Carnforth to Wennington, passenger traffic following on June 6. In February, 1864 Richard Moon of the L.N.W.R. had tried to talk the Furness into abandoning the project; with his company's awakening interest in the lines of West Cumberland, he can have had little taste for a probable Midland incursion into the Barrow district. To the Furness, of course, Midland traffic would be bound to bring benefits and in any event the company was already looking ahead to the expansion of its steamer services which would accrue therefrom. Moon was told that the line would be built, and Messrs. Benton & Woodiwiss were awarded the contract at an estimated cost of £102,850. In February, 1865 the Midland began to think of enlarging Wennington station and in May, 1866, the company agreed with the Furness to provide a galvanised iron engine shed to hold four locomotives, with turntable and water column, at Carnforth. The Midland was to erect the signals along the line, except at the junction at Carnforth. The three intermediate stations of Melling, Arkholme, and Borwick were built on the Furness pattern. There was one tunnel—Melling, of 1,230 yards—and two viaducts over the River Lune. By an agreement in August, 1868 the Furness undertook to maintain the line, the Midland to work all the traffic. For a short period the station at Carnforth was situated at about the site of the present Carnforth East Junction; in fact part of the old structure still stands. It was closed by July 1, 1868, when the short remaining portion of the line not yet opened, across the Carnforth-Warton road and the River Keer, and making a junction with the Furness Railway, was brought into use. With the closure of the temporary station a new one came into use at the West Junction. This in turn was made redundant when, by the Furness Railway Act of 1879, the loop line from the East Junction to the L.N.W.R.'s Carnforth station was constructed and brought into use, together with a new joint L.N.W.R./F.R./Midland station, on August 2, 1880.

On New Year's Day 1868 Charles Langton, of Wiltshire, wrote to *Herepath's Journal*. His letter put into a nutshell some of the other worries concerning the construction of the Settle and Carlisle line, which had not so far been touched upon. Before such a hostile thing against the L.N.W.R. as the Settle line was made, he said, should not the Midland shareholders ponder on what retaliatory measures Euston might take? The L.N.W.R. was now able to use the Midland's station at Derby, it had the right to use the M.S.L.R. into Sheffield, and it had penetrated the woollen district. There seemed nothing to stop it making a line via Derby and Sheffield to join its system in Yorkshire at Dewsbury, thus enabling it to compete with the Midland for the Yorkshire-London traffic. Having cast a shadow over the Settle line Langton turned his attention to the proposed amalgamation between the Midland and the G.S.W.R., still presumably going ahead in the session of 1868, if Hutchinson's word was anything to go by. Having got to Glasgow, he asked, what was there to stop the Glasgow directors from using the joint capital to extend the system north and east? By the time the letter was published the shareholders were already working along the lines he had inferred.

On Tuesday, December 31, 1867, there was a meeting of the Midland proprietors at the 'Queen's Hotel' in Leeds to consider how best they could protect their interests, and to agree a policy to put before the directors at the next Midland meeting at Derby on January 15. They were particularly concerned about the company's intention to raise the additional £5 m., already referred to. With Edward Baines in the chair, they decided to press for the setting up of a committee of consultation to discuss with the directors the possibility of relinquishing or at least

154

postponing the outstanding works of the company. These were listed as the Settle and Carlisle line, taking £2,200,000; the Mansfield lines at £650,000; the Ashby and Nuneaton railways at £220,000; lines authorised by the 1865-1866 Acts, excluding the Settle line, and costing £200,000; the Midland proportion of the Liverpool and Cheshire lines, at £835,000; works in progress or ordered on the existing system at £100,000; rolling stock additions at £200,000; and finally the London station, hotel and offices at £200,000. In all £4,605,000.

Four days later a meeting was held of the Manchester shareholders, with Henry Rawson in the chair. Joshua Fielden of Todmorden called for a general revision of the existing arrangements of the Midland Railway. Rawson said that he wished to pay tribute to the views that Baines had expressed at Leeds. He only feared that Baines had too kindly a nature and too intimate an acquaintanceship with some of the Midland directors to 'pursue that rigorous course which any man who undertakes to reform railway matters must assume'. Henceforth, said Rawson, the shareholders should not accept at face value any statements of future expenses issued by the directors—the consulting committee which had been requested by Baines must be chosen from people not under the directors' influence. By January 15 the committee was in being. Its first act was to agree that the £5 m. capital required by a Bill to be shortly introduced to Parliament, to cover the existing commitments of the company, should be called up over a period of years, and not all at once. By this time the Midland board had gracefully bowed to the inevitable; the committee was promised full support in making its enquiries.

Besides trouble with its shareholders the Midland had difficulties in other directions. Early in February a forged letter bearing on the Settle line problem was attacked by the company in the railway press and the daily papers :

MIDLAND RAILWAY

A letter, copy of which is given below, purporting to be signed by me as secretary to the Company, having been sent to the several Stock Exchanges, which letter is a forgery, notice is hereby given, that a reward of £50 will be paid to anyone who will give such information as will lead to the detection of the author or authors of such letter. By Order of the board, G. N. BROWNE, Secretary. Derby, Feb. 5, 1868.

(copy of forged letter)

Midland Railway, Derby Station,
Feb. 1, 1868.

Sir,—I am requested to state a committee of shareholders and Midland Directors had a meeting this afternoon, when a resolution was passed to abandon the Settle and Carlisle line, the London and North Western board having made very reasonable offers for the working of the Scotch traffic over the Lancaster and Carlisle line. A second resolution was passed to postpone several other projects for five years; this will reduce the amount of new capital required to very narrow limits. Further, the auditors have nearly completed our accounts, which indicate a dividend at the rate of £6 10s. per cent. per annum for the past half year,—Yours respectfully,

G. N. Browne, Secretary.

M. Slaughter, Esq., Stock Exchange, London.

The letter was quite probably an attempt to make a quick kill on the market; in that case the choice of addressee used by the writer conveys a certain humour. The point of interest to the Midland was that to all intents the letter was substantially true, and at the half-yearly meeting later in February it was learned just how true when the report from the committee of consultation, which had been accepted by the directors, was read out. It appeared that there had been some considerable correspondence between the committee and the L.N.W.R.; Richard Moon, the L.N.W.R. chairman, had written from Euston on January 28 that though there had always been differences between his board and the Midland over the Settle-Carlisle line, he thought that some arrangement could be made to terminate them. He reminded the Midland that it was about to spend some £2 m. to make the line and it would require about £5 per cent per annum—say £100,000—to make it pay. If the Midland would guarantee an annual payment for net toll of £50,000 for the use of the Ingleton-Carlisle line, the L.N.W.R. would be prepared either to give the Midland running powers thereover, or make the line into one owned jointly by both companies, with rights of joint management and equal rights to fix their own rates and fares. The L.N.W.R. was also prepared to join with other companies to fully recognise the Ingleton route as a line within the English and Scotch Agreement. This was, of course, a complete climb-down from the original position adopted by Euston. The L.N.W.R. had at last realised that the Midland had been pushed just that little bit to far. To ensure a sympathetic reception to these revised terms, Moon also hinted at the end of his letter that it was possible that there might be other arrangements which could be agreed at the same time, and in this connection mentioned the Ashby and Nuneaton line, already authorised to be constructed jointly by both companies by an Act of 1867. On receipt of this letter Baines realised its importance and immediately passed it on to Hutchinson. Hutchinson had had a meeting with the other directors and all had agreed that this time the L.N.W.R. terms appeared worth discussion. A letter was hastily sent to Euston asking for an agreement from the L.N.W.R. to keep the offer open for three or four months. As was to be expected, Euston replied that it would do so. After some desultory discussion on the feasibility of continuing with the Settle line the February meeting terminated. There was a general vote of thanks to the committee; some sort of harmony between the board and its shareholders was once more apparent, the committee having agreed to let the money Bill for £5 m. go ahead without further trouble. Powers were obtained by an Act of June 25, 1868, to raise an additional £3,750,000 in shares and £1,250,000 on loan. With the possibility of abandonment so much in the air, and thus the likelihood of Ingleton retaining its importance as an interchange station, the 1868 Act also empowered the Midland to purchase a considerable amount of land at the town. As it turned out the powers were allowed to lapse.

Throughout July and August Derby and Euston talked terms. It was rather difficult for the Midland to be pinned down at this particular moment. Quite a lot depended on the present session of Parliament. There was first the question as to whether the company should seek an extension of time for the construction of the Settle line without at the same time offending Euston and prejudicing the discussions. The company's solicitor put the matter squarely before the board in August. If the Midland wished an abandonment Bill to go through, he intimated, the outcome would not be known until the following May and this, if the Bill was unsuccessful, would leave hardly any time to serve the notices on the landowners for the construction. The time for the compulsory acquisition of the lands expired on July 16 next and if the instructions to the company's engineers and surveyors were not immediately put in hand the Midland might have no option but to apply for Bills for extension of time and abandonment at the same time. If, however, the abandonment Bill was passed by Parliament the company would only have incurred the expense of preparing the notices.

The board was in a dilemma. Any delay could be fatal, yet to prepare the notices now would need some explaining away to both the L.N.W.R. and the shareholders. In the event some very careful expounding on the part of the board reassured the latter that such a move was only in the nature of an insurance. As to Euston, with its pre-eminent knowledge of the devious ways of railway Parliamentary procedure, there was no difficulty. Richard Moon must have seen that to object would have forced the Midland directors to take the sure course of making the line.

By November agreement had been reached between Derby and Euston to let the Midland use the Ingleton-Carlisle line. The L.N.W.R. had promised to drop the England-Scotland traffic provisions which had been the undoing of the 1865 talks, and had given an undertaking not to oppose an application for an extension of time on the Settle-Carlisle line should the abandonment Bill fail. Moon tried to get as much as he could from the prevailing concord between the two companies by asking for running powers over the Bristol and Birmingham line, but was told that they could not be written into the new agreement. This document, dated November 11, 1868, permitted local Midland passenger traffic between Low Gill and Carlisle, out of which 15 per cent. for working expenses was to go to the Midland, and the rest to the L.N.W.R. The Midland was also to pay an annual minimum mileage proportion of rates and fares totalling £40,000 to use the line. Euston was to support the abandonment Bill in the 1869 session. The agreement, which was to be for a period of fifty years, was dependent on ratification by Parliament and the success of the Bill. Meanwhile, in August 1868, pending the proposed amalgamation with the G.S.W.R., now of course shelved, the Midland had agreed with that company that each should afford to the other complete facilities for the interchange of traffic. They were, in effect, to work in mutual co-operation.

On Thursday, October 1, 1868, the Midland's extension to London had been opened through to St. Pancras. The line from Moorgate Street to Bedford had been taking local passenger traffic from Monday, July 13. The St. Pancras opening terminated the working of main line trains over the G.N.R. to Kings Cross. On October 24 it was reported that over the past four months the traffic had increased by £57,000. *Herepath's Journal* remarked at this time that it was probable that the Midland directors would be able to inform the shareholders in the following February that the company's affairs were now on the turn, with an increased net profit of at least £60,000 for the six months ending December, 1868. By March of 1869 the net receipts in the current half-year had advanced about £150,000 over the previous year, mostly due to the London extension.

The Midland and London and North Western Railway Companies (Lancaster and Carlisle and Settle and Carlisle Railways, &c.) Bill came before the committee of the House of Commons, chaired by Myles William O'Reilly, on Thursday, April 8, 1869. Messrs. Venables and Hope-Scott appeared as counsel for the Midland and L.N.W.R. respectively. Venables started by stating the case for the Bill. Much of what he said covered the history of the Midland's attempts to reach Carlisle, and the build-up of the company's system. Some of the points made, however, have not so far been dealt with. Referring to the North British Railway, Venables said that in 1859 that company had received powers to make the 'Waverley Route'—Edinburgh to Carlisle. When the line was made the Midland had agreed to work in concert with the N.B.R. as to the Scotch traffic, even though the two companies were at the time separated by the Lancaster & Carlisle. Having provided a third route not contemplated in the original Octuple Agreement, the Midland claimed it to be outside its provisions. In a suit in Chancery, when the Midland was the plaintiff and all the other parties to the Agreement the defendants, it had ultimately been decided by Vice Chancellor Kindersley that the Midland was correct in its contention and that the company should not be compelled to divide the proceeds from traffic on the route to the terms laid down in the Agreement. After dealing with the blocking tactics of the West Coast companies which followed from this decision, Venables outlined the subsequent abortive talks between Derby and Euston, and the agreement made between the Midland and the North of England Union which had led to the Settle line project. Referring to the Settle-Carlisle Bill, Venables said that the Midland had never represented the line to be one for local traffic; it was to be mainly for the purpose of a new through route, and if the abandonment was authorised he felt that the people living in the Hawes area would be no worse off as they already had a new line under construction by the North Eastern Railway. After dealing with the events of 1868, which led to the resumption of negotiations between Derby and Euston, Venables came to the petitions against the present Bill.

He dealt first with the North of England Union, saying that even if its Bill had been passed in 1866 the money panic of the following year would have killed it. Such was the feeling for abandonments in 1867, he said, that a special Bill had been prepared to facilitate them. (It received the Royal Assent on August 11, 1869.) As to a precedent for the present Bill he cited the case in 1866 when the South Eastern and London Chatham & Dover Railways had promoted a line from Beckenham to Brighton, not as long as the Settle-Carlisle line but necessitating some £3 m. capital. The promoters had said at the time that the line would be of great use and despite the fact that Parliament knew of the poor financial state of the L.C.D.R. the Bill had been allowed to proceed. By the time it had reached the House of Commons the Chatham company had become practically insolvent. Even so the Bill was passed. Venables reasoned that this showed that lack of capital alone could not have been the reason that Parliament permitted the line's abandonment in 1868. In that year the London Brighton & South Coast, and the South Eastern, had gone to Parliament with an amalgamation Bill as part of which both agreed to abandon some of their proposed lines, which were to have been competitive but were now rendered superfluous, including that from Beckenham to Brighton. Though the amalgamation Bill was withdrawn in the Lords at the insistence of the South Eastern, for various financial reasons, the abandonment went through.

Venables next turned to the North British petition against the Bill. That company had supported the original Settle-Carlisle Bill of 1866, arguing that it had constructed the Waverley route at an expense of £5 m. to compete for through traffic. It was restricted by the combined attentions of the L.N.W.R. and Caledonian companies. But, Venables pointed out, the N.B.R. had recently agreed on a common purse agreement with the C.R. As to the company's claim that with regard to its access to the Midland at Ingleton it was continually interfered with by the L.N.W.R., Venables stated that 'all this refers to the past and not to the future, and to nothing in this Bill'. What the North British really wanted, he thought, and the reason why it supported the Settle-Carlisle Bill of 1866, was that not being on friendly terms with Euston, it wished to meet the Midland at Carlisle—a company with which the N.B.R. saw eye to eye on Scotch traffic. But—and here was the crux of the abandonment case—as by the abandonment Bill now being discussed the Midland would still be at Carlisle by as free a right and with as full powers as the L.N.W.R., the North British would be just as well off. The North British was also arguing that the abandonment of the Settle line would deprive it of access to the important districts which that line was intended to traverse. To this Venables replied caustically, 'It would furnish a means, no doubt, of getting from Aberdeen to Hawes, but whether anybody ever wants to get from Aberdeen to Hawes I think may be doubtful.' The counsel continued by demolishing other N.B.R. claims, especially one dealing with the fear that the Midland might yet still amalgamate with the G.S.W.R. if the present Bill was passed. Venables did not agree—if anything he thought the reverse applied. The G.S.W.R. amalgamation Bill was rejected partially because the Settle line had not then been constructed. He thought that its total abandonment would surely diminish the chance further. As to the N.B.R. charge that 'the proposal to hand over the exclusive control of the Lancaster & Carlisle to the London & North Western and Midland companies is pregnant with great danger', he felt that the N.B.R. would have to accept a *fait accompli;* in any event it would be able to put pressure on each company in turn as to the southbound traffic.

When dealing with the L.Y.R.'s petition against the Bill, Venables could not see why the company was objecting at all; it was some ten to twenty miles away from Settle; it would be able to send traffic over the Midland via Ingleton just as well as by the Settle line. The company had an agreement, with seven years unexpired, for traffic to the north over the L.N.W.R. This meant, said Venables, that any grievance it might have would not start for seven years, and at the end of that time it would be no grievance at all since it would be able to choose between going via the Midland or the L.N.W.R. as both would have equal rights over the L.C.R. As part of its petition, the L.Y.R. had objected to the 'evil precedent' of giving a company powers to make an important new railway merely so that it could strike a better bargain with another company and then abandon the line. Turning to the chairman, Venables effectively dealt with this : 'Here, sir, is a piece of morality which the Lancashire & Yorkshire indulge in . . . I really think, though I respect the fine moral sentiments of the Lancashire & Yorkshire company, that it had better have considered before its advisers framed that paragraph whether it might not at some future date itself become liable to some similar remark.'

The next L.Y.R. charge was that the whole Bill was based upon the groundless assumption that the L.N.W.R. had rights of use and control over the L.C.R. between Ingleton and Carlisle. To this attempted spanner-in-the-works Venables replied that the Midland certainly did assume that the L.N.W.R. had some rights in the matter, when it knew that Euston had a lease of the L.C.R. for fifteen years, that nobody had tried to interfere so far, and that the line carried L.N.W.R. traffic every day. 'We do not ask to see their title deeds, but we rather take it for granted that they must have something to do with that line, and we do not assume anything in this Bill.' The object of the Bill was not to confirm the L.N.W.R.'s title to the L.C.R.; it was to enable its rights to be shared. After some more destructive attention to the L.Y.R. petition, which must be admitted was at times quite naive, Venables ended by saying that having had to read it again he was more than ever at a loss to see how the L.Y.R. could possibly be injured by the Bill.

Venables was followed by Hope-Scott, another counsel for the promoters. He examined William Cawkwell, general manager of the L.N.W.R. and the first of the many witnesses to be heard. His answers to Hope-Scott's careful questioning gave a picture of sweet reasonableness towards the L.Y.R. and N.B.R. He really could not see how either could be harmed by the Bill. He thought their traffic worth cultivating. He wished particularly to be on good terms with the N.B.R., even though its trains were sometimes just a little late into Carlisle. One can imagine him smiling paternally at the N.B.R. party at this point. Cross-examined by Mr. Pope, for the L.Y.R., he expressed surprise at the gross value of the English-Scotch traffic in which the L.Y.R. was interested—over £600,000—and their share—£84,840—which was larger than he cared to admit. He agreed, however, that there was another traffic agreement in the making, and that the Midland, by virtue of its own right into Carlisle, would claim a larger stake. Having apportioned the proceeds, Pope, with knowledge of the Ingleton land powers, asked him what guarantee there was that the Midland would ever work a pound of traffic north of Ingleton. To this Cawkwell said he thought the Midland trains would work right through to Carlisle but asked in turn what harm there would be if they did not. To Pope the answer was clear—if the company built its Settle line it would be forced to. Pursuing Cawkwell's line of reasoning Pope demanded what would then become of the N.B.R. and L.Y.R. if faced with the L.N.W.R. in sole charge of the L.C.R. Cawkwell replied that the same position would apply then as it did at the moment—four goods trains daily between Ingleton and Carlisle to work the traffic of the two companies. Cawkwell hedged over the question of traffic north of Carlisle. Pope argued that with the L.N.W.R. and Caledonian in sole control at Carlisle all the other companies would go to the wall. He called for the agreement between the L.N.W.R. and C.R. At first the committee would not agree to this but as question and answer progressed it became clear that the L.N.W.R. did not want the document produced, probably because it excluded N.B.R. traffic. If this was so, said Pope, it was imperative that the Midland should be in Carlisle, and the only way of making certain that this happened was to have it build its own line. Apart from a brief argument over the question of whether to produce the L.N.W.R. and C.R. agreement—a question left to the committee to decide—Pope's cross-examination brought the proceedings of the first day to a close. In all, the L.Y.R. and N.B.R. had good reason to be hopeful. The promoter's case had been somewhat dented by the damaging admission from Cawkwell that the Midland need not actually run anything north of Ingleton, in order to benefit from its new-found compatibility with the L.N.W.R.

The second day's hearing on April 9, 1869, brought to an end Cawkwell's ordeal at the hands of Mr. Pope. He was still in the stand, however, when Sir Mordaunt Wells, for the petitioners, rose to cross-examine him on his evidence in 1866 when speaking against the Settle and Carlisle Bill. He admitted that at that time he had thought the present arrangement sufficient for working the L.C.R., that he knew nothing of the arrangements made between the Midland and the N.E.U. prior to the Settle and Carlisle Bill being lodged, and that though he may have been present at Allport's evidence on this subject, he remembered nothing of it. This led to the final question from Sir Mordaunt—'And you come to give evidence in support of the abandonment of a line without knowing anything of the arrangement between the Midland company and the landowners?' Replying to questions from Mr. Merewether, on behalf of the promoters, Cawkwell defended the agreement with the Caledonian by arguing that the Midland had had at the time arrangements with the G.S.W.R. and N.B.R. Charles Mason, the general manager of the G.S.W.R., followed Cawkwell and after Mason came Hutchinson of the Midland. In both cases the evidence was designed to set in perspective the history of the events leading up to the abandonment Bill.

The third day, Monday, April 12, brought a cross-examination of Hutchinson by Sir Mordaunt Wells. The Midland chairman explained that his company had already started work on the Settle line, that £40,000 would be paid yearly for the use of the L.C.R., and that the N.B.R. would be as well off without the Settle line as it would had it been made. Edward Baines, as chairman of the Midland shareholders' committee, was called and gave evidence on the right or otherwise of a company to abandon a line after a pledge to build it, when the shareholders considered the line unnecessary. Following him came Thomas Elliot Harrison, engineer to the North Eastern Railway. His company apparently hoped that the Settle line would not be made. The N.B.R.'s Waverley route had already diverted N.B.R. traffic from the East Coast route. He considered the construction of the Settle line a waste of time. To this last remark he was asked what he thought, therefore, of the N.E.R.'s York-Doncaster direct line, promoted in 1864—a rather uncomfortable question, seeing that its purpose was to secure an admission that independence had its uses. Thomas Kenworthy Rowbotham, general manager of the N.B.R. from 1852 to 1867, said that when the Waverley route had been completed the L.N.W.R. had become antagonistic—N.B.R. passengers had to change at Carlisle for the south as the L.N.W.R. would not take on their carriages. The North British had looked to the Settle and Carlisle line as a means of giving some return on the outlay on the Waverley route. If the abandonment Bill was passed he did not think that the Midland would be able to accommodate them as well.

On the following day Mr. E. B. Denison for the N.B.R. addressed the committee. Pointing out that it had been agreed that if the Settle line was made the Midland stood to get a return of 5 per cent., he asked what the company's pretext was for now abandoning it. If the Midland did not make it, then the company would get £54,000 a year from the old line. Less working expenses, he thought the amount very small. He had not called Allport because it would have been unfair to subject him to the awful arithmetic of the matter, but out of the Midland's £200,000 worth of yearly traffic he had worked out that the L.N.W.R. would get 73 per cent. and the Midland 27 per cent. At this point Venables, for the Midland, queried this statement but agreed, after examining clause three of the Bill, that Denison's calculations were indeed correct.

Denison: 'This is beautiful: Here are these people believing that they are going to bag 73 per cent, and the North Western 27 per cent, instead of its being the other way—Now, I said at the beginning of the case that I fully admitted that it was a very good bargain for the North Western, and I said that I would prove it to be so; and it is a precious good bargain for them.'

Denison finished his speech by telling of the urgent wish of the N.B.R. to get free of the L.N.W.R. If the Midland had to expend some £2 m. to get to Carlisle he thought the company would search for every bit of traffic it could, including that of the N.B.R.

Rowbotham returned, on April 14, to give a new slant on the proposed joint use of the L.C.R. if the Bill was passed. Trains, he said, would inevitably race each other. The number envisaged meant that if the Midland was to work in competition with the L.N.W.R. from Ingleton to Carlisle it would need to run two trains over that portion, against those of Euston, and fit them into existing traffic. After a journey of some three hundred miles they would probably not be to time and this could lead to dangerous working. One of the companies would be bound to give way and he thought it must be the Midland. He was sure, as Cawkwell had suggested, Midland trains would terminate at Ingleton. If not there would be a series of very fast competing trains, at irregular times, mixed up with the local traffic, on gradients of 1 in 75, in notorious weather conditions on a line not built with the capacity to take them. He forecast that the reverse would apply if the Settle line was built; both companies would be able to travel unhindered and safe to Carlisle. In Rowbotham's view it had become obvious that between them the L.N.W.R. and the Midland would be able to cut up the traffic to the exclusion of other companies. Terminating his evidence, he said that the Midland had only agreed to extend its working arrangement with the N.B.R. if the G.S.W.R. amalgamation Bill was passed. It had not been and the Midland had since refused to extend the arrangement. He hinted darkly that it looked as if Derby was once more taking orders from Euston.

Some interesting facts about the prevailing traffic working were brought out in the evidence of Peter Macpherson, the N.B.R. goods manager. Speaking of his company's southbound traffic, he remarked that the L.N.W.R. took all it could carry unless it was to a place to which that company had no access. Very little traffic was returned, however; the N.B.R. sent some 17,000 tons of freight to Liverpool in eighteen months and got back only a tenth. At the present time there was no unconsigned traffic from the L.N.W.R. getting on to the N.B.R. despite the fact that three-quarters of it originated in Liverpool for Scotland. This was flouting the English and Scotch Agreement the terms of which were now known to have been set aside by a private arrangement between the L.N.W.R. and the Caledonian. At Carlisle the L.N.W.R. made things very awkward for North British traffic. Cattle arriving from the south for Dalkeith were kept waiting *en train* in the yard for some hours. Though the N.B.R. delivered southbound traffic into the L.N.W.R. yard the latter did not return the compliment—the North British locomotives had to work down into the L.N.W.R. territory, root about, marshal a train, and take it out. During his evidence Macpherson gave some figures showing the deplorably poor service given by the L.N.W.R. for through N.B.R. carriages on to the Midland system. Out of the 39 occasions in 1864 when through carriages had been run from the North British to the L.N.W.R., only 6 had gone via Ingleton. Out of 34 in 1865, 4 only; out of 26 in 1866, the same number; out of 27 in the following year, a mere 2; and out of 34 in 1868, none.

Macpherson's evidence was reinforced on the following day by that of Samuel L. Mason, general manager of the N.B.R. since May, 1867. He told of trains arriving at Carlisle from the south. Frequently late, they had to be broken up to be sent on by either the G.S.W.R. or Caledonian. The North British passengers had to get out and walk along the platform into the N.B.R. train, which was not allowed to leave until the Caledonian train had departed. Not content with generalities, Mason gave actual instances, and recent ones at that. On August 7, 1868, the last train from the south arrived at Carlisle at 6.39 p.m. The Caledonian left at 7.04, and the North British at 7.10. The N.B.R. train had been quite ready to leave at 6.45 but the passengers had been kept waiting twenty minutes or so, notwithstanding the fact that the arriving train was already half an hour late at 6.45 and nearly an hour late when it left. On the following day the train from the south arrived at 6.29 p.m. The North British was ready to go at 6.35 but was kept back until 6.56 when it left, 3 minutes after the Caledonian. Mason said that such practice was the ruination of the N.B.R.'s competitive traffic. It also meant that when eventually the N.B.R. express was able to leave Carlisle its passing disrupted the company's local trains for miles.

Following Mason came William Thorley, traffic manager of the L.Y.R. He said that the Settle and Carlisle line was essential for the L.Y.R.'s Scotch traffic. As soon as the current agreement with the L.N.W.R. to take freight northwards from Preston came to an end, the company would send its traffic on to the Midland from Colne. If the Settle line was constructed he expected that the L.Y.R. would then make the thrice-tried line up Ribblesdale to join the Midland. (After the unsuccessful L.Y.R. attempts in 1861 and 1862, such a line had been authorised by the Ribblesdale Railway Act of June 23, 1864. In the session of 1866 the Craven Junction Railway proposed constructing a link from the Ribblesdale Railway to the Midland at Earby. The Ribblesdale faded away in the early 1870s and the Craven Junction was rejected in Parliament.)

Next to give evidence was John Hawkshaw, engineer to the L.Y.R. Speaking of the Ribblesdale line he said it would provide the shortest route from Manchester to Carlisle. As to the proposed joint use of the L.C.R., Hawkshaw echoed the remarks of Rowbotham, made the previous day. He came down heavily against the proposed running of Midland expresses over the L.C.R. and thought that if this had to be, then a 15 minute interval margin should be adopted. Lord Wharncliffe was called and reminded the committee of the Midland's proposal to break its promise to make the Settle line—an undertaking only given after the N.E.U. had agreed to quit the field.

Mr. Pope, on behalf of the L.Y.R., terminated the proceedings for the day. His speech was lengthy. It dealt with the already laboured point of the loss to the L.Y.R. if the Settle line was not made. This theme was summarised in his closing sentences :

'The case therefore of the Lancashire and Yorkshire company is a very plain and simple one. Abandon this Settle and Carlisle line and you deprive the Midland company of any interest to cultivate friendly relations with the Lancashire and Yorkshire at Colne. It is essential to the interests of the Lancashire and Yorkshire company that such relation should be possible, because though at present they are on friendly terms with their neighbours at Preston, they may not be so ultimately, and they desire to have agreed friendly relations with the Midland company. It is no use having agreed friendly relations with the Midland company unless it is in the interest of the Midland company to cultivate them in future. It would not be the interest of the Midland company to cultivate them if they passed any of the mileage to the Lancaster and Carlisle line—it would be the interest of the Midland company if they had the whole mileage in their own pockets; for I say it is clear that, so far as the Lancashire and Yorkshire interest is concerned, it is a bona fide case, it is a perfectly plain and straightforward argument. Whether it is to weigh with the committee or not is not for me to judge, but it is as plain and straightforward a case as could be submitted—that you deprive the Midland company, by abandoning this line, of all interest in cultivating the best portion of the Scotch traffic, because you deprive them of such a share of the mileage of such traffic as to make it not worth their while to touch it at all.'

Friday, April 16, saw the end of the evidence. Counsel appeared for the landowners and the L.C.R., and Hope-Scott summed up the case for the promoters of the Bill, at the end of which the committee room was cleared. After some time of tense waiting the various parties were re-called and informed that the committee had found the preamble of the Bill not proved. From that moment the Midland was committed without further question to making the Settle and Carlisle line. Had the result not gone as was hoped, the landowners along the route had prepared a petition to Parliament which set out their objections to the abandon-ment. Now in the possession of the Archivist to the Railways Board, the signatures took up some 40 feet of linen, in a double column.

It would appear that the Furness too was pleased with the result for when the proposal for abandonment had first been put forward there was some consternation in Barrow. The Furness minutes of the time noted that one of the directors, Lord Frederick Cavendish, M.P., had heard that the Midland rights over the Lancaster & Carlisle, which would result from the abandonment, would include powers to run over the L.N.W.R.'s Windermere branch. His Lordship straightway wrote to Derby, reminding the Midland that the Furness was 'at considerable inconvenience constructing a branch to Newby Bridge mainly with a view to provide good access to the Lakes from the Midland District. There is certainly not any actual Agreement between the Companies on the subject but there can be no doubt we have undertaken the line on such an honourable understanding with you as justifies me in expressing a confident hope that our interests will not be disregarded but will be fairly protected in any arrangement you may make with the London & North Western Railway.'

To all this Hutchinson merely replied that it was nothing to do with him—the shareholders were cooking up the arrangement with Euston. However, he said, the Midland would, if it came to anything, look after the Furness interests as to the Newby Bridge line.

Powers for the branch had been obtained by the Furness in 1866, while the Carnforth-Wennington line was under construction. It was opened from Plumpton Junction to Windermere Lakeside on June 1, 1869. In passing, reference was made by Mr. George Taylor in the February, 1957 issue of the *Journal of the Stephenson Locomotive Society*, of a proposed Midland scheme in the 1870s for a line from Keswick to Ambleside and Newby Bridge.

On May 18, 1869, the Midland Railway company met at Derby. The shareholders were informed, as if they didn't know already, of the result of the Parliamentary contest. They were told that as the line had now to be made instructions had already been given for the surveys and land purchases to be resumed. As the railway would take a long time to build the heaviest works would be started first and at an early date. Edward Baines summed up the general feelings of the meeting. He said that though he knew that Hutchinson had had a hankering after the Settle and Carlisle line from the start, he, Baines, had nothing but praise for the way he had fought for its abandonment in Parliament. Apparently the L.N.W.R. directors, when leaving the Houses of Parliament after the Bill had been rejected, had called out to Hutchinson, 'It's not your fault; you have done all you could to carry the Bill.' The meeting terminated by voting the company the right to raise £550,000 towards making a start on the line.

XI

Settle and Carlisle

Seven Years Hard

With the rejection of the abandonment Bill, action became the order of the day. On June 1, 1869, Messrs. Benton & Woodiwiss approached the Midland board with an offer to start work on their contract on the Settle line on the same terms as originally agreed. They were told that this was not possible as the contracts were not to be the same as before. On August 3 applications were invited for tenders for the first contract —Settle Junction to 17 miles 18 chains at Dent Head—and for 20,000 tons of steel rails, 20 feet long and 80 lb. to the yard. Deliveries were to commence in January of 1871 and were to be continued over the following eighteen months at a monthly average of 1,200 tons. By the end of the month the tenders were in for contract No. 1. Crossley's estimate for the works was £336,523. Fourteen firms tendered; Benton & Woodiwiss made an offer for £375,496 but were unsuccessful for on September 14 John Ashwell's tender of £349,226 was accepted. By October 5 this had been amended to £348,318, Ashwell, of Highgate Road, Kentish Town, agreeing to take half the money during the sinking of the shafts at Blea Moor tunnel, and the remainder when they were finished. The Midland appointed two resident engineers for this contract; R. E. Wilson took the first part and E. O. Ferguson the second. The second contract, from the termination of the first just south of Arten Gill on land belonging to Lord Bective to 34 miles 19 chains near the South Durham & Lancashire Union line at Kirkby Stephen, about 17 miles in length, was let in November to Benton & Woodiwiss. As before, the firm had asked that their original 1866 quotation should stand but this was not allowed; the amended price of £334,880 was agreed instead. John S. Storey was appointed as resident engineer to contract No. 2 and James Hay was the contractors' agent. Earlier in the month the tender for rails, to be delivered at Carnforth, was accepted from the Barrow Haematite Iron Company at £9 5s. 0. per ton.

In view of what was to happen later, some further details of Ashwell's contract are of interest. Dated November 6, 1869, it bound him to provide all labour and materials (excepting the station buildings and permanent way) required for constructing a double line of railway from Settle Junction to Dent Head. The line had already been staked out. The contract stipulated that the workmen were to be paid once every fortnight at least, in an office to be erected for that purpose. The contractor was to provide all necessary police for the contract as required by the local magistrates and there was to be no Sunday working, except when specifically permitted by the company's engineer. As to the time limits for construction—and these must have worried Ashwell as much as financial troubles—the first 12 miles from Settle Junction was to be completed by June 30, 1871, and from there to the end, through Blea Moor, by May 1, 1873. These time limits could be extended at the discretion of the Midland's engineer, but Ashwell faced a penalty of £20 per day for every day they were not completed after the relevant dates.

While the works had not actually been started the L.N.W.R. made one last attempt to stop construction. On August 3, 1869, Richard Moon had informed Derby that as from the beginning of next month Midland rights over the Ingleton-Carlisle line would be restricted to whatever the company could legally enforce, and no more. This had the effect of bringing the Midland, N.B.R., and G.S.W.R. into discussions for the use of Carlisle when the Settle line was built—not quite what Euston had intended. Now, on January 22, 1870, Moon penned a letter to Derby stating it was his belief that one of the proposals which had been made when the terms for a new English and Scotch traffic agreement were being discussed might still offer a basis for a settlement of the dispute, and that he was willing to withdraw his original letter regarding the use by the Midland of the Ingleton-Carlisle line. Derby did not respond. The company was in fact very busy with land purchases for the new line, and was already engaged in the preliminary work on the new junction and temporary sidings at Settle, the first sod of which had been cut in November at Anley.

In March 1870 contract No. 3 for the next 14½ miles, to 48 miles 62 chains at New Biggin, went out to tender. Crossley's estimate was £258,980; the contract was awarded to Joseph Firbank at a price of £278,813. The resident engineer was Jesse Drage and the agent J. Throstle. In April Crossley reported progress to the directors. On contract No. 1 some 7,000 yards of fencing was up; 45,000 cubic yards of earth had been excavated from nineteen of the thirty-two cuttings; and nearly all the land required was in the contractor's possession. One of the shafts at Blea Moor had already gone down some 78 feet of the 90 required, and it appeared that the tunnel would pass through grey limestone and black marble. As eventually worked there were to be seven shafts, four being permanent; No. A 100 feet deep, No. 1 232 feet, No. 2 370 feet, and No. 3, 385 feet. The actual strata met with in the tunnel were limestone, gritstone, gritstone beds, and shale. Crossley was particularly happy that so far there had been no trouble with water in the one shaft already started. He mentioned that huts were being built at various places along the line. On contract No. 2 twelve out of the forty cuttings had been commenced, the contractor having taken possession of the land in mid March. At Smardale viaduct trial boreholes had got some 20 feet down into the rock. Eight miles of the land were in the contractor's hands, equipment was rapidly being delivered and, as in the case of No. 1, huts were springing up alongside the works. Contract No. 3 had, of course, only just been let and the works had not started. As to the final length, contract No. 4 completing the main line to the junction with the N.E.R. at Petteril Bridge, tenders were in hand, Crossley's estimate being £347,402. The best of these, from Eckersley & Bayliss for £329,905, secured the contract on April 23, 1870. There were two resident engineers for this length, John Allin and Samuel S. Paine, and two agents, J. Lambert and E. Williams.

About this time the inhabitants of Stainforth approached the company for a station to serve the locality. They were asked to wait until the question was being generally discussed. Crossley also reported to the committee that Ashwell had been to see him regarding the proposed appointment of a 'scripture reader'. To this suggestion the committee agreed—provided that Ashwell paid half the man's wages.

By May of 1870 works were well under way on the first three contracts. Ashwell, however, was making but slow progress with the tunnelling on No. 1. He was called before the committee and told to hurry the work up. Towards the end of the month a temporary road had been laid over Blea Moor and round-the-clock work was in progress on the tunnel. There were by now two temporary shafts, one being already down to formation level, and the headings had been commenced. On contract No. 1 there were by now some 530 men employed, ten less than on No. 2. On the latter the stone for the viaducts was being quarried, the bridge-work started, and shafts had been commenced at Rise Hill tunnel (also known at various times during the next few years as Cowgill tunnel or Black Moss tunnel). On contract No. 3 the shafts of Helm tunnel were being bored, and out of the 368 men employed, some 240 were already allotted to temporary huts. Ashwell, on No. 1, was still finding the work slow going. The company's solicitor took him to task but it was becoming obvious by this time that Blea Moor was not going to be an easy proposition. Presumably with the idea of keeping the minds of his men on higher things, Ashwell's scripture reader, James Tiplady, from the Bradford Town Mission, started his ministrations in July. He was paid a yearly salary of £100 and granted a free pass from Bradford to Settle and back once a month. Instructions were also given at this time for the electric telegraph to be installed on No. 1. It was in operation by December 6, 1870.

Meanwhile Crossley had been pondering over the question of the sleepers to be used on the line. Those then employed on the Midland main line measured 11 ft. 10 in. x 11 in. x 5 in. and were of Baltic redwood, used without preparation. They had been adopted for general use in 1860 and, at a cost of 2s. 4d. each, and unprepared, lasted up to fourteen years. Crossley weighed the merits of creosoting at 1s. a sleeper and worked out satisfactorily to himself and the board that it would be best to stick to the existing type and method, the redwood being probably the most economical to use.

The engineer's report for July 1870 gave a hint of the setbacks to come, for heavy rain had hindered the work. Some 1,400 men and 170 horses were at work on contract No. 1 and the tunnel shafts were being excavated in three shifts, extra men being set to work as they arrived. Some progress had been made on the foundations of Ribblehead viaduct and it appeared that Ashwell was going full tilt at Blea Moor. There was an inclined plane up the moor to the head of the working shafts and the stationary engines for this were being erected after a muscle-pulling haul up the temporary road to the top. A tramway was under construction from the Ingleton road at Ribblehead to the south face of the tunnel; on the north side a similar arrangement operated from the mouth to the Dent Head road. Four locomotives and 440 wagons were trundling along these temporary ways taking away the spoil and bringing up the supplies, including some 2,000 tons of 45 lb. rail. On contract No. 2 the Rise Hill tunnel was under way and one of the headings started, but water from the heavy rains of early June had got into the works which were stopped, waiting the arrival of pumping engines. August came and with it the news that 'the works have suffered much derangement from a violent storm of rain—causing serious injury and loss of life'. Crossley was not explicit about this but it seems that the rainwater had carried away some of the temporary works bridging the River Dee. This was not his only trouble. There began, to his great annoyance, the yearly exodus for the hayfields. Most of the trouble was confined to No. 3 contract which was on a length of the line through agricultural country far different to the first two. Though there was plenty of work to be done on the line in the thirteen cuttings 'the men have left in droves'. There was nothing he could do to stop them.

Crossley's report for September was better. On contract No. 1 over four miles of the formation had been made. The men were improving in their work—there were now 1,952 of them and 178 horses. Operating the temporary railway were five locomotives and four 'portable' engines. On top of the moor September 5 was a red letter day, for steam was got up on one of the stationary engines and the others only required connections before coming into use too. The other contracts were in full swing also, and there were 5,391 men and 552 horses at work on the line by the end of August, 1870. These figures improved during September to 6,250 and 549 respectively (did they, perhaps, eat some of the horses?); that month also saw work started on the viaducts at Crosby Garrett and Ormside. Either Mr. Tiplady's readings on contract No. 1 were bearing fruit, or the men of No. 2 were thought to be sorely in need of like edification, for on October 4 the committee appointed for the latter William Fletcher as scripture reader, also from Bradford Town Mission, at a salary of £100 per annum. During October Crossley was able to release some of the men employed on making the temporary works and draft them to the permanent ones. The effect should have been to increase the tempo but it was nullified by bad weather. There were now 2,208 men, 184 horses, and six locomotives working flat out on contract No. 1. The tunnel was still proving a slow business; since starting on the heading only 238 yards had been driven through the moor. As to contract No. 2, heavy rains had turned all the clay workings into quagmires—only those through rock were workable, most of the others being completely unapproachable. 1,419 men, 106 horses, and eight locomotives did the best they could in the poor conditions. To get food and clothing to the men through the heavy clay and peat, the only vehicle which could be used was a cart with a massive roller in place of the wheels. Frederick Williams, on a visit to the workings, was told that as many as three horses had to be used to get it moving and even then they often sank up to their bellies and had to be pulled out. On one occasion four horses had to be employed to pull one telegraph pole along. So glutinous was the clay that one animal had its hoof torn off.*

Crossley's remarks on contract No. 4 are of interest—'The difference in material and climate are strongly shown on the work done on contract No. 4—1,543 men . . . having done 110,114 yards as compared with 1,419 men on contract No. 2 having done only 42,963 yards.' The year ended in a period of almost continuous rain. Water got into Blea Moor tunnel; all work stopped in the cuttings on No. 2, it being impossible to move horses and wagons in the wet clay; Nos. 3 and 4 were also adversely affected, though to a lesser degree and then only where the clay was encountered. The minutes of the Midland's Settle and Carlisle construction committee note at this time that a Mr. Parker was appointed as scripture reader to No. 4. This was probably the Rev. I. D. Parker, Vicar of Hawes, who wrote to the company on November 26, asking the Midland to erect a building at the Moorcock for Sunday services. The company replied that £10 was to be offered to the contractor for this purpose—the words 'for use on Sundays' being added to the note, rather implying that it was feared that the work might be interfered with if the Rev. Parker was given a free rein.

It would, perhaps, be best to leave the works for a moment. Crossley had had a year of it and could see by now that there were difficulties unimagined when his original estimates for time and cost were drawn up. It is doubtful if he had realised that the weather conditions could be quite so bad. What was worse, though he was at the time happily ignorant of the fact, the elements had so far dealt with him pretty mildly. As to the main events during 1870, a new and improved fast service of trains was inaugurated on Tuesday, February 1 when the Chesterfield-Sheffield line was opened. At the half-yearly meeting Hutchinson gave notice of his impending retirement. Edward Baines, still mindful of Hutchinson's performance during the time of the abandonment Bill, put a motion which was carried to vote £1,000 towards a portrait of the chairman to hang alongside those of his predecessors in the board room at Derby. The new chairman elected by May, was William

* *The Midland Railway*. Frederick S. Williams. 1878.

171

Philip Price; his deputy, Edward Shipley Ellis, was the son of the late John Ellis.

The weather which was bothering Crossley had a general effect during February of 1870; it was so severe that there was a temporary decrease in traffic receipts—over £800 less during one week. This was far out-balanced by the very large increase generally of £51,398 in two months of the half-year over a similar period the previous year, in itself an increase over the preceding year. At that time Price did not share Crossley's more hopeful forecasts; the chairman stated in May, however, that he thought the Settle line would be completed within the new time limit sought by a Bill then before Parliament. The resulting Act of June 20, extended the time for the completion of the line until July 16, 1873. One of the main happenings during 1870 was the final purchase of the little North Western. In May that company decided to sound the Midland as to terms. After considerable argument it was agreed on Tuesday, July 19 that the transfer should take effect from January 1, 1871. On August 10 a meeting of the N.W.R. shareholders formally approved the terms, though actual transfer of management did not take place until July 1, 1871.

1871 started with bitter cold weather and work on the Settle-Carlisle line almost at a standstill. Frost had stopped all masonry work on the viaducts, and the clay, so treacherous in the wet weather, was frozen hard. By February the two southern contracts were deep under snow; No. 2 was virtually inaccessible, the works being some 800 to 1,200 feet above sea level. Only in the bowels of Blea Moor did men still sweat as they hacked and shovelled through the headings, 'from Sunday night at ten till Saturday night at ten; relays of men relieving one another at six in the morning and six at night.'* For this they received an average of 10s. a day. The end of the month brought a thaw, and with it a sea of mud. There were, nevertheless, some 28 miles of formation finished by now, and with the better weather that came with March Crossley hoped to gain ground during the coming months. In February the Midland decided to purchase about 28 acres of land at the junction with the N.E.R. at Carlisle for engine sheds and exchange facilities—the birth of Durran Hill sheds.

By April the men were drifting back to the workings. The weather was much improved and in a report to the construction committee Crossley was able to say that work on the cuttings was again in progress and that staging had been erected for the Ribblehead viaduct (then known as Batty Wife Moss viaduct). To the committee he said, 'Good weather and men alone are wanted'. He had left out luck—something he was to find more than ever elusive during the coming years of construction. On May 3 work on the Arten Gill viaduct was started and the staging was completed within the month. Altogether things had the appearance of going well but there were misgivings over the state of Ashwell's finances.

* *The Midland Railway*. Frederick S. Williams. 1878.

The contractor for No. 1 had been asking for heavy loans to tide him over the bad weather and his latest request had led the committee to examine his books. For the time being it was satisfied, however; his initial expenses had of necessity been very costly but it was thought that the contract could be quite safely left in his hands if proper care were taken. June brought a split in the firm of Eckersley & Bayliss. Again financial difficulties similar to those of Ashwell resulted in John Bayliss, the partner who remained on the job, asking for and getting a loan of £20,000 on the security of his plant.

So far the Hawes branch had not figured in any of the construction. This line, contract No. 5, was let out to tender in mid 1871. The engineer's estimate was £75,837 12s. 8d. and once again Crossley's idea on cost seems to have been on the low side. The contractors, remembering the weather conditions, obviously thought so as the lowest tender received, and accepted, was from Benton & Woodiwiss for £83,913 12s. 6d. The resident engineer was Frank Lynde.

August saw a return of the wet weather. This caused the men to leave the works as short time only could be made. Even though Crossley thought the wage rate was good the earnings per week were hardly satisfactory when the number of hours worked was limited by the elements. In May there had been 6,980 men at work—in July 5,722. The contractors had hoped for an increase of 2,000 in the labour force; they got instead a decrease of 1,258. Continual efforts by the contractors to get men were proving of no use. On contract No. 2 there was as much as a 73 per cent. turnover of men in one month. Crossley wrote to the committee that he was becoming disheartened—the works could not be completed within the time at this rate. Contract No. 3 was having trouble of a different kind. The towns of Kirkby Stephen and Appleby went in mortal fear of some of the navvies—the committee got a wigging from the Chief Constable of Carlisle for this; he wrote on two occasions in August that several barrels of ale had been seized in the men's huts on Firbank's contract. There was of course a logical remedy—the Rev. J. Clarke of Great Ormside was appointed as a scripture reader. Despite all the petty strife, and Crossley's worst expectations, it was, however, a fact that work was still progressing, even if at a slower rate than could be wished for. In September the committee asked the Barrow Haematite Iron Company to deliver 3,000 tons of rails. Tenders were also to be got for twenty miles of single line permanent way, together with 36,000 sleepers and 110 tons of chairs. At the same time Allport, Crossley and Kirtley were asked to report to the committee on the sites and sizes of the engine sheds and stations which would be required on the line. Meanwhile John Ashwell had finally had to bow to the inevitable and hand over contract No. 1 to the committee, receiving £10,000 in discharge. This meant that the Midland would finish work on No. 1 and accordingly the company appointed W. H. Ashwell as its agent. (His capability is indicated by the fact that in 1875 he took the post of consulting engineer to the Queensland Government.) Crossley's report for October 3 noted that the general management of No. 1 had already been much improved since the take-over. The other contracts had suffered in varying degrees the annual harvest walk-out but were now benefiting from a steady stream of men returning to the workings. Apparently money troubles were still bothering Benton & Woodiwiss and Joseph Firbank. They approached the committee in October to ask for a revision of terms only to be told that such heavy works were bound to have an element of difficulty attached to them and that they should have thought of this at the time of tendering. Considering Crossley's undoubted surprise at the ferocity of the North Yorkshire and Westmorland weather this remark was rather unjust. Things got worse during October. It was a month of short, dark and wet days. On contract No. 1, however, all was action—Crossley gave orders during the month for the purchase of a hundred second-hand tip wagons and four portable cranes. If any of the contracts should be in difficulty it would not be his.

Ashwell's contract was cancelled by an agreement dated October 26, 1871. One of the main reasons for the trouble on No. 1 was the severity of the conditions met with while attempting the most difficult part of the line. In their early stages most works of that nature would be naturally awkward; as the main earthworks get completed, however, and as an established order of working comes into being, with perhaps temporary railways taking over from the cart tracks and local roads, an easier though probably no less strenuous time arrives. It was Ashwell's misfortune that he tendered for the worst contract on the line at prices based on virtually the 1866 levels. The second 'Railway Mania' of 1866, the money panic consequent on the failure of one of the main banks, Overend Gurney & Co., and most of all, the Franco-Prussian War, all contributed to thrust prices and wages 50 per cent. above the 1866 level. An example of an early wage increase can be seen by studying various contracts for works, made now and later. On contract No. 1, in October 1869, for instance, the day rate for a navvy was 3s. 6d. By April 1870 when Eckersley & Bayliss signed their contract it had risen to 4s. 6d. Miners went from 4s. to 8s. in one year. (A table of day rates for various contracts appears in Appendix No. VII.)

As has been seen Ashwell was not alone; the other contractors were also feeling the pinch. Frederick McDermott, Firbank's biographer, writing in 1887, said that men could only be persuaded to work on the line by paying them double the usual rates. Cartage costs were high and the local roads appalling. When Firbank took the contract coal was priced at 11s. a ton. It rose to 32s. before the line was finished. Apparently Firbank's friends advised him to do the same as Ashwell and face a loss of some £100,000 but the contractor's personal determination helped pull him through. It also encouraged the others to stick it out. McDermott told how when Firbank got the job he decided to base his headquarters at Appleby. 'At the time the contract was let there was only one house empty, and that was in Chancery.' The first necessity, before any work could be attempted, was the construction of numerous huts. 'Later on, also, as the works were pushed further from Appleby, huts had to be built in wild districts far from the bare necessities of life. At these advanced posts provisions had to be brought from distant towns, and a visit from the butcher was quite an event.' After describing the inadequate road system he continued—'The laws of supply and demand, however, act even in the wilds of Westmorland, and, before long, these outworks were supplied by a wholesale grocer from Carlisle, who started a store at Helm . . . Here, also, the contractor provided a reading-room, coffee-house, and hospital for the men—the last-named being, unfortunately, a much-needed addition to the colony.' One of the bigger navvy settlements north of Appleby was near Long Marton at Battle Barrow Bank.

To add to the general danger and discomfort there came an epidemic of smallpox which ravaged the navvy population so much that the Rev. E. Smith found it necessary to write to the Midland company in July soliciting a subscription towards the enlargement of the burial ground at Chapel-le-Dale. The company gave £20. By December there was mutiny over the scripture readers. With their resources drastically impaired, and the Midland refusing to assist, the contractors banded together in a refusal to pay any more towards the upkeep of the readers. Perhaps a more useful contribution to the navvies was the sum of £20 voted by the committee—after a personal appeal to Crossley from Lord Bective—to help pay for the enlargement of Cowgill school, much overcrowded by navvy children. At the end of the year Crossley was asked to report specially on the major works on the line and to give an estimate of the time they would take to complete. These included the Ribblehead viaduct, Blea Moor tunnel, Arten Gill viaduct, the Moorcock embankment, Birkett tunnel, Smardale viaduct, and the slip at Eden Brow. Before coming to his report, however, let us see what had been happening to the Midland during 1871.

There were two wars in being. The first was that between France and Prussia, and the second—if one can be permitted to mention it in the same breath as the first—was between Derby and Kings Cross. Both affected the Midland traffic, the first indirectly. While the Franco-Prussian War hit all railways to some extent by reducing continental business, the battle with the G.N.R. was a strictly partisan affair over coal rates which did neither company any good; the Midland lost over £2,000 worth of traffic weekly. It was in this atmosphere that complaints at the inordinate time being taken to construct the Settle line began to be heard from Midland shareholders. Of course one of the main shiers at the chairman's head was Hutchinson's old acquaintance, Mr. Hadley of Birmingham. That gentleman found that Price was a different customer to Hutchinson, however, for whereas Hutchinson was a rather grave and solemn man, Price was an inveterate leg-puller, giving as good as he got.

Frederick Williams, in his Midland history, tells of Hadley how 'That gentleman, with lugubrious accents and manner, deplored (he appears always to be deploring something) the slow progress made on the Settle and Carlisle line, the works on which had been retarded by the weather. Mr. Price assured Mr. Hadley that he deeply regretted that the directors could not control the climate; but added, "I have no doubt if we had Mr. Hadley among us we should be blessed with perpetual sunshine".'

Three Bills which were to go before Parliament for the session of 1872 might well have altered the balance of railway power and affected the later history of the Settle line. The first, despite all the vitriolic things said by the L.Y.R. against the L.N.W.R. in 1869, was for nothing less than a complete amalgamation between the two companies. Not to be outdone, the Caledonian started courting the N.B.R., which in turn had the not unexpected result of pushing the Midland into a repeat performance of the amalgamation Bill with the G.S.W.R., which the latter's shareholders formally approved at a meeting on February 24, 1872. If passed, the amalgamation was to come into operation on July 1, 1872; it provided for the ordinary stock of the two companies to receive equal dividends from the first quarter-day after the opening of the Settle and Carlisle line. The Bill for the C.R. and N.B.R. amalgamation was not deposited; the others went ahead. As to the station at Carlisle; this had been occupying the attention of the Midland board throughout 1871. In May of that year the North British Railway's Carlisle Station Bill failed in Parliament due to the action of the L.N.W.R. It was perhaps to the good, for the N.B.R. decided to put a more extensive scheme to Westminster during the next session. To this end the company met the Midland and G.S.W.R. in November, 1871, and hammered out an agreement whereby the construction of the new works would be carried out by all three concerns. (Fuller details of events at Carlisle are given in a later chapter.) On the same day as the agreement, and perhaps suddenly aware that the additional traffic would need containers for its conveyance, the Midland ordered another 2,000 goods wagons. As to Bills from other companies, there was an attempt by a small independent concern, the Lothersdale Railway, to get powers during the session of 1871 to make a line nearly five miles in length from Raygill House, about a mile west of Lothersdale, to join the Leeds & Bradford Extension line on the east side of the bridge over the latter immediately adjacent to Kildwick & Cross Hills station. The Bill was withdrawn.

Crossley's report on the major works reached the committee on January 2, 1872. One of the most interesting points to emerge was that he had not at that time made up his mind as to the number of arches to comprise the Ribblehead viaduct. According to the workers available for either earthworks or masonry the number of arches could vary between eighteen or twenty-four. Crossley thought the latter figure more desirable; the decision to go ahead with this number was not made until December, 1872. With regard to Blea Moor tunnel, he told the committee that its original length was to have been 2,112 yards; it had been increased by 308 yards at the south end and 66 at the north to shorten the amount of cutting and also to provide an aqueduct over the line for two streams. This made a new total to date of 2,486 yards. 609 yards were complete and progress was at the rate of 70 yards a month. Crossley pointed out that as soon as he could get more shafts down and increase the working headings this rate would substantially improve. The work, however, was subject to almost poltergeistic influences. 'Shaft 2,' said Crossley, 'has proved to be near some disturbance in the strata—the motion of the rock having produced the very unusual condition of pieces of rock of considerable size being projected from the face roof and floor with a very loud report and with considerable and dangerous force—this has now abated and work at this shaft is resumed.' For explosives for blasting the company was beginning to use dynamite—new to the Victorians and held in some awe by the men—instead of gun-cotton. It cost £200 a ton and, as no railway company would carry it, was brought by road from Carlisle or Newcastle. Superintending the construction of the tunnel and Ribblehead viaduct was the company's inspector from the Ingleton Road to Dent Head, a Mr. Davidson.

Crossley was of the opinion that the tunnel would probably take another two years to complete. As for Dent Head viaduct; this was some 21 months from completion. At Arten Gill viaduct there was a shortage of men. Stone was plentiful, however, and though progress was slow it was sure. There had been some considerable trouble at the Moorcock embankment; for months all the earth tipped there had sunk into the moss. By this time, however, the seat of the embankment had been thoroughly drained and a trench cut through the peat for all the length and half the width to the solid bottom. Birkett tunnel had not been started; Crossley had a party of miners from Wirksworth—some forty men—driving the working shaft down to the tunnel floor and hoped to have the headings started within three weeks. In all, most of the works were suffering from a dearth of navvies. Heavy rains and the Christmas holidays had not helped; as to the former, Crossley calculated that Westmorland had recently had about four times as much rain as in the midlands. He told the committee point blank that another 5,000 men would be necessary to finish the line by July 1873.

Early in March of 1872 the Midland board received a letter from Mr. Lister, the clerk to the Settle Union, requesting a subscription to the Settle smallpox hospital. Edward Shipley Ellis decided to satisfy himself as to the state of the epidemic and his investigations prompted the board to send Mr. Lister a cheque for £100. It seemed the very least the company could do, for its own navvies had brought the disease to the town. At the end of April the Rev. A. Pitcher, Vicar of Horton-in-Ribblesdale, asked the company for a schoolroom for the navvy children on contract No. 1. The company gave £50 towards the cost. By this time there were considerable settlements of navvies all along the line. A regular township, albeit makeshift, had formed itself at Ribblehead, alongside the Ingleton Road. Named Batty Wife Hole—some said after the wife of a local ne'er-do-well who sought peace in one of the nearby potholes by throwing herself into the deep waters it contained, it was described by the *Lancaster Guardian*, which for the benefit of its readers did a tour of the line in 1874, as follows :

> 'Making our way to Batty Green one could not but look with astonishment at the numerous huts which cover the moor, and are known as Batty Green, Sebastopol, Jerusalem, Jericho, and Tunnel huts. At the first mentioned place there are Sunday and day schools, a mission house, a public library, post office, public houses, and shops for the sale of a variety of merchandise, and a new and neat looking hospital with a covered walk for convalescent patients. All is life and bustle at this moorland town of huts, potters' carts, traps and horses for hire, drapers' carts, milk carts, green grocers' carts, butchers' carts, bakers' carts, and brewers' drays; in addition to which may be seen numerous pedestrian hawkers plying from hut to hut their different trades.'

Among the 'civic buildings' described above, were the engineer's offices and huts and the mixed assortment of navvy homes, crudely built some of them, with local stone for the walls and with wood and felt coverings.

By October of 1872 Crossley and Kirtley had agreed on a report to the committee on the proposed engine shed and station sites. A small station was recommended to be constructed south of Settle Junction to serve as a traffic exchange point between the new line and the little North Western. At Settle itself a large passenger traffic was expected and the report suggested that besides a good sized station there should also be ample sidings. It stipulated that the station platforms should be at least 300 feet long and that the goods shed should be able to take five wagons at a time. There were to be horse and cattle docks, and cattle pens for twelve trucks. As to station masters' houses and cottages for the whole line, these varied from station to station. One of the main difficulties was that of water supply both for the locomotives and the stations. At Settle the report suggested that a pumping station should be set up on the River Ribble to take water to the station. At Horton and Selside, the next two stations in the report, the passenger traffic was expected to be much lighter and it was thought that small station buildings would suffice. For freight there were to be coal and goods sidings and a cattle dock for three trucks at each station. That at Selside was, of course, not constructed. Ribblehead was not considered for a station in the report. The station at Hawes, at the end of the branch line, posed a bit of a problem for it would also connect with the N.E.R. in Wensleydale. The report recommended a small station with sidings for goods and coal traffic. The goods shed was to take four wagons and there were to be horse and carriage docks and a cattle dock to take eight trucks, together with an engine shed for two locomotives. Hawes Junction was to be provided with a small passenger exchange station with sorting sidings and shed accommodation for twenty-four engines, with an adequate water supply. Kirkby Stephen and Crosby Garrett were to have a station and coal and cattle facilities approximating those at Settle. It was considered likely that a station might be required at Asby—or Breaks Hall —about ½ mile south of Helm tunnel; the report thought that only a small structure would be required with goods and coal sidings and a cattle dock to take four trucks; Great Ormside was not considered as a site. Appleby and Long Marton stations were to be roughly the same as that at Kirkby Stephen. Water at Appleby was to be obtained from the North Eaden reservoir. New Biggin was to have a small station; Culgaith was not mentioned; Langwathby and Lazonby were to approximate to Kirkby Stephen, with Lazonby having the additional facility of a water supply for the engines. As for Little Salkeld, it had not been finally decided whether or not have a station there. Armathwaite and Cotehill were not included in the report, whereas Cumwhinton and Scotby were both to have small stations. Having arrived at Carlisle, Crossley and Kirtley agreed that Petteril should have a goods shed to hold ten wagons, exchange and sorting sidings, and a marshalling yard, together with a shed to hold twenty-four locomotives. Water was to be obtained from the River Petteril. The report concluded with a note that it might become necessary to make a station for Dent Dale between the north end of Blea Moor tunnel and the Dent Head viaduct. Having determined the sites it soon became apparent that additional lands would be required and in the company's Bill deposited in November 1872 powers were sought for lands at the north end of Culgaith tunnel, at Settle Junction, Stainforth, Garsdale, and Skipton.

In November the committee agreed to pay a bonus of 15 per cent. on all the agreed prices to the contractors on Nos. 2, 3 and 4, provided they pushed the work with all possible speed. As to contract No. 1, Crossley was able to tell the committee in December that with the exception of two short gaps he would soon have a temporary line laid all the way from Settle to Ribblehead. This would assist in the problem of carting materials from Settle to the Ingleton road throughout the coming winter months. To cut the expenses he was proposing to weed out the indifferent workers. It appeared that contract No. 1 was employing the largest number of men but that it was losing more money per cent. than the others. During the month the chairman and deputy chairman of the company toured the works. Quite a number of the major items were nearing completion but the main difficulties were still to be found in the tunnels. Heavy rainfall over the preceding four months, and the difficulty in finding labour, had slowed the works appreciably; 60 ins. of rain fell at Kirkby Stephen in 1872, compared with the usual average of 37, and 92 ins. at Dent Head compared with 68. Price instructed Crossley that henceforth he was to report monthly to the committee. On New Year's Eve the Rev. G. W. Atkinson, and some of the landowners of Culgaith, asked for a station. They were told that Culgaith was not considered suitable. At the same time there was an application for a station in the parish of Wetherall. This brought a different response; there were some large plaster works to be built nearby which could, if the Midland was lucky, bring some 25,000 tons of traffic on to the line annually and the station—that of Cumwhinton—was eventually built about a mile to the north of the works.

As to the general events of 1872, the Midland and G.S.W.R., and the L.N.W.R. and L.Y.R. amalgamation Bills both failed. To be more correct they were bound over to await the findings of a Parliamentary Joint Committee then engaged in discussing the whole question of railway amalgamations. Both of the Bills were withdrawn; both were redeposited for the session of 1873, though this time the joint Midland and G.S.W.R. company was to take the title of 'Midland Railway'. Accompanying them was a Bill deposited by the L.N.W.R. and Caledonian—the Carlisle Citadel Station Bill—which proposed considerable works at the station with an almost entirely new layout of approach tracks and with an avoiding line for goods traffic. Like the others, it had already been unsuccessful in 1872. The works authorised by the Carlisle Citadel Station Act of 1873, discussed more fully in Chapter XIV, included the demolition of the Caledonian engine sheds at West Walls which also housed the G.S.W.R. locomotives at Carlisle. Though the Act provided for a replacement of this accommodation at the new Etterby shed of the C.R., the Glasgow company, with its lean towards the Midland, opted to use the latter's sheds at Durran Hill instead, when completed. Also deposited for the 1873 session was a Bill from the N.B.R. for branches at Carlisle. A brief appearance was made during the year by a proposed new concern—the Cumberland & Cleveland Junction Railway. This proposed a line, some 25 miles long, from the N.E.R. at Alston—the branch to the east of Carlisle, running south from the Newcastle & Carlisle line —to join the N.E.R.'s Tees Valley Railway at its terminus at Middleton-in-Teesdale, thus giving the N.E.R. new access to Carlisle from the south. Apparently the authorities at York cannot have been over enthusiastic as the Bill was withdrawn early in the session for lack of money.

One of the main domestic events of the year was the introduction, from April 1, of third class accommodation on all Midland trains, to a howl of protest from other companies. This was mainly Allport's doing and was but the precursor to a general betterment of the company's policy towards its passengers which was to become a byword in later years. In fact on January 1, 1873, the board instructed Kirtley, and E. M. Needham, the passenger traffic superintendent, to conduct exhaustive tests to ascertain the cause of the jerk always experienced in the carriages when the trains started to move. In many ways passenger comfort was becoming of great importance. It is discussed further in Chapters XII and XVIII.

Once again, as in the previous years, 1873 saw the rejection and withdrawal of the two amalgamation Bills. Once again it was the principle which was under fire, not the companies. For the Midland it meant only one thing—that with the time limit for the completion of the Settle line supposedly drawing near it was not advisable to wait for yet another Parliamentary refusal. It became of the utmost importance to get a working arrangement with the G.S.W.R. and by July a new traffic agreement had been drafted. To keep on good terms with the North British the Midland joined with that company in an agreement with the Forth Bridge Railway, incorporated during the previous session to bridge the Firth. Within the Midland company itself Price resigned on May 20 to take up the post of one of the three commissioners to be appointed under the provisions of the Railway & Canal Traffic Act of 1873. His place was taken by Edward Shipley Ellis, Matthew William Thompson becoming the new deputy chairman. It was agreed, in the now time-honoured fashion, that a suitable portrait of Price should be hung in the boardroom.

Meanwhile, away to the north, Crossley's men still toiled on the Settle and Carlisle line. The earnest pleadings to the contractors to hurry the works seemed to be having some effect. Bayliss's contract, south from Carlisle, had managed to acquire an additional 1,000 men by January 1. To house them he erected huts with boarded floors, iron bedsteads and bedding provided. He also supplied coal and put up a provision stores where food and clothing could be bought. The men were paid completely in cash and no obstacle put on them buying their goods away from the store. They also had a sick fund. Mr. Bayliss must have been something of a psychologist. By June the weather conditions had been fairly good for some time but labour problems were still taking much attention. Though there were more men on the job those working on piece rate were leaving the work after about 3 p.m. by which time they had earned an average between 6s. 4d. and 6s. 9d. As to the others—according to Crossley—'The day men stay their hours but do not work to hurt themselves'. The tunnels were still behind schedule mainly because Crossley could not find enough miners to do the work. At Birkett tunnel someone had had the idea of using a drilling machine but it had been for ever breaking down. Meanwhile, the residents of Culgaith had refused to accept the adverse decision on the station question, and the committee asked Crossley to report his views. These must have been favourable as a station was eventually constructed. During June and July work on No. 1 was principally on the viaducts and the tunnel, the men from the finished portions being turned on to these as they became free.

At the company's half-yearly meeting in August, Ellis called for yet more speed from the contractors. He also announced that £1,000 was to be given towards the portrait of Price. In the same month the Vicar of Cowgill, the Rev. D. Adams, wrote asking for a subscription to enlarge the churchyard. His current difficulty was the same as that of his colleague at Chapel-le-Dale, who had already drawn a sympathetic response from the company. The Rev. Adams, however, came off better by £30;

he was perhaps more isolated than at Chapel and in any case could claim to be nearer Blea Moor tunnel, where many of the accidents occurred. The sort of thing he had to contend with was violently illustrated in September when there was a bad runaway on the rope hauled tramway near Rise Hill which killed two women riding in the wagons. Despite the average of nearly one death a week on the workings—whether from accidents or from vicious navvy feuds—the daily grind went remorselessly on. Towards the end of the year nearly the whole length of contract No. 1 had a single line of rails laid down. Some of the old rails and iron, used for the temporary line, were disposed of at about this time together with one of the locomotives, the *Sedbergh*, which was sent to Derby.

Of the contractors' locomotives used for the making of the line, details are hard to come by. In 1872 the Hunslet Engine Company supplied one of its engines, works No. 72, and named *Wellington*, to Firbank at Appleby.* According to the *Journal of the Stephenson Locomotive Society*, for February, 1957, an 0-6-0 saddle tank built by Messrs. Manning, Wardle & Co. and named *Derby* was also delivered at Settle during 1872. The *Journal* surmised that some half a dozen other engines—about which little is known but which were taken into Midland stock at this time—may well have come from the contractors working on the Settle line. The engine *Sedbergh*, mentioned above, appears in the Midland locomotive committee minutes as being contractors' engine No. 328, used for ballast working immediately prior to its purchase by the committee in November, 1873, for £870. On July 4, 1876, Samuel Johnson, the Midland's locomotive superintendent, reported to the committee that a small six-wheeled coupled tank engine *Queen*, then numbered 1326, was transferred from No. 1 contract to the committee for £650 in the previous January. Finally, Williams mentioned locomotive No. 568 as working between Settle and Blea Moor during the latter stages of construction.

There were two Bills in the session of 1874 which concerned the Midland's line from Leeds to Skipton. One was promoted by the company itself, in opposition to the Great Northern, for a line from Huddersfield to Halifax and Bradford via Queensbury, and the other was deposited by an independent company to make a railway from Ilkley to Skipton. The first only deserves mention in that it might have offered through running from Huddersfield to Carlisle at some future date. Planned to leave the Leeds & Bradford line at Manningham by a triangular junction it would have given the Midland an alternative route to the south via its powers over the Huddersfield and Sheffield line to Beighton, thus avoiding Leeds. The Bill did not pass. The solicitors for the Skipton & Ilkley project approached the Midland on January 7, 1874, suggesting that if the Bill received the Royal Assent the new company would be prepared to hand over the sole control and virtual ownership of the line to the Midland and the N.E.R. To this attempt at a quick return the

* *A Hunslet Hundred,* L. T. C. Rolt. 1964.

Midland replied that far from wishing to take over the concern, it would oppose it in Parliament. The Bill was rejected.

By February of 1874 the expenditure so far on the Settle and Carlisle line amounted to £1,913,579. Work was again almost at a standstill. Heavy floods, followed by deep snow and the Christmas holidays, had combined once more to keep the few men on the site shivering in their huts. Nevertheless some 62 miles of the formation were now constructed, on 36 of which the permanent way was already laid. While the weather had the line in its grip the locomotive committee in Derby finally decided on the accommodation it required. Kirtley—a sick man for some time —had died in the previous June shortly after making his report on the carriage jerkings, a report which showed that he had taken a personal interest in the tests made on the line with different trains so much so that he may well have overworked. In his place the board had appointed Samuel W. Johnson. Together with Crossley and Allport, he decided to cut the proposed locomotive establishment at Hawes Junction by half. Water tanks of 36,000, 20,000 and 12,000 gallons capacity, each with a pumping engine and a cottage for the man attending, were to be installed at Hawes Junction, Appleby, and Lazonby respectively. The shed at Carlisle was still to house twenty-four locomotives but a more specific instruction than Kirtley's indicated that as to water supply at Carlisle, this was to be of similar nature to that at Hawes Junction. For the enginemen there were to be twenty cottages at the latter place, and twenty-five at Carlisle. During February the construction committee ordered that Crossley should start getting tenders for the stations and for a temporary goods shed at Carlisle. He was also to lay a further 25 miles of single line. By March there were over 6,000 men at work on the line and though frost had again stopped most of the masonry work, progress was considered to be reasonable. Early in the month the station designs were approved by the committee and sent out to tender, and on March 31 the remaining 50 miles of single line, together with all the points and switchwork, were likewise offered out. By early May the tenders were in for Settle, Settle Junction, Helwith Bridge, and Horton. Contracts were awarded in each case to J. Thornton of Bradford, the first for £2,828 and the last three for £2,259, though the station at Helwith was not built. Settle station site at this time was being made up to rail level by tipping soil brought from Ingfield, nearby. On the part already firm there stood contractors' huts, a temporary engine shed, store huts, and masses of assorted equipment.

Early in June Crossley was recommending the tenders of Benton & Woodiwiss of £5,739 and £5,050 for stations and warehouses at Kirkby Stephen and Arten Gill. As to the latter he suggested that the design of the station at Arten Gill be used for that at Hawes Junction. The committee was not sure, however, whether it wanted a station at Arten Gill or Dent Head and for the time being it decided to stall. At the end of June John Bayliss put in a successful tender for the locomotive sheds and fitting shops at Carlisle—by far the biggest building item—at £29,099. Meanwhile Joseph Firbank, on contract No. 3, had agreed to construct the necessary stations at a pro rata scale to those on No. 2, agreed with Benton & Woodiwiss. In mid July George Black of Carlisle was successful in obtaining the contracts for Scotby, Cumwhinton, Armathwaite, Lazonby, Little Salkeld, Long Wathby (sic), Culgaith, and Duncowfold. The station at the latter place was later to be named as High Stand Gill during construction, but received its present name of Cotehill before its opening. In effect all the stations then agreed upon were by now let out to contract.

The death roll among the navvies on contract No. 1 led the men to raise a subscription among themselves during mid 1874 to erect tablets in the churches at Settle and Chapel-le-Dale in memory of their dead comrades. The company gave £25 towards the fund.

By August the tunnels on contracts 3 and 4 were finished. Crossley's report in early September told of more bad weather. Many of the men were again away at the harvest; out of the 7,000 at work in June, some 1,000 had left. Of the 145½ miles of single track to be laid 70¼ were complete; a temporary line had been laid over Ribblehead viaduct and the arches were being keyed in. At Carlisle Messrs. Cowans & Sheldon had agreed to supply and fix a 42 ft. engine turntable for £685. Crossley mentioned that a petition for a station at Selside had been refused. By October most of the earthworks on No. 1 were finished, and only the parapets were now wanted on the Ribblehead viaduct. At Dent viaduct only one arch and the parapets remained to be completed. On the other contracts things were not so advanced. Earthworks lagged behind as did the ballasting on the finished lengths. On the Hawes contract it was decided that a deviation should be made to reduce the cutting of the drift which had proved to be almost impracticable. Generally the tenor of the report was good, however, Crossley telling the committee that rails could now be laid to almost any extent. The committee took him at his word and ordered more permanent way equipment, by far the largest amount going to Petteril. The year ended with a request from Ellis that Benton & Woodiwiss be prodded into more action. Ellis had been badgered by shareholders into a tour along the line a short time previously and was not impressed with the speed of construction.

On June 2, 1874, almost a year after he had retired from the chair, Price was given an official farewell at the 'Midland Hotel', Derby. There he was brought face to face with his portrait painted, like those of John Ellis, Beale, and Hutchinson, by John Lucas of St. Johns Wood. It brought the tradition to an end; Lucas had died shortly after completing his commission.

Towards the end of 1874 Crossley fell ill. The report to the committee dated January 5, 1875, was taken over by John Underwood. It was thought that contract No. 1 would be finished by the end of March. On No. 2 there were several heavy cuttings yet to do. The viaducts were also behind and Underwood hoped to complete them as soon as the weather permitted bricks from Bradford to get to the site via Kirkby Stephen. These were to be used by as many bricklayers as could be got together on the Dandry Mire and Lunds viaducts so as to release stone-masons for work at Arten Gill, one of the few viaducts which had its arches turned in stone. Smardale had ten arches completed and it was hoped that the viaduct would be ready soon—as always it all depended on the weather. Tunnelling was almost complete on No. 2 except at Rise Hill where a fair amount of lining still had to be done. Dealing with No. 3, Underwood pointed out that the viaducts were almost complete. Coming to the northern end of the line, 'The temporary engine house, goods warehouse, and yard for the Glasgow and South Western traffic at the Petteril station Carlisle, as promised, were completed by 1st of this month under very adverse circumstances as regard weather'. Besides the major construction works, which were within spitting distance of being operational, steady progress had been maintained on the stations and signalling. By this time the ballasting on No. 1 was ready for the track, about 27¼ miles of which had been laid as a single line. The completion of this to the end of the contract was hoped to take place shortly so that contracts 3 and 4 could be fed direct from the Midland system and not be so reliant on good weather.

The company's half-yearly meeting of February, 1875, reflected the general feeling about the Settle line. It had ceased to be a great event —it had become a bore, and an expensive one at that. Expenditure by this time had reached well over £2½m. and throughout the time of construction the L.N.W.R. was still happily milking away further profits by taking an average of £70-80,000 annually from tolls over the Lan-caster & Carlisle line. Once more urged on by an impatient group of the shareholders Ellis toured the line early in February. He travelled most of the route on the new permanent way and came back to Derby with the expressed hope that at least goods trains might be able to use it in six months' time.

Underwood's report for February revealed his frustration. Though he expected double track to be laid throughout contract No. 1 by the end of March, there was still an annoying series of delays and reversals to account for the slow progress elsewhere. In Rise Hill tunnel the rock had suddenly been found to be less firm that was expected; at the Moor-cock cutting 'it is impossible to make any progress here during the wet weather, it was ankle deep in mud when I walked through but there is not a large quantity of work to do and two months of fine weather should enable the contractor to clear this and get a road through'. There had been a slip at Birkett tunnel, blocking it for about a fort-night which prevented materials getting through to the other side. The viaducts were still abysmally slow to complete. He had seventeen masons at work on contract No. 2, and a further ten arriving from Scotland. Nearly all the stations were under way but here again the pace varied;

whereas Settle and Horton stations were ready for slating, that at Hawes Junction had not been started as the branch to Hawes was far from ready. An example of the sort of thing Underwood was up against came at the end of his report. 'At the Carlisle goods station during the gale on the night of the 20th ultimo, the temporary engine house was blown down, one half has been rebuilt, and is ready for the Glasgow and South Western engines and the remainder will be complete early this month.'

In March the company received a clarion call from Scarborough to extend to the town. With such commitments on its hands as the Settle line, the board regretted its inability to comply. On April 7 there was a letter from a Mr. R. French of Brampton on the subject of a diversion of a line apparently under consideration between Scotby on the Settle line and Gretna. Mr. French not unnaturally wanted it to go through Brampton. Nothing more was heard of the matter but the construction committee minutes inferred that at least it was under discussion, presumably as an avoiding line for Carlisle. This scheme at least may or may not have been a furtherance of an earlier proposal, the Brampton & Longtown Railway—a joint N.B.R. and G.S.W.R. project, which got powers in 1866 for a line $12\frac{1}{2}$ miles in length to terminate at Brampton, thus taking the two allies of the Midland part way towards the Settle line. The idea was allowed to die a natural death when the time limit for construction expired. Just to tidy up the matter of proposals affecting the Brampton area, there was a curious Bill deposited for the session of 1872, the Carlisle Brampton & Milton Railway. The intending shareholders, headed by the Rev. W. Dacre, proposed constructing a railway just over 12 miles in length from near the Brampton station of the N.E.R.'s Newcastle & Carlisle line to Corporation Road in Carlisle. The gauge was to be to the engineer's discretion but not more than 4 ft. $8\frac{1}{2}$ in., or less than 3 ft. This Bill also was withdrawn. One can guess what the N.E.R. thought of it. Incidentally one of the two engineers was R. Fairlie, which may have accounted for the idea of the line having a narrow gauge.

During April there was a spell of fine weather and the line hurried to completion. The following month Messrs. C. & I. Armstrong tendered successfully for twenty-four cottages at Petteril. By this time Crossley was back. In March he had asked to be relieved of his post and the Midland agreed, provided he undertook to stay on until the Settle line was completed. He was then to be retained as consultant engineer to the company at a nominal annual salary of £100. As a mark of appreciation of all his work he received a very munificent golden handshake of £10,000. His report to the committee in May indicated an early termination of the works on the line. Only $1\frac{1}{2}$ miles of single track remained to be laid on contract No. 1 and he had thirteen wagons working on the last cutting. Work at Settle Junction was in progress though somewhat slowed down by non-possession of some of the land. On the other contracts work was going on very well but Rise Hill tunnel was still being difficult. The signalling throughout was well advanced. 'There is every reason,' he ended, 'to expect that by the 1st of July, goods trains may be carried over the lines and after a few months testing passenger trains may be run. The directors passed over the entire line on the 29th April without break and on permanent way except for one mile of temporary road.' Apparently the scripture readers on contract No. 1 had been given three months' notice that they would no longer be needed. They each received a gratuity of £10.

June 29 saw the company's current Bill passed. This authorised the Appleby South Junction, land at Cumwhinton near the Eden Brow embankment, at Culgaith, at Garsdale for the station at Hawes Junction, and at Blea Moor, Ribblehead, Horton-in-Ribblesdale, and other places on the main line.

On August 3, 1875, Crossley wrote to the construction committee, no doubt with a sigh of relief, 'I have the pleasure to report that goods trains have this day travelled over the line'. There were still some minor works to be completed, including doubling the then single line between Mallerstang and Hawes Junction, but at long last THE DAY had arrived. The date given conflicted with the announcement in the directors' half-yearly report for August that goods workings had commenced from Monday, August 2. The report told the shareholders that double track had now been laid throughout (this was not strictly true—Mallerstang to Hawes Junction was still single at this time) but that it was not expected that passenger traffic would commence until the following Spring. In fact the opening of the line to goods traffic preceded the inspection by the Board of Trade by almost a month; the junctions at Settle were inspected almost fortuitously by Colonel Rich on his way from Leeds to a job at Lancaster. Some of the Midland officers, knowing that Colonel Hutchinson was booked to inspect the junctions at a later date, took the opportunity of Colonel Rich being in the area to suggest that he did it instead. Apart from a locking bar at the junction the Colonel found nothing wrong.

The local paper, the *Craven Herald,* in its issue of Saturday, August 14, 1875, noted that the 'luggage traffic' had commenced on the previous Monday—thus possibly adding yet another date—and took the opportunity to hope that the Midland might now extend into Durham. 'There the North Eastern Railway holds undisputed sway at present, and as a consequence is very independent. We think a little competition would do good in this instance . . . The Midland Railway is undoubtedly the best railway in the kingdom, and no benefit will accrue to the travelling public by the Midland company leasing their line from Colne to Skipton to the Lancashire & Yorkshire company.' Just where the paper had got this last idea from was not disclosed. The first goods timetable over the Settle line shows that the service operated on weekdays only with eight trains each way. Monday was an exception; there were six down freights and four up.

The remaining works were mostly confined to buildings for operating the passenger and goods services. Cottages for the operating staff and carriage and wagon shops were to be built at Durran Hill. On August 31—the day Colonel Rich was at Settle Junction—the committee received the following breathless report from Crossley: 'I beg to report that the line has been maintained and the traffic carried safely with one exception and the running off of the train was caused by the too sudden stopping of the engine by reversing before the rear brakes were on—the derangement of the road which alarmed the driver was caused by expansion from the heat of the sun and when the rails became cool the road became straight and so continued and when the ballast is laid on no further expansion will occur.' Thus the first recorded accident was a minor affair. A later chapter will tell how from small beginnings the Settle and Carlisle line was to loom large in the annals of railway mishaps. The report went on '. . . the lining of Rise Hill tunnel is going on as fast as men can be induced to work in it, they complain of the smoke and leave the work'. According to *Wildman's Almanack* of 1877 there was single line working through the tunnel at this time because of the lining work. The same source notes that on account of the horizontal strata in the tunnel it was found necessary to place wrought iron ribs across the roof, at distances of 6 feet apart. They sprung from the side walls of the tunnel and, after being fastened with tie rods, they formed an arch to support the roof. There was still a village of huts above the tunnel in which some 350 of the navvy people had lived during its construction.

On October 5 the committee decided to postpone its decision as to the site of Dent station. Crossley reported that month that the banks at Mallerstang had been widened and raised to permit of the second line from Mallerstang to Hawes Junction to be used on October 4. He was pleased to say that heavy rains during September had not damaged the works in any way—in fact the combined attention of the rain and the goods trains was consolidating the formation in a very effective manner. As a point of interest, mineral trains from the Craven Lime sidings had been using the southern end of the line for about two years before through working had commenced; at the end of 1875 Allport had agreed to additional sidings at the Blea Moor or Ingleton Road station for the company's use—the Midland traffic committee had not yet made up its mind as to the station's name. The remaining works were still in varying stages of completion. Some of the stations stood mutely awaiting traffic and a few of the cottages were already inhabited —those at Moorcock for instance. At Settle Junction the platform walls had been built but work on the station buildings was in abeyance. Paling fences had been erected between the road and the railway so that the engines should not startle horses, as the original line had been widened and deviated nearer the road, and two signal boxes to control the junction were being constructed. At Settle the buildings were nearly complete; at

Horton only the foundations were in. Hawes Junction engine establishment had in the meantime been much altered and the work considerably reduced. Appleby station was complete and painted while in the case of Kirkby Stephen the foundations were not even finished. The stations on to Carlisle were all at different stages. With the southern end of the line virtually complete, Batty Moss was by now almost deserted; it was about to be permitted to return to its natural state.

On November 30 the construction committee finally decided on the site of Dent station. It also determined to transfer all the buildings, in whatever state of completion, to the way and works committee. The difficulty of obtaining sufficient ballast easily and cheaply had also decided the committee to buy some land adjacent to the line at Lazonby for this purpose; Bayliss was to lay in the tracks for the sidings and was then to hand over the maintenance of the whole of No. 4 contract to the company. As to the permanent way, the rails were held in chairs secured to the sleepers with two trenails and two spikes. A considerable amount of the ballast was prepared by Marsden stone breakers, portable six-wheeled railborne stone breaking machines then being made—in this instance for crushing limestone—by the firm of H. R. Marsden of Leeds.

At the end of 1875 there was a complaint from the enginemen that in the cottages built for them at Petteril someone had committed a *faux pas*; an anti-traditionalist had been at work. Oven boilers and grates had been fixed in the front rooms and only an ordinary grate in the back. Very hastily the locomotive committee, which had heard of the desecration of the front parlour with horror, ordered a switch to be made or for there to be a cooking range put in the back room too. One hundred and forty-nine cottages were being or had been built. One hopes that the episode was not repeated elsewhere. (A list of the cottages appears in Appendix VIII.)

On December 14, 1875, it was decided that as from New Year's Day contract No. 4 should be taken over by the way and works committee, together with Bayliss's workmen and their huts and tools, including nine platelayers' huts, purchased from the contractor at £30 each. To look after these works, now under its direct responsibility, the committee appointed Edwin Westerman as superintendent of the Settle and Carlisle line, at £180 per annum, the appointment to commence from January 1, 1876, the date when contracts 1 and 3 also passed to the committee's care. The large number of men in the company's employ who now began to work on the line all needed housing. This meant additional accommodation to that which had already been provided for the operating staff and on January 4 the way and works committee ordered 50 wooden cottages for the permanent way men. On February 1, Robert Lander & Co. were given the job of supplying ten pairs of wooden cottages at £175 11s. 8d. per pair, delivery to be at Leeds, the Midland to transport them to their ultimate sites. On April 1 the maintenance of contract No. 2 also passed to the committee. Meanwhile at the end of February

Crossley reported that Colonel Rich of the Board of Trade had devoted a week, commencing on February 14, to inspecting the line. He had, Crossley said, been favourably impressed. Though Crossley agreed to the way and works committee taking over the line, a sort of passing out parade affair, he warned the committee not to make the mistake of treating the Settle and Carlisle in the same way as it would an old line; there was much continuous packing and ballasting still to be done. He thought that this alone warranted all the available men being kept on for some time. In any case, even though he had reported Colonel Rich as being satisfied, the B.O.T. report, dated February 22, showed the line to be not yet fit for passenger traffic. After telling the board that the Midland had used 80 lb. rails and 40 lb. cast iron chairs and that there were 15 stations ready, 85 overbridges, 150 underbridges, 25 viaducts having 168 openings, and 13 tunnels, the Colonel stated that in the matter of the smaller details the work was not complete. Clocks, name boards, lamps, and sleeper crossings were required at the stations and catch points for runaways at Settle and the Craven sidings at Stainforth, at Horton, at Blea Moor lie-bys, at Kirkby Stephen and at most of the stations on to Carlisle. He was not at all happy at the height of the bridge parapets at some of the stations (was this, perhaps, an echo of the old business at Oakley?). He noted that there were to be additional stations at Stainforth, Rise Hill and Hawes Junction. Various small clearing, cleaning and draining jobs were outstanding. In all he was not quite as pleased as Crossley's message had intimated. His report ended that the line 'cannot be opened for passenger traffic without danger to the public using the same in consequence of the incomplete state of the works'. A copy of the report was sent to Derby accompanied by an instruction which forbade the opening for one calendar month. On March 21, having had no intimation from the company that it was complying with the Colonel's requirements, the Board of Trade further postponed the opening for another month. As an indication both of the unreadiness of the line, and of the fact that it traversed such hilly terrain, there was only one level crossing —at Low House—and as late as March 14 C. H. Leas was awarded the contract to supply the crossing gates.

Meanwhile, leaving the Board of Trade to its own devices, the Midland directors decided to inspect the works. According to the *Carlisle Journal* of May 2, 1876, the inspection took two days, Tuesday and Wednesday, April 25 and 26. The directors travelled in a brand new Pullman car, the *Venus*, which was not actually put into service for another week. On the Tuesday the construction committee decided to tour the line. The *Sheffield & Rotherham Independent* reported on this outing, noting that amongst the party were Edward Shipley Ellis, Sir Isaac Morley, James Allport, Carter, Thompson the vice-chairman, Messrs. Mappin and Thomas—two of the directors, Crossley and his successor Johnston, and I. H. Sanders the architect of the stations and other buildings. The party scorned the soft comfort of the *Venus*—it wanted to see the line properly, and a cattle truck, fitted out with wooden benches for the occasion, was put behind an engine and towed all the way to Carlisle. The paper ran away with itself in its description of this seemingly novel mode of travel. 'There, in appropriate wrappings and in close-fitting caps, with nothing to obstruct their view of the line —they were enabled to appreciate the glories of land and sky, the ranges of mighty mountains, intersected by wild gorges or divided by lovely valleys, through which ran the rivers and their tributary streamlets and rills, in a way denied to those travelling in any closed carriage.' It went on to say that it did not recommend open trucks for entire journeys but suggested that in summer-time all the trains ought to have a little truck attached to the rear so that passengers might enjoy the scenery. Someone, one hopes, cut this article out and put it on Clayton's desk, for the company's carriage and wagon superintendent had spent, as will be seen, the last five years or so perfecting the Midland's carriage stock to a point hitherto unknown, mainly for the opening of the Settle line.

In April Colonel Rich made another inspection and his report, dated April 25, stated that though the station at Hawes Junction was not complete, all the other works were, and subject to a careful watch being kept on the cuttings the line might now be opened with the exception of the link to the N.E.R. at Appleby.

There had been delay over the letting of the contract for the south curve at Appleby. In 1875 it was thought that through running with the North Eastern would be possible and as the original plans of 1866 had not provided for the south connection the necessary powers had been obtained in the Midland Railway (Additional Powers) Act of June 29, 1875. Firbank was given the contract for the Appleby South Junction line at a price of £8,346 on April 4, 1875. (See Appendix IX as to previous plans for junctions at Appleby and Kirkby Stephen.)

Engineer's report dated May 1, 1876: "I have to report that the line from Settle to Carlisle is ready and will be opened this day for the traffic of passengers and is in good condition. The station buildings are nearly completed, two or three small buildings are incomplete but will soon be finished. The final accounts for works are in forward progress and I do not recommend any payments on account to contractors until the accounts are agreed upon.'

It had taken just under seven years from the time of the defeat of the abandonment Bill. In the end the line was found to have cost the Midland close on £3 m.; it took three extensions of time, granted by Parliament in Midland Acts of 1870, 1873 and 1875. The works at Arten Gill and Cow Gill had run into such trouble that powers to deviate the line had been obtained by an Act of 1871, incidentally reducing the planned height of Arten Gill viaduct by some 50 feet. At Wetherall the line had not been constructed in accordance with the plans of 1866 and another Act of 1874 had been needed to legalise the position. Finally the Hawes branch had run into difficulty and deviations and extension of time were authorised by an Act of 1875. The men who had built the railway had been drawn from many previous callings and were of many nationalities. Mostly they were attracted by ready work on the piece rate basis. They came from a vast army of skilled and semi-skilled labourers on the railways who had built up a tradition of hard work and tough living from the time when the navvies had made the first canals. Not all, however, were from a navvy background. Amongst the men who came from other professions to earn their way on the Settle and Carlisle line was Edward Coates of Derby. At the age of nineteen he was the Midland's station master at Haworth and later he went to Ingleton, then, of course, a reasonably important post as the main interchange station for the Scotch traffic. In 1870 he severed what must have been a promising career with the railway company and joined Benton & Woodiwiss on the Settle and Carlisle line.

Before coming to the general preparations for the opening of the line, it would perhaps be best to finish with the construction details of the Hawes branch and the Appleby South Junction line. On August 3, 1876, Colonel Yolland of the Board of Trade reported that, though lacking a clock, Hawes Junction station had just been opened. By the following month the Midland and the N.E.R. had agreed as to the layout and details of the station at Hawes. Nearly three hundred and fifty men were at work on the branch in September; progress at Appleby was held up by the dearth of men because of the harvest. About $2\frac{1}{4}$ miles from its junction with the main line the Hawes branch passes through the short Moss Dale Head tunnel (245 yards) and shortly after crosses Moss Dale Gill viaduct. A further two miles brings the line to Appersett viaduct and another $1\frac{1}{4}$ miles to the joint station at Hawes. By December of 1876 the branch and the Appleby curve were well under way but the engineer's report for January of 1877 told of excessively stormy weather which had retarded all operations on the latter. Meanwhile on the branch line the second arch of Moss Dale Gill viaduct had suddenly collapsed, injuring three men—one fatally. Heavy rains throughout February almost stopped any progress on the branch but at Appleby things had improved so much that only a little earthwork remained to be done, together with some masonry to the one bridge on the short junction line, about $\frac{3}{4}$ mile in length. By March the weather in Wensleydale was no better but the following month saw the Appleby line ready for ballast. The engineer noted that as soon as the signalling arrangements were in order at Lazonby the ballast could be brought from the new sidings. By May he reported that the line was virtually ready; it could be in use by mid-month if the N.E.R.'s junction to the South Durham line was completed. On June 5 he reported that '. . . the Appleby South Junction curve is quite finished and the final certificate appended . . . the use of the curve is retarded by the non completion of the North Eastern company's junctions and as the management of the affair has been removed from the engineer to the general manager I can offer no information respecting it.' Neither, apparently, could anyone else. As far as can be ascertained the N.E.R.'s junctions were never completed. The Midland junction was removed after a while and the rails were lifted in 1902.

Through almost continuous rain work on the Hawes branch slithered through 1877, the tunnel being bored throughout by September. On June 1, 1878 the first N.E.R. goods train from Askrigg entered Hawes, passenger traffic starting on the following October 1. Meanwhile, in late July of 1878, Underwood got permission for the Midland line, which was nearly ready, to be handed over to the way and works committee. It was opened for traffic on August 1. Four days later Crossley died at his home at Barrow-on-Soar.

His was an achievement out of the ordinary for, in his latter years, often far from well, he had laboured successfully with the aid of his lieutenants J. Underwood and J. T. Thompson, and the teams of resident engineers, to complete what must have been one of the most difficult of lines to construct. Crossley had been associated with the Midland since its earliest days. Born at Loughborough on Christmas Day, 1812, he was left an orphan two years later. At the age of twenty he was appointed engineer to the Leicester Canal Company, and almost immediately started work on the surveys for the Leicester & Swannington Railway. In 1835 he had been with Vignoles, assisting on the preliminary work connected with the Midland Counties line. After this there was a gap of about a decade when Crossley's career did not touch the Midland but in 1852 he started surveys on the Leicester-Hitchin branch. He was apparently a man who drove himself hard; this time he went too far and over-work produced a paralytic stroke on November 30, 1852. It did not stop him; by September 1853 he was back as resident engineer on the Leicester-Hitchin line and four years later he was appointed engineer to the Midland. There had followed all the engineering works from then on culminating in the Settle and Carlisle line, a task which obviously had required a man like Crossley to complete it. He knew of his achievement; on reaching Carlisle on that boneshaking inspection in an open truck the week before the line was opened he was heard to remark 'Finis coronat opus'. The line is his memorial, and his name, or rather that of his wife, is inscribed into it; on completion of Smardale viaduct the contractor thoughtfully asked Mrs. Crossley to lay the last stone. This she did and there it remains : 'This last stone was laid by Agnes Crossley, June 8th, 1875.'

One cannot hope to do justice to the building of the Settle and Carlisle line without calling on the work of Frederick S. Williams. In his history of the Midland he relates how he visited the works in their latter stages. He toured the whole route and with fine reporting journalism managed to present an eye-witness account that cannot be bettered in detail about the men and the countryside in those mid-Victorian years.

In this chapter the chronology has been attempted rather than the detail; and for whose who wish for the latter the sixty-five pages of Williams' book devoted to the construction can be read with enjoyment. As to dates for the commencement and termination of various individual works details may be found in Appendix IX.

XII

Preparations for the Opening

Way and Works, Carriages and Locomotives

1870 – 1876

For some time before the opening of the Settle and Carlisle line the Midland sought to improve both the approach lines and the stations of the Leeds & Bradford and the little North Western, together with the locomotive and rolling stock, in time for the independent Scotch service which would be ushered in by the new route.

Dealing first with the general improvements along the line from Leeds, it was decided in 1870 that Shipley should have a new station more fitting with the better service which was to come and with its position as an important junction station. Throughout the late 1860s a series of small ameliorations had been made in the Leeds & Bradford line, mostly passing loops and lie-by sidings, all of which assisted the through traffic. Early in 1871 complaints from local passengers led to improvements at Apperley Bridge and six months later Kirkstall Forge station also qualified when the bridge over the Leeds & Liverpool Canal was renewed. A series of widenings of the Leeds & Bradford took place during the mid 1870s. Though there were no widening powers sought, the Midland's Acts of 1871 and 1873 authorised various land purchases. Bridge drawings which have been inspected, to do with the widenings, are dated 1874, and construction took place during the following year.

One of the most important of the alterations, however, concerned Skipton. There the old level crossing was to be done away with and a new station and exchange sidings completed north of the old in time for the opening of the Settle line. In charge of all these works was the traffic committee. On a tour of inspection made between July 10 and 14, 1871, it was decided that Armley station should be converted to cottages and new station buildings constructed on the up platform with an approach from the overbridge. At Kirkstall waiting rooms were to be provided on the down side of the line, adjoining the new station, built like that at Armley on the overbridge. The existing station and station master's house—the latter being too damp—was to be removed. At Bingley and Keighley the committee decided that entirely new stations should be constructed south of the road overbridge to replace those on the north side in each case. With November of 1871 came approval for the lengthening of the platforms at Apperley Bridge. Side by side with these improvements came the introduction of the block telegraph system and in July, 1872, approval was given for alterations at Thwaites Crossing, Keighley, Steeton, Kildwick, Cononley, and Robinson's Sidings made necessary thereby, in an effort to get the block system in operation before the Settle and Carlisle line was opened. Meanwhile in March, 1872, it had been agreed to make a new station at Frizinghall in response to appeals from local people who otherwise had to go into Shipley or Manningham, a station having been opened at the latter place on February 17, 1868. The 1870s saw a considerable programme of platform raising; this was not tied to any particular new scheme but was the result of a wearying and unflagging campaign by the Board of Trade. Not all companies complied straight away. The Midland did, however, eventually carry out the improvement over its whole system, the activity coinciding with the building of the Settle line.

At the end of May, 1872, the committee made another tour and was put out to find that no attempt had been made to start work on the new stations at Bingley and Keighley; that at Skipton was still in the planning stage. The committee decided that when the L.Y.R.'s line to Hellifield was completed the Midland station, a small affair about $\frac{1}{2}$ mile south of the present station, should be re-sited immediately north of the junction. As to Settle Junction it was on this tour that the decision was reached to provide a passenger station and exchange sidings. It was also thought at the time that when the Settle line was opened the existing Settle station, that now known as Giggleswick, could be removed. October of the following year saw the committee still concerned on this point, debating whether to construct a new curve to enable the old station at Settle to be closed without affecting passengers on the little North Western. Skipton too had need of a new curve for where the little North Western joined the Leeds & Bradford Extension the former veered away to the north at an alarming radius totally unsuited to the new rolling stock and high speeds the company was planning. Land for the curve, sidings, and new station was authorised to be purchased by the company's Act of 1873. In November of that year it was briefly mooted that a new north curve from the Colne line to the little North Western should be put in, making a triangular layout at Skipton North Junction, but the idea seems not to have progressed further. The following March it was decided to extend the block system as quickly as possible from Saltaire just north of Shipley, where it terminated, to Settle, and on to Wennington and Morecambe in May. As a matter of policy the company decided in July 1874 to provide henceforth the block system as a necessary part of all new lines and in November the Furness and Midland line from Wennington to Carnforth was included in the programme. Meanwhile the plans for the new station at Skipton had been sent out to tender, and in December 1874 the firm of Kirk & Evans got the contract for the station buildings on the up side at £4,572 15s. 3d.; the platforms and roofing contract went to W. Macfarline (some records give this as W. M. Farlain) & Co. for £11,174 6s. 11d. nine months later. In November 1875 the way and works committee gave instructions for a 46 ft. turntable to be provided at Skipton, and four months later a wooden engine shed was ordered from W. Nicholson & Sons.

In October 1874 the Midland directors decided to abolish second class travel on their system with effect from January 1, 1875. The reason for this was tied directly to the Settle and Carlisle line. On Tuesday, November 17, a special meeting was held at Derby to thrash out the proposed abolition of second class and the reduction of the first class fares to 2d a mile. The meeting was told that the directors had come to their decision on October 4; they had been considering at that moment the rolling stock which would have to be ordered for the Settle line and whether it should be in three classes or two, something which had been frequently discussed over the past years. It had been decided that there would be substantial economies by operating only two classes of carriage and, once the principle had been accepted, it was a logical move to apply it to all trains.

As might have been expected there was criticism from a number of shareholders but the directors maintained that if the second class was abandoned receipts would go up. The chairman, Edward Shipley Ellis, pointed out that in 1850 the earnings per train mile were 4s 10d. Soon afterwards the Great Northern extension northwards had swept away a considerable amount of the Midland's north-south traffic and by 1852 the receipts were at about 4s 1d a mile, by 1862 3s 10½d a mile, and by 1870 3s 6d. However, Ellis said, the first year that the company took third class passengers by all trains, including the expresses, the receipts had risen to 4s 8½d, the highest since 1850.

The abolition of second class on the Midland drew the G.N.R., G.W.R., L.Y.R., L.N.W.R., M.S.L.R., and N.E.R. together in a pact of mutual desperation; they issued a statement that they would not discontinue second class carriages, and that differential fares between first and second class would be maintained. This did not deter Derby. *Herepath's Journal* for December 12, 1874, noted that the company, in view of the fact that second class season ticket holders would be disenfranchised under the new arrangements, had decided to issue third class seasons. The journal's issue one week later informed its readers that the Midland was making all possible progress converting the rolling stock to suit the third class, in which the old compartments were being fitted with comfortable leather cushions so as to be almost identical with the existing seconds, with the exception of leather backings. The new thirds were to be furnished with footwarmers in winter and with partitions sufficiently high to prevent draughts.

All this was not before time. Over a period of years the company had been reminded at intervals that its coaching stock was not all that it should be. A letter from a Mr Walter Leith, written in January of 1870, may be taken as an example of what the public must have been thinking all too often. His experiences in travelling over the G.N.R., L.N.W.R., and Midland, he said, had led him to think that the latter's coaches were the least comfortable and smooth. This situation the Midland endeavoured to rectify and by September of that year the locomotive committee—then the authority for coaching matters as well as motive power—was providing all new second class carriages with racks, hat strings and blinds. The existing stock was to be so fitted as it came into the shops. With winter coming on the second class stock was also given footwarmers, the company's stock of these now long-forgotten articles growing at a prodigious rate so as to be able to serve all the carriages in the cold weather. This was as much to do with outside example as to any new-found generosity towards the passengers. The following year there was a meeting at the Railway Clearing House at which the L.N.W.R. virtuously said that it was going to provide everyone with footwarmers—even the menial thirds. With the continuous spirit of competition then prevelant the Midland had to follow suit.

The company was not averse to looking outside for new ideas. One of the L.N.W.R.'s new saloon carriages caught the eye of the general manager late in 1870 and particulars were discreetly taken so that something similar could be knocked up in the shops at Derby. It has been seen how the company was concerned at the jerking experienced when the trains started and stopped and of Kirtley's tests to eliminate the trouble. It had been found that the best results were obtained from carriages fitted up with a continuous drawbar and india-rubber packings so arranged as to give a play of $1\frac{1}{2}$ inches, and in early April of 1873 a test train was fitted up so that the idea might be thoroughly put through its paces. The experiment was tried out on May 17 and proved so successful that the locomotive committee was ordered to fit up all the company's carriages on this principle. Other matters under active consideration at this time included a supposedly improved mode of cord communication between the passenger and the train crew, and the question of the type of brake to be employed in future rolling stock. Both of these problems took several painful years to sort out and appear later in Chapter XVIII.

Matters were not helped by the fact that at a time when the Midland was expanding the system it was notoriously short of both carriages and locomotives. By 1873 it was becoming apparent in both spheres that a considerable programme of new stock was imperative. In early February of 1874, in time for the coming summer traffic, the carriage and wagon committee was told to provide thirty additional train composites and one hundred thirds, twenty of the former to have two first, one second, one third, and a luggage compartment and ten to have two firsts, two seconds and one luggage. The third class carriages were to have the division of each compartment carried up to the roof. Only seven months later the committee was told to produce fifty twin composites, one hundred and fifty thirds, fifty brake-thirds, fifty brake vans, fifty horse boxes, ten covered carriage trucks, ten large parcels vans, twenty fish and poultry trucks, six milk vans, six family carriages, and four invalid carriages.

At the end of 1874, Thomas G. Clayton, the company's carriage and wagon superintendent, submitted plans of proposed bogie carriages with comparative estimates showing their cost as against ordinary four-wheeled stock. One 60 ft. bogie carriage containing seven firsts and a luggage compartment, to accommodate forty-two passengers, was priced at £1,419 compared with two ordinary 29 ft. first class carriages each containing four first class compartments and accommodating forty-eight passengers with no luggage accommodation at a total cost of £1,302. These in turn compared with another 60 ft. first class bogie carriage, with a through passage, accommodating thirty-six passengers and without a luggage compartment, at £1,357. Coming to the third class carriages, Clayton compared a 60 ft. bogie carriage containing nine thirds and a luggage compartment, to accommodate ninety passengers, for a cost of £884, with two ordinary 29 ft. coaches each having five thirds and taking one hundred passengers with no accommodation for luggage, at a price for the two of £768. Lastly, he instanced a 60 ft. third class bogie with a through passage and taking seventy-two passengers and no luggage for £827. These details were, of course, merely Clayton's ideas to put before the board for its decision when contemplating new stock. For the time being, however, nothing more was done, for the whole question of bogie carriages was under discussion as was the principle of six-wheeled versus four-wheeled stock.

Meanwhile the earlier orders to the carriage and wagon committee had borne fruit and some of the results had already found their way into train formations. *Herepath's Journal* of February 20, 1875, was distinctly pleased :—

'A number of greatly improved first class carriages have, the *Leeds Mercury* says, been added to the rolling stock of the Midland Railway. One difference is that they are much larger than those hitherto used, the body of each carriage measuring 28 feet in length, and consisting of four compartments instead of the customary three. The exterior presents a handsome and substantial appearance, with several improvements, including the greater safety afforded by a larger footstep. It is in the interior, however, that the changes for the better are most numerous and apparent. The new carriages have, in the first place, the advantage of being more commodious than the old ones. They are at least 8 inches higher in the roof, measuring 7 feet in height from the floor, which leaves room for even a tall passenger to walk out or in without damage to either his head or his hat. Each compartment is 7 feet 6 inches broad from side to side, by 6 feet 4 inches wide from end to end. When only a single seat on one side is occupied the passenger can lie down comfortably full length over the whole width of the carriage, arm rests being turned up. In order that travellers may more easily see the country through which they pass, the side windows have been much increased in size—being 2 feet 6 inches in length by 1 foot 5 inches in breadth.'

The accolade was well deserved; with Clayton in charge of the carriage designs, and with James Allport backing him, the Midland coaching stock was to undergo a rapid metamorphosis. Some of Clayton's work for the Settle and Carlisle line M. & G.S.W. joint stock in particular is discussed in Chapter XVIII. As to the Midland's own stock for the opening of the line the traffic committee decided in July 1875 to recommend that as a start twenty composite carriages, 54 ft. long and on bogies, should be constructed, together with forty ordinary composites and twenty-four brake vans. This was very good but it still left Clayton short of all kinds of passenger accommodation. On the same day that the committee ordered the Settle and Carlisle stock he was addressing a *cri-de-coeur* to the carriage and wagon committee. '. . . the traffic department are so short of carriages—first class, third class and vans, that they are complaining very much of my detaining them for repairs although we are not stopping many which require to be stopped and are thereby running greater risk and incurring more responsibility than we ought to be called upon to bear.' Half finished alterations were running on the system with two-hued coverings—paintwork and patchwork. 'Every week', he continued, 'they are imploring me to let them have carriages that are under repair . . . and I am letting them have all that are safe to run irrespective of their general condition and appearance'. The trouble was that Clayton just could not get them out of traffic to complete them. Deliveries over the past year, with the slow rate of growth of the Midland, had only just been sufficient. Now, with the much increased tempo, matters were worse, and on August 3 Clayton stated that he required an additional two hundred carriages. At the same time he suggested that six wheels should be put in all non-bogie carriages exceeding 27 ft. 6 ins. in length or nine tons in weight. Though this latter suggestion was agreed to at the time, just over four months later Clayton had changed his mind. On December 1, 1875, he and E. M. Needham, the superintendent of passenger traffic, had reported to the board with their recommendations for future policy as to the passenger stock. These were, briefly, that it should consist of four-wheeled and bogie carriages only; six-wheeled vehicles were out. The four-wheeled carriages were to be made as large as was consistent with the efficiency and safety of such a type, up to 26 ft. in length. Anything over this length was to run on bogies, and as a general principle it was decided that the bogie carriage should be adopted to a much greater extent than before. It was recommended that one bogie carriage be provided for every two of the old four-wheeled carriages broken up in the future. The report was accepted; its theme of re-equipping the rolling stock with bogie vehicles was probably in no small way due to the success of the recently introduced Pullmans, though as will be seen shortly, their performance made Clayton switch from four-wheeled bogies to six-wheeled when designing the Scotch stock.

But it was with the Pullmans that the Midland hoped to attract custom to the Settle and Carlisle line. They were not a brand-new idea; Pullmans had been running on the Midland for just on a year when the Settle line was opened and they were considered to be the ultimate in luxury—it was with the Settle line, however, that they came into heavy and sustained use. Their early teething troubles were at first invaluable to Clayton as to the design of his bogie rolling stock, and later a constant annoyance as a repeated source of operating difficulties.

James Allport had toured America in 1872 to see what the New World had to offer in rolling stock design. He met George M. Pullman and travelled in the parlour and sleeping cars then being turned out by the Pullman Palace Car Company. He was impressed—more so than with the European versions of the same idea. His views were made known and on November 5, 1872, the Midland traffic committee discussed the whole question of adopting American carriages for special trains and referred the matter to the board. Price, the chairman, was also interested and it was decided to invite Pullman to the next shareholders' meeting where both he and models of his vehicles could be unveiled to what was hoped would be rapturous cheers. This event took place in mid February of 1873. The shareholders were first told all about him and then informed that he was in the room with them—at that point Pullman bowed to the cheers—to show them how the Midland would, by his aid, be able to run coaches 'equal to a first-class hotel'.* So as to allay any fears that the Midland, then straining every financial muscle to get the Settle line built, should be called upon to bear the cost of the new carriages, George Pullman had undertaken to build the cars himself. He merely asked the Midland to attach them to its trains. This seemed fair enough but on the same day that the idea was brought out in the open the traffic committee became worried about the 'attach' part of the bargain. A hurried rethink on the matter of couplings was necessary as the Pullmans had an entirely different central coupler and buffing gear to that employed on the Midland's ordinary coaches. The committee decided that some sort of match carriage and van would be necessary for each train taking a Pullman, and instructions were given that one of each sort, with similar bogies to those on the Pullmans, should be constructed.

By May of 1873 the scheme was under way. In fact events became somewhat hectic as it was decided that the Pullman cars would be constructed in Detroit, taken to pieces, sent over to Derby, and re-erected by the Pullman company in a shed to be allotted solely to its use at the carriage and wagon works. No such shed was available and a rush job had to be done in time for the first shipment.

On January 20, 1874, with the first cars nearly ready, Allport reported to the board that Pullman cars—he must have meant their clearances—had been tried out on every portion of the system over which they were to be introduced, with the exception of the Ambergate–Leeds section, and the road bridges and tunnels had all been found of sufficient width to allow the cars to pass each other, except in Marple tunnel which he recommended should be altered. This was, of course, for the Manchester service, and as it was on the Sheffield and Midland Joint

* *Herepath's Journal*, February 18, 1872.

201

line the Sheffield's engineers had already given an estimate for the alterations of some £23,000. This, however, is no part of our story.

When George Pullman agreed to construct his new-fangled American style vehicles with their cumbersome appearance—at least compared with British railway vehicles—Allport had been concerned with the aesthetic look of the mixed trains which would be running as a result. For one of the conditions was that Pullman should be permitted to attach one sleeping car and one parlour car to each of the agreed ordinary scheduled services, the remainder of the train to be made up of Midland stock. So Allport made a further condition; that the Pullman Palace Car Company should construct at Derby works some more coaches—called by the Midland 'day coaches'—having the same exterior appearance as the regular Pullman cars, but with interiors composed of ordinary seats for those passengers who merely wished to use the trains and not the Pullmans, or, more likely, who just did not wish to pay the supplement. This Pullman agreed to do, the Midland to purchase the cars as soon as they were completed, the Pullman company retaining ownership of all its own cars.

The first Pullman car to issue forth from Derby works was the sleeping car *Midland* on January 25, 1874, followed by another sleeping car, the *Excelsior* on February 15. Others followed in rapid succession, *Enterprise*, another sleeper, and *Victoria*, *Britannia*, and *Leo*, parlour cars, were all ready for traffic by June of 1874. Side by side with these came the Midland day coaches. It would appear from the Midland's traffic committee minutes that the Pullman company did the upholstery work for all the cars, their own, and those of the Midland, but one cannot be sure as the minutes are disconcertingly vague in distinguishing between the two. A description of how the Pullmans appeared to a contemporary observer is given in the next chapter. The details of the stock already constructed concluded the programme for 1874, all the day coaches being constructed that year.

On March 17, 1874, the first trial trip took place when *Midland* and *Excelsior* carried directors and officers of the Midland from Derby to St Pancras behind a Kirtley 2-4-0 locomotive, No. 906, the tender of which had been fitted with a Miller automatic coupling to fit those of the Pullmans. Four days later, joined by the parlour car *Victoria,* the train ran to Bedford and back, its distinguished passengers and representatives of the press enjoying a meal provided by Messrs Spiers & Pond, the caterers.

Preparations now got under way for the inauguration of the first regular passenger service to use the Pullmans. On May 19 the traffic committee approved the timetable for a Pullman service between Bradford and London to commence on June 1, thus making the Leeds & Bradford line the first to be so honoured. The *Railway Fly Sheet* of June, 1874, tells how the train left Bradford at 8.30 a.m. and arrived at St Pancras at 2.05 p.m. It remarked upon the pleasant, quiet journey and told of a rubber of whist played comfortably and with hushed voices during the trip, the inference being that one usually had to shout to be heard above the noise of the wheels in ordinary stock. The return train left St Pancras at midnight and arrived in Bradford at 5.50 a.m. it was noted with evident satisfaction that since the Pullman sleeper stood ready at St Pancras from 10 p.m. onwards, revellers in London could retire at any time within two hours before midnight and catch up on their sleep. They were likewise catered for at the Bradford end for the car was shunted off to a quiet spot to allow them to sleep through to 8.00 a.m. Harold Behrens in his *Pullman in Europe* gives the marshalling of this first Pullman train. There were five vehicles; cars Nos. 1 and 2 were Allport specials—a third class and baggage vehicle, and a first and second class composite. Then followed a Pullman sleeping car and a parlour car, and the last vehicle was similar to car No. 1.

By the end of June it had become apparent that the difference in couplings was going to be of increasing annoyance. Several of the Midland locomotives had been temporarily fitted with the central coupler to take the Pullmans but it was obvious that to alter all the existing stock would be ridiculous. On June 30 Clayton told the carriage and wagon committee that he wished the Pullman couplings to be altered to the usual Midland pattern and this was carried out by 1876.

According to Ahrons the Bradford–London Pullman trains ran at first via Derby, but from July 1, 1874, the departure time from Bradford was put back to 9.20 a.m., and the train ran via the Erewash Valley route to arrive at St Pancras at 2.35 p.m. August saw the stops at Chesterfield and Trent deleted from the timetable which showed a new arrival time at St Pancras of 2.15 p.m. A year later, from September of 1875, the train called again at Trent and arrived at St Pancras at 2.20 p.m. and this final timing was kept until, as will be seen, the service terminated with the opening of the Settle line. It was, in fact, one of the few Midland attempts to compete directly with the Great Northern for the Bradford and Leeds to London traffic; for the most part all the Midland trains called at the centres of population on their way between the West Riding and the metropolis.

On October 20, 1874, the traffic committee reported to the board that it considered a dozen more day cars were necessary, all first/third composites (the coming abolition of second class of course affected the day coaches), six to have side entrances and six with a central passage. In fact they were not constructed. The public did not like the day coaches. Hamilton Ellis has put forward the probable reason : 'One can only suppose that the change from riding in an oblong box, probably facing five complete strangers, to travelling in a sort of chapel, possibly regarding the backs of some dozens of necks, was too drastic.' * In any event only the eight cars of 1874 were constructed. Edward Shipley Ellis, speaking at the meeting of November 17, 1874, when the abolition of

* *The Midland Railway.* Hamilton Ellis. 1953.

second class was discussed, made the point that at that time the Midland regarded the whole idea of Pullmans as an experiment. The day coaches lasted only until 1884 when four of them were withdrawn and the others rebuilt; further details of their history after 1876 will be found in Chapter XVIII. Almost as soon as they were in service the day coaches underwent alterations. Allport, in a memorandum to the carriage and wagon committee dated January 19, 1875, requested that the second class compartments be altered and trimmed with blue cloth and made first class, and that all the smoking compartments in the composite cars should be done away with and provision made for first class smokers at one end of the third class cars, which were to be trimmed and fitted up as first class. All eight cars were taken out of traffic for these alterations in July of 1876. The coaches were purchased from the Pullman company in March of 1875, the cost of the four first/second class composites being £7,875 17s 1d, and the four third class baggage cars £4,730 4s 10d. The cost of the shed used by Pullman at Derby was noted as being £1,624 13s 5d. In May of 1875 the Pullman company asked to rent a second shed.

On April 1, 1875, the Pullman sleeper service was extended to Liverpool, via the newly opened Marple curve, and a St Pancras to Manchester service was commenced in March of 1878. As to the Liverpool trains, the L.N.W.R. was obliged to make a similar effort and sleeping saloons were put on the night trains between Euston and the northern city on the same day as the Midland service commenced. The Bradford service was augmented, from November 1, 1875; an additional Pullman was run attached to the up night mail leaving Leeds for St Pancras at 10.05 p.m., Sundays excepted.

It has already been mentioned that Clayton was concerned at this time with plans for the new Midland passenger stock for the opening of the Settle and Carlisle line. It had not gone unnoticed that the Pullmans, for all their flamboyance, tended to be unfortunately prone to hot boxes and on July 6, 1875 he reported to the carriage and wagon committee that from observations of the working of the four-wheel bogie he recommended that the new carriages already ordered should have six-wheeled bogies substituted for the four-wheeled ones then being fitted.

On April 29, 1876, the *Railway News* reported that the Metropolitan Carriage Company of Saltley had just turned out the first two of the new Midland carriages ordered the previous summer. Their length was quoted as being 'immense'; they had eight compartments, four thirds, three firsts, and one for luggage. The six-wheeled bogies were remarked upon as was the clerestory roof, 'giving an air of lightness and space refreshing and novel'. The firsts were well upholstered, with movable arm rests, and the woodwork was of sycamore divided into panels by maple mouldings. The *News* noted that there were many more under construction and that Mr Rawlings, the manager of the works, was only too pleased to let anyone in to see them. On May 2, 1876, the day after the Settle line was opened to passenger traffic, the *Carlisle Journal*, quoting another newspaper, noted that the two carriages were at that time in the paint shop at Derby, and gave some more details :—

'The roof of the first-class is *à la* Pullman, raised in the centre, and illumined with some of the most artistic distemper painting, while the airy and light build gives it a handsome general appearance. In length the carriage is 60 feet or within a foot of the length of the Pullman; and the others of the same build making at Saltley Works, Birmingham, will contain four first, four third, and a luggage locker. The carriage is but half the weight of the Pullman, though capable of carrying about as many passengers, and it will have the appearance of being more in character with the general English carriage. . . . The directors tried the two new carriages mentioned above on the Derby to Burton line, and ran them to the speed of over 70 miles an hour, the result of which crucial test was highly satisfactory. They are stated to be less oscillatory than even the Pullman, which claims to be the easiest car in the world.'

Altogether Mr Rawlings' firm turned out 32 of these coaches, another 12 coming from the Ashbury Railway Carriage Company.

To end these details of the Midland's carriage stock and the doings of the Pullman company immediately prior to the opening of the new line, it would be wrong to suppose that Derby was completely sold on the idea of Pullmans. The Midland was still inclined to be a little suspicious of its general manager's American friend. On April 5, 1876, less than a month before the opening of the Settle line, the board asked Allport to furnish a statement showing the number of Pullman cars running on the Midland, the number of cars for which requisitions had been made, and the receipts to the railway company from those in service. There was indeed to be a very careful watch kept on all aspects of the Pullman phase in the company's affairs, and it was not to be long before the operation of these vehicles on the crack trains was causing some doubt as to their retention.

If the situation in the 1870s was bad in the carriage department, it was about the same in that of motive power, where Samuel Waite Johnson was wrestling with the mixed bunch left behind by Kirtley. There had been a dearth of suitable engines for some time and in November of 1873 Johnson reported that in consequence of the greatly increased traffic it had become necessary to obtain one hundred and fifty new engines, at an estimated cost of £450,000. He suggested that out of these one hundred should be for the main line goods, thirty should be passenger tanks, and the remaining twenty for shunting. To give weight to his argument he followed this up in February of 1874 with a report on the state of the locomotive engines. The picture presented was very unsatisfactory for not only were there insufficient engines, but some of those that were running on the system were in a decrepit condition. It appeared that there were as many as eighty-nine sets of drivers and firemen without engines, having to work other engines as soon as their crews left them. This meant that a very high percentage of the total number of engines was kept almost non-stop in steam. Johnson pointed out that their condition could only be described as 'average good order', it being impossible with the very high usage to service them properly.

The published total locomotive stock as at June 30, 1873, was 1,012 which was classed in the following condition in the stock-taking:—in general good order, 894; in moderate order, 97; in bad order, 3; in the shops rebuilding, 8; and broken up for rebuilding, 10. In addition to these there were 46 duplicate engines, making a total of 1,058. The average age of the 1,012 was only 6.47 years, and that of the duplicate engines 19.3. Out of the 97 moderates, however, 37 were almost ready for breaking up. These, including the bad stock gave a total of 40 engines which, plus the duplicates (most of which were nearly worn out), gave no fewer than 86 engines shortly to be unavailable to traffic.

This was not all; whilst Johnson considered that to permit of proper maintenance there should only be 75 per cent. of engines in steam as a maximum, figures that he had extracted showed that in four years since 1869 the percentage had in fact risen from 88 to 94. His request for additional engines was granted. Meanwhile, with the opening of the Settle and Carlisle line looming closer he did what he could to liven up the existing stock. Perhaps the most successful of these was the Kirtley 800 class, 2-4-0s having 6 ft. 8 in. coupled wheels and with outside bearings. Their work on the main line had proved itself to be uniformly good and, as a holding operation pending the arrival of new engines, they were given larger boilers and cylinders and an increased grate area. Ahrons mentions in his *The British Steam Railway Locomotive from 1825 to 1925*, that the 800 class could stand continuous hard work with ease. As rebuilt, the locomotive's weight was increased from 36 tons 3 cwt to 40½ tons, in working order. The 800 class numbered 48 engines, thirty built by Neilson's in 1870 (Nos. 800–829), and twelve built at Derby in the same year (Nos. 165–169 and 60–66). To complete the class Derby built six more the following year (Nos. 3, 22, 23, 93, 138 and 139), the first four of which were sent to work the little North Western. With wider tenders and bigger cabs, the latter replacing the apology provided by Kirtley, the engines were given a new lease of life. All worked on the Midland for many years after; No. 827 lingered on until 1936, thirteen years after the Midland itself had ceased to exist.

Another Kirtley design, the 890 class, also of 2-4-0 wheel arrangement and having 6 ft. 8½ in. coupled drivers, was given larger cylinders and had other minor alterations made, including the provision of a decent cab, and outside bearings to the leading wheels. The first twenty of the class (Nos. 890–909) were built by Neilson's in 1871, the firm turning out five more the following year (Nos. 2, 90, 92, 95 and 125). During 1873–1874 Derby built a further thirty (Nos. 5, 7, 12, 19, 21, 40–49, 67–69, 72, 78, 91, 120, 121, 123, 124, 127, 131, 132, 151 and 152), and another six were added by 1875 (Nos. 126, 128, 130, and 134–136). Like the 800 class they survived many years of work, the last being scrapped in 1938. Of the remaining passenger engines at the Midland's disposal in the year preceding the opening of the Settle line mention should be made of twenty engines designed by Kirtley and built by Sharp, Stewart & Co. in

1874. Again 2-4-0s, they had 6 ft. 2½ in. coupled wheels and were numbered 1070-1089.

As to the better goods engines there were a number of Kirtley 0-6-0 tender design already available. Thirty-six of this type were built at Derby between 1872-1874 and these were supplemented in 1875 by a further one hundred and twenty (Nos. 1142-1251, 381-385, and 400-404). With 4 ft. 10 in. coupled wheels and 17½ in. by 26 in. cylinders, these locomotives were later produced in great numbers for goods working and many survived up to the Grouping of 1923. Fifty of the 1875 batch were built by outside firms; on May 19, 1874, tenders from Dubs & Co. and Kitson's were accepted for thirty engines at £2,375 each and twenty at £2,920 each respectively. To work the goods traffic on the Settle line Nos. 1222-1251 were sent to Carlisle and Leeds.

To complete the picture up to the early part of 1875, the following details, though not strictly applicable to the Settle line, nevertheless show the current locomotive position in the light of Johnson's report of April 1875, as under. On December 15, 1874 tenders were accepted from the Vulcan Foundry and from Neilson's for five engines at £2,135 each, and fifteen at £2,285 each respectively. These were to be goods tank engines for the South Wales traffic. In February of 1875 the Vulcan Foundry was given a further order for ten more of the same type, presumably destined for South Wales though the same class of engine was frequently put to work on shunting duties on the main lines. As to local passenger traffic, Neilson's were given an order in the same month for thirty 0-4-4 passenger tank engines at £2,325 each. These were mostly delivered in 1876 and had 5 ft. 6 in. driving wheels and were provided with cabs —the latter point differentiating them from a series of ten similar engines (Nos. 6, 15, 18, 137, 140-144, and 147) built with 5 ft. 3 in. wheels the previous year. These engines, designed to work the Metropolitan lines from the Midland into Moorgate, were at first cabless. The Neilson tanks of 1876 were numbered 1252-1281.

In April of 1875 Johnson reported again on the locomotive stock. 'The increase in train mileage this half year is greater in proportion than the estimate of it, as made at the beginning of the half year, and there is little doubt that the Liverpool and Settle and Carlisle working will maintain at least the present rate of increase. . . .'. He estimated the number of engines required by the end of 1876 to be 1,375. 'This estimate is based on bringing up the present stock to 1,375 by the end of the year 1876, which I propose should be ordered as under :

For delivery in first half of 1876	Goods engines to be ordered on 4th May 1875	40
	ditto 10 additional	10
For delivery in first half of 1876	4-Coupled express engines	
	to be ordered in June 1875	25
	4 ditto ditto (bogie)	25
For delivery in second half of 1876	Goods engines to be ordered in August next	50
and to be completed in that year		
	Total	150

'This, if carried out, and the increase of mileage is not greater than estimated, will bring our engines in steam to 89% of the stock, and place us in a better position than we now are . . .'.

On May 4 the tenders were in for the forty additional goods engines. Beyer, Peacock & Co. and Neilson & Co. were each given an order for twenty engines. On June 1 Kitson's, Beyer Peacock, and Neilson's were each asked to supply ten goods engines. As to the passenger locomotives, ordered predominantly for the Settle and Carlisle line, thirty were tendered for by Dub's on August 3, 1875, each costing, including their tenders, £2,690. Two were to be delivered within six months, and the rest at four per month thereafter. In actual fact the firm only delivered twenty-eight locomotives. These were 2-4-os, based on the successful Kirtley design and had 6 ft. 6 in. coupled wheels and 17½ in. by 26 in. cylinders. They were numbered 1282–1311. Meanwhile Derby works was concentrated on producing more of the same design and during 1876 ten modified Kirtley 890 class were delivered from the shops (Nos. 1, 9, 10, 13, 70, 71, 73, 74, 96 and 146). With 6 ft. 2½ in. coupled wheels, they were designed specifically for the Settle and Carlisle line, the smaller wheels being thought best to tackle the gradients with the heavy trains the company was preparing to run. As will be seen they did not live up to their designer's expectations. Five more engines, similar to those building by Dubs, came out of Derby, this time with 6 ft. 6 in. wheels (Nos. 50–54), and these were closely followed by a further five of the same 2-4-0 design (Nos. 55–59), but with 6 ft. 8 in. wheels. These, together with the Dubs engines, brought the number of new engines to forty-eight. It will be seen from the report of engines required that twenty-five four-coupled express bogie engines were to have been ordered in June of 1875 but it was not until January of the following year that the locomotive committee noted that ten of such type were required for the Settle and Carlisle line. On February 1, 1876, Kitson's tender was accepted at a price of £2,750 each, delivery to be two within five months and four per month thereafter. The engines were 4-4-os with 6 ft. 6 in. driving wheels and 3 ft. 3 in. bogies. The cylinders were 17½ ins. by 26 ins. The point about the Settle line is interesting as Ahrons says that they were specially intended to run over the heavy gradients and tight curves of the Peak District line from Derby to Manchester. In any case they were the first leading bogie design on the Midland but for some reason were considered unsuccessful as apart from a further twenty of the same type, built the following year by Dubs with 7 ft. drivers for the London–Leeds service, the Midland reverted for some time after to its favoured 2-4-os. The Kitson engines of 1876 were numbered 1312–1321, and the Dubs 1327–1346. With the prospect of the necessity of stabling locomotives at the southern end of the Settle line in the near future, the locomotive committee, as mentioned earlier, gave orders in January, 1876 for a temporary wooden engine shed to be erected at Skipton.

One other item which took much of Johnson's time was that of coal for the new locomotives. In August of 1874 *Herepath's Journal* pointed out that this commodity had cost the Midland, in its locomotive department during the last half-year, £207,163 as against £144,873 in the corresponding previous period. The half-yearly report of the directors noted this point but explained that the reduction which had recently taken place in the price of materials had enabled the company to enter into reduced price contracts for the current period. Whereas the average price per ton was 18s 5¾d, the new contracts, dating from June 30, had reduced this amount by about 7s a ton. Despite the gratification at Derby this was not necessarily a wise decision as the quality of the new coal was sometimes questionable.

Contemporary with putting its internal affairs to right, the Midland was involved in arranging with the Lancashire & Yorkshire Railway the services which would be instituted between the two companies on the opening of the Settle and Carlisle line. The L.Y.R. was at this time slowly disassociating itself from the L.N.W.R. with which it had carried on a coy courtship for some time as already mentioned in an earlier chapter. With the coming of the Settle line it saw great possibilities for new traffic and a complete break from the overbearing attitude of Euston.

On June 2, 1875, Allport met William Thorley, the L.Y.R.'s traffic manager, at Derby. There they hammered out a temporary suggested arrangement for the through traffic pending the opening of the L.Y.R.'s Chatburn and Hellifield line. The main points were that the Midland traffic between the Settle and Carlisle line and L.Y.R. stations was to be exchanged at Skipton, the L.Y.R. to work the traffic between Skipton and Colne at 33⅓ per cent. of the working expenses. The Midland was to have carting agents at L.Y.R. stations. Through passenger fares were to be worked out, the L.Y.R. to carry the local passenger traffic between Skipton and Colne. With these points tentatively agreed it was arranged to leave further discussion to the two companies' superintendents and goods managers, a meeting to be held as soon as possible.

On June 10 T. Collin for the L.Y.R. and Messrs Newcombe and Harrison of the Midland met at Skipton. Collin asked if all the north-south traffic exchanges between the two companies would now take place at Skipton. Newcombe said that he thought at the time that only the Scotch traffic would be exchanged at Skipton but that Allport had not yet made up his mind on this point. In any event it was arranged that the Midland would place representatives at Bolton, Blackburn and Preston. Newcombe asked Collin if he would undertake a service of goods trains in connection with the Settle line and the latter agreed to the proposal, subject to approval by the L.Y.R. board. The services were thereupon agreed in principle. (They are summarized in Appendix X.) The schedules thus minuted to the meeting of June 10 were only intended as a rough outline. They gave the idea though, of what was intended, and a goods service based thereon came into operation on November 1, 1875. Unfortunately the L.Y.R. had a series of chronic bottlenecks in its system which frequently led to delays to the Midland connections. In December the two companies bickered about this, the L.Y.R. countering Midland complaints of general inefficiency by pointing out that L.Y.R. engines were frequently held up at Skipton by the non-appearance of the Midland freights from Carlisle. Harrison remarked quickly that this was nothing to do with the Midland; the fault lay with the northern connections to the Midland at Carlisle. Despite these petty troubles over the goods traffic, there was an overall atmosphere of co-operation, and in any event agreement had been reached during July of 1875 to let the Midland passenger trains into Liverpool from the Settle line as soon as the Chatburn-Hellifield route was ready. This of course meant that Derby would now be able to operate fast through Liverpool–Manchester–Glasgow trains in direct competition with Euston.

From 1873 the Midland and the Glasgow & South Western had been preparing for the opening of the Scotch service. A joint committee had been formed to make overall policy in conjunction with the North British company and in October of 1873 it was decided to seek powers to purchase land for stations in Glasgow. The G.S.W.R. traffic, hitherto worked at Carlisle by the Caledonian, was to be taken over by the Midland as soon as the agreement between the two Scottish companies expired on January 31, 1875. It was agreed that the G.S.W.R. should extend its line to a new and already authorised station at St Enoch, and that a joint goods station at College Street should be constructed, a temporary station to be erected immediately. As to the Glasgow terminus, the City of Glasgow Union Railway—in which the G.S.W.R. and N.B.R. had a joint interest—had received powers in 1864 to make railways which terminated on the north and south banks of the River Clyde. By an agreement between the companies, confirmed in the C.G.U. Act of 1865, on October 6 of that year the G.S.W.R. requested the C.G.U. to make a station at St. Enoch Square, a short distance to the north of the latter's Dunlop Street station, the G.S.W.R. to use Dunlop Street in the meantime. In order to assist the C.G.U. to carry out the works the G.S.W.R. subscribed heavily towards them, the money to be used exclusively on the station. By a further agreement made in August, 1870, the proposed station was to be enlarged, presumably because by then the G.S.W.R. knew that the Settle line was going ahead and the traffic would warrant a larger station. Of course the G.S.W.R. paid a handsome rent for all this and for the time being the Union company, under the direction of the joint Midland and G.S.W.R. committee, went ahead. Meanwhile, at the Carlisle end, an agreement was sought with the N.E.R. as to access over the latter's Newcastle & Carlisle line for G.S.W.R. engines into the Midland's goods yard at Petteril.

On Friday, October 9, 1874, the committee met and recorded that the price of the works at St Enoch, up to platform level, had been agreed with Thomas Brassey, the contractor to the C.G.U. There had been a response from the N.E.R. on the question of G.S.W.R. access to Petteril; Henry Tennant, the N.E.R. general manager, had written from York on September 25 to say that his company was not prepared to grant running powers to the Glasgow company over the N.E.R. but had no objection to its engines working traffic over the line instead of the Midland engines, when the latter company so desired, on arbitration terms. (These were 1s for each loaded vehicle, and 1s for each light engine.) It was therefore agreed to provide temporary accommodation for six G.S.W.R. locomotives at Durran Hill and, as has been seen in the last chapter, this was ready by January 1, 1875, only to be blown down within a month. Perhaps a bit too temporary.

In April of 1875 work at St Enoch had progressed to the point where Brassey had arranged for the roof to be completed by Messrs Handyside & Co. of Derby by July 1, 1876. College Street was another matter. Work there was so slow that William Crouch, the engineer, was told to get a move on. It appeared that the contractor on the job was having some difficulty finding men. Three months later with James Blair, the C.G.U.'s engineer at St. Enoch, reporting that all was going ahead to schedule, the committee decided that the coaches for the new service should be provided by the Midland, the first being the forty-two 54 ft. twelve-wheelers shortly to be constructed, and already mentioned. By October St Enoch was half completed. Blair, who attended a meeting of the committee on October 14, was told to get the station ready for the English and Scotch traffic by March 1 of the following year, the date then fixed for the opening of the Settle line. On December 14 Allport and W. J. Wainwright, the latter the general manager of the G.S.W.R., reported that their respective boards had approved of some 'pictorial placards' which had been prepared and they were authorized to get these ready in time for the start of the service.

January of 1876 was not so happy for there was trouble between the two companies. The Midland was in the process of coming to an agreement with the N.B.R. to hand over a portion—undefined as yet—of the unconsigned traffic for Glasgow to that company, in contravention, according to the G.S.W.R., of the existing G.S.W.R. and Midland traffic agreement. There was a reason behind the Midland's policy; if it did right by the N.B.R., the latter undertook to withdraw its traffic canvassers from England. The North British had frequently managed to consign considerable traffic to the L.N.W.R. which originated west of Leeds and which could have gone by the Midland. The G.S.W.R., however, considered this encroachment into Midland preserves as nothing compared with the loss the Midland and G.S.W.R. joint service would face if the traffic, instead of going to Glasgow by the G.S.W.R., the most direct way, was to be tamely handed over to the N.B.R. to wander all round that company's system. If the Midland dropped the idea, said the

Glasgow board, then the G.S.W.R. would be prepared to join in discussions as to an equitable division of the traffic to and from the Midland system and Scotland, via Carlisle. The idea was contained in a G.S.W.R. board minute read out to Ellis at a slightly strained meeting of the joint committee held on January 13. He accepted it. From the resulting talks stemmed the triple partnership which successfully ran the 'third choice' England–Scotland service from the opening of the Settle and Carlisle line right up to the Grouping of 1923, when the joint committee came to an end. Barring the completion of St Enoch station, everything was now ready for the joint service to start and on March 28 the committee held its last meeting to agree the proposed timetable before it came into effect on May 1. The discussion included the N.B.R. within its scope and hinged on the speeds with which the trains could work over the two companies' systems.

During this time the traffic committee had been getting out details of the train arrangements and stock required to work the Scotch trains. Interest in the new route was high. In the immediate locality of the Settle line people were looking forward to emancipation day. Elsewhere on the system demands were made from local people along the line for new stations. In August, 1875, the Midland received a request for a station again at Low Bentham, on the little North Western, which it agreed to provide; one made the following December for a station at Crossflatts, near Bingley, was not so fortunate.

With the idea of getting the Leeds and Bradford local service into order in time for the through running of the Scotch expresses, the traffic committee decided on February 1, 1876, to arrange it so as to consist of nine trains, each having four first class carriages with three compartments, three third class with five compartments, and two thirds with three compartments and a brake. The trains were to be fitted up with short buffers and drawbar gear similar to that used by the Midland Metropolitan traffic. The line also acquired a new station; that at Frizinghall, opened on February 1, 1875. It was at about this time, by the way, that travellers on the Leeds and Bradford line might have been excused if they had thought they had been suddenly transported to the continent. For the Midland had introduced as an experiment a quite peculiar looking item of rolling stock which must have stuck out like a sore thumb amongst the red coaches. This was a 'continental-green' German railway carriage. Built by Klett & Co. of Nuremberg and supplied in 1872, it contained two first and two second class compartments, was 24 ft. long, 8 ft. 6ins. wide, and 6 ft. 6 ins. high. All the fittings were distinctly Teutonic and possibly with a view to toning down the overall effect it disappeared into Derby works in April of 1873 for some discreet alterations. According to G. A. Sekon it continued running into 1880 and was scrapped in 1886.*

By March of 1876 preparations were in full swing; new sidings at

* *Railway Magazine*, June 1925.

Skipton, for the interchange traffic, had been laid down by the previous October, the timetable was nearly agreed, and on March 14 Allport was able to report to the board on the formation of the trains, the stops and certain speed modifications necessary. There had been some apprehension about the latter aspect; in February it had been reported that some of the goods trains had been delayed at Appleby due to continual failures with the pumping engine for the water supply, sand from the river having got into the pipes. In April agreement was reached with the two northern companies on the timetable to be adopted for the opening; it had also been decided, on the previous January 14, that fares on the Settle and Carlisle line would be calculated on the same principle as the rest of the Midland system. Another request for an additional stop, this time at Low Crossing on the Settle line, was rejected on April 4.

On April 15, 1876, *Herepath's Journal* remarked upon the coming opening of the line :

'This new route to Scotland will be opened for passenger traffic on 1st May next, and a new and efficient service of express and fast trains will be established. A morning and a night express train will be run between St Pancras, Edinburgh and Glasgow, with Pullman cars attached. Express trains will also run to and from Bristol, Bath, Gloucester and Birmingham, in connection with the through service between London and Scotland, and likewise between Liverpool, Manchester, and stations on the Lancashire and Yorkshire line and Skipton in connection with the through service via the new route.'

Just over a fortnight later the line was opened for passenger traffic; the culmination of a sustained campaign for freedom which had lasted nearly twenty years.

XIII

Opening the Line

May Day, 1876, and the start of a new era for the Midland Railway company. At St Pancras station there is a quiet air of optimism and excitement. Far away to the north work is still in progress at St Enoch station but all is ready for the first train to arrive from the south later in the day. At Leicester arrangements are complete for the reception of orders for lunch which the passengers will eat at Normanton, where the fine station refreshment rooms in which it will be served are in readiness. At Skipton, the previous day, a new station has been opened, on which the Midland has expended, together with the new curve and sidings, some £15,000. Beyond Settle Junction the line stands quietly waiting, the wind humming through the telegraph wires, a line which is still new with the spring grass—the contractors' regulation rye grass and white clover—creeping slowly over the raw earthworks. Only goods trains have used it so far; today its fulfilment is to come. Of the stations, with their staff in readiness, Culgaith, Hawes Junction, Dent, Ribblehead, and Settle Junction are not yet completed; Ribblehead is even lacking a name, being known, for the want of something better, as Batty Green. The new line is two miles longer than that via the old Ingleton route, from this day relegated to the status of a mere branch, and one that in Midland eyes leads nowhere. At the same time as the termination of the Ingleton through service comes a parallel withdrawal of the Bradford Pullmans, now wanted for greater work.

As the clock at St Pancras nears the hour of 10.30 a.m. we can follow the correspondent of the *Railway News* as he joins the first train to run right through to Scotland by the Settle and Carlisle line. His account is of interest as it gives an impression of what the public thought of the new Pullmans—the best contemporary Victorian mode of travel. 'A train', he wrote shortly afterwards, 'such as had not before been seen in this, or, indeed, in any other country, for the perfection of its appointments, and for the luxurious ease and comfort provided for the passengers, started from St Pancras precisely at 10.30. It consisted of two Pullman drawing-room cars, resplendent with gilding and colour, named respectively *Juno* and *Britannia*,—and two of the new composite carriages. . . . These are 54 feet in length, and have eight compartments, and (are) supported by two "bogie" kind of six wheels.' The train was drawn by two locomotives.

There appeared to be no outward demonstration that this run was to be anything out of the ordinary. The Midland board had apparently decided to treat the opening service in a quiet and businesslike manner—

'preferring to await the result of experience in working the line rather than indulging in glowing anticipation as to the future'. There followed a laborious description of the scenery through which the train passed until it reached Normanton, the running thereto being 'highly satisfactory'. 'Making allowance for some slight delays, due to the heated axles of some of the new carriages, the run from St Pancras was all that could be desired.' At Normanton the train halted, the Midland having undertaken to guarantee a stop at the station of half an hour for lunch. This interval was considered enough, provided the traveller went 'straight to business'. Messrs Spiers & Pond, the caterers, had things organized with precision efficiency; small handbills, distributed in the train before leaving St Pancras, set out the table d'hôte at Normanton, and the passengers were requested to note, in a space on the bill, the number in each party who wished to have lunch. This was handed to a uniformed attendant on the platform at the Leicester stop and then, while the train continued north, the number was telegraphed ahead to Normanton and the appropriate lunches prepared. In fact the company was engaged in extending the dining facilities at Normanton; in April John Garlick's tender for a new dining room had been accepted at a cost of £3,081, and a further extension was to be ordered on May 16, presumably the popularity of the luncheon stop having taken the company unawares.

As the bogie Pullmans and carriages, with their new and strange wheel rhythm, slowly glided into Normanton station the soup was already hot in the plates. A general bustle in the direction of the refreshment rooms followed, though some sought the toilets, as the new Midland Scotch stock had as yet no such facilities. Meanwhile, in the lofty refreshment rooms, neat waitresses—remarked upon with pleasure by the *News* correspondent as being a sight better than 'greasy waiters'— tripped to and fro putting the next courses ready on the table. Not a minute was lost as the steadily munching Victorian faces disposed of :

SPRING SOUP

SALMON CUTLETS	SAUCE TARTARE
LAMB CUTLETS	GREEN PEAS
FILLETS OF BEEF LARDED	SAUCE PIQUANTE
JELLIES	CREAMS
CHEESE	SALAD

In fact everything went so smoothly that the correspondent hoped, in an apparently heartfelt way, that Spiers & Pond would now begin to turn their attention to reorganizing railway station breakfasts in similar manner. The rest of the description covered the route to Carlisle, where the train divided, a Pullman for each part, to Edinburgh and Glasgow. A locomotive exchange must have taken place at Leeds, where the train would be reversed, but the *News* man did not comment on this.

After his description of the run, during which it is of interest to note that the hot boxes which were to plague Scotch expresses for some time had appeared right at the start, the correspondent got down to describing the rolling stock. He noted that an important feature in connection with the opening of the new line was that Pullmans were to be attached to several of the trains and run through the whole distance. They were seen for the first time, he said, by hundreds of spectators along the route. One wonders what the people of Kirkby Stephen and Appleby must have thought as these magnificent vehicles purred through, so used as they were to the archaic coaches of the North Eastern Railway. The correspondent harped again and again on the luxurious feeling of the two Pullmans. Though neither was a sleeping car, he felt impelled to describe for his readers what such a conveyance was like. It had, he said, one large compartment and two smaller ones, the latter serving as private sitting and bedrooms for those wanting 'exclusion'.

'The large compartment, a beautiful saloon about 26 feet long, exceedingly well lighted, and equally well ventilated, has during the day two rows of seats, with a table between the seats of each pair. By a series of very ingenious mechanical appliances all that is necessary to transform the saloon into a sleeping carriage is to remove the tables and convert each pair of opposite seats into a bed, while a second bed is formed above by letting down a shelf, which, looking like a part of the ornamental ceiling, hangs obliquely against the roof of the carriage. The mattresses and bed linen, all exquisitely neat and proper, are, during the daytime, stowed away on the upper shelf, while a box below the seats holds the pillows. All the seats and couches are covered in Utrecht velvet, while the whole of the woodwork is of American walnut, which looks very chaste as a background of much tasteful gilding and painting. Numerous other comforts, great and little, including a system of warming by hot water pipes, and abundance of curtains, and lavatories for both ladies and gentlemen, raise travelling in the Pullman Palace Train from a fatigue into a positive pleasure.
'But, apart from all the luxurious upholstery and the many contrivances which add to the comfort of the temporary inhabitants of the travelling palace, there are two other things which make the Pullman Train the perfection of all railway trains. The first is the admirable service of the carriages. There are no porters taking delight in opening and slamming doors, either playfully or dutifully asking for tickets, but in their stead act well-trained servants in livery, polite and courteous, obeying the behests of Mr Pullman's guests and patrons as if waiting upon Mr Pullman himself. This is a change which must be felt to be appreciated.'

His second point was that of the great smoothness and quietness due to the bogies. There was, as remarked on when the Bradford Pullmans began running, a virtual freedom from the usually inescapable noise of the ordinary railway carriage of the time, compared with which a Pullman in motion, to the Victorian ear, could only be, according to the correspondent, 'faintly described in words'. He continued : 'A bed in a Pullman car means an actual place to sleep. Indeed it is asserted on good authority that there are persons who, like the great German Chancellor, suffering from insomnia, find immediate relief during a night's trip in a Pullman sleeping car.' There was complete tranquility at high speed. Even at stops, where some of the passengers alighted, there was an absence of the usual shouting. The Pullman attendants were always softly hovering about, whispering assurances to sleepy passengers, and quietly awakening those who had to leave the train at some dim, dark station during the journey.

He was no less enthusiastic about the sleeping cars' sister vehicles :

'The drawing room car is a large saloon, fifty eight feet long and nine feet broad, divided into several compartments, a main or general saloon upwards of thirty feet long, two private rooms with couches and armchairs, each about six feet long, and various smaller chambers forming lavatories. The main saloon, an altogether magnificent apartment, superbly painted, decorated, and mirrored, with plate glass windows, from the ceiling to the bottom (*sic*), has sixteen arm-chairs, eight on each side, with a passage between them. The chairs, covered in scarlet velvet, with handsome anti-macassars against the backs, swing on pivots all round, and the sitter, therefore, may turn his face whichever way he chooses, towards the windows on either side, backward or forward, the seat fastening, by the touch of a spring, whenever desired. By the touch of another spring the chairs fall back to any angle down to forty-five degrees, allowing, with feet on stool, any amount of comfortable position or change of position. Thus, reclining in the most luxurious ease, with the daylight moderated or increased at will by self-acting curtains (roller blinds)—one of the thousand cunning devices to be found in the Pullman cars, which really show the strain of ingenious thought in every nook and corner, being, so to speak, brimful of brains—the traveller may survey the landscape under a sense of enjoyment from which nothing detracts.'

This then, was the end product of all the struggle and anxiety of past years; the Midland had at last got its independent service to Scotland. And it had got it in style. From May 1 the L.Y.R. ran connecting passenger and goods trains to the new Scotch service. Notes on the passenger side were given by Mr Walter Laidlaw, writing in the *Railway Magazine* of November, 1930 :

'Upon that date through carriages were run from Liverpool at 9.00 a.m. and 2.00 p.m. to Glasgow, returning at 10.15 a.m. and 2.30 p.m., and from Man-chester at 9.25 a.m. and 2.20 p.m. for Edinburgh, returning at 10.25 a.m., 2.35 p.m. and 4.25 p.m. The trains from Manchester ran through to Skipton, the through carriages for Edinburgh being at the front of the train. At Accrington the Glasgow coach from Liverpool was attached in front of the Edinburgh one and placed next to the engine. After arrival at Skipton (by the morning train) these two vehicles were attached in the rear of the 10.32 a.m. train from Leeds to Carlisle, and this arrangement continued until the end of May, 1880.'

June of 1880 was to see the opening of the L.Y.R.'s Chatburn–Helli-field line and a consequent alteration in the connecting services. This was in the future though, and will figure later in the story. In 1876, wor-king in partnership with the N.B.R. and G.S.W.R., the Midland had produced a service which appealed to the public, and provided such comfort, as well as an attractive scenic route so beloved by the Vic-torians, that King's Cross and Euston cannot have been other than extremely apprehensive that their long-standing pre-eminence in the East and West Coast routes respectively would suffer. It was Euston that was bound to feel the draught the most though and, to digress for a moment, it is of interest to trace the steps the L.N.W.R. had taken, in alliance with the Caledonian Railway, from the first moment it had become certain of the growing threat from Derby, back in 1869.

The West Coast companies had formed a committee, called the West

Coast Conference, and an examination of the minutes of its meetings since 1869 shows a steady attempt to forge a traffic pattern inimical to Midland interests, one which the committee obviously hoped would be able to withstand the lure of the latter's Settle and Carlisle service. That this policy failed was as much due to the disenchantment which the L.Y.R. began to feel towards Euston after the two companies' amalgamation hopes had been dashed by Parliament in the early 1870s, as to the Midland's own traffic arrangements.

On April 29, 1869, barely a fortnight after the L.N.W.R. and Midland joint Bill for the abandonment of the Settle line had been thrown out in Parliament, the West Coast committee met and instructed J. Fitzsimons, the L.N.W.R.'s district goods manager at Lancaster, to meet officers of the L.Y.R. in an attempt to agree a method of working the Yorkshire–Scotland traffic via Preston. At the same time the Caledonian representatives at the meeting agreed to remove their canvassing agent from Derby—the heart of what was now enemy territory but not so important trafficwise—to the neighbourhood of Leeds, a far more dangerous area for the Midland. There they were to solicit for Scotch traffic from the Leeds and Bradford district, to be sent north via the L.Y.R. and Preston. By July 1, 1869, the arrangements had been completed and as much traffic as could be legitimately cajoled into going north by this route was soon on its way. Thus early on was the struggle started. Meanwhile, at a meeting in Liverpool on June 1, George Findlay, the L.N.W.R. goods manager, and Messrs Kay and Taylor, the company's district goods managers for Manchester and Liverpool, met Collin—a gentleman from the L.Y.R. whom we have already met—to fish some more waters in Yorkshire, those of Halifax, Bradford, and Wakefield, and as before it was agreed to divert all the traffic from these areas via Preston. In fact an overall policy was agreed that traffic between Scotland and L.N.W.R. stations east of Manchester should be forwarded via Preston instead of Leeds. As to the Sheffield, Rotherham, and Barnsley traffic, this was to be sent via Guide Bridge to Preston. There, for the time being, the matter rested.

Two years later, with the Settle line being pushed doggedly forward, and with the unpleasant knowledge that something new was stirring in the Midland carriage department at Derby, the committee was forced to reconsider its own carriage stock. It decided on twenty-two new vehicles, to be added to the existing stock, thus bringing it to :

No. of vehicles	Description	Compartments			
		1st	2nd	3rd	Luggage
18	Double composites	2	2	—	1
6	ditto	3	1	—	1
30	Tri-composites	2	1	1	1
7	ditto	1	1	2	1
14	Third class	—	—	4	1
25	Guard's brake van	—	—	—	—
100					

Considerable care was taken to see that the new coaches rivalled those of the Midland. Much was made of the arm rests, fixed and folding, to be found in the new first class stock. When constructed, however, the new vehicles caused some irritating delays at Carlisle for a time; they were too long to use the traversers. To get in first with sleeping cars became of prior importance. In November, 1871, the committee noted that a new sleeping carriage was being constructed experimentally by the L.N.W.R. for the Holyhead traffic and it was agreed to watch how the public responded. By mid 1873 it was obvious that the West Coast route would have to have its quota of sleeping cars if it was to hope to compete with the Midland, and in September the L.N.W.R. and Caledonian agreed to make a coach each, the vehicles to become part of the West Coast joint stock. Meanwhile, though some of the committee were not too happy with the design of the Holyhead vehicle, it was agreed to transfer it to the Euston–Glasgow run from October 1, the coach to be attached to the up and down limited mail train and the fee per seat to be 10s. In mid November it was reported that the number of passengers using this carriage during the month of October was, down to Scotland 53, and up from Scotland 44, giving a return of £48 10s in addition to the ordinary fares. At a meeting of the committee on November 14 Finlay stated that the L.N.W.R. was building a second sleeping saloon, to be part of the West Coast joint stock, with a view to inaugurating a nightly service in both directions between London and Glasgow. It appears, however, that this particular vehicle took some time to construct; at a meeting on October 31, 1874, the committee noted that only three vehicles were then in use and one was being built. It was recommended that two more should be made, bringing the total to six, all on the West Coast joint account. Just to show that the committee meant business it was decided to run up the colours, for on the same day orders were given for the West Coast arms and monogram to be painted on all its passenger stock, 'including third class carriages'. By this time receipts from the sleeping vehicles were averaging £75–80 per month on the down journeys, and £35–40 on the up.

Having, it hoped, catered for the first class passenger, the committee proceeded to consolidate its position respecting the third class. Almost exactly a year before the Settle and Carlisle line was due to be opened, the committee decided to counter the Midland's avowed intention of permitting third class passengers on all its through Scotch trains by speeding up from June of 1875 the L.N.W.R. main line trains and putting third class accommodation on to the 10 a.m. up and down expresses between London and Edinburgh. (In fact the Midland's joint assault on the established Scotch routes—the Settle and Carlisle line, and the abolition of second class—had a similar effect on the Great Northern for that company speeded up the 'Flying Scotsman' in response.) Euston was facing a kaleidoscope of change all the time now. On July 22, 1875, the committee read a letter it had received from the G.S.W.R. which imparted the news that on and after the coming August 2 goods traffic between the G.S.W.R. and the Midland would be exchanged at Carlisle, instead of at Ingleton. 'Resolved : Midland and Glasgow & South Western to pay tolls.' Any tolls, that is, which could be got from the two companies at Carlisle. Turning to the Caledonian, as if it too, old faithful as it was, seemed about to desert, Euston made quite sure that the latter's traffic would continue to use the Ingleton line when necessary. On the same date that the G.S.W.R. letter was read, another horrid thought struck the committee; perhaps the opening of the Settle line would necessitate a general reduction of fares. November of 1875 came, and the committee noted that the Midland was to start a regular goods service in connection with the L.Y.R., now gone way beyond recall, between Liverpool, Manchester and Scotland, from November 1. Finally, knowing that Pullmans were to be introduced on the Settle line from the very first, the L.N.W.R. traffic committee decided on January 19, 1876, to attach something similar to the 10 a.m. up and down trains already mentioned and the West Coast committee gave its approval on February 8, 1876, for the building of four experimental saloon coaches.

To the Midland all this, with memories of Captain Huish, must have been sweet revenge. Here was the L.N.W.R. chasing about, reducing its fares to Carlisle and scratching around for Scotch traffic in a way that was delightful to see. One final little march was stolen; on May 12, just over a week after the Settle line came into operation for passenger traffic, the committee agreed that as the Midland had adopted a charge of 8s per sleeping berth in the Pullman cars, the 10s charge made by the West Coast route would have to be brought into line. Further, bed linen and sheets were to be provided and, from the following June 1, an attendant allotted to each West Coast sleeping car. Here then, in the Midland Railway company, was personified for a short time a fine example of a latter day nineteenth century pace-setter.

The question of the fares was brought up by the *Railway News* of May 6, 1876, in an article which gave the up-to-date position of the English-Scotch services of the three contending companies :

'As will be seen from the table below there are now fourteen trains running each way daily between London and Edinburgh and Glasgow. The daily mileage of these trains would be about 15,000 miles, and to carry on the service at least one hundred locomotives and seven hundred carriages are employed. A few years since the travelling between London and Edinburgh was represented by little more than the stage coaches, which started each evening from the Post Offices of London and Edinburgh, performing the journey in about fifty hours, instead of the nine and a half as at present.'

The article went on to give the table as follows; the arrival times shown being for Edinburgh :

LONDON AND NORTH WESTERN
From Euston—Six Trains

	1	2	3	4	5	6
Dep.	5.15 a.m.	7.15 a.m.	10.00 a.m.	11.00 a.m.	8.40 p.m.	9.00 p.m.
Arr.	4.40 p.m.	5.50 p.m.	8.25 p.m.	9.00 p.m.	6.50 a.m.	7.50 a.m.

(Fastest train 10 hrs. 10 mins.; slowest 11 hrs.)

GREAT NORTHERN
From Kings Cross—Five trains

	1	2	3	4	5
Dep.	5.15 a.m.	10.00 a.m.	10.35 a.m.	8.30 p.m.	9.00 p.m.
Arr.	8.35 p.m.	7.25 p.m.	8.45 p.m.	6.00 a.m.	7.40 a.m.

(Fastest train 9 hrs. 30 mins.; slowest 15 hrs. 20 mins.)

MIDLAND
From St. Pancras—Three Trains

	1	2	3
Dep.	5.15 a.m.	10.30 a.m.	9.15 p.m.
Arr.	5.10 p.m.	9.15 p.m.	7.45 a.m.

(Fastest train 10 hrs. 30 mins.; slowest 11 hrs. 55 mins.)

From the above it will be seen that the Midland took third place in the race to Edinburgh and, in the case of Glasgow, the result was the same, the fastest train running from Euston in 10 hours and 30 minutes while both the Midland and the G.N.R. took 20 minutes longer. The *News* was quick to point out, however, that though there were sleeping saloons by the 8.40 p.m. from Euston to Glasgow, and by the 8.30 p.m. from King's Cross to Edinburgh, neither company could run anything better to compete with the Pullmans. And there, as Allport had known it would be, was the Midland's strength. There had been threatened at one time, said the *News,* another rate war as soon as the Settle and Carlisle was opened but the good sense of the companies had prevailed and the fares during the first week of May were steady as follows :

	Edinburgh	Glasgow
First single	57s. 6d.	58s. od.
Third single	32s. 8d.	33s. od.
First return	109s. 6d.	110s. 3d.
Third return	62s. 8d.	62s. 11d.

Supplements were: for the Pullmans and sleeping coaches 8s. extra, and for the Pullman drawing room cars 7s. extra.

At the end of the first week's operating *Herepath's Journal* came out with a statement of the traffic carried on the Midland as a whole during the period. On the goods side there was a loss showing over the same period of the previous year, due in the main to coal strikes in Derbyshire and Yorkshire. On the passenger side, however, there was an increase of £2,000. The journal thought that this must be a reflection on the opening of the Settle line. As to the competitors, the L.N.W.R. showed a decrease of £3,273 while the G.N.R., which was not affected so much, showed a general increase of £3,722 in the week. No great point can be made with these figures, however; they are altogether too general. Much more pertinent are the figures given by George Findlay to the L.N.W.R.'s traffic committee on May 17, 1876. These were the returns of the receipts between Euston and Edinburgh and Glasgow during the first fortnight in May and they showed a falling off, compared with the same period in 1875, of £443 in the Glasgow passengers and an increase of those to Edinburgh of £22. In a later statement made in June, and covering the whole of May, it was seen that the number of passenger receipts booked from Euston, Birmingham, Liverpool, and Manchester, to Carlisle, compared with the 1875 figure, had fallen by £1,321. The L.N.W.R. was without doubt worried; in October of 1876 the traffic committee was even to suggest speeding up the West Coast trains by increasing the rate of ascent over Shap summit, the idea being to withdraw the banking engines from Tebay and let them get a run at the gradient all the way from Oxenholme. For the time being, however, having seen the almost immediate effect that the Settle and Carlisle line had upon the authorities at Euston, let us see how it was received in the southern part of the area through which it ran.

The *Craven Herald* of April 22, 1876, noted that during the past week the London and provincial newspapers had announced the intended opening. Apparently an experimental train with Pullman drawing room and sleeping cars attached and hauled by one of the Midland's new engines, fitted with the Westinghouse brake, had run over the line on the previous Thursday, April 20. The paper considered it remarkable that the trip from Skipton to Carlisle, done in 2 hours and 5 minutes, had averaged a speed of 43 m.p.h. At Skipton, the town was pleased with its new station. A reporter from the *Craven Herald*, writing in the issue of April 29, had quite a lot to say on the subject :

'The Skipton new railway station has attained a stage of completion sufficient to warrant the directors in opening it tomorrow (Sunday) when the business of the station will be transferred to it from the old building. The opening of the Settle and Carlisle line on the following day, and additional trains to Colne &c., necessitate the adoption of such a step, perhaps earlier than otherwise would have been the case, and we doubt not from the general appearance of the new building, the change will be as beneficial as its want has hitherto been felt. Since its commencement the erection of the new building has progressed rapidly, although it is only recently that this has been more apparent.'

The reporter was shown round the station by Mr Vicars, the clerk of works, and obviously gained a good impression. He noted the bass relief of a 'Griffin' on the station front and remarked that this—the company's crest—was one of the only 'pretensions to ornament' that the station could boast of. He thought that as regards architectural beauty, the new station was inferior to the old in point of its size but 'the contractor seems to have concentrated all his energies in making the place commodious and convenient, rather than ornamental'. It was indeed much more fitted to the coming traffic than was the old. 'The platform ... is very spacious, its length being between 700 and 800 feet. It is covered with glass set in an iron framework. There is also a middle platform similar to that at the old station, from the off side of which, we were informed, the Colne trains will start.'

A week later the paper reported upon the opening of the station and remarked that a large crowd assembled to see the first train leave. 'The station master's son, Fred Wilcock, booked the first passenger and with this slight exception, all ceremony was dispensed with.'

This lack of ceremony was a feature which ran through the next day too, the opening day of the Settle and Carlisle line. In fact one detects a note of antagonism in some of the articles which appeared in the *Craven Herald* of May 6. Not necessarily against the company but against any form of bally-hoo. The line had, after all, been an awful long time coming. The main article dealt with the factual history of the need for the line, the L.N.W.R. versus the Midland, and the Parliamentary struggles which had lead to the Settle line being built. It went into a long travelogue, detailing the views and scenery that could be had from the line, and it fully covered the civil engineering details, making much play with Ribblehead viaduct. The total length of the structure was given as being 1,328 feet. The loftiest of the 24 arches measured 165 feet from the foundations to the parapet. The viaduct was said to contain 34,000 cubic yards of masonry and 6,000 cubic feet of concrete. The piers, nearly all 45 feet apart, were 13 feet thick at the base and 6 feet thick at the springing of the arches. For the most part they rested on a bed of concrete 6 feet thick and laid on to solid rock. 'Every sixth pier, however, partly as a means of increasing the strength of the work and partly for increasing the beauty of its appearance, is eighteen feet thick at the top instead of six.' The extra thickness of these piers seemed to the paper to break what would otherwise be a monotony and greatly improved the appearance of the viaduct when viewed at a distance. A note of interest as to Blea Moor was that the paper claimed that £50 a month had been spent on candles to light the working faces of the tunnel during construction. In its local news section the paper noted that there were now no fewer than 52 trains passing through Skipton daily. There was not too much interest evinced though; this item was placed hidden away next to one which remarked that the cuckoo had been heard in many parts of the district. Further up the line the reception was altogether better, people crowding on to the stations to cheer the trains.

At Settle itself there was no public demonstration. The reporter was indeed slightly cynical; he evinced the symptoms of having had a headache at the time :

'The national standard on Castleburgh, and two or three private colours were the only signs that the day was recognized as being more noteworthy than the dull routine of its fellows. Still the first train was received by a pretty numerous company at the station, and each succeeding train during the day had its select knot of admirers. A few enthusiasts made the trip to Carlisle, and they speak of the wonders of the road. The local passenger traffic is still of very meagre dimensions, many of the trains passing Settle with almost as many carriages as passengers. The Pullman trains, however, seem to be well patronized, and heavily laden goods trains follow each other at very short intervals. The junction is not ready for use, consequently the old station has had its life lengthened for a short time, and Longpreston (*sic*) is used as a junction at present.'

After saying that the proximity of the new Settle station to the town was a boon the reporter got the following of his chest :

'We hear great complaints of bad arrangements made at Settle for the goods and cattle traffic. It is patent to the most ordinary observer that the goods warehouse and the cattle docks have both been formed without the slightest regard to their easy working. The plans cannot possibly have been made or inspected by anyone having the slightest pretensions to being practically acquainted with goods or mineral traffic. The oversight no doubt will lead at no distant period to a large outlay of money, which half an hour's conversation with any of the humblest officials at Settle would have prevented. The entrance to the booking office is also planned as awkwardly as it well could be, being out of sight, round a corner, and nothing to guide a stranger to its whereabouts. The simple removal of the door to the opposite side would remedy this defect at small cost.'

And there he stopped. Nothing about the town now being on the Midland main line to Scotland, a position which could bring nothing but benefits; just a general beef about the facilities offered. Perhaps it wasn't a headache; perhaps he had shares in the L.N.W.R. In any event, regarding Settle, his comments were at variance with an article which had appeared in *The Engineer* the previous July : 'A commodious station and extensive yard have been erected at Settle, much more convenient to the public and the grazing business than the old station above a mile from the town'.

We will leave the *Craven Herald* at its issue of May 13. This noted two events : the first was the opening of the Appleby Agricultural Auction Market on the coming Monday, May 29, 1876, an event advertised in the paper by John Kidd of Appleby, with details of the Midland company's new goods and cattle service which would afford many better facilities; and the second dealt with one of those people who, for the satisfaction of some vague enjoyment in useless statistics, nearly always turn up to declaim on some aspect of new versus old. This one concerned himself with Skipton station :

'Some people have been puzzling themselves a good deal of late as to the difference of time in walking to the old railway station and to the new one. A gentleman on whom we can place some reliance took the trouble the other morning of walking over the distance to both stations making the Ship Corner his starting point, and he found that it took him exactly a minute and a half longer to go to the new station than it did to the old one.'

So there it was. Perhaps the local papers in Cumberland and Westmorland dealt slightly less flippantly with the new line. One of the reasons for the seeming lack of official enthusiasm was that the Craven district had always had a service of sorts to the north. This may be so; it is also likely that the further north the line went the more welcome it became. In any event we will return now to the affairs of the Midland, particularly the early years of the Settle line's operating.

I (*Top*) Leeds Wellington station, c.1910; (*centre*) Calverley & Rodley station, looking east, with 2–4–0 No 80 on a down express, c.1908; (*bottom*) Thackley tunnels, west end, c.1905. (*D. F. Tee collection*)

II (*Top*) Bradford Forster Square station and Midland Hotel, c.1905; (*bottom*) Bradford Forster Square station, looking north, with No 42145 shunting, May 6, 1967. (*Author's collection; D. F. Tee*)

III (*Top*) Leeds–Morecambe DMU train leaving Shipley main line platform, April 3, 1986;
(*bottom*) Morecambe–Leeds train leaving Saltaire station, April 3, 1986. (*Author*)

IV (*Top*) Last day of the old station at Bingley, closed 1892; (*centre*) Bingley station, looking north, c.1905; (*bottom*) Keighley station main line platforms, looking north-west, c.1910. (*D. F. Tee* collection)

V (*Top*) Steeton & Silsden station, looking east, c.1902, 0–4–4 tank arriving on down train; (*centre*) Kildwick & Crosshills station, looking west, c.1910; (*bottom*) 4–4–0 No 449 on up passenger train near Cononley, c.1923. (*D. F. Tee collection, top and centre; L & GRP/David & Charles*)

VI (*Top*) W. H. Smith bookstall at Skipton station, thought to be October 1908; (*bottom*) Class 4 No 75041 passing through Skipton station on up tank train, DMU for Colne at Platform 3, September 19, 1966. (*D. F. Tee collection; Author*)

VII Hellifield in its prime, c.1906: (*top*) South Junction and signal box, looking north-west; (*bottom*) down platform, looking north-west, showing Midland Railway monogram in the canopy ironwork. (*D. F. Tee collection*)

VIII (*Top*) Old Midland Railway Pullman car body at Hellifield, August 1964; (*centre*) Long Preston station, looking south-east, with unidentified Class 5 heading the 11.58 ex Hellifield stopping train to Carlisle, March 19, 1965; (*bottom*) Settle Junction, looking north, with remains of old station, September 3, 1964. (*Author*)

IX (*Top and centre*) 'Rationalisation' at Giggleswick: the up platform looking south on September 24, 1963, and as the 17.11 Leeds commuter train (15.50 ex Hull) arrives on April 3, 1986; (*bottom*) Ingleton Midland station, looking north, with the branch freight (Class 4 No 43042), June 22, 1964. (*Author*)

X (*Top*) Bentham station, looking east, c.1905; (*centre*) Wennington station on August 7, 1965: No 45204 on 11.05 Leeds City–Barrow, D5201 on 12.30 Morcambe Promenade–Leeds City, 12.20 Carnforth–Leeds City through carriages in bay to be attached to 12.30 ex Morecambe; (*bottom*) Halton station, looking east, August 19, 1967. (*D. F. Tee collection; D. F. Tee, centre and bottom*)

XI (*Top*) Lancaster Green Ayre station, looking south-west, April 28, 1965; (*bottom*) the Midland's Lune viaduct at Lancaster, with former LNWR Siemens three car open set EMU, re-equipped for 6,250V ac operation, September 24, 1963. (*Author*)

XII (*Top*) Morecambe Old Pier and railway; (*bottom*) Morecambe Promenade station (to right), signal gantry and box, October 1907. (*Martin Bairstow collection; Roy Anderson collection*)

XIII (*Top*) Morecambe Promenade station, October 1907; (*bottom*) Heysham station, c.1905. (*Roy Anderson collection; D. F. Tee collection*)

XIV (*Top*) Settle station, looking north, June 22, 1964; (*bottom*) With Pen-y-ghent in the background, 47 589 heads south at Helwith Bridge with a return special from Carlisle to Yarmouth, March 31, 1984. (*Author; Dr W. A. Sharman*)

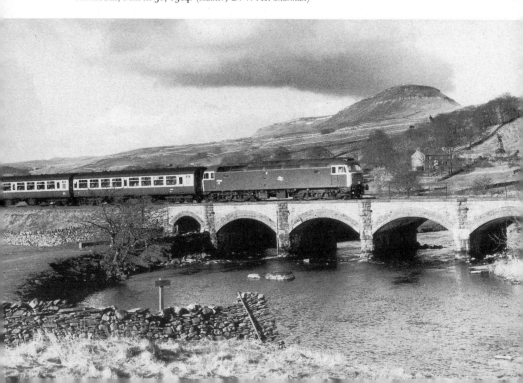

XV Ribblehead viaduct is dominated by Whernside as the 09.55 ex Liverpool to Glasgow headed by a Class 47 travels north on its diverted route, April 2, 1983. (*Dr W. A. Sharman*)

XVI (*Top*) After emerging from Blea Moor tunnel 45 107 heads north over Dent Head viaduct with the 09.07 ex Leeds to Carlisle, April 28, 1984; (*bottom*) 47 413 crosses Arten Gill viaduct with the diverted 07.10 ex Glasgow to London on April 2, 1983. (*Dr W. A. Sharman*)

XVII The seasons at Dent: (*top*) the cutting north of the station during the great blizzard of February 1947, looking south; (*bottom*) with snow fences a mute reminder but now in mid afternoon summer sunshine 40 158 heads a down mineral train through the station, July 8, 1977. (*By courtesy of the National Railway Museum, York; Martin S. Welch*)

XVIII (*Top*) 2–6–2 tank No 41206 on 12.46 Bradford Forster Square to Hawes at Garsdale station, April 24, 1954; (*bottom*) 47 442 leaves Garsdale station past the old turntable with the 15.55 Leeds–Carlisle, July 5, 1984. (*A. C. Gilbert; Dr W. A. Sharman*)

XIX (*Top*) No 47 537 heads the 06.55 ex Glasgow to Nottingham past the derelict Ais Gill signal box, Wild Boar Fell beyond, January 23, 1982; (*bottom*) on April 30, 1966, Class 5 No 44902, complete with snowplough, takes an up freight over Ais Gill viaduct. (*Dr W. A. Sharman; Martin S. Welch*)

XX (Top) '1282' class 2–4–0 piloting '2203' class 4–4–0 on an up express approaching Ais Gill, c.1901–2; (*bottom*) Two preserved locomotives, Midland Compound 4–4–0 No 1000 and LMS 'Jubilee' class 4–6–0 No 5690 *Leander*, double-heading the southbound 'Cumbrian Mountain Pullman' through Kirkby Stephen on February 12, 1983. (*D. F. Tee collection; Martin S. Welch*)

XXI (*Top*) Kirkby Stephen West, looking north, June 10, 1967, with the 16.40 Skipton–Carlisle passing the 16.41 Carlisle–Skipton; (*bottom*) 45 132 takes a special charter train south through Culgaith bound for Leeds, April 21, 1984. (*D. F. Tee; Dr W. A. Sharman*)

XXII Carlisle Citadel station; (*top*) at the turn of the century two immaculate Midland locomotives, a 2–4–0 piloting a 4–4–0, wait to leave with an up Scotch express; (*bottom*) 'Jubilee' class No 45705 *Seahorse* with the 08.05 for Hellifield, September 24, 1963. (*Author's collection; Author*)

XXIII Successful preservation: (*top*) Keighley & Worth Valley Railway oil-burning 0-6-0 saddle-tank *Brussels* with Keighley-Oxenhope train at Haworth station, March 1984; (*bottom*) the magnificent Stanier Pacific, No 46229 *Duchess of Hamilton* thunders north at Blea Moor on the 'Cumbrian Mountain Express', October 29, 1983. (*Martin Bairstow, Dr W. A. Sharman*)

XXIV 'By public demand': (*top*) at Lazonby on August 3, 1985 the crowded DalesRail DMU arrives from Carlisle at 17.40, heading south; (*bottom*) down DMU enters busy Appleby station, April 4, 1986. (*Dr W. A. Sharman; Author*)

XIV

The Early Years

1876 – 1883

The Settle and Carlisle line had only been open a short time when on June 20, 1876, at a meeting of the Midland traffic committee, the question was raised of excluding local traffic from the Scotch expresses. After some discussion it was agreed that during the summer months local traffic should not be carried between London–Bedford, Bedford–Leicester, Leicester–Trent, Leicester–Nottingham and the north eastern district, Sheffield and Leeds–Bradford, by the down day train; or between Nottingham–Leicester, Trent–Leicester, and Bedford–London by the up day train. Also the down night train would not carry local traffic between London–Bedford, and Bedford–Leicester.

It might perhaps be best before describing the further general history of the company regarding the Settle line to look at the timetable as shown in *Bradshaw,* and the motive power as it was in July of 1876, the first summer of operation. Fuller details of the locomotives mentioned have already been given to an extent in Chapter XII. Though not distinguishing the Leeds and Bradford service from the strictly Leeds to the north and Bradford to the north trains, but looking at the service from the passengers' point of view, the July timetable provides a base on which later alterations can be noted.

Taking the down trains first, the earliest on weekdays to travel over the Leeds & Bradford line and on to the Settle and Carlisle section was the Pullman sleeping car express which left St Pancras at 9.15 p.m. the previous evening, reached Derby at 11.55, departed from Leeds at 2.08 a.m., and connected at 2.27 at Shipley with the 2.15 a.m. from Bradford. On reaching Skipton at 2.49 a.m. the train split, the Edinburgh portion leaving at 2.55 and running non-stop to Carlisle, which it reached at 4.55 a.m. Engines stationed at Skipton which would have been available to take either this or the following Glasgow portion on to Carlisle included any of the ten 1876 built modified Kirtley 890 class. As already mentioned the wheels were of a smaller diameter than was usual, this being thought better for a heavily graded line. In fact, however, these particular engines seem never to have done well on the Settle line, breaking crank axles at an alarming rate, and were removed in about 1879 and sent to Nottingham. Between Normanton and Skipton the Scotch trains were worked by the 890 class Nos. 900–904, fitted with the Westinghouse brake for the purpose. They were heavy trains, the usual load being two Pullmans, three 12-wheeled bogie carriages and three eight-wheelers, three six-wheelers, and several vans.

Having arrived at Carlisle, the Edinburgh portion was then handed over to the North British Railway and taken on to its destination where it arrived at 7.35 a.m., making connections for Dundee (arr. 11.20 a.m.), Perth (arr. 10.00 a.m.), Aberdeen (arr. 4.05 p.m.), and Inverness (arr. 6.25 p.m.). That it got even as far as Edinburgh in reasonable time was due to the fact that the North British locomotive department had been desperately getting together some motive power which could tackle the Pullmans ever since they had first been mooted. The department was concerned about the problems involved in running a heavy train over the Waverley route, at competitive speeds, when the line itself had heavy gradients, 1 in 70 being the steepest, and sharp curves; Ahrons called it the hardest express route in the country. When Dugald Drummond became locomotive superintendent of the N.B.R. in the early part of 1875 he had immediately put his mind to the Pullman problem. The result was a bogie 4-4-0 design with 6 ft. 6 in. coupled wheels. Four such locomotives were delivered from Neilson's in 1876 and ran the Waverley route Pullmans, though whilst awaiting their appearance the company had perforce, for a few weeks after the opening of the Settle line, to entrust the Edinburgh portion to an earlier 4-4-0 design of 1873, N.B.R. No. 421, specially fitted with the Westinghouse brake so as to take the Midland coaches. The whole question of brakes and rolling stock for the Scotch service is dealt with separately in a later chapter. Suffice it to say now that in 1876 the Midland was experimenting with various types of brake and had decided on the Westinghouse for its Scotch trains. As this particular chapter takes us up to 1883 it will not go amiss to clear the North British locomotive deck at this stage, as four more of the Drummond 4-4-0s were built by Neilson's in 1878, two of which were sent on to the Waverley route, and a further four were turned out by the N.B.R. works at Cowlairs in the same year. The locomotives available for the Waverley connection to the Midland Scotch expresses for the first twenty years or so were, therefore, as follows :

Year Built	Builder	No.	Name
1876	Neilson & Co.	476	Carlisle
1876	,,	477	Edinburgh
1876	,,	478	Melrose
1876	,,	479	Abbotsford
1878	,,	488	Galashiels
1878	,,	489	Hawick
1878	North British Railway	490	St. Boswell's
1878	,,	491	Dalhousie
1878	,,	492	Newcastleton
1878	,,	493	Netherby

(They were joined in 1879 by Nos. 486 *Eskbank*, and 487 *Waverley*, which with the same numbers but named *Aberdeen* and *Montrose* respectively, had been working for a year on the Aberdeen-Dundee run up to the time of the fall of the Tay Bridge.)

Returning to the down Pullman sleeping car express, the Glasgow portion left Skipton at 3.05 a.m., and also ran non-stop through to Carlisle, reached at 5.05 a.m., from where the G.S.W.R. took it on to St Enoch to arrive at 8.00 a.m. For this service the Glasgow company used its 7 ft. 1 in. coupled 4-4-0s, the 6 class, a bogie design of James Stirling numbering twenty-two locomotives and brought into service between 1873 and 1877. At the time we are discussing, July of 1876, there were several of the class stationed at Carlisle and Glasgow, and to work the Scotch expresses they were equipped with the Westinghouse brake. Between 1879 and 1880 the Stirling engines were for the most part replaced on the Carlisle–Glasgow run by 2-4-0s, the 18 (or sometimes 157) class, with 6 ft. 9½ in. drivers, designed by the company's new locomotive superintendent, Hugh Smellie.

Between the Pullman and the arrival of the next train out of St Pancras, there was an early morning local on the Leeds & Bradford, the 5.20 a.m. from Bradford, which missed Frizinghall, and then called at all stations to Keighley which was reached at 5.50 a.m. The next main line connection with London was a slow which left Leeds at 5.35 a.m.—with passengers off the midnight train from St Pancras (Mondays excepted)—and called at Kirkstall, Newlay for Horsforth, Apperley, and Shipley. At the latter place there was a connection with the 5.50 a.m. stopping train from Bradford which ran, calling at all stations except Saltaire, to Skipton, which it reached at 6.51 a.m. From Skipton a train left at 7.30 a.m. for all stations to Colne, reached at 8.00 a.m. The 6.51 arrival at Skipton, meanwhile, had departed six minutes later for the little North Western line, stopping at all stations to Lancaster and making connections at Clapham for Ingleton, and at Wennington for Barrow and Windermere.

Most of these Midland local trains were worked by 2-4-0s, either of the 156, 800, or 890 classes. Of the 800 class, Nos. 812-819 were stationed at Leeds during the 1870s and worked the services between Carnforth, Leicester, Leeds and Derby. In 1871 they were joined by Nos. 3, 22, 23, and 93 at Skipton. Nos. 19 and 21 of the 890 class were at Lancaster from the mid 1870s until 1878 when they were sent to Nottingham. Whilst in the West Riding they worked the Lancaster–Leeds–Bradford service. In 1876, however, a change came to the Leeds & Bradford local service for whereas over the past years the line had been worked by 2-2-2 or 2-4-0 tender engines, mostly of early vintage, the Neilson 0-4-4 tanks, then being delivered, quickly ousted them, some twenty of the new engines being sent post haste to Bradford. Another addition to Skipton shed was a batch of five locomotives, Nos. 55-59, which worked the little North Western and the Leeds & Bradford lines from 1876 to 1883 when they were sent to Hull.

Following the 6.57 a.m. out of Skipton, at 7.15, there came a stopping train for the Settle and Carlisle line, calling at Long Preston at 7.35, and then Settle new station at 7.45, Horton at 8.00, Kirkby

Stephen * at 8.41, Crosby Garret at 8.51, Ormside at 9.02, Appleby at 9.09, Long Marton at 9.19, New Biggin at 9.27, Longwathby (sic) † at 9.38, Little Salkeld at 9.43, Lazonby ‡ at 9.50, Armathwaite at 10.01, Cotehill at 10.09, Cumwhinton at 10.16, Scotby at 10.20, and arriving at Carlisle at 10.28 a.m. from where a connection could be made to reach Glasgow at 4.00 p.m. The foregoing Settle–Carlisle stations were, of course, all that were open at the time.

After these first two trains down the Settle and Carlisle line there was a pause until mid-day. Meanwhile there were seven various trains in a down direction over the Leeds & Bradford lines, the first of which was the 6.25 a.m. stopping train out of Bradford to Skipton which connected with the 7.30 to Colne already mentioned. Following this came the 7.05 stopping train out of Leeds, which connected with the 7.30 a.m. from Bradford at Shipley, and called at all stations to Skipton, making a connection thence to Colne by a stopping train which reached the latter place at 9.05 a.m. Next came the 8.05 local from Bradford to Kildwick & Cross Hills; the 8.10 stopping train from Leeds to Saltaire; and the 8.55 from Leeds, similar in all respects to the 7.05 already mentioned, which made connection at Skipton to reach Colne by 11.00 a.m. There had in the meantime been a stopping train from Skipton to Colne, leaving at 8.10 a.m. and arriving at 8.40. After the 8.55 from Leeds came the 10.05 slow from Bradford to Skipton, reached at 11.05. Of the six trains already noted, all those from Leeds missed Kirkstall Forge, and only the 8.35 from Bradford called at Frizinghall. The last of the seven was a long distance train which left St Pancras at 5.15 a.m. and which, on arrival at Leeds, split into two trains, the 10.30 and the 10.40, both of which met up at Shipley with Bradford portions and arrived at Skipton at 11.15 and 11.27 a.m. They in turn met at Skipton with the 9.00 a.m. and the 9.25, from Liverpool and Manchester respectively, which had come in off the Colne line. At Skipton the train which had arrived at 11.27 split, one portion leaving at 11.32 to run fast down the little North Western, making connections with the Furness and Midland joint line at Carnforth, whence Windermere and Barrow trains ran, and the other portion following the first at 11.40 and calling at all stations to Lancaster, with a connection at Clapham for Ingleton. The L.N.W.R. service on the northern end of the Ingleton line was worked at the time by the L.N.W.R. engine No. 1191, *Ingleboro,* shedded at Tebay. This locomotive had been built in the late 1850s by W. Fairbairn & Co. and belonged originally to the Lancaster & Carlisle; it was scrapped about 1884. The 11.32, just mentioned, was shown as stopping conditionally at Settle old station to pick up Isle of Man passengers only.

To get back to Skipton, however, before either of the little North Western trains left, the 11.15 arrival from Leeds departed from Skipton

---

* Renamed Kirkby Stephen & Ravenstonedale in August, 1900.
† Renamed Langwathby in 1877.
‡ Renamed Lazonby & Kirkoswald in July, 1895.

as a semi-fast at 11.23, calling at Settle new station at 11.47, Appleby at 12.50 p.m., and arriving at Carlisle at 1.36, from where connections were made to Edinburgh (arr. 5.40 p.m.), Glasgow (arr. 4.45 p.m.), Dundee (arr. 10.55 p.m.), and Perth (arr. 9.30 p.m.). Ahrons mentioned that this particular train—the 5.15 a.m. from St Pancras—was invariably worked from Leeds to Carlisle by Leeds engines 811 or 819. The semi-fast was followed out of Skipton by the 11.50 a.m. which called at all stations to Settle new, which it left at 12.34 p.m. and then stopped at Horton at 12.50, Kirkby Stephen at 1.31, Crosby Garrett at 1.42, Ormside at 1.53, Appleby at 2.00, Long Marton at 2.10, New Biggin at 2.18, Longwathby at 2.29, Little Salkeld at 2.34, Lazonby at 2.41, Armathwaite at 2.52, Cotehill at 3.00, Cumwhinton at 3.07, Scotby at 3.11, and arrived at Carlisle at 3.20. There it made connections with Glasgow St Enoch (arr. 8.26 p.m.), Dundee (arr. 12.50 a.m.), Perth (arr. 11.35 p.m.), Aberdeen (arr. 3.20 a.m.), and Inverness (arr. 8.55 a.m.).

Another gap of three hours or so followed on the Settle line during which there was an 11.05 a.m stopping train out of Leeds to Keighley, reached at 12.15 p.m. This train was the first in the day to call at Kirkstall Forge, and was the slow connection at Leeds for the 5.15 a.m. from St Pancras. It was followed at 12.20 p.m. by another stopping train from Leeds to Keighley which missed Kirkstall Forge and arrived at 1.35 p.m. Again, this connected at Leeds with a train from the south, the 9.30 a.m. from Derby. The Keighley & Worth Valley line was, of course, run in connection with the local service and was operated by 0-6-0 tanks which had arrived the previous year. They were essentially a goods design, however, and were replaced in 1883 by new locomotives, Nos. 218, 219, and 1397–1399. These latter had 4 ft. 6 in. wheels and boasted a proper cab.

The next train from Derby, the 10.25 a.m., also connected at Leeds with the next local, the 1.10 p.m. This called at all stations except Holbeck and Kirkstall Forge, making connection at Shipley with the 1.40 p.m. from Bradford which connected at Skipton with a train to Colne, reached at 3.20 p.m. and stopping at all stations. This train was followed on the Colne branch by the 3.30 non-stop from Skipton, arriving at Colne after a twenty minute journey. The next local out of Leeds was a semi-fast to Bradford. It left Leeds at 2.00 p.m., ran non-stop to Apperley and then continued to Bradford. Passengers for the Leeds & Bradford Extension line changed in this case at Manningham on to the 2.30 p.m. from Bradford which terminated at Keighley at 3.00 p.m. It was followed by another semi-fast, the 2.50 p.m. from Leeds, which picked up passengers from the 8.30 a.m. train out of St Pancras. The semi-fast ran non-stop to Shipley where it met the 2.55 p.m. from Bradford and arrived at Skipton at 3.32 p.m. It stopped at Keighley on the way, only to set down, passengers informing the guard at Leeds. It left Skipton at 3.38 p.m. and ran fast to Clapham and then to Wennington. There it connected with the 4.25 to Carnforth for Barrow and

Windermere. This train ran non-stop but would halt at Arkholme, when required, to set down from Bradford, Leeds, or stations south of Leeds, on informing the guard at Wennington. The 3.38 from Skipton then left Wennington at 4.22 and ran slow to Lancaster, arriving at 4.55. A connection was shown to Castle station on the L.N.W.R.—as this did not arrive at the latter until 5.30 it was probably quicker to walk.

The Carnforth-Wennington line service had been operated since its commencement by Nos. 138 and 139, two of the six 800 class turned out by Derby in 1871, the other four going to Skipton as already mentioned. Nos. 138 and 139 left Carnforth for Derby a few years later and were replaced by four of the 890 class 2-4-0s, Nos. 2, 5, 7, and 12, built between 1872 and 1874. They stayed at Carnforth until about 1878, working to Leeds and Bradford.

After the 2.50 p.m. from Leeds there next came the remaining heavy north-bound train of the day, the Pullman drawing room car express. This left St Pancras at 10.30 a.m., Derby at 1.00 p.m., and Leeds at 3.10 and made connection at Shipley with the 3.15 from Bradford. The Pullman left Shipley at 3.30, called at Bingley at 3.38, Keighley at 3.45 and arrived at Skipton at 4.02 where it made connection with Liverpool and Manchester passengers who had arrived from the Colne line off the 2.00 and 2.20 trains from those cities respectively. As in the case of the sleeping car train, the drawing room car train split at Skipton. The Edinburgh portion and its Pullman car left Skipton at 4.18 p.m. and reached Carlisle exactly two hours later from where the N.B.R. took it on to arrive at Edinburgh at 9.15 p.m., connections being made thence to Dundee (arr. 12.50), Perth (arr. 11.35), Aberdeen (arr. 3.20), and Inverness (arr. 8.55). The Glasgow portion and Pullman coach left Skipton at 4.30 p.m., also taking exactly two hours to run non-stop to Carlisle. From there the G.S.W.R. took it on to St Enoch to arrive at 9.20 p.m.

The next train along the Settle line was a slow. It left Leeds at 3.50 p.m., taking passengers from the Pullman from London who were bound for the local stations. Only stopping at Holbeck and Apperley, it connected at Shipley at 4.17 with the 3.58 from Bradford and then stopped at Bingley and Keighley before arriving at Skipton at 4.47. From Skipton there were three connections; the 4.51 semi-fast to Lancaster which stopped at several stations when required to take up for Barrow and the Belfast boats, connection with which was made as usual at Wennington, the 5.00 p.m. stopping train down the Settle and Carlisle line which called at all stations and arrived at Carlisle at 8.30, and finally the 5.10 p.m. stopping train from Skipton to Colne, reached at 5.40. For local passengers along the Leeds & Bradford Extension line there was a train which left Bradford at 4.10, stopped at all stations, and arrived at Skipton at 5.05 p.m. Similarly for local passengers between Leeds and Shipley, etc., there was a slow train which left Leeds at 4.10 p.m. and, even calling at Kirkstall Forge, arrived at Keighley at 5.10. There were, therefore, a whole series of connections from Leeds, Shipley, Keighley, and Skipton, to lines radiating from the Midland main line, which passengers from the 10.30 Pullman could take.

Continuing towards the close of the weekday down service, there was an isolated evening train which left Wennington Junction at 6.00 p.m., called at Melling, Arkholme, and Borwick, the three intermediate stations on the Furness and Midland joint line, and arrived at Carnforth at 6.25, making connections for Windermere and Barrow. Two trains left Bradford in the late afternoon, running on Mondays and Thursdays only, at 5.00 and 5.20 p.m. The first ran fast to Skipton, arriving at 5.31 and leaving four minutes later to run non-stop to Hornby and Lancaster, reached at 6.18 and 6.35 respectively. The 5.20 called at Bingley, Keighley, Steeton, and Kildwick & Cross Hills, arriving at Skipton at 6.06 from where a train left five minutes later for Colne, reached at 6.35 p.m. After this came the 5.10 p.m. stopping train to Keighley, passing Kirkstall Forge. From Keighley it ran fast to Skipton, arriving at 6.32. Next was the 5.25 p.m. from Leeds—taking passengers from the 11.30 a.m. from London—which ran fast to Apperley and connected at Shipley at 6.12 with the 6.05 from Bradford. It then stopped at all stations to Skipton, arriving at 7.05 p.m. Incidentally, this train stopped conditionally at Newlay for Horsforth, and at Calverley, to set down London passengers on informing the guard at Leeds. Next came the 5.40 p.m. from Leeds, also taking London passengers from the 11.30 a.m., which stopped at Kirkstall, Apperley, Bingley, Keighley, and arrived at Skipton at 6.38. At Skipton, therefore, there were two arrivals within six minutes; the 6.32 and 6.38. They were joined by passengers from the 3.30 from Liverpool and the 4.45 from Salford which arrived from the Colne line. At this point the last two northbound trains of the day left Skipton; the 6.50 which stopped at all stations to Lancaster and gave a connection at Clapham for Ingleton, and the 6.45 which ran fast to Settle new station and then called at Kirkby Stephen at 7.57, Appleby at 8.18, and arrived at Carlisle at 9.05 p.m. No northward connections were shown. After these two, the next train out of Skipton was the 7.20 p.m. stopping train to Colne, arriving at 7.50.

To complete the local service there were six more trains remaining in the day. The first was the 6.41 p.m. from Apperley which stopped at all stations to Keighley, arriving at 7.20 and picking up Bradford passengers at Shipley. This train, as were others which appeared to start or terminate at Apperley, originated from the Apperley–Guiseley–Otley–Ilkley lines. After it came the 7.45 p.m. from Leeds which, with the exception of Kirkstall Forge, stopped at all stations to Kildwick & Cross Hills, where it terminated at 9.00 p.m. This train continued on to Cononley and Skipton on Saturdays. There was then a 9.15 p.m. from Leeds—with London passengers from the 3.15 p.m. from St Pancras—which called at all stations, except Kirkstall Forge, to Keighley, arriving at 10.45 p.m., and picking up the Bradford connection at Shipley. The last train out of Leeds was the 10.20 p.m.—with London passengers off the 4.30 from St Pancras—which ran similarly to the 9.15 and arrived at Keighley at 11.20. The Shipley–Keighley stops were omitted on all but Saturdays. There remained two more trains; the 7.55 and 10.45 p.m. trains out of Skipton which ran fast through to Colne, arriving at 8.15 and 11.15 respectively.

Having given a complete list of the down weekday services, those in the up direction can be briefly summarised. On the Settle and Carlisle line the first train of the day was the Pullman sleeping car train which left Carlisle at 12.08 a.m. (dep. Inverness at 10.18 a.m., Aberdeen at 12.23 p.m., Perth at 4.20 p.m., Dundee at 3.03 p.m., and Edinburgh at 9.20 p.m.). It reached Skipton, after a non-stop run, at 2.08 a.m. and waited there for the Glasgow Pullman to arrive. This left Carlisle at 12.18 a.m. (dep. Glasgow at 9.15 p.m.) and reached Skipton after a similar run to the Edinburgh train, at 2.18. There both trains were joined, and left at 2.25 a.m., stopping at Shipley at 2.47 for the Bradford connection which arrived at 3.00 a.m. The up sleeping car Pullman reached Leeds at 3.10 and St Pancras at 8.00 p.m.

The Midland locomotives stationed at Carlisle for the up trains at this time were Nos. 1302–1311, 2-4-0 Dubs engines, built in 1876 and having the Westinghouse brake fitted specially for the Scotch trains. The rest of the class were fitted with a different brake and ran mostly on the London to Manchester service. In 1882–1883 Carlisle got its first Midland 4-4-0s, Nos. 1572–1581, with 6 ft. 9 in. coupled wheels. These engines were also on the Westinghouse system and stayed on the northern end of the Settle line until 1894 when they came south to Skipton.

After the up Pullman there followed a stopping train which left Carlisle at 7.30 a.m. and, calling at all stations, reached Skipton at 10.55. There it picked up a connection from the Colne line and arrived at Leeds, after stopping at all stations, at 12.35 p.m. A London connection could be caught to reach St Pancras at 6.30. The next train out of Carlisle was a semi-fast, leaving at 9.00 a.m. and only calling at Cumwhinton, Armathwaite. Lazonby, Little Salkeld when reauired to pick up for stations beyond Skipton, Longwathby, Appleby, Kirkby Stephen, Settle new, and Skipton, which latter it reached at 11.40. There it connected with a train from Lancaster and the Furness and Midland joint line, and one from Colne, and then ran as a semi-fast to Leeds which was reached at 12.40. The next two trains on the up Settle and Carlisle service were the two portions of the Pullman drawing-room car train. The first left Carlisle at 1.05 p.m. (dep. Glasgow at 10.15 a.m.) and ran non-stop to Skipton, arriving at 3.05. The same arrangement as before applied, the Edinburgh portion leaving Carlisle ten minutes later (dep. Inverness 7.35 p.m., Perth at 6.00 a.m., and Edinburgh at 10.25 a.m.), and reaching Skipton at 3.15. As before both portions were joined at Skipton and left at 3.28, calling at Keighley at 3.42, and making a connection at Shipley (to set down only), to arrive at Bradford at 4.10

p.m. The Pullman arrived at Leeds at 4.10 and at St Pancras at 9.05 p.m. The next train on the Settle line was the 4.10 p.m. which, with a Glasgow connection (dep. St Enoch at 10.40 a.m.), stopped at all stations to Skipton where it arrived at 7.25 p.m. Connection could be made thence over the Colne line to Manchester and Liverpool, passengers for Leeds picking up the 7.55 p.m. from Skipton which was the 5.30 fast from Carlisle. This train, which had connections from the north (dep. Aberdeen 6.30 a.m., Perth at noon, Dundee at 11.00 a.m., Glasgow at 2.30 p.m. and Edinburgh at 2.35 p.m.), ran fast from Carlisle, calling at Appleby at 6.15, Settle new at 7.18, and arrived at Skipton at 7.45 p.m. It left ten minutes later and arrived at Leeds at 8.50 p.m., running as a semi-fast. According to Ahrons it was usually hauled by any of the Leeds engines Nos. 812–819, already mentioned. The last train of the day was a semi-fast from Carlisle at 8.05 p.m., also with northern connections, (dep. Aberdeen at 9.15 a.m., Perth at 1.55 p.m., Glasgow at 4.35 p.m., and Edinburgh at 4.25). This train called at Appleby at 8.50, Kirkby Stephen at 9.12, Settle new at 9.58, and arrived at Skipton at 10.25 p.m. It left as a fast ten minutes later, calling at Kildwick & Cross Hills when required to set down, Keighley at 10.50 p.m., Shipley when required to set down for Bradford (reached at 11.25 p.m.), and arrived at Leeds at 11.22 p.m. From Leeds a London connection could be made, to arrive at St Pancras at 5.15 a.m. The Leeds & Bradford, Colne line, and little North Western services were virtually the reverse of those described for the down trains.

On Sundays, both up and down, the Settle and Carlisle line had only one train each way—the Pullman sleeping car express—though Settle at least was served, since Settle old station had two trains which called in each direction. The down Pullman left St Pancras at 9.15 on Saturday nights and arrived at Skipton at 2.49 a.m. on Sunday. According to *Bradshaw* it did not split but left Skipton as one train and arrived at Carlisle at 4.55 a.m., taking exactly two hours for the journey. As usual, from Carlisle the Edinburgh and Glasgow portions went their separate ways (arr. Edinburgh 7.35, Glasgow 8.00, Dundee 11.20, Perth 10.00 a.m., Aberdeen 4.05, and Inverness 6.25 p.m.). The up Pullman sleeping car train left Carlisle at 12.18 a.m. (dep. Inverness at 10.18 a.m. Saturday, Aberdeen 12.23, Perth 4.20, Dundee 3.03, Glasgow 9.15, and Edinburgh 9.20 p.m.). The Pullman train arrived at Skipton at 2.18 a.m. and as one train left at 2.25 a.m., stopped at Shipley at 2.47 for the Bradford connection (arr. Bradford at 3.00 a.m.), and arrived at Leeds at 3.10 and St Pancras at 8.00 a.m. As to the local Sunday services, there were two morning and five afternoon trains which left Leeds for Bradford, Skipton or Lancaster, and virtually a similar service the other way. The Colne line had a morning and afternoon stopping train which called at all stations each way.

Such then is a summary of the opening service over the Settle and Carlisle route and its adjoining lines. Nothing, of course, has been said of the connections with the North Eastern Railway at Appleby and Kirkby Stephen and these will be dealt with briefly in their turn. In mid July it was suggested, but turned down by the traffic committee, that an additional Scotch train should be run each way. To end, a note on the Midland service at Lancaster : the trains between Green Ayre and the L.N.W.R.'s Castle station were discontinued from November 1, 1876. They recommenced running on July 1, 1881.

It would appear, in 1876, by the way, that Midland drivers at about that time were swinging their trains along in a style considered excessive by the locomotive committee as it decided that, come the next working timetable, the traffic department should insert the times at which all passenger trains were to pass signal boxes nearest to the summits and foot of all heavy banks on the main line. On the principle that the further you are from home the less it matters, one wonders whether a good bit of this nineteenth century 'ton-upmanship' was practised on the fine 1 in 100 grades of the Settle line.

Of course they could not do so well with the goods trains. Indeed according to the minutes of the Midland and L.Y.R. meetings on this aspect of operating there appeared to be a slight chill between the two companies in that each still accused the other of bad connections. At a meeting on July 19, 1876, it was noted that the 11 a.m. express goods from Skipton to Salford was to be taken off because of light loading, though it was agreed that if at any time the 6.40 a.m. Midland goods from Carlisle had twelve or more wagons for Manchester they would be worked through as a special train from Skipton to their destination as quickly as possible, provided that Carlisle telegraphed the L.Y.R.'s agent at Accrington, a Mr Gooder, to produce the necessary motive power. Various complaints were made at the meeting by the Midland about the L.Y.R.'s working of the Scotch traffic. The locomotives frequently were just not up to their job. The recent case of the late arrival of a Dewsbury-Skipton train was instanced, where the L.Y.R. locomotive provided to run it had just expended all its energy on working a pick-up goods from Knottingley. Goods trains tended to grow roots if not prodded; apparently Dewsbury traffic often stood for hours at Mirfield. On October 26 it was suggested by the Midland that owing to the accelerated train services put into force by the L.N.W.R. between Glasgow and Manchester, the L.Y.R. should run the 8.20 a.m. Skipton to Salford train in 2½ hours, the same as was done in the opposite direction, to which the L.Y.R. replied that if only the Scotch trains arrived at Skipton at anything approaching the correct time it might be possible to comply. The Midland was complaining in this instance that Scotch potatoes for Oldham road were frequently delayed after leaving Skipton.

To leave this ineffectual bickering for a while, the Midland goods engines assigned to the Settle and Carlisle line were Nos. 1222–1251, stationed at Carlisle and Leeds; 0-6-0s, with 4 ft. 10 in. wheels, they have already been described in Chapter XII. To quote from Ahrons, they 'worked the whole of the Scotch express goods traffic between these points for nearly 30 years. The Carlisle goods drivers were noted for the high speed at which they worked their trains, and with the 1222 class they used to do some very fast running. The signalmen between Carlisle and Leeds would always give the Carlisle goods drivers "the road" even when they were within measurable distance of a following express passenger train, because the signalmen knew that the goods train would keep clear, but when the Leeds goods drivers came along they were promptly shunted into the nearest siding until the passenger train had passed.' *

In July of 1876 Johnson was still on the prowl for more engines. In a memorandum to the locomotive committee he said he considered it necessary to order 30 goods and 20 passenger engines for delivery by June of 1877, and if the winter workings of 1877 were considered the number of goods should be brought up to 50. He still had about 91 per cent of engines in steam. In June of 1876 the company had a stock of 1,120 locomotives, of which 876 train, and 244 shunting and ballast, were in steam. To reduce the percentage to 75 in steam the stock should be 1,493, this showing a deficit of 265. The 30 goods and 20 passenger locomotives were authorized on August 1. It would be well off our subject to follow the locomotive history of the Midland much further, except where it occasionally directly concerns the Settle line. It has been attempted, however, to show how the company's new lines outstripped its motive power department. In the matter of the locomotives just mentioned though, it may be noted that 20 new goods engines were delivered from Dubs & Co. in 1877-1878. They were 0-6-0s and had 5 ft. 2½ in. wheels. Nos. 1357–1371 went to Bradford where, for some years, they worked the night express goods to London. Most of the new passenger engines delivered during the period covered by this chapter went on working the Leeds–London expresses. All were of the 2-4-0 express passenger type with 6 ft. 9 in. coupled wheels. In 1879 Derby turned out Nos. 1400-1409, in 1880 Nos. 1472-1491—the first three being stationed at Leeds for some time, and between 1880 and 1881 Neilson's produced Nos. 1502–1531, of which 1502–1526 were also at Leeds. Incidentally, in 1883 Nos. 1400-1409 went to Carnforth and Lancaster for the little North Western service and the Furness and Midland joint line. They were later renumbered 207–216. As to details of the renumbering which took place on the Midland in 1907, reference should be made to Ahrons's study of the Midland train working, without which much of the foregoing would have been impossible to record.*

It was during the early 1880s that the famous "Derby Red" colour was adopted. The question of changing the engine livery had been occupying the locomotive committee since October, 1881, when it was noted in the committee's minutes that ten engines had been painted red instead of the

* *Locomotive & Train Working in the Latter Part of the Nineteenth Century.—* E. L. Ahrons.

usual green, the reason being that the former colour was thought to be less expensive to maintain. On November 1, 1881, Johnson explained to the committee that the cost of painting engines red or green was about the same, though the red was a few shillings cheaper. He estimated that the oxide of iron paint now being tried out—not being such a fugitive colour as green—would stand wear and tear about twice as long as green before the locomotives needed repainting. The cost of engine painting for 1880 had been £5,176; if the engines were to last twice the time in red paint, he thought the annual saving, when all were painted in oxide of iron, would be at least £2,000. After a trial period, it was agreed by the committee on October 18, 1883, that all engines should henceforth be painted red. Some of the first to be so decked out were Nos. 1657–1666, 4-4-0s with 6 ft. 9in. wheels, which followed on Nos. 1572–1581, already mentioned. This policy continued until 1910. On February 4 of that year the locomotive department decided that goods engines—then painted "engine lake" every two years at £11 each—would from then on be painted black every four years, at £13.

The following shortened summary of the down goods traffic north of Leeds is extracted from the Midland's working timetable of February 1877 :

12.40 a.m.	(MX)	Hunslet sidings to Keighley, arr. 1.50 a.m. (Mineral from Normanton)
2.25		Leeds Wellington to Carnforth, arr. 4.30 a.m. (Empty carriage train from Normanton)
2.35	(MX)	Hunslet to Carlisle, arr. 9.45 a.m. (Semi-fast)
2.43		pass time through Leeds, Sheffield to Carnforth, arr. 7.25 a.m.
2.55	(MX)	Bradford to Lancaster, arr. 8.50 a.m.
3.20	(MX)	Hunslet Lane to Bradford, arr. 4.35 a.m.
3.30	(MX)	Hunslet sidings to Bradford, arr. 7.10 a.m. (Pick-up goods)
4.50		Hunslet sidings to Guiseley. Pass Newlay at 5.25 a.m. (Normanton-Guiseley train)
4.55		Hunslet Lane to Skipton, arr. 7.30 a.m.
5.45	(MX)	Skipton to Carlisle, arr. 10 a.m. (Express goods)
6.05		Hunslet Lane to Skipton, arr. 12.30 p.m. (Pick-up goods)
6.10	(MX)	Hunslet sidings to Bradford, arr. 7 a.m. (Liverpool-Bradford goods)
7.05	(MX)	Hunslet sidings to Bradford, arr. 7.55 a.m. (Express goods London-Bradford, bearing three lights)
8.35		Hunslet sidings to Ilkley. Left L.B.R. metals at about 9.40 a.m.
8.50		Hunslet sidings to Carnforth, arr. 12.50 p.m. (Express goods)
9.00		Bradford to Keighley, arr. 9.20 a.m. (Empty carriage train)
9.25	(MX)	Hunslet sidings to Carlisle, arr. 3.30 p.m. (Express goods)
9.30		Skipton to Carnforth (Pick-up goods)
9.40		Skipton to Carlisle, arr. 6.05 p.m. (Pick-up goods)
10.00	(MX)	Skipton to Carlisle, arr. 2.45 p.m.
10.40	(MX)	Hunslet sidings to Carlisle, arr. 4.20 p.m.
11.00	(MX)	Hunslet sidings to Bradford, arr. 12.05 p.m. (Burton-Bradford goods)
11.15		Bradford to Colne, arr. 2.55 p.m.
11.15		Hunslet sidings to Stainforth, arr. 3.05 p.m.
11.30		Hunslet sidings to Keighley, arr. 12.55 p.m. (Mineral from Whitwood)

12.20 p.m.	(WO)	Hunslet Lane to Bradford, arr. 1.20 p.m.
		(Cattle train from Wakefield)
12.25		Hunslet sidings to Kirkstall Forge, arr. 12.55 p.m.
		(Goods and mineral)
12.40	(WFO)	Skipton to Lancaster, arr. 4.20 p.m.
1.25		Skipton to Carnforth, arr. 4.20 p.m.
1.25	(MX)	Hunslet sidings to Carlisle, arr. 7.40 p.m. (Express goods)
2.45	(MX)	Skipton to Carlisle, arr. 7.30 p.m. (Express goods)
3.02		Hunslet sidings to Bradford, arr. 4.35 p.m.
		(Cattle train from Wakefield)
3.45	(MX)	Skipton to Carlisle, arr. 9.20 p.m.
4.40		Hunslet sidings to Carnforth, arr. 9.10 p.m.
5.05		Hunslet sidings to Carlisle, arr. 12.05 a.m.
6.20		Bradford to Skipton, arr. 7.55 (SX) and 8.30 (SO)
6.34		Shipley to Bradford, arr. 6.55 p.m.
		(This was an Ilkley-Bradford train off the Baildon line.)
6.45		Skipton to Carlisle, arr. 10.45 p.m. (Express goods)
7.10	(SO)	Bradford to Shipley stone sidings, arr. 7.20
		(Shipley shunting engine)
7.40		Hunslet sidings to Keighley, arr. 9.15 p.m.
8.30	(SX)	Bradford to Carlisle, arr. 2.05 a.m. (Express goods)
8.35		Hunslet Lane, arr. Carlisle 2.20 a.m. (Express goods)
8.45		Hunslet sidings to Carnforth, arr. 1.05 a.m.
9.20		Shipley shunting engine to Bingley, arr. 9.27 a.m.
		There it performed shunting after which it returned
		to Shipley.
9.20		Hunslet sidings. Sheffield-Carnforth goods, arr. 2 a.m.
10.40		Hunslet sidings, arr. Bradford 11.40 p.m.
		(Mineral from Barnsley to Bradford)
10.50		Skipton to Carlisle, arr. 2.40 a.m. (Express goods)
11.00	(SX)	Bradford to Colne, arr. 2.05 a.m.
11.05		Hunslet Lane to Skipton, arr. 12.15 a.m.
11.06		pass through Hunslet. Mineral from Normanton to Bradford,
		arr. 1.15 a.m.
11.25	(SO)	Bradford to Carlisle, arr. 4.45 a.m. (Express goods)
11.40		Skipton to Carlisle, arr. 3.40 a.m. (Express goods)
MX	Mondays excepted	
SX	Saturdays excepted	
SO	Saturdays only	
WO	Wednesdays only	
WFO	Wednesdays and Fridays only	

On Sundays there were a dozen goods, on the above pattern, including the express goods from London to Bradford and eight arrivals at Carlisle :

2.30 a.m.	from Hunslet sidings, arr. 9.20 a.m.
5.45	Express goods from Skipton, arr. 10 a.m.
9.15	Express goods from Hunslet sidings, arr. 3.05 a.m.
9.35	from Skipton, arr. 2.15 p.m.
10.25	Scotch express goods from Hunslet sidings, arr. 4 p.m.
12.20 p.m.	from Hunslet sidings, arr. 6.50 p.m.
1.35	from Skipton, arr. 6.15 p.m.
3.35	from Skipton, arr. 8.20 p.m.

The above are of course greatly simplified. A considerable number of goods on the Settle line stopped at Skipton, Settle, Kirkby Stephen, Appleby, Little Salkeld, etc., to take water. Details of one run will suffice. The 2.35 a.m. from Hunslet stopped to shunt at Shipley between 3.14 and 3.50 a.m., stopped at Keighley at 4.10, at Skipton at 4.35 where it watered and left at 4.55. It then stopped at Gargrave at 5.10 a.m., Settle at 5.44 for eleven minutes, during which time it took water, Kirkby Stephen between 7.16 and 7.21 and Appleby between 7.55 and 8.05, both of these times only to take water. Its last stop before Carlisle was Langwathby at 8.50.

At the time of the opening of the Settle line the rules to the working timetable then in force had last been revised in 1869. Presumably with the experience gained from the first year's operating, a further revision was made in 1877. Extracts from engine load tables, headlight codes, and speed restriction tables are given in Appendix XII.

The connecting G.S.W.R. and N.B.R. goods trains at Carlisle were shown in February 1877 to arrive and depart at the Midland yard as under :

Weekday Arrivals

N.B.R.	12.15 a.m.	(MX)	N.B.R.	5.00 a.m.	(MX)
G.S.W.R.	1.50		G.S.W.R.	5.45	
G.S.W.R.	2.20		N.B.R.	5.50	(MX)
N.B.R.	2.30		N.B.R.	3.00 p.m.	
G.S.W.R.	2.55		G.S.W.R.	4.00	
N.B.R.	3.00	(MX)	N.B.R.	4.45	
N.B.R.	3.30	(MX)	G.S.W.R.	7.05	
G.S.W.R.	3.35		N.B.R.	7.45	(SX)
N.B.R.	4.00	(MX)	G.S.W.R.	8.25	
G.S.W.R.	4.30		G.S.W.R.	9.20	
			N.B.R.	10.15	

Sunday Arrivals

N.B.R.	12.15 a.m.		G.S.W.R.	4.30 a.m.
G.S.W.R.	1.50		N.B.R.	5.00
G.S.W.R.	2.20		N.B.R.	5.50
G.S.W.R.	2.55		G.S.W.R.	6.10
N.B.R.	3.00		G.S.W.R.	7.45
N.B.R.	3.30		N.B.R.	5.45 p.m.
N.B.R.	4.00		N.B.R.	7.15
			N.B.R.	9.00

Weekday Departures

G.S.W.R.	12.00 midnight		G.S.W.R.	7.20 a.m.	
N.B.R.	12.45 a.m.	(MX)	G.S.W.R.	10.10	
G.S.W.R.	2.55		G.S.W.R.	11.50	
N.B.R.	3.00		G.S.W.R.	3.25 p.m.	(MX)
N.B.R.	3.30	(MX)	N.B.R.	3.30	(SO)
N.B.R.	4.00	(MX)	N.B.R.	6.15	
N.B.R.	4.30	(MX)	G.S.W.R.	7.30	
G.S.W.R.	4.35		N.B.R.	8.15	(SX)
G.S.W.R.	5.35		G.S.W.R.	8.20	
N.B.R.	5.55	(MX)	G.S.W.R.	8.45	(SO)
N.B.R.	6.15	(MX)	N.B.R.	10.45	

Sunday Departures

N.B.R.	12.45 a.m.		G.S.W.R.	8.45 a.m.
N.B.R.	3.30		G.S.W.R.	5.15 p.m.
N.B.R.	4.00		N.B.R.	6.00
N.B.R.	4.30		N.B.R.	7.45
N.B.R.	5.55		G.S.W.R.	8.20
N.B.R.	6.15		N.B.R.	9.30

By early 1877, with the Settle line 'run-in' and beginning to be accepted by the travelling public as a third route to Scotland, the other companies started to put on the pressure. As has been noted, the L.N.W.R. Manchester–Glasgow goods was speeded up; in January the company reduced its charge for sleeping cars. Of course, the Pullmans had to do the same. Their chequered career is described later in Chapter XVIII. Publicity as we know it now was then still in its infancy but in early April of 1877 the Midland's traffic committee decided to bring out a special timetable and general information book about its Scotch trains, similar to ones already issued by the East and West Coast companies. From May 1, the date an improved Midland service was to come into effect, the L.N.W.R. speeded up its trains, cutting as much as forty minutes from their timings. The Midland replied by raising its speed over the Settle and Carlisle line from an average of 43.9 miles per hour to one of 45.25, at which it stayed for ten years. In fact on June 19, when the revised timetable was being considered, Johnson submitted to the locomotive committee a return on the train services of the L.N.W.R., G.N.R., and M.R. for three days, May 31 and June 1 and 2 of 1877, from which it appeared that the number of carriages on Midland trains averaged 15, L.N.W.R. 12, and G.N.R. 11. The average speed on the three lines was 45.6 m.p.h. on the M.R., 45.5 on the L.N.W.R., and 49.3 on the G.N.R. The average booked speed for the whole journey of the Midland Scotch expresses was 47 m.p.h. and it was agreed that this should remain as the maximum for the moment. As to the locomotives, by mid July of 1879 Johnson reported that there were now 1,400 engines and 60 duplicate engines, of which total 973 were in good condition, 209 were moderate, and 278 under repair. Out of the total, engines were stationed as follows on June 30, 1879; Leeds 72, Bradford 42, Skipton 19, Carnforth 14, Lancaster 9, and Carlisle 32.

As to Midland internal affairs at this time, there was still some criticism of the expenditure that had been made on the Settle and Carlisle line and at the half-yearly meeting in August of 1877, Mr Garnett of Leeds asked for details of both this and the traffic returns to date, especially of the Pullmans. In reply Edward Shipley Ellis said that the board was satisfied with the returns but was doubtful about the Pullmans. They were not doing as well as they should. He pointed out that there had been, and still was, a severe trade depression and that this was undoubtedly a cause of the lack of custom. Another reason was that the Midland had made its ordinary coaching stock of such comfort that the passengers were loth to pay the extra Pullman charges. Asked again about the cost of the Settle line he said that there were some wild rumours going about, noticeably among the meetings of some southern companies, that the figure was something like £6m. In fact, he said, it was about £3,800,000.

The half-yearly meeting of February 1878 was more optimistic for, despite continuing bad times, receipts over the half-year had increased generally by over £75,000. The majority of the shareholders, however, called for a halt to any increase in the size of the Midland system. As to the Pullmans, the returns were still poor; the agreement with George Pullman still had some thirteen years to run and the board hoped to get a revision of the terms. What happened will be seen in a later chapter dealing with the rolling stock. On the passenger traffic side, a circular from Needham dated June 29, 1878, noted that now the new Tay Bridge of the N.B.R. was open it had been arranged that from July 1 that company would run a service of trains between Edinburgh and Aberdeen via Stirling, Lady Bank, Tay Bridge, Dundee and Arbroath. The Midland's night Scotch express which left St Pancras at 9.15, was to be in direct connection at Edinburgh with the Arbroath train. Other traffic arrangements were in being or under discussion when the bridge fell on the night of the great gale of Sunday, December 28, 1879.

Though of course it was the North British that suffered from the calamity, the Tay Bridge disaster was gloomily seen at Derby as but the final setback in a series of events which made 1879 a poor year for the Midland. There had been a seventeen day strike among the goods guards who, using the revision of hours worked per week from 60 to 66 as an excuse—or so it was said—came out in protest against the trip system. This was a revision of the terms of pay whereby a man was paid per number of trips made and not by the hours worked. Its introduction had already provoked one abortive strike in 1876. There was a general feeling of discontent among the men. Circulars, recently issued from Derby and signed by James Allport, had a lot to do with it. One such read as follows :

Order No. 304

General Manager's Office,
Derby,
Nov. 22nd, 1878.

PORTERS' WAGES

The Directors have decided that the Wages of all Passenger and Goods Porters, Parcels Porters, Parcels-delivery Porters, Cloak-room Porters, Lamp Porters, Carriage Cleaners, Number-takers, and Policemen, in receipt of 17s per week and upwards, shall be reduced one shilling per week from the morning of December 13th. You will please communicate this to the men under your supervision, and carry out the arrangement, commencing with Pay Bill week ending December 19th.

JAMES ALLPORT,
General Manager.

There can be no doubt that this little Christmas bonus was the logical end to the vast expenditure on the Settle line, and the increasingly tough attitude taken by some of the shareholders had also compelled the board to revise the goods guards' workings. At the beginning of 1879 Mr Allcock, the station master at Settle, received the following gem from the superintendent's office at Derby. Having been, according to Mr Garnett and others, pound foolish, the board was literally trying its hardest to be penny wise :

Superintendent's Office,
Derby Station,
January 16th, 1879.

Mr Allcock,
Settle.

Dear Sir,

Giggleswick Tickets

You may allow tickets to Giggleswick from stations south thereof to be made use of to Settle without extra charge in the case of third class tickets, but as regards first class, as such fares to Settle are 1*d* in excess of those to Giggleswick, where passengers used tickets issued to the latter place to your station, you must call upon them to pay this difference, except in the solitary case of Bell Busk, when the first class fare to Settle is 1*d* less than that to Giggleswick, and you need not make any charge in this instance.

Yours truly,
pro E. M. Needham,
E. A. Pakeman.

(As will be seen Giggleswick was the new name for Settle old station.)

Despite all this, and the very bad summer and non-existent harvest of 1879, with only mineral receipts up and all the others down, the Midland was still able, and proudly, to pay a dividend of 5 per cent. at a time when most other companies were doling out to their shareholders sums much less than usual.

By the end of 1883 there had been a whole string of general improvements along the line. As to the goods traffic, in June of 1876 the Craven Lime Company asked for a new siding at Ribblehead, then known as Ingleton Road. The firm's mineral traffic was expected to grow—for the year ending March 1876 the amount sent by rail from their nearby Langcliffe works had amounted to 6,797 tons. In fact, as will be seen in the station working figures in Appendix XI there was a remarkable growth in limestone and other mineral traffic in the first few years. In August, 1876, it was decided to lay down additional interchange sidings at Carlisle; during June of that year 9,403 wagons were exchanged between the Midland and the N.B.R. and G.S.W.R. At Bradford, a new down goods line was opened between Manningham and Shipley on August 20, 1876, and a complementary up line on the following December 3. Just over a fortnight later it was decided that Ormside should have goods facilities; the inhabitants had said that the station would be able to produce as much traffic as at Little Salkeld, which latter had dealt with some 1,362 tons in the six months up to October. On New Year's Eve, 1876, the Skipton south to north junction down goods line came into operation, and five days later Ribblesdale lime sidings were opened for traffic. Besides these additional facilities the Midland increased the traffic over the line in May of 1877 by an agreement with the N.B.R. whereby the Highland Railway would undertake to send over the Waverley route and the Settle and Carlisle line a fair share of its unconsigned traffic, and the following August 7 saw the opening of the new Carlisle goods traffic committee lines. As has been seen there had been trouble at Carlisle, with delays to trains. Some blame for this could be attached to the system whereby G.S.W.R. engines had to run into and out of Petteril and in July of 1878 plans were agreed for alterations in the layout which would cut this down. The history of the Carlisle goods and passenger stations is summarized later in this chapter. The first recorded closures on the line took place on July 28, 1879, on which day the signal boxes at Salt Lake and the Craven Lime sidings became redundant.

By far the most important development, however, was the opening of the L.Y.R.'s Chatburn–Hellifield line. There had been some initial disagreement between the L.Y.R. and the Midland as to the cost of all the work at Hellifield which included the laying out of exchange sidings and the provision of a joint station. By February 5, 1879, it had been agreed that the station, to cost about £18,000, should be built by the Midland and that the L.Y.R. should pay rent to use it. On July 2 the Mayor and inhabitants of Clitheroe, not knowing that agreement had at last been reached, appealed to the Midland—they had apparently given up the L.Y.R. as a bad job—to get the line open. Derby replied that there was nothing it would like more. Meanwhile work progressed and on August 19 a tender from Messrs Cowans & Sheldon was accepted for the supply of a 50 foot turntable for the sheds at Hellifield, at a cost of £325. In fact it did not arrive in time for the opening and for some while engines working traffic from the L.Y.R. northwards had to run back light. The Chatburn–Hellifield line was opened for traffic on June 1, 1880, the date that the new station at Hellifield came into use. Powers for the line had been obtained by the L.Y.R. in 1871 and during the latter stages of construction, as has been seen, the Midland was told that it could have access thereover to Manchester and Liverpool, thus shortening the route to Carlisle by about 12 miles. This, however, immediately posed a problem, for the tunnels on the L.Y.R. line at Sough and Farnworth were not large enough to take the proposed Pullman service. This, despite the fact that the Midland's structure gauge was generally tighter than that of the L.Y.R. The Lancashire company therefore undertook to lower the track through Sough tunnel and to bore a new tunnel parallel with that at Farnworth, so that the old tunnel could be used for single track. Though this work was completed by the opening of the line, and the lowering of Sough tunnel was done by February of 1882, it was to be another six years before the Midland Pullmans took advantage of the new route.

At the Midland's half-yearly meeting in August, 1880, the cost of the works at Hellifield was given; £20,718 had been expended on the station, sidings, engine shed, and the company's cottages. Meanwhile Hellifield exchange sidings had come into use on March 1, 1880, so that when the Chatburn–Hellifield line was opened L.Y.R. Scotch goods trains ceased running to Skipton and switched to Hellifield. As before, however, they frequently arrived late. At a meeting held on March 25, 1880, at a time when the L.Y.R. goods were still running to Colne and the actual exchange was effected at Hellifield, the Midland complained that traffic from the Oldham and Werneth branch, and some of the Liverpool traffic, was not being received in time for the Carlisle connections. Even when the new line was opened the Midland still had cause for complaint. In February of 1881 the L.Y.R.'s excuse was the bad weather. The argument culminated in the Midland informing the L.Y.R. in March, 1881, that it intended running through traffic between Colne and Liverpool. L.Y.R. trains over the Chatburn line were not stopped, however, and in April of 1882 it was still obvious that the Midland would have been badly put out had the former ceased operating the through Scotch service; Noble of the Midland persuaded the L.Y.R. to keep running two of the night trains which the Midland were anxious not to see discontinued, as threatened, and only got L.Y.R. agreement on the payment of 1s. per mile between Liverpool and Blackburn. As to the question of bad weather, George P. Neele, in his *Railway Reminiscences,* remarked that snow storms in 1881 "caused the Midland Line to be entirely blocked at Blea Moor, and once more the Ingleton route had to convey their obstructed Scotch traffic."

On the passenger side on the Settle and Carlisle line, the years 1876–1883 saw several additions to the facilities provided when the line was opened. On June 19, 1876, the Rev. E. H. Woodall of Settle wrote to the Midland Railway suggesting that the new station at Batty Green, previously known as Ingleton Road, should be called Ribblehead, and this was agreed to. Emboldened by this the Reverend gentleman wrote a further letter, shortly after, suggesting that the Rev. Father Hill should be given a gratuity for his ministrations to the Catholic workmen during the making of the line. This did not find favour. On August 1, 1876, Hawes Junction station was opened, the Board of Trade inspecting officer, Col. R. E. Yolland, visiting it two days later and giving his blessing—all that was missing was a clock and the Colonel did not seem too worried about that. On the following November 10 his colleague, Col. Rich, inspected the new station at Settle Junction and pronounced it fit for use. There were now three stations at Settle; Settle old, Settle new, and Settle Junction, a situation calculated to infuriate booking clerks all over the system and one which was soon put right. In July, 1877, it was decided to rename Settle old as Giggleswick, to take effect from the following November 1. Meanwhile, in the previous May, with Settle new dealing with all the goods traffic, it had been agreed to take up the sidings at Settle old, and to lengthen the platforms. It would seem that clerics have a penchant for naming stations. In April, 1877, the Rev D. Adams, Vicar of Cowgill, wrote to the Midland suggesting that the new station to be opened at Dent should be known simply by that name. To this the company not unnaturally agreed; as we have seen, at one time it had been proposed to erect it at a point some distance south of its present site, with the name of Dent Head. The station was opened on August 6, 1877. The problem of still having two stations with the name of Settle was ended in November of 1877, when it was resolved at a meeting of the Midland traffic committee that as Giggleswick had in fact been retained there seemed little use for Settle Junction station and, 'as an experiment', the latter was closed. It must have had one of the shortest lives of any Midland main line station; its buildings still stand, in the style of its more fortunate contemporary namesake, further north, on the down side of the line. Well to the north, plans were prepared in early 1879 for a station at Culgaith, and passenger trains first called there on April 1, 1880.

Improvements were planned for the two main stations on the Leeds & Bradford Extension line. In mid 1877 a Mr Whittaker had a fatal accident at Bingley station, in circumstances which must have been thought to be the Midland's fault as the Board of Trade saw fit to write a letter of complaint about it in October. The company replied that it was shortly to rebuild and re-model the station. In fact it did nothing for several years. It did, however, have plans ready by July of 1878 for a new station at Keighley. And that, for the time being, was as far as it got. In March of 1880 there were vigorous complaints about both existing stations from the respective local authorities. These were followed in April by a letter from the Halifax Chamber of Commerce calling for a joint station at Keighley with the G.N.R. In fact the latter had approached the Midland in 1878 with an offer of joint ownership of its Halifax Thornton and Keighley lines, authorized in 1873. Midland directors, including the chairman and deputy chairman, and accompanied by Allport, had inspected the lines on June 6, 1878 and, while agreeing that joint ownership with the G.N.R. would be of interest, they had declined the offer on the grounds that connections to the H. T. & K. lines, particularly at the Halifax end, to be of any use, would be too costly for the company to consider at the time. The Halifax High Level Railway had a go at the Midland in September of 1883 with like result. As will be seen later, the Chamber of Commerce had been pushing the idea of a Midland/G.N.R. pact in Yorkshire for some time. Its present suggestion about Keighley, however, was the only one that had so far borne fruit, and by an agreement between the Midland and the G.N.R. dated June 1, 1881, the former undertook to construct a new junction station and to permit the G.N.R. to run into it over the metals of the Keighley & Worth Valley line in exchange for a traffic agreement as to goods and passengers between Keighley and Halifax. While Bingley had to wait, therefore, work at Keighley went ahead and the new station —on the south instead of the north side of the main road, and with a new overbridge to replace the previous level crossing—was opened on May 6, 1883. The works also necessitated an alteration to the curve between the river bridge and the road on the K.W.V. line, which company, by the way, the Midland had decided in June, 1880, to purchase, powers to this end having been obtained in the Midland Railway (Further Powers) Act of 1876. The further history of the K.W.V. can be shortly disposed of at this point. The Keighley company vested in the Midland in 1881, though it did not lose its identity and was paid an annual rent of £4,200 from July 1 of that year. Powers for the new Keighley station and the widening of the K.W.V. between the station and the junction with the G.N.R., together with the right to the latter to use the K.W.V. and the station in perpetuity, were granted in the Midland Railway (Additional Powers) Act of 1882. The widening was opened as a double track on June 8, 1884, and the G.N.R. started using the station from the following November 1. By the Midland Railway (Additional Powers) Act of 1885 the capital of the K.W.V. was consolidated, a further Act of 1886 dissolved the small company, and in 1891 the Midland got powers to deviate the line at Oakworth and to make the New Vale viaduct. The latter was opened on November 6, 1892, and loops at Oakworth and Haworth came into use on April 4, 1900. The valley line was on the block system as early as 1877, and was worked on the electrical train tablet system from 1900.

To complete the story of the main line up to 1883, by July of 1877 St Enoch station was virtually ready. As we have seen the station came into use concurrently with the Settle and Carlisle line but was not officially opened until October 17, 1876, at a ceremony attended by the Prince and Princess of Wales. There were, of course, alterations to the structure from time to time in the years ahead but for all practical purposes the station can be said to have been completed when the hotel was opened on July 3, 1879, the G.S.W.R. headquarters staff taking up residence in the office buildings on New Year's Day, 1879. By late July of 1882 a figure of £1,388,731 10s 10d had been spent on the station, general offices, hotel, and land by the C.G.U. company, much in excess of its authorized capital for the station which was £1,200,000. As the small company had obvious difficulties in meeting its creditors, the only solution was for the G.S.W.R. to take over the station and pay the difference. This it did by its Act of June 29, 1883, the station, hotel and offices becoming part of its undertaking from the following August 1, though the existing N.B.R. rights in the station were protected.

Meanwhile at Carlisle the Midland had been successful in resolving some of the major difficulties inherent in running its trains through a station which was nominally in the hands of hostile companies. As has been seen the Settle and Carlisle Act of 1866 had given the company the right to run into Carlisle Citadel station. The joint owners of the station were the L.N.W.R. and the Caledonian and the 1866 Act provided for a rent to be paid by the Midland as a percentage upon the money which would have to be expended by the owning companies in providing such extensions and enlargement to the station as would be necessary to take the increased traffic. If there should be disagreement between the owners and the Midland as to the extent of these additions the Act had provided for an arbitrator to be appointed to give a fair opinion. Of course difficulties had arisen almost immediately and the L.N.W.R. and C.R. companies had asked to go to arbitration. The arbitrator appointed by the Board of Trade was Joseph Cubitt and though he was able to hear some of the evidence put forward by both parties he fell ill, was unable to continue, and eventually died without having made an award. Faced with going through the whole business again the Midland and the owning companies came to an agreement as to the works and in pursuance of this the L.N.W.R. and Caledonian companies obtained the Carlisle Citadel Station Act of 1873 which both sanctioned the new station and confirmed their agreement with the Midland. This situation had seemed satisfactory so long as the Midland was still battling northwards with the Settle and Carlisle line but as soon as traffic from the new railway had begun to use Carlisle there had been trouble. It has been seen how the authorities at Derby had often to excuse the late arrival of their Scotch trains at Skipton to the L.Y.R. In fact precisely the same tactics as were employed by the Carlisle station committee against the N.B.R. and the G.S.W.R. in earlier years, and which were publicised at the time of the Settle line Bill, were being used again. By 1882, despite personal interviews by the company's new chairman— Matthew William Thompson—with the Carlisle station committee and with Richard Moon of the L.N.W.R., at all of which he was received very pleasantly, but which achieved nothing, matters had reached a point where Derby had to act to protect the traffic; the Midland went to Parliament with its own Carlisle Citadel Station Bill in that session seeking to become a member of the joint station committee and thus have a say in the conduct of the station business. The preamble of the Bill accused the two companies point blank of having rigged the station arrangements and signalling so as to favour their traffic at the expense of the Midland, N.B.R., and G.S.W.R. The two owning companies each had four members of their respective boards on the committee and the Midland suggested that it too should provide four. Any disagreement between the members of the committee was to go before the Railway Commissioners for arbitration. The threat was enough. There was some lengthy correspondence between Derby and Euston and rather than be forced to take Midland members on the station committee—members backed by the opinion of the Board of Trade, the L.N.W.R. and Caledonian had to give way and agree to certain basic rights.

The 1873 Act had also had the effect of nullifying preceding N.B.R. efforts to construct new lines at Carlisle. That company had originally gained access to Citadel station from the north by the Carlisle Extension Line—authorized by the Border Union (North British) Railways Act of 1859—which joined the old Port Carlisle Dock & Railway line at Canal Junction. As to the company's legal right to use the station, this rested upon agreements, made together with the Maryport & Carlisle and the G.S.W.R., with the Carlisle Citadel station committee and confirmed in the latter's Act of 1861, the N.E.R. being let in by an Act of the following year. In 1862 the N.B.R.'s extension line was opened and because of the difficulties encountered by the company in its relationships with the L.N.W.R. and C.R., already mentioned, it attempted to better its access by a Bill of 1864 which failed, Acts of 1865, 1867 and 1868, and another Bill of 1871. The coming of the Midland's line into Carlisle brought about the events related above, and the Citadel Station Act of 1873 empowered the N.B.R. to abandon its authorised lines in exchange for guaranteed rights over those to be built by the L.N.W.R. and C.R. The Act of 1873 also provided for a joint goods traffic committee, composed of the L.N.W.R., C.R., M.R., G.S.W.R., and in certain instances which need not be detailed, the N.B.R. and N.E.R. The goods committee was to make an avoiding goods line leaving the Caledonian main line north of the station at the bridge over the River Caldew to join the N.E.R.'s Newcastle & Carlisle line at Rome Street Junction. From there the latter was to be abandoned as far as London Road Junction, at which place the new line ceased. On to this new goods line, with the idea of remaining independent, the Midland, G.S.W.R., and N.B.R. received powers by the latter's Act of 1876 to make yet another line leaving the first south of Bridge Street and terminating at a new goods yard at Dentonholme, a scheme which had been in cold storage since 1865.

To ease congestion at Carlisle the 1873 Act authorised the removal of the level crossing of the L.N.W.R. and N.E.R. south of the station. The L.N.W.R. line was to be raised and the new line, between Rome Street Junction and London Road Junction was constructed so as to permit it to pass under the former. These alterations were long overdue. The level crossing had dangerous possibilities and though it had operated without mishap for some twenty years the inevitable accident occurred when, in the early hours of July 10, 1870, a North Eastern goods with an intoxicated crew rammed the middle of an up Scotch night mail train resulting in the deaths of six passengers and the injury of some thirty more. The old crossing was removed between 1875 and 1876 and the new layout made; two very interesting photographs, taken at the time, were reproduced in the January and February 1949 issue of the *Railway Magazine*.

The rebuilt Carlisle Citadel station came into use on July 4, 1880. As to the works at Dentonholme, Messrs Ireland & Co. successfully tendered at a price of £15,250 in October, 1880, and the goods station was opened for Midland traffic on October 1, 1883. Perhaps in order to keep Carlisle well under surveillance a new Midland director was appointed in 1881 to succeed Grosvenor Hodgkinson, a member of the board who had recently died. The new man was Robert Andrew Allison of Scaleby Hall, near Carlisle.

Leaving Carlisle and returning to the Settle line, it is of interest, remembering the earlier reference to religious services held at Ribblehead station until recent years, to find that these dated back almost to the beginning of the line. In April of 1880 the Midland board received a letter from the Rev. A. Relton telling of the difficulties experienced by the company's servants and others in the Parish of Chapel-le-Dale in attending a place of worship, and asking for permission to use either the booking hall or the waiting room at Ribblehead station for services on Sunday afternoons, probably twice each month. The board resolved that permission should be granted, 'on condition that no damage shall accrue to any of the company's property nor shall the company be put to any expense and that the permission be withdrawn at any time on notice from the company being given to that effect'.

Turning now to the more general history of the Midland company during the period under discussion, on the personality side by far the greatest event was the death on December 3, 1879, of Edward Shipley Ellis. No comment is necessary, as his career has been touched upon many times already. In January the board voted, as it had done so many times before, for a portrait to be painted so as to perpetuate the likeness and memory of a lost colleague. This time, of course, there was no Lucas to do the honours. Being a well-known artist his work had usually cost the board about £1,000 a portrait. In May, 1881, the board minutes noted that a cheque was to be drawn in favour of Mr T. Blake Wirqman in the sum of £441 for the portrait of Ellis and its frame. In December of 1882 William Evans Hutchinson followed Ellis. Save to say that he had been a director of the Midland Counties Railway before 1844, and had sat on the Midland board ever since, there is no need to recall his career as it too has come into focus from time to time in connection with the Settle line. Following Ellis's death, the board elected Allport a director in his stead, the office of general manager being taken by John Noble, and that of assistant general manager by Richard Speight. It appears from the half-yearly meeting of February, 1880, that Allport had asked to be relieved of his duties and reluctantly the board had had to comply with his request. It was, however, unthinkable that such a man should be allowed to fade away. Hence the directorship which, by an irony, was proposed by Mr Garnett at the meeting on February 17. Richard Speight, by the way, only stayed with the Midland until 1884 when he left to become chairman of the Commissioners of Railways in the Colony of Victoria. To succeed Ellis the Midland board had, as we have seen, chosen Matthew William Thompson of Guiseley, near Leeds and, as his deputy, Timothy Kenrick. Thompson had, of course, been the deputy chairman for some years and his appointment was significant in that he was also a member of the G.S.W.R. board. He became its chairman on March 21, 1883.

On August 24, 1883, the board met to fill the position vacated by Crossley, as engineer to the company, though the post was now designated as chief engineer. Three men appeared before the board; Kennett Bayley, chief engineer of the Great Southern & Western Railway of

Ireland; a Mr Footner, one of the L.N.W.R. district engineers; and Alfred A. Langley, the Great Eastern's engineer. Langley got the job, at an annual salary of £2,000. His northern divisional engineer on the Midland, Henry Bolden, had been appointed in January, 1878, at £500 per annum.

Before coming to the last heading of this chapter, that of the foreign Bills which affected the Midland during the period up to 1883, note can be taken of the connecting N.E.R. services to the Leeds–Settle–Carlisle line. Dealing with the southern part first, the Midland's Shipley and Guiseley branch came into use on December 4, 1876, and shortly afterwards talks between Derby and York resulted in an agreement that the N.E.R. should work a through service of trains between Harrogate and Bradford via Guiseley, Menston Junction, Milner Wood Junction, the Otley and Ilkley line and the N.E.R.'s Otley branch, and the Leeds Northern line from Arthington Junction. It was decided that the service should commence from July 2. In fact it started on August 1, 1877, with four trains each way, and for the next twenty years was worked by N.E.R. Fletcher bogie tank engines. In July of 1878 the Midland approached the N.E.R. regarding the possibility of the latter putting on a connecting train service between Appleby and Penrith, to compete with the L.N.W.R. for the Lake District services, but the following month the matter was dropped for the time being. Meanwhile, the Northallerton–Tebay line, connecting with the Midland at Kirkby Stephen, operated a service of four trains daily, worked by N.E.R. engines Nos. 1238–1241 and 1265–1270, 4-4-0s with 7 ft. driving wheels. Designed by William Bouch, the Stockton & Darlington locomotive engineer, and inherited by the N.E.R. on the take-over of the Stockton company, these engines were not a success and were known collectively and euphemistically as 'Ginx's Babies', a polite way of terming them as unwanted children.* By about 1882 they had been rebuilt as 2-4-0s, and continued in service for many years after. As to the Hawes branch, it was agreed in September, 1878, that the N.E.R. should work a service connecting the main line trains of the N.E.R. at Northallerton with those of the Midland at Hawes Junction, the N.E.R. to receive an annual payment of £500 for the Hawes–Hawes Junction trains. Lastly the Ingleton branch : regarding the connecting L.N.W.R. service to the north, Euston must have felt that its line to the town was in danger of stagnating and with a view to getting at least some benefits from its existence it was agreed in April of 1881 that an improved service of trains should be put on to provide a resurrected Leeds–Penrith–Carlisle service, in co-operation with the Midland. Regarding all these arrangements, and the state of the Midland train service generally, the *Railway News* of August 21, 1880, observing that the Midland was a company remarkable for its progress, had the following to say :

* *Locomotives of the North Eastern Railway.*—O. S. Nock.

'Several important improvements have recently been made in Midland affairs. The completion of the Nottingham and Melton, and of the Manton and Kettering lines has provided the directors with a duplicate route and a better gradient over the most crowded part of their system; and the new service of express trains runs from London to Kettering, and from Kettering to Nottingham, and the North in half an hour less time than formerly. Nottingham itself, with its 160,000 inhabitants and its thriving industries, is now, and for the first time, on the main line of a great railway company. Additional expresses have also been arranged to bring the Northern and Midland counties of England into more direct access to Bristol, Bath, and Bournemouth, and the South and West of England generally; and the stopping of the express at Appleby, and a fresh service of trains between Appleby and Penrith, put the vast populations resident on the main line of the Midland in immediate communication with Keswick and with the whole of the northern part of the Lake District, from which they have hitherto been practically excluded. An improved service also connects Leeds and Bradford with Ben Rhydding and Ilkley, and the beautiful district of Wharfedale generally; and another unites the cities of Manchester and Liverpool, and the Central station at Manchester is now in full operation. The speed of several trains has also been considerably increased, and others stop at fewer stations. Fifty miles an hour is the speed for which the trains are timed; and the punctuality which they have so far shown leaves nothing to be desired.'

(Outline timetables for the Hawes branch and South Durham & Lancashire Union line as at July 1879, for the Eden Valley line for July of 1879 and 1880, and for the Ingleton branch showing the improvements as in force on the latter in July of 1881 as compared with the previous year, are given in Appendices XIII–XVIII.)

The fresh service of trains between Appleby and Penrith was the outcome of the 1878 talks with the N.E.R. and consisted of three additional fast connecting trains over the Eden Valley line from July 1880. The service lasted some thirteen years, for the first six of which the N.E.R. received a rate per mile payment from the Midland.

Lastly we come to the various schemes which were put forward by outside parties between 1876 and 1883, some of which would undoubtedly have affected the Leeds–Settle–Carlisle line had they come to fruition. First among them was the proposed West Riding & Lancashire Railway. This scheme ante-dated the arrangement between the Midland and the G.N.R. as to the Keighley–Halifax service, and was the start of the series of attempts by the Halifax Chamber of Commerce, already mentioned, to push the two companies together. November of 1875 saw the start of the campaign when the W.R. & L.R. appeared for all too brief a time with what seemed like the answer to Halifax's prayers. As proposed, the W.R. & L.R. was to leave the Leeds & Bradford line south of Manningham by a triangular junction, run west for about a mile and then join the G.N.R.'s City Road, Bradford, branch. Where the latter joined the G.N.R.'s Bradford & Thornton line, the W.R. & L.R. intended putting in a connection at Horton Park Junction so that through running could be had westwards through Queensbury to a point just south of Holmfield tunnel. There the main line of the W.R. & L.R. was to leave the G.N.R. and run south for about 5 miles to a point just south of Dryclough Junction on the L.Y.R.'s Manchester & Leeds line. There it divided; one line was to go south-east for about 6 miles to

Huddersfield, and the other was to meander about in a generally south-westerly direction, passing through Ripponden and Oldham on its way to Manchester, where it joined the M.S.L.R. near Openshaw. With a bit of luck this would have put Halifax in a better position to kick against the monopolistic L.Y.R. Halifax–Manchester service then, and for some years past, of doubtful quality. The earthworks on the proposed line and the gradients involved would have been very heavy. To give some illustrations; the climb to the City Road branch was intended to be at 1 in 56, and the descent on to the G.N.R. at Horton Park at about 1 in 50. After leaving the G.N.R. at Holmfield there was to be a drop into Halifax at a ruling gradient of 1 in 80 which included a viaduct, 200 yards long and 142 feet high. Getting out of Halifax, and climbing through Greetland and Barkisland, the ruling gradient was to be 1 in 92, with a viaduct 836 yards long and 275 feet high over the L.Y.R. and the River Calder, and a 990 yard long tunnel at Barkisland. These were followed, a few miles further on, by a tunnel, 3,355 yards long and passing 400 feet below Rishworth Moor, the summit of the line. The descent into Manchester, on a ruling gradient of 1 in 66 and including four more viaducts and another tunnel, concluded the main line. There were also to be several short branches. The Bill gave running and other powers to the Great Northern, and to the Midland and the M.S.L.R. in the event of either of them becoming a joint owner with the G.N.R. of the Halifax Thornton & Keighley line; it also sought running powers into the Manchester stations of the Midland and M.S.L.R. The railway was planned by John Fraser & Son, engineers who had carried out much work for the G.N.R. It was hardly likely, in any event, that the Midland would have been interested. The company had just spent twice as much as it had thought it would have to on the Settle line and in any case the works contemplated by the W.R. & L.R. were expensive; the capital required was estimated to be £1,967,000 with borrowing powers of £665,000. The Bill was thrown out by Parliament. Another apparent G.N.R. attempt, this time to get into Huddersfield from the south, with John Fraser again as engineer, appeared in the guise of the Huddersfield South & East Junction Railway. This proposed a line just over 17½ miles long from Hemsworth on the West Riding & Grimsby Railway, and from Sandal on the North Midland line, to the Huddersfield & Manchester Railway of the L.N.W.R. about a mile north of Huddersfield joint station. With an intended capital of over £½m, and loans of £190,000, the proposed company sent a deputation, accompanied by the Mayor of Huddersfield, to the Midland asking for assistance in May, 1880. It was turned down flat and the Bill was rejected by Parliament. In any case the Midland had its own ideas on reaching Huddersfield and these are mentioned in a later chapter when the whole matter of shortening the company's route mileage to the north is discussed.

Schemes around Skipton were well to the fore in the early 1880s. The first was the Skipton & Kettlewell Railway, a company which got powers for its line by Act of August 26, 1880. In the previous April it had written to the Midland asking for a working agreement but this had been declined. Originally the company had wanted to construct a railway leaving the Midland at Gargrave to run some 14 miles through Flasby, Hetton, Threshfield, and Conistone to Kettlewell, terminating in a field with the name of 'Priest's Rain'. Local opposition, however, cut it to a length of about 9 miles ending at Threshfield, and it was in this form that the Bill was passed, as mentioned above. The company had also sought to run over the Midland from Gargrave to Keighley but this was not granted. The next session it deposited a Bill not only to continue to Kettlewell but to extend northwards through Buckden in Upper Wharfedale and then to tunnel under Buckden Pike into Bishop Dale by a line 9 miles long to join the N.E.R.'s Wensleydale line just west of Aysgarth station. Running powers were sought over the N.E.R. into Leyburn and over the Midland into Shipley, so as to make a junction both there and at Keighley with the G.N.R. These proposals fairly put everybody's back up and the Bill was so hacked about in Parliament that the promoters withdrew it. Nothing daunted, the small company bounced back yet again in 1882, this time with an even bigger scheme; nothing less than a full-scale attempt to reach Darlington. At the same time a new concern, the North Yorkshire & Lancashire Railway, deposited a Bill for 1882 proposing a line from the L.Y.R. and the Midland by a double junction at Hellifield to run some 33 miles, in a north-east direction, to join the N.E.R. at Fingall in Wensleydale, with two branches to the Skipton & Kettlewell, the existing powers of which it aimed to take over. Both lines, therefore, threatened Darlington and the N.E.R. was quick to react. Both Bills failed but whereas the N.Y. & L. accepted defeat the S.K.R. tried yet again in 1883 with a modified Bill, still aimed at Darlington but cutting out many of the branches deposited in the previous session and concentrating on a direct thrust into the N.E.R. hinterland with a line some 47 miles in length from Threshfield to Darlington with three small branches at the northern end. Any attempt at running powers was dropped, presumably to placate its enemies, and an effort was made to try and tempt the N.E.R. into working and traffic arrangements. It was to no avail. Perhaps with the view that a change of image might bring success, the S.K.R. went back to Parliament in the session of 1884 with a Bill to revive its land purchase powers of 1880 and to rename itself, again undoubtedly with one eye on York, as the Skipton & North Eastern Junction Railway. This time the powers it sought, to make an extension to the 1880 railway, were limited merely to a scheme very similar to its earlier and unsuccessful Aysgarth line. Once more Parliamentary approval was withheld and at last the penny dropped. In the session of 1885 the S.K.R. did succeed in Parliament but only to get an Act for the abandonment of the 1880 line and the winding up of its affairs. It might be thought that all this activity north of Skipton would have exhausted the market, so to speak, and yet in the session of 1883 there came another proposal to tap the Midland main line to the north, this time from the Richmond & Hawes Junction Railway. This concern sought to construct a railway some 25 miles in length from Richmond to the Hawes branch, which it intended to join by a double junction near to Hawes Junction station. Once again John Fraser was the engineer. The Bill failed. The wonder of it all was that most of these attempts to break into territory already spoken for relied on the naive assumption that the big companies would welcome them with open arms. The truth was that if the lines had been really wanted they would have been promoted by the latter; for the most part they were nothing more than an attempt to get powers and then negotiate a profitable arrangement whereby the idea was taken up, for a price, by the major companies. Another such attempt, and one of those most unlikely to have succeeded, was made by the aspiring Mid Cumberland Railway. Early in 1882 it approached the Midland with an idea for a line 25 miles in length which it intended to construct westwards out of Penrith. It can only be assumed that with the N.E.R. conveniently connecting Penrith with the Settle and Carlisle line, the Mid Cumberland saw rosy chances of getting a through Midland service over its metals, no doubt built by the Midland too. It was quickly disabused; on May 3, 1882, the Midland board replied very shortly that it was not interested.

Coming south again, and back to something more substantial, there had, as has been seen, been attempts in the past years to get a railway constructed between Skipton and Ilkley, and in the session of 1882 two separate proposals were put to Parliament by local parties, both named as the Skipton & Ilkley Railway. Both got to committee stage in the Lords and were then scotched. In fact there appears to have been a private arrangement between one of the schemes and the Midland as in early September the Midland board received an appeal from the promoters of one of the defunct concerns to make the line. It was the Midland's view that, being at either end of the line, it should come to terms and it was therefore agreed to go ahead. As surveyed by John Underwood, by now the company's new works engineer, the Skipton and Ilkley line was planned to be double tracked and to be about 11½ miles in length at an estimated cost of £302,661. Powers were obtained in the company's Act of July 16, 1883, and in the following December the Midland board gave the green light for construction to start.

XV

Expansion

1884 – 1890

On February 15, 1884, the Midland board confirmed the appointment of Matthew William Thompson as chairman of the company, a position he had held since Ellis's death. Within the past year Thompson had also become the chairman of the Glasgow & South Western and both moves indicated the present and growing affinity between the two companies. The Midland's deputy chairman, Timothy Kenrick, resigned in the following October to make way for Ernest George Paget who was to succeed to the chairman's position on Thompson's resignation in 1891. Thompson's tenure at the head of both companies was to cover a period during which the Midland essayed a general expansion of its system in the north. The Settle and Carlisle line had, in fact, provided a pad from which launches were to be made towards Northern Ireland via Portpatrick, to Liverpool and Manchester via the Hellified line of the L.Y.R., and to a final and nearly successful attempt to amalgamate the G.S.W.R. with either the Midland or the North British systems.

A detailed history of the first of these moves, that of the pre-Midland story of the Portpatrick line, would be out of place here but as the Portpatrick & Wigtownshire Railway was to form part of the Midland system from 1885 onwards, held jointly with other companies, a brief survey of its history is of interest in that it was, in effect, the northernmost extension of the Midland from the Settle line. The line first came into Midland history as far back as 1857 when, as mentioned in Chapter VII, the little North Western had supported the British & Irish Grand Junction scheme in that session. Its interest in the B. & I.G.J.—which came through Parliament as the Portpatrick Railway—was naturally passed on to the Midland when the N.W.R. came under Derby's wing. The origins of the Portpatrick line were tied up with the hope of a regular mail service from the south of Scotland to Northern Ireland. As far back as the mid seventeenth century there had been a weekly sailing from Portpatrick to Ireland. A pier had been built at the harbour at Portpatrick in 1774, and in 1790 the service became a daily one. In the 1820s the Government decided to improve the harbour works for the mail service and though progress in this direction was slow they were substantially completed by the early 1860s. A few years earlier, as told, the B. & I.G.J. proposal had been put forward, and on the strength of Government backing—a promise was made that by the time the line was built the harbour works would be complete—the Portpatrick Railway received the Royal Assent on August 10, 1857. The Lancaster & Carlisle, Glasgow & South Western, and Belfast & County Down companies all contributed towards the Portpatrick Railway. The main line, 61 miles in length, commenced at Castle Douglas by a junction with the Castle Douglas & Dumfries Railway—opened on November 7, 1859, and worked by the G.S.W.R. The Portpatrick Railway was opened from Castle Douglas to Stranraer on March 12, 1861, and on to Portpatrick on August 28, 1862, the latter station being at the termination of the main line, and that at Stranraer on a short branch. The government works, however, had not come up to expectation. Indeed they were never to be completed. The Act of 1857 had authorized the G.S.W.R. to work the Portpatrick Railway but before the opening the Portpatrick quarrelled with the G.S.W.R., purchased its own engines and rolling stock, and did the job itself. The Portpatrick Railway was constructed as a single line with passing loops.

From the opening of the line the company repeatedly requested the Admiralty to complete the harbour, but to no avail. Meanwhile, with the object of bringing Irish traffic on to the railway, and with the coming into operation of the Belfast–Larne line, the Portpatrick, in conjunction with the Irish company, the Castle Douglas & Dumfries, and the L.N.W.R., established a daily service between Stranraer and Larne. By 1864, however, this was showing a loss and it was only because of the ultimate potential of the Irish traffic that the railway kept it going, in conjunction with private companies. By two Acts of July 29 of that year the Portpatrick was empowered to run over the Castle Douglas and Dumfries line and was authorized to carry out certain works, to arrange with the L.N.W.R. and C.R. to work the line—with facilities to the G.S.W.R., and to establish a steamer service between Portpatrick and Donaghdee as well as the Belfast–Stranraer–Larne run. As to the working, it was also decided that the Caledonian, which had reached Dumfries on September 1, 1863, via the Dumfries Lochmaben & Lockerbie Railway, should work the Portpatrick for 21 years from October 1, 1864, for 38 per cent. of the gross receipts, the latter company selling its eight locomotives and the rolling stock to the C.R. for this purpose. In 1867 the Corporation and Chamber of Commerce of Belfast added their voices to the pleadings of the Portpatrick Railway in trying to get the Government to send the mails by the Portpatrick line. It was a forlorn hope, for by now the authorities had realized that not only were the rival steamer mail routes of Holyhead–Dublin and Glasgow–Belfast sufficient; they had turned the Portpatrick venture into something of a white elephant. It was an expensive one, as the harbour works so far carried out totalled around the £½m mark. *Bradshaw's Shareholders' Guide* of 1868 noted that :

'The directors regretted being still unable to report any setttlement of the mail question. Every effort had been made to prevail on the Government to carry out the arrangements proposed . . . but although the obligations incurred . . . had been duly recognized, no definite arrangement had yet been made, and the loss to the company was every year increasing.... The County Down, finding that the official reports of the Board of Trade and Post Office were adverse to the establishment of the mail service at Portpatrick, because the harbour had been reported insufficient for a night passage, had obtained from the Treasury a minute, dated the 8th of July last, admitting their claim to compensation, and agreeing to give them a loan . . . in the event of the Portpatrick and Donaghdee route being finally abandoned. In the event of Portpatrick being abandoned the next best arrangement would be to establish the service via Stranraer, but via Portpatrick was the most expeditious route.'

The following year the Portpatrick directors decided that they had waited long enough. There being no Government mail service to Ireland, the company accepted a payment of £20,000 and a long term loan in compensation for its wasted time, the sorry end to its hopes being made the subject of a special Act. With the government steamers withdrawn and the sea crossing at a standstill the company decided, with its colleagues in northern Ireland, to put some of the £20,000 towards a new Stranraer–Larne service. To this end the Larne & Stranraer Steamboat Company was formed in 1871 and by mid 1872 the new two-funnelled paddle steamer *Princess Louise* was doing the daily trip, in under three hours, run in conjunction with a special connecting train put on by the Caledonian. Five years later the Portpatrick Railway Act of 1877 authorized the company to take over the east pier at Stranraer, a structure that the Stranraer Town Council had undertaken to keep in order so that the trains could run alongside the steamer berth, but which was in such bad repair as to have become positively dangerous. The Act also permitted the Girvan & Portpatrick Junction Railway to make use of the pier.

The Girvan & Portpatrick Junction—about 31 miles in length, had been authorized by an Act of July 5, 1865, to make a line from the Maybole & Girvan Railway to join the Portpatrick line about 2 miles west of Glenluce. Having got its powers the company went into hibernation, only showing sufficient signs of life to get its second Act, on June 20, 1870, which gave it a renewal of powers and an extension of time. In August, 1871, a heavy issue of shares was made and the works were commenced; the line was to be operated by the G.S.W.R. The following year, by an Act of August 6, the G. & P.J. was empowered to use the Portpatrick into Stranraer and to become joint owners of the portion so used, provided payment was made within a specified time. Work still proceded slowly, however, mainly because of some difficult tunnel construction and on July 7, 1873, the company received a further extension of time. It is at about this point that the Midland enters the picture; the formation of the joint committee between the company and the G.S.W.R. and the ever-present thought of amalgamation, naturally brought Derby into any new moves made by the Glasgow company. On October 12, 1876, the committee discussed the proposed working of the G. & P.J. and it was decided that the G.S.W.R. should offer to do the honours for the first year while the traffic potential could be accurately assessed. The line was opened on October 5, 1877. The Midland had, of course, by now got a vested interest in the G.S.W.R. share of the Portpatrick Railway. On October 9, 1879, the Midland representatives on the committee told the G.S.W.R. that their company intended applying to the Railway Commissioners for through booking from the Midland system to Ireland via Stranraer and Larne. In the following April the committee read a letter from the secretary of the Wigtownshire Railway asking on what terms the G.S.W.R. would work that company's line.

The Wigtownshire Railway Act of July 18, 1872, had authorized the construction of a line from Newton Stewart, on the Portpatrick Railway, to Whithorn—about 19 miles, and a tramway of $1\frac{3}{4}$ miles to Garliestown. The company was to be closely tied in to the Portpatrick line by working agreements. The line was opened from Newton Stewart to Wigtown on April 3, 1875 (*Bradshaw's Shareholders' Guide* of 1876 gives the date as both April 3 and 7, and later years as April 3), and on to Millisle near Garliestown on the following August 2. By the Wigtownshire Railway Act of June 28, 1877, the company was authorized to abandon the tramway and to construct a branch to Garliestown harbour. New working arrangements were to be made with the Caledonian, Portpatrick, G.S.W.R., and L.N.W.R. Millisle to Garliestown came into operation on April 3, 1876, and the Millisle–Whithorn line followed on July 9, 1877. The line was single throughout.

Though the Caledonian was currently working the Portpatrick line negotiations for an agreement to operate the Wigtownshire too fell through and Thomas Wheatley, who had been locomotive superintendent of the N.B.R., was given the job of manager of the Wigtownshire in 1875. He was to provide the locomotives and rolling stock and was to maintain the line. The first engine to work the Wigtownshire at its opening—engine No. 1—was a 2-2-2 well tank of the N.B.R. which had been purchased and converted to a 2-4-0. An interesting photograph of this engine appeared in the August 1951 issue of the *Railway Magazine*.

Leaving the Wigtownshire Railway for a moment, and returning to the Girvan & Portpatrick Junction, in 1879 that company received powers to borrow the necessary money to enable it to become joint owner with the Portpatrick of the 'Stranraer Section' of the latter's line—the part over which the G. & P.J. had running powers. In 1881 the Midland and G.S.W.R. joint committee noted that it was entering into negotiations for the purchase of the smaller company. As will be seen these came to nought, the G. & P.J. evidently having ideas about its own potential which were a direct challenge to the G.S.W.R.

As to the Portpatrick Railway, the joint committee met in October, 1883, to agree a Bill whereby the company should be vested equally in the Midland, G.S.W.R., C.R., and L.N.W.R. The current arrangement for working the line by the Caledonian was due to end in 1885. On Friday, February 15, 1884, the Midland Railway company held a special meeting at Derby to discuss the Bill. Thompson, who with his joint interest in the Midland and the G.S.W.R. was undoubtedly whole-heartedly behind the idea, told the shareholders that the Midland board had been pressed by people living in northern Ireland to give them a connecting train and boat service to London. It was a logical outcome of the Settle and Carlisle line. He thought that the Irish traffic would mutually benefit the through receipts to Euston and St Pancras and emphasised that the idea was sound. The meeting voted in favour of the Bill. There was, however, a doubt that the Bill would go through, as terms of access for the L.N.W.R. and Caledonian could not be agreed, and in fact it failed. By January of 1885 agreement had been reached and the Bill redeposited, this time to include in the purchase the Wigtownshire Railway. The Portpatrick & Wigtownshire Railways (Sale and Transfer) Act received the Royal Assent on August 6, 1885, and from the first day of that month the Caledonian working agreement was terminated and the Midland company had a quarter share in the joint undertaking, to be known as the Portpatrick & Wigtownshire Joint Committee. The Midland was given running powers over the Caledonian from Carlisle to Gretna Junction where the rails of its ally the G.S.W.R. took over to Castle Douglas. The Act also provided for agreements with the Irish companies as to the Stranraer–Larne steamer service, and for the Girvan & Portpatrick to have through booking and other facilities between the south and north of both Ireland and Scotland. The Portpatrick line was henceforth worked by the Caledonian and the G.S.W.R., each of the English companies being content to leave this to its Scottish partner.

To bring the Portpatrick story to the end of the period covered by this chapter, a meeting of the Midland board early in 1885 anticipated the company's rights over the Portpatrick. It was decided that from July 1, in lieu of the 'Highland' train which had for some years past operated between London and Carlisle during three months of the summer, a new train should be run from St Pancras to Carlisle which would have connections there with Glasgow and the north of Scotland, and with which a connection to Stranraer could also be established immediately after the passing of the Portpatrick Bill. There was also to be a corresponding train in the opposite direction, together with a new Bristol–Trent train in both directions to give a connection with the London–Carlisle service and the West of England. The main reason behind this move, as given at a meeting of the Midland and G.S.W.R. joint committee on April 9, was an attempt to parry the accelerated L.N.W.R. Scotch service which had recently been put on. The committee also hoped that by providing a competitive train service from London to Stranraer it would be able to tender for the mails if the Post Office decided to adopt the route for that purpose. Again, to boost the Midland's Scotch service, the Pullman Car company was to make available an additional coach for the night train to Greenock. It was also decided that the Pullman charge for sleeping accommodation from St Pancras to Scotland, then standing at 8s., should be reduced to 6s. Almost immediately afterwards this was cut to 5s., the Midland agreeing to pay the Pullman company the difference of 1s. per passenger. When in August the winter timetables were discussed, it was obvious that the new night service was either popular or a political necessity as the board decided to retain it and the connecting services at Trent, except for the northern connections to the North British and Highland Railways. By 1891, however, the 'Highland' express was fully back in business, leaving St Pancras at 7.15 p.m. and arriving at Carlisle at 2.20 a.m.

Before continuing with the Midland story the fate of the Girvan & Portpatrick as it affected the G.S.W.R. and Midland interest in the Portpatrick line can be shortly told. We left the company in 1881, being approached by the G.S.W.R. for purchase. In 1882 and 1886 it got powers to borrow more money, some of which was to help pay off the Portpatrick and some to go towards new lineside equipment and the purchase of rolling stock. It had, in fact, decided to break away from the G.S.W.R. and go it alone, the agreement by which the latter company worked the line being terminated on February 27, 1886, and from the following day the G. & P.J. worked the line itself with locomotives and rolling stock hired from the G.S.W.R. This use of G.S.W.R. stock was short-lived for the line closed on April 12, 1886, while the G. & P.J. gathered its breath and its own stock prior to a re-opening on the following June 14, now completely independent. To remain alive it had to expand, but first it changed its name, selling itself to a nominally new company, the Ayrshire & Wigtownshire Railway whose Act received the Royal Assent on May 23, 1887. With its new name and independence it thumbed its nose at the G.S.W.R. and went for powers in the sessions of 1889 and 1890 to run over that company's line from Girvan to Glasgow, and with rights for any other companies running over it to do likewise. This piece of sauce was justified by the A. & W. with the argument that together with the Stranraer portion of the Portpatrick line it formed the shortest Scotland to Ireland route, though as will be seen later in this chapter, this was not the true reason. In 1889 Parliament found the Bill's preamble was not proved, and in 1890 it was again defeated. It had shot its bolt. Ayrshire was looked upon by the G.S.W.R. directors as something being peculiarly theirs, and they would defend it against all comers, something the Caledonian was finding out to its cost at the same time. After a fruitless attempt to sell to the Caledonian in 1891, the Ayrshire & Wigtownshire Railway was acquired by the G.S.W.R. in 1892 by the latter's Act of June 20 of that year. The locomotive stock thus inherited by the G.S.W.R. included three old worn-out North London Railway tank engines.

Turning now to the Liverpool and Manchester via Hellifield route, the Midlands aspirations in that direction were made plain in the company's half-yearly meeting of February 20, 1885. Speaking to the shareholders, Thompson said that for many years the Midland had had a

259

right to run over the E.L.R. line to Liverpool and Salford. Despite the entreaties of local people the company had never made use of its powers. Now, the L.Y.R. had the Blackburn–Hellifield line too, and the Midland again had running powers. The company was, therefore, seeking permission for a short branch at Ardwick, near Manchester, to connect the L.Y.R. with the G.C.R. and Midland joint line from New Mills, thus permitting the Midand to run through London and Bristol trains to the L.Y.R.'s Manchester Victoria station, and to Liverpool Exchange when the latter was completed. Services between Scotland and London and Bristol via Manchester would also be possible. The Ancoats Junction, as the Ardwick line was called, received the Royal Assent on June 16, 1885. As to the Hellifield route, Midland passenger trains from the Settle line began running to Manchester and Liverpool in 1888. Details of the services are dealt with later in this chapter.

By mid 1885 works on another extension or offshoot of the Leeds–Settle–Carlisle line—the Skipton to Ilkley branch—were well under way. The *Railway Times* of April 25 recorded that the contract had been let to Mousley & Co. of Bristol. There were some seventy bridges and small viaducts required on the line and a short tunnel, Haw Bank (219 yards), near the Skipton end. Three stone-built stations were to be erected, at Addingham, Bolton Abbey, and Embsay. The paper remarked that the line was already staked out. There was quite a considerable force of navvies employed on the works and on August 21 the board read a letter from the Rev A. C. Downer of the Vicarage, Ilkley, asking for a subscription towards a mission for the men. The board sent him £50. By August of 1887 the viaduct at Ilkley was complete, Haw Bank tunnel half-finished, the permanent way and stations commenced, and a good portion of the earthworks finished. A year later the line was opened; Ilkley to Bolton Abbey on May 16 (*Bradshaw's Shareholders' Guide* gives June 1), and Bolton Abbey to Skipton on the following October 1. It followed a circuitous route : leaving Skipton, where an additional platform seemingly divorced from the main station had been provided, it curved south and then climbed in a north-easterly direction over the Leeds & Bradford Extension line to curve round towards Embsay. From there it skirted most of the high ground so that gradients were kept reasonably easy. To work the line the Midland used engines Nos. 14 and 20. They were of a series of ten early coupled locomotives built in 1863 and numbered 50–59. Eight of them were rebuilt and renumbered between 1877 and 1881. Nos. 14 and 20 went to Colne to work the Midland trains over the branch and on the opening throughout of the Skipton and Ilkley line they ran through to Otley with one train. For some time the L.Y.R. also ran through Manchester–Ilkley trains over the new line, in exchange for the Midland's Scotch service over the Hellifield line. The Skipton–Ilkley line also gave the Midland access to Harrogate via Arthington Junction and a service to Colne–

Harrogate trains commenced. The N.E.R. gained to the extent of being granted running powers from Ilkley to Bolton Abbey.*

As to the Colne line, a meeting of Midland and L.Y.R. officers at Colne station on May 11, 1887, learned that there were many complaints from the public about the delays at the station and at the inordinate amount of what seemed like unnecessary shunting which went on, presumably into the small hours, as a result of the heavy increase of mineral traffic. It was decided to put in more sidings and to re-arrange the carriage working so as to relieve stabling room at night. This was to be done by taking the carriages which arrived at Colne from the L.Y.R., and which were usually stabled there for the night, and forming them into the 8.30 p.m. train from Colne to Skipton, to be worked there by the Midland as was the current practice. The carriages forming this train were to be provided by the two companies in alternate periods of nine months to the L.Y.R. and three to the Midland, so as to regulate the mileage account. The three carriages which formed the Midland arrival at Colne at 6.32 p.m. were to be worked back to Skipton by the engine which would then return light to Colne, thus relieving Colne of their stabling. It transpired that there were twenty carriages kept at Colne for strengthening L.Y.R. trains on Saturdays and it was agreed that sixteen of these should be farmed out to other stations.

Various improvements took place during the late eighties. In December of 1886, with a respite after the summer traffic to Morecambe, the board instructed that the Lancaster–Morecambe line should be doubled in time for the next season's excursion traffic. At an estimated cost of £7,885 the work was completed and double track opened on April 3, 1887. The line had been on the block system from January 1, 1876. (A note of the little North Western line opening dates and widenings will be found in Appendix IV.) Suffice it to say that by 1890 the line had assumed practically its present state. There were still requests for new stations on the Settle and Carlisle line; one in December of 1887 wanted trains to stop at Mallerstang. Considering there was practically nothing to stop for at such a bleak place it is not surprising that the board turned it down. On the following October 19, there came a memorandum from the inhabitants of Penrith and Pooley Bridge for the company to extend its system to those places. Again the answer was no. At Bradford the new passenger lines and station came into use on March 2, 1890. It was during the period under discussion that the idea of having station garden competitions was put forward. A board minute of July 18, 1884, noted that on the recommendation of the traffic committee the sum of £100 per annum was to be appropriated as prize money to 'promote the cultivation of neatness and order in the maintenance of gardens as an ornament to the stations'. Apparently the scheme

* *Locomotive & Train Working in the Latter Part of the Nineteenth Century.*— E. L. Ahrons.

was successful; on October 19, 1888 the board upped the amount to £150. It would seem that the board was taking a new interest in the 'image' of the Midland. On March 18, 1887, Allport, recently become Sir James Allport, produced a treasure he had found. Laid on the boardroom table, this resolved itself into three books of engravings—one containing views of cities and towns, and two with views of palaces, abbeys and castles—many of which, he pointed out, were on the Midland system. They were, he said, taken from engravings made by Messrs Buck about the year 1730 and could be purchased for £45. This the board resolved to do, and instructions were given to have the prints of scenes on the Midland system mounted and framed for the company's use.

Coming now to the locomotives and train services, in 1882 and 1883 Derby turned out the first of the 4-4-0 locomotives which were henceforth to be constructed in preference to the old 2-4-0 designs. Of these 4-4-0s Nos. 1572–1581 were sent to Carlisle. They had 6 ft. 9 in. driving wheels and were fitted with the Westinghouse brake for the main line workings. They were joined four years later by Nos. 1748–1749 which, like the others, were 4-4-0s but had 7 ft. driving wheels and improved boilers. They came from a batch of twenty engines and Ahrons rated them as perhaps the best that ever ran on the Midland. Incidentally the last of the class, No. 1757, was one of the few Midland named engines. Bearing the name *Beatrice* it was exhibited at the Saltaire Exhibition in 1887. By 1884 Skipton shed had acquired Nos. 801–811 of the 800 class as rebuilt by Johnson with enlarged cylinders and boilers. They joined Nos. 22 and 800 which were already at Skipton. Of the Leeds engines 812–819, Nos. 818 and 819 went to London at about this time to work the Scotch trains between St Pancras and Leicester.*

1888 was the first year of the Scotch races between the G.N.R. and L.N.W.R. Though the Midland stood aloof—it could hardly have competed—the company was forced drastically to rethink its schedules in order to retain traffic. The result was a decided improvement to the Scotch expresses. Up to this time the down morning Scotch express—the 10.35 a.m. from St Pancras—had run as one train, but in order to speed it up the company decided to split it into two separate trains from St Pancras. First to leave was the Glasgow portion. With the dining stop at Normanton cut to 25 minutes, it left St Pancras at 10.30, Leicester at 12.29 p.m., Normanton at 2.38, Skipton at 3.27, and arrived at Carlisle at 5.16, averaging 47.8 m.p.h. over the Skipton–Carlisle portion. The Edinburgh train went via the Nottingham line. It left St Pancras at 10.40 a.m., Nottingham at 1.09 p.m., shot past the Glasgow portion standing in Normanton station for the luncheon break, and arrived at Leeds at 2.47 where the passengers were allowed a luncheon time similar

* *Locomotive & Train Working in the Latter Part of the Nineteenth Century.—* E. L. Ahrons.

to that at Normanton. The train left Leeds at 3.12, Hellifield at 4.10, and arrived at Carlisle at 5.47, averaging 47.3 m.p.h. over the Settle line. The heavy loading of this train necessitated assistance between Leeds and Hellifield and in 1889 one of the old 2-2-2 engines, No. 39, was transferred from Derby to Leeds to act as pilot.* Another threat to the Scotch trains in 1888 came from the Bristol–Scotland service of the G.W.R. and L.N.W.R. Using the new Severn tunnel route the two companies shaped up to disturb the Midland traffic with a new fast timing. This was countered by Derby by the introduction of a new service which left Bristol at 9.35 a.m. and, avoiding Birmingham, arrived at Normanton and Leeds to connect with the Glasgow and Edinburgh portions of the Scotch trains just mentioned. According to Ahrons this Bristol Scotch train had the unenviable task of ensuring connection with the main line; it would have wrecked the London–Carlisle schedule had it been late.

To work the Hellifield–Manchester–Liverpool trains the Midland constructed a series of fifteen 4-4-0 locomotives at Derby. Numbered 1808–1822 and with 6 ft. 6 in. driving wheels, they were in operation by September and were stationed as follows: 1808–1813 went to Newton Heath on the L.Y.R., and later to the Midland establishment at Belle Vue, 1814–1818 went to Liverpool (Sandhills) and worked the Liverpool–Blackburn portions—the trains dividing at the latter station, and 1819–1822 went to Hellifield. In 1891 ten more of the class, Nos. 80–87, 11, and 14 went to Hellifield to work the Leeds–Carlisle and Carlisle–Manchester trains. Besides the locomotives mentioned, Carlisle engines Nos. 1572–1581 also ran through to Manchester as well as some of the 2-4-0 engines stationed at Hellifield, though according to Ahrons these latter were looked upon with disapproval by the L.Y.R., who preferred the Midland 4-4-0s over its line, and they were withdrawn shortly afterwards.

To arrange the new service Needham of the Midland had met John Maddock, his opposite number on the L.Y.R., on June 18. On August 4, 1888, their respective general managers had a meeting during which, as was becomingly boringly usual, there were disagreements. For the Midland John Noble told William Thorley of the L.Y.R. that he thought the traffic for the north of Hellifield from Midland stations in Lancashire and Cheshire could be worked over the L.Y.R. via the new Ancoats Junction line and that traffic to and from Midland stations previously exchanged with the L.Y.R. at Oakenshaw, could be more easily dealt with at Ancoats. He urged that Midland trains from the north of Hellifield should as far as possible terminate in the Midland stations at Manchester and Liverpool, and not those of the L.Y.R. To this Thorley disagreed; it was apparently more convenient to the L.Y.R. if a large proportion of the Midland trains used L.Y.R. stations. It was a good try

* *Locomotive & Train Working in the Latter Part of the Nineteenth Century.—* E. L. Ahrons.

but it annoyed Noble who tartly pointed out that the Midland was entitled to deal with its own traffic at its own stations. The Midland trains over the L.Y.R. were to consist of first and third class only, the company not seeing its way to take L.Y.R. second class traffic in its own trains. This problem was solved, however, by an agreement that the Midland trains should attach L.Y.R. second class coaching stock which that company had specially provided for the new Scotch service. The L.Y.R. was also to be at liberty to attach extra carriages on the 4.35 p.m. from Manchester on Tuesdays and Fridays—market days—'up to the limit of the engine'.

One cannot do better, referring to these Midland services over the Hellifield line, than to quote Mr Laidlaw again :

'On Monday, July 2, 1888, the Midland Company, with their own engines and carriages, commenced to work the service from Liverpool and Manchester to Hellifield, and *vice versa,* and continued to do so until Saturday, December 30, 1916, five trains in each direction being worked by them. The departure times from Liverpool were 12.50 a.m., 9.45 a.m., 2.25 p.m., 2.50 p.m. and 4.25 p.m. Four drivers worked the trains, and on the opening day they were respectively worked by H. Hingley, 1342, at 12.50 a.m.; I. Horn, 1751, at 9.45 a.m.; R. Halling, 1335, at 2.25 p.m.; H. Hingley, 1342, at 2.50 p.m., and L. Loweth, 1752, at 4.25 p.m. and again at 12.50 a.m. (Tuesday). Engine 1344 was the spare engine. By the end of August these were replaced by 1814, 1817, 1816 and 1815 respectively, and 1813 as spare. In July, 1889, these left, and 1811, 1808, 1810 and 1809 respectively worked the service with 1812 as spare engine. In July, 1890, a further change was effected, and 1321, 1316, 1320 and 1318 were given the job, and continued to have it until the end of 1916. The Midland Company took over the working of the goods traffic on August 1, 1888, and have continued to work it to this day: there were two trains so worked, leaving Huskisson at 7.40 p.m. and 12.5 a.m.

The Liverpool passenger engines in July, 1888, went as far as Hellifield with the 2.50 p.m. train, returning with empty coaches as far as Blackburn, and after working the 9.45 a.m. to Blackburn, went forward to Hellifield with empty coaches, and returned with the 3.34 p.m. train, due Liverpool at 4.55 p.m.

There were also four sets of drivers at Newton Heath, Manchester, and with the 4.35 p.m. train they went to Carlisle and returned with the 12.20 a.m. train, due back at 3.55 a.m., but the 4.35 p.m. train only ran until the end of September. The trains from Manchester were 1.5 a.m., 9.55 a.m., 2.30 p.m., 2.45 p.m., and 4.35 p.m., and on the opening day were respectively worked by J. Oddie, 1330, at 1.5 a.m.; W. Beardsley, 1341, at 9.55 a.m.; A. Denison, 1576, at 2.30 p.m.; G. Roberts, 1808, at 2.45 p.m., and J. Oddie, 1330, at 4.35 p.m. 1579 was the spare engine. Shortly afterwards 1330, 1341, 1576 and 1579 went away, and 1809, 1810, 1811 and 1812 replaced them, 1812 being the spare one.' *

(Outline timetables of the Midland service for July 1888 are given in Appendix XIX.)

By 1891 the timing over the Hellifield–Carlisle route was 96 minutes; the Carlisle–Appleby time was 38 minutes and in the reverse direction 40. The L.Y.R. connecting passenger trains on the Hellifield line were mostly operated by that company's engines Nos. 55, 56, 60, 61, 71, 74, 79, 83 and 85. These were 0-4-4 bogie side tank locomotives, fitted with the Westinghouse brake, delivered by Dubs & Co. in 1878 and stationed at Newton Heath. In 1881 they were joined by several of the 4-4-0 express engines, among them Nos. 668 and 681, out of a series of 16

* *Railway Magazine.*—November 1930.

built by Sharp Stewart & Co. The best timing over the Manchester-Hellifield line in the early 1880s was about 1½ hours. The Midland service cut some 10 minutes off this with its best train.

North of the Border, there had been another change in the motive power supplied by the G.S.W.R. Between 1886 and 1889 Hugh Smellie brought out a series of 20 4-4-0 express engines, with 6 ft. 9½ in. driving wheels, and numbered 153, 154, 79, 52–57, 65–70, 86–89 and 109. They replaced the 2-4-0s of the early 1880s on the Scotch expresses and remained the principal motive power on the route for about a decade.

Leaving the run-of-the-mill services, an article in the *Railway News* in 1887 gives an idea of the special services put on for the summer season :

'The Midland Summer Tours to Scotland and the North

'The Summer service of express trains to and from Scotland, via the Settle and Carlisle route of the Midland Railway is now in operation. Two trains per day—one at 8.25 a.m., and the other at 9.15 p.m.—leave St Pancras Station and reach Greenock in time for the passengers to join the *Columbia* or *Iona* steamers for the Highlands. There is no change of carriage by these trains. Saloon and family carriages, and family sleeping saloons can be attached on application at the London station to run through to any railway station in Scotland. Arrangements can be made for the despatch of heavy luggage in advance of passengers, who will be spared all trouble and annoyance in respect to the usual impedimenta of travel. A very liberal and complete service is provided for Matlock, Buxton and other places of seaside or pleasure resort in Yorkshire, Lancashire, and the Lake District. Tourist tickets are issued at temptingly low rates available for two months. Care has been taken to provide adequately for the important service of refreshments. A dinner of five courses, with dessert, and no fees to waiters, is prepared at Normanton, and half-an-hour is allowed for the discussion and disposal of the good things so liberally provided. A telegram handed to the guard—no charge for transmission—will secure a special dinner, which will be served for family parties in the saloon or compartment which they occupy. Carriages are supplied, on application, for invalids, which may be attached at any station on the company's line. Compartments of carriages may be retained by four first-class passengers. It is difficult to discover a want in the shape of creature comfort, or luxury of travelling, which is not at the command of passengers by the Midland Railway. In no other country in the world does such a service of trains exist as that which is provided by the Midland, Eastern, and Western routes to Scotland and the north. There are eight up Midland trains to Carlisle in the day, and seven to Glasgow and Edinburgh, and the same number of down trains. There is a service of five trains daily each way for Dundee and Perth, and two to Aberdeen, via the new Tay Bridge—and Inverness has its contingent of three trains daily each way. It remains to be added that all trains on the Midland are first and third class. The programme of the season does credit to the organizing powers of Mr Noble, the general manager of the company.'

It is more than likely that this particular rosy picture was disrupted, for in August of 1887 the Midland had to withstand a serious strike among the enginemen. Once again the *Railway News* was well to the fore. On the night of August 4 an excited reporter telegraphed to his office that a strike was in being for the next day. So far, he said, the men had been paid weekly, even if there was no work for them to do. The company now intended to pay them for the turns actually worked. The old pay averaged out at 7s 6d a day for drivers, 4s to 4s 6d a day for firemen, and both grades had a lodging allowance. The new system was rather more complicated but the gist of it was that henceforth the men would receive graded payments. It meant, in effect, that security of income was to go; that is it went if the men would not work, which the company had claimed it had difficulty in getting them to do—knowing that their rate was guaranteed. Thompson and Paget had met the men's leaders on the night of Wednesday, August 3, and the talks had resulted in the present crisis. The men were backed by their unions who appealed to drivers in other companies not to answer a call from the Midland for assistance. Robert Weatherburn, writing in the *Railway Magazine* of August, 1914, was able to tell how he was personally involved in what followed. He was at the London end of the affair and, after having satisfied himself that there were quite a few of the men who would not strike, he went to Stratford to see James Holden, locomotive superintendent of the Great Eastern, to beg some men off him to go to Derby. Holden tried to avoid an interview but was finally pinned down in a train bound for Liverpool Street, after having tried to give Weatherburn the slip. The latter pointed out that what the Midland was doing could only benefit all companies if it came off, but that if the men won then the Great Eastern and others would have similar trouble. By the time Liverpool Street was reached he had the help he wanted. Not only from the G.E.R. did assistance come; various southern companies also sent parties of their drivers and firemen. Their arrival at Derby added fuel to the fire, for the Midland men had been confident of backing. On August 5 Derby was in a state of siege. The strikers resorted to raking out the fires of engines in the yards and sheds, and Midland officers and clerks were kept hard at it directing the stumbling newcomers to the locomotives thus disabled. At Child's Hill, near London, the strike was broken by Weatherburn offering all the passed firemen immediate upgrading to driver, on full pay, if they would get the trains moving. They did. By Friday night it had become clear what was happening. Although up to now the passenger trains had mostly been getting through with the scratch crews, the situation was threatened by a new move made by the goods drivers and firemen. Foiled to a large extent at the sheds, they pretended to have accepted defeat. Supposedly trusted once more, they took out the goods trains to isolated signals and left them under their protection, having raked out the fire. Numbers of dead engines littered the system. The *Railway News* told how the Scotch mail, arriving at Derby some 40 minutes late, brought the news that this plan had been carried out on many parts of the main line. All the Midland drivers who had not struck were by now on the passenger train workings, and the 'foreign' crews were despatched to collect the abandoned goods trains. A report from Glasgow on the Friday evening said that Midland trains were arriving about an hour behind schedule, which was not bad as apparently the Settle and Carlisle line had its quota of disabled goods.

Actually about 74 per cent. of the men had returned to work within a week. The Midland kept open the posts of some of those still out, particularly if they were senior men, in the hope of getting them back. The strike was undoubtedly broken by the quick response of other companies; it was remarkable with what speed the recruits were brought in. As usual, in Victorian times, the railway press and national papers were bitterly hostile towards the railway unions. It was the second serious strike within a decade. On September 16, 1887, the board decided to reward all the men who had remained on duty. The amount paid out was £2,698 8s 5d. There were two sequels. At the half-yearly meeting on August 12 one daring spirit, Alderman Scarr, spoke up in favour of the men. 'A policy of paltry economy to a large extent has forced on this strike.' This was too much of a home truth and he was not permitted to continue. Thompson silenced him with an appeal to the heckling crowd of shareholders to vote on whether they wished to hear more. They did not and Mr Scarr sat down, but not before he had shouted out that the strike had cost the company about £100,000. On February 21, 1890, the traffic committee recommended to the board that new wage scales for station porters and others should be as follows : passenger shunters and parcels porters at the principal stations 20s a week for the first year, rising by annual increments of 1s a week to 24s; parcels porters at other stations were to get 17s a week for the first year and 18s a week for the second and following years; shunters at Derby were to get a special scale of 24s a week for the first year, 25s for the second, and 26s for the third and following years, this being an advance of 1s a week on the current wages; Sunday work was to be paid as if for a twelve hour day; and all porters, parcels porters, and lamp porters were to have an overcoat issued every three years. The annual cost to the company of these 'concessions' as they were called, was £1,230 11s 6d.

Of the Bills sought by other companies for new railways which could have affected the Midland during the period covered by this chapter, all were more or less unrelated to the Leeds–Settle–Carlisle line. Three of them, however, will be discussed in the next chapter for they are part of the background to the Midland's efforts to shorten the route mileage to the north in the 1890s.

By far the most important schemes on other fronts, and ones which could well have affected the Settle line and its traffic, came late in the 1880s. On August 9, 1889, the Midland board gave its approval to the proposed amalgamation of the G.S.W.R. with the N.B.R. The *Railway News* of September 21 remarked upon the current report from the directors of the G.S.W.R. There had been a serious decrease in revenue, whereas the N.B.R. receipts had steadily grown. The two companies had gone for powers to amalgamate, provisionally fixed for August 1, 1890, the new concern to be known as the North British Railway. Scheduled to the Bill was an agreement between the G.S.W.R., N.B.R., and the Midland that the latter would support the amalgamation in Parliament. The amalgamated company was to forward over the Midland route a minimum proportion of English traffic under its control and to maintain the express passenger and goods connections with the Midland at Carlisle. It also agreed to run passenger trains between Balloch, Helensburgh, and St Enoch stations in connection with the Midland morning and evening up and down expresses between Glasgow and St Pancras. The Midland already had an interest in the Forth Bridge Railway and in accordance with the provisions of the latter's Act of 1878 the amalgamated company agreed to give the Midland running powers over its lines to Perth and Dundee. Finally, a 'Midland and North British Through Traffic Committee' was to be set up to manage the joint and common interests at Carlisle.

So far as Derby was concerned the idea must have seemed a good one, but by November 2 the *Railway News* was reporting heavy Caledonian opposition to the move. Ignoring the North British altogether, the Caledonian proceeded to bombard the G.S.W.R. with letters claiming that it, and not the N.B.R., was its rightful partner, a situation, said the *Railway News* that was in question. 'We do not find', the paper said, 'the competitive traffic from St Pancras on the one hand, and Euston on the other, is treated at Carlisle by the Caledonian on the footing of "Partnership" '. The *Scotsman* also had some trenchant remarks to make :

'It will be seen that the basis of the Caledonian complaint against the Glasgow and South Western is that the two companies are united at the ownership of certain lines, and that the Glasgow and South Western has, from Carlisle to Gretna, running powers over the Caledonian. On this ground the companies are spoken of as "partners", and in a tone of injured innocence, surprise and regret are expressed that an agreement to introduce a different partner with hostile interests should have been made without communication with the Caledonian. To those familiar with Scottish Railway history this view of the relative position of the two companies may be criticised in the words of Lord Beaconsfield used regarding the invective of an assailant—it lacks finish.'

The *Scotsman* went on to point out that the Caledonian had stolen marches on the G.S.W.R. and the N.B.R. whenever and wherever it could. The Caledonian invasion of Ayrshire—always a touchy subject to the G.S.W.R.—probably provided the main reason for the latter's choice of the N.B.R. with which to amalgamate.

To the letters from the Caledonian the G.S.W.R. replied that that company had no right to interfere. In return the Caledonian said that the G.S.W.R. should come jointly to it and the N.B.R., but that since the N.B.R. seemed determined to go ahead regardless of the consequences, the Caledonian would oppose the scheme. By November it had put forward its own Bill for amalgamation with the G.S.W.R. Entitled quite bluntly as the Caledonian Railway (Acquisition of the Glasgow & South Western Railway &c.) Bill, it re-stated the supposed affinity between the C.R. and the G.S.W.R. and threw out a crumb to the N.B.R. to the effect that if Parliament thought the N.B.R. worthy of the occasion it should be permitted to come in as a joint owner. The Bill intended that the G.S.W.R. should completely vest in the C.R. from

February 1, 1891, and it claimed for the Caledonian the right to work the Ayrshire & Wigtownshire Railway which company, as we have seen, was attempting a break-away from the G.S.W.R. at the same time. As to the N.B.R. side of the story, the company was to be given just one month to decide whether or not it wanted to join in, after which time it would not be considered. If the N.B.R. did join, however, the two companies were to form a 'Glasgow & South Western Joint Committee' to run the joint system.

To all this the *Railway News* commented: 'If the Glasgow and South Western is to be wed at all it must enter into a "bigamous" contract with the Caledonian and the North British. Failing this, the Caledonian gives notice that it will forbid the banns'. By February of 1890 the paper was reporting that representatives of the N.B.R. and G.S.W.R. were canvassing support for their amalgamation Bill; the G.S.W.R. shareholders formally approved the proposal on February 18. The Parliamentary evidence on both the rival Bills does not concern this story. It is sufficient that both were rejected, the Caledonian by the House of Commons committee on May 13, and though the N.B.R. Bill was passed by the Commons on the same day as its rival's defeat, it was thrown out by the Lords on July 11.

It was only for a breather, however, for both Bills were to be redeposited in 1891 for a further attempt. In the meantime an interesting crossplay of words took place at the G.S.W.R.'s half-yearly meeting in September, 1890. Thompson, by now Sir Matthew William Thompson, addressed the meeting as chairman of the company and found himself under fire. After some mutual commiseration about the fate of the amalgamation Bill with the N.B.R., the question of the Parliamentary expenses arose. One of the shareholders, a Mr Buchanan, rose to speak:

Mr Buchanan: I respectfully submit that the Midland should pay the whole amount.

The Chairman: The Midland had nothing to do with it except that the Glasgow and South Western did what they wanted.

Mr Buchanan: The Glasgow and South Western never sought amalgamation.

The Chairman: The Midland had nothing to do with the expenses. How much has the Midland paid the Glasgow and South Western company?

Mr Buchanan: I don't know.

The Chairman: It was given in evidence before the Parliamentary committee.

Mr Buchanan: I suppose the Midland have been very generous to the Glasgow and South Western, but the Glasgow and South Western have paid for everything they got. They are quite prepared to do without the Midland. There are other companies prepared to carry their passengers and goods, and I do not know why the Midland should control the Glasgow and South Western.

The Chairman: They do not control it.

One can imagine that the last utterance was probably shouted out. In truth there were quite a few G.S.W.R. shareholders of the same opinion as Buchanan.

On January 2, 1891, Sir Matthew resigned from the Midland chairmanship through ill-health. He had been chairman for eleven years—the longest tenure so far. He had left the G.S.W.R. chair on the previous September 16, to be succeeded by Renny Watson a fortnight later. His position had been one of some difficulty. His last years were filled with trouble; there had been the strikes and then the intense activity of the amalgamation Bills. During his term of office the G.S.W.R. and the Midland had developed many mutual bonds, and his purpose of uniting the companies completely was to die with him, though not for a few years yet were its effects to be entirely dispelled. When in January of 1887 William Lister Newcombe had retired he was succeeded by G. H. Turner, who came from the G.S.W.R. where he had been goods manager since April 29, 1885. Turner was one of those self-made thrusting Victorians who appear to have thrived career-wise on setbacks and his appointment was yet another move to bring the companies together. Incidentally in July of 1890 Langley retired as civil engineer of the Midland. He was succeeded by the then resident engineer, J. A. McDonald.

In February of 1891 the Midland's half-yearly meeting approved the fresh attempt to be made that session by the N.B.R. and the G.S.W.R. to amalgamate. Watching wearily from a director's seat was Sir Matthew William Thompson. There were, in fact, three Bills which affected the issue. First was the Caledonian which was a rehash of that of the previous session. Next, the N.B.R. and G.S.W.R. proposal, with some additional provisions designed to placate the L.N.W.R. and the C.R., in that the former was to be permitted running powers to St Enoch with originating L.N.W.R. traffic and the latter, if successful in its current application to take over the Ayrshire & Wigtownshire, would not be debarred from extending its running powers from that line on to some of the amalgamated company's lines. As to this latter point, the third proposal, the Ayrshire & Wigtownshire Bill, sought powers for the Caledonian to take over the company and to run over the railways of the G.S.W.R. between Girvan and Paisley via Dalry and Johnstone, and between Barassie and Kilmarnock and on to the Glasgow Barrhead & Kilmarnock Joint Railway.

Once again the Bills failed to get through Parliament. It was perhaps as well. The C.R. and G.S.W.R. amalgamation would have been disastrous for the Midland; the N.B.R. and G.S.W.R. proposal was obviously looked upon by many in the G.S.W.R. as being merely a child of the Thompson era. And so it was, for after his death in 1892, there was only to be a last half-hearted attempt, this time between the Midland and the G.S.W.R. It will be dealt with in the next chapter.

Finally, there is note of another possible Midland scheme which comes to light in the company's minutes for 1890. On May 13 of that year, at a meeting of 'ratepayers and others' at Bowness, a resolution was passed at which the Midland was asked to extend its system to the Lake District by constructing a line from the Furness Railway, between Carnforth and Grange, up the Winster Valley to Bowness. At the same time the Bowness-on-Windermere Association passed a similar resolution, and both were sent to the Midland board. They were followed on May 15 by a deputation to Derby, representing the inhabitants of Kendal. The board promptly referred the matter to the traffic committee for a report on the proposal. The committee let the matter stew until October 17, 1890, when it replied that it was unable to recommend compliance with the request. Meanwhile the board had already made up its mind; a Furness Railway board minute dated October 3, 1890, noted : 'Read letter from the General Manager of the Midland Railway stating his Directors had decide not to promote an extension of their line to Kendal in the Lake District.' The Midland's decision is not surprising. The Newby Bridge line—though a longer way round —already took the company's trains to the south shore of Lake Windermere and in any event Kendal passengers had ready access to the Midland system at Carnforth.

XVI
Times of Endeavour
1891 – 1899

The 1890s saw the height of Midland empiricism, but at the end of the decade the coming termination of the Victorian era paralleled the beginning of the end of the company's high fortune for though all looked well the first signs were to be seen of the coming slump in railway property. The early nineties swept away many of the figures who had dominated the company's affairs for years past. Three notable men who had done much to lead the Midland's northern advance quit the stage. Thompson's death has been noted in the last chapter. Following his resignation in 1891 the board elected as the new chairman of the company his deputy, George Ernest Paget. The new deputy chairman was Charles Thomas. After Thompson's death the board, in March of 1892, voted for the usual portrait, painted by Professor Herkomer at a cost of £540.

On the evening of Monday, April 25, 1892, Sir James Joseph Allport died from acute inflammation of the lungs, at the age of 81, in the Midland Hotel at St Pancras. Following his retirement from the office of general manager in 1880 he had been elected to the board and knighted four years later. His services to the Midland had been beyond measure. On the completion of the Settle line he and his wife had been presented with their portraits by a grateful board. Williams noted an extract from his speech of thanks in which he had reflected upon his part in the making of the Settle and Carlisle :

'I shall not forget as long as I live the difficulties that surrounded us in that undertaking. Mr Crossley and I went on a voyage of discovery—"prospecting". We walked miles and miles; in fact, I think I may safely say, we walked over a greater part of the line from Settle to Carlisle, and we found it comparatively easy sailing till we got to that terrible place, Blea Moor. We spent an afternoon there looking at it. We went miles without seeing any inhabitant, and then Blea Moor seemed effectually to bar our passage northward. But to the skill and energy of the Engineer we are indebted for overcoming the difficulty. But such is my recollection of the afternoon, that when Mr Williams, the painter, said he should like to paint in the background of the painting something illustrative of the Midland Railway, I then gave him the *History of the Midland Railway* by Mr Williams of Nottingham, and pointing to the engraving of Blea Moor contained therein, told him to put that in it; and you will fine Blea Moor in the corner there. If I have had one work in my life that gave me more anxiety than another, it was this Settle and Carlisle line.'

On May 20, 1892, illness forced John Noble to resign from the general managership. Like Allport before him, he was elected to the board, filling the place of John Wakefield Cropper who had died on

June 3. Cropper had been a director since 1869 and for many years had been chairman of the locomotive and carriage and wagon committees. The new general manager was G. H. Turner. On July 16, 1896, William Noble, writing from the Temple, London, told Paget that his father was now too ill to remain a director, and on July 17 John Corrie Carter was elected in his place. On Sunday, November 15, 1896, Noble died. He had started as a clerk in the Railway Clearing House in 1847, had joined the Midland in 1866 as traffic accountant, had become assistant general manager two years later, and then general manager in 1880.

It has been noted that with the death of Thompson the amalgamation issue between the Midland and the G.S.W.R. had taken a back seat. Within two years it was brought to an end. In September 1892 a provisional agreement was made between the two companies to try yet again for amalgamation. On October 21 Paget reported to the board that on the invitation of the G.S.W.R. he had made an inspection of that company's lines on September 28 and 29. On the last date the Midland and G.S.W.R. joint committee had met in the evening at Carlisle to discuss terms and he had told the committee that the Midland had decided to go ahead on the basis of a fixed 4 per cent. dividend on ordinary G.S.W.R. stock. Sir William Renny Watson, the G.S.W.R. chairman, had urged at the meeting that the results over the past years justified a higher rate than 4 per cent. He sowed the first doubt about the amalgamation by pointing out that the G.S.W.R. directors on the committee had no authority from their board, by whom the subject had not been discussed, but said he would make a statement after the G.S.W.R. board meeting on October 11, and would probably consult with some of the larger G.S.W.R. shareholders in the meantime. Since then, Paget told the Midland board, he had received a letter from Sir William on October 13 which read as follows :

Glasgow & South Western Railway,
Board Room, St Enoch Station, Glasgow
12th October, 1892.

G. E. Paget Esqre.

Dear Mr Paget,
    Before our Board meeting yesterday I called on one or two of our largest shareholders and found that in one case while the inclination was towards amalgamation the basis mentioned was considered hardly sufficient and in so far as I can learn this feeling is very general.
    I then saw Sir John Burns who pointed out that most of his friends held our stock as an investment and to these a guarantee of four per cent was not so attractive as the larger dividend which they had received over an average of past years.
    As a trader I found Sir John decidedly against amalgamation but he asked time to consider the general question and he subsequently wrote me that he did not see his way to agree in the views I had courteously communicated to him.
                                                    , Signature.

The letter ended by saying that the G.S.W.R. board had had a full discussion and wanted to let the amalgamation matter rest. If it had thought that this might have increased the Midland offer it was mistaken, for after a brief discussion the Midland board agreed that the negotiations were now terminated. They were not to be resumed.

'From eight or nine o'clock in the morning until far into the evening the fate of the Midland Station and the Queen's Hotel hung in the balance.' Thus spoke the *Yorkshire Post* of Thursday, January 14, 1892, telling of the great fire which had broken out in the arches under the Midland and the joint L.N.W.R. and N.E.R. stations in Leeds at about 4 a.m. the previous day. The old Midland Wellington station and the joint 'New' station—the latter built in the mid 1860s—had been constructed on a series of brick arches over the River Aire—'a labyrinth of arches some hundreds in number—'. Known then, and today, as the 'Dark Arches', they had in 1892 'a questionable reputation for two things, viz., that here when the days are warm and the river low the full pungency of the waters of the Aire may be best experienced, and that they are to some extent a resort at night for questionable characters'. Also, then as now, the arches were used for warehousing—those that is which abutted on the river—and in 1892, of the 10 acres of available storage space, $1\frac{1}{2}$ were let to Messrs Joseph Watson & Sons, soap manufacturers. There the firm kept tallow, resin and oils, under the west end of the stations.

The fire which broke out among this combustible mass and which was actually spread by the application of water which carried the oil with it, caused the collapse of the arches carrying several of the approach lines to the west of the stations and totally disorganised L.N.W.R. and N.E.R. traffic so that both companies had to claim the hospitality of the G.N.R. and L.Y.R. at the Central station for some time afterwards. The fire lasted until about 1 a.m. on January 14 and was extraordinarily fierce; hours after the flames had been beaten back the walls of the arches where it broke out remained at white heat. At its height the centre of Leeds from the stations to the town hall was in the shadow of an immense pillar of smoke. One fireman died in the blaze.

The Midland was more fortunate than its neighbours for, though the fire got a hold on the carriage shed and thus for a time threatened the Wellington station, the company's own brigades from Leeds, Bradford, and even Derby, contained it with between 30 and 40 hoses by soaking the station structure. By 11 p.m. on the Wednesday the company had managed to restore working over four of its six approach lines to the station.

At a meeting in February of 1891 the joint committee had been concerned about a falling off in passenger receipts between Glasgow and London. To help offset this it was decided to cut out the lunch stop at Normanton and put on a service of mid-day dining car expresses. The up train left Glasgow at 12.30 p.m., and Carlisle at 3.03, a dining car being attached from Leeds to London. The down trains, however, continued for the time being to call at Normanton but in December, 1892, the Midland traffic committee recommended that they too should be provided with dining cars. This was agreed, the passengers to travel in the coaches throughout the journey, instead of just during meals. The decision to run dining cars on the Scotch trains was spurred on by their introduction on the L.N.W.R. Euston-Glasgow service in the same year, that company providing sets of twin cars comprising a 50 ft. 6 in. kitchen/dining car to seat eighteen passengers in two compartments, and a 47 ft. 9 in. dining car with two saloons taking twelve and four passengers, with lavatory accommodation. The Midland cars are described in Chapter XVIII. They started running on the down service on July 1, 1893, with the Normanton down stop cut out, the morning train leaving St Pancras at 1.30 p.m. and arriving at Carlisle at 8.05 p.m. Shortly after, the departure time was altered to 2.10 p.m. with a correspondingly later arrival time of 8.55, intermediate stops being Nottingham 4.37, Sheffield 5.41, Leeds 6.34, Hellifield 7.22, with the pass time at Ais Gill of 8.00. By December of 1893 the G.S.W.R. was receiving complaints from passengers that the arrival time in Glasgow of the 2.10 p.m. was too late to admit of them reaching their homes in the suburbs. It was suggested that the Midland departure time should revert to 1.30 p.m. but Derby did not comply. The company did undertake, however, to consider the matter in time for the new timetable in April 1894, and though nothing was done for a while the old departure time was eventually reinstated.

In February, 1894 the joint committee decided to put more dining carriages for first and third class on the day expresses between London and Glasgow. From July 1 the Glasgow express was to leave St Pancras at 10.30 a.m., to arrive at Glasgow at 7.35 p.m., the Edinburgh train being booked to depart at 10.35 a.m. By the following December the need had arisen for increased first class dining accommodation. The pressure put on the Midland by the current rivalry between the East and West Coast route racing, already alluded to, and the continual need to keep the service competitive, was remarked upon in the August half-yearly meeting of 1895. Paget, addressing the shareholders, replied to criticisms of the Midland Scotch trains, and put the Midland philosophy clearly :

'Several letters have appeared in *The Times* criticising adversely the policy of the Midland board in not joining in what is called "the race to Scotland". I hope the writers of these letters are not Midland shareholders—(hear, hear)—for we always wish to be in accord with you, and we cannot endorse the views of these writers, nor can we follow their advice. (Applause.) The Midland between London and Carlisle runs through such towns as Kettering, Nottingham, Leicester, Derby, Sheffield, Leeds, and Bradford. In all of those towns we have excellent customers who cannot be neglected. Beyond that, on the other side of the Border, there are towns between Carlisle and Edinburgh which are unfortunately connected in business with the towns of the Midland Counties. Now it is impossible by any acceleration of train service to serve all these towns. It becomes therefore our duty to consider whether it would be wise to put on an entirely new service of trains between London and Carlisle, and asking our friends, the North British, to put on a corresponding service between Carlisle and Edinburgh, to ignore all, or nearly all, the towns on the way in order that we might get what is called our share of the Scotch traffic. Now that would involve, to the Midland, the running of over 3,700 miles a week of extra passenger traffic. We do not think that that is desirable. (Hear, hear.) Our neighbours have not the same considerations to face, at all events, to the same extent, and it is not for me to criticise their action, but for ourselves we are anxious rather to restrict our passenger running so as, if possible, to get a better return per passenger train mile, and to aim at punctuality by booking our trains at a moderately high rate of speed, rather than put in our time bills that which we cannot accomplish.' *

Quite what he meant by the words 'unfortunately connected in business' is not clear.

In the February meeting of 1896 Paget outlined the company's scheme to build a new harbour at Heysham for the Irish traffic. Heysham will be discussed later in this chapter but it is mentioned now in that it triggered off some complaints about the Portpatrick line. One of the shareholders, a Mr McLean, asked that as Paget had brought the matter up, was he aware that passengers to Belfast, via Stranraer and Larne, had to wait six hours at Carlisle between 9.00 p.m. and 3.30 a.m.? Paget pointed out in reply that it was merely a matter of running more trains but, as the service did not pay, more trains meant less dividends. Another shareholder brought up the question of speeding up the Scotch traffic. Apparently *The Times* was still saying that the Midland was not as efficient as the other two companies in the matter of Scotch expresses. He suggested that if the company was incapable of making locomotives able to do a sustained 60 m.p.h., then it should buy half a dozen outside. He also thought water troughs should be provided. This drew a sharp retort from Paget who defended Johnson's engines and repeated what he had said the previous August. There was no doubt, however, that the company was facing ever increasing competition. Both the East and West Coast lines were putting on more than just fast trains; their coaching stock had vastly improved over the past few years. On April 24, 1896, the Midland and G.S.W.R. joint committee discussed the train arrangements to be made for the July timetable. Two trains were to run from London to Glasgow leaving St Pancras at 9.15 p.m. and 10 p.m. and arriving at Glasgow at 7.10 a.m. and 7.20 a.m. In the opposite direction trains were to leave Glasgow at 9.15 p.m. and 10 p.m. arriving at St Pancras at 6.55 a.m. and 7.55 a.m., as against one train in 1895 which left at 9.30 p.m. and arrived at 7.35 a.m. A new express would also leave Glasgow at 11 a.m. for the L.Y.R. line. It was also decided to work independently the train from the L.Y.R. line from Hellifield to Glasgow instead of attaching it, as hitherto, to the 10.30 a.m. train from Leeds. The usual acceleration was to be made to the 10.30 a.m. express from St Pancras for the summer season so that it arrived at St Enoch at 7.35 instead of 7.45 p.m. Not only on the London-Scotland run was the pinch of competition felt; the L.N.W.R. and G.W.R. Bristol service also had to be watched. On August 2, 1897, the Midland extended its dining car service by the addition of two new afternoon dining car expresses, one each way between Bradford and Bristol, leaving at 1.25 and 2.05 p.m. respectively.

* Railway News.

Despite the chairman's remarks at the February, 1896, meeting, some of the locomotives employed were not built at Derby, though they were of a Johnson design. In 1892 some new 4-4-0s, with extended wheel base to permit of a larger firebox, were built by Sharp, Stewart & Co. Numbered 2183–2202, Nos. 2183–2192 were stationed at Nottingham for some time and worked one of the Scotch expresses as far as Hellifield. With them at Nottingham were five more of the same class, having 7 ft. coupled wheels, and built at Derby in 1896. When in 1893 the Dore and Chinley line was opened a class of fifteen new locomotives was employed to operate the service, Nos. 2203–2217, again built by Sharp, Stewart & Co. 4-4-0s, they had 6 ft. 6 in. driving wheels and were tested out on the Settle line for a short time before going to the Dore and Chinley route. So successful were they on the Settle and Carlisle road that sixteen out of a further thirty of the class that were built in 1894 went to Carlisle. Numbered 184–199, they replaced the old 1572 class. The following year ten more were constructed, Nos. 230–235 going to Leeds, and Nos. 236–239 to Hellifield. In 1891 the G.S.W.R. also provided some new motive power for the Scotch trains for, with the advent of a new chief locomotive engineer in the person of James Manson, the company's works at Kilmarnock started turning out a new series of 4-4-0s which went on to the main line, several being stationed at Carlisle. In December, 1894, the G.S.W.R. ceased stabling its engines at the Midland sheds and began using its own accommodation at Currock Junction, on the Maryport & Carlisle line, immediately south of Carlisle.

We will come back for a last look at the train services before the end of the chapter but a note here on the improvements on the Leeds–Settle–Carlisle line which were the precursors to far-reaching alterations and widenings in the early 1900s, will bring the history of the line itself to the turn of the century. In 1891 the Midland got powers to widen the North Midland line at Holbeck south of the Leeds & Bradford. In August, 1896, work started on widening the Leeds & Bradford from Apperley to Calverley. A year later it was reported that the small bore of Thackley tunnel, combined with the ever-increasing traffic through it, was becoming more and more difficult to ventilate. A second tunnel was recommended and the board decided to go for widening powers in the session of 1898. In fact the company intended, with the West Riding Lines, to be discussed later, to make an all-out attempt to shorten its main line and iron out all bottlenecks. The Midland Railway Act of July 1, 1898, empowered the company to carry out the following widenings : Bingley to Thwaites (2 miles 4 furlongs and 1 chain) on the Leeds & Bradford Extension; Apperley Bridge & Rawdon to the west end of Thackley tunnel (2 miles and 6 furlongs) on the Leeds & Bradford line; Waterloo and Stourton, Cudworth and Royston, Wath and Darfield, and Beighton and Treeton, totalling over 10½ miles of widening on the North Midland line, together with widenings at Brightside, Sheffield,

Whitacre, and Leicester. It was not to be until the twentieth century that these works were ready for use but their assistance in the operating of the line was to permit the company to revise its schedules to include some much faster running. As to stations on the line, on June 1, 1892, a new station was opened at Thwaites, an occurrence which elicited a formal vote of thanks from the local people. Meanwhile in September of 1889 the Midland board had decided to build a new station at Bingley and the present structure was opened at 6 a.m. on July 24, 1892. At Skipton the Skipton–Snaygill up and down goods lines came into use at the beginning of 1899. The permanent way also was extensively renewed during the late nineteenth century. In February, 1898, Paget alluded to the Settle line when discussing the high cost of working and maintenance expenses which were causing some disquiet at the time. It appeared that half of the Settle line had at one time or another been relaid since 1875 with rails mostly of 85 lb weight, but about 80 miles, or nearly half of the total track mileage, had not been touched. This the company now intended to relay at an estimated cost of about £1,000 a mile. Ahrons has some interesting observations to make on Midland rails at this time. Noting the faster times which came in with the late nineties, with the same engines as had been doing slower times a few years back, he remarked that this was probably caused by harder steel rails, 100 lbs weight to the yard replacing the old 85 lb rails. This, combined with an increase in the tensile strength of tyres, he thought caused less bending of the rails and flattening of wheel rims which in turn led to a decrease in friction. In any event it would appear that at least half of the rails on the Settle and Carlisle line had lasted twenty years which, according to Paget, was not bad. Especially so since he pointed out that he had authorised their purchase from the Barrow Haematite Company in 1869 for the very low price of £9 5s per ton.

On the Morecambe Irish traffic question the company had for some time been finding the accommodation for the private steamer service to Ireland to be far too limited and at the half-yearly meeting in February, 1896, Paget told the shareholders that the harbour was now totally inadequate to deal with the traffic. A very large expenditure would be necessary to make any improvements and in any case the harbour was silting up. It had already been decided some four years earlier that it would be best to try for a new pier about 3½ miles south of Morecambe, at Heysham. The company had obtained powers in June, 1892, to make a new railway to Heysham, and work had started straight away, there being an Act to deviate part of the Heysham branch in 1895. Now, in 1896, it had been decided to build a completely new harbour. It was some years before the works were to be complete, however, and the further outline history of Heysham and of the Midland's Irish services are dealt with in the next chapter.

The various railway promotions in the area of the Leeds–Settle–Carlisle line during the 1890s can be quickly disposed of. On

August 14, 1890, a new and potentially dangerous company—the North West Central Railway—had appeared with an Act empowering it to make a series of thirteen railways connecting Preston, Whalley, Colne, and Keighley. In effect the latter portion was to leave the G.N.R. south of Keighley by a triangular junction and run north-west towards Colne where spurs made junctions with the L.Y.R. East Lancashire line, and the Midland's Skipton–Colne branch, the main N.W.C. line continuing on to Whalley. It was another of those schemes which had appeared from time to time with a novel route and which hoped to gain a backer later. It would appear from the Act that the company had close associations with the Manchester Sheffield & Lincolnshire and West Lancashire Railways, for working and maintenance powers were permitted to the two companies; running powers were also granted over the West Lancashire line into Preston station. If this supposed affiliation was so then it was unlucky, for the M.S.L.R. was to become very busy quite soon with the extension to London and was to have neither time nor thought for reaching Preston, even though it had sought powers for a terminus at Preston in 1884 and was still casting covetous eyes towards Blackpool. The proposed works on the N.W.C. were such as so to daunt the new company that it never commenced construction; the capital authorized to be raised was £2m and the estimate of expense not much less. In the session of 1893 it went back to Parliament for an extension of time to construct the line but its Bill was rejected and replaced by one authorising abandonment. If the line had been made it would, despite a ruling gradient of 1 in 50, have adversely affected the Midland's Bradford–Keighley–Skipton–Colne traffic, and would have made serious inroads into the Bradford–Manchester traffic via the Colne line. On March 5, 1892, the Colne Local Board asked the Midland for a line from Colne to Manchester via Nelson, Burnley, Rawtenstall and Bury. When the Midland replied in the negative the Local Board turned to the G.N.R. for help but to no avail.* In the early 1890s there were rumours of yet another scheme, nothing less than the building of a new line to Glasgow via Burnley, Leyburn, Darlington and Newcastle, to be known as the Manchester Newcastle & Glasgow Grand Trunk Railway. For some time it stayed dormant but the *Railway Magazine* of January, 1898, attempted a forecast of its eventual building, tying it up with the Great Central which, having got to London, the magazine thought, would now back the Glasgow line and challenge the existing companies for the Scotch traffic. Perhaps luckily for the Midland such an idea was about twenty years too late, about as much too late as the G.C.R.'s London extension. Given an earlier start, a better financial condition, and no threat to revenue from tramways and the internal combustion engine, the Manchester Newcastle & Glasgow Grand Trunk might have come off. As will be seen, the Midland's finances were in poor enough shape

* *Railway Times.*

by the early 1900s without the rivalry of another main line from London to Scotland.

Three small concerns became tied up with the Midland system north of Leeds before the end of the century. In 1885 the Guiseley Yeadon & Rawdon company obtained powers for a short line, the route to be as its title suggests. Unable to make progress it subsequently went through a bewildering series of name changes and attempted to extend its line through the centre of Horsforth to the N.E.R. at Headingley, the latter thus being connected with the Midland's Shipley-Ilkley line. Though the necessary powers were obtained the company was eventually taken over by the Midland as a near bankrupt concern in March of 1896. Just over a mile in length, it was opened for goods and mineral traffic as a single line on February 26, 1894. Following this, in September of 1896, the Midland board declared itself interested in a proposed railway to run from the Skipton-Ilkley line about 9 miles into Upper Wharfedale to Grassington, and on July 5, 1897, it agreed to work the line—to be known as the Yorkshire Dales Railway—for 60 per cent. of the net earnings. The Yorkshire Dales Railway was actually a smaller version of a line, put forward by the same promoters, which had come before Parliament in 1895, proposing to construct railways connecting the L.Y.R. and Midland at Hellifield, and the Midland south of Embsay on the Skipton-Ilkley line, with the N.E.R. at Darlington. The railway would have been about 59 miles in length and included, among some very heavy works, a tunnel some 6,000 yards long north-east of Arncliffe. The Hellifield line, and its two junctions mentioned, totalled about 7 miles and ran due east to connect with the line from Embsay, 4¼ miles in length, at Rylstone. From there it was to continue in a generally northward direction passing near Carlton, Middleham, Spennithorne, Leyburn, Hauxwell, Richmond, and Middleton Tyas to join the N.E.R. south of Darlington. It was planned to have a ruling gradient of 1 in 100. Running powers were sought over the L.Y.R. to Blackburn, over the Midland to Hellifield, Skipton, and Ilkley, and over the N.E.R. to Darlington and Middlesbrough. The estimated cost of construction was £1,489,207. The Bill was withdrawn, doubtless due to opposition, and after a decent interval, and with the scheme reduced to the Grassington line, the company approached the Midland as mentioned above. This time it was successful —the Midland receiving confirmatory powers to work the line by the Yorkshire Dales Railway Act of 1897. Whilst works were progressing the Midland's Act of 1900 authorised the company to contribute towards the Y.D.R., and when in July, 1902, the first trains started running they were worked by Midland engines, on the train staff without ticket system with one engine in steam. Two years later the Y.D.R. was equipped for operating with the electrical train tablet system. As will be seen, though the Yorkshire Dales company remained quiescent, operated without fuss by the Midland until 1923, when its independent existence came to an end with the Grouping, the grandiose scheme of 1895 set off a series of attempts in the early 1900s to succeed where it had failed. The line was closed to passengers on September 22, 1930. Finally, of the schemes absorbed in the 1890s, we come to the Barnoldswick Railway. This had been authorised as far back as 1867 to make a line about 2 miles in length from the Leeds & Bradford Extension just south of Earby. It had been opened for traffic on February 8, 1871, and the Midland had worked the line from the beginning. In March, 1898, the Barnoldswick company asked the Midland if it would buy. As the line was trouble-free and regularly paid out a reasonable if fluctuating dividend —on June 30, 1897, it was 5 per cent.—the Midland agreed and the necessary powers were obtained in 1899. These three small additions then, the Guisley Yeadon & Rawdon, the Y.D.R., and the Barnoldswick, together with the new Heysham line shortly to be in service, completed the build-up of the Midland system north of Leeds.

The story of the company's attempts to make a cut-off route, which avoided Leeds and shortened the Scotch trains' journey time, forms the last major effort made in the north. To tell it we need to go back to the early 1880s and a scheme made by a small outsider, the Hull Barnsley & West Riding Junction Railway & Dock company, to get into the big-time league. The Hull company first got powers for a main line from the North Midland line near Cudworth to Hull in 1880. It directly challenged the North Eastern's hegemony in the East Riding, and in consequence was thought at York to be beyond the pale. It was, in fact, the outward and visible sign of the inward determination of the citizens of Hull to get shot of the North Eastern monopoly. It soon became obvious that to live the Hull company must expand. Its main *raison d'etre* was to carry coal, but if the industrial West Riding should become attainable then the company stood a good chance of making a steady profit instead of just surviving. In 1882 it managed to persuade Parliament to grant powers for an 18 mile extension from South Hiendley to Huddersfield, and a further 5 mile line on to Halifax.

At this point the Midland came on to the scene. For some years past it had viewed the business heart of the West Riding with some longing, for its main line to the north neatly circumnavigated a very lucrative area which was only touched at Leeds and Bradford. The leading light of the Hull company was Lieut. Colonel Gerard Smith, M.P. An astute man, he saw that by agreeing running powers to the Midland into Huddersfield and Halifax, he would gain an ally of considerable use and by February of 1882, some months before the extension powers were obtained, the Midland board had agreed to permit an exchange station at Cudworth in return for the running powers mentioned. Late in 1883 Colonel Smith wrote to the Midland to the effect that the Hull company was about to call for the capital to make the extensions. He asked for an assurance that the Midland would make use of its powers. The board answered that it would. All this must be seen against a background of still as yet vague Midland thoughts of a cut-off route. On the same day as its reply to Colonel Smith the board arranged to meet the Town Clerk of Bradford to discuss the possibilities involved in another new scheme—the Bradford Central Railway. This proposed connecting the L.Y.R. and Midland lines at Bradford by a viaduct through the centre of the town. A new central station was to be built and the scheme would undoubtedly have prompted still further the Midland's hopes of a through north-south route. By January of 1884, however, the Bradford Central idea was dead. With a good many irons in the fire elsewhere at the time, the Midland could do little to support it. The virtual gift of access to Huddersfield and Halifax, however, was another matter altogether. By January 18 it had been agreed that Colonel Smith might publish the Midland's intention to use the new line, so as to help the raising of capital, and arrangements had been made to discuss the details of the coming Cudworth–Halifax workings. By February agreement on these had been reached. Two years later, however, the whole picture had changed. Unable to raise sufficient money the Hull company abandoned the Huddersfield–Halifax link and turned the Cudworth–Huddersfield line over to a new concern, the Hull & North Western Junction Railway. This company intended running the 1882 line into the L.N.W.R.'s Kirkburton branch, and though running powers were still available to the Midland into Huddersfield this meant that it would now come face to face with that company. As it happened the H. & N.W.J. was as penurious as the Hull Barnsley & West Riding Junction. In February, 1888, with the latter company in Chancery, the Midland briefly thought of taking it over and Thompson even toured the line so as to report to Midland shareholders. Nothing came of this, however, and with the eventual abandonment of the H. & N.W.J. by an Act of 1894, the Midland was left with no alternative but to plan its own route.

The increasing competition on the London–Scotland run made it quite apparent that any delay would be harmful. The demise of the Hull schemes had also left a number of frustrated and dissatisfied people in the West Riding who had been hoping for a new southern access out of the area and preferably one which would get their traffic on to the Midland. Late in 1895 a deputation came to Derby with a plan for a Barnsley–Bradford line. The particular route chosen did not please the Midland board but the concept did, and instructions were given for surveys to be made of a number of different routes. On August 7, 1896, with the results before it, the board could not agree on any one scheme and it was decided not to go to Parliament that session. In May, 1897, deputations from Huddersfield and Halifax appeared before the board and after considerable discussion the engineer was asked to prepare surveys for either a through line from the North Midland at Royston to Bradford, to serve Huddersfield en route, or for a branch to terminate in the Spen Valley. This latter idea was not proceeded with; it had the disadvantage of doing nothing towards the required through line. The

Royston–Bradford proposal was quite acceptable on this score, however, and in August the engineer was told to add Halifax to the scheme.

Such a heady plan, no less than to invade a territory jealously held by the L.Y.R. and L.N.W.R., would obviously be most expensive. It is ironic, bearing in mind that the new line eventually petered out through lack of funds, to note that at the Midland's half-yearly meeting of February, 1897, a dividend of 7 per cent. was announced, occasioning much mutual congratulation. The following meeting, in August, told the same story; receipts were up by no less than £240,000 of which £58,000 were attributable to passengers. So prosperous appeared the future that the company had actually made some recent pay awards, but—needless to say—not before it was pushed into doing so. At the February meeting of 1898, with the traffic returns up yet again by £153,448, Paget spoke to the perhaps over-confident shareholders about the new line. The *Railway News* reported it in full and from the chairman's remarks it can be seen that the paramount reason behind the proposal was the shortening of the route for the Scotch trains :

'In the north and west and especially on the northern part of the line we are not so well situated as we are in the south and, therefore, we are today to ask for additional powers in order to make future accommodation in the north. As I have said, with regard to the deficiency being filled up with traffic, that has happily got to be the case in the south but still we can get more business than we have now under our present facilities and therefore it seems a right time to give a favourable response to the very many kind invitations which have been made to us from the West Riding of Yorkshire. It has been urged upon us for many years past that the Midland Company should be physically represented in the district which it is not at present. It has been urged upon us by almost all those who live in the district that we should come and be welcome, that we should come and do our business at first hand instead of at second hand as we do now. Deputations from Corporations and from Chambers of Commerce of the many large towns in the district have been good enough to wait upon us, each of them suggest also that unless the line passes through their particular town or through a particular district it would be of very little use to the Midland shareholders. Well, you know, that of course was very encouraging but at the same time it was rather embarrassing because one of our objects in going through the West Riding of Yorkshire is to get a line to Bradford and the north which is shorter and not worse in the matter of gradients than our present line. It was therefore obvious that the two things were incompatible, that is to say, we cannot serve all the towns on the way north and at the same time get a line to Bradford which was short and had good gradients. What we had to do, therefore, was this : to instruct our Engineer to give us a line up the Spen Valley to Bradford fulfilling as to shortening and as to gradients, and which would call upon the best towns en route upon its way. The result leaves our present main line at Royston, continuing in a north westerly direction to Thornhill where there will be another line up to Huddersfield and one to Halifax. The distance from Royston to Thornhill is 8¼ miles and from Thornhill to Bradford the line runs north by north calling at Heckmondwike, Clackheaton (*sic*), and Dewsbury on the way and finally arriving at Bradford and meeting our present line in the Bradford station at a dead end. This continues its course to Manningham and Shipley and joins the line again at that point for the north. Mr McDonald has been very successful, I think, in arranging a line that has as good gradients as possible under the circumstances. The first half of the Royston and Bradford line has a ruling gradient of 1 in 200; for the remaining distance the ruling gradient is 1 in 132, or the same as your Leicester and Bedford line, so I think that must be a very satisfactory thing to the shareholders for I am sure that Mr Johnson's engines will be able to accomplish 1 in 132 considering you have them groaning over some of the worst gradients at present on the Midland system. Coming back again to Thornhill, the line goes to Huddersfield and Halifax—$7\frac{1}{2}$ miles, and here unfortunately our gradients are not so good. The ruling gradient between Thornhill and Huddersfield is 1 in 100 and that between Huddersfield and Halifax 1 in 60. The saving in distance by the new line from London to Bradford will be $11\frac{1}{4}$ miles, the distance being $197\frac{1}{2}$ as against $208\frac{3}{4}$ miles as at present. The distance to Scotland by the proposed line will be $5\frac{3}{4}$ miles shorter than by the existing route. I have talked about Bradford but let me say one word about Huddersfield and Halifax. We are perfectly alive to the importance of these; we know what very important towns they are. The Mayors and Corporations of these towns were particularly anxious that we should carry our line through Huddersfield and Halifax up that way to the north than by Bradford but it was found to be absolutely impossible by our Engineer to give us a line through these towns at anything like the cost which the Midland shareholders should be willing to grant. That is to say we would not get a line with reasonable gradients through these towns. Years ago—I think it was in 1867—we applied for powers or rather powers were applied for—I ought to say—to Huddersfield and land was actually bought in that town for the position of the station. That land we still retain and that land we now hope to use when this line is made. I think when I speak of Huddersfield and Halifax I ought also to mention Batley. We have had a petiton from the Mayor and Corporation of Batley and they expressed a very great deal of disappointment that the line cannot take a course through Batley. Exactly the same thing happened in the case of Batley as in the cases of Huddersfield and Halifax. We could not get a decent gradient. They have suggested that we make a loop line through Batley and they are rather anxious to pin me to say that we will do it. But I have not declared that. All I can tell them is—when we see our way we shall be very glad to consider the question when the proper time comes but I am not giving on behalf of myself and my Board any pledge whatever in that direction.'

Despite all the talk of Huddersfield and Halifax, within two months the towns had been jettisoned. The L.Y.R., by now thoroughly alarmed, agreed with the Midland early in April that if the latter would drop its connecting lines into the towns, the Lancashire company would grant it running powers from Low Moor to Halifax—the Midland to construct a short connecting line on to the L.Y.R. for this purpose, and to Huddersfield from Barnsley via the Clayton West branch, which the L.Y.R. would extend to its line at Darton. (Powers for the L.Y.R. to do this had been obtained in 1893.) The Halifax arrangement was subject to the Midland building its own station at the town, and as to Huddersfield the Midland reserved the right to promote a better access in the future. In return the company was to give the L.Y.R. running powers over the new line from Low Moor to Bradford and thence to Skipton as well as Shipley to Ilkley and Otley. Facilities were also granted to the L.Y.R. from Colne to Bradford and Leeds.

The Midland Railway (West Riding Lines) Act of July 25, 1898, authorized the Royston–Thornhill–Bradford line. It was to approach Bradford through a long tunnel under Bowling Park and then run beneath the city, mainly in tunnel or covered way, to make a junction with the Leeds & Bradford about 130 yards north of the existing Bradford station. With the West Riding Lines Act came the other Act which authorized all the widenings already mentioned. In the same month as the Royal Assent to the two Acts there was an ominous little sentence in the half-yearly directors' report: 'The increased earnings have been absorbed by the increased cost of working and by charges for new capital'. The law of diminishing returns was catching up with the Midland. Nothing daunted the company marched into 1899 with a Bill for the Low Moor Junctions, the necessary branch to the L.Y.R. for access to Halifax; the Halifax Connecting Lines, these being for the Midland's own station at the town; the Huddersfield Railway, a line 4½ miles in length from Mirfield on the L.Y.R. to the land at Huddersfield already held by the Midland; and the Thornhill Junction, a connecting spur from the Royston–Bradford line on to the L.Y.R. at Thornhill. The reasons behind the last two lines were simple. The Midland had originally intended a direct Thornhill–Huddersfield line for the 1899 session, with no contact with the L.Y.R. Once again the latter had come forward and suggested the amended arrangement which, though it meant the Midland would have to run over the L.Y.R. between Thornhill and Mirfield, permitted a considerable saving in construction costs. The Act received the Royal Assent on July 13. The further history of the West Riding Lines and their subsequent sorry diminution into being merely a branch line to Dewsbury does not concern us here, save to say that if they had been promoted just five years earlier then, with the Settle and Carlisle line, the Midland could well have effectively challenged the L.N.W.R. between London and Carlisle for speed as well as comfort. The distance from Euston to Carlisle is 299 miles; that from St Pancras via the West Riding Lines and the Settle and Carlisle would have been 302½. And, of course, the L.N.W.R. had Shap to contend with. That this point was not lost on the authorities at Euston is borne out by their Bill for the 1898 session which included a railway at Shap forming a deviation from the Lancaster & Carlisle line about 9 miles in length. Heavy earthworks and a tunnel about 1½ miles in length were to be carried out to reduce the gradients over Shap to one of 1 in 135. The Lancaster & Carlisle line was also to be widened at some points. Euston evidently intended to make a fight of it. The L.N.W.R. Act received the Royal Assent barely a month after the Midland's West Riding Lines, and with the remedy in its pocket if needed, the L.N.W.R. was enabled to sit and watch the game out.

Before leaving the nineteenth century a last look at the train service from St Pancras to Scotland might be of interest. With the Leeds and Normanton stops out all the Scotch expresses carried first and third class restaurant cars. The fastest train of the day was still the 10.30 a.m. from St Pancras, departing from Leicester at 12.30 p.m., Chesterfield at 1.35, Skipton at 3.12, and arriving at Carlisle at 5.00 p.m. It was due to reach Glasgow 9 hrs. and 5 mins. after leaving St Pancras and carried through coaches to Ayr via Kilmarnock and to Greenock. This train did not call at Sheffield or Leeds; it went via the Staveley line and the Whitehall Junction curve. Close after it from London came the 10.35 a.m. for Edinburgh, calling at Bedford, Nottingham, Chesterfield, Sheffield, Leeds, Skipton, Hellifield, Lazonby, and Carlisle. It also called conditionally at Appleby. Despite the greater number of stops it arrived at Carlisle at 5.45. The next train, the 2.10 p.m., with four stops, arrived at Carlisle at 8.55. There were also, of course, the two night sleeper trains to Glasgow and Edinburgh. On the Manchester–Glasgow run the fastest train took 5 hours and 40 minutes to do the journey. Regarding the 10.30 a.m. from St Pancras, Ahrons mentions that from St Pancras to Leicester it was usually worked by one of the Midland single engines. From Leicester to Skipton it was taken over by one of the Nottingham engines 2183–2192, or 156–160, all 4-4-0s. At Skipton one of the Carlisle engines, Nos. 184–199, already mentioned, took it over the 'Long Drag'.

XVII

Up to the Grouping

PART I

1900–1914

The turn of the century. In London that winter of 1899–1900 people groped about under dank dripping trees and begrimed buildings in an atmosphere of unrelieved greyness. Victorian London in the last-but-one year of the old Queen's reign, with its gaslights and hansom cabs, was enshrouded in dense fog day after day. In fact all the country was affected. From Thursday, November 6, the whole of the Midland Railway line as far north as Carlisle had been enveloped in fog until the following Sunday afternoon. On the Saturday afternoon it was so thick that 55 of the company's passenger trains did not run. The February half-yearly meeting was held in an atmosphere of resigned gloom which matched the weather, for the news imparted to the shareholders was not good. Apart from the fog—which had caused losses enough, increased competition and the rising price of coal had combined to produce a net operating loss of close on £40,000. The company was beginning to find that the Great Central main line was making inroads in the south, taking away former Midland passengers from the Sheffield to London route. As to the Midland main line to the north it had become imperative to get the widenings opened as soon as possible so as to speed the traffic. Nearly 1,000 yards of the new Thackley tunnel were completed and the viaduct at Apperley was almost ready for use. At the August meeting, though the tale was one of expanding traffic, it was found that working expenses had not only absorbed receipts but had led to a diminution of the dividend. Paget, by now Sir Ernest, told the meeting that the company was anxious to defer the construction of the remainder of the West Riding Lines until building costs returned to normal.

There was some relief to the main line when the Bingley and Thwaites widening was opened during the year. The Marley-Thwaites down goods line came into use on May 25, and between Marley and Bingley North on October 21, the same day as the up goods line from Bingley North to Thwaites. Most of the remaining widenings on the Leeds & Bradford line became operational during 1901. On January 27 Thackley tunnel and the Shipley and Apperley widening between Thackley and Apperley North were opened. The widening was extended to Thackley Junction and Apperley Junction on November 17, and two additional lines opened between Thackley Junction and Leeds Junction a week later. Work continued on the remainder of the widenings towards

Armley and on July 31, 1903, Kirkstall Forge station was closed when the line was diverted over the new canal bridge nearby. A new station was opened at Kirkstall itself on July 7, 1905. In January, 1904, the traffic committee ordered that the up and down goods lines between Snaygill Junction and Skipton South Junction should be converted to common use. May 15, 1904, saw the removal of the short Laithes tunnel, near Newlay, preparatory to the opening of the Newlay and Calverley widening on the following August 21. It was in 1901, incidentally, that Appleby got its footbridge, in response to a petition from local people, who did not like using the sleeper crossing. Lye-by sidings such as Delaney's at Gargrave were also brought into use at about this time. A more detailed chronology of the various widenings and signalling alterations since 1890 will be found in Appendix XXII.

Despite the troubled outlook of the early months of 1900 the Midland was gearing itself to provide a better Scotch passenger service to challenge the East and West Coast routes. A start was made on May 1, with the introduction of four new Pullman sleeping cars on the Scotch trains to replace some of the old ones. They were put on the 9.15 and 10.15 p.m. trains from St Pancras for Edinburgh and Glasgow respectively, and on the 9.30 p.m. from Glasgow, and 10.00 p.m. from Edinburgh to London. New corridor stock was introduced on the morning trains from St Enoch and St Pancras the following July. These improvements, however, were but forerunners to a complete revision of the timetable for the July services of 1901. A supreme effort was made to recapture some of the lost traffic which had been seeping back to the East and West Coast lines over the past few years. 1901 was the year of the Glasgow Exhibition and the new service came into operation from July 1. It was advertised on timetables as being 'Revised and improved Express Service between England and Scotland by the most interesting route, via the Settle and Carlisle, etc.' The first Scotch train of the day left St Pancras at 5.15 a.m. and called at Leicester, Nottingham, and Sheffield. The Edinburgh portion left Sheffield at 9.00 a.m. and, calling at Leeds and with a connection with Bradford, arrived at Carlisle at 12.40 p.m. whence Edinburgh was reached at 3.25, Perth at 6.20, Aberdeen at 8.40, and Inverness at 11.25 p.m. For the first two months this train also had connections to Oban and Fort William. The Glasgow portion of the 5.15 left Sheffield at 9.10 a.m., and running not far behind the Edinburgh train, reached Carlisle at 1.15 p.m. and Glasgow at 4.00 p.m. The next train was the 9.30 a.m. dining car express from St Pancras which called at Leicester, Chesterfield, and Leeds. This ran as one train to Carlisle, with a through dining car from St Pancras to Edinburgh. At Carlisle the Glasgow portion took a dining car on the remainder of its journey. Arrival times in the northern cities were Edinburgh 6.05 p.m. and Glasgow 6.20. Out of St Pancras there followed at hourly intervals two more dining car trains, the 10.30 which ran via Leicester, Nottingham, and Bradford, and the 11.30 calling at Kettering,

Chesterfield, Leeds and Appleby. The arrival times at Carlisle of these two trains were 5.38 and 5.48 p.m. respectively, the Edinburgh and Glasgow portions both reaching their final destinations at 8.25 p.m. The 9.30, 10.30, and 11.30 all had connections to Perth, Aberdeen, and Inverness, and the last mentioned train had through carriages from St Pancras to Windermere Lake Side which were detached at Hellifield and worked forward via Carnforth and over the Furness Railway. The 5.15 and the 10.30 both connected at Hellifield with the Manchester and Liverpool service. The first afternoon train out of St Pancras was the 1.30 p.m. dining car train to Glasgow. With stops at Leicester, Leeds, and Hellifield, it reached Carlisle at 7.55 p.m., and Glasgow at 10.20. From Carlisle a connection reached the northern capital at 10.25, and one from Glasgow arrived at Greenock at 11.35. There was a long gap until the next departure from St Pancras, the popular Highland Express which left, Saturday nights excepted, at 7.20 p.m. with a through sleeping car to Inverness via Edinburgh, and with a dining car as far as Trent. It reached Carlisle at 1.30 a.m., Edinburgh at 3.50 a.m., the Inverness coach arriving at 9.10 a.m. Connections were also given to Oban, Fort William, Mallaig, Perth, and Aberdeen. At 9.30 p.m. another train left St Pancras for the north—this was the 9.15 of the old timetable retimed. It had sleeping carriages through to Edinburgh and arrived at 6.45 a.m. The Glasgow passengers alighted at Carlisle to await the arrival at 4.32 of the 8.00 p.m. Bristol Scotch express. This got into Edinburgh at 7.05 and Glasgow at 7.10 a.m. The 1.30, 7.20 and 9.30 p.m. expresses all connected at Hellifield with the Lancashire trains. The last two trains were the 10.30 p.m. with sleeping cars from London to Glasgow and Edinburgh calling at Leicester and Leeds and arriving at Carlisle at 4.45, Edinburgh at 7.05 and Glasgow at 7.25 p.m., and the 11.55 out of St Pancras which called at Leicester and Leeds and got to Carlisle at 8.45 a.m. From the three last-mentioned trains connections were available to stations further north.

On the up service a new train left Carlisle, with Edinburgh and Glasgow connections, at 11.45 a.m. and arrived at St Pancras at 6.00 p.m. As regards the night trains to St Pancras, the 1.45 a.m. from Carlisle, which had left Edinburgh at 11.25 and Glasgow at 11.00 p.m., arrived into St Pancras at 8 a.m. One thing may be noticed about the new trains—the non-appearance of Normanton in the schedules and the frequent appearance of Leeds. The reason was simple. In 1899, following a policy of passing Leeds non-stop via the Holbeck curve, the Midland even went so far as to halt the morning express at Cudworth for a short time during 1899; Cudworth in preference to Leeds. Quick advantage was taken of this shortcoming by the N.E.R., however, which threatened to take away many of the Leeds–Carlisle passengers. The 1901 timetable remedied this situation. By September of that year the St Pancras–Leeds trains bettered even those of the G.N.R. Though the latter company soon reduced its timings between London and Leeds to about $3\frac{3}{4}$ hours, the Midland service stood the test well. In fact W. J. Scott, writing in the *Railway Magazine* for September of 1901, remarked that the 9.30 a.m. from St Pancras was 'almost inconveniently full' north of Chesterfield with both its dining cars having at least a paying load. In the matter of competition the service payed off—just. The 9.30 a.m. from St Pancras usually made Carlisle ahead of the 10 a.m. from Euston, and the 1.30 also succeeded in beating the rival 2 p.m. This despite speed restrictions between Trent and Leeds and an additional route mileage of some 9 miles.

The new timings did not please everybody, however. A reported speech extract from the *Railway News* of August 17, 1901, dealt with the Midland's half-yearly report :

'There had been a good deal of sensational writing in the newspapers of the excessive speed at which the Midland were running to Scotland and the enormous addition to train mileage; but shortly, it amounts to this: from London to Carlisle the company are running this year at an average speed of 51.7 miles per hour, as compared with 49.1 miles per hour a year ago. That is an increase of 2.6 miles per hour, and considering the splendid road and magnificent rolling stock that speed cannot be called excessive. There is no racing going on, and nothing in the nature of racing, so far as the Midland are concerned, and the same may be said for their competitors. The addition to the mileage by the new timetable is about 3,000 miles per week, and supposing the directors keep their Highland train on for six months, there will be run 78,000 miles more than in the corresponding half last year. . . .'

The North British contributed but little to the new service, having as it did a particularly awkward time with delays at Carlisle due to the difference of braking system between it and the Midland, and the difficult nature of the Waverley route. In fact the N.B.R., with virtually nothing to gain from the new timings in that it already took Scotch traffic on the East Coast route, asked for a financial guarantee from the Midland as to the revenue from some of the trains on the new service. As to the G.S.W.R., the late R. E. Charlewood, writing in the *Railway Club Journal* for June, 1902, thought the Glasgow company carried out its share of the new timings 'very creditably', although it sometimes arrived late into Carlisle with the up trains. He mentioned that the 'Midland arrivals at Carlisle were extremely erratic even after the press of the Scotch traffic was over', some very good and some very bad timekeeping being displayed.

In 1902 and 1903 the traffic increased so much that the 9.30 a.m. from St Pancras, mentioned above as being full in 1901, ran as two portions to Carlisle; in the following year there was an even greater speed-up on the Settle line with the introduction of a start to stop booking between Appleby and Carlisle of no less than 59.5 miles per hour, albeit on a mainly down grade. The summer of 1903 saw the 11.30 a.m. treated the same way as the 9.30. As to the train loading, the comments of R. E. Charlewood again, writing in the *Railway Magazine* of July and August, 1947, are of interest. 'The Midland had, of course, in 1901, a virtual monopoly of traffic to Scotland from its provincial towns south of Leeds, but this was really a very small business, and a census taken early in 1902 indicated that 78 per cent. of Midland-Scottish traffic originated in London (or south thereof), while 15 per cent. of the remaining 22 per cent. joined at Leeds, and although the new trains loaded well between Leeds and London, they were never all paying propositions over the Settle and Carlisle line. Far too many of them neglected Sheffield (then just beginning to be influenced by Great Central competition) for the sake of a very small gain in journey time, and their mileage bill was so heavy that their running restricted development in other directions.'

Let the *Railway News* tell of the Midland's summer service for 1903; it included a new venture north of Leeds :

'The Summer arrangements of the Midland Railway . . . include an improved service of through expresses, worked by their own locomotives and vehicles, between St Pancras and Harrogate. It was only last year that the Midland Company took up its running powers to the famous Yorkshire Spa, and now four through expresses on the up journey and three on the down are running daily, the 10.27 a.m. out of Harrogate carrying a luncheon car, and the 5.0 p.m. from St Pancras a dining car. The Company's arrangements for the Scotch traffic include two new evening expresses, leaving St Pancras at 7.30 (Saturdays and Sundays excepted) and 8.30 p.m. (Saturdays excepted) respectively, the former for Edinburgh and North Scotland, carrying through carriages for Perth, Aberdeen, Inverness, and Fort William, and sleeping car for Perth and Inverness. The second is a through train to Glasgow, but also includes through carriages and a sleeping car for Stranraer Harbour, connecting at the latter point with the early morning boat to Larne for Belfast and other parts of the North of Ireland. Supper cars will also be run from London to Leeds by these trains. No less than five trains will leave St Pancras before noon with through carriages for Scotland, two of which afford connections to the principal Clyde watering places, and three give through connections to Glasgow, Edinburgh, and the Highlands. . . .'

Excursions out of Leeds during 1903 included a weekly tourist return to Belfast for 12s 6d and a return ticket to Ambleside via Carnforth, which included a trip by boat on Lake Windermere, a 12 mile drive, and a hot dinner, for the remarkably low price of 12s 9d. Morecambe of course, was the Bradfordian's home from home, and a considerable number of excursion trains ran from the West Riding stations over the Midland route during the summer months. Returning to the Scotch trains for a moment; the quickest Leeds–Glasgow trip took 4 hours and 45 minutes, and that to Edinburgh 4 hours and 27 minutes, the distances respectively being 227 and 210 miles.

1903 was distinctive in another way; it saw the introduction on the Settle line of the first of the new compound locomotives. They were mentioned in the February report. After telling the shareholders that 1902 had been a better year, with receipts up and fuel costs down, Paget said :

'. . . on the locomotive question you will see that during the half-year there have been fifteen engines added to the company's stock. Two of those engines are very large compound passenger engines, which have been designed and built by Mr Johnson in the locomotive shops at Derby; and they are capable of hauling longer trains and heavier loads over our somewhat difficult gradients at high speeds, and loads which have never been attempted on our line. The result has been, between Leeds and Carlisle, so satisfactory that we have ordered Mr Johnson to build more of them. I believe that these engines are superior to perhaps anything at present running in this country. We know, at the same time, that the Great Western Company are building some engines of the type adopted by the Northern of France, which may be, for all I know, equal to, and perhaps superior to, the engines which Mr Johnson has built. I am quite sure that Lord Cawdor will allow his locomotive superintendent to give Mr Johnson every information on this subject, and in return Mr Johnson will, I am sure, give his locomotive superintendent every opportunity of investigating his engines.'

The greater weight of the compounds over that of the usual locomotive types threatened restriction of their use at first to certain routes. In February, 1902, a month after the prototypes came out of Derby, the way and works committee was instructed to strengthen no fewer than 108 bridges under the line at an estimated cost of £96,000. Details of such work on the Settle line, and the dates when it was ordered to be put in hand, will be found in Appendix XXIII.

The February report of 1903 also told of the imminent take-over by the Midland of the Belfast & Northern Counties Railway, with the object of ensuring an efficient development of the Heysham services to Ireland. By May of 1903 the *Railway News* noted that the B. & N.C. was now in Midland hands and it thought that the company would take a more positive interest in the Belfast–Larne–Stranraer route. As has been seen the summer timetable bore this out. Actually the paper's announcement was rather premature; the vesting Act received the Royal Assent in July.

In October of 1903 the winter timetable came out. The surprising thing about it was that instead of running until December 31 as was usual it went right through to April, and several of the important trains usually withdrawn at the end of September remained in operation. The evening Highland train was kept on, carrying dining and supper cars as far as Leeds and with sleeping cars from London to Edinburgh, Perth, Dundee, and Aberdeen. Also retained was the 8.30 p.m. for Glasgow and Stranraer, with its sleeping car to the latter place and dining and supper cars between St Pancras and Leicester. In the up direction the 11 p.m. from Glasgow and 11.30 p.m. from Edinburgh, for St Pancras, continued to run. Also remaining was the St Pancras–Harrogate service, with a journey time of a little over $4\frac{1}{2}$ hours. This was, of course, a vast improvement on the usual Midland winter timetable for the Scotch trains.

With regard to the progress at Heysham, we left this in the last chapter at the stage where the branch railway had been authorised. Though it had been intended to construct a pier at Heysham this part of the scheme was not carried through. Instead, due to the increasing difficulties at Morecambe, powers were got in the session of 1896 for construction of a fully-fledged harbour. In fact over-fledged would better describe it, for the scheme originally provided for an enclosed water space twice the size of the present harbour. Two giant breakwaters were built out from the shore to enclose by pincer movement a large area of the sea. A temporary dam was built between the two arms and when the area had been pumped dry the main works commenced. A centre pier was then built on which was the passenger station and cattle docks. To the south of this there were to have been further docks, both wet and dry, but somehow, though money was easy at the time, the whole scheme slowed down with the onset of harder times and this part of the original plan never materialized. Messrs Godfrey & Liddelow were the contractors for the railway and Messrs Price & Wills for the harbour works. A table of the day rates applicable at the time appears in Appendix VII. Details of the construction would be out of place here; it was to have been an ambitious project, however, with large tracts of land bought for future development of the town around the port. When this refused to take place, or at least while it was being confidently expected, the grasslands were used to refresh sea-sick and weary cattle off the Irish boats for priming for the English market. To attract patrons to Heysham the Midland acquired the Heysham Tower Hotel in 1896. It never really paid though, and as early as 1900 was closed during the winter season. With the railway and harbour not yet operating this was not surprising. Even so, the hotel led a halting existence until the First World War when it briefly served to house officers commanding troops in the district. On July 17, 1919, the Midland's hotels and refreshment rooms committee decided to call a halt, noted that there had been a perpetual loss on the venture, and gave instructions to sell.

To return to the beginning of the century, the Heysham branch railways were opened for contractor's traffic only in November, 1898, and were worked by Midland engines. A year later the contractor took over the working until the line was opened to ordinary traffic in September, 1904. There was to be one intermediate station—at Middleton Road. Meanwhile, by the Midland Railway (Steam Vessels) Act of July 31, 1902, the company was permitted to provide and work a steamer service between Heysham and Belfast, Larne, Londonderry, and the Isle of Man, and between Barrow and Belfast and the Isle of Man. Power was also given to enter into an agreement with the Furness Railway as to the latter's share in the Barrow boats.

So far the history of the Midland's steamer interests has been excluded so as not to befog the main theme. With the Act of 1902, however, some back history is due, if only to explain the existing situation at Barrow. This of necessity involves delving back into the 1840s.

The Midland's Irish connections start at the point where the little North Western Railway was in control at Morecambe. The N.W.R. Act of 1852, it will be recalled, virtually re-organised that company. It also legalised the construction of the stone jetty and 'tramways' at Morecambe which had been built with only a vague similarity to the harbour works authorised by the Morecambe Harbour & Railway Act of 1846.

With the jetty nearly complete by February of 1851 the N.W.R. board had resolved that arrangements should be made with the Whitehaven & Furness Railway and the Midland for the joint working of a steamboat service between Piel Pier at Barrow, and Morecambe. Four months later it had been decided to lengthen the jetty and construct a breakwater from rubble taken from Denny Beck, and in September further improvements to the jetty had been authorized and the construction of a landing stage ordered. So far, however, there were no boats actually in the company's ownership though it was noted in the minutes that the steamer *Albion* was then operating a service. This vessel must shortly after have come into the company's hands, however, as by May it had been agreed to purchase 'another' steamer from Denny Bros. of Dumbarton.

By the 1852 Act the necessary powers to operate the service between Morecambe and Piel had been obtained and by that time the Midland had agreed to work it. It was stated in the N.W.R.'s half-yearly meeting in August that the shipping traffic at Morecambe continued to increase both in character and quantity; the Irish trade had steadily improved and arrangements had been completed for the sailing of 'first-class iron steam packets' for passengers and goods twice weekly between Morecambe and the north of Ireland.

By July, 1852, the new steamer, the *Plover*, had arrived at Morecambe and the outright purchase of the *Albion* was completed. During the past few months the Irish service had been operated by the Belfast Steam Packet Company.

In August it was reported that a goods warehouse and crane had been erected on the pier at Morecambe. Three months later it was agreed that Denny Bros. should build another steamer for the Morecambe–Piel run. Meanwhile the *Albion* was to be repaired by her builders—Messrs Gibson & Butcher of Fleetwood. It was noted in the minutes that a further £25,000 expenditure at Morecambe was being held back because of the current fear of the proposed amalgamation of the Midland with the L.N.W.R., an occurrence which would have switched the former's operating interests from Morecambe to Fleetwood. Additional lamps and another crane had, however, been added to the jetty. Also, a pile lighthouse was to be built on the shoulder of Clarke's Wharf. This decision was reached after a derogatory report about the harbour approaches from the 'Captain of the Belfast steamer'.

In January of 1853 there was a crisis of some sort—the minutes of the N.W.R. are vague as to details—over the Irish service. Apparently the outcome of recent talks with the Londonderry & Sligo Steam Packet Company had convinced the Midland and the N.W.R. that unless they took immediate steps to place an independent steamboat on the 'Morecambe and Belfast station' the large traffic which had been developed would be lost to them.

Whereas powers to operate the Morecambe–Piel service had been obtained, however, there was no statutory authority for either the Midland or the N.W.R. to work any steamers to Ireland. Nevertheless the minutes make it clear that the N.W.R. offered to advance half the sum towards a new steamer if the Midland would do the same. To this the latter agreed, at a meeting in Derby on January 5, 1853. This occurred at a time when amalgamation between the Midland and the L.N.W.R. was still in the air and when the Midland and the little North Western were arguing over traffic. The local Morecambe–Ireland and Fleetwood –Ireland services were supposed to be arranged to minimise conflict between the Midland on the one hand and the L.N.W.R. and L.Y.R. on the other. There was, however, no definite agreement concerning competitive steamer services outside the Irish run and it seems from the minutes that the Midland was concerned as to its backing of the N.W.R.'s Irish venture lest the latter decided to kick over the traces and try for a Morecambe–New York run. This would, said the minutes, annoy the L.N.W.R.

Even so, Derby decided to take the risk and three weeks later the N.W.R. board ordered the steamboat pier at Morecambe to be lengthened, two turntables to be put on the jetty and the breakwater to be raised. There was a commotion at this time when the company's engineer laid before the board a false bolt which, together with several others, he had taken out of the timber jetty contracted for by John Storey and then in course of erection. Such practices were dangerous and the directors expressed 'their great indignation at such gross dishonesty'. Despite this sort of thing the works were in the main of a substantial nature as was proved when the great gale of December 27, 1852, created havoc elsewhere. Reports were circulated of great loss of life, and of vessels being driven from their moorings and foundering, but Morecambe harbour passed through unscathed.

In February the N.W.R. directors' report noted that opposition offered by 'parties interested in the Fleetwood steam packets' had hitherto curtailed the advantages accruing to the N.W.R. from the steam packets plying between Morecambe and Belfast. However, it continued, the directors in conjunction with the Midland board would 'continue to use every legal means for securing to Morecambe a fair proportion of such large traffic to and from the north of Ireland'. And in that statement lay hidden the method by which the two companies were to get over the difficulty of not being legally permitted to run the service. It was, quite simply, that though the Midland and the N.W.R. might purchase the necessary vessels these would be registered in the names of private individuals who happened to be directors of the two companies, and operated by an apparently independent concern.

While the steamer needed to start the service was on order the Drogheda Steam Packet Company's vessel *St Patrick* was chartered. In March there was a proposal from the L.Y.R. for an agreement to stop the present competition between Fleetwood and Morecambe for the Belfast traffic but a meeting held on May 10 achieved nothing, except to prod the N.W.R. to suggest to Derby that an additional boat be obtained to enable there to be three sailings a week from Morecambe in the event of the Fleetwood sailings being reduced to that number.

A year later, with the L.Y.R. intransigent, it was agreed that another steamer should be obtained. In July, 1854, Whelon and Kirtley went to Newcastle and looked over a boat in course of completion for the Russian government which was now prohibited from sale due to the Crimean War. The steamer was purchased for £9,000 and, named the *Arbutus*, was registered in August under the names of W. E. Hutchinson and G. B. Paget on behalf of the Midland. At Morecambe it joined another steamer, the *Laurel*, apparently purchased recently, and these two boats ran the Morecambe–Belfast service for some time, relieved when under repair by the *Stork* in 1857 and the *Lyra* in 1860, both apparently specially chartered.

In October, 1860, it was agreed that a new boat was required. This was to be a paddle steamer in lieu of the *Arbutus*, which was a screw driven vessel. It would appear that the *Arbutus* was in fact sailing on the Morecambe–Londonderry route, for a minute of January 22, 1861, noted that she was to be taken off the run from February 1, an occurrence which when it happened raised a storm of abortive protest from the merchants of Londonderry. Also on January 22 it was agreed to purchase two new boats, the *Talbot* and *Shelburne*.

In August, 1862, the *Arbutus* went back on the Londonderry run but only as a chartered vessel to the private firm who had taken over the working from the railway.

In this state the Irish service continued for about three years until September of 1865 when the Midland board, which now had the direction of affairs completely within its own hands, resolved that the old vessels *Laurel* and *Arbutus* should be sold and replaced by a new boat equal to the *Talbot* and *Shelburne*. A month later Allport reported that he and Kirtley had contracted, subject to the board's approval, to purchase from Messrs G. & T. Burns of Glasgow a paddle steamer named the *Roe* for the sum of £25,000 payable upon delivery at Glasgow, Burns' taking in part exchange the *Arbutus* at £7,000, to be delivered at Glasgow. On October 31, 1865, the Midland traffic committee minutes recorded 'Read letter from Messrs McLean & Son, dated 26th instant, reporting that the *Roe* made her first voyage from Morecambe to Belfast on the 25th in ten hours, and that in the face of severe weather and a heavy gale of wind the vessel behaved admirably'.

Note has been made in an earlier chapter of the 1863 Act for the Carnforth–Wennington line linking the Midland system direct with that of the Furness. This was at a time when the latter's works on the Barrow docks were well in hand. From the outset, however, it was agreed that Piel Pier was to be the first target for Midland trains and on May 31, 1867, the Furness board noted its agreement with the Midland for the transfer of the latter's Irish steamers to Barrow and the intention to modernise Piel Pier so as to take Midland boat trains. There had been intermittent services from the pier since the mid 1840s but with the coming of the Midland's Irish service Barrow was to enjoy considerable traffic up until the opening of Heysham harbour.

In May, 1868, an agreement was completed between the Midland, the Furness, and Messrs James Little & Co. It noted that the Midland was the owner of the *Roe*, the *Talbot*, and the *Shelburne*, and that James Little & Co. owned the steamer *Herald*. It was agreed that the three companies should operate a partnership to run the steamers between Barrow and Piel and Belfast and the Isle of Man, in connection with the trains of the Furness and Midland systems. Again, the steamers were registered in the private names of directors of the three 'partners'. James Little were to manage the partnership and act as ships' husbands with powers to appoint crews, etc. The partnership, frequently noted in agreements and minutes merely as 'the firm' was in fact the Barrow Steam Navigation Company. The *Roe, Talbot,* and *Shelburne* started the Barrow–Belfast service on September 2, 1867, the paddle steamer *Herald* doing the Isle of Man run.

A Furness and Midland joint committee minute of March 3, 1870, noted that a new paddle boat was to be provided, with compound engines, and that the *Herald* was to be retained for the Isle of Man service. Subject to this, said the minute, 'any of the old boats for which a proper offer can be obtained may be disposed of'. In 1871 the new steamer, the *Antrim,* was purchased; it was slightly larger than the *Talbot* and *Shelburne*. November of 1872 saw the committee debating the question of opening communication with Dublin, 'where a steamer is available'. Though a detailed proposal was approved, it was shelved for further consideration. In 1881 the five steamers of the Barrow Steam Navigation Company, and their connecting trains, ceased using Piel Pier and switched over to the Ramsden Dock at Barrow. Meanwhile the *Talbot* and *Shelburne* had been renamed as *Armagh* and *Tyrone* respectively, while the *Antrim* became the *Manxman* and went over to the Isle of Man service. Also in 1881 two new vessels, the *Londonderry* and *Donegal*, were purchased. These had been the Burns' paddle steamers *Camel* and *Buffalo*. The following year saw another arrival, the South Eastern Railway's ship *Duchess of Edinburgh,* constructed in 1881. She was renamed *Manx Queen*. With the sale, early in the 1880s, of the *Tyrone* the Barrow Steam Navigation Company's vessels now numbered seven. Of these the *Roe* was scrapped in 1887 and the *Herald* disposed of soon after. A new vessel was then acquired, the twin screw boat *City of Belfast*, built at Birkenhead in 1893. Four years later *Donegal* was scrapped, the *Armagh* following in 1898. In 1897 another new vessel, built by Vickers for the Barrow Steam Navigation company and named *Duchess of Devonshire* started operating. In 1902 and 1904 the *Manxman* and *Londonderry* were scrapped. By the time of the beginning of the Heysham service, therefore, the Barrow route was operated by the *City of Belfast*, the *Duchess of Devonshire*, the *Manx Queen*, and one other, the old

Rouen of the London Brighton & South Coast Railway, renamed *Duchess of Buccleuch*, and purchased in 1903.

To return to strictly Midland doings, in 1903, with Heysham harbour nearing completion, the company ordered three boats for the Irish traffic, and one for the Isle of Man run. The first three were the twin screw ship *Antrim* of 2,100 gross tons—a non turbine vessel capable of 20 knots and built at Clydebank, the *Donegal*—a similar vessel but built at Greenock, and the triple screw turbine ship *Londonderry* built by Denny Bros. The Isle of Man vessel was ordered from Vickers. Named the *Manxman* it was a triple screw turbine ship of 2,174 gross tons. At the company's February meeting of 1904 Paget was able to say that three of the steamships would be ready for launching by April. The company's financial position had greatly improved over the past year and the coming Heysham service would, he hoped, open out new traffic. As to the Morecambe–Heysham line two steam rail motors had been ordered to do the local shuttle service.

The chairman's main announcement, however, concerned Johnson, who had retired from the Midland on December 31, 1903. 'Mr Johnson has the satisfaction of leaving with us what I believe to be the finest passenger engines that are running in the United Kingdom.' Charles Rous-Marten, writing in the *Railway Magazine* of November, 1903, thought them good too. He reported that he had recently travelled behind one of the new compound engines on the Settle line. The train described was the 11.50 a.m. from Carlisle to Leeds, a total load of 240 tons behind a double-bogie tender, and hauled by No. 2632. The trip outdid his expectations. His commentary contained phrases such as 'I had no previous experience of equal merit up that severe incline'—that was Kirkby Stephen to Ais Gill, and 'along this length'—the Blea Moor to Settle Junction stretch—'we made some splendid running, breaking all my Midland records, and coming very near to lowering all my records of mere speed either in this country or abroad'. He recorded a speed of 91.8 miles per hour and, thoughtful man, ensured that driver Killan would not be admonished for running the train so fast, by obtaining written permission from the Midland authorities before publishing.

The coming of the Midland compounds followed closely on the appearance late in 1900 of five new express passenger engines which were vastly different to any of Johnson's previous designs. 4-4-0s, they were known as the 'Belpaires' after their fireboxes of that type, and heralded a change in style and power for the Midland locomotive 'image'. The first five, Nos. 2606–2610, were stationed at Leeds and worked the trains on the Carlisle run. Meanwhile, two years earlier, W. M. Smith, the N.E.R.'s chief locomotive draughtsman, had brought out a 3 cylinder 4-4-0 compound engine which in its design enabled better results to be obtained on hilly runs than was possible with 4-4-0 simple engines. Johnson was a friend of Wilson Worsdell, the N.E.R. locomotive superintendent, and the latter's favourable reports on the workings of his company's compound came at a time when the Midland was actively seeking increased motive power for the same wheel arrangement, that of the 4-4-0, to carry the increasingly heavy trains on the St Pancras–Manchester and St Pancras–Carlisle runs. It was apparent that, failing some new approach, the practice of double-heading must increase, since the only foreseeable alternative to compounding—that of constructing much larger locomotives, of the 4-6-0 wheel arrangement—was not looked upon with favour by the Midland's civil engineer. The 'Belpaires' of 1900 had about reached the limit in standard Midland design for 4-4-0 simple engines.

The first two compound engines out of Derby were numbered 2631 and 2632. The former went to Leeds and the latter to Carlisle. They were essentially to the same working design as the Smith compound of the N.E.R. but had a generally larger scale and the Derby trimmings. Between August and November of 1902 the two engines carried out an exhaustive series of tests on the Leeds–Settle–Carlisle line. Fitted with hair-raising indicator shields for the engineers observing the runs—the shields were housed either side of the smokebox—they roared up and down the Settle line in all weathers. The results, as mentioned by Paget in the February report of 1903, were highly satisfactory. We have heard Rous-Marten's comments on the performance put on by No. 2632. Other runs were equally good. On September 5, 1902, No. 2631 took the 5.33 p.m. Leeds–Carlisle train, 229 tons, to a speed of 86 m.p.h. through Kirkby Stephen, doing the 76.7 miles from Hellifield to Carlisle in 79 minutes. On one of the up runs with the same engine, that of the 3.55 p.m. from Carlisle on September 16, No. 2631 took the 174 ton train up to Ais Gill—a distance of 48.4 miles—in 57 minutes and ran at over 80 m.p.h. from Blea Moor to Settle. In all the 76.7 mile run took just 81 minutes. The other three compounds in existence at the time of the February meeting of 1904, and the last built before Johnson's retirement, were Nos. 2633–2635. They went almost immediately on to the St Pancras–Manchester trains. All five of the first compounds had massive 8-wheel bogie tenders, for these were the days before water troughs—or just before, since the first on the Midland system came into use about 1901. Taking No. 2631 as an example, the weight of the engine and tender in working order was 112 tons 3 cwts, the total length over the buffers was 60 ft. 10 ins. and the water capacity of the tender was 4,500 gallons. The driving wheels were 7 ft. in diameter and were driven from one 19 in. high pressure, and two 21 in. low pressure cylinders. The working pressure was 195 lbs to the square inch.

Johnson was succeeded as locomotive superintendent of the Midland by his understudy, Richard Mountford Deeley. Under Deeley—an uneasy arrangement this—was Cecil W. Paget as works manager, the only surviving son of the Midland's chairman. On the carriage side Clayton left the company in 1902; his successor was David Bain of the North British Railway. Practically the first joint design of new locomotive superintendent and new carriage and wagon man was that of the two little steam rail cars for the Morecambe line. As with other rolling stock, details of these will be found in Chapter XVIII. They operated from July 11, 1904.

Before leaving the compounds, it is of interest to note that on May 19, 1904, Deeley reported to the locomotive committee that the results from the five engines already built warranted the construction of others of a similar kind. He pointed out that as the compound design was the patent of W. M. Smith he would require permission to consult with that gentleman concerning the royalty fees to be paid to him for future engines. This was agreed to, and in August Deeley reported that he had arranged for a payment of £300 to cover the next ten engines. The following month the committee minutes noted that Smith had issued a general licence— to construct as many engines as might be required (according either to Patent No. 20769 of 1890 or Patent No. 14721 of 1898 either alone or in any combination with one another) for the sum of £30 per engine. The early compounds had opened up a new era in Midland locomotive engineering, and Deeley was to add a series of modifications and improvements to the Johnson engines, as well as producing some forty more compounds himself.

In September of 1904 came the opening of the new Irish service via Heysham. The *Railway News* gave an account :

'The first ordinary train from London to Heysham ... left St Pancras at 5 o'clock on 1st September, and there were a large number of passengers by it. Four carriages—first class and third class dining-cars and two composite carriages—ran through to Heysham with stoppages at Kettering, Nottingham, Sheffield, and Leeds, the carriages being drawn from the Company's newest stock. On the sides of the through carriages were boards bearing the words 'Heysham for Ireland'. Mr John Elliott, outdoor assistant to the superintendent of the line, travelled in charge of the train, which was due to arrive at Heysham at 10.45 p.m. At 11 o'clock the new steamship *Antrim* was timed to leave Heysham for Belfast, and the vessel was due to arrive at Donegal Quay at 5.30 next morning. At 9 o'clock on Thursday night the new turbine steamer *Londonderry* was due to leave Belfast for Heysham, and the train in connection with it was timed to arrive at St Pancras at 11.20 Friday morning. There will be one service in each direction every weekday. Three boats will sail between Heysham and Belfast, the third being the *Donegal*.'

This brought the company's steamer services to five : Heysham– Belfast, Heysham–Dublin, Heysham–Londonderry, Barrow–Belfast, and Stranraer–Larne. The first has been dealt with; the second operated daily; the third left Heysham every Tuesday and Saturday at 11 p.m. and Londonderry every Monday and Friday at 5 p.m. The Barrow–Belfast service ran every evening except on Sundays, leaving Barrow at 8.30 p.m. in connection with the 1.30 p.m. train from St Pancras. In the reverse direction the steamer left Belfast at 8.30 p.m. and connected at Barrow with the 7.10 a.m. to St Pancras. On the Stranraer–Larne service, which was operated by a new vessel, the *Princess Maud*, the down train has already been mentioned. In the up direction, however, the return working left Stranraer harbour at 9.08 p.m. The opening of the Heysham route hit the Barrow steamers hard and the Furness Railway was quick to sell out its interest in the service for the sum of £45,000. Some hard bargaining on the part of Alfred Aslett, the Furness company's secretary and general manager, ensured that the Midland should keep the steamers operating. He also got a guarantee that a portion of the competitive traffic to and from Ireland should continue to go by Barrow—either that or a cash equivalent.

In November, 1906, the Midland agreed with the Furness to substitute as from January 1, 1907, a three days a week service for the daily sailings between Barrow and Belfast. Departures from Belfast were on Mondays, Wednesdays, and Fridays, and from Barrow on Tuesdays, Thursdays, and Saturdays. In 1907 *Manx Queen* was broken up, and three years later the *Duchess of Buccleuch* was disposed of. The two other vessels, *City of Belfast* and *Duchess of Devonshire,* ceased sailings from Barrow early in the First World War when requisitioned by the Government.

For pleasure trips and towing purposes at Heysham the Midland acquired in 1905 another vessel. It was considerably smaller than the others and was the twin screw ship *Wyvern* which operated for some time between Heysham, Blackpool and Fleetwood. Its name prompts the remark that all the Midland owned vessels displayed the company's flag—a red wyvern on a white background.

The history of the Stranraer–Larne service since its commencement as told of in Chapter XV can be briefly related. Following the introduction of the *Princess Louise,* another paddle steamer, slightly larger and named the *Princess Beatrice,* was built by Harland & Wolff. In 1890 the Larne & Stranraer Steamboat Company went out of business. It was taken over by the constituent companies of the Portpatrick & Wigtownshire Joint Committee, and the Belfast & Northern Counties Railway, the first group taking ⅘ths of the old company, and the Irish railway the remaining ⅕th. The eventual vesting of the Belfast & Northern Counties in the Midland in 1903 was to increase the latter's holding in the steamer interest to ⅖ths. Following the demise of the old steamboat concern the joint companies and the B. & N.C.R. formed the Larne & Stranraer Steamship Joint Committee. By that time there was another steamer employed on the run—the *Princess Victoria*—and this was followed by the last paddle steamer to be used by the committee—the *Princess May.* All four of these vessels had been scrapped by 1921. The *Princess Maud,* referred to in the summary of 1904 services as given above, was a triple screw vessel built in 1903 to replace the *Princess Beatrice,* scrapped in the following year. In 1909 the second *Princess Victoria* was built, also a triple screw ship, to take over from its namesake, scrapped in 1910. By the time of the First World War, therefore, the Stranraer–Larne service had three vessels.

To return to general Midland affairs north of Leeds, during 1904 there was another attempt by a new concern to build a railway connecting the Midland and the L.Y.R. at Hellifield with the N.E.R., though this time the junction with the latter was to be at two places, near Spennithorne on the Wensleydale line, and at Scorton on the Richmond branch. In all, the North Yorkshire Dales Railway Bill of 1904 sought powers to make twelve railways totalling some 51 miles in length. Connecting by two loops to both the Midland and the L.Y.R. south of Hellifield station, the proposed line ran east towards Rylstone, making a connection north of that station with the Yorkshire Dales Railway, and then crossed and re-crossed the latter south of Grassington where another connection was made. Between Grassington and Kettlewell the proposed railway parallelled an intended extension of the Y.D.R., deposited in May, 1903, by the Upper Wharfedale Light Railway. The N.Y.D. line continued from Kettlewell in a northerly direction as far as Buckden where it turned north-east and burrowed under the high ground near Bishop Dale by a tunnel 3,100 yards long. After this it ran through West Burton and West Witton to pass under the Northallerton–Hawes line of the N.E.R. near Spennithorne, where it threw off two connecting lines to east and west. From Spennithorne the line continued by West and East Hauxwell, Hornby, and Catterick, and joined the Richmond branch immediately south of Scorton station. The ruling gradient was to be 1 in 100 and for the most part the curves were good. This was to be no ordinary railway, for the Bill included provision for working the trains by electricity, and sites for generating stations were planned at Threshfield, Barton-cum-Walden, and East Hauxwell. The estimate for the line was £886,581. It would appear from the siting of the stations that there was a possibility it might have been worked as a hydro-electric system. Before petitions against the Bill could be lodged, however, the promoters withdrew it; the same thing happened to the Upper Wharfedale Light scheme. The North Yorkshire Dales Railway was the forerunner of two other attempts, both variations—like that of 1904—of the original Yorkshire Dales scheme of the mid 1890s. They will be mentioned again in their turn. In 1907 and 1908 the Upper Wharfedale Light Railway again tried to get the sanction of the Light Railway commissioners. Despite the support from Skipton Council in 1907 the commissioners rejected the proposal—for an extension to Buckden—mainly because of Midland opposition. Mention earlier of the Hawes line prompts a note that early in the century the Midland began operating two of the daily Hellifield–Hawes trains. Up to 1900 the station at Hawes Junction was known by that name but in that year it was altered to Hawes Junction & Garsdale.

Commenting on the current service over the Settle line, in the March, 1904, issue of the *Railway Club Journal*, R. E. Charlewood noted:

'The standard bookings between Hellifield and Carlisle (76¾ miles) are now 88 mins. on the down and 95 on the up journeys, representing average speeds of 52.3 and 48.5 m.p.h. One train—the Edinburgh portion of the 11.30 a.m. from St Pancras—is still booked to cover the 30¾ miles from Appleby to Carlisle in 31 mins., an average start to stop speed of 55.9 m.p.h., and until last September there was an almost equally fast run from Hawes Junction to Hellifield, 25⅜ miles in 26 mins. The trains are not very heavy. Except in a few cases, the loads do not exceed 13, but piloting is very seldom resorted to in spite of the severe weather often encountered on the section. The older types of engines—the various branches of the 6 ft. 6 in. and 7 ft. four-coupled classes—are occasionally assisted to Ais Gill from Hellifield or Carlisle in which case a special stop is made to detach the pilot engine. The locomotive work in general affords a striking contrast to that which prevails on the parallel line of the L. & N.W. between Preston and Carlisle, and the Midland are at last reaping the reward of their very liberal policy in a slowly but steadily increasing Scotch traffic.'

In 1905 the Midland Railway appointed a new superintendent of the line—John Elliott, whom we met in September, 1904, on the first Heysham boat train. He had joined the company in 1864 as a booking clerk at Nottingham and on the opening of the Settle line had attained the position of superintendent of traffic at Leeds, becoming station master there a year later. This was followed by various jobs in London which culminated in 1903 with his appointment as outdoor assistant to the superintendent of the line at Derby. The new appointment was the first of a series made by the company which were to lead to the streamlining of the traffic departments. The directors' half-yearly report of February, 1905, had told of the death of the company's chief engineer, J. A. McDonald. He was succeeded by William B. Worthington, the chief engineer of the L.Y.R.

Financially, 1905 was a bad year. In February, Paget told the shareholders that it was still not possible to construct the West Riding Lines. The Act had been obtained at a time when prospects were better. Now it was necessary to obtain an extension of time. In April, deputations from Bradford were told that not only were trade and traffic bad but that difficulties had arisen as to the engineering of the line as planned through Forster Square, Bradford. Though they were told that the board had no doubt that in a modified form the line would eventually be made, its original impetus had been lost. The company was, however, going ahead with the widenings and in August it was stated that the remaining portion of the Leeds & Bradford line, between Kirkstall and Leeds, was under discussion. Since the utility of this last improvement to the L.B.R. was beyond question it was decided to go ahead. For the time being, however, any larger works took a back seat. Again, at the August meeting, it was said that if 1905 was going to be the pattern for years to come the Midland dividend would be impossible to maintain.

Besides lack of funds, one reason for the board's apparent reluctance to do anything further about the West Riding Lines could be found in the seeming importance of stopping the Scotch trains at Leeds. As has been seen the policy had been to cut the Leeds stop prior to 1901 but with the renewed traffic from the northern city and the greater speeds resulting both from the widenings and Johnson's and Deeley's engines, the expensive saving of a mere 5¾ miles by the proposed West Riding Lines had become less attractive. Another point—a minor one—was that the company's chief rival on the Scotch run was finding the heavier trains of the period an ever increasing embarrassment over Shap. Charles Rous-Marten noted in the *Railway Magazine* of November, 1905, that after a trip behind L.N.W.R. engine No. 66, *Experiment*, the first of a new series of 4-6-0s just turned out of Crewe, he had misgivings about the future of the L.N.W.R. winter schedules :—

'. . . excellent as was the performance of *Expermient*, on the occasion under notice, it did not convince me that it will be possible during the winter for even this powerful locomotive to keep time on the best expresses without assistance up Shap when the load exceeds 300 tons behind the tender.'

He thought that some form of electric traction would eventually have to be employed. Rous-Marten's death three years later was a great loss to the recording of locomotive history. Pens as good as his took over but his vision of electric traction was a far-sighted one for the time—so much so that it is only now that the Shap incline may be added to the already partially completed electrification of the West Coast main line. In 1905, though Euston had the powers for a Shap tunnel as an answer, it seems that the necessary goad of the West Riding Lines was awaited. Meanwhile, during this waiting game, on balance the Midland probably came off better. For a short while, in mid 1905, however, there was some talk on the Midland board of at least extending the West Riding Lines into the Spen Valley from Dewsbury, utilizing some of the authorized route, but nothing came of it.

The year saw little change in the passenger services over the Settle line. A feature of the July service, however, was the running of new dining and sleeping cars on the main Scotch trains, the 1.30 p.m. each way from St Pancras and Glasgow having the dining cars, and the 8.30 p.m. from St Pancras to Stranraer, and the return 9.58 from Stranraer, the sleeping cars. They are described in the next chapter. The fastest train over the route was the 4 p.m. out of Leeds which did the run to Carlisle in 2 hours 7 minutes at an average speed of 53.2 m.p.h. In June the Midland and G.S.W.R. joint committee met to consider the goods workings. The committee was concerned at recent announcements by the East and West Coast routes of new express goods services between England and Scotland and it was agreed that the joint route should be put on a footing of equality. To this end instructions were given to fit several of the goods engines and a number of covered wagons and vans with the continuous brake so as to run the trains at higher speeds. The G.S.W.R. had also been affected by recent bad returns; the receipts for the half-year ending January 31, 1905, showed a decrease on all branches of traffic. January of 1906 saw discussions between the L.N.W.R., Caledonian, Midland, and G.S.W.R. on the subject of fitted freight trains. There had been some talk previously of pooling the traffic and a recent idea had been that economies could be effected by each of the two routes taking it in monthly turns to run a single joint fitted freight in lieu of acting separately as before. All had boded well until examination of the problem showed that there were now too many wagons conveyed by the express goods on each route for them all to go on one train. It was agreed that no economies would result from trying to operate the scheme and the decision was reached that extension of 'piped' trains between England and Scotland should only take place, by mutual consent, where the East Coast companies were competing.

In July, 1906, the general manager, John Matheison, retired through ill-health and was replaced by Guy Granet, the then assistant general manager. Matheison had taken over from Turner in 1901 and had come to the Midland from the position of general manager of the Victorian Railways in Australia. He had had much to do with the Midland before that, however; as an official of the G.S.W.R —which he had joined as a booking clerk in 1859—he had been present, in his then capacity of superintendent of the line, at the opening of St Enoch station and had worked closely with the Midland officers regarding mutual interests at the time of the construction of the Settle and Carlisle line. His retirement sadly was of short duration; he died at Harrogate on Thursday, August 9. The appointment of his successor was another of the steps in the alteration of the Midland hierarchy which was to revolutionise the company's standing. William Guy Granet was born in 1867. He had been called to the Bar in 1893 and in 1900 was appointed as secretary to the Railway Companies' Association. Five years later, well prepared for the post, he went to the Midland as assistant general manager, and it seems likely that he was so groomed that when Matheison retired he could promote new management policies, taking over much of what had previously been the chairman's business, relegating the latter to being more of a figurehead, while letting some of the more detailed day-to-day work, previously the charge of the general manager, pass to the chief departmental officers. Granet was, in fact, one of the few officers who had not risen from the ranks. Another such was Cecil Paget, the chairman's son. As Deeley's assistant, he was at this time waiting in the wings for bigger things.

There was an attempt by a new company in 1906 to get powers for a line south of Lancaster to bring the Midland and the Great Central systems to Blackpool. The Wigan & Heysham Railway was to have consisted of six lines. The first, 15¾ miles in length, was planned to commence by a junction with the Great Central at Wigan Central station and then to run north and north-west, crossing the Lancashire Union line near Boar's Head, to Preston where it was to terminate on the south side of Fishergate Hill, by a junction with Railway No. 2 and adjacent to the West Lancashire Railway's station. From there No. 2 was to run north-west to a point north of Kirkham where it joined Railways 3 and 4. No. 4 went due west to terminate at Blackpool, and No. 3 north to join the Midland by a semi-circular curve on the north bank of the Lune immediately to the east of the Lancaster & Carlisle line river bridge. Railway No. 5 completed the triangular junction north of Kirkham, and No. 6 was to be a spur at Wigan. Though this venture was in all probability yet another attempt by the Great Central to get to Blackpool—it had supported the Blackpool Railway for a line from Preston to the town in the 1880s but the powers had been allowed to lapse—the extension on to Lancaster and thus Heysham is of interest, as running powers to the port and to Morecambe were sought in the Bill as well as over the G.C.R. to Glazebrook on the Cheshire Lines Committee. Another clause in the Bill provided for the Wigan & Heysham company to enter into traffic, maintenance, and working agreements with the Midland, G.C.R., and C.L.C. The scheme did not prosper. Intense opposition, not only from the entrenched railways in the area, caused the Bill to be withdrawn in March, 1906. It does not seem to have been re-deposited. The episode might well have a bearing on correspondence in the *Railway World* where Mr J. P. Bardsley recalled in the March, 1965, issue that Midland surveyors were in the Blackpool area in 1906.

The *Railway Club Journal* for July 1906 had the following comments on the Midland summer service for that year : —

'The Midland time-table contains several novelties, and a fair amount of additional mileage, for nearly all of which Heysham is responsible. A new train leaves London at 6 p.m. in connection with the Belfast boat, runs without stop to Sheffield in 3 hours, and reaches Leeds in 3 hrs. 52 mins., and Heysham in 5½ hours; an excellent service is provided for passengers from the south to the Isle of Man, for not only is the mid-day express from Sheffield and Hellifield to Heysham (connecting with the 8.30—now 8.15 a.m.—from St. Pancras) reinstated, but a new train runs on Fridays and Saturdays until the middle of September at 8.30 a.m. from London, with advertised stops only at Leicester, Nottingham, Chesterfield, and Skipton. This train, as well as the corresponding up train from Heysham to Sheffield, has luncheon-cars attached. The up service from Heysham is very similar to that of 1905; there is however a new early morning train on Mondays connecting with a Sunday night sailing from Douglas, and passengers by the morning boat from the Isle of Man can reach St Pancras at 7.15 p.m. by changing at Leeds, though the through carriage does not arrive till 7.40.

'In the Scotch services the alterations are of an unsettling nature. The only novelty is a morning express at 8.40 from Leeds (7.55 a.m. from Manchester and 7.50 from Liverpool), which leaves Hellifield at 9.37, and reaches Carlisle at 11.5, Glasgow 1.45, and Edinburgh 1.35. The second (Glasgow) portion of the 9.30 a.m. from St Pancras again runs non-stop to Sheffield, in 3 hrs. 2 mins.; the second portion of the 11.30 a.m., via Nottingham and Sheffield, avoids Leeds but calls at Hellifield, and of the night trains, the 7.15 p.m. Highland express is retimed, ceases to call at Hellifield (thereby losing a very useful connection from the L. and Y. line), and runs non-stop in 127 mins. from Leeds to Carlisle, which it reaches as before at 1.25 a.m. In the up service, minor alterations take place in the night trains; the 9.30 a.m. from Edinburgh again runs independently from Carlisle, but via Nottingham instead of via Leicester, and the 1.12 p.m. from Carlisle is accelerated by 13 minutes between Leeds and London, making the 196¼ miles non-stop run in 213 mins., and becoming practically a 6 hours train from Carlisle to St Pancras.

'We note an advertised "Cheap Third-class Scotch Corridor Express" (with luncheon-car)—on Saturdays only, and during the height of the season—at 11 a.m. from St Pancras. Its only advertised stop is at Nottingham, and the arrivals are Carlisle 5.30, Glasgow 8.10, and Edinburgh 8.17 p.m.'

The 11 a.m. was in fact a relief train; it went some way towards easing the overcrowded weekend Scotch trains. The Nottingham stop was from 1.25 to 1.30 and it also halted briefly at Leeds Engine Shed Junction at 3.10 p.m. to change locomotives. The *Journal* remarked that on July 28 —the first day it ran—the train got into Carlisle 14 minutes late hauled by a 'Belpaire' with a load of 16, 'extremely well-filled'. No. 828 brought it in on the following Saturday with a load of 18½, 'so that as far as loading is concerned the experiment has been a complete success'.

Remembering that the Hawes Junction smash was but a few years ahead and that it was caused by a rear collision, an interesting note concerning the dispatching of two trains from Hellifield for the north with only two minutes between them, was made by R. E. Charlewood in the October issue of the *Journal* :

'At Leeds I waited for the 9.45 a.m. from London, which arrived punctually with a compound = 11, or 185 tons. We started away at 1.46 (engine No. 813, Belpaire) and should no doubt have reached Hellifield punctually had the road been clear. But a slow train had only just preceded us out of Keighley, and we consequently made some non-advertised stops between there and Skipton, and reached Hellifield at 2.39, 10 minutes late. The delay had even wider results than this, for the authorities at Hellifield, seeing the 9.45 a.m. from London reported as passing Shipley on time, decided with unusual caution to detain the slow train (2.22 from Hellifield) to Hawes Junction— which the time-table squeezes in between the 9.30 and 9.45 from London—until after the passing of the latter express. But they reckoned without Keighley, and in consequence the 2.22 left Hellifield at 2.47, the 9.45 from London having departed at 2.45, at an interval of fully 20 minutes after the 9.30 a.m. I have outlined this little occurrence rather fully, as it is very typical of the Company concerned.'

Adverting to the Wigan & Heysham scheme, this was discussed at some length in the December, 1906, issue of the *Railway Club Journal* by the Rev. J. T. Lawrence. At the end of his article there appeared the following item of interest which may well tie in with the previous statement regarding Blackpool :

'Another scheme involving Blackpool has recently been revived, an extension of the Midland from Colne. This would be a more heroic undertaking than the other'—the Wigan & Heysham—'for the new line would have to traverse a country that hitherto no railway company has had the courage to penetrate into, across Pendle Forest and Longridge Fell. Seeing that the Midland have nothing on that coast but Morecambe, which is very far indeed from being a Blackpool, it might pay them, and certainly the Leeds and Bradford trippers would hail such an alternative line with joy, for it would provide them with a route much more picturesque, and much less complicated, and therefore less liable to unpunctuality.'

Finally, to quote the *Journal* for the last time, there appeared in the February, 1907, issue an article by R. A. Selby on 'Christmas Traffic on the Midland Railway'. It started with 'How the other lines fared I do not know, but the state of things on the Midland Railway was, to say the least of it, painful.' It seems that St Pancras station was virtually in a state of siege, with many extra coaches having to be found for an abnormally large and ever-growing number of passengers. Apparently Mr Selby travelled to Nottingham.

'We returned by the "Leeds and Bradford Luncheon Car Express" leaving Nottingham at 2.38, booked to run to Kettering in the even hour, and then fast to London, 72 miles in 77 minutes. This train has connections from Carlisle and the Furness line, and was badly delayed in the north, as it did not come into Nottingham until after 3.0. We were over half an hour late leaving the latter place; further delays ensued, and Kettering was not reached until 4.15. Here tickets were taken. The load, by the way, was equal to 14, and our engine was No. 1020, one of the newest compounds.'

After Kettering the train managed to get up to nearly 90 m.p.h. on Sharnbrook bank and ran at average speeds of nearly 70 m.p.h. all the way to St Pancras. There it waited eight minutes outside the station and eventually pulled in 68 minutes late.

At a Midland board meeting in July, 1906, it was decided to electrify the Lancaster–Morecambe–Heysham lines. Sir Ernest Paget made it clear at the August half-yearly meeting that he thought electricity to be the motive power of the future. He said that this was partly the reason why the new scheme had been introduced—to give the company's officers experience in this field. He also announced that the line to Huddersfield was going ahead and that there were two Bills for the next session of Parliament; one to abandon further construction of the West Riding Lines, and the other to authorize an extension of time for their building. As it turned out the Act of 1907 authorized extensions of time both for the West Riding Lines and the Thornhill Junction line, until 1912 and 1913 respectively. Previous extensions had already been granted for the first in 1901 and 1904, and for the second in 1902 and 1905. There had been some trouble with the Bradford Dyers' Association at about this time over the water rights under the town, but by January, 1907, this was over.

On March 24, 1907, the company opened a new station at Morecambe. The contractors, Coates, Murgatroyd & Son of Bradford, put up the buildings, the Midland staff constructing the platforms. At the same time a new 60 foot engine turntable was provided, together with independent running lines between the station and the Heysham branch. By this time the old harbour had been leased to Messrs Thomas Ward, the Sheffield ship-breakers. On April 6 a special meeting of the board appointed Cecil Paget to a new position, that of general superintendent of the Midland Railway. At the age of 32 this was an extremely responsible position to have attained, and the appointment, in other circumstances, might have smacked of nepotism. Cecil Paget had, however, all the necessary qualifications. He was a fully fledged locomotive man and, like Granet, had been carefully prepared beforehand. The new position was created with the object of bringing together the running or operating departments and the traffic department, so as to concentrate under one officer all the train movements. The need for some sort of reform had become increasingly apparent during the past few years. The fact that the superintendent of the line, John Elliott, had apparently been unable under the old system to ease the traffic difficulties—especially among the mineral trains—was obvious from the appointment. Nevertheless Elliott must have been highly thought of as the board retained his services and even increased his salary. This might, of course, have been construed as a 'kick up-stairs' but in fact Elliott had one valuable asset. At a time of increased friction between management and the uniform staff he held the confidence of the men. By 1910, however, agreement with the staff over current problems had been reached whereby Elliott was enabled to retire. There has been considerable study elsewhere of the further policies and effects concerned with the new Midland headquarters set-up as first laid down in the mid 1900s, and much further discussion here would be out of place. By November of 1907 Cecil Paget's moves were beginning to pay off, with improvements to train timings all over the system. The gradual swing in power towards the general superintendent was backed wholeheartedly by Granet and the taking of the locomotive running department out of Deeley's hands in August of 1909 and merging it into the traffic department under Paget has been advanced as one of the main causes of Deeley's resignation that month.

A minor event during the year was the destruction by fire on Easter Tuesday of Halton station, apparently caused by the sparks from a down express to Heysham igniting a cask of naphtha. Most of the station buildings were gutted.

Regarding the 1907 train services on the Leeds–Settle–Carlisle line, Cecil Paget's improvements in train timings had already begun to take effect. 'Brunel Redivivus,' writing in the *Railway Magazine* of July, 1907, had the following to say :—

'The Midland Railway is taking time by the forelock. . . . There is a new express from Bristol at 8.10 a.m. (with connection from Bath) for Malvern, Worcester, Birmingham, the North and Scotland, the arrival at Edinburgh being at 6.5 p.m. Last year the earliest train from Bristol for Edinburgh left at 9.45, and arrived at the modern Athens at 8.42 p.m. . . . . Accelerations are to be found in the Midland's Scottish services; the train which left St Pancras last July at 5.15 a.m., now starts at 5.10, and is due at Edinburgh at 3 p.m.; Glasgow, 3.20 p.m. Last summer the arrivals at both places were timetabled at 3.30 a.m.; five minutes is gained on the up train due at St Pancras at 6.10 p.m. It now leaves Edinburgh at 9.35 a.m., instead of 9.30 . . . . From the above information readers will see that, even in 1907, a notably lean year in improvements in train services, the Midland is amongst the railways that are to be credited with a few ameliorations.'

And turning to the North British Railway he commented :

'On the Waverley route the 10 a.m. train from Leeds, with connections from Manchester at 9.35 and from Liverpool at 9.30, will be accelerated, and be due to reach Edinburgh at 3 p.m. instead of 3.30. This will give first-class connection with these important places for Edinburgh and also for Dundee, Aberdeen and the Great North of Scotland Railway by the 3.20 p.m. non-stop corridor vestibule express from Edinburgh. There will also be a connection for the West Highland Railway by the 4 p.m. train from Edinburgh, the passengers changing at Cowlairs into the 4.50 p.m. from Glasgow to Fort William.'

Nevertheless the fastest train on the Settle line still took, as in 1905, 2 hours and 7 minutes, though this time it was the 11.18 p.m. down train from Leeds to Carlisle. Generally, however, the overall improvement was high. One particular addition to the Settle line which was of undoubted assistance was the installation of water troughs at Garsdale during the first half of 1907. Apart from anything else it permitted the compound engines to jettison the large bogie tenders so necessary before to keep speeds up. The new troughs and their attendant apparatus cost the company £4,396, and another £1,707 was spent on fitting up locomotive tenders with the water pick-up apparatus. In all there were but four other places where water troughs were installed on the Midland system, besides that at Garsdale, these being at Oakley, Melton Mowbray, Loughborough, and Tamworth. As laid, they were all 1,670 feet long, and held between 5 and 6 thousand gallons, about 2,000 of which were taken up by a tender at one 'sitting'. Each trough was laid in 167 lengths of 10 foot galvanized steel. Cut-off valves kept the troughs filled from the water tanks and the troughs themselves communicated with each other so as to keep a constant level. It appears a use was found for some of the old tenders; a locomotive department minute of June 18, 1908, recommended that four snow ploughs for the Hellifield–Carlisle section should be built on disused bogie tenders. By this arrangement it was hoped to liberate four goods engines for general traffic which had until then been kept standing during the winter months with snow ploughs attached.

Returning to the 1907 timetable, on the Hawes branch there were five trains daily each way, nearly all of which connected with trains on the main line. (An outline timetable for the branch will be found in Appendix XX.) The 1907 timetable for the main line showed that an experimental train, the 8.40 a.m. from Leeds to Carlisle (reached at 11.15), with arrival times at Edinburgh and Glasgow of 1.35 and 1.45 p.m. and connections at Hellifield with the Manchester and Liverpool service, instituted in 1906, had been withdrawn. This had been run in addition to the ordinary 10 a.m. out of Leeds and was presumably an attempt to challenge the N.E.R. Leeds–Scotland service.

The July timetable of 1908 contained a surprise packet, for the 11.30 a.m. train from St Pancras was shown as running non-stop to Carlisle. This was not strictly true, however, as the train called at Shipley for the purpose of changing engines. Even so it represented the longest non-stop run so far on the Midland—a distance of 206 miles between St Pancras and Shipley. The timings were as follows : St Pancras depart 11.30 a.m., Shipley arrive at 3.27 p.m. and depart at 3.32, Carlisle arrive at 5.29. 'Brunel Redivivus' commented in the *Railway Magazine* for July, 1908, thus :

'Dealing with the Midland-Scottish services, we find that the 7.15 p.m. Highland express has 10 min. added to its running time, and will leave St Pancras at 7.10 p.m.; the 1.30 p.m. is timed to Leicester in 106 min., and has extra running time thence to Leeds; 9.45 a.m. ex St Pancras will not run via Sheffield, and is due at Carlisle 4.04, 4 min. later than last summer.

'The 9.30 a.m. is due Carlisle at 3.50 p.m., and, therefore, takes 5 min. longer on the journey. We have already referred to the 11.30 a.m., which is for Glasgow only; the second portion leaves St Pancras at 11.36 a.m., and runs via Leicester and Leeds; it is divided at Hellifield and the two portions are due at Carlisle at 6 and 6.10 p.m. respectively.

'In the up direction the 11.47 ex Carlisle arrives at St Pancras at 6.15; but the second portion (12.5 ex Carlisle) is not due till 6.30 p.m., and is therefore again decelerated.

'The 1.12 p.m. ex Carlisle runs non-stop from Leeds to London in 3 hrs. 38 min., as against 3 hrs. 33 min. in 1907; 1.30 p.m. ex Carlisle is slowed 5 min., and arrives at 8.10 p.m.; 3.55 p.m. ex Carlisle leaves at 4, runs via the Trent direct line, and so omits the Nottingham stop, but still arrives at 10.21 p.m.'

He also mentioned that the fastest run that summer was again between Appleby and Carlisle, but that 32 minutes instead of 31, had been allowed for the 30¾ miles.

On the first day of the new timetable the 11.30 a.m. from St Pancras did a smart piece of engine changing at Shipley saving 2 minutes and arriving at Carlisle 7 minutes early. The engines concerned on this trip, which was with a train of 139 tons, were compounds Nos. 1033 and 1028. From Carlisle the G.S.W.R. took the train non-stop to St Enoch, a change from the usual practice which was to call at Dumfries and Kilmarnock, though this working soon came back as passenger loading was low enough without the stops to make the G.S.W.R. portion un-economic. In fact the new schedule was not so extraordinary as it seemed; the time from St Pancras to Carlisle of just under 6 hours compared with runs in 1903 and 1904 when the 9.30 from St Pancras, usually a train of some 220 tons, did the journey in 6¼ hours, calling at Leicester, Chesterfield, Leeds, and Hellifield, on its way. For a short time the national press followed the doings of the 11.30 a.m. train, partly de-luded by the fact that the timetable did not show the Shipley stop, and so gave the impression of the reality of a through non-stop run. At the Ship-ley stop the trains normally halted on the curve between Leeds Junction and Shipley North box. A fresh engine waited in the platform on the north curve and, after the London engine had uncoupled, run forward, and backed into the station, the Shipley engine went through the reverse movement. The venue of the actual exchange, carried out on a line with-out platforms, gave the excuse for not showing the stop in the timetable.

It was widely canvassed that summer, following the press publicity, that the racing days on the Scotch routes might be reviving, and stop-watch brethren girded their loins for action. But it was not to be. If Euston felt any inclination to slap the Midland and G.S.W.R. venture down, it kept the impulse well hidden. In any event there were two good reasons why such an event was improbable; the trains in question were no longer the small affairs that could be light-heartedly whisked about as in the 1880s and 1890s; they were heavier and their schedules were such that the ultimate speed with the engines of the period had about been reached; secondly, there were various backstairs meetings in progress which were shortly to lead to an 'understanding', notably between the L.N.W.R., Midland, and L.Y.R. as to working arrange-ments, which put racing out of court. The 'pooling' agreement which resulted was really in answer to the 1909 Parliamentary sanction that the G.N.R., G.C.R., and G.E.R. should be worked as one concern—in lieu of amalgamation refused by Parliament in 1908. The West Coast companies' agreement meant in effect that goods trains could be diverted so as to give route availability preference to the passenger traffic of the three companies where an alternative was possible, and it was the main reason behind the Midland's non-stop London–Carlisle run. It also effectively stopped such schemes as the West Riding Lines. As to the latter, there had been angry discussions in September of 1907 between the corporation of Bradford, and the Midland. According to the *Railway News* of September 14, the Lord Mayor had hinted at support being given to a scheme for a new line from Sheffield to Newcastle unless the Midland abandoned its dilatory attitude on the West Riding Lines. As before, Paget pointed out that the time was not right, but that the idea had not been shelved.

Before leaving the 1908 services note can be taken of two unusual workings north of Leeds. For the duration of the summer timetable, and for subsequent summers until that of the First World War, the Saturdays only third class cheap ticket express from St Pancras to Glasgow was diverted to run via the Apperley Junction–Menston Junction–Skipton line, calling at Ilkley *en route*. This tied in with a policy started by the Midland in the summer of 1908 to attract hikers in some of the districts served by the line. Ordnance maps showing the surrounding locality were supplied to many stations, for display in the booking offices, in the scenic parts of the system. Some of those north of Leeds included Lazonby, Appleby, Kirkby Stephen, Settle, Clapham, Ingleton, Lancaster, Morecambe, Grassington, Bolton Abbey, Ilkley, and Skipton. Another innovation concerned Bradford. The city had always been something of a headache with regard to the Scotch trains in that connections were usually via Leeds, but in 1908 an attempt was made to better the up service by slipping Bradford coaches at Saltaire from the 1.30 and 2.20 trains from Glasgow and Edinburgh respectively. Though a half-measure, it may have placated the Bradford people somewhat.

By May of 1908 the contract for the final widening on the Leeds & Bradford portion of the Scotch route—that from Holbeck to Kirkstall—had been let (it was brought into use on May 29, 1910), land for the Huddersfield line had been acquired, the viaduct at Apperley carrying the fast lines had been strengthened, and the company was arranging to construct a jetty at the harbour at Heysham. Apparently there was some trouble at Heysham; the harbour was already beginning to silt up. Local people wagged their heads knowingly at this, remembering why the Midland had pulled out of Morecambe, and the company acquired a dredger or two to keep the harbour clear. The July timetable also saw the opening of the new electrified lines between Lancaster, Morecambe, and Heysham. The scheme covered about 20 track miles and was operated on alternating current at 25 cycles, supplied at 6,600 volts on the overhead system, with a motor voltage of 300 at normal running speed. It operated as such until 1951 when for a short time it was replaced by a steam service before coming back into operation as a single phase 50 cycle A.C. system.

The summer timetable for 1909 showed a further slowing of some of the main trains, and the introduction of a service by the Midland and the L.Y.R. over the Royston–Thornhill line, opened for passenger traffic on July 1. As to the latter the line had been opened for goods traffic as follows : Royston Junction to Crigglestone, July 3, 1905, Crigglestone to Thornhill, November 10, 1905, and Middlestown Junction to Dewsbury (Saville Town) on March 1, 1906, the same day as the opening of the goods stations at Crigglestone and Middlestown. As before, let 'Brunel Redivivus', writing in the July, 1909, issue of the *Railway Magazine* comment on the summer service :—

'The (advertised) non-stop 11.30 a.m. express St Pancras to Carlisle, does not re-appear this year, but in place of the 11.30 Glasgow, and 11.35 Edinburgh and Glasgow trains, we have one booked to leave St Pancras at 11.50, and shown (as last year) non-stop to Carlisle, where it is due at 5.57 p.m., a slowing of 8 min. on last summer's meteor to Carlisle, and of 15 min. to Glasgow, but an acceleration of 23 min. on the Edinboro' time of the 11.35 train of 1908. The 7.10 p.m. down Highland Railway sleeper does not appear till July 12th. The 10.30 a.m. ex "Auld Reekie' will still run non-stop Leeds to St Pancras, but is allowed 2 min. longer for the journey. The 11 a.m. from Glasgow is also slowed 5 min., although the Hellifield stop is eliminated.

'The new through service from the Lancashire and Yorkshire Railway consists of three trains in each direction, the through vehicles working on the 9.45 a.m., 1.30 p.m. and 6 p.m. from St Pancras being detached at Sheffield. At Thornhill they bifurcate to Bradford and Halifax. The best time between St Pancras and Halifax is 4 hrs. 32 min. down, and 4 hrs. 27 min. up. Bradford's bests are 4 hrs. 28 min. down, and 4hrs. 30 min. up, a quickening of 10 min. of the Midland's best to Bradford on last year's timing, but of only 2 min. on that of 1907.'

Incidentally, Thwaites station was closed immediately before the commencement of the summer timetable. In May Granet had told a meeting of the board that the station had only been lightly used for some years past; the total coaching receipts over the past four years had only amounted to between £70 and £90. With the possibility of the Keighley Tramway coming out to Thwaites there seemed no justification in keeping the station open.

Though the 1909 timetable can be said to have been the template for the remaining years up to the First World War, in that in the main the pattern stayed the same each year, there were variations and additions. Perhaps the most interesting occurred in 1910. As we have seen, the Midland, L.Y.R., and L.N.W.R. had reached an agreement by that time to work co-operatively. The *Railway News* of July 2, 1910, had an item which told of a new Midland service :—

'On the 17th June a special express train composed of two Midland Railway restaurant cars, two first and third class carriages, a brake van, and a composite slip carriage was experimentally run between Hellifield and Carlisle over the London and North-Western Railway, via Ingleton, Low Gill, Tebay, Penrith, and Carlisle, in order to test the bridges and platforms in readiness for the regular Midland daily service over the same route, commencing July 1st, which is intended to connect Leeds, Bradford, Nottingham, and other large centres direct with Keswick, the northern capital of the English Lake District, which has hitherto not enjoyed the same advantages of communication with popular centres as Windermere.'

The July, 1910, Midland timetable noted that 'The 10 a.m. train from Leeds to Scotland and 10.30 a.m. Express from Edinburgh to Leeds, etc., will run via Penrith, with connection to and from Keswick. An improved Service will be given with Kendal, Windermere, etc., via Carnforth'.

The down train—described in the timetable as the 'Lake District Express'—left St Pancras at 5 a.m. and called at Leicester, Nottingham, and Sheffield. From Leeds it ran non-stop via the Ingleton branch, arriving at Penrith at noon, from where connections over the Cockermouth Keswick & Penrith Railway arrived at Keswick at 12.50 and Cockermouth at 2.28 p.m. The up connections left Cockermouth at 11.12, Keswick at 12.35, and caught the Midland train at Penrith at 1.42, arriving at Leeds at 3.35 and St Pancras at 7.15 p.m. This up train was the 10.30 a.m. out of Edinburgh Waverley which left Carlisle at 1.10 p.m.

All this was done with Euston's blessing The friendship between the two erstwhile opponents led to other improvements; from July 16 to September 17, 1910, the Midland operated a new North Wales service from Sheffield to Llandudno via Buxton, and in October the two companies improved their through joint service between Manchester and Bournemouth. Though this is well away from our subject it is nevertheless indicative of the growing affinity between Euston and Derby. Early in the summer season the L.N.W.R., L.Y.R., and Midland extended their working arrangements so that return tickets between England and Scotland were made available over either of the main routes.

To return to the Ingleton-Penrith services, the October, 1910, timetable noted that the down train would run on April 15 and June 2 and 3 only, during the first half of 1911. The up train was shown as running only on April 18 and June 6, 7, and 10. The July–September timetable for 1911 showed both trains fully back in business and though the departure time from St Pancras was put back to 4.50 a.m. the other times were similar to those of 1910. The October, 1911, timetable again limited the running to three days in April and May on the down service, keeping the same times as the summer; and three on the up, with the Penrith stop altered to 2.40 p.m., and arrival times at Leeds and St Pancras of 4.50 and 10.25 p.m. respectively. This particular train started at Carlisle. Thereafter the fortunes of the "Lake District Express" fluctuated, and its short career ended in 1913 when the trains reverted to the Settle and Carlisle route. That it had been something of a success, however, was shown by the concurrent introduction of a new train which ran four days a week over the Ingleton line fulfilling the same function.

Bearing in mind the earlier reference to the sharp curve at Low Gill and the controversy aroused in 1858 by the L.C.R.'s proposal to make it of such radius as to preclude fast running at the junction, coupled with the Midland's airy assurance to the little North Western that it had just such a curve on the main line at Derby—and put up with it—it is of interest that the appendix to the Midland's working timetable, for the instruction of staff working over the L.N.W.R. at the time of the "Lake District Express" venture, noted two special speed restrictions which the trains would have to observe :—

Sedbergh-Low Gill—both lines—limit of 45 m.p.h. Low Gill Junction—to and from the Ingleton Branch—limit of 15 m.p.h. And these, of course, were immediately before the climb to Tebay, with Shap looming ahead.

These years before the war were busy ones on the Settle and Carlisle line. In 1909 there were no fewer than thirteen down expresses daily between Hellifield and Carlisle. The fastest long distance train over the route the following year was the 11.12 p.m. from Leeds which took 2 hours 13 minutes to Carlisle, averaging 50.9 m.p.h., the next fastest being the 1.56 p.m. from Shipley to Carlisle (the 11.50 a.m. from St Pancras), taking 1 hour 56 minutes at an average speed of 50.1 m.p.h. Higher speeds were obtained on the local runs; that made by the 5.33 p.m. from Appleby to Carlisle was done at an average of 55.9 m.p.h., nearly all on the down grade of course. In October, 1910 the evening train from St Pancras to Stranraer ceased to run north of Leeds, the practice henceforth being to restrict it to summer working only. Likewise the Highland express was also relegated to summer working; it ceased altogether in the summer of 1914. This Highland express was a very fast train—it took only $6\frac{1}{4}$ hours from St Pancras to Carlisle. The relegation in effect meant its withdrawal for April, May, and June of 1909. This was one of the trains which the N.B.R. watched warily as to revenue. R. E. Charlewood, writing in the *Railway Magazine* of July and August, 1947, pointed out that before its withdrawal, for reasons of economy, 'it had achieved the distinction in the previous winter of running non-stop from Leeds to Carlisle with fewer than ten passengers on several days. On the "guarantee" to the North British for this train (its earnings had to be brought up to $2s\ 1\frac{1}{2}d$ a mile till 1912 and afterwards to $1s\ 0\frac{3}{4}d$), the Midland actually paid £6,097 between 1903 and 1907, and on the Edinburgh portion of the 1.30 p.m. from St Pancras £5,090 was paid in respect of the four years to June, 1908.' As to the Stranraer train, Euston took over the traffic from the time of the cessation of the Midland service.

Between 1901 and 1914 Hellifield station reached its peak of activity. In 1910 it was handling some 90 passenger trains daily, including the Leeds–Carlisle service, the trains off the L.Y.R. line, and those on the Lancaster and Carnforth routes. Added to these were numerous goods trains which exchanged wagons on the two sets of sidings—just under 200,000 wagons being dealt with yearly. The engine sheds housed 28 engines and two snow ploughs. In command at Hellifield was the station master, Edwin Hooper Russell, with a uniform staff of about 60, as well as the goods and passenger guards. Russell's time at Hellifield lasted from 1905 till 1917 when he became station master at Chesterfield.

On October 15, 1911, a new viaduct was brought into use over the River Lune at Lancaster. It was the third on the site. The first had been replaced in the 1860s when by an Act of 1861 the Midland had got powers to deviate the line from Skerton bridge to the junction of the Castle branch with the Morecambe line. The old rail bridge over the Lune was replaced by one immediately to the north, 461 feet in length. By the Midland Railway Act of 1909 the present bridge was authorized, virtually in the same position as the 1846 structure. It is 413 feet in length and has nine spans, the same number as the 1861 bridge. (The 1909 day rates for the construction are given in Appendix VII.)

The locomotive working over the Leeds–Settle–Carlisle line during this period was mostly in the hands of the 990 class, a batch of ten 4-4-0 non-compound super-heater locomotives with 6 ft. 6 in. driving wheels. They were designed by Deeley and came out of Derby works in 1907. They quickly proved their worth on the Settle road and for the most part replaced the earlier compounds, of which the last were produced in 1909, and these latter began to work south of Leeds. Some of the earlier Johnson engines were also worked over the Settle and Carlisle line from time to time. In 1898 Johnson had produced, prior to his first compound design, a number of 4-4-0s known as the 60 class, this being the locomotive number of the first arrival. In 1901 twenty of the type, with 7 ft. driving wheels and 19 in. cylinders, were built at Derby and included Nos. 805–809 and 2636–2640. The first five went to Carlisle and the others to Leeds, all to work the Scotch trains. The remaining ten engines, built by Neilson, Reid & Co., were shedded at Leicester and Kentish Town, the Leicester engines being numbered 2591–2598, and working the Scotch trains south of Leeds. They joined four of the Johnson singles, Nos. 2601–2604, which were built in 1900 as part of the last batch of ten of this design.

The rolling stock on typical Midland Scotch trains was as follows : the main train of the day, the 11.50 a.m., included eight of the joint stock coaches, the first five being labelled M. & G.S.W. and the next three M & N.B., for Glasgow and Edinburgh respectively; as to the evening Highland express, this consisted of an assortment of two dining cars for Leeds, three vehicles—including a sleeping car—for Inverness, then a coach and a sleeper for Aberdeen, and finally a through carriage for Fort William.

In all, the Midland service between London and Scotland, though never quite able to match the speed of the L.N.W.R., was, prior to the First World War, extremely creditable. That it was marred by two disastrous accident, at Hawes Junction and Ais Gill, detailed later, did not detract from its image. Ghastly though they were, in their very magnitude, they fitted the size of the line. In both instances they pointed to very serious operating trouble from which until then the Settle line had been remarkably free, with the notable exception of the early teething troubles of the first Pullmans. Perhaps the two most important assets of the Midland service were comfort and reliability. As to the former, the *Railway News* noted in April of 1907 that the company had even introduced games of chess and draughts for passengers on the Scotch trains. The car conductors kept sets of the games which could be had at no charge. Apparently many a game of chess, started somewhere south of Carlisle, eventually ended hours later in the lounge of the St Pancras Hotel.

Before coming to the end of the first part of this chapter, note can be taken of the two main Parliamentary proposals which might have affected the Midland in 1911 and 1913. The failure of the West Riding Lines has been mentioned. In 1911 the Midland brought out a variation —the Bradford Through Lines, proposing substantially the same end result but with a certain saving of expense.

Briefly, the scheme consisted of dropping the idea of a separate line up the Spen Valley south of Bradford, using the L.Y.R. as far as Low Moor, to which access could of course be gained from the constructed portion of the West Riding Lines between Royston and Thornhill, and then making a new line commencing with a triangular junction from the L.Y.R. at Low Moor and running north to the Leeds & Bradford near Manningham. To do this the Bradford Through Lines would have had to tunnel some 3,600 yards under Bierley Top to get into Bradford, the depth of the tunnel reaching 265 feet. The ruling gradient on this section was planned to be about 1 in 300. The line was to cross over Bradford partly on embankment and partly by viaduct. Forster Square station was to be passed over at a height of 18 feet above rail level and at a point near the end of the station platforms the line was to revert to embankment and drop at an incline of 1 in 100 for 7 furlongs, making a junction with the Leeds & Bradford line immediately south of Manningham station. The route north of Low Moor was substantially the same as the former scheme; the viaduct at Bradford obviated any further difficulty with local parties such as had held up the original tunnel idea. As a perk to stimulate construction the Corporation of Bradford agreed to assist in every way, even to the extent of relieving the Midland of payment of rates for a time. The scheme would have been costly. A new high level station planned for the city was estimated to cost over £40,000, viaducts £73,000, tunnelling £272,000; and the grand total came to £815,667. Like its forerunner it was doomed. This time the war killed it off and the Grouping of 1923 reduced its importance. One can only wonder whether the Midland ever meant it to succeed, especially after the L.N.W.R., L.Y.R., M.R., pact of 1909 when only a short time before Bradford had threatened to support a hostile scheme if the Midland attempted to go back on the West Riding Lines proposal. As a holding operation the Bradford Through Lines scheme was a success. It was, incidentally, Sir Ernest Paget's swan song,

317

for he retired through illness in the autumn of 1911. The new chairman was George Murray Smith, who had been a director of the company for ten years or so.

The other proposal during the pre-1914 war period was concerned with the last attempt on two occasions made by the North Yorkshire Dales concern to construct a line through the so far untapped country between Skipton and Northallerton. In the session of 1911 it deposited a Bill for an extension to the Grassington line of the Yorkshire Dales company. The scheme north of Grassington was almost identical to that deposited under the same name in 1904 but with the Grassington–Hellifield portion omitted. Four railways were to be made totalling some 34 miles. From Grassington to Spennithorne—railway No. 1—the line was to be single; from Spennithorne to Scorton—Railway No. 2—it was to be double. Two short connecting lines, as in the previous schemes, were to join the Northallerton–Hawes line near Spennithorne. Running powers were sought over the Midland to Skipton and Colne, and over the N.E.R. to Darlington and Middlesbrough. Though not as bad *vis-a-vis* the L.Y.R. as the previous project of 1904 the line would have hit that company and the Midland and N.E.R. hard if it had been constructed as the distance between Manchester and Newcastle via Burnley and the N.Y.D. would have been about 20 miles shorter than by the existing route through Normanton. All three ganged together to oppose the Bill but, as before, it was dropped, this time before Parliament met. A final attempt was made in the session of 1913, with the 1911 proposal in its entirety, except for a slight alteration to the running powers over the N.E.R. and with the addition of a clause offering agreements with the three main companies and the Yorkshire Dales as to construction, maintenance, and operation. This time the Bill got as far as a first reading in Parliament before, once again, it was withdrawn.

Though strictly off the main line, one further scheme can be mentioned at this point as it completely clears all the proposals affecting the Midland north of Leeds during the period. In May, 1904, the Barnoldswick & Gisburn Light Railway sought powers to make a short single track line leaving the L.Y.R.'s Chatburn and Hellifield branch just north of Gisburn station and connecting after a run of 3¾ miles with the Midland's Barnoldswick branch. It was scotched by the L.Y.R.'s refusal to allow a junction at Gisburn. Actually, the L.Y.R. pulled a fast one over the engineer to the line, E. O. Ferguson, by appearing to agree to all the clauses and then turning up at the inquiry, held by two of the Light Railway Commissioners in the 'Ribblesdale Arms' at Gisburn, and denying that it would permit the junction. The company had, it appeared, been too busy to look at the scheme properly. Shattered by this bland effrontery, the promoters withdrew the scheme. Nine years later, presumably having had enough time to reason out where they had gone wrong, the idea was again put forward, on a slightly amended route, and without the junction to the Midland. This time the L.Y.R. was all smiles, provided it was permitted to work the line. This time the Order was granted but again it seems as if the war got there first. Without the junction it would hardly have made any difference anyway.

PART 2

1914 — 1923

The summer of 1914 saw the end of the best years of the Settle line while still under the direction of the Midland Railway. The Great War was to reduce it to being a route of secondary importance to its near neighbour—the West Coast main line. And at the end of the hostilities, with the ravaged general economy that was all-pervading, the line never returned to its previous glory. With the Grouping only four years distant there was to be no time for the Midland to rebuild the service as it would have wished.

Let us take a last look at the Midland's summer service—that of 1914, published a month before the Great War broke out. It shows that several of the trains which have already figured from time to time in this narrative as tentative proposals had firmly ensconced themselves in the July timetable. The extract comes from the July, 1914, issue of the *Railway Magazine:*

'The summer train services on the Midland will, as usual, take effect from July 1st, when additional and improved services will come into operation affecting Scotland, the Lake District, the Isle of Man, Buxton, Matlock, Harrogate, Ilkley, the Eastern Counties, North and West of England, etc. The 11.50 a.m. express will again leave St Pancras for Scotland and run without advertised stop to Carlisle, engines being, however, changed at Shipley as heretofore. . . .

'The through train from Leeds to Keswick at 9.35 a.m., returning at 12.35 p.m. on Mondays, Tuesdays, Fridays and Saturdays, will run from July 13th to September 19th. This train will stop at Kirkby Lonsdale and Sedbergh. A much improved service will be given from Newcastle and other important towns on the North Eastern line to the Isle of Man by the Heysham route via Harrogate, Otley and Skipton, by the 3 p.m. boat from Heysham and 9.30 a.m. boat from Douglas. Through trains will be arranged between Harrogate and Skipton conveying the through carriages for Heysham. A new train will be run from Ilkley to Harrogate in connection with the 8.35 a.m. through train Manchester to Ilkley. A return train will connect with the 6.30 p.m. Ilkley to Manchester (through train). This will improve the service between Colne, Burnley, Accrington, etc., and Harrogate. . . .'

And these were in addition to the regular daily service on the main line. The summer service was to be short-lived, however. On August 4, 1914, the railways in Great Britain passed under the control of the Railways Executive Committee. Though at first the process was slow, there began a period when the British railway companies had to take the tremendous strain of a full wartime traffic.

Thirteen days after the declaration of war, and with a good propor-

319

tion of the summer holiday traffic over, the Scotch train service, in common with other main line services on the Midland, was cut to a winter footing. The summer Isle of Man services had virtually ceased on August 5 and the Heysham–Belfast boats started sailing on alternate nights from August 8, reverting to a daily service on August 24. On February 22, 1915, a further cut in the Scotch service was made with the permanent withdrawal of the 1.30 afternoon express from St Pancras, passengers being permitted, by an arrangement of inter-availability of tickets, to use the L.N.W.R. afternoon train instead. Two more general timetable alterations to Midland services were made in 1915, on July 12 and October 1.

In common with all the major railways, the Midland played a large part throughout the war in providing a vital through link for essential military and civil traffic. It jumped in at the deep end. Edwin A. Pratt, in his *British Railways and the Great War*, published in 1921, gave details of many aspects of the Midland's war service. At the outbreak of hostilities, on mobilisation, there was an immediate and immense volume of troop traffic. As regards the Settle line, between 5 p.m. on Saturday, August 15 and 10.30 p.m. on Sunday, August 16, there were no less than 67 special trains carrying naval and military personnel worked between Carlisle and Bedford. To a great extent these overlapped with 65 special trains, operating between 7 a.m. on August 15 and 1 a.m. on August 16, from Derby and Burton to Luton.

'As indicating the real nature of the situation occupied by the Midland . . .', said Mr Pratt, 'the fact may be mentioned that, in the event of an invasion or a threatened invasion of this country by the enemy, the Midland Company's line had been selected under the scheme of "Standard Routes and Timings" as the trunk railway over whose system the greater part of the special trains conveying troops, etc., would have passed.'

Apparently troop traffic over the Settle line—after the initial stage—was not particularly heavy, but as regards the transit of war material between England and Scotland, exclusive of coal traffic for the Admiralty, some 45,000 wagons were hauled over the three main routes in a typical week. 29 per cent of these went by both the L.N.W.R. and the Midland, 38 per cent by the N.E.R., and 4 per cent by the Maryport and Carlisle line.

A great volume of exports and imports, beforehand dealt with at East Coast ports were, during the war, switched to the West Coast. The Midland, with its own port at Heysham, and its interests at Barrow, etc. took a good proportion of this traffic. The iron mines of West Cumberland, working at full tilt, poured huge quantities of iron and iron ore onto the Furness and Midland systems for Sheffield and other centres of steel production. Special trains of cordite paste were worked over the Settle line from Carlisle to Brent *en route* to Faversham, and to Bath *en route* to Wareham. Later in the war there was an increase in troop trains over the Settle line; American troops from Glasgow to the south travelled via

Edinburgh and Carlisle. All this was but a small proportion of the total extra traffic carried throughout the Midland system as a whole, and during the heaviest war year the company carried 18 million more 'passengers' than in 1913 and 3,220,000 tons more of goods and minerals, increases of 14 and 6 per cent respectively.

This must be seen against the loan to the Government, for foreign service, of 78 locomotives, 6,000 wagons, and 50 brake vans, and the loss of 21,813 staff for war service, 6,541 of whom were killed, wounded, or posted missing. In addition, Derby works turned out a phenomenal amount of direct war material on government contract. In the case of the lines north of Leeds, one additional station came into being as a direct consequence of the war, that at the Torrisholme munitions factory at Morecambe. Platforms for munitions workers were constructed by the works and the Torrisholme Sidings signal box and connections were opened on March 5, 1916. The platforms were removed on December 23, 1921.

As to the company's steamships, the *Antrim, Donegal* (mentioned later), and *Londonderry* were put to troop transporting; the *Duchess of Devonshire* and *City of Belfast* were used as armed boarders, the *Manxman* became a sea-plane ship; and even the little *Wyvern* did its stint as an Admiral's tug and boarding steamer.

1916 saw the Bank Holidays abolished, tourist tickets discontinued, and the ending on March 6 of the Heysham–Belfast passenger service. The tourist tickets were stopped as from May and at the same time charges on the sleeping cars were raised from 7s 6d to 10s with a further 5s rise in September. As to dining cars the Midland was fortunate. While the L.N.W.R. were no longer permitted to take them the Midland was, though a reduced number. The *Railway News* of December 2, 1916, reported that this particular aspect of Midland affairs had led to a question in Parliament which both gave the Government policy quite clearly and also indirectly mentioned the Settle line.

'In the House of Commons on Wednesday, Mr Pretyman in answer to Mr Robinson, who asked whether the President of the Board of Trade had official information showing the approximate costs of running a railway dining car per 100 miles; and whether, in the interests of economy, he would take steps to stop the running of these cars, said: I am unable to give the figures asked for by my hon. friend, but I understand that it is doubtful whether any real economy would be effected by the withdrawal of those dining cars still remaining in service. Mr Wiles asked whether the Ministry of Munitions had not required the Board of Trade to try to prohibit, as far as possible, the use of engine power, and whether the suspension of dining cars would not lead to economy. Mr Pretyman: No Sir, it would not. That is the purport of my answer. Mr Pringle: Why is it economical for the Midland Railway to run dining cars, but not for the London and North Western Railway to do so? Mr Pretyman: I do not think that that need be an incompatible propositon. The two lines which go to the north are to a certain extent interchangeable, and it is unnecessary to have dining cars on both.'

In fact, throughout the war, only six companies continued to run restaurant cars; the Midland and G.S.W., G.C.R., L.S.W.R., G.E.R. and the G.N.R. of Ireland. In the Midland's case, whereas there were 64 pre-war daily summer trains with restaurant cars and 55 in the winter, these were reduced to a mere 20. Likewise, in an effort to cram more passengers into less trains, there was a marked switch to non-corridor stock, though once again the Midland, with the G.W.R. and the East and West Coast companies, escaped this, at least on their long distance trains.

As the conflict wore on there was a general increase in goods traffic. The Settle line had its share and to facilitate the marshalling of trains at Carlisle several signalling improvements were carried out at Durran Hill and Petteril in 1916. Nothing has been said so far about signalling and communications and there had in fact been a general improvement along the line since the early days of the century. Indeed the telephone had revolutionised traffic control. By 1916 it was a far cry from the days of 1899 when it was noted by the traffic committee that the traders in Skipton were deserting the railway for the Leeds & Liverpool Canal because the Midland had held out stubbornly against subscribing to the Skipton telephone exchange. The build-up in communications had been gradual. In October, 1903, the traffic committee resolved that a telephone circuit should be provided between the Settle South Junction and Blea Moor signal boxes, with intermediate instruments at Settle Junction, Settle Station, Stainforth sidings, Helwith Bridge, Horton, Selside, and Ribblehead. The circuit was to replace the existing block bell telephones. Two years later this was followed by a telephone system between Manningham, Shipley, and Saltaire. In April, 1907, the main line circuit was extended north from Blea Moor box to Kirkby Stephen, the intermediate instruments being at Dent Head, Dent, Hawes Junction South, Ais Gill, and Mallerstang. Four months later outer home signals and track circuiting were provided at Settle Junction and Skipton Junction, in each case so as to protect the main line from the branches. An innovation was the traffic committee's decision in November, 1907, that the block sections between Hellifield and Bell Busk, Bell Busk and Gargrave, and Steeton South and Keighley North Junctions should be divided by providing electro-motor automatic signalling. In September, 1909, orders were given for the two signal boxes at Hawes Junction to be replaced by one; this was ready by 1910 and was very soon to be the centre of one of the line's worst accidents.

With Cecil Paget's traffic control reforms well into their stride it became of some importance to get the private residences of the chairman, general manager, and general superintendent on the telephone system; all three were connected by the end of 1910, the first two on to the company's own line between Derby and London, and Paget who lived at Kings Newton direct on to the National Telephone Company's exchange at Derby, the Midland providing the wire alongside the railway. The Hawes Junction crash, which led to the site of the accident being track circuited in 1911, also prompted Granet to ask the board for authority to spend £100,000 on the protection of passenger trains on fast lines, the works to be spread over five years.

In February, 1913, the traffic committee ordered that a telephone circuit be installed between Carlisle control office and Kirkby Stephen, with intermediate instruments at Cumwhinton, Armathwaite, Lazonby, Langwathby, New Biggin, Appleby, Ormside, and Crosby Garrett, thus completing the through link over the Settle line. Also in 1913 the Leeds–Bradford, Leeds–Skipton, and Skipton–Colne communications were perfected and in the following year the Skipton–Morecambe–Heysham link was improved. In February, 1916, a direct circuit was ordered to be made between Leeds control and Skipton. Finally, though it is a little ahead of time yet clears the permanent way alterations, the siding connections and crossover road at Settle South Junction, together with the South Junction signal box, were all ordered to be removed in October, 1922.

On December 15, 1916, the Midland board noted that in consequence of the War Office calling for rolling stock and locomotives for France, all railway services would be restricted, and from January of 1917 many more cuts were made. (There had, by the way, been no Midland October timetable.) The 9.30 and 11.30 morning trains from St Pancras were replaced by one leaving at 9.15 a.m., which arrived at Glasgow at 7.20 p.m., exactly one hour later than the arrival of the 9.30 timing of July, 1901. This new train was part of an allocation made by the Railway Executive as to the Scotch traffic. King's Cross took the Edinburgh and Aberdeen traffic by the 10 a.m. train, and passengers for Perth went from Euston on the 9.30 a.m. Cancellations included all remaining slip carriages as well as many of the through coaches. Cheap fares were discontinued and ordinary fares raised by half, all with the object of restricting unnecessary travel. One of the smaller cancellations was that of the service by the L.Y.R. over the Thornhill–Royston–Sheffield line. Despite the January timetable, the Settle and Carlisle line was able to boast the fastest time on the whole system—an average of 52.8 m.p.h. by the 12.15 p.m. between Appleby and Carlisle. This fastest time was one of a number noted of different railways by Cecil J. Allen, writing in the June, 1917, issue of the *Railway Magazine*. In the list the Midland was eighth in place of honour, number one being attained by the N.E.R. with a speed of 58.8 m.p.h. on the racing ground between York and Darlington.

Leaving the train services for a moment, and looking at the picture overall, there are two events of note about 1917. The first was the loss of the Heysham–Belfast steamship *Donegal* which, while acting as a hospital ship, and while being escorted by destroyers, was torpedoed on the night of April 17 with the loss of forty-one lives. The other event was the retirement of Worthington as chief engineer and the appointment as his successor of James Briggs, until then the assistant engineer. A minor occurrence was the burning down, on October 7, of the engine shed at Hawes Junction.

323

In March, 1918, there were more cuts, the Railway Executive demanding a reduction of passenger services to half those of the 1914 level. A month later, with the current restrictions in force regarding unnecessary travel, there was an awkward question in Parliament, again concerning the Settle line. The *Railway News* of April 19 reported :

'SPECIAL TRAIN. Mr Gilbert asked the President of the Board of Trade whether he was aware that a special train, consisting of Midland brake, bogie composite, three horse vans, eleven carriage trucks, and bogie van, was run by the Midland Railway company between Appleby and Clifton on Wednesday, March 27; how many miles this train was run both full and empty; whom it was run for; if it was paid for at the usual rates; and would he state why it was run, in view of the general knowledge of railway stock and the appeals to the public to give up all unnecessary travelling generally and during the Easter holidays? Sir A. Stanley: I had not previously heard of this matter, but I am making enquiries and will let the hon. gentleman know the result.'

Unfortunately the *News* did not print his eventual reply so we are left to wonder for whom, or for what, the train was run. The company's minutes appear to be discreetly silent and a search through *Hansard* has brought forth no further information. The Clifton referred to must have been that at Bristol; the only other one would have been on the Eden Valley line and it is beyond the bounds of possibility that a sneak train running those few miles would have metaphorically terminated at Westminster. What seems incredible about this affair is that it got as far as it did. The crime must have been a heinous one for a war Parliament to have discussed it. It is indicative though of the strict government control which was at that time in force.

By October, 1918, the Settle line had relinquished its tenure of being the possessor of the fastest time. Thirteenth down the list of all the companies, the Midland fastest time now went to the 9.25 a.m. Mangotsfield to Gloucester train with an average speed of 48 m.p.h.

1918 saw what must have been the last attempt by an outside concern to construct a railway which might have affected the Leeds–Settle–Carlisle line. As in many previous occasions this scheme was aimed at Hellifield. The Longridge & Hellifield Light Railway, with E. O. Ferguson as its engineer—a gentleman who apart from the Yorkshire Dales line had been singularly unfortunate with various light railways in the area—proposed to construct three lines totalling about 24 miles in length. The first, and the longest, was to leave the Longridge branch of the L.N.W.R. and L.Y.R. just north-east of Longridge station whence it was to run in a mainly north-east direction through Chipping, Slaidburn, and Wigglesworth, to terminate a short distance west of Hellifield station. Two short lines at the Hellifield end were to be made; one to join the Midland about ¼ mile west of the station, and the other to terminate in a field about 300 yards south-west of Hellifield junction. On the main line of the proposed railway the ruling gradient was to be at 1 in 75 spread over a total distance of 5 miles out of 23. There were to be four viaducts totalling fifteen arches. The single track scheme was estimated to cost £233,856. It seemed as if the line was really thought of as being in connection with the new Fylde waterworks, authorized in 1912, and situated between Wigglesworth and Slaidburn. The light railway company offered to conclude agreements with all the three railways with which it connected as to construction, maintenance, and operation, and sought to run into both Hellifield and Longridge stations. The scheme did not go forward. At a meeting at Slaidburn on May 9, 1918, the Railway Commissioners, though noting that none of the main line companies had any objection to the scheme in principle, that such a line was wanted in the district, and that the promoters hoped to get the backing of the local authorities, nevertheless reserved judgment. In September the promoters were told that the traffic prospects did not appear to justify a greater expenditure than £6,000 per mile and that unless they could construct at that figure there seemed little point in going on with the scheme. It was the kindest answer the Commissioners could give for, undoubtedly, the line would never have paid. In December, 1919, the waterworks concern settled for sidings at Long Preston instead.

The extent of the general curtailments in train services during the war is brought out in a comparison of the fastest times on the Midland Scotch services between 1914 and 1918. The following extract is from a table of comparisons prepared as part of an article by 'Voyageur' in the *Railway Magazine* of February, 1919 :

Distances and Fastest Times between London and Provincial Towns in 1914 and 1918

Town	Distance miles	1918 Fastest Time h.m.	Direction	Route	1914 Fastest Time h.m.	Increase 1914 over 1918 h.m.	per cent
Bradford	208	5.55	Down	Midland	4.13	1.42	40
Bradford	203½	5.00	Up	G.C. & L.Y.R.	4.42	0.18	6
Carlisle	299	6.45	Up	L.N.W.R.	5.45	0.57	16
Carlisle	308¾	7.28	Down	Midland	6.05	1.23	23
Edinburgh	393	9.40	Down	East Coast	7.45	1.55	25
Glasgow	401½	9.30	Up	West Coast	8.00	1.30	19
Glasgow	424¼	10.40	Down	M.R. & G.S.W.	8.45	1.55	22
Inverness	567¾	15.55	Down	West Coast	12.50	3.05	24
Leeds	185¾	4.32	Down	G.N.R.	3.25	1.07	33
Leeds	196	4.47	Down	Midland	3.40	1.07	30
Perth	449¾	11.05	Down	West Coast	9.00	2.05	23

In March, 1919, with the Scotch train allocation still in force, the Midland put on a new service timed to leave St Pancras and Glasgow at 10.45 a.m. each train taking 11¼ hours on their respective journeys north and south. In the same month the East and West Coast routes restored restaurant car facilities to their main Scotch trains. Generally, timings on all the main railway companies in the after war period remained at a low level. With shortage of staff, a backlog of repairs, and the still attendant restrictions, the services were to be some time before returning to anything like the pre-war condition. The fastest Midland Scotch timing

of the summer service of 1919 between St Pancras and Carlisle was 7 hours
28 minutes, the same as in 1918, and in 1919 the Midland had no non-
stop runs which exceeded 100 miles. With respect to restaurant cars the
twenty trains which carried those vehicles in 1918 were augmented the
following year by a further twelve. Out of this total of thirty-two trains
in 1919, twenty-eight were worked by the Midland, and four jointly
with the G.S.W.R.

At the end of October, 1919, Sir James Bell, the chairman of the
G.S.W.R., called the attention of the Midland and G.S.W.R. joint committee to the desirability of an early improvement in the London–Scotland service. The Midland representatives undertook to look into various
suggestions made by Sir James and on April 20 they were able to report
that a new service would commence from May 1 (in fact May 5). It was
further hoped to make other improvements in the following October.
The new summer timetable brought the timing of the fastest Midland
train between London and Carlisle down to 6 hours 45 minutes, 40
minutes longer than that of 1914 but 43 shorter than the 1919 time, and
only 13 minutes longer than the current fastest train of the L.N.W.R.
The best through Glasgow timing was 9 hours 45 minutes, 55 better than
the previous period. 1919 also saw the addition on the Midland and
G.S.W.R. service of two more restaurant cars, the total number of these
vehicles run on the Midland system that year having reached forty-
four. May of 1920 saw the re-appearance in the timetable of the
Heysham–Belfast service. In February, 1922, the 9 a.m. from St Pancras
to Leeds was continued on to Carlisle. This was apparently done because
it had proved impossible to get the 9.50 from St Pancras to arrive at
Glasgow in time to make connection with the East Coast route's 10
a.m. train at Edinburgh Waverley. To get over the difficulty a through
Aberdeen carriage was put on the 9 a.m. instead. The following July
saw the Leeds–Lake District service restored, via the L.N.W.R. The
Leeds trains were routed to call at Bradford and travelled via Carnforth
instead of through Ingleton as in the pre-war services. A new train
introduced in July 1920 was the 'East Lancashire Express', a restaurant
car train which left St Pancras at 1.30 p.m. and travelled via Chinley,
Manchester, and then over the L.Y.R. via Bolton and Blackburn to
Hellifield. The return workings left Hellifield at 11.5 a.m. and Manchester Victoria at 1.15 p.m. The train was worked north of Manchester
by L.Y.R. locomotives, in this respect being different to a rather similar
service put on by the Midland in earlier years which had been withdrawn in 1911. This had been operated throughout by Midland engines
as far as Blackburn, where it had terminated.

On August 15, 1921, the railways of Great Britain were released
from control by the Railway Executive but in the same year the Railways Act provided that they should be grouped into four main companies as from 1923. From January, 1922, the Lancashire & Yorkshire
Railway became amalgamated with the L.N.W.R. and a year later the

Midland, with the North Staffordshire, Furness, Caledonian, Glasgow & South Western, Highland, and a host of subsidiary companies, joined with them to become the London Midland & Scottish Railway Company. The Settle and Carlisle line, from being the lifeline of the Midland Railway, and providing a competitive service between Scotland and the English capital, became merely a duplicate line to the West Coast route, with both under the same ownership. The Grouping ended the seventy-nine years' existence of the Midland Railway, most of which had been concerned with the struggle for Scotch traffic as one of the predominant requirements to the increasing growth of the system.

As to the traffic carried by the Midland north of Leeds between 1900 and 1922, tables of passenger, mineral, and livestock returns for various selected stations and years are to be found in Appendix XXI. From them it can be seen that there was a marked decline in minerals in and out of Carlisle over the period—as distinct from through trains of course—and a lesser decrease through Horton-in-Ribblesdale. What is of interest, however, is the tremendous increase through Ingleton from the beginning of the First World War, from 3,132 tons in 1914 to 29,997 in 1915. Other years for Ingleton were 52,081 in 1916, 52,672 in 1917, 83,041 in 1918, and 67,916 in 1919. By 1922 it was back to the pre-1915 level. As to livestock the traffic appears not to have been unduly influenced by the war. On the passenger side, however, the situation is markedly different, all traffic showing the expected decrease in 1917. Of interest are the figures for Hellifield and Carlisle, the best year of the former, 1922, being well over the figure for the worst year of the latter, 1917. In fact Carlisle did not have as many passenger bookings as might have been expected from its size. This was due, of course, to the fact that the L.N.W.R. provided the competition that was lacking at Hellifield. Next to Hellifield in the number of booked passengers came Settle (later giving way to Skipton) and then Ingleton and Appleby. The peak year for passenger traffic was 1920. Figures are : Carlisle 58,519, Appleby 15,663, Kirkby Stephen 6,852, Settle 31,946, Ingleton 21,574, Hellifield 44,412, and Skipton 374,151—over six times more than at Carlisle. As a cross-roads on the railway system the Midland station at Leeds Wellington gives a good indication of the traffic fortunes of the company in its last years : 897,798 in 1900, 790,733 in 1907, then yearly from 1913 until 1922 as follows : 850,672, 811,795, 788,345, 863,903, 633,481 (the 1917 figure), 782,558, 1,020,169, 1,165,350 (the 1920 figure), 1,002,608, and 983,757 in 1922.

The last meeting of the Midland and G.S.W.R. joint committee before the Grouping was held on October 27, 1922. There had been some important changes in the direction of the Midland since the war, changes which, with the early death of Sir Guy Calthrop of the L.N.W.R., were to deprive the new-born L.M.S.R. of some able officers. Sir Guy Granet had retired from the general managership of the Midland at the end of 1918, and the directors appointed in his place the deputy general manager, Frank Tatlow. Tatlow had served under all the previous general managers since Allport's time and had been assistant general manager since 1915. In May, 1919, Lieut. Colonel Cecil W. Paget retired from the post of general superintendent of the company. Paget was an outstanding railway officer whose original operating ability had, with the introduction of train control on the Midland, revitalised the train service in the hectic competitive days before the war. Through his ideas and leadership the Midland was one of the pioneers in running almost all its system by an organisation of district controls working under the central guidance of Derby. With the introduction of the 'path' system which enabled the line to be used to its greatest capacity, Paget had been able to remedy a chronic state of congestion, which had come into being, without the necessity of a whole new series of costly widenings and other improvements. During the war his talents had been at the disposal of the government in clearing up the operating difficulties of the military railways in France. While away from the Midland his place had been taken by John Henry Follows, and on Paget's retirement Follows was appointed to succeed him. David Bain, the carriage and wagon superintendent, retired at about this time and was succeeded by Robert Whyte Reid. The Midland also ended its separate existence with a new chairman; George Murray Smith died in May, 1919 and was succeeded as chairman by Charles Booth who had been deputy chairman for a year. Booth was also the chairman of the Booth Steamship company of Liverpool. Lastly, the Midland bequeathed to the L.M.S.R. its chief mechanical engineer, Sir Henry Fowler, who had succeeded Deeley on January 1, 1910. His adoption by the new company was to spark off a trial of strength between the Midland and L.N.W.R. basic locomotive designs. The story of this and the later locomotive working on the Settle line are briefly noted in Chapter XX.

As to the engine allocations and diagrams concerning the working of the Leeds–Settle–Carlisle line, a very comprehensive article, entitled *The Leeds–Carlisle Road at the Close of the Midland Era,* appeared in the September, 1961, issue of the *Railway World.* In it Mr. Norman Harvey gave a complete list of individual engine allocations to the various sheds, and working diagrams, the latter being those in force from May of 1922, and the allocations being given as at December 31. To quote the article would be invidious; it stands on its own and should be studied by those who wish to find the engine turns on the route during its last months in the ownership of the Midland Railway.

To end this chapter, a few details of the Ingleton branch in its later years before the Grouping may be of interest. Mr G. Milne, writing in the December, 1955, issue of the *Journal of the Stephenson Locomotive Society* has some interesting 'Ingleton Memories'. He tells, among other things, of the two stations divided by the viaduct, both called Ingleton, but the L.N.W.R. one being known locally as Thornton. It was possible to book between them, and enjoy a rooftop view of the town, for the price of one penny. Apparently for many years the Midland line was operated by an o-6-o tank, No. 1420 (renumbered in 1907 as 1692). Its train consisted of three six-wheeled carriages, two being brake/thirds and one a composite. 'The Midland water column at Ingleton used to dry up in hot summers, when the Midland engine had to cross the viaduct to get its supply from the L. & N.W., a privilege, I believe, which had to be paid for. There was no water column at Clapham'. Mr Milne tells how the two station masters at Ingleton hardly fell over themselves to be co-operative about connecting trains from Tebay with those from Clapham. Of the times when Midland trains went through to Penrith for Keswick, Mr Milne mentions that a L.N.W.R. 'Jumbo' took them on from Clapham—not Ingleton. Nevertheless, Midland engines did occasionally do the run, and he remembers 'hearing that Midland drivers having occasion to take the Ingleton–Penrith route laughed at Shap which they regarded as a mere flea-bite compared with their own "Long Drag" from Settle Junction to Blea Moor'. At the Grouping the Thornton station was closed down and now virtually nothing remains of it. Of the flavour of the Ingleton line, now possibly doomed to complete extinction, there is much more in Mr Milne's account, purloined as it has been, than can unfortunately be found space for here.

XVIII

Rolling Stock

The opening of the Settle and Carlisle line came at a time when the Midland Railway, and other companies, were involved in examining the possibilities available in the matter of brake power, and the early years of the line's operating were to bring an amount of running difficulties associated with current brake trials. In order to appreciate the Midland's position at this time, and its difficulty in deciding on the brake it was to adopt, it is necessary to go back a few years prior to the opening of the Settle line.

On October 16, 1872, a tyre broke on a train travelling between Dronfield and Dore & Totley. The report by the Board of Trade's officer, Captain Tyler, was read to the Midland traffic committee on October 31, and it was decided to follow the Captain's suggestions and make some experiments with a form of continuous brake. Such a brake would of course apply a retarding force so as to slow a train safely and uniformly, as against the sudden front-end application from the engine which had caused the Dronfield accident. The appliance currently being produced by the Westinghouse Brake Company was chosen and it was decided to fit this to several of the company's trains operating on the Metropolitan lines in London. Various trials with the Westinghouse brake took place in the months following, notably between London and Bedford on April 10, 1874.

On February 15, 1876 the Midland locomotive committee read a report from Johnson and Clayton on the subject of brakes. There were two methods by which the driver could be given more power to stop a train. The first was by a direct brake, either steam, hydraulic, or air, applied direct to the engine; the second was the application of a continuous brake to the carriages as well as to the engine and tender. The report stated that the ideal continuous brake had not yet been found. There had been a recent series of brake trials at Newark, held under the aegis of the Board of Trade, and pending any action the Midland directors might be making thereon, Johnson and Clayton thought it unadvisable to introduce the Westinghouse brake further than could be avoided. There was, however, so little time left before the Settle and Carlisle line expresses would start running that the only way to provide adequate brake power at that moment was to fit the necessary minimum number of locomotives and carriages with the Westinghouse to work the trains. With an eye on the future the report pleaded for uniformity in the type of brake to be adopted—a request that was to be only partly heeded. The report ended :

'Our present view is that an efficient steam brake can be arranged for the engine and tender, and that this, together with the ordinary guard's brake power, would be found to meet the requirements of ordinary passenger working.

'We also recommend that the block system be so worked that no express or fast passenger train shall be permitted to pass a station until the main line through the station in front, at which it is not booked to stop, is clear of trains; that is—trains, if shunting, must be clear of the main line before block is released, or if not shunting they must have left the station.

'With these precautions we see no fear of working the trains with safety.'

Exactly a week after the report, Johnson informed the committee that in consequence of the opening of the Settle and Carlisle line for passenger traffic on May 1 next he had ordered fittings for five engines from the Westinghouse Company, and would require eleven more to complete the engines for the service. On March 1 the board learned from the carriage and wagon committee that in order to fulfil the requirements of the traffic department in the fitting up of carriages for the Scotch traffic with the Westinghouse brake, 88 carriages would have to be altered at a cost of £2,904.

The story of the rolling stock so far has been brought up to the time of the opening of the Settle and Carlisle line. The number of Pullmans was obviously not enough as on June 7 Allport told the board that requisitions had been issued for 24 drawing room cars and 12 sleeping cars. He had in fact allowed his enthusiasm for the American cars to run away with him, for the board immediately made it clear that he was not to order any more of the vehicles until a statement of the earnings was available. On July 4 eight Pullmans, of a design which had not proved popular with the public, were taken out of service for extensive alterations and on August 2 the board instructed the accountant to make a statistical analysis of Pullman car earnings.

At about this time the locomotive committee received a letter from George Westinghouse junior, saying that he foresaw no difficulty in fitting up the Scotch trains with brakes, provided a set of instructions he issued in his letter as to their use and maintenance was carried out. That work in this direction was proceeding slowly was borne out in a report from Johnson and Clayton on October 17 in which they said that on account of the foreign and Midland carriages, not fitted with the Westinghouse brakes, being introduced into the Scotch trains during the past six weeks, no proper opinion could be formed as to the working of them as continuously braked trains. The locomotive committee, to whom the report was made, ordered that records should be kept of the different workings, and on November 14, 1876, Johnson and Clayton were back with some results. They were still of the same opinion as before, however; they did not like the Westinghouse. The return of carriages running on the Scotch expresses from October 19 to November 11, showed that out of 84 trains running, 15 were effective throughout, 65 partly effective, and four ineffective throughout. Out of all the carriages running in the trains, 443 were not fitted with the Westinghouse brake, 340 were fitted but not at work, and 1,838 were fitted and at work. The performance was obviously erratic and the two officers pointed out that the brake's natural tendency was to stop the train whether wanted or not. There had been several occasions recently when it had gone on partially, unknown to the crew, and some of the wheel tyres of the carriages had as a consequence become so heated and expanded as to endanger the train. Despite the advantage the brake had in stopping breakaways, Johnson and Clayton still thought the direct steam brake was best. They asked, and got permission, to try out two test trains with the Smith's Vacuum brake—this being the simplest available brake. 'Pending the settlement of the continuous brake question,' they said, 'we are of opinion that with the addition of a steam brake to the engine and tender, as well as the present hand brake on the tender, together with two guard's van brakes to each train of more than ten vehicles, the passenger trains may be worked with increased safety.'

Despite this the locomotive and carriage and wagon committees gave orders on December 4 for eight Pullman parlour and six sleeping cars to be fitted with the Westinghouse brake for the Scotch traffic. The year ended with the introduction on the Settle line of a carriage fitted with Pintsch's gas lighting. In August 1876 one of the new bogie carriages then under construction had been given the system as an experiment, following its successful use on the St John's Wood line of the Metropolitan Railway. On December 5 the locomotive committee switched the coach to the London–Glasgow run for a week or so prior to examining the possibility of fitting all the Scotch trains with the new lighting.

The first year's operating of the Settle line had attracted the public to the new route and on February 6, 1877 the traffic committee noted the desirability of having additional family carriages for the Scotch traffic. It ordered six 'of the most improved design' to be made. The saloons used over the previous year were to be put into the ordinary traffic. Early in April Johnson and Clayton were asked why the use of Clarke's chain brake had been suspended. They reported that 29 carriages were fitted with the brake and that after experiments had been made in April 1874 it had been found undesirable to put the train into traffic. Apparently it applied unevenly, breaking the train into sections, and was considered unsafe. The Midland method of working the brake was to have each vehicle in the train fitted and then to work it in three sections simultaneously. This differed from the standard L.N.W.R. practice with the same brake; three vehicles and the van next to the tender were worked by the driver or front guard, and three vehicles in the rear similarly worked. This had apparently proved successful as the L.N.W.R. was reported to be happy with it. At the same time Johnson and Clayton had something to say on the Barker's hydraulic brake :

'We beg to report that we have two engines (Nos. 132 and 135) and 24 carriages fitted with Barker's Hydraulic Brake. One train with engine No. 135 worked on the Leeds and Bradford section for nine months, and for the past seven months two trains have been working with the two engines above named on the line between Bedford and London.

'Barker's brake is very powerful, works smoothly and well, and has given less trouble than any other brake we have had at work; it is, however, complicated on the engine and carriages, and this forms, so far as our experience goes, the only objection to it.'

The Barker's brake was a sideline, however. In the previous November the board had given instructions for the fitting up of two trains and the engines for working them with the Smith's vacuum brake for trial purposes, and on May 1, 1877, the directors ordered that monthly returns were to be made to the board on the working of the Westinghouse and Smith brakes in use on the Manchester and Scotch expresses, showing the daily composition of the trains and the number of vehicles in which the brakes were in action, together with an explanation for any failures of the brakes and the costs of the repairs. The vehicles so fitted included some of the Pullmans, and Allport was asked to report on the best trains with which to carry out the experiments. By June 6 it had been decided to put the Smith's vacuum on the 12 noon from London to Manchester and the 1 p.m. from Manchester to London, these trains being composed of Pullman cars and ordinary stock. The Westinghouse system operated on the Scotch trains. By August the results were beginning to come in, and after reading the reports from the officers, the board ordered that two of the most important trains each way were to be fitted with the vacuum brake, in addition to those already fitted, and that one additional train each way be fitted with the Sander's brake, the trains to be agreed by the operating companies.

The report of the working of the continuous brakes for the month ended August 15 showed the following: Westinghouse—out of 169 trains run, 63.7 per cent. using the brake, there were 29 failures causing 43 minutes delay and costing £55 8s 2½d in maintenance; Smith's—54 trains ran having a percentage of 67.71 vehicles fitted with the brake, with one delay causing two minutes wait. The maintenance of the brake had cost £8 19s 4d. The September returns showed that out of 171 Westinghouse trains, with 78.07 per cent. of the carriages using the brake, there were failures on 17 occasions causing 37 minutes delay. The Smith's system, however, with 54 trains run and 74.89 per cent. of the vehicles fitted, had no failures or delays. For the month ended October 15 there were six Westinghouse failures out of 136 trains run while four Smith's trains failed out of 50. This time the percentage in each train of carriages using the respective brakes was about equal.

Leaving the question of brakes for a moment and returning to the Pullmans, by November 1877 the Pullman company had completed construction of all the cars at Derby, dispensed with its workmen, and withdrawn the manager and foreman to America. The names of the Pullman cars and the dates when put into service are as follows:

Parlour Cars	Date	Parlour Cars	Date
Victoria	—.6.1874	Albion	9.10.1876
Britannia	„	Comet	31.10.1876
Leo	„	Ariel	„
Jupiter	23.8.1875	Apollo	19.1.1877
Saturn	10.9.1875	Adonis	„
Mercury	28.4.1876	Aurora	1.5.1877
Juno	„	Ceres	„
Venus	3.5.1876	Eclipse	10.7.1877
Vesta	28.7.1876	Alexandra I	„
Minerva	„	Globe	(Still in shops
Planet	27.9.1876		at Nov. 6, 1877—
			not yet in traffic)

Sleeping Cars	Date	Sleeping Cars	Date
Excelsior	—.6.1874	Scotia	28.4.1876
Enterprise	„	Norman	2.6.1876
St. George	28.6.1875	Australia	20.6.1876
Princess	17.7.1875	India	28.7.1876
Transit	13.10.1875	Germania	26.8.1876
Saxon	4.2.1876	Midland	—.6.1877
Castalia	28.4.1876		

(Note: The above list is extracted from the Midland carriage and wagon committee minutes, and shows the Pullman stock in the company's service as at November, 1877. Remarks at the foot of the list note that *Midland* went on the continent in July, 1874, returning on June 20th, 1877. *Mars* went to Brighton on October 26th, 1875, as did *Alexandra II* and *Albert Edward* on October 10th, 1877; none of these vehicles is noted above of course. Further developments as to alterations and transfers are dealt with later in this chapter as they arise.)

As to the car *Midland,* Clayton reported to the carriage and wagon committee on November 19, 1877, as follows :

'This car which has been over on the continent for about three years was brought back to England in June last, and the first I heard respecting it was from my London foreman, the Pullman people having applied to him to render them assistance in getting the car on to the rails at the docks at Poplar. He asked my permission which was given, but in the interval the car was got on by someone else and brought round by the North London Railway to St Pancras station. Upon the application of the Pullman Car Company we made the car that it would couple up with our trains that it might come to their shops at Derby and we charged them with the cost. The Pullman Car Company then put the car into good order, altered the draw-gear and buffers to our standard in their own shops, after which the car was sent to work in the Scotch traffic. The first trace we have of its working was on 30th August last, it has been on these trains since that date.'

During its time in the shops at Derby the *Midland* was altered to conform with the standard pattern of the other cars, since as originally built it had been a 'non standard' car. George Behrens, in his book *Pullman in Europe,* mentions that it had ten sofa sections and two cross-sections.

Early in January, 1878, when the monthly returns came through, the traffic committee was told to take two of the cars earning the least return per mile out of service though presumably they were to be retained in store. The car *Ohio,* not mentioned in the above list, but built by the Midland on behalf of the Pullman company, returned to Derby from the G.N.R. later in 1878 and was rebuilt as a dining car and renamed *Prince of Wales*. Another car, this time on the list, which left the Midland, was the *Victoria*; renamed *Alexandra*, it went to the London & South Western Railway.

With the Midland board still wondering whether the continuous vacuum brake was a necessity in any brake eventually adopted by the company, the returns for the month ended February 15, 1878, became available. By now the Sanders' brake was in use; it had been accepted on a licence arrangement for the sum of £2,000. Out of 12 short trips with this brake there were seven failures causing 15 minutes delay. The brake was, however, much cheaper to maintain, or at least it appeared to be. It was also quite annoyingly independent—out of 16 trips made during the month ended March 15 it failed six times yet a month later it ran 1,400 booked stops without a murmur compared with 35,983 miles of booked Westinghouse stops, 417 miles of which were made, somehow or other, with the brakes totally inoperative, and a further $101\frac{1}{4}$ with partially operative brakes. Obviously no decision could yet be made.

In December of 1877 a meeting of officers from the Midland, G.S.W.R., and N.B.R. agreed on a joint rolling stock in the proportions of one third each, a fund to be created by a mileage charge contribution out of which the repairs and maintenance should be paid, the balance to be divided equally between the three companies. The carriages for the London traffic were to be constructed on the bogie principle with smaller carriages for short distance traffic. With the policy thus sketched out the traffic committee met on March 5, 1878 to consider what could be done in the interim period before the new carriages came into service. The committee noted that the third class carriages on the East and West Coast routes were being fitted with cushions and stuffed backs on the Scotch trains and as a start it was decided that the Midland thirds should be brought up to this standard at an estimated cost of £9 9s 7d per compartment.

On March 19, 1878 the traffic committee read and approved the following minutes of a meeting held six days earlier between the three companies at which the joint stock was discussed:

'The question of the class of carriage stock to be adopted for the joint service was discussed, and it was
  AGREED to recommend that the following stock be provided.
10 (ten) 54 feet carriages with six wheel bogies containing three 1st class and four 3rd class compartments and a luggage compartment at each end.
20 (twenty) 40 feet carriages with four wheel bogies containing two 1st class and three 3rd class compartments and a luggage compartment, the latter to go at the end of the carriage.
10 (ten) brake vans.
  'The carriage stock to have ordinary roofs and the compartments to be 7 feet 2 inches high (this is the figure given in the Midland and G.S.W. joint committee minutes—the Midland traffic committee minutes give it as a plain 7 feet) as recommended by the Locomotive and Carriage Superintendents of the three companies.
  'The question of the disposal of the 54 feet carriages when they become unfit for the Scotch service was considered, and as Mr Wainwright and Mr Walker stated they could not be very well utilised for the ordinary local traffic on their

branch lines Mr Allport said that he should be prepared to recommend the Midland company to take such stock at a valuation, the other companies taking under the same circumstances a share of the 40 feet carriages at a proportionate price.

'It was agreed that water closets should not be provided in any of the new stock, and that the matter should now be referred to the Locomotive and Carriage Superintendents to prepare the necessary plans for the consideration of the directors.'

While these deliberations were going on the Midland was constructing for its own use a number of additional bogie carriages and by April 16, out of 150 under construction, 30 had been fitted with a clerestory roof. It was decided to abandon this roof on the remainder except some 40 which were half completed and could be modified. At the same time all the thirds in the new carriages were to be brought up to the same standard as had already been applied to the Scotch traffic. Of these carriages, which were ordered in November 1876, 50 were to be exclusively third class, 50 to have two firsts and four thirds, and 50 to have three thirds and three firsts.

On July 11, 1878, eleven days after the Midland & Scotch Joint Stock arrangement came into force, the general managers of the Midland, G.S.W.R. and N.B.R. reported to the Midland and G.S.W.R. joint committee that the proportions of the first and third class passengers booked at St Pancras and St Enoch to stations on the G.S.W.R. and Midland respectively, during the two years ended April 12, 1878, were 32 per cent. first class and 68 per cent. third class and that the accommodation provided in the carriages proposed was in the proportion of 30 per cent. and 70 per cent. respectively. Allport submitted drawings of the proposed carriages, the cost of which was estimated to be :

54 ft. six wheel bogie	@ £1,083 each
40 ft. four wheel bogie	@ £721 "
Brake van	@ £275 "

These estimates were revised, however, and on January 9, 1879 it was reported that the following stock had been ordered and was being constructed at the Midland works at Derby :

10	54 ft. carriages	@ £1,029	= £10,290
20	40 ft. carriages	@ £681 10s.	= £13,630
10	Brake vans	@ £275	= £2,750
			£26,670

It was expected that the vehicles would be ready for next season's traffic and instructions were given as to the preparation of an agreement for their joint use. On November 6, 1878 it had been agreed that all the joint stock should be fitted with the Westinghouse brake, though not necessarily on a permanent basis.

The new stock could not come quick enough, for behind the doors of the traffic departments of the Anglo–Scotch companies there was an air bordering on panic. The Pullmans, supposedly the mainstay of the Midland Scotch service and the cynosure of all eyes, were doing terrible things to their careful schedules with a series of minor disasters. Clayton told of the trouble in a report to the carriage and wagon committee early in April, 1878 :

'I have to report that ever since the Pullman cars commenced running upon the railway we have had great difficulty with the journals running hot.

'Everything has been done that could be to make them run cool from the very first, both by the Pullman people themselves and also by us.

'All through the time they have been in traffic, oils of the very best description have been obtained and used without the desired effect. Mixtures of oil, sulphur, black lead, and plumbago, all of which have a tendency to keep the journals cool, phospho-bronze and other special kinds of bearings have been tried and every possible care has been taken. Men have travelled with the cars for weeks together to pay special attention to them, and at our various terminal stations the Pullman cars have received more attention and given us more trouble than all the other stock. At intermediate stations the cars have had special attention and taken up the examiners' time which has on very many occasions been to the detriment and neglect of the other vehicles on the train.

'I attribute their running hot to two causes :

FIRST The bad construction of the axleboxes and mode of lubrication.

SECOND To the great weight there is upon the journals.

'The number of hot journals in proportion to the number of cars in traffic is the same now as when the first few cars began to run, and I really see no way to cure it without going to the expense of making a different class of axle box, but this is a difficult matter because it involves other alterations in the bogie frame and axleguards and the cost of which is estimated at £27 10s per car.'

So far the image of the Midland Scotch service was not good. After the initial runs over the Settle line with admiring journalists in attendance the whole effort had lost its momentum in a series of trains coming to a stop either with their brakes clamped obstinately on or in an awe-inspiring mixture of sparks and smoke from the hot boxes. The matter of the axle lubrication was quickly followed up. On April 30, 1878, the carriage and wagon committee discussed the idea of using oil instead of grease. Clayton pointed out that this had all been gone over $2\frac{1}{2}$ years ago. He argued that the traffic department was claiming the trouble was caused by grease and was asserting that neither the East or West Coast routes got hot boxes. The G.N.R. used oil and L.N.W.R. grease. Previous to the year 1874 the Midland had moved backwards and forwards twice in the use of grease and oil for axleboxes. He had talked to Patrick Stirling of the G.N.R. and had got at the truth. On a pro rata basis the G.N.R.'s hot boxes were 300 per cent. of the Midland's. The Midland was also better in this respect than the L.N.W.R. Clayton was convinced that grease was cheaper and better than oil. He backed this by saying that after exhaustive tests the L.N.W.R., G.W.R., L.Y.R., M.S.L.R., C.R., G.S.W.R., N.B.R., L.B.S.C.R., and S.E.R. all used grease, whereas the G.N.R., L.S.W.R., N.E.R., and G.E.R. used oil. He ended by saying that hot boxes would always occur due to carelessness but if grease was used properly it was excellent. Needless to say all this soon got to the ears of the Pullman Car Company and on May 1, 1878 it asked the Midland if it might do the lubricating of the axles. The board agreed subject to two conditions : the Midland staff was to have the ultimate responsibility for taking cars off the trains in the interests of safety; and the company reserved the right to terminate the Pullman company's maintenance of the cars at any time.

Matters were not helped on July 2 when Clayton reported that the car *Globe,* which was the last of the Pullmans to be constructed at Derby and had been standing in the works there since it was built, not having been in traffic, had been 'taken away without our knowledge and worked up to London on 29th June, the car had not been inspected by this department since November, 1877'. (The *Globe,* renamed *Beatrice,* eventually found its way over to the L.B.S.C.R.) The following day, with another batch of returns relating to the Pullman earnings before it, the traffic committee reported to the board that it was about to withdraw the cars between Birmingham and Bristol, and Birmingham and Leeds. It was resolved that the existing agreement whereby the Pullman Car Company greased the cars in the Scotch trains be extended —to expire at any time—to the Pullmans running on the London and Manchester and Liverpool trains. Allport stated Mr George Pullman would be in England in a few days and the board arranged a deputation to meet him and discuss the agreement as well as a proposition from Pullman that he should become the company's agent in America.

By August 7 Pullman and the board had agreed that a Mr Rapp should be appointed to use the two sheds at Derby, formerly occupied by the Pullman company, to be set aside for repairs to the cars. The Midland was to supply all the wages and materials but the cars were to be maintained, oiled and greased to Rapp's satisfaction. It was also agreed that the Pullman company could erect cars in the sheds for use by other railways so long as such activities did not interfere with the primary object of keeping the Midland cars up to scratch. By this time the Midland had decided to discontinue the Pullman service between Leeds and London—this did not mean the Scotch trains—as well as the Leeds and Bristol service, and any of the cars so redundant could be taken back by Pullman at valuation. The agreement was to run for three years. On August 19 Clayton reported that the Pullman company wished to withdraw the cars *Germania* and *India,* and that after meeting with the Pullman representative it had been agreed that repairs were to be carried out at Midland expense before releasing them—the amounts being £31 5s and £40 6s respectively. The two cars went to work on the East Coast route.

Clayton was a busy man at about this time, keeping a check on what Allport's American friends were doing. In late September he reported to the carriage and wagon committee that Rapp would be starting his work on October 1 and would have an assistant, who would be paid £3 10s a week, to keep the accounts and overlook the shop and stores during his absence. The foreman in charge of painting and repairs was to get £2 15s a week as was an 'out-door man' who would take charge of the running of the cars. Besides this the Pullman company was employing the requisite number of men at ordinary wages. Apparently in an attempt to solve the lubrication problem, Rapp intended placing two additional men at St Pancras, two at Leicester, one at Derby, one at Liverpool, one at Manchester, two at Normanton and one at Carlisle. They were to be employed on lubricating the boxes, and replaced the travelling staff. By October 15 Rapp had asked the Midland train examiners to attend to the lubricating at Bedford, Stockport, and Skipton.

It soon became apparent that Rapp was in difficulties for on November 5, 1878 Clayton, obviously in a bad frame of mind, pointed out that Rapp had had charge of the running of the Pullman cars for over a month and with eleven additional men to attend to lubrication there had been 39 cases of hot boxes during the month, necessitating the taking out of service of 19 cars, whilst on the journey, with a total train delay of 123 minutes. But this was only on the Midland line; the disease had now spread to Scotland with the detaching at Kilmarnock of two others. 'During the corresponding period of 1877', said Clayton, 'we had one car detached and two others ran hot causing 10 minutes delay to the trains'.

Even if the Pullmans did not fail with the Westinghouse brake, or begin to smoulder quietly while coasting down from Blea Moor, they had yet another trick—that of coming uncoupled from the ordinary stock. Apparently they broke loose at odd times, relying for the remainder of the journey upon the tenuous link of the side chains. This clearly would not do and at the end of 1878 Clayton suggested that 'elastic or spring buffers' should be fitted on the sides with ordinary draw-gear in the centre. It was decided to fix up six of the vehicles as an experiment. It seems that nothing could go right at this time, but at least one minor puzzle was solved for in the same month someone, presumably wondering at the frequent damage to the brake gear of the carriages, came up with the answer; a good number of the buffer stops along the line came incorrectly into contact with the gear when the stock was shunted against them.

Returning to the question of the brakes, at a meeting of the board on November 6, 1878, it was decided that the automatic action brake should be adopted in principle; which kind it was to be, however, was left open. The summary of the working of the continuous brake for the month ending November 15 showed that 117 Westinghouse trains with 76.6 per cent. of the carriages using the brake made 962 booked stops and had 11 failures causing 44 minutes delay; 162 using Smith's vacuum with 76 per cent. made 1,296 stops, had 3 failures with 3 minutes loss of time; and 128 Sander's automatic vacuum trains, with 81.8 per cent. of the carriages fitted made 2,036 stops with 6 failures causing 26 minutes loss. Sander's brake was being fitted to all the Midland bogie carriages then under construction though this, of course, did not include the Scotch joint stock. The returns for the month ending December 15 showed that 111

Westinghouse journeys with 78 per cent. of the stock using the brake made 901 stops and experienced 15 failures causing delays amounting to 74 minutes. This contrasted badly with 1,205 stops made by the Smith's brake with no failures, and 143 by Sander's with 7. Allport called attention to the fact, while reading this report, that delays charged against the Westinghouse brake were of such a nature as to suggest—the Boffins had been busy—that the defect was caused not by the brake but by the drawbars of the carriages. This was better news and it was decided that one of the directors, C. H. Jones, should investigate these cases and report to the board. Returns for the month ending January 15, 1879, were just as bad. Jones, however, had received a letter from Clayton :

'Referring to the board minute . . . dated 1st January, 1879.
'Where all the vehicles in a train were fitted with continuous brakes which were in operation throughout and drawbars were broken from rebounding or jerking, such cases have been entered against the brake.
'We have records of a number of drawbars broken on trains fitted and working throughout with the Westinghouse Automatic Brake but none with either Smith's or Sander's, the cause for which on the Westinghouse Brake trains is the unevenness with which the brake applies on different vehicles in a train, for whilst upon one vehicle a pressure of nine tons is obtained on the brake blocks in three seconds, it takes six seconds to get six tons on the next vehicle and oftentimes upon other vehicles the brake has not been applied at all owing to the triple valves not acting properly, and this brake acts just as unevenly in releasing as it does in applying.
'There have been a number of drawbars broken on passenger trains when only part of the vehicles have been fitted and in operation with the continuous brakes, owing to the vehicles not fitted over-running those that were, and rebounding when trains come to a stand, but such breakages of the drawbars have not been entered as a defect against the brake because the fault was owing to the manner in which the trains were made up and worked.'

With all this additional work on the rolling stock to bother him it is not surprising to find Clayton suggesting on February 18, 1879, that a telephone—invented in 1876—should be installed between the carriage works and the locomotive and stores departments.

With more bad returns for the month ending February 15, 1879, the board resolved that a monthly return should be made of the engines and vehicles fitted with the Westinghouse and Sander's brakes, with date, weight and cost details together with repairs done. In the following March and April consideration was given to the desirability of attaching continuous brakes to such of the fast trains as had not already been supplied. Following this, on May 7, Allport reported that there was considerable inconvenience in working the carriage stock in consequence of the application of more than one type of brake. At the same time Johnson and Clayton recommended the alteration of 114 carriages from the Smith's system to the automatic vacuum at a cost of £4 each, and the alteration of 36 engines likewise at £30 each. This was to enable the running of 24 out of a number of 29 additional trains to be fitted with the continuous brake in consequence of the board's policy originating from its discussions during March and April. The effect of the change would be to do away with the Smith's vacuum brake on the main line and convert it into an automatic brake interchangeable with the stock fitted with the Sander's brake. Their recommendation was approved. The Sander's brake, by the way, was a source of annoyance to the Westinghouse people who contended that it was an infringement of their patent and the Midland's solicitors were kept busy on this matter for some time.

By mid 1879 the delays to the Scotch trains caused by the failure of the Westinghouse brake had reached a point where Allport felt bound to protest. He wrote to the traffic committee on August 5 :

'The detentions of our Scotch trains in consequence of the failure of the continuous brakes on the new joint stock have become so numerous that I feel it necessary to call your attention to the subject.

'These cases, during the past month of July have amounted to 42 . . . a number very much in excess of anything we have previously experienced.

'I need not enter into the controversy which has taken place between the Westinghouse company and our Carriage Department but I feel compelled to ask that some immediate action be taken to remedy the very serious evils we are now subjected to.

'It will be in the recollection of the Directors that we had a very large number of Pullman carriages taken off the trains in consequence of the heating of the axles, and that after considerable discussion it was thought advisable that the Pullman Company should send one of their own men to attend to the repairs of their stock. Since they have been put in order by the Pullman Company's manager there has been a great improvement in their running, only 11 carriages having been detached with hot boxes between January 1st and July 31st, 1879, as against 39 for the corresponding period of 1878, and if the period between April 1st and July 31st be taken, when it may be assumed the whole of the carriages had been overhauled by the Pullman Company, a still more marked improvement has taken place, no carriage having been detached during the four months of 1879 as against 23 detached in the same period of 1878.

'This fact suggests to me whether it would not be advisable for the Directors to take a similar course with regard to the Westinghouse Company and allow the fitting up of the Westinghouse brake to be under the supervision of someone whose experience would qualify them for the duty.'

This was blunt talking from a general manager to his directors, and the implied criticism of the carriage and wagon staff cannot have gone unnoticed. Apparently, since Clayton's report on Rapp's difficulties the previous November, the Pullman people had made good to the extent of showing up the Midland's own staff. Clayton too had something to say, this time to the carriage and wagon committee, on August 4 :

'Referring to the reports of the failure of the Westinghouse brake during the month of July.

'I ask your attention in particular to those failures which have caused the tyres to become heated so much as to burn the wood disk, because I am afraid that some accident may occur to a train.

'We have had several cases in which the vehicles have been detached from the trains with wheels burned more or less, we have here now No. 1 M.S.J.S. passenger brake van with one pair of wheels with the wood disk destroyed, No. 13 M.S.J.S. bogie carriage came in with all the wheels, I am afraid, badly burned.'

These two notes found their way to the board on August 6 and at the same time it was reported that the locomotive committee had agreed in principle to Allport's suggestion and had fixed up a meeting between the Westinghouse people and Johnson and Clayton to inspect the new Midland & Scotch Joint Stock carriages, which had been completed by June 17, 1879. It was made clear that the firm was only to be allowed to point out defects in the present servicing arrangements; the committee was absolutely opposed to it actually maintaining the brakes. The board agreed to the first proposal but reserved its opinion on the second.

Following the meeting with Westinghouse the locomotive committee felt able at the end of September 1879 to make a firm recommendation to the board as to the type of brake best suited for general adoption. It plumped for the non-automatic vacuum brake, and was satisfied that 'were this brake fitted on the carriages and worked in combination with the steam brake on the engine and tender, the driver would have a perfectly efficient brake with full controlling power over his train'. However, said the committee, since the board had already spoken its mind against the non-automatic brake the committee had only dealt with the automatic brakes. Of these it favoured the 'Sander's Improved Brake'. Its power to stop a train was fully equal to the Westinghouse; it had a simpler mechanism and was less likely to become inoperative by disuse or exposure to the weather; and it combined efficiency in working with simplicity in construction and was economical in first cost and maintenance. Having heard this fulsome eulogy the board resolved, while still not definitely committing itself to a final decision, to adopt the Sander's brake on any trains thereafter fitted with an automatic brake. And to show it was in earnest it started off by ordering that the 5.15 a.m. newspaper train from London be so supplied as soon as practicable.

Meanwhile, hot boxes were still causing trouble. For the month of September 1878 there had been 19 Pullmans and 11 ordinary carriages taken off the trains. September of 1879, however, saw the Pullmans apparently cured while the number of ordinary carriages offected by hot boxes had risen to 26, of which 12 had to be taken off. As to the rolling stock generally during 1879, as already noted, the new carriages ordered for the joint service in the early part of the year were completed by mid June. They were put into service with the letters 'M.S.J.S.'—Midland & Scotch Joint Stock—on their sides.

Reference has already been made as to the difficulty in distinguishing in the various minutes of the company between the Pullmans proper and the day coaches constructed specially for the Midland. It would appear from a minute of the carriage and wagon committee that the original eight day coaches constructed in 1874 had not proved successful, for on July 1, 1879 the committee noted that they were altered in 1877 with a view to making them 'more suitable for main line traffic'. The alterations had apparently not proved a success and the day coaches had been taken off again. The committee noted that before they could be used for either excursion or branch traffic the Pullman lamps had to be replaced by ordinary carriage roof lamps and fittings. At the same time—July 1879—the traffic department reported that there was not sufficient hand power on the brakes on the cars to enable them to be worked on branch trains without passenger brake vans being attached and it was agreed that increased brake power should be provided. It would seem that these references must have been to the cars actually owned by the Midland— the day cars—as on September 3, 1879 the board decided to approach the Pullman company to ask if it would sell all its cars and the rights to the Midland. For the time being nothing came of the idea. From the previous April 26 the car *Midland* had been loaned to the G.N.R. for test purposes on the East Coast route. The car returned to the Midland on July 10, 1879, having run 33,592 miles during its service with the G.N.R. The accountant worked it out that as the Pullman car was equal to two ordinary first class carriages the G.N.R. should be charged twice the ordinary Clearing House rate for its use, amounting to £209 19s. The *Midland* must have been a decided success on the G.N.R. as that company commenced running the Pullman dining car *Prince of Wales,* rebuilt as mentioned, between King's Cross and Leeds in November, 1879. In fact, however, the Pullmans were expensive vehicles to run and were not viewed with quite such enthusiasm by the Midland's allies. In the autumn of 1879 the North British wrote to the Midland :

Kippenross, Dunblane.
September 18, 1879.

Dear Sir,
      We have been looking into expenses and one point we all agree upon is too many carriages are run in the trains. It increases the cost of fuel, the wear and tear of the road, and particularly our carriage repairs. Our through passengers are very few in winter and I am asked to write to see if the Midland would drop the day Pullman from Edinboro' to Carlisle on the 1st of October for the winter months. We are carrying very few passengers in it and I do not believe we shall have two a day, even now we have not much more, I would not propose this if the East Coast run a day one but theirs is only at night.
      Please let me hear from you soon,
Yours truly,
J. Stirling.

It was agreed to discontinue the day Pullman from November 1, 1879 for the duration of the winter months.

1880 started with more hot boxes. Five cases of vehicles being taken off the trains were reported in the three months up to March. In June the board received a letter from the solicitors to R. D. Sanders calling attention to the increased number of failures recorded against his brake and attributing them to various mechanical additions made by the Midland to the brake without his permission. Sanders asked for all the impedimenta to be removed. This was followed shortly afterwards by a letter from Westinghouse claiming improvements to the firm's brake, and the board decided to let them fit the necessary additions to the brakes already in service. It was becoming more urgent as time went by to get the question of the brakes finally settled. In March Needham had alerted the carriage and wagon committee to a proposal to run several new expresses on and after June 1, entailing the provision of a hundred additional vehicles all to be fitted with the continuous brake. The trains in question were eight extra between London and Leeds and four between Leeds and Bristol. In September the locomotive committee suggested that Westinghouse should be given full facility to fit and test the improved brakes. When this was done, and the vehicles were operating properly, the firm was to certify each vehicle and was then to touch it no more without permission. This suggestion was agreed. Two accidents, at Blea Moor and Wennington—dealt with in the next chapter—further impressed the need for adequate braking. That at Blea Moor was caused by the uncoupling of the hose on the Westinghouse brake, and at Wennington the trouble was partly lack of braking. In November the board agreed that invalid and family carriages, horse boxes, carriage trucks, milk vans, fish trucks, and other vehicles run with passenger trains should be fitted with a communication tube so that they might be attached to trains fitted with either the air brake or the vacuum brake without disturbing the connection. This followed on as a direct result of the Wennington accident after which, on reading the report of the coroner's jury, it had been decided to fit the continuous automatic brake to the whole of the company's carriages and other vehicles which ran in passenger trains, and also to fit the engines with steam brakes.

In September 1880 the carriage and wagon committee took another look at the hot box problem. The summary to date was that in 1874 the number of cases had been 1,273, in 1875 it was 833, in 1876 there had been 466, and in 1879, 291. This was in the face of a 40 per cent. increase in passenger train mileage and increased weights and speeds. It appeared that the first axle of each of the bogies of the six-wheeled bogie stock tended to heat up the most due to the application of the continuous brake reaching those wheels slightly before the others. On January 4, 1881 Johnson and Clayton reported on the current position regarding brakes:

'We beg to report that during the half year ending 31st Dec., 1880, the following increase has taken place in fitting up the engines and carriages with continuous brakes:

Westinghouse	— engines	3 carriages
Sanders & Bolitho's	54 engines	701 carriages

and the following decrease has taken place:

Smith's	2 engines	— carriages
Barker's	— engines	3 carriages

'The following trains are now working with a continuous brake:

Kind of Brake	Train	From	To
Westinghouse	10.35	London	Carlisle
(Automatic)	9.15	,,	,,
	12.10	Carlisle	London
	1.10	,,	,,
Total	10.32	Leeds	Carlisle
11 trains	3.00	,,	,,
	8.40	Carlisle	Leeds
	5.36	,,	,,
	1.18	Carlisle	Skipton
	8.02	,,	,,
	11.28	Skipton	Carlisle'

From the report it appeared that there were 47 trains working on Sanders and Bolitho between London, Liverpool, Manchester, Nottingham, Bedford, Bradford, Bristol, Birmingham, Leeds, York, and Sheffield, plus six engines working the Bradford–Leeds omnibus trains daily—25 trips. There were 12 engines working with the Smith's brake (non-automatic) on the Metropolitan trains daily—about 125 trips with the brake. Finally, the Barker's brake was worked on the 7.45 a.m. Bedford to London train and on the 4.40 p.m. from London to Bedford, this being a non-automatic. The totals were 11 main line trains using the Westinghouse, as given above and concerning the Settle and Carlisle line; 47 on the main line (excluding the Settle line) using Sanders & Bolitho and 25 on the Leeds & Bradford using the same brake, making a total of 72 for the Sanders & Bolitho; 125 using the Smith's brake on the Metropolitan service; and two using the Barker's brake on the main line. The grand total was 210. This broke down as to stock :

Westinghouse	57 engines	155 carriages	56 through pipes
Sanders & Bolitho's	122 ,,	940 ,,	325 ,,
Smith's	20 ,,	115 ,,	—
Barker's	2 ,,	20 ,,	—

In August, 1881 it was agreed to put two new Pullman sleeping carriages into traffic and to convert two of the parlour cars to diners, the work to be done at the cost of the Pullman company. Clayton was asked to value the Pullman parlour cars then running on the company's lines. On the original cost of £1,640 each for 14 cars the total was £22,960. As the cars had been in traffic for about five years he estimated their present value to be £1,301, totalling £18,214. With this figure in mind John Noble was requested to resume his negotiations with Pullman on the question of purchase. The fourteen cars valued by Clayton were *Alexandra, Jupiter, Saturn, Venus, Mercury, Juno, Vesta, Minerva, Planet, Albion, Comet, Apollo, Aurosa,* and *Eclipse.* He prefaced his remarks by saying that he thought the Midland could build its own cars exactly similar to the Pullmans for £1,640 each. In the autumn of 1881 Rapp left for America. His place at Derby was taken by his assistant Joseph Monck who had come over from America some time ago to help set up the Pullman plant. The parlour cars converted to diners—noted in the minutes by Monck as 'hotel cars'—were *Britannia* and *Leo.* They went into traffic in 1882 renamed *Windsor* and *Delmonico* respectively.

On August 8, 1881 there had been an accident at Blackburn on the L.Y.R. When the Board of Trade report—dealt with in the next chapter —reached the Midland board the following February it was decided to join with the G.S.W.R. and N.B.R. in an effort to improve the Scotch joint stock braking power as well as any other carriages of the two companies which might have occasion to use the Midland main line. In effect an attempt was to be made to jettison the Westinghouse system. A communication was sent to the two companies which drew a reply from the North British a fortnight later that it had never had any trouble with the Westinghouse brake and did not want to change. If the Midland wanted to fit an additional brake on to the Scotch joint stock it was welcome to do so but at its own cost. From the G.S.W.R., however, there was a better response; that company agreed to fit the automatic vacuum in addition to the Westinghouse. To assist in this operation, and for the better working of the G.S.W.R. stock, the Glasgow company suggested that 25 six-wheeled composite carriages and 10 brake vans should be fitted with both brakes as an additional new stock to that existing. It would also fit the alternative piping, so that either system could apply, on various vans if the Midland did the same. It was immediately agreed that Clayton should fit the automatic vacuum brake to all the joint stock but as to the G.S.W.R.'s proposal for new vehicles, it was decided that there must be complete agreement between all three companies. On April 13 Noble reported that the stock required for the through trains as marshalled for the coming summer service was : eight 54-ft. bogie composites, 16 40-ft. bogie composites, 43 ordinary composites, eight five-compartment thirds, and 30 vans. The present Midland & Scotch joint stock consisted of 10 54-ft. bogie composites, 20 40-ft. bogie composites and 10 vans. It was agreed to recommend an addition to the joint stock of 25 composite carriages, 10 five-compartment thirds, and 10 passenger brakes, at an estimated total cost of £17,000, exclusive of continuous brakes. By mid October, 1882, after some show of reluctance, the N.B.R. agreed to construct the 25 composites, the 10 thirds to be built by the G.S.W.R., and the passenger brakes by the Ashbury Carriage Company at a cost of £299 each.

In May, 1882, the agreement with the Pullman company was renewed as to the two sheds at Derby. On the question of selling any of the cars to the Midland, however, the Pullman company refused to part with any of the day or night cars or to reduce its charges. It did agree to relieve the Midland of one of the parlour cars immediately, however, an agreement having been made with the London Chatham & Dover Railway to run it on their line. This car, the *Jupiter*, left that month. The previous winter had also seen the departure of the parlour cars *Ceres*, *Ariel*, and *Adonis* to the London Brighton & South Coast Railway. In order to make the remaining parlour cars more attractive the Pullman company declared itself willing to introduce buffets for light refreshments. Thompson, the Midland's chairman, reported that he had pointed out to Mr Pullman the unfairness of the arrangement whereby the Great Northern was permitted to operate Pullman sleeping cars between London and Scotland without being put under the same restrictions as the Midland with regard to the running of other sleeping cars on the line. Pullman had suggested as a solution to the difficulty that he should be allowed to furnish to the Midland 'a somewhat inferior description of sleeping car, for the use of which the same fares might be charged as are charged by the Great Northern and London & North Western companies'. Four such cars were apparently under construction at Derby. By this the Midland refused to be drawn. As to the position regarding sleeping cars, Monck reported to the carriage and wagon committee in April, 1883 that during the previous quarter the cars *Australia* and *Castalia* had been sent to Italy. They were replaced by the two new Pullman sleeping cars on February 1, 1883, *St Andrew* and *St Mungo*. These were followed by two more similar vehicles during the following quarter, *St Louis* and *St Denis*. By October, 1883 Pullman had turned out two more sleeping cars, *Missouri* and *Michigan*, which were at that time still in the sheds at Derby. During this period Pullman also built at Derby, for the G.N.R., sleeping cars *Culross* and *Balmoral*; they were sent into traffic on January 2, 1883. Also in October one sleeping car, the *Enterprise*, was destroyed by fire at Hunslet in tragic circumstances—an event dealt with in the next chapter. Several of the Pullmans which left Derby for work on other lines ended their days in a more or less violent fashion. First was the *Prince of Wales*, mentioned earlier, damaged by fire at Leeds in the year before the *Enterprise* affair. In 1884 yet another fire destroyed the *Castalia* while working on the state-owned South Italian Railway. The *Jupiter* was in the Norwood Junction accident in May 1891 and in November of the following year the car *India* was severely damaged in a bad smash on the North Eastern at Thirsk. It had to be broken up later. Another 'fatality' was the *Ceres* which, renamed *Maud*, was badly knocked about in the Wivelsfield collision of 1899.

In September 1882 the Midland board decided to fit the automatic vacuum brake to 352 horse boxes and 316 carriage trucks—the only vehicles so far not fitted which ran in passenger trains. Vehicles of every description running in the joint services connecting with the G.S.W.R. and N.B.R. at Carlisle were also to be supplied with the Westinghouse brake, though for all intents and purposes the Midland was now a fully automatic vacuum line.

The Pullman parlour cars running on the Midland system—the board minutes give the number as 15—were purchased by the Midland in the autumn of 1883 at a price of £1,600 each. One of the cars was sold three years later to Cooks Tours for £700.

During 1884 there were some alterations to the original eight Midland day cars. No. 1, an eight-wheeled brake third, was remodelled as a diner by July 1884 and named *London*. Nos. 2 to 4, similar in origin to No. 1, were withdrawn from service. No. 5, an eight-wheeled 1st/2nd composite parlour car, was retained but renumbered as 19, eventually being withdrawn a few years prior to the turn of the century. Nos. 6 and 7, of the same type as No. 5, were rebuilt as twelve-wheeled dining cars and renumbered as 18 and 17 respectively. Lastly, No. 8, similar again to No. 5, was rebuilt as a twelve-wheeled dining car in July, 1884 but was not renumbered—as No. 16—until the autumn; it was eventually withdrawn, with Nos. 17 and 18, in 1900. All of the original day cars had clerestory roofs and measured 58 ft. by 8 ft. 7 ins. By October

1884, *Windsor*, one of the original parlour cars—now a diner—had been deprived of its name and was numbered 15. All these alterations had left vacant numbers from 1 to 14 and it is presumed from the following letter from Noble to Clayton, dated March 10, 1888, that they were allotted to the fourteen sleeping cars taken over by the Midland that month :

'We have purchased the 14 Pullman Sleeping Cars now running on the Midland line and as we are under an obligation to take off the "Pullman" names, I shall be glad if you will do so, and substitute the word "Midland" for it (*sic*), also renumbering the cars and removing the names "St Mungo", etc., by which they are at present known.'

The sleeping cars cost the Midland £20,000. On May 4, 1888 Clayton reported that Monck had accepted the job of foreman in charge of the Pullmans—the cars to be henceforth designated as being of parlour and sleeping varieties. (With the last American influence gone, the 'u' in 'Parlour' had crept back into the minute books.) Incidentally, as to dining cars, the Revenue Act of 1884 made it lawful to sell tobacco on trains and on September 19 of that year the Midland board approved a suggestion from the traffic committee that licences at 5*s* 3*d* per annum for each dining carriage be applied for. (Tobacco kiosks and refreshment barrows did not appear on Midland stations until early 1905.)

Up to this time the G.S.W.R. coaching stock, as distinct from the M.S.J.S. vehicles, had been dark green in colour. As G.S.W.R. coaches frequently ran through in the Scotch trains over the Midland lines, Wainwright of the G.S.W.R. wrote to Noble in August of 1884 to ask if the Midland would have any objection to the Glasgow company's coaches being painted the same colour as those on the Midland. The latter was only too pleased to agree and the G.S.W.R. board formally assented to the adoption of the new livery at a meeting on September 16. Within the next few months, as the G.S.W.R. coaches went through the shops, the varied colour of the Scotch trains was diminished somewhat. It was something after Allport's heart. Another event which must have interested him occurred at the Midland half-yearly meeting of 1888. The *Railway News* reported that 'As usual there was a little wordy war on the question of classes. Mr Frost thought that, as 92 or 93 per cent. of the passengers were carried in the third class carriages, the time had come for the institution of one class only.' This was out-Allporting Allport, and must have caused some smiles. The idea was argued backwards and forwards, and though no decision was reached it appeared that quite a few of the shareholders were of similar mind to Mr Frost.

Early in 1880 it was decided to convert 18 of the 40 ft. composites and two of the six-wheeled composites of the M.S.J.S. so as to afford lavatory accommodation in each—something not hitherto available except in the Pullmans. At the same time it was proposed to alter the mode of lighting in the joint stock working the Liverpool and Manchester to Carlisle service from petroleum to oil gas. By the end of 1890 it was agreed to provide more lavatory accommodation, this time in the night Scotch expresses, and 22 Midland and 12 M.S.J.S. vehicles were altered accordingly. There must have been an abundance of private patience displayed by Victorian passengers who had supped too well at Normanton or Leeds in the early days, while the train made the haul over the 'Long Drag.' One can imagine the bated breath with which successive stations were viewed as trains neared Carlisle, and the concerted rush on to the platform as soon as they arrived. The new accommodation was to alleviate what had for years been an unfortunate contingency to be dreaded on a long journey.

Another question of comfort was under discussion in late 1890; that of train heating. Again, the Pullmans were the only vehicles which could boast adequate warmth in winter, the other stock making do with foot warmers. As much as possible had been done to ensure that these articles—'feet warmers' as they were then called—functioned properly, as is shown in the following circular to station masters issued by Needham as far back as March 3, 1875 :

'I beg to call your particular attention to the supply of Feet Warmers to Passenger Carriages, which is not at present being satisfactorily carried out.
'Complaints are made by Passengers of the difficulty of obtaining Feet Warmers, and defective and leaky Feet Warmers are frequently placed in the Carriages, causing the mats to be saturated with water, and making the Carriages very uncomfortable, besides damaging the mats.
'I have therefore to request that you will give this matter your personal attention, and take care that the service is in future properly performed.
'Feet Warmers must be placed in all Carriages whether asked for or not. The greatest care must be taken that no damaged or leaky Feet Warmers are used, but only those which are perfectly sound, and also that the outsides of the Feet Warmers are dry before being placed in the Carriages.
'All defective Feet Warmers must be immediately forwarded for repairs, to Mr Johnson, Locomotive Department, Derby, each Warmer being labelled with the name of your Station to ensure its being returned.'

This conjures up a delightful picture. Having considered the alternatives to 'feet warmers', by then presumably lying about in all sorts of odd corners at the locomotive works, Johnson and Clayton reported on December 17, 1890 that the system of heating by hot water appeared to be the most practical and effective, and it was recommended that one train of ten carriages should be fitted up with the necessary piping at a cost of £60, for experimental purposes. Some of the earliest vehicles using the new system of heating were two dining cars built for the Scotch service and put into traffic in 1893, as described in chapter XVI. The decision to construct the cars for the mid-day service was made at a meeting of the Midland and G.S.W.R. joint committee held on January 5, 1893 and in the following April it was noted that they would cost £7,835. With the onset of autumn, it was decided in September that £116 should be expended in fitting 13 M.S.J.S. vehicles with hot water heating apparatus in order that the new dining car trains might be heated throughout. Each of the Midland dining sets consisted of a first class car seating 12 and 9 passengers in two compartments, with kitchen, pantry, and lavatories, and a third class car seating 30 and 9 in two compartments, with luggage, pantry, and lavatory accommodation. The small compartment for nine passengers in each car was for smoking, and the larger for dining. The length of each vehicle was 63 feet 2 inches over the buffers, and each body, which weighed 33 tons, was carried on two six-wheeled bogies. The cars were lit by compressed oil gas.

A carriage and wagon committee minute dated December 4, 1891, is of interest as it throws a sidelight on passenger train livery : 'Mr Clayton drew the attention of the committee to the uselessness of lining the parcels vans, carriage trucks, and many other vehicles that work on passenger trains, with gold leaf, inasmuch as such vehicles are not washed, and the dirty condition completely hides the gold lining, and he proposed to only use gold leaf lining on the passenger carriages and guards vans'. The proposal was agreed.

In January 1894 it was reported that the traffic committee had withdrawn the Pullman parlour cars from service and had placed them in Spondon carriage sheds. There were, by then, only 13 of these vehicles, all averaging 18 years of age, and they had done fine service. Apparently their internal condition was still good as Clayton, who obviously had a liking for them, reminded the carriage and wagon committee that the cabinet work should not be allowed to get damp.

The following month the joint committee authorised the construction of three more dining cars to be run in the forthcoming summer services on the day expresses between London and Glasgow, and in April it was agreed to make various alterations to the existing dining stock to give greater comfort to passengers in the afternoon Scotch expresses. In the same month, 'following public demand', the committee gave orders that the middle compartments in each of the ten third class five-compartmented M.S.J.S. coaches should be converted into two lavatories. On December 14 the committee discussed the need for increased first class dining accommodation on the morning expresses from St Pancras to Glasgow. Three of the existing M.S.J.S. bogie composites were to be provided with gangways to connect with the first and third class coaches, and were to be altered internally to provide facilities for dining twelve passengers.

Mention of the heating for dining cars has already been made; as to the three new cars ordered in February 1894 it would appear that there was some trouble on this score for it was reported to the Midland's hotels and refreshment rooms committee on August 8, 1895 that 'great complaints were made last winter of the extreme cold in these cars'. The traffic committee was asked to remedy the situation in time for the next winter.

The method of lighting the joint stock came up for discussion in February 1895, and an expenditure of £790 was authorised for fitting 28

M.S.J.S. vehicles with appliances for burning oil gas. It was mentioned that when this work had been carried out, the whole of the joint stock vehicles would then have been fitted up for using this illuminant.

A year later Clayton was becoming increasingly concerned at the age of the carriage stock operating on the Midland system and he suggested that there should be a large scale rebuilding programme. He called for new ideas in carriage design. Too many old carriages were running on important trains; 82 first class vehicles were over 20 years old and few new carriages had been constructed during the past ten years. He mentioned that there were at that time (1896), 627 lavatory compartments in Midland trains. In October of 1896 he reported on some new stock :

'The three new trains of carriages consisting of a composite-first class dining carriage 60 feet long; a third class dining carriage 60 feet long, with a kitchen, pantry, and luggage compartment in a separate vehicle 31 feet long; one first class bogie carriage 60 feet long with lavatories; one bogie compo brake carriage 60 feet long with lavatories, and one passenger luggage van 31 feet long; that is, five carriages in each train, which have been arranged and approved by the joint committees and ordered to be got ready for next summer's traffic, have been put in hand.'

Early in 1898 the joint committee discussed the need for replacing the original M.S.J.S. vehicles which were nearly life expired, and on the following June 21 the general managers of the Midland and G.S.W.R. reported as follows :

'The existing passenger rolling stock working on the Midland, Glasgow & South Western, and North British services comprises the following:—
(a) 40 ordinary carriages and vans built in 1879
(b) 45 ordinary carriages and vans built in 1883, three of which were converted into dining bogie composite carriages in 1894.

  ——
  85

'NOTE.—In addition to these 85 vehicles the Midland and Glasgow & South Western companies have the following dining carriages :—
     5 dining carriages built in 1893
     3 dining carriages built in 1894.

  ——
  8
  ——

'The Midland Company's Carriage and Wagon Superintendent reports that the 40 vehicles (a) will require renewal within the next three or four years; and the 45 (b) in seven or eight years' time.

'The Passenger Superintendents of the three companies concerned consider that 175 new vehicles, including six composite diners, should be constructed, but that instead of one joint stock as now, separate sets of coaches should be provided for the Midland and South Western, and Midland and North British services respectively, as under :—
    Midland and South Western — 104 carriages and vans, including three bogie dining cars.
    Midland and North British — 71 carriages and vans including three composite dining cars.

'We propose that the new coaches be built on the bogie corridor principle, with clerestory roofs, and be fully equipped with lavatories.

'The method of heating and lighting the carriages to be considered later on.

'The stock running over the Glasgow & South Western line to be fitted with the Automatic Vacuum Brake.

'The renewal to be proceeded with gradually, the coaches in certain agreed trains being first replaced with new vehicles.

'The old stock as it is put out of service to be taken over in equal third proportions by the Midland, Glasgow & South Western, and North British companies.'

The report ended, after some discussion of the financial details between the three companies as to proportional costs, with a list of the suggested new stock for the M. & G.S.W. and an estimate of the cost :

Number of Vehicles	Description	Estimated Cost Per Vehicle £	Total £
45	50 ft. bogie composite carriage	1,572	70,740
12	50 ft. bogie composite brake	1,548	18,576
12	50 ft. bogie third class	1,255	15,060
10	50 ft. bogie brake van	862	8,620
22	31 ft. bogie brake van	431	9,482
3	50 ft. bogie dining carriage	1,980	5,940
104			128,418

The recommendations were approved and it was agreed to put them into effect as soon as possible. After various discussions, the following was agreed on December 9, 1898 :

'All new carriages to be made by the Midland Railway Company. The first to be made to be those required for working the expresses leaving Glasgow and St Pancras at 1.30 and 2.10 p.m. respectively, viz :—
   6 guard's vans, each on three pairs of wheels.
   3 lavatory bogie thirds.
   3 lavatory bogie composites.
'Carriages to be arranged so that all first class compartments shall be together at end of train nearest first class diner, and third class similarly.
'Dimensions should be as under :—

Outside measurements :	ft.	in.
Height from rail to top of lamp cover	13	4
,, ,, clerestory	13	1
Height at side	10	8
Width of body (dispensing with observatories)	8	6
Width over step boards	9	0
Length of carriages	50	0
(Each carriage to be on two four-wheeled bogie trucks)		

Inside measurements :		
Back to back. First class	7	9
,, Third class	6	6
Width of corridors	2	1
Width of seats, with 2 in. slope	1	8
Width of seats at front	1	6
Distance between seat rails	2	3

'That the interior fittings of the carriages be as follows :—
   First class to be trimmed with blue cloth.
   The arm rests to be made broader, and to turn up higher, than those in
      the existing coaches.
   The cushions to be covered with cloth on one side and leather on the
      other, and to be reversible.
   The head rests to be circular shape.

The sides of the carriages to be padded from the top of the arm rests to
the bottom of the window. The woodwork above the upholstery and the
parcel rack to be of sycamore, and the roof to have lincruster or millboard
panels, with polished walnut mouldings, the panels to be painted white
and decorated with gold lines.
Oil gas to be used for present as illuminant.
Heating to be by hot water apparatus.
Pneumatic system of communication between passengers and officers in
charge of train (as is in use on the G.C. line) to be adopted.
The existing dining cars, which will run with the new stock, to be fitted
with gangways so as to afford communication with rest of train.'

Meanwhile, bearing in mind the current uncertainty *vis-a-vis* the
M.S.J.S. set-up, two composite diners and six bogie composite thirds
were ordered in February 1898 for the London–Edinburgh service; as
will be seen they became part of the new M. & N.B. stock. In January
1899 the general manager reported to the traffic committee that the
N.B.R. had assented to the provision of a separate M. & N.B. coaching
stock, consisting of 68 carriages and vans, and three composite dining
cars. The Midland was to construct all the vehicles, the character and
dimensions of the coaches to be similar to those already ordered for the
M. & G.S.W. trains. The estimated cost of the 71 M. & N.B. vehicles
would be £95,720, of which the Midland would bear two-thirds. It was
agreed that the trains first to be marshalled with the new stock should be
the 10.35 a.m. from St Pancras and the 10.5 from Edinburgh, for which
the undermentioned vehicles were required :

Number of Vehicles	Description	Estimated Cost £
15	50 ft. bogie composites (lavatory)	23,940
3	50 ft. bogie composite brakes (lavatory)	4,716
3	50 ft. bogie thirds (lavatory)	3,837
3	bogie vans	2,676
3	ordinary vans on six wheels	1,386
3	composite dining cars	5,940

(Note: Two of the Pullman cars, the reconstruction of which had already been
ordered, were to be appropriated as two of the three dining vehicles.)

In February 1899 four Pullman sleeping cars were ordered. As in the
case of previous Pullmans, they were to be constructed at Derby. The
Midland was to provide the bogie trucks, drawgear, buffing gear, and
connections. A month later the carriage and wagon committee told
Clayton to fit all first class carriages with blue cloth seats and reversible
cushions. In the following December the Midland and G.S.W. joint
committee decided that the Midland should construct 25 milk and
parcels vans for the committee's trains, and on the same day it was
agreed that the passenger vehicles then under construction for the
morning expresses to and from Glasgow, by then numbering 30, should
be illuminated with Stone's electric light system. On the following February 23 this latter decision was rescinded, the carriages to be 'oil gas' lit
as previously arranged. This adherence to a potentially dangerous form
of lighting was to have disastrous consequences later. By February 22,

1901, the number of vans under construction for the M. & G.S.W. service had risen to 32, and orders were given for them to be fitted with a through electrical communication wire.

On Thursday, January 9, 1900, the chairman and two members of the carriage and wagon committee, accompanied by Clayton, walked round to the shops at Derby to examine two vehicles. These were a M. & N.B. corridor bogie composite, No. 108, 50 ft. long on eight wheels, with one luggage, two first class and three third class compartments, and separate first class and third class lavatories; and a Midland 'lavatory bogie composite', No. 3145, 48 ft. long, on eight wheels, and containing similar accommodation. Standing shiny with new paint, the two vehicles were submitted by Clayton as patterns for comment, so that a decision might be reached as to future design and on various points which had cropped up over the years. The following discussion ranged over many aspects, and some of the more interesting points included the agreement to use 'Smoking' labels in lieu of frosting the glass of smoking compartments—it was evidently something one had done in private until then; metal wash basins were to be fitted in future in the lavatory compartments, and catches were to be provided to prevent W.C. seats from falling—a practice the reinstatement of which would find favour today. The lamps in the first and third compartments in the Scotch joint stock, and in all Midland main line carriages including saloons, were to be fitted with coverings. Of further note was that the carriages had six doors, as indicated on the sketch; it was decided that in future they were to be provided with three doors less, on the corridor side. A month later, as an afterthought, it was agreed that the dividing door between the first and third class compartments should be labelled 'To First Class' and 'To Third Class' respectively.

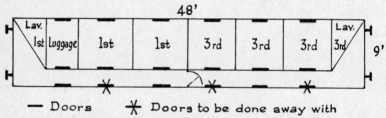

— Doors   ✳ Doors to be done away with

The new Scotch stock was speedily constructed. On July 6, 1900 Clayton reported that the 57 carriages forming the following trains had been sent into traffic and had commenced running on July 1, the first day of the summer timetable, on the following trains :

10.30 a.m.	St Pancras to Glasgow
10.00 a.m.	Glasgow to St Pancras
9.15 p.m.	St Pancras to Edinburgh
10.00 p.m.	Edinburgh to St Pancras

The old livery for the joint vehicles had undergone a slight change; in place of the original 'M.S.J.S.' along the carriage sides, there now appeared the initials 'M. & G.S.W.' and 'M. & N.B.'. The division of the joint stock thus into two separate lots had much to recommend it. The N.B.R. was still obstinately a Westinghouse line, while the G.S.W.R., of course, had long since come over to the Midland's idea of the automatic vacuum. Besides this, the N.B.R. had always been parsimonious about the joint stock. It had only come into the 1879 arrangement because it objected to the hire charge of Midland carriages.

Meanwhile, the new Pullman sleeping cars had been delivered. On May 5, 1900 the *Railway News* reported :—

'The Midland Railway company announce that, commencing May 1, new and luxurious sleeping carriages will be run on the night expresses between London (St Pancras) and Glasgow, and Edinburgh. The carriages, which have been constructed by the Pullman Company in America, and put together by their representatives at Derby, comprise all the latest improvements, and are of the best design. In length the new vehicles measure 60 feet, supported upon two six-wheeled bogies of the most improved type for ensuring smooth, easy, and quiet travelling. Gas lamps will be used for illumination. Automatic vacuum and high pressure brakes are attached. Smoking saloon, lavatory compartments, also a buffet for light refreshments, such as tea and coffee, form part of the accommodation. The interior of the cars presents an arched appearance, with green and gold decorations, folder curtains, and plush drapery. The internal decorations include mahogany carvings and inlaid work, all being produced so as to present neatness of effect. The carriages are fitted with bevelled mirrors, and electric bells are provided in each berth, giving communication with the conductor. Provision is also made for private compartments capable of holding one or two persons. The carriages are warmed by self-contained heating apparatus. Accommodation is provided for eleven sleepers, there being no top berths as in the old cars, thus securing a larger measure of air space for each occupant; in fact, everything possible seems to have been done to ensure the comfort of travellers. The carriages are painted in the Midland style, and the contour has been kept in accord with the Midland stock, so that the artistic uniformity of the train should not be interfered with. Covered entrances are provided at each end, an improvement upon the old style of open entrance. . . .'

The question of the actual accommodation needs slight clarification. Each vehicle had what were termed as three 'staterooms' each taking one passenger, and one which took two, which together occupied half the length of the car. The other half was a day saloon with three Pullman sections which could easily be converted to night travel. The extract also gives the impression that the cars were more like the standard Midland stock than the Pullmans of the past but this was not so; their appearance above the belt, so to speak, was much like the old Pullmans, but with the refinements of closed ends.

Two months later, on July 7, the *Railway News* found more copy in another development concerning the Midland and G.S.W.R. service, when it came out with an article concerning a new corridor train for the Glasgow–London run. The accommodation was a compromise between the large general car and the old compartment stock, but the *News* was pleased to note that the compartments still retained their privacy—something peculiarly prized by the Victorians, and to a lesser extent in the present day. The article continued :

'It is not a dining train in the sense in which that term has hitherto been understood, but a train with dining facilities throughout. The service car, with electrical connections to each compartment, occupies a central position, and meals may be served in any part of the train. For this purpose each compartment is equipped so as to admit of a table being placed between the seats and removed when not required. In this way all the passengers may be served simultaneously, an arrangement which entirely obviates the inconvenient delays which not infrequently occur under the special car system. Apart from the very welcome improvement which will thus be effected in the comfort of the passengers, the train possesses several features of novelty which are of general interest. The vehicles, which are of great weight, are 50 ft. in length, and are mounted on bogie carriages ensuring smoothness and the minimum of oscillation in running. Internally, the arrangements and appointments, which are remarkably complete, include the most approved appliances for heating, lighting, and ventilating; and all the compartments are upholstered and decorated in excellent taste. In the first-class carriages the woodwork is in walnut, the doorways being of a massive ornamental design, while the upper walls and the clerestory roof are panelled in cream-coloured materials, enriched with tracings in gold. An equally decorative and ornate, though less elaborate scheme, is adopted in the third-class carriages. The communication cord is inside the carriage, and is arranged to act upon the brake, so that in the event of being used the train is speedily brought to a stand, a disc indicating the carriage from which the signal has been made. An experimental trip of the new train has just been made from Dumfries to Glasgow ... The train will leave St Enoch station at 10 o'clock on Monday morning, and a corresponding train from London to Glasgow will also be run for the first time on the same day.'

New destination boards for Midland trains were agreed upon in June 1901, to consist of a white background with black lettering. Later in the year it was noted that there had been complaints about the bad running of the six six-wheeled family carriages, and though they were not due for renewal until 1905 it was agreed to replace them immediately with new vehicles. The old family carriages were converted to first class excursion stock.

During 1902 meetings had been held with other companies to try and decide upon a uniform type of vestibule communication to assist the marshalling and coupling of foreign vehicles on through runs. The L.N.W.R., with its many corridor vehicles, had refused to entertain any alteration and a short time later the Great Western decided to change to the L.N.W.R. pattern. In September 1902 the Midland agreed to do likewise. Three months later the Midland and G.S.W. joint committee noted that there was a deficiency during the summer season of third class accommodation on the through Scotch corridor trains, and that carriages of the parent companies had had to be used. At the same time there was a surplus of composites. It was agreed to provide fifteen additional third class 54 ft. bogie corridor carriages, each containing seven compartments 6 ft. 5 ins. wide, with a lavatory at each end. The Midland was to take over ten of the existing composites at valuation from the joint committee. In fact, these ten vehicles were retained in the joint stock until the new carriages became available, and were not taken over by the Midland until January 1906.

During 1903 there were several occurrences of note concerning the rolling stock. In February the committee's 104 coaches were ordered to be fitted with by-pass rods, which could be worked from either side of the carriage, for regulating the consumption of gas. At the same time alterations were to be made in two of the dining cars, Nos. 1 and 2, so that passengers could pass through the corridors between the saloons and the other portions of the trains, without having to go through the kitchens as was then necessary. A lurch at Shipley, and one was literally in the soup. The scheme was approved by the committee provided that the alterations did not conflict with the existing lavatory accommodation. There had also been complaints of insufficient lights in the cars, and it was decided to change to electricity. Another reason noted in the minutes was that 'the heat from gas lighting is very undesirable in dining cars'. In June the committee considered more complaints about the lack of ordinary first class accommodation in the 1.30 p.m. up and down expresses. There were in fact only two ordinary first class compartments available, apart from those in the dining cars, on the two trains. A plan was submitted of a proposed carriage containing three firsts and a brake compartment, and also of a vehicle with three thirds and a brake compartment required to compensate for the third class seats in the present composites which it was decided to withdraw from the two trains. The idea was approved and instructions given to make three of each and add them to the joint stock. On December 11 more vehicles were ordered, three first class cars with kitchens, and two third class without kitchens. They were to replace Midland vehicles running in the through service, and would also afford passengers taking meals the convenience of a car on the morning expresses in place of the existing corridor carriages. Finally, on the same day, the committee ordered 1,200 antimacassars for the first class compartments in through trains between London and Glasgow. In May 1902 the board ordered that there should be a trial of a steam heating apparatus on one train on one journey each way between London and Manchester. With footwarmers still very much in use—1,500 new ones had been ordered in 1900 and 7,515 new acetate of soda type a year later—it was becoming essential to better the heating arrangements. In 1903 talks were held with other companies to agree on a standardised carriage heating system and on June 19 of that year the Midland board ordered that steam heating apparatus should generally be applied to all stock, Lord Belper, a member of the board, pointing out that no system was satisfactory which did not permit of its being regulated by the passenger in the compartment. Following its success on the Midland, it was decided in February 1904 that the joint stock should also be heated by this method, and 66 carriages and 28 vans already supplied with piping for the old hot water system were converted, together with 14 carriages and four vans not fitted with any means of heating.

There was also a crying need for yet more joint stock. Once again not enough had been available and the ordinary non corridor coaches of the parent companies had had to be employed, incidentally destroying the unity of the through corridor and putting the Midland's Scotch service in a bad light compared with the East and West Coast routes which had almost a surfeit of corridor stock. To equip adequately the through Scotch service 22 additional coaches were required but, with the financial position of the times being awkward, it was decided to scrape along on a mere dozen. By April it was agreed that these should consist of two bogie brake composites, four bogie thirds, and six bogie brake thirds, at an estimated cost of £15,568. By December the committee, with the summer rush behind it, decided to go the whole hog and order the other 10, to consist of eight corridor bogie composites, and two corridor bogie thirds, at an additional £14,034.

A note here about the Morecambe–Heysham rail motors which had just been introduced. Their total length was 60 ft., their width 9 ft., and they were divided into four compartments—a vestibule for the guard, and for the driver when driven from that end, a saloon to seat 56 passengers, a luggage compartment, and the engine room. The saloon was finished in birch and oak and the seats were of performated syca-more. The boiler of the engine was of the multitubular vertical type with a steam pressure of 160 lbs and there were two 11 in. cylinders, having a 15 in. stroke. The rail motor ran at an average speed of 30 m.p.h.

Getting back to the joint stock, the renewals for the North British service were discussed in July 1905. The N.B.R. agreed to the construc-tion of two more dining cars for the M. & N.B. stock, and to the provision of 39 new vehicles, the expenditure to be spread over two years, and the dining cars to replace two Midland cars on the service.

Number of Vehicles	Description	Estimated Cost £
15	Bogie composites	21,750
6	Bogie brake composites	8,802
6	Bogie thirds	7,752
12	Bogie brake thirds	15,324

The new dining and sleeping cars introduced into the Scotch service in July 1905, as mentioned in Chapter XVII, were described by the *Railway News* on June 24 :

'The new sleeping cars are 65 ft. long and 9 ft. wide. This exceptional width admits of spring mattress beds 6 ft. 2 ins. long being arranged trans-versely with a corridor the full length of the vehicle for access to lavatories and other portions of the train. Particular care has been taken to ensure smooth running by reducing to a minimum all vibration and the tendency to roll while at high speed. The flooring is a double one, and has been specially arranged with a view to deaden sound, the upper floor being covered with Axminster pile carpet. All the interior doors have been made to slide, so as not to block the corridor, and to obviate the possibility of disturbance through banging. Efficient roof ventilation is provided, and the cars are built with a clerestory roof, which makes the compartments lofty and airy. In winter the cars are heated with steam pipes, which can be regulated by the passengers in the compartments to suit their convenience. Passengers by the Midland Company's night trains will therefore have everything in their favour for ensuring a good night's rest. The first class dining car consists of one dining and one smoking saloon to dine eighteen passengers, and another compartment to dine six passengers, both finished in walnut suitably relieved with sycamore and gold, and upholstered in blue cloth. A portion of this car is set aside for service, and comprises a spacious kitchen fitted with a large and specially designed range, two pantries, linen cupboard and lavatory, with ice chamber for keeping food sweet and wines cool. The third class car will dine forty-eight passengers, being divided into three compartments, two accommodating eighteen each and the third twelve. The whole design and arrangement of both dining and sleeping cars is adapted to give the maximum amount of convenience and comfort during long journeys.'

By this time, of course, Clayton had left the Midland, and the new coaches, and others built since 1902, were designed by the new carriage and wagon superintendent, David Bain. They had what Hamilton Ellis has described as 'clipper or tumblehome' contours and had recessed vestibule doors. The sleeping cars were actually built for the Midland and all six of them, then operating on the London–Edinburgh run, were turned over to the M. & N.B. stock by a traffic committee minute of June 1905. As to the ordinary joint stock, incidentally, a serious accident at Cudworth on the North Midland line in January 1905 destroyed five of the joint vehicles. According to a Midland and G.S.W.R. joint committee minute of February 26, 1906, they were replaced by five other suitable vehicles of an improved design. In December 1906 it was agreed that the three joint stock third class diners built in 1894 were unsuitable for modern requirements. The kitchens were inadequate and the absence of side corridors meant that passengers still had to pass through the kitchens to get to other parts of the trains. It was agreed that the vehicles should be replaced by three new third class diners, with kitchens, fitted with steam heating apparatus, and lit by electricity. They were to be constructed by the Midland and, on their going into service, the Midland was to take over two of the old diners, and the G.S.W.R., one. The vehicles were in traffic by October 1909. Still with an eye to perfecting the heating arrangments it was ordered in June of 1908 that 13 joint stock milk and parcels vans be supplied with the apparatus. This was necessary because owing to the vagaries of marshalling it sometimes occurred that the vans divided one portion of the passenger accommodation on long distance trains from another, with the consequence that passengers emerged either baked in their jackets or blue with cold.

There were two small developments regarding carriage livery in 1906; in July it was decided that the company's coat of arms should no longer adorn its carriages, and in the following month it was resolved that the figures '1' and '3' should be painted on the outside and inside of coach doors of Midland carriages in place of 'First' and 'Third'. Also in 1906 heating was again discussed and in October the decision was taken to fit steam heating apparatus to the 59 engines and 200 carriages and vans working on the Leeds and Bradford district local trains.

In view of the later terrible disasters at Hawes Junction and Ais Gill it is of interest to note a minute of the traffic committee dated March 14, 1907 :

'Resolved that the undermentioned Midland and North British Joint Stock carriages which form part of the additional stock (already) sanctioned—and which are in course of construction be fitted with electric light instead of gas at an additional estimated cost of £1,813 :—

    8 bogie corridor compos
    3   „   „   compo brakes
    2   „   „   third brakes
    6   „   „   thirds. . . .'

Following the Hawes Junction crash of 1910—described in the next chapter—in which four of the M. & G.S.W. vehicles were destroyed by fire, it was agreed in 1912 that tools, rescue equipment and fire extinguishers should be provided in long distance trains, both on the Midland proper and on the joint services. The tools were supplied to the brake vans and brake compartments. Their advent was immediately prior to the second of the two accidents—that at Ais Gill, likewise dealt with in the next chapter. In January of 1911 two 65 ft. sleeping cars were ordered to be built in place of the two destroyed at Hawes Junction, Stone's electric lighting system to be installed.

October of 1912 saw the need for a further addition to the M. & G.S.W. stock so as to enable the joint committee's service to provide properly for excursion traffic. It was agreed to construct 10 bogie thirds and two bogie brake thirds. On April 25, 1913 the joint committee agreed that the 135 M. & G.S.W. vehicles, then lit by flat flame gas burners, should be altered to use inverted incandescent lights. At the same time three of the M. & G.S.W. first class carriages containing a compartment for an attendant and luggage, were authorised to be converted to provide a brake compartment. As to the M. & N.B. stock, 91 carriages were also to be given the new form of lighting. This latter decision was taken three months before the Ais Gill disaster.

In January 1913 there was a collision at Hurlford on the G.S.W.R. in which one of the 50 ft. carriages was destroyed, and it was decided to replace it by a 54 ft. vehicle, having seven compartments. The Ais Gill accident accounted for two more of the M. & G.S.W. stock. The 8-wheeled third class coach was replaced by a similar vehicle but the brake van's replacement was four feet longer than the original.

With the lesson of Ais Gill in mind, the Midland took action to improve the strength of the stock. In April 1914 the traffic committee reported (inter alia) as follows :

'The General Manager submitted a report dealing with the various suggestions and recommendations made by the Government Inspector in his report on the collision which occurred between two passenger trains near Ais Gill on September 2nd, 1913.
'Sir Guy's proposals, including the following recommendations, were approved and referred to the Board :—
'That specially strong headstocks and shock-absorbing buffers be fitted to the following vehicles :—

    Wooden underframe corridor and vestibule stock
    15 years of age and under
    184 M.R.   vehicles at £23 6s. od. each   £4,287
     81 M. & N.B.   „   „   „   £1,887*
    116 M. & G.S.W.   „   „   „   £2,703*

Steel underframe corridor and vestibule stock
not already so equipped

276 M.R.	vehicles at £20 14s. od. each	£5,713
41 M. & N.B.	„ „ „	£849*
27 M. & G.S.W.	„ „ „	£559*

* (Agreed that M.R. bear two-thirds of the cost.)

Other recommendations were that in order to gain experience with steel coaches, 10 passenger vans and 10 carriages were to be constructed with steel bodies instead of timber. Additional tools were to be supplied and the outside doors of corridor vehicles were to be fitted with a steel or iron loop, at a cost of about 1s each so as to afford sufficient leverage in opening carriage doors after an accident. The bulk of the timber to be used in new carriages was to be fireproofed. As to train lighting, it was agreed that all vehicles were to go over to electricity. On April 24 the orders were given for all carriage stock in the joint service then running or under construction to be fitted with electric light and with improved buffers and headstocks.

In April 1915 it was decided to order some new dining cars to replace five vehicles—two firsts and three thirds—which had been operating on the Scotch trains for some 21 years. The new cars were authorised as follows:

2 First class dining cars with kitchen at estimate of £2,154 each—£4,308
3 Third class dining cars (non kitchen) at estimate of £1,880 each—£5,640

Of the old cars one first and two thirds went to the Midland and one first and a third to the G.S.W.R.

The Midland board decided in October 1915 to adopt a new standard type of elliptical roof for all future carriage stock including dining and sleeping cars instead of, in the case of the main line vehicles, building the roofs as clerestories. Some of the first vehicles so fitted were the eight joint stock carriages then under construction, these being the two 54 ft. bogie thirds and one 54 ft. bogie van authorised as accident replacements, and the five dining cars. In all probability these particular vehicles suffered postponement due to the increasing demand, as the war progressed, on the Midland's carriage and wagon department. In the case of the diners it seems that they did not materialise until October 1921. They were the most likely vehicles to be held back, however, as dining cars generally were in short demand at this time. Some of the new Midland main line elliptical stock, however, 169 of which were ordered in October of 1914, were in service between St Pancras and Manchester by September 1917.

As has been mentioned, 1917 brought many restrictions. It soon became apparent that seating problems would become acute and in November of that year the joint committee gave orders that the central arm and head rests should be temporarily removed from the first class compartments in the joint stock. For a time in 1918 it seemed as if a number of the committee's coaches would be handed over to the United States Government for use as ambulance trains but the end of the hostilities came in time to stop this happening. With the end of the war came the lifting of restrictions on carriage construction. There was, however, no urgent need for new stock and except for alterations made to three of the joint stock vehicles in October 1920 nothing of note occurred until October 1921 when the joint committee decided to fit all the lavatory compartments with water heating apparatus. Of interest, however, is a decision of the Midland carriage and wagon committee in April, 1921 that a family sleeping carriage should be converted into a club day car, for the Bradford–Morecambe service. Finally, on November 16, 1922 the traffic committee authorized the fitting of steam heating apparatus in the nine carriages and two engines working the Barnoldswick branch service, nearly twenty years after the main line coaches had been so fitted and barely a month before the Midland ceased to exist.

The further history of the rolling stock would take this chapter into the era of the L.M.S. when standards, and the stock itself, with the exception of the M. & N.B. vehicles which remained in operation until 1928, became merged in a concern somewhat removed from the best days of the Midland. That company, in conjunction with its northern allies, had been able to pioneer a degree of comfortable travel, with magnificent carriages, that was perhaps second to none, and which will probably not be bettered in certain respects. With the passing of the Midland ends the story of the joint stock constructed to take the traveller over the Leeds–Settle–Carlisle line to the north.

Some of the accidents on the line, which occasionally had a bearing on the design of the rolling stock through the years, are dealt with in the next chapter.

XIX

Accidents

1875 – 1923

Some of the mishaps which occurred on the Midland line north of Leeds in the years before the advent of the Settle and Carlisle line have already been detailed. This chapter tells of the accidents on the Leeds–Settle–Carlisle route from its opening throughout in 1875. Compared with some railways the Midland was not particularly accident-prone and the line from Leeds to Carlisle had probably less misfortune in this respect than did others on the system. Up to 1910 it could claim a fairly good record of safe running but in that year the accident at Hawes Junction, and the later terrible affair at Ais Gill, redressed the balance somewhat.

In 1875 there were three accidents on the line, all south of Skipton. The first occurred at Calverley on the Leeds & Bradford on June 22. In view of what happened it was ironic that the layout at Calverley was in the process of being arranged to concentrate all the points and signals in one box, and to interlock them. At the time of the accident, however, the up home and distant signals were worked from a hut on the station platform, while the manual goods yard points, at the south end of the station, and the signal protecting them, were controlled by the points-man at the yard. The accident was caused by the wrongful shunting of a goods train of 37 wagons and brake van on the main line at a time when it fouled the path of an oncoming up Scotch express. When the goods arrived at the station the platform signalman called out to the guard to shunt clear of the main line but instead of doing so the goods continued through the station to stop at the goods yard points, where it proceeded to detach the brake van and leave it on the main line, while it ran back into the siding to pull out 12 wagons which were to be coupled to the brake van. Following this the engine detached 28 wagons of bricks, put them into the siding, and then ran out solo and coupled on to the train. It was only at this point that the goods driver decided to clear his train from the main line by putting it back, already marshalled to continue its journey, into the siding.

When the platform signalman saw that despite his warning, shunting was being carried out at the yard, he threw his signals to danger to stop the express. This had left Clapham from the Ingleton line six minutes late and was running fairly fast to make up time. It consisted of engine, tender, five composites, four first class carriages, four brake vans—two of which had a guard in them—two fish vans and a horse box. Even at this late stage the accident might have been averted but for two things: the distant signal was faulty and though put to danger still appeared to be in the off position; and the home signal, which was properly at danger, was obscured from the express driver until he was within 400 yards of it by the smoke and steam from an Ilkley train leaving Calverley station. Under these circumstances nothing could stop the express from tangling with the goods. Though the driver claimed he had seen the home signal, the Calverley station master insisted that the engine did not whistle for brakes until it passed the platform signalman who was frantically waving a red flag. Even so the speed was down to about 16 miles an hour when the engine of the express hit the second vehicle of the goods, forcing three wagons and the tender off the rails and propelling the goods engine some 80 yards along the line by the force of the impact. The engine, tender and several coaches of the express were derailed and much damaged. Twelve passengers, and the driver and fireman of the express, were injured. When Colonel Rich of the Board of Trade got to Calverley on August 24 he found that the goods guard and the yard pointsman had already been dismissed for permitting the goods to shunt in defiance of the platform signalman, and when knowing the express was signalled. Though they were undoubtedly at fault, Colonel Rich put some of the blame on to the express driver who, he said, should have had his suspicions aroused by the ambiguous position of the distant signal. Criticism was also directed against the brake power on the express.

Two months later there came another accident, this time at Kildwick on the Leeds & Bradford Extension, where again the combination of bad signalling and staff disobedience to the working rules caused the collision of one passenger train with another resulting in seven deaths, and injury to about 40 passengers. Though by this time the line from Leeds to Keighley had gone over to block working the rest of it on to Morecambe was still on the old time interval system. As in the case of the Calverley crash, however, it was currently being equipped for block working and in fact the Keighley–Settle Junction portion was almost ready.

The night of August 28, 1875 was damp; mist and rain caused the rails to be greasy and the signals to be but dimly seen from a shorter distance than usual. Late in the evening two trains approached Skipton station from the north; both were running late. The first, a return excursion from Morecambe, ran past Skipton North signal box at 11.04 p.m. and stopped in the station. Six minutes later the 10.15 p.m. up mail from Ingleton, which had left at 10.25 due to the late arrival of the Scotch train, was held up at the north box to await the departure of the excursion train from the station. Hauling the mail was engine No. 819 with driver Harrison Palfreeman and fireman William Dobson. When his train stopped at the box Dobson shouted out to know what was standing in the station and was told of the excursion. Apparently drivers of the regular trains were not informed officially of the existence of individual special trains. In answer to a further question from Dobson, the signalman, Thomas Breward, ascertained that the excursion was not going to shunt and that it was leaving the station. He then told driver and fireman that it was going on from Skipton and that they were to draw ahead into the station. The excursion, meanwhile, had left at 11.12.

When the mail arrived at the station there was a considerable movement of passengers which took up all the attention of the platform foreman, Thomas Moss, to the exclusion of his warning the driver of the presence of the excursion ahead. The latter train was booked to run through Kildwick station, $4\frac{1}{4}$ miles south of Skipton, but the mail was to stop there. At the intermediate station at Cononley, Jonathan Baldwin was in the signal box; his colleague at Kildwick was Richard Staveley. When the excursion passed through Cononley Baldwin noticed that the tail lamp was out and sent seven beats on the telegraph to Kildwick to 'stop and examine the train'. From his box he could see the distant signal at Kildwick set at danger to protect the excursion and knowing that in any case the mail was due to stop at Kildwick he did not consider it necessary to halt it at Cononley. Accordingly, even though the interval of five minutes had not elapsed since the passing of the excursion, he set his distant signal to 'alright', and his home to caution, so as to give the mail good warning of the obstruction ahead. (The signals in use on the line at the time were of the old pattern which showed three positions : stop, caution, and 'alright', with the respective lights of red, green, and white.)

Meanwhile the mail had left Skipton five minutes after the excursion. Palfreeman noticed that the Skipton signals were only lowered to caution but as he had never known them show 'alright' he and other drivers always assumed that the way ahead was clear. At Cononley he saw the distant showing of a white light—'alright'—and also, and this is where the trouble started, the Cononley home showed a white light. He passed the Cononley box at about 40 m.p.h. and ran on towards Kildwick. There the excursion had been brought to a halt. It was being drawn forward for examination at the same time that the mail was approaching the Kildwick distant signal which was at danger. Palfreeman complained afterwards that he did not see the signal till within 300 yards of it since besides the night being misty the signal was obscured on the curve by some trees. In any event he was slow in applying the brake until he got under the bridge at Kildwick and saw the right hand light of the excursion's brake van ahead. The company's regulations provided for drivers to shut off steam when approaching a distant signal at danger so as to be able to stop at the signal but, if they could see that the way ahead was clear, they could proceed with caution. Palfreeman could not see ahead because of the Kildwick bridge and so he, like Baldwin in the Cononley box, erred in assuming that all would be well. Despite several attempts by the fireman to get the brake to hold on the slippery rails, the engine of the mail crashed into the rear of the excursion at a speed of about 10 to 15 m.p.h. The tail van of the excursion took the blow well but the two preceding carriages were almost completely destroyed. Captain Tyler was the B.O.T. inspecting officer at this affair and at the conclusion of his report he censured Baldwin for not stopping the mail train, and Palfreeman for having run through the Kildwick distant at an excessive speed. As to the matter of whether the home signal at Cononley had shown a white or a green light, the evidence was conflicting and Captain Tyler decided to let it pass. The whole sorry business was just another fruit of the bell, book, and candle, and by guess and by God method of working by the time interval system. Captain Tyler took the opportunity, as he and his colleagues had been doing for some years, to call for the introduction of the block system. He was fair to the Midland, however, pointing out that the line would probably have the block system within the next two months, and that on the Midland as a whole, out of 975 miles of railway, the company had already installed the system over 627 miles and intended to operate it on all passenger carrying lines. In this respect the Midland was a model line.

The third accident on the Leeds–Settle–Carlisle line in 1875 took place on September 27 at Keighley. This was before the rebuilding of the station, and at the time of the accident the junction of the Worth Valley line was situated about 100 yards south-east of the station. The Keighley & Worth Valley Railway was worked by the Midland by one engine only on the line at any one time and it was not then provided with the telegraph system. Early on the morning of the accident Abraham Welch, a goods guard who had been on the Worth Valley line for six years, worked a train from Keighley to Kildwick and back before getting aboard the 6.00 a.m. goods train from Keighley to Oxenhope. This consisted of a tank engine, six goods wagons, five coal wagons, a brake carriage, five passenger carriages, and a goods van. It left Keighley at 6.13. After dropping off a wagon at Ingrow, the train arrived at Oakworth at 6.51, where a wagon next to the engine was to be dropped. The procedure at Oakworth, where the gradient was at 1 in 60 down towards Ingrow, was to stop the train and screw and pin down brakes and sprag the wheels of any vehicles left standing on the line. Welch told his under guard, John Wigglesworth—who was actually a porter at Keighley station, to screw down the brake in the rear goods van, while he—Welch—walked along the train, got into the third class brake carriage and screwed that down. He made no attempt to sprag the wheels or to pin down any of the wagon brakes. Having ensured what he obviously thought was sufficient brake power for the sixteen loose vehicles he called to the driver, Benjamin Whitfield, to ease back so that he could uncouple the front wagon from the rest of the train. This done he remained on the wagon whilst it went forward with the engine to be shunted into the siding, but on looking round he saw that the vehicles were slowly on the move down the incline towards Keighley. Jumping off, he raced back and ran alongside the wagons in an attempt to sprag the wheels. In a last despairing gesture he threw a sprag which did not connect and then made a jump for the engine which was on its way back to the train, having parked the wagon. A hair-raising chase followed, with whistle blowing, down the three miles or so to Keighley in a vain attempt to catch the runaways. With the little group of three men on the foot-plate of the tank engine anxiously peering ahead, it rocked over the curves and into the straight at the intermediate station at Damens.

Meanwhile Wigglesworth, who had not left the train all through the short time at Oakworth, had seen it started, apparently by a very strong wind blowing downhill towards Keighley, and had managed to thrust a sprag between the wheels. The sprag had broken, however, and he had clambered into the goods van with the intention of screwing down the brake yet harder. This had no effect and he was now in the van, in more senses than one. As the engine bucketed down the line close up to the front wagon of the train—at one point it got to within four yards—there was an argument between the men on the footplate as to whether it was possible for one of them to clamber over the bunker and on the buffer beam in an attempt to couple the engine to the train. Understandably they decided it was not. At Ingrow there was a chance that the runaways might be switched into a siding but the porter at the station, Jeremiah Laycock, heard the engine whistling and thought the train was running correctly and that the driver was calling for a clear road. The view from Ingrow, looking towards Damens, is obstructed by a short tunnel at the down end of the station and it was only after the train had passed through the station that he saw the engine, now about 150 yards behind.

At 6.20 a.m. a passenger train had left Bradford bound for Colne; it reached Keighley at about 6.55. At about that time the goods was running through Ingrow. Seconds later the signalman at Worth Valley Junction saw what was happening and called to the level crossing keeper, about 25 yards from him in the direction of Keighley station, to get the Colne train on the move. At the same time, attracted by the whistles coming from the branch, the Keighley station master, Ralph Singleton, and the station signalman, Eli Mitchell, both called to the Colne driver to get away. Indeed Mitchell had heard whistling in the distance as soon as the passenger train had arrived and had told the driver not to linger. The latter, James Kershaw, attempted to start his engine twice but each time it was on dead centre. Now he tried twice to reverse it, and had just managed to move his train forward a short distance when the collision occurred. Perhaps the luckiest man was Wigglesworth, who with a head-on view of the line, roared round the bend at the front of the train into Keighley station. Just before the impact he threw himself to the floor, and was knocked unconscious. When he recovered a few minutes later, he found himself unhurt. His van had run in under the van on the passenger train, which reared up destroying the station roof for about 30 feet. The underframe of the passenger van chewed into the goods brake to about floor level but did not quite reach Wigglesworth. The only other major damage was to a composite carriage in front of the passenger van, which had its end stoved in, and to the headstocks of a few of the preceding coaches. Luckily for the passengers, the engine whistles from the branch had sufficiently alerted the station staff in time and most of them had obeyed with alacrity repeated calls to jump out. Twelve who remained in the train were injured. From the accident came the loop at Oakworth, mentioned in another chapter, and the installation of the telegraph along the branch. The culprit was, of course, the unfortunate Welch, who had disobeyed the current instructions for working the branch by leaving a loose train without ensuring that it was properly braked and spragged.

The next accident to occur on the line took place at Kirkstall on March 1, 1876 and it brought to light a serious defect in the new block arrangements which were now in operation. Forty-two yards west of the station at Kirkstall there was a crossover road from the up line to the down line, the points for the latter's connection being another 50 yards beyond the station. Opposite them stood the up home signal, protecting the crossing, and beyond that, in the direction of Kirkstall Forge and 756 yards distant, was the up distant signal. The position of the up home signal, so near to the crossing, combined with the rule that when an up train had passed the signal, the signalman in the box at Kirkstall was allowed to give the 'line clear' to Kirkstall Forge station so that a second train might come up to the Kirkstall home signal from Kirkstall Forge without being checked, even when the station was holding the first train on the same line, was the direct cause of the accident. For two days before the morning in question a ballast train had been working at the station and its surrounds, avoiding regular passenger and goods trains either by using the siding accommodation or the crossover. At 10.55 a.m. a local train left Bradford for Leeds. It consisted of a tank engine, six composite and two first class carriages, a third class brake carriage and a luggage van. The driver, Joseph Willey, had been 12 years on the run without mishap, but had been accustomed up to three days previous to driving a small 'four-wheel coupled' engine; he was now on something bigger. Meanwhile at Kirkstall, the ballast train was still dodging about. At 11.17 a passenger train from Leeds arrived at the station, the ballast train having been moved to the up line. With the knowledge that the Bradford–Leeds local was due the guard of the ballast asked the signalman to let his train on to the down line behind the passenger, by means of another crossover at the Leeds end of the station. The signalman replied that he had a goods due to run up to the station on the down line behind the passenger train and that he would rather the ballast train backed over the crossover at the Bradford end. This was agreed to and after the Leeds–Bradford train had left at 11.18, the points were turned for the ballast to trundle over to the down line to clear the up road for the 10.55 from Bradford. With distant and home signals set at danger to protect the crossing, the ballast train moved back. Meanwhile Willey's train had gone through Kirkstall Forge at about 45 miles an hour, and steam had been shut off for the usual booked stop at Kirkstall station. On sighting the distant and the home signals set against him, Willey slowed down. He was not quick enough. Used to working a smaller engine, and with the rails very greasy that morning, he could do nothing except whistle for the guard's brake, sand the rails, and do all possible on the footplate. It is evident that he really thought he would stop inside the home signal but at a speed of about three miles per hour his engine nudged into the ballast, throwing three of its wagons off the rails. Three passengers on the local complained of slight injury. The point of collision occurred a mere 15 yards beyond the home signal, where the crossover left the up line.

Captain Tyler in his report to the Board of Trade drew attention to this. The line was professedly worked on the block system, he said, but the space between trains which the system was meant to ensure for safety's sake was reduced in this case to 15 yards—a totally insufficient amount. He censured Willey for not having approached the home signal at a slower rate but pointed out that if he had had continuous brakes under his control the accident would not have happened. His main argument, however, revolved round the interval between trains on the block system. It was the third case within the past few months that he had had to report upon collisions on the Midland from the same cause— where the reduction in the interval of space in block working had been reduced to the 'thickness of the signal-post or a few yards beyond it'.

The first accident to happen to a passenger train on the Settle and Carlisle line took place on August 15, 1876. At 8.45 the previous evening a goods train left Bradford for Carlisle. After some shunting at Skipton, it consisted of engine, tender, 37 wagons of which nine were loaded, and a goods brake van. As the goods was passing Crosby Garrett station the signalman there noted that the train was divided at about the middle and sent a message to that effect to his colleague at the next station— Ormside. The line between the two boxes is on a falling gradient towards Carlisle of about 1 in 100. At the same time as he received the warning, the signalman at Ormside also had notice from Appleby of the presence of an oncoming Carlisle–St Pancras express. This consisted of engine, tender, brake van with guard, a Pullman, three composite carriages, and a brake van at the rear with another guard. According to the Board of Trade accident report the time this train left Carlisle is given as '8.12, four minutes late'. This does not seem correct, however, since an evening train from Carlisle at 8.12 could not possibly—unless it was drastically held up on the way—pass at Ormside a goods train which had left Bradford at 8.45 p.m. and shunted at Skipton in between. The possibility of the 8.12 being a morning train, thus putting the accident time at about 9 a.m., is discounted by the report saying that 'the night was dark and foggy'. Examination of the timetable, however, shows an express leaving Carlisle at 12.8 a.m., and as this had a Pullman it seems likely that this is the correct departure time of the train in question, thus putting the accident more realistically at about 1 a.m.

Acting perhaps too hastily the Ormside signalman decided to stop both trains and immediately put his up and down signals to danger. The first train to draw to a halt at his box was the express. At this point the signalman made the mistake of permitting the express to proceed on to Crosby Garrett with caution. The express driver set off but had not gone more than 150 yards when he saw the engine of the goods—which was then pulling up at the Ormside home signal—run past him and almost immediately afterwards heard the two halves of its train come together. Some of the goods wagons were thrown off the rails and though the engine of the express passed clear, the van next the tender fouled one of the wagons, tearing the off side and one of the ends of the van. The off side and end of the Pullman were also damaged as were the off sides of the three following composites and the rear van. Eleven goods wagons were damaged—so much so that it was not possible to find the cause of their breaking away. The front guard of the express and two of the passengers were injured. Blame was attached to the Ormside signalman, for under the regulations he should have held the express and let the goods through, giving its driver a hand-lamp signal that his train was divided. The express should only have been permitted to continue after he had satisfied himself that the goods had not done any damage to the permanent way ahead, or left any obstruction in its wake.

On September 27, 1876 another Pullman was damaged in a collision at Whitehall Junction, Leeds. The Glasgow portion of the 10.30 a.m. Midland down express from St Pancras was due to pass Whitehall Junction at 3.50 p.m. This, of course, was one of the Midland's trains which did not call at Leeds but took the Water Lane and Whitehall Junction curve of the Leeds triangle. Shortly before 3.50 p.m. a North Eastern goods train, in the charge of driver Charles Hickinson, left Copley Hill and started down the 1 in 90 gradient towards Whitehall Junction where it would join the Midland metals as far as Leeds Junction. There it was to run on to the joint L.N.W.R. and N.E.R. line through Leeds New station and on to the N.E.R. proper for its eventual destination of Milford Junction on the N.E.R.'s Leeds & Selby line. As the N.E.R. goods train came down the slope, the down Scotch express was rounding the curve between Hunslet and Water Lane. The N.E.R. driver, knowing that he might have to stop at the signal before Whitehall Junction, came fairly slowly down the slope but his first view of the signals at the junction misled him. The signals were arranged as follows : those for trains coming from the north and from Copley Hill were on two posts, about 36 yards from the points, the top arms on each post referring to the line on which the train was approaching the junction, and the bottom as to the direction they were to take when past the junction. For

Hickinson, then, the top arm on the right hand post and the bottom arm on the left would have given him the road. As he came round the curve he could not see the top arm of the right post but assumed, as the top arm of the left was set to danger, that the former was clear. According to his evidence later, a brief glance showed him that one of the bottom arms was in the off position, and this, he said, confirmed his supposition; when next he looked he saw that all the signals had gone to danger. They had been against him all the time and were only set for an up Scotch express which had left Skipton at 3.23. The N.E.R. driver realized his mistake immediately and attempted to pull up short of the junction but the weight of the train on the incline, and the inadequacy of the brakes—the goods brake at the rear had skidded with the brake full on all the way down the slope because the guard thought the driver was going too fast—made it impossible. The N.E.R. engine, which was running tender first, struck the passing down Scotch express engine, whose driver had seen the goods ahead of him and had already applied the brake, separated its tender from the rest of the train, and smashed the front van and a composite completely, as well as slightly damaging the front end of the Pullman next to it. At this moment the up Scotch express was running through Armley. The signal at Wortley Junction was set in the off position for it as were those at the Whitehall Junction, but when almost up to the Wortley signal it went to danger and the driver saw the Holbeck station master come out on to the platform waving his arms. The train was travelling at about 16 miles per hour at this point, and the driver's immediate application of the Westinghouse brake pulled it up in less than 150 yards.

Colonel Hutchinson, who reported on the accident, said much against the N.E.R. driver who, incidentally, had seemed to be quite ignorant of the signalling arrangements at the Whitehall Junction. Recommendation was made that a dead end siding should be provided, as well as another set of rails, on the slope from Copley Hill, so that trains could be arrested if necessary. Criticism was made that the N.E.R. engine had only a tender brake but the Westinghouse was warmly commended, for on both Scotch trains it had worked extremely well, stopping one altogether and substantially reducing the speed of the other before the collision. There was no criticism of the signals at Whitehall Junction.

Another up Scotch express had a narrow escape on August 10, 1877 when the locomotive of the 1.05 p.m. from Carlisle, running at a speed of about 50 miles per hour, suffered a broken crank axle while passing through Kirkstall Forge. The engine concerned was No. 9 and the fracture caused the right hand driving wheel to drop off and fall foul of the down line. It was retrieved before any train passed. The quick action of the Westinghouse brake was sufficient to pull the train up short of the same crossover south of Kirkstall station where the previous accident with the ballast train had occurred. Had it had to negotiate the crossing it is doubtful whether the locomotive would have remained on the rails and as the train consisted of eleven vehicles, including a Pullman day car and two bogie carriages, the resulting smash would have been bad. As it was nobody was injured and the train only suffered superficial damage, mostly caused by ballast thrown up by the loose wheel.

Another junction collision on the Leeds & Bradford occurred on the wild and stormy morning of Christmas Eve, 1877. The 7.15 a.m. Leeds to Harrogate train of the N.E.R. was leaving the Midland metals at Wortley Junction when it was run into by the Midland's 6.45 a.m. passenger train from Bradford to Leeds. A new down home junction signal for Bradford and a new up home junction signal for Leeds had been installed only the previous day, and it seems probable that the driver of the Midland train, who with the fireman was killed in the crash, mistook the back light of the down signal for the front light of the up, the latter's lamp having been blown out by the wind a short time before. It was also obvious that the company was still permitting trains to approach dangerously near to each other at junctions—a point made by the B.O.T. inspector. Five passengers and the two guards on the Midland train were injured, and two passengers, the driver, fireman and guard on the N.E.R. train.

In 1878 there were two more junction accidents. The first happened at Settle Junction on June 26. At 12.28 p.m. the 8.35 up goods train from Carlisle, hauled by engine No. 1183, driven by Samuel Trow and fired by Thomas Beale, left Settle station six minutes early to proceed towards Settle Junction. As it passed Settle box the signalman, William Ball, called out that the train was to proceed at caution to Settle Junction, where Edwin Allard was the signalman on duty at the junction north box. He had received a 'be ready' signal from Settle regarding the goods train at 12.07 but had not given permission for the goods to come on at caution until 12.18. Two minutes later he received the 'be ready' and 'train approaching' signal from Giggleswick box on the little North Western line, for the 11.15 a.m. passenger train from Morecambe to Leeds but did not answer until 12.25 so as to let the 11.50 a.m. down passenger train from Skipton to Carlisle clear the junction. At 12.33 he received the 'train on line' signal from Giggleswick, and sent the 'be ready' and 'train approaching' signal to Settle Junction south box. The position now, therefore, was that two trains were approaching Settle Junction, the passenger under clear signals, and the goods with distant and home signals set against it. Both home signals for the junction were set close together and, as in the case at Whitehall Junction, the goods driver mistook one for the other. Though he swore at the enquiry that the left hand signal had been in the off position, the interlocking of the points and signals at Settle Junction made it impossible for this to be so when the junction was set and signalled for a train leaving the Morecambe line. As in other cases, the driver discovered his error too late and fouled the junction just as the passenger train approached. W. Jarvis, the driver of the passenger train, and fireman W. Harling, stayed on their engine as long as possible when they saw that the goods was not going to stop, and managed partly to screw down the tender brake and reverse the engine but the momentum carried it on. Both drivers and firemen leaped from their footplates. The goods engine was knocked off the rails and its tender overturned, narrowly missing fireman Beale. The passenger train engine suffered considerable damage, as did a van, third class carriage and a composite. Six passengers were injured. In his report Colonel Yolland put the blame on the driver of the goods but also criticised the sending on of a train, which was actually running some four minutes early, so as to bring it up close to a junction when another train was due. This was something that other companies had already remedied—but not the Midland. He also remarked that had the passenger train been fitted with continuous brakes the accident might well have been avoided or its effects mitigated. Considering the efforts being made by the Midland during this time to find a reliable brake it would seem that this last remark was in reality probably addressed *en claire* more at some of the recalcitrant companies which were then lagging on that score. Even so, it was not until the later Wennington accident that a determined attempt at adequate braking was to be instigated—and then only after a tongue-lashing from the Board of Trade.

In the early morning of September 25, 1878, another collision took place at Whitehall Junction. The up and down lines on the Leeds & Bradford at this point were double tracked from Wortley to Whitehall Junction and the junction was controlled by two home signals, each having the upper and lower arms, the latter being route indicators as already mentioned. At 3.46 a.m. signalman Robert Thomas Taylor, in the junction box, received the 'be ready' call from Wortley Junction box for the 2.20 a.m. up goods from Bradford to Burton. He gave permission for it to approach the junction and at 3.47 got the 'train on line' signal. It arrived at the box and stopped at the home signal on the inside of the two up lines, where it was to be held to await the passing of an up Scotch express, hauled by engine No. 901 and consisting of two guards vans, the Pullman car *Enterprise*, five carriages, and another guard's van in the rear. Only the first three vehicles were fitted with the Westinghouse brake. At 3.56 Taylor received the 'be ready' for the express and a minute later 'train on line'. As soon as the 'be ready' was received he told the next box at Water Lane of the express, and after seeing the Water Lane distant come off, he lowered his own home signal for the outside up line to let the express through. At this point the driver of the goods, who later admitted that he had been debating whether to call the signalman because he was not sure which of the signals referred to his train, made up his mind in a hurry and set off. Seconds later the goods engine passed over the points in front of the express. Taylor immediately threw his signals against the express but by that time it was too late. The night, though clear, had been foggy earlier and the rails were greasy. Despite the fact that the Westinghouse brake was immediately applied by the express driver, it seemed not to take effect. Unfortunately he did not whistle for the guard's brakes because, as he later said, he was confused by the fact that when the signal went to danger, the Water Lane distant stayed in the off position. The resulting clash of trains was not serious. The engine of the express was derailed but the remainder of the train kept on the road. Several of the goods wagons were severely damaged.

Major Marindin conducted the enquiry and had some strong remarks to make about both drivers. He thought the goods driver had made a stupid mistake but the express driver was also to blame. He had no business, said the Major, to pay any attention to the Water Lane distant until he had passed the junction home signal. It also turned out that the additional up and down roads between the two junctions had been in use since the previous May but had not yet been submitted for inspection to the B.O.T. as there were still some works to be carried out. Major Marindin took the opportunity to criticise the position of the junction home signals which, he said, could only be seen for a distance of 75 yards by a train on the outside up line, owing to obstructions. What puzzled him most was the express driver's statement that the Westinghouse had failed to act properly, and the report concluded with the disturbing information that after an examination of the vehicles concerned it had been found that the brakes on one of the front brake vans, and those on the Pullman car, would not act at all for the simple reason that no air was getting into the brake cylinders. The triple valves in each case were so clogged with oil and dirt that they could not operate.

Three accidents occurred in 1880. The first concerned the running down of two passengers at Bell Busk station. At about 7.15 on the morning of April 2, two elderly men, intending to catch a down train standing in the station, were on the up platform waiting for the train to draw forward clear of the sleeper crossing connecting the up and down platforms. Despite the warning from the station master that an up goods train was due they got on to the crossing and were killed by the goods. Both men were deaf and did not hear either the verbal warning or the whistles of the goods train. It was an unfortunate accident; the station master was censured for having crossed over to the down platform, leaving the crossing unprotected whilst knowing that another train was due to run through.

August saw a really bad accident. The scene was Wennington, the junction station for the Furness and Midland Joint line with the little North Western. On the day before the accident John Bee, a foreman platelayer, and two men under him, were engaged in doing repairs to the junction crossing. This was constructed on through sleepers for the down Lancaster and down Carnforth lines so that there was no cant or elevation for the curves. Indeed, due to the way the crossing ballast was packed it seems that on the Lancaster line the cant was slightly the

374

reverse of what it should have been. As will be seen there were other things wrong with this crossing. On August 11, the 12.15 p.m. train from Leeds to Morecambe was headed by one of the Midland's biggest engines, No. 813, used on the Leeds–Carlisle and Leeds–Morecambe runs, but frequently on the Scotch expresses between Skipton and Normanton. Her driver was John Whiteoak, a native of Skipton, where the engine was shedded. He appears to have had an affection for the locomotive, and immediately after the accident did some sleuthing on its behalf which was to be very useful in evidence. The train, which consisted of a front brake van, seven carriages, and a rear brake van, left Leeds 16 minutes late owing to the late arrival of a connecting train. Whiteoak apparently made no effort to make up time but ran at a speed of about 35 miles per hour during the journey, with stops at Shipley, Keighley, Skipton, Hellifield, Giggleswick, Clapham, and High Bentham stations. On approaching Wennington station he shut off steam so as to slacken speed slightly. He did this on his own initiative because he knew that the works had only just been completed at the junction. As it was he saw the three plateplayers standing by the side of the line to let the train pass. As the heavy locomotive went over the crossing it was felt to jump and become derailed; first the right leading wheel got in the six foot, and the left in the four foot. A few yards further on the driving wheels also came off. Whilst this was happening Whiteoak got the engine's brake on. All the train was derailed at the crossing following the engine, and though the latter was equipped with the Westinghouse, the remainder of the train could only rely on the two brake vans. The engine, tender, and half of the leading brake van churned along the sleepers and safely negotiated a stone overbridge 160 yards from the crossing. Not so the remainder of the train, which proceeded to pile itself up in a hideous mess. The first two carriages caught the bridge abutment, the third swung broadside on across both up and down lines and was rammed by a third class coach. Miraculously, the last three coaches and the rear brake van stayed on the line. Eight passengers died in the smash and 24 were injured, many severely and one fatally.

Leaving his fireman to rake out the fire in the engine, Whiteoak immediately went to help the passengers get out of the train and then ran back to the crossing, his sole concern at the moment seeming to be to prove that the engine was not at fault. Judging by eye, but later proved to be correct, he found the crossing was tight to gauge and that the inside curve check rail was at too great a distance from the running rail, so permitting the front wheels of the engine to ride too far over onto the wing rail. For a short distance before the point where the wing rail of the down Lancaster line came up to the fixed point of the crossing, the wood keys in the chairs were loose. The fixed point appeared to have been struck hard by the engine wheel. The evidence given before Colonel Yolland of the Board of Trade seemed composed largely of a battle of words between the locomotive and civil engineering departments of the Midland as to the cause of the accident, the former saying that the crossing was at fault and the latter that the train went over it at too high a speed. By careful examination of the crossing and the witnesses, Colonel Yolland found that the cast iron box crossing, in which were fixed the right rail of the down Lancaster line and the left rail of the down Carnforth line, was cracked right across immediately under the fixed point. The gauge of the down Lancaster line opposite the fixed point was $\frac{3}{16}$ inch tight and the check rail was 2 inches distant from the left stock instead of $1\frac{3}{4}$ inches—the standard distance on such crossings on the Midland. Besides this, the cant of the outer rail should have been elevated by about $\frac{1}{2}$ inch but was found to be depressed by $\frac{1}{4}$ inch. The Colonel criticised the work on the crossing, the fact that trains were permitted over it at what he considered excessive speeds, and the lack of a good continuous brake which, if used in time, might well have stopped the progress of the derailed train before it struck the bridge. During the evidence Samuel Johnson had alluded to the lack of brakes on the train but had added that the progress of fitting up the stock was going on as rapidly as possible. Colonel Yolland was short with this statement :

'It is all very well for the Midland Railway Company now to plead that they are busily employed in fitting up their passenger trains with continuous breaks (sic), but the necessity for providing the passenger trains with a larger proportion of break power was pointed out by the Board of Trade to all Railway Companies more than 20 years since; and with the exception of a very few railway companies that recognized that necessity and acted upon it, it may be truly stated that the principal Railway Companies throughout the Kingdom have resisted the efforts of the Board of Trade to cause them to do what was right, which the latter had no legal power to enforce, and even now it will be seen by the latest returns laid before Parliament that some of those Companies are still doing nothing to supply this now generally acknowledged necessity.'

He had also worked out that the speed of 37 miles per hour at which the train ran over the crossing was far too great, and recommended to the Midland that a speed restriction should be applied at Wennington. The practice of using joint sleepers for such points, where a cant was obviously necessary, and therefore made impossible, was also condemned. His strictures regarding brakes were noted and as mentioned in Chapter XVIII the Midland board gave instructions shortly afterwards that all passenger stock was to be provided with the continuous automatic brake.

Only eight days after the Wennington accident two trains were involved in a collision in Blea Moor tunnel. In 1878, the Westinghouse Company had found that the means of connecting the flexible hoses to the iron pipes on the vehicles by the use of brass collars was insecure. That July the firm had sent, free of charge and carriage paid, 400 hose clamps of a new pattern—made of malleable iron and far stronger than the flat brass bands then in use—to the Midland with a request that they be fitted in place of the old type. The railway company was slow to carry out the alterations, however, despite several letters from Westinghouse pointing out that vehicles were still operating with the old pattern clamps. At the same time, the Westinghouse people had recently altered the driver's brake valve with the consequence that not only did it work better but the pressure was so great as sometimes to blow off the hoses. Thomas Clayton was later to point out that three such incidents had occurred with the new malleable clamps. The mix up over the brake hoses, and the Midland's dilatoriness in fixing the new clamps, were the main factors in the tunnel collision, but the strange behaviour of the signal-men at Blea Moor and Dent Head on the day in question was another.

On August 19, 1880 the 3 p.m. train from Leeds to Carlisle, hauled by engine No. 819 and driven and fired by Philip Silcock and Arthur Wroe respectively, left Hellifield for the next stop at Appleby, with nine vehicles and two vans each with a guard, eight minutes late at 4.14. The train's brake was the Westinghouse, applied to the tender and to all the wheels of the carriages except the centre wheels of the six-wheeled coaches. Near the south end of the tunnel stood Blea Moor signal box. The signalman, Daniel Hewitt, received the 'be ready' for the Leeds train at 4.37 and 'on line' at 4.42. It passed his box at 4.45 and ran into the tunnel at a speed of about 45 miles an hour. When within sight of the northern end of the tunnel, the brake suddenly went on and pulled the train up short, against steam. Silcock remained on the footplate while Wroe went back and found that the hose connection on the tender had come adrift. He screwed the hose back on again and Silcock opened the tap to try and let some more air in so as to release the brakes, but the hose again flew off. There was obviously no use in trying to fix the hose, so it was decided that the fireman, the front guard and a ticket collector should open all the taps on the coaches, a procedure which entailed crawling under the vehicles. At the same time George Beevers, the rear guard, who had come up to see what was the matter, an-nounced that he was going back to protect the rear of the train.

Meanwhile, at the south end of the tunnel, the 10.35 a.m. train from St Pancras, with a pilot engine from Skipton, was toiling up to Blea Moor from Ribblehead. Hauled by train engine No. 1307 and consisting of brake van, two bogie carriages, two Pullmans, two more bogie carriages, two composites and a rear brake van, it found the signals against it at Blea Moor and drew to a halt, where it was decided to detach the pilot engine instead of at the then usual place—Dent Head. The Scotch express stopped at Blea Moor cabin at 4.49, and the pilot was duly taken off for its journey back to Ribblehead. What happened next between signalman Hewitt at Blea Moor and signalman Arthur Samuel at Dent Head is confused, for their evidence was contradictory. It certainly seems, however, that not having received the 'line clear' for the Leeds train from Dent Head, Hewitt became anxious and called the latter's attention by sending one beat on the bell. He got one beat back. At this point, despite the fact that both boxes were supplied with a speaking tube, should there be need for verbal communication, Hewitt called

Samuel's attention by moving the up line needle about, there being no 'train on line' pegged at the time. Seeing the needle moving in his box Samuel did an extraordinary thing; knowing that the Leeds train had not passed he nevertheless unpegged the down needle for 'train on line'. Samuel later insisted that he had then imediately repegged the down line. The train register, in his box, however, referring to down trains, was later found to have the relevant page torn out and all the entries copied into the next sheet, so proof of his statement was lacking. Samuel said he had torn out the sheet because it had got dirty when the guard of one of the trains rushed into his box to write a telegram message to Carlisle on it. The guard denied this completely and all Samuel's evidence was suspect. In any event, Hewitt obviously thought the needle was unpegged and is then supposed to have received all the necessary signals from Dent Head to send on the Scotch express. He lowered the starter signal for it at 4.53. One minute later Samuel came through on the speaking instrument with 'Where is the first express?'. To this Hewitt replied, 'What express do you mean?'. As this fatuous exchange was going on, guard Beevers had covered about 300 yards along the line behind the Leeds train and had laid four fog signals, when he heard a rumbling noise in the tunnel. At first he thought it was water which was rushing down from a shaft a few yards back but he soon realized it was the second train, with steam on, and picking up speed from its start at the other end of the tunnel. Fortunately, though the driver did not see Beever's hand lamp he heard the detonators. Quick application of the Westinghouse brake reduced the speed of the train to about 10 miles per hour at the time of the collision, and though the rear vehicles of the Leeds train were damaged, there was no injury to any of the passengers. The driver of the London train said at the enquiry that if he could have had another 20 yards warning he would have pulled up in time. As it was, Silcock on the footplate of the Leeds train heard the express approaching and tried to get away. The brake held him fast, however, until the moment of impact when the couplings between the tender and his train parted and his engine shot forward for two carriage lengths. By this time the tunnel was indescribably choked with fumes and escaping steam but after a short while he was able to draw ahead to Dent Head to warn Samuel of what the latter had done.

There were three direct causes of the accident, any one of which was bad enough. Taking the matter of the malleable iron collars, it seems extraordinary that Samuel Johnson, when asked to comment on the Westinghouse letters and the supply of free improved clamps, should remark that at no time had Westinghouse advised him that the brass collars were dangerous or that he should replace them with the new ones. He had only heard indirectly, he said, of Clayton's side of the story—that the carriages were being so fitted—and had recently ordered eleven new hose connections for locomotives. This was tantamount to shifting responsibility on to Westinghouse to run the brake side of the Midland locomotive and coaching stock itself—something the firm had suggested it should do but which had been strenuously rejected by the Midland authorities. It was, to say the least, a peculiar attitude for Johnson to adopt. The matter of signalling irregularities was plain to see; neither of the men could be fully believed. Samuel's destruction of the all-important page in his book was matched by a statement in evidence from Hewitt that 'the cause of the erasure of the receipt of the "line clear" (from Samuel—and which was probably never sent) for the second express was owing to my having entered the receipt of the "line clear" for the light engine from Ribble Head (*sic*) by mistake in the down line column. The time I entered was 4.59, the time at which I received "line clear" from Ribble Head for the pilot engine. I cannot explain why I omitted to attend to the instructions directing me to draw my pen through an incorrect entry instead of erasing it.' Another gentleman who had some explaining to do was guard Beevers. It was calculated that eleven minutes had elapsed from the time the Leeds train stopped to the moment of collision. During that time Beevers wrongly went 100 yards up to the front of the train before setting out to protect the rear. The inspecting officer, Major-General Hutchinson, remarked that in too many cases of abrupt stops the guards were loth to go back, thinking that the block system would be sufficient protection, as well as not wishing to be left behind if the train suddenly restarted. In all, Blea Moor was a small accident; like the others though, it pointed to some bad practices which might well have proved fatal.

The year ended with a very bad collision at Leeds and though not strictly part of the story in that it did not involve any of the Leeds–Settle–Carlisle trains, it is worth brief mention. Due to some misunderstanding as to the number of carriages required on the 5.30 p.m. passenger train from Leeds to Sheffield on the evening of December 21, one of the carriages was taken off and fly shunted, coming to rest fouling the points and preventing the signalman from releasing the starting signal. At about this time the signalman learned of the approach of the 2.55 Derby to Leeds train. Unable to lower the starting signal for the Sheffield train and thinking that the points were set right for the departure line, the signalman then proceeded to destroy the value of the block system by waving it out with a hand lamp at the same time as lowering the arrival signal for the Derby train to come up to the station. It was not until he had got well on his way towards Leeds Junction that the driver of the Sheffield train realized that he was running on the arrival line, and though he at once attempted to stop, there was an almost immediate headlong collision with the incoming Derby train. Considerable damage was done to the Sheffield train; the engine, No. 56, had a damaged buffer beam, cylinder levers and hornplates, the smokebox and frame were buckled and some of the rivets on the boiler sprung. The carriages were in various stages of partial disintegration, with some amount of telescoping. As to the Derby train, the engine, No. 104, suffered similar damage to the other, and there was also some telescoping in the centre of the train. One passenger died immediately, one later, 15 passengers were taken to Leeds Infirmary, some of them badly injured, and 57 other passengers and eight Midland employees were injured less severely. Though the signalman was undoubtedly to blame the shunter also came in for criticism as it was part of his duties to ensure that loose wagons did not foul points. He was warned that the starter signal could not be moved, for the reason given, but if the coach had been moved off the points it would still have been impossible to lower the signal without setting the right road.

On August 8, 1881 there was a severe accident at Blackburn on the L.Y.R. Again, this is somewhat off the main line of the Leeds–Settle–Carlisle route but as it concerns one of the connecting Midland trains from Manchester to Hellifield operated by the L.Y.R. with some Midland stock, and as the Westinghouse brake was partly the cause of the accident, an outline account is of interest. The 2.10 Liverpool to Todmorden express passenger train arrived at Blackburn station at 3.09 p.m., three minutes late. From the head of this train there was to be removed a saloon carriage, and from the rear a Midland coach which was to be attached to the 2.25 p.m. Manchester to Hellifield train. The front saloon was uncoupled and run into the sidings by the front engine which then returned to its train, while L.Y.R. engine No. 682 *Vesuvius* went to the rear of the train to take off the Midland coach. During this time the Manchester–Hellifield express was approaching Blackburn. Though absolute block was in operation up to Blackburn Old Junction, permissive block was in use from that point to Blackburn West cabin and through the station to the Tunnel End East signal cabin. It was the practice under this system, when a train was standing in the station on the same line, for the West box to keep its distant ·and home signals in the danger position until a following train came up to the Old Junction home signal. The signalman in the latter box took his cue from the position of the West box signals. When, with the station line still occupied, the West box lowered its home signal, keeping its distant to danger, the Old Junction home signal followed suit, permitting the oncoming train to run up to the West box at reduced speed past the West box distant—still on—and the West box home whence it would be cautioned to approach the station platforms by a green flag shown from the West box. On the day in question, as the Manchester express approached Blackburn—hauled by eight-wheeled tank engine No. 74, and consisting of a L.Y.R. composite, a N.B.R. composite, a brake van, two L.Y.R. composites, and two third class carriages—the driver, William Stansfield, was experiencing difficulty with the Westinghouse brake. It had been acting quite well on the journey so far but by the time he reached Bolton Junction he realized that the hand brake would be necessary. He also whistled for the guard's brakes and put the engine in reverse, giving it steam. With wheels frantically spinning and the engine whistling to clear the station, the Manchester train bore down past the West box into the station. There was considerable damage. The Midland coach was knocked off its bogies and *Vesuvius* was put out of commission for some time. The force of the collision pushed the Liverpool train forward by about two coach lengths. Two passengers were killed immediately, five died later, and over 60 were injured. There was the usual inquiry and coroner's hearing, but after a series of exhaustive tests carried out at the request of Colonel Yolland, in which a similar train, with Stansfield as driver, was run over the same length of line, using the same combination of brakes, the exact cause of the accident remained something of a mystery. The signalling arrangements at Blackburn were such that the Colonel expressed surprise that there had not been an accident there before, but as to the driver, fireman, and guard of the Manchester train, there was no blame attached. The driver's explanation that in some peculiar way the Westinghouse brake had failed between Over Darwen and Blackburn on all the vehicles except the engine, and that having realized this he did all he could to stop by reversing the engine, was accepted. There were ugly stories that the Westinghouse firm had tried to 'persuade' him to take a long paid holiday in America so that he need not give evidence, but it seems that as the suggestion was made to him in a railway carriage at a time when he was crying and saying that the company would not keep him as a driver after the accident, there is no doubt that it was meant kindly and in good faith. Indeed the Westinghouse office in London went to great trouble to assist Colonel Yolland. The firm agreed that if, as sometimes happened, the brake hoses were coupled in the wrong way, this could result in the engine alone receiving its benefit. It has been seen that the firm was very concerned for its reputation at this time and during the preceding years, and it does not seem possible that the authorities in the railways using the brake would not have been fully aware of this possibility. As it was, evidence from various L.Y.R. men brought to light the disquieting fact that they were not always instructed in fitting the brake when first introduced to it. Though Westinghouse was vindicated—just, Colonel Yolland urged that where the brake was used the permissive block should not be worked, for though the brake was, as he put it, 'a very clever, ingenious piece of mechanism', its very intricacy made it prone to failure. It was, after all, still in the teething stage.

Once again Leeds Wellington is the scene for the next accident. At about 8.50 on Wednesday night, January 4, 1882, a train from Carlisle arrived at platform 4. The usual practice after getting the passengers out was to pull the coaches back out of the station and then propel them into the carriage siding between platforms 2 and 3. This night, engine No. 1253 was attached to the rear of the train and the starting signal for the north departure side, worked by the Leeds Junction box, was lowered to permit the train to draw forward. At this point the signalman in the station box mistook the signal, and thinking the south departure signal had been lowered in error, sent the quite irregular and ambiguous call of six beats, 'signal in error', to the junction box. According to the station signalman the signal was sent to the junction signalman by the south bell but the latter swore later that he thought it was received by him on the north bell and that he had, therefore, signalled the empty carriage train out in error. At any event, the starter signal was then put to danger and the engine of the carriage train came to a halt on the crossing of the north departure and south arrival lines where it stood for some four or five minutes. Assuming that this train was still safely in its platform, the junction signalman with the block now clear to permit him to do so, proceeded to signal out on the south departure line a shunting engine, taking as his authority the four beats he received on the south bell from the station box following the previous six beats of 'signal in error'. He also received a signal at the same time from Whitehall Junction box of the approach of the 8.30 p.m. Bradford–Leeds local and, on getting assurance from the station box that it could come forward, the signals were lowered. By now the driver of the empty carriage train had seen the approaching light engine. He climbed down from his train and ran up to warn the driver that his own engine was fouling the latter's road but before he could get back to it the Bradford passenger train loomed up out of the darkness and rammed it. The driver of the Bradford train, Frederick Willoughby, had acted quickly, given a full application of the vacuum brake to his train, composed of nine short-buffered coaches, and had managed to reduce his speed to about four miles per hour at the moment of impact. Both engines were considerably damaged but none of the Bradford coaches was derailed and only five passengers and three Midland employees were slightly injured. In his report Major Marindin criticised all concerned except the driver of the Bradford train; the two signalmen were clearly negligent, the driver of the empty train should have whistled to the light engine and backed when he saw the Bradford train.

At 1.57 a.m. on Sunday, October 29, 1882, the 9.15 p.m. down night Scotch express from St Pancras left Normanton, bound for its next stop at Skipton. It consisted of engine and tender, a horse box, front guard's van, a N.B.R. third class carriage, a bogie composite, two Pullman sleeping cars—the *Enterprise* and *Excelsior*, two more bogie composites, a G.S.W.R. third class carriage, a Midland covered carriage truck, and the rear guard's van. Both vans had a guard and the two Pullmans were in the charge of Pullman company conductors Robert Donaldson and Andrew Baillie. The *Enterprise* was bound for Edinburgh, and the *Excelsior* for Glasgow. As the train approached Hunslet the driver heard the whistle of the safety cord apparatus and on looking back down his train he observed a light above one of the cars. He immediately shut off steam and brought the train to a halt near the Hunslet South Junction signal box. Conductor Baillie in the *Excelsior*, occupying one of the end vacant berths in his car, at the end nearest the *Enterprise*, had also become aware of a light reflected in one of the headboards of his

Pullman and on looking out of the window had seen that the *Enterprise* was on fire. Rushing out on to the platform of his car, he found that the end door of the Edinburgh vehicle was shut, and so pulled the communication cord. He then saw that the window in the rear door of the *Enterprise* was broken and that smoke and flames were belching from it. Thinking that for some reason the communication cord had not worked, he passed through his own car, telling all the passengers to get up, and went out to the other end when a pull at the cord appeared to bring the brake into play. As soon as the express had stopped he ran forward and joined in the division of the train so that the *Enterprise*, whose roof was now well alight, might be drawn clear of the adjacent Pullman and the preceding coaches. This was soon done and buckets of water brought up in an attempt to put out the fire. In the meantime, his colleague on the *Enterprise* had been having a hectic time. Shortly after leaving Normanton, Donaldson had passed through his car and had seen a Mr Cranston, who had boarded the train at Sheffield and had gone to bed in berth No. 8, almost in the centre of the vehicle, in bed with a reading lamp burning. This was not, strictly speaking, against the rules of the Pullman company, but Donaldson pointed out the danger to him, only to be told by Cranston that he was used to having a reading light and would blow it out before going to sleep. Just what occurred next is uncertain as the evidence of Cranston and Donaldson differed, Cranston saying that after a time he thought the atmosphere had become very close and that he went out and found Donaldson and that both of them discovered that the coach was on fire, whereas Donaldson maintained that after leaving Cranston he had taken off his cap and gone and stood by the stove at the rear end of the car to warm himself. While there he had thought it had got very close in the car and then discovered that it was on fire. According to Donaldson, he then turned about and raced through the car screaming out that it was on fire and saw Cranston still in bed. At this point he tried to get into the Glasgow car to get help from Baillie but found the end door too hot to touch. Meeting Cranston on his way back to the front end of the car, Donaldson went out to the front platform and tried to pull the cord, but it did not appear to work. He then knelt down on the platform and turned off two taps on the Westinghouse brake. Shortly afterwards the train stopped.

There were three other passengers in the *Enterprise* besides Cranston. One of them, a Mr Dove, succeeded in leaving the car by the orthodox method while a Mr Main broke the window in berth No. 5 and was pulled out. The third passenger was a Doctor Arthur. Witnesses later described seeing a tall gentleman enter the train at St Pancras. Donaldson said that he saw a tall man walk down the platform at St Pancras, apparently in a state of intoxication, for he reeled about before getting into the front part of the train. At Leicester he had got into the Edinburgh car and asked for a berth and a brandy and soda. Donaldson had diplomatically told him that he only had soda water left but was nonplussed when the doctor took it and added to it a concoction which he said was Egyptian brandy. After this the doctor had got into his berth without taking his shoes off but Donaldson had removed them to prevent damage to the headboard. After producing a cigar and demanding a light—an action which ended with Donaldson taking the cigar away—the doctor had been helped out of his jacket, had asked for his overcoat and had then gone to sleep. In the confusion of the fire it was assumed that he had got out of the car, especially as someone said that he had answered to a call.

When it was found impossible to douse the flames, the *Enterprise* was moved 876 yards down the line to the water crane near the Hunslet station signal box, but on being found to be too high to permit the hose to reach the roof, it was pushed back a few yards in front of another hose from Nicholsons Chemical Works. There the fire was eventually put out. A short time later two police officers went into the burnt sodden shambles and found the doctor's body. When last seen at Trent he had been in berth No. 3; when found he was in No. 7, next to the one where Mr Main had climbed through the window.

Colonel Yolland conducted the enquiry and could find no other cause for the fire than that Cranston's reading light must have set light to the blind. The main gist of his report, however, related to the wrongful action of the driver in pulling the train to a halt immediately the alarm was given, when for a few extra yards it could have been brought into Hunslet station where the fire could be efficiently tackled and the doctor's life saved. The rule book was explicit that if the driver saw nothing which, when the alarm was sounded, really necessitated the immediate stopping of the train, he was to proceed to the next station. If, however, on looking down the length of the train, something was visible, such as vehicle oscillation, then the train was to be halted as speedily as possible. This rule, Colonel Yolland said, had been framed at a time when continuous brakes were rare. He continued :—

'It is urged on the part of the Midland Railway Company that this rule . . . was partly based on a recommendation of mine when reporting on the terrible accident which occurred at Shipton-on-Cherwell on the Great Western Railway on the 24th December, 1874; but in my report dated the 27th February, 1875, I pointed out that the train in question was not a properly equipped train, having an entirely insufficient amount of break (*sic*) power fitted to it, and having no less than six vehicles behind the last break-van; that the cord communication (Harrison's) failed on that occasion to act, and that the drivers of the two engines at the front of the train at once reversed their engines without actually looking back and observing that the vehicle next to the last tender was running partly off the rails, and they thus applied a heavy retarding force at the front of the train, and thus pushed that vehicle altogether off the rails, as there was no retarding force at the tail of the train to keep it properly stretched on the line.

'Now the circumstances in this case are entirely different. Here a well-appointed train with the Westinghouse continuous automatic breaks fitted throughout the length of the train, and running on a main line of railway worked on the absolute block system, suddenly has the alarm whistle sounded on the engine, to give notice that something was wrong. If that alarm whistle had been

384

sounded by the communication cord being broken by the separation of the train into two parts, the automatic action of the breaks would at once have acted on the separated parts, have reduced their speed, and thus brought both parts to a stand, without, as far as I can see, the slightest risk to any individual in the train, passenger or servant of the Company; but as no such stoppage did take place, the driver must have known that it was an alarm whistle sounded by some passenger or servant of the Company giving him notice that something was wrong in the train in order that it might be stopped.'

So, Donaldson had been wrong in not seeing that Cranston's reading light was put out, and the driver was wrong in pulling up so soon. As to the Harrison communication cord, it appeared from what the Colonel said later in the report that it was not of a pattern sanctioned by the Board of Trade, and it bore one very bad point in that as regards the Pullmans it could only be reached from the platforms of the cars. In this instance, the opening of the end doors to get at the cord had so increased the draught through the body of the car as to give the fire a complete hold on the vehicle. It was of small consolation that Doctor Arthur was probably already only semi-conscious from alcohol and was overcome by smoke and fumes before the flames reached him.

1885 saw two accidents, at either end of the line. The first, at Carlisle, was slight, and only two passengers complained of minor injuries. It occurred on August 29 when the 10.30 a.m. Midland passenger train from Leeds was standing at the down home signals near the Crown Street signal box. Waiting in the station were the carriages of the 2.15 p.m. train from Carlisle to Appleby. Out of the Midland sheds came a light engine, No. 907, for attaching to the train, driven by Charles Burton. Seeing one of his signals in the off position, he assumed that the others were also clear and with great negligence failed to note that the advanced signal, worked from the cabin at the rear of the stationary Leeds passenger train, was at danger. At a speed of about five miles per hour the light engine ran into the rear of the Leeds train. Major-General Hutchinson censured Burton but noted that if the Carlisle Citadel Station rule No. 39 had been carried out by the signalman in No. 7 cabin—a rule which prohibited a junction home signal being lowered to permit a train to draw forward to an advanced signal at danger—Burton would have had his attention automatically drawn to the danger. It was unfortunate that the signalman in No. 7 cabin was exempted from this rule, but the General noted that henceforth it would apply.

Midland drivers, and indeed most drivers on the railways, were a lordly race. Their locomotives were smartly turned out and a genuine pride was taken in the ability to drive them to their maximum efficiency. This pride in the job had its counterpart in a vanity which showed itself in many small ways, one of which was to make a 'smart' stop in a station. The idea was to run in at about 10 miles per hour and to make, with a flourish, a quick application of the brakes, a procedure at terminal stations which frequently entailed the engine buffers coming to a rest a few inches from those of the station stop blocks. In the early

morning of December 8, 1885 driver George Rutherfort, in charge of the
1.57 a.m. train from Normanton to Leeds—the Leeds portion of the
down Scotch express—sadly misjudged his ability to stop his train in
Leeds Wellington station. Coming in with steam shut off he found himself well along the platform with no response from the Westinghouse
brake. It was later found that the triple valve had frozen. This was not
sufficient excuse, however, as Rule No. 293 clearly stated that trains
should only enter stations at speeds at which the crew could bring them
safely to rest while operating the hand brake alone. When about half way
down the platform Rutherfort had given up with the brake, and had put
his engine into reverse. It was of no avail, however, for the train slid
majestically into the buffers, causing minor damage to the platform and
the front of the locomotive, No. 102. Rutherfort was not the first driver
to do this. Napoleon Charles Simmonds, 19 years a driver and Josephus
Milward, only one year less, were drivers of the pilot and train engines,
Nos. 1510 and 93 respectively, on the 1.25 p.m. from Derby to Leeds on
August 2, 1884. They managed to so muddle the timing of the application of the brakes as to hit the buffers at Leeds Wellington. The speed
was only about half a mile per hour but six passengers were slightly
injured.

Another buffer stop collision occurred in 1888, this time at Crosby
Garrett. On July 12 a return excursion train from Edinburgh to Roch-
dale, consisting of an engine and tender and nineteen ordinary L.Y.R.
carriages, left Carlisle at 11.35 p.m.—30 minutes late. It left Appleby at
12.40 a.m. having lost a further 12 minutes. Behind it was the 12.08 a.m.
up Scotch express from Carlisle, running 18 minutes late. Though the
excursion was due to shunt either at Kirkby Stephen or Mallerstang to
clear the line for the express it was decided to run it into a siding at
Crosby Garrett, and at 1.04 a.m. it started to shunt back. Due to the
fact that the excursion was longer than an ordinary passenger train and
that the guard did not inform the signalman, the latter continued to
show a white light—indicating clear—from the box until the rear of the
train came into violent collision with the buffers at the siding end. There
was also some muddle on the train. The rear guard, having given a
cautionary advance signal with a green light and seeing that the driver
was coming back too fast, called to a L.Y.R. inspector in the rear brake
van to put on the brakes and then jumped out and waved a red light. It
was not seen. The inspector attempted to screw down the hand brake
but neglected the continuous brake, which application would undoubtedly have slowed the train considerably. Despite the fact that the train
staff were somewhat negligent though, the driver was in no way to
blame. He could only expect to be shunted into a siding which would be
long enough. It was also agreed that the staff were operating a train of
unusual length on a strange line in the middle of the night and could be
excused up to a point. The signalman was the real culprit; he knew the
length of the siding and should have enquired from the guard the

length of the train. 'The whole affair', said Major Marindin, 'was a blunder from beginning to end, for there was really no necessity for shunting the excursion train at all at this station, as the express was signalled as running 18 minutes late.' The collision threw the inspector off the rear van and stove in the last compartment of the rear carriage; seven passengers and the L.Y.R. inspector were injured, all only slightly. Two of the carriages were considerably damaged, however, and panes of glass were broken in other parts of the train.

Three years later, on July 22, 1891, there was virtually a repeat performance of the Settle Junction collision of 1878. A goods train, shunting at Clapham Junction, was run into by the 6.35 p.m. up mixed train from Ingleton. Just before the latter was due to leave Ingleton, the signalman, George French, gave the 'Is line clear?' to Clapham and received 13 beats on the bell in return—'Section clear and station or junction blocked'. He then signalled the 6.35 out of the station and as it was passing his box he held out a green flag and called to John James, the driver, to go at caution. The latter should then have expected to find the distant and home signals at Clapham against him and ought to have worked the train at a sufficiently low speed near Clapham so as to stop in time. He saw the distant signal at danger, put his brake on, and slowed the train from 30 to 20 miles per hour. On approaching the home signal, however, he left it too late and when he applied the brake again the wheels skidded. Despite sanding by the fireman, the engine of the mixed train ploughed into a rake of wagons being drawn out of the sidings at Clapham. Having regard to the steep gradients from Ingleton down to Clapham, Major Marindin condemned the practice of allowing the 'Section clear but line blocked' signal at this location and suggested that it should be forbidden at Clapham for trains coming from Ingleton even though it would probably necessitate the introduction of a block signal box at about the position of the existing up distant signal, near Newby Moor crossing. Though the Major's recommendation was carried out it was for a limited period; a traffic committee minute of March 1908 noted that in order to close the signal box near Newby Moor crossing signalling alterations were to be carried out and a portion of the up line track circuited. The box was closed on June 4, 1908.

The next accident is the first of two that occurred at Hawes Junction and it introduces the tragic figure of Alfred Sutton who was later to be the unwitting cause of perhaps the worst disaster on the line. This time, however, he was not at fault—it was to be another nineteen years to the awful night when he would send the down night Scotch express to its destruction. In 1891 Hawes Junction had two signal boxes, the north and the south. Sutton was then in the south box. At about 4.36 p.m. on August 22, 1891, he accepted from Dent box a down excursion train from Bradford to Aysgarth on the Hawes branch. The train, headed by No. 1367 and consisting of 11 passenger vehicles, ran into the down main platform while an up goods train passed through the station. The points were then set for the excursion to back on to the up line where it stopped, and ran forward on to the Hawes branch. The engine was then detached and run onto the turntable, before coming back to the train at the north end of the station on the branch platform line. At this point Sutton had quite correctly re-set the up main points for the main line which, through interlocking, had also opened those for the dead end at the south end of the branch platform. The driver of the excursion then informed the Hawes station master, William Henry Bunce, that he required water and the latter, instead of checking that the points had been re-set for the train to back on to the up main again, this being necessary for the engine to get to the water column at the south end of the station, assumed they were still in the position when the train had originally run off the main line into the platform, and gave the driver permission to back. To make matters worse, the disc signal at the points, which clearly showed they were open on to the dead end, was invisible to the driver. The latter accepted the station master's word and backed with some force into the dead end doing damage to all the vehicles, so much so that the engine had its side framing and footplate bent, and the buffer beam distorted. Out of the 150 passengers, 18 were injured, one severely. An unpleasant part of the case was that immediately after the crash Bunce came over to Sutton's box and asked him what he thought he was doing, saying that the driver had said he had arranged with Sutton to back the train. The driver himself pointed out later that he had only asked for the engine to be turned but said that he had sent the fireman to tell Sutton that he also wanted water. Sutton is supposed to have replied that water could be obtained at the turntable but as there never had been a water column at that point the driver's or the fireman's evidence on this issue was not only false, it exonerated Sutton from blame. He would hardly have suggested a location where no column existed, and Major Marindin accepted his word that the fireman had not told him that the train would need to back on to the main line again. In fact, evidence showed that the fireman had gone to the north box. Bunce, of course, was negligent in not making sure that the points were set correctly for such a move.

There were two accidents during 1892 which though not on the Leeds–Settle–Carlisle line, deserve passing mention. The first took place on the fine hot afternoon of June 9 at Esholt Junction where the Apperley Bridge to Guiseley line meets the Shipley and Guiseley branch, a short distance south of Guiseley station. The 3.07 p.m. Midland train from Leeds to Ilkley was due to pass over the junction at 3.21, and the 3.10 p.m. North Eastern Railway train from Ilkley to Bradford was due eleven minutes later. The approach from the Leeds line is through a sylvan setting on an upward gradient of 1 in 60. A short tunnel at the north end of the line terminates at a point about 254 yards from the junction home signals which were then on separate posts in the fork between the two lines, both visible from the tunnel to the driver of a train approaching the junction from Leeds. Unfortunately the view on this occasion was partially obscured by a bush on the cutting slope and at a time when both trains were approaching the junction, the N.E.R. train having just left Guiseley for Bradford, and the Midland running late and coming up the gradient from Apperley, there was a third train coming from the south along the Shipley and Guiseley line. On approaching the pair of home signals, the left hand one, relating to the Shipley to Guiseley down road, was at clear whilst that for the Midland train on the Apperly line was set at danger, protecting the junction. At the same time the up signal from Guiseley for the N.E.R. Ilkley to Bradford train was in the off position. Archibald McLay, the driver of the Midland train, had joined the company at the time of the strike about $4\frac{3}{4}$ years previously, and had been driving passenger trains on the Leeds–Ilkley run ever since. At Apperley Junction box on the Leeds & Bradford line the signalman carried out the usual procedure for a junction blocked at the next post and stopped the Leeds train. He then lowered his signal for the train to take the branch up to Guiseley and showed a green flag which the driver correctly took to mean 'Section clear, but junction blocked'. Acknowledging this with a wave of the hand, McLay then opened the regulator of his engine—No. 179—so as to start the climb up to Guiseley. Coming to the Esholt Junction distant signal he saw it was at danger, but on glancing at the home signal a few seconds later he thought he saw it at clear. Only when he was almost at the junction did he see that it was the down Shipley line signal that was clear; his was against him. Too late to stop, he ran forward on to the junction and rammed the Ilkley–Bradford train, badly damaging the fifth, sixth, and seventh vehicles so much that five passengers were killed, one outright, and 26 injured, as well as one of the guards in the Ilkley train and the driver, fireman, and guard of the Leeds train. McLay was commended by Major-General Hutchinson for his completely frank confession of negligence and it seemed from the General's summing up in his report that the driver had been unlucky as well as careless. The bush which had obscured his own signal while ensnaring him with a view of that for the Shipley line was mentioned as being the real culprit. It had been hurriedly removed by the time the inquiry was held. The General recommended that the down Shipley line home signal should be moved to the left hand side of the down line so as to be invisible from the Leeds branch, and he once more condemned the continuing Midland practice of allowing two trains to approach a junction on a fouling course at the same time. McLay's fireman, Walter Bolton, was also censured for not keeping a better lookout.

The second accident in the year occurred at Leeds five days later. As in other cases of station collisions at Leeds, this one happened at night. The Bristol portion of the down Scotch express, due at Leeds at 2.07

a.m., came into collision, on entering the station, with a light engine. Four passengers and five of the company's servants were injured. The cause of the accident was that the signalman in the Leeds Junction box had mistakenly lowered the wrong signals, which could not have been set for collision if he had noticed that the block instrument was showing 'line blocked', and sent the express into the south, instead of the north, arrival platform. The unattached engine, No. 1512, was thrust forward about 150 yards by the force of the collision and was badly knocked about; the train engine, No. 1492, was converted into what was more like a poorly knit collection of pieces of metal. Nearly all the rivets were loose on the frames, which were bent and broken. Three of the coaches were derailed and five out of the six on the train were damaged. General Hutchinson thought that to avoid such accidents in the future, the signalman at the station cabin should have control of the home signals for the north and south arrival lines.

Frost, or the break-up of it, caused the next accident, between Clapham and Giggleswick on March 16, 1895, when the 7.30 p.m. passenger train from Hellifield to Morecambe became derailed between the two stations when running at about 40 miles per hour. It was thought a recent thaw, and the passing of an express train a short time before, had spread the road slightly before the passage of the local. The engine, No. 1408, kept on the rails but probably contributed to the spread so that the wheels of the tender and the following three coaches left the rails. Damage was slight and the passengers only complained of a shaking. The line, which was composed of 24 ft. 77 lb steel rails and 40 lb chairs with inside keys, had only been inspected a short time before and had been found in good order. The Board of Trade inspecting officer, Major G. W. Addison, found that no-one could be held accountable for the accident but remarked that the driver of the preceding express who later reported that his engine had rolled when passing over the spot, should have mentioned this straight away instead of throwing it out later as an afterthought.

We now come to the first of the two really disastrous accidents which have taken place on the Settle and Carlisle section. Hawes Junction was the venue, and the chief actor was signalman Alfred Sutton. On Christmas Eve, 1910 the junction was to acquire a name among railway accidents which, for high drama has not often been equalled. It will be recalled that in the earlier accident at Hawes Junction there had been two signalboxes and that during the summer of 1910 these had been done away with and all the signalling concentrated into one box. This was situated on the down platform with the floor of the box about 8 feet above the platform level. Early in the morning, with a high wind buffeting the windows in the box, signalman Sutton was a busy man. He had come on duty at 8 p.m. the evening before and by early morning, besides the regular through trains, he had five light engines in the small yard to contend with. Two of them, Nos. 448 and 548 had arrived earlier and were waiting to run back light together to Carlisle. At about 5.20 a.m., immediately after a down special express had cleared the junction, Sutton signalled the two light engines to run across from the back platform road on to the down main line where they came to a halt at the advanced starter signal. It was Sutton's intention to send them on to Carlisle, coupled together, as soon as the down express ahead of them had cleared Ais Gill. On No. 548 there was a red tail light on the right hand lamp iron. While the engines were crossing over to the down main, at about 5.21, Sutton accepted an up goods train from the box at Ais Gill, and having done this began to move three other light engines. Two, which were bound for Leeds, came off the stockaded turntable line on to the back platform line, while the third ran back to a lie-by siding. While these movements were taking place, at about 5.25, Ais Gill box advised Sutton that the down special had cleared the section but at about this moment he was dealing with the preliminaries for the dispatch of the two Leeds engines, Nos. 247 and 249, and appears to have forgotten the two for Carlisle still standing at the advanced starter. The next train through the junction was the up goods from Ais Gill which rumbled past the box at 5.29. Hardly had its echoes been swallowed up by the wind than Ais Gill offered him another. Before accepting, Sutton asked Ais Gill how close the goods was as he wanted to get the two Leeds engines away in front of it. Ais Gill, however, wanted the goods to go through first and so Sutton accepted it at 5.32. During this time he was also concerned with arranging a relief for one of the Leeds enginemen besides sorting out by telephone the movements of two Hellifield engines on the turntable line.

So, the picture comes into focus. A very busy signalman, with relief trains and a number of light engines to deal with, as well as the normal traffic, all taking place on the eve of Christmas in a lonely box shaken by the winds which howl through the night over the northern Pennines. On the evening before, the down Scotch express had left St Pancras for Glasgow. As it roared out of Blea Moor tunnel and on towards Dent and signalman Sutton at Hawes Junction, the train, weighing about 378 tons, and travelling fast, consisted of a 2-4-0 pilot engine No. 48 and the 4-4-0 train engine No. 549 with, behind them, M. & G.S.W. 8-wheeled bogie brake third coach No. 237 with the brake compartment leading, M. & G.S.W. 8-wheeled bogie third class coach No. 225, two Midland 12-wheeled bogie sleeping cars Nos. 2765 and 2767, M. & G.S.W. 8-wheeled bogie first/third composite coach No. 227, M. & G.S.W. 8-wheeled bogie third class coach No. 203, M. & G.S.W. 8-wheeled bogie brake van No. 208, and Midland 6-wheeled brake van No. 337. The train had left Leeds about six minutes late and despite the fact that the load was a light one for two engines, a further ten minutes had been lost by the time it left Skipton. There were 56 passengers, 17 of whom were in the two sleeping cars under the charge of attendant Thomas Butlin. The passenger guard, John Mills, was in the seventh vehicle.

391

At 5.39 a.m., with the express approaching Dent station, the signalman there offered it to Hawes Junction and Sutton immediately accepted. As the second up goods from the north was running past his box, Sutton offered the express on to Ais Gill and on it being accepted he lowered all his down line signals to let it through. During all this time, for some 23 minutes, drivers Edwin Scott and George William Bath on the two Carlisle light engines had been waiting patiently—too patiently —at the down advanced starter signal. They must have known that they were only waiting for the previous down express to clear Ais Gill—which had happened 18 minutes earlier, though without them knowing the exact time—and as soon as they had run across from the down main they must have been expecting to see the signal come off for them almost immediately. But as has been seen, it was not until 5.43 that red changed to green—for the midnight express to pass.

Seeing the signal come off, both drivers gave a short whistle and set off for Carlisle. Even at this late stage catastrophe might have been averted if Sutton had heard the whistles for he might have been able to throw the signals to danger in front of the express. As it was the whistles were lost in the wind and in any event he would probably not have associated them with the two engines in question since the remaining three engines at the Junction were giving occasional whistles as they moved about.

The two Carlisle engines rounded the curve away from Hawes Junction and entered Moorcock tunnel at a speed of about 25 miles per hour. When about 500 yards north of the tunnel, driver Bath in the rear engine, No. 548, happened to glance back up the line, and through the dark of the night and into the tunnel he saw a sight which galvanised him into activity. For there, emerging from the tunnel, and coming up fast behind him on his road, were the headlights of a train. As it came out into the open he was appalled to see that it was gaining on them at what seemed a tremendous speed; fire seemed to be flowing from the smoke stacks of the two express engines. Spinning round he pushed his regulator wide open, shouted to his fireman to keep the whistle going full blast. It made no difference.

Driver Richard Johnston Oldcorn, on the pilot engine of the express, a man who was a passed fireman stationed at Carlisle but who had acted as a driver for over nine years in winter time, had noted that his train was still about 16 minutes late at Hawes Junction so it seems that there had been no excessive running done to make up time. Standing on the bucking footplate of No. 48 as it fumed through the tunnel, he had only about six seconds warning of the two engines ahead before the collision took place. The shock threw the two light engines forward about 190 yards in front of the eventual resting place of the pilot engine. In so doing, No. 548 and its tender were derailed on the outside of the down line and tore up the track for about 366 yards. The leading light engine, No. 448, kept the rails except for the leading and trailing wheels of the tender. In the next few seconds the Scotch express was turned into a hideous funeral pyre, for as the two leading coaches telescoped into each other, killing twelve passengers, fire from the engine coals lying about immediately took hold of the gas in the cylinders under the coaches. It consumed the whole train with the exception of the last two brake vans. Nine passengers were injured and thirteen more complained of shock. With the exception of the two sleeping cars which were electrically lit, all the remaining coaches were lit by Pintsch's gas light. The gas cylinders measured 6 feet by 4 inches and were filled to a pressure of 105 lbs. Only the frames, wheels, and axles of the first six coaches escaped destruction and from their position it was seen that they had all been derailed towards the outside of the line.

Major Pringle held the inquiry into the accident and Sutton was censured for forgetting the presence of the two light engines. He should, the Major said, have looked out at the line before setting the signals for the express and in any event ought to have entered the movements of the two engines into his train book. From his and another signalman's evidence, the enquiry heard that a poker or a piece of telegraph wire were sometimes used to latch the lever of a signal in the rear of a waiting train to remind the signalman of its presence. In the case of light engines, however, these 'homely devices' were not used since there were so many of them. For some time the Board of Trade had been pressing the Midland to introduce into its signal boxes collar clips for this same purpose, but the company had done nothing about it. 'There seems, therefore,' said the Major ruefully, after hearing about the uncertain use of the pokers and wire, 'to be some ground for the position the company have taken in respect to the supply of collar clips.' He also said that the two light engine drivers should have obeyed rule 55 which had been framed to cover just such an event. In short, this was that the firemen of light engines, and the guards of trains, kept waiting at a signal for longer than a certain period, were to go to the signal box and wait there until the signal was lowered. The fact that in this case they had not done so was bad enough; that they had waited silently in the darkness beyond the box without even bothering to whistle was worse. Their excuse was that they had thought the preceding special was in fact the Scotch express. Besides the recommendation that the company should adopt collar clips, the Major strongly advised the fitting of cut-off valves on the type of gas cylinder which had contributed so disastrously to the fire. Nearly two years later the Midland started to supply rescue equipment and fire extinguishers in the brake accommodation on long distance trains and the Midland and G.S.W.R. joint committee agreed that the 58 joint stock brake vans or the brake compartments should be similarly supplied.

The public might have had reason to hope that the Hawes Junction accident would never be repeated and so it was with shock and considerable anger that it was to learn within three years that something just as bad had happened—and within two miles of the first disaster. Again it was a rear collision and fire ensued.

Two southbound express trains were due to leave Carlisle at 1.35 a.m. and 1.49 a.m. on Tuesday, September 2, 1913. The first train from Glasgow, with a Stranraer portion at the back, was headed by 4-4-0 engine No. 993 driven by William Nicholson and fired by James Metcalf. It consisted of rolling stock in the following order : M. & G.S.W. 8-wheeled composite brake No. 254, two 8-wheeled Midland sleeping cars Nos. 2770 and 2777, M. & G.S.W. 8-wheeled third class coach No. 237, M. & G.S.W. 6-wheeled brake van No. 204, M. & G.S.W. 8-wheeled composite brake No. 250, Midland 8-wheeled third class coach No. 79, Midland 8-wheeled sleeping car No. 2785, M. & G.S.W. 8-wheeled third class coach No. 227, and M. & G.S.W. brake van No. 208. Before leaving Carlisle, Nicholson had expressed misgivings about the power of his locomotive to take the train over the summit at Ais Gill and had asked a station inspector for a pilot engine. He was told that there was not one available. This was not an unusual occurrence and it was said later at the inquiry that the company stipulated that when a driver had asked for assistance or was known to have an engine that might be overloaded, he would not be penalised for any resultant late running. Carlisle drivers at this time were continually harassed by a fear of running out of steam, for the locomotive fuel supplied was known to be inferior. The coal came from Naworth and though it was of good potential steam raising quality, the colliery had been told time and again that it was not being screened properly with the result that slack and small coal was getting into the locomotive tenders. Amends had been made during the summer but by September the poor quality was again evident, making it difficult to raise steam to a high working pressure. The matter, according to the Midland, was being actively taken up again with the colliery company by the stores department. Nicholson, in evidence later, told how on the very evening of the crash, so he had heard, another express had to stop twice for lack of steam on the bank.

At any event, the train left three minutes late and got as far as Ormside without any appreciable difficulty, but it was at this point that Nicholson began to have trouble in keeping sufficient steam raised to be able to make the correct time over the heavy gradient up to Ais Gill summit. As he approached Mallerstang, despite the fact that he had taken a turn at firing, the speed was down to about 20 miles per hour, and he was about 10 minutes behind time. By the time he had got past Mallerstang, with the regulator wide open, he found that the vacuum had dropped to 15 inches and he had to use the large ejector to keep the brakes off. Nothing could be done to help and slowly but surely the express came to a halt, at about 2.57 a.m. with only about 80 pounds of steam pressure, 185 yards north of Ais Gill down distant signal. Only half a mile further on was the level road of the summit stretch, with the long run down to Settle beyond.

Sixteen minutes after the Glasgow train left Carlisle it was followed out by the up Edinburgh Scotch express, running five minutes late, headed by 4-4-0 engine No. 446, driven by Samuel Caudle and fired by George Herbert Follows. Caudle was a man of considerable experience; he had been driving over the Settle line for most of his 29 years as a driver and had worked over the route for 37 years, the time in fact that the line had been open. His fireman, Follows, however, though also fairly experienced, was new to the type of engine. The Edinburgh train consisted of all 8-wheeled M. & N.B. rolling stock in the following order behind the tender : third class brake No. 123, composite sleeping car No. 155, composite brake No. 143, sleeping car No. 171, composite brake No. 142, and composite coach No. 122. The whole train only weighed 245 tons compared with Nicholson's train of 349 tons. For some reason the second express did a slower time to Ormside than the first but there the similarity ended for the lighter weight told, and No. 446 made easy going of the rising gradients. After passing through Kirkby Stephen, driver Caudle performed the usual duty of moving off the footplate at a point where he knew the road would be steady, to oil his engine, leaving Follows in charge. He found the wind to be stronger than he had expected and was therefore longer than usual on the job.

Meanwhile the fireman, still feeling his way on the strange engine, was having difficulty with the right-hand injector. Both men were there-fore busily engaged and the duties of looking out for signals were largely forgotten. As soon as the first express had passed his box, signalman Sutherland at Mallerstang had put all his signals to danger. The first of these to be encountered by the second train was the Mallerstang up distant, and as he swept up to it on his exposed position on the engine framing, driver Caudle thought he saw it in the clear position. Almost immediately afterwards he groped his way back to the cab and tried to assist Follows with the injector. At about this time, at 2.56, signalman Sutherland became aware of the train's approach. He immediately got through to Ais Gill to ask what had happened to the first express. His colleague there, Thomas Clemmet, replied that the train had not passed. So far everything was alright, however, as far as Sutherland was con-cerned, but at this point he made a bad mistake; he looked out of his box at the approaching train and assumed, or thought he saw, that it was not steaming. Remembering that all his up signals were at danger he imagined that the driver had slowed in obedience to the distant signal, and so he lowered his home signal so that Caudle could proceed slowly up to the starter which he had left at danger. Caudle, however, was still blissfully ignorant of any danger—still thought he was running under clear signals all the way. Almost as soon as he had lowered the home signal, Sutherland saw with consternation that the express was in fact steaming hard and was moving at speed. Throwing the home signal to danger, he violently waved a red lamp at the driver but without success. With mounting horror the signalman watched the train run past the starter signal, still mutely at danger, and then dashed over to the bell to warn Clemmet at Ais Gill that he had a train running away on the right line. The signal was immediately acknowledged but Clemmet was powerless to do anything. Away in the dark, somewhere between the two boxes, certain devastating destruction was coming to two trains.

When the Glasgow express had crawled to a halt the guard, David Charles Donnelly, had gone along to Nicholson and asked him how long it would take to get up steam. Though Nicholson later admitted that he knew it would take at least 10 minutes, he had replied 'only a few minutes'. Donnelly also said that the driver advised him to 'go back to your van'. Turning on his heel, Donnelly walked back to the rear of the train and called out to the guard there, Oliver Whitley, that the driver had said he would be about a minute. Almost as he spoke the two men heard the noise of an approaching train. At this last moment Whitley decided that the rear of his train ought to have been protected and set off walking down the line. A second or two later he realized the noise was from a train fast approaching on his line and he started to run forward showing a red lamp. He was much too late. Anyone of these experienced men should have known that a stoppage for lack of steam took longer than a mere few minutes, and in any case Whitley should immediately have taken steps in the case of any breakdown or failure, to protect the rear of the train. It had, in fact, been standing for no less than seven minutes.

Meanwhile, a few seconds before, Caudle had got the injector working satisfactorily but had suddenly realised that he had gone through Mallerstang without noticing the signals. Instead of stopping, or at least slowing, he kept the regulator open and watched Follows put some more coal on the fire. The fireman, with eyes still dazzled through the white heat of the firebox, peered ahead through the night and thought he saw two red lights ahead which he took to be the distant and home signals at Ais Gill. After giving a short whistle to warn the signal-man he suddenly realized that they were the back lights of a train. Caudle, still wondering why Follows had sounded the whistle, heard the latter shout 'Look out, Sam, there's a red light in front of us'. He immediately applied the brake and closed the regulator. There were only 50 yards between engine No. 446, travelling at about 30 miles per hour, and the M. & G.S.W. brake van ahead of it. They met at about 3.04 a.m., the line's worst accident, brought about by a whole catalogue of negligence.

Seconds earlier signalman Sutherland heard the sound of an engine whistle near Ais Gill and then a rumbling sound of collision. Signalman Clemmet listened from his box too; when Sutherland had asked him about the first train he had listened for it but a strong north-east wind carried into oblivion any sounds it might have been making. A few seconds later he saw 'a light rising and falling like a red mist away beyond the distant signal'. Seven or so minutes later fireman Metcalf stumbled out of the darkness into Clemmet's cabin. By this time both Kirkby Stephen and Hawes Junction boxes had been warned of the collision by the two signalmen and within half an hour the Hawes station master, William Henry Bunce, was on the scene. To detail what he found would be unpleasant; passengers were trapped in burning wreckage, others were vainly trying to drag them out in the blistering heat of a terrible fire that had got a hold on the last three vehicles of the first train. Doctors were soon on the scene; their evidence to the inquiry was harrowing. The whole of the first train had been driven forward about 13 or 14 yards by the force of the collision. The last two vehicles were reduced immediately to a mass of wreckage piled up on the smoke box of engine No. 446 which, with its damper open, scattered red hot ash underneath it. There seems to have been an attempt to remove the next vehicle, the sleeping car, but this was given up when it was found that it was buffer locked with the rear vehicle. At first, according to some witnesses, all the lights in the carriages went out, followed almost immediately by a burst of flame and explosion from the gas cylinders. In fact, however, the enquiry seemed satisfied that the fire extinguishers on the train and the cut-off valves on the cylinders—fruits of the Hawes Junction accident—had enabled the fire from the cylinders to have been brought under control. Too free a play with the extinguishers, however, meant that there was nothing left to deal with the really sudden and bad outbreak which came from the ash under the firebox setting light to the tinder dry wreckage strewn around. When Bunce arrived on the scene all the carriages of the first express, except the last three, had been drawn forward. Up to about then passengers and staff had been working in a nightmare darkness after the gas was put out but the steadily rising glare from the real fire soon gave them all the light they wanted. As the injured were taken out they were sent off to Kirkby Stephen and Hawes Junction. Two doctors who came on the scene within a short time found that all the injured were out but that the fire still burned in what had been the rear carriage of the first express. It was with some small degree of thankfulness that the enquiry heard that from the doctors' examination of some of the charred human remains in the wreckage, they were certain that death had taken place before the fire had reached them. 14 passengers died and were burnt, two more died later, and 38 suffered from injury, some in the first vehicle of the second train.

Since there was an idea that the inquiry might lead to criminal proceedings against one or more of the railway staff it was decided, according to precedent, to hold it in private. The first sitting was at Kirkby Stephen but as the public obviously thought, according to Major Pringle, that matters were being hushed up, he decided to hold the second and subsequent sittings in public, in Leeds and later in London. He found that in some way or another many people had contributed to the disaster. Driver Caudle, however, was singled out as the chief culprit, and signalman Sutherland was censured for not making sure that the second train was slowing before lowering his home signal. As to this latter issue, it was pointed out in mitigation that it would not have made any difference anyway. Such was the outcry against the Midland that Guy Granet thought it best to give a full account of the progress made by the company in implementing the Board of Trade Inspector's recommendations after the Hawes Junction crash. His evidence showed that the company had done all it could. (A brief summary of the signalling improvements put into force appears in Chapter XVII and a chronology of permanent way and signalling alterations since 1890, in Appendix XXII). Recommendations from the Ais Gill inquiry were many; though the rescue tools were sufficient it seems that in the confusion following the crash few people knew with certainty where they were kept; notices of their location should be positioned in the corridors. Automatic appliances on the track to warn a train running through signals were suggested as were flares for stranded trains to fire off. Instructions should be given to enginemen that when absent from the footplate they must ensure that the fireman watched the signals. Steel under-frames for rolling stock with shock absorbing buffers and with woodwork to be rendered non-inflammable were strongly advised, and finally a further recommendation was made that gas should be replaced by electricity as a means of train lighting. (These points are discussed in Chapter XVIII.) Major Pringle thought that the poor grade of coal, though a contributory factor, was like the absence of a pilot engine at Carlisle, merely part of a chain of events which led inexorably to the tragedy. In the interim before the report was published the Midland board decided to make the following donations to those involved in the crash : to doctors 350 guineas, to infirmaries 300 guineas, to passengers 800 guineas, and to staff 350 guineas .About a week after the report came out the doctors' sum went up to £420.

Press and public were not at all satisfied with the report, and a campaign was launched against the Midland and the Board of Trade. Individual s were roused to a fury; a postcard at present in the custody of the Archivist to the Railways Board typifies public feeling. Addressed in block capitals to 'Sir G GRANET MID Ry DERBY', and postmarked from Kilburn, it carried on the back a newspaper cutting :—

'LATEST OFFICIAL MESSAGE

'Late last night the Press Association received the following telegram from the general manager of the Midland Railway Company:

"The fire was confined to the three last coaches of the first train, and was started by the fire scattered from the engine of the second train on collision.

"The doctors who have made the post-mortem examination have given us authority to say that in their opinion there is no doubt that those passengers who lost their lives were instantly killed by the collision.

"Owing to the impossibility of removing the bodies whilst the fire was burning, identification is extremely difficult.

"The total number of lives lost is fourteen." '

The writer of the postcard heavily marked the second paragraph of

Sir Guy's statement and then added, again in block capitals, the following :

> 'WHAT A LYING
> STATEMENT TO MAKE.
> WHAT HAVE YOU DONE
> SINCE THE LAST
> DISASTER, NEARLY
> NIL.
> Signed   A PASSENGER'

On the whole the Press faithfully reported the inquiry. There were remarks upon the public misgivings that after the Hawes accident the Midland had again killed a number of passengers under similar circumstances. Comparison was made with one of the big Canadian lines which apparently could boast that it had never had a fatality. Arthur Henderson, M.P., chairman of the Labour Party, spoke for many when he wrote the following in the *Derby Daily Telegraph* of December 8, 1913 :

'The report of the Board of Trade inquiry into the Ais Gill disaster is published, and anything more disappointing could scarcely be imagined. The inquiry opened with a deliberate attempt to conceal the facts from the public, and only a strong remonstrance from the Press served to defeat that proposal. As the evidence proceeded it became manifest that the refusal of a pilot engine and the continued use of cheap coal had contributed largely, if not entirely, to the cause of the collision. There were other obvious irregularities which helped to swell the horrors of that terrible calamity. The use of gas at a time when most other companies had discarded it showed, too, that the Midland company put profit before safety. The public, I repeat, constituted the jury in this matter, and the verdict did not await the "touches" of a Board of Trade official to complete its significance. On the principal points England had one mind, and it is therefore interesting, at all events, to know now that the inspector's opinion was opposed thereto.'

Henderson thought the report was worthless; the B.O.T. had no power to compel and the inquiry was therefore little more than a farce. The coal question was made to seem unimportant but Henderson claimed the company had changed the supply immediately after the accident. It was, he said, untrue that drivers were allowed more time if a pilot engine was not provided; as to drivers being advised not to oil their engines while trains were in motion, it was well known that if certain results followed from a dry axle the driver was punished. Henderson's article reflected the public's view. The railwaymen, however, had a different spokesman. Great anger had been aroused by the report amongst the Midland locomotive men, and J. H. Thomas, M.P., made a statement at the headquarters of the National Union of Railwaymen, to the *Morning Post*. It was published on Thursday, November 27, and completely refuted the statement that if a pilot engine was not allowed the driver was given extra time to do the journey.

'It was clearly pointed out at the inquest and not denied by the locomotive superintendent at Carlisle', said Mr Thomas, 'that prior to the accident there was a notice to drivers posted informing them that they must keep time with their trains even if they had more than their allowance load. That notice was posted at the Carlisle sheds, but was taken down immediately after the accident.'

He described the coal as being like dust and remarked that when water was added it turned to liquid. He thought the coal was definitely the major cause of the crash; it had as much to do with the trouble experienced on the second train, with steam shortage and water low in the glass, as it did with the first. As to oiling, Major Pringle had pointed out that, due to recent improvements in lubrication, there was no need to oil the engine during the journey.

'This is not true. The engine that Caudle had and every engine of the same class has had the "well" for lubrication purposes stopped, and Caudle was most emphatic in stating his only object in leaving the footplate was to prevent the engine getting hot. There is not a driver on the Midland system today working this class of engine who does not have to leave the footplate every run to do similar work.'

Referring to the B.O.T. report, Mr Thomas ended 'A factory inspector can insist upon his recommendations being carried into effect but in the case of the Board of Trade these reports of their inspectors are merely pious expressions of opinion, whilst what shall be done is left entirely to the discretion of the railway company'.

There can be no doubt that these two attacks on the Midland were but samples from a number which had a veiled political motive behind them. Nevertheless the evidence pointed to a disquieting state of affairs. It was true that the Midland had been making progress towards remedying some of the bad points brought out by the Hawes Junction crash before the Ais Gill disaster, but it took the latter to produce a coaching revolution in which wooden stock was rejected in favour of steel.

The three main points at issue throughout this awful business—those of the lack of a pilot engine, oiling locomotives in motion, and the supposedly bad coal—will bear a little more examination. The first was touched upon by Granet in his report at the inquiry. Pilot engines were supposed to be supplied to trains when they were definitely thought to be overloaded for the class of engine hauling them. On this occasion, however, two factors had combined to negative Nicholson's request for assistance; his train was only just overweight, and it would have taken some time to get the pilot engine coupled on, though there was one available despite the evidence. The station inspector had thought it unnecessary. What Granet did not say, and what the inquiry could not know, was that there had for some time been a campaign against piloting. Indeed, in 1898, Johnson had inveighed against the practice as being altogether too common, and had introduced a premium scheme to reward drivers who took the highest number of vehicles and kept the most correct times, with the least assistance from pilot engines. Later, Deeley thought the awards—made up partly from fines taken from their erring mates—so paltry as to be not worth the enginemen striving for. He had scrapped the system in 1904, and had put the money towards deserving cases on retirement. Nevertheless, with the big engine policy which had transformed the locomotive working it is quite certain that, to put it no stronger, piloting had come to be considered *infra dig* in official circles.

Oiling engines in motion. Here the minutes give a clear lead on official thinking. In January, 1901, two accidents, at Melton and Birmingham, in which enginemen were injured while off the footplates of their moving locomotives, resulted in a recommendation being made to Johnson that the company should issue instructions to drivers and firemen that they must not leave the footplate while their engines were in motion. Also, neither of them should move the engine while the other was engaged in working off the footplate. Finally, arrangements should be made for sufficient time to be allowed for the enginemen to oil their locomotives while at rest. In his reply, noted in the locomotive committee minutes for April 4, 1901, Johnson stated that, in his opinion, it was not advisable to issue such instructions '—as they could not be rigidly enforced without seriously interfering with the working of the traffic, and without causing engines to fail on the road much more frequently than they do now'. He thought the current instructions warning engine crews against running unnecessary risks were quite sufficient.

On the question of coal, let us hear Granet in his own words to the inquiry. He is defending the Midland against insinuations convicting it of 'blameworthy parsimony' :

'The coal used by the two engines in question was a mixture of Naworth and Blackett coal. The latter coal had been used on the engines working the Scotch express trains for a period of over two years. The Naworth coal had only been used since July 1st last (this being the first contract the company had made with this colliery company), and is the coal to which these criticisms have been applied. Let me say at once that the Naworth coal was only bought after a satisfactory analysis made by the company, an analysis which showed that it was better as regards calorific value, and, indeed, in every other respect, than the coal which we have always regarded as the best English coal, viz., the South Yorkshire.

'The price we paid was 6d. higher than the price we paid at the same time for the best South Yorkshire coal, and was 1s. 6d. higher than the price we were then paying for Derbyshire and Nottinghamshire coal. The contract was not made until after careful tests had been made on locomotives running between Carlisle and Leeds. The report on these tests was excellent.

'When the contract was made it was stipulated that the coal should be screened through ¾ inch bars. The delivery of this coal commenced on July 1st, and on August 1st a complaint was received at Derby that the coal was giving trouble. An inspector was sent down on August 5th to enquire into the matter, and he reported that the coal was not of the size contracted for. The matter was immediately taken up with the colliery people by telegram on August 6th, followed up by a letter on the same date, and the colliery managers agreed to, and did, put matters right. On August 21st the inspector was again sent down to inspect the coal at Carlisle, and he reported that the deliveries were then in every way satisfactory.

'After that we had no further complaints as to the coal, and we assumed, and had the right to assume, that deliveries were being made according to contract. I must, however, make this admission—that on the night in question the coal supplied to the engines working the two trains was, by reason of its smallness, but only for that reason, such as to make it very difficult, if not impossible, for the drivers to keep a full head of steam. So far as the size of the coal was concerned, therefore, it was a bad coal, and it was undoubtedly very difficult for driver Caudle to keep the steam pressure up in his boiler with that coal. I do not know that I have the right to say so, but, in my opinion, whatever blame that driver has incurred for the faults he has admitted, the circumstance I have referred to is one which should be taken into full account in weighing the amount of blame which should be laid upon him.' *

* *Railway Engineer,* October, 1913.

Granet resented the suggestion that the coal had a poor calorific quality or that it was in any other way unsuitable. It had a calorific value of 15,150 British thermal units per pound, '—which makes it equal in steam-raising value to good Welsh coal, and better than the very best South Yorkshire coal'. He thought it quite possible that a wagon of small coal might well, quite unintentionally, have got mixed in with the others at the colliery and gone unnoticed.

On the face of it Granet's reasoning seems fair enough, but once again the minutes—this time of the stores committee—bring some interesting facts to light; facts which give a more balanced picture. They show that the Midland was partly the victim of its own current experiments to cut costs. It had to do with internal economies—hardly a subject to be appreciated as evidence at the inquiry. There had for some time been an argument in progress between the locomotive and traffic committees. For years the latter had been hauling the locomotive coal and had been debited with the cost of conveying it from the collieries to the coaling points. When the Settle line was opened the Midland was using predominantly South Yorkshire and Nottinghamshire coals. From the nearest point of supply, therefore, there was an almighty journey to be made for the tenders to be filled at Durran Hill. With the traffic people making their point, it became clear to the locomotive committee that a source much nearer to hand should be found. All this took time, and there was no real sense of urgency about it. However, when an offer was made in June of 1913 by Messrs J. Fenwick of Newcastle, to supply 100 tons of 'Naworth' steam coal at 13s. per ton, pit, from July 1, 1913 to December 31, 1913, the stores committee received approval to complete a contract. The colliery was but a few miles from Carlisle, on the Newcastle and Carlisle line. On June 26 a further contract was entered into for an additional 200 tons per week. A fortnight later, things began to go wrong. A stores committee minute dated July 10, 1913, tells that :

'It was reported that J. Fenwick (Naworth Colliery), being unable to supply the 100 tons per week of coal, screened over $1\frac{1}{4}$ inch screens, at 13s. per ton, pit, as reported on June 5th—in addition to 200 tons per week, screened over $\frac{3}{4}$ inch screens, at 13s. per ton, pit, as reported on June 26th—, it has been agreed to accept, in place of the first contract, 100 tons per week of coal, screened over $\frac{3}{4}$ inch screens, at 12s. 9d. per ton, pit.'

So, an inferior grade of screening to that which must have been agreed upon as being suitable was knowingly accepted at a cheaper price. Up to a point, the dashing about of an inspector between Derby and Carlisle, to look at the grade of coal being supplied, was something of a red herring. Despite the fact that Granet mentioned in the first instance that the $\frac{3}{4}$ in. screening was the contracted amount, he knew that it had already been taken as second best. Further, despite all the talk of the coal being so wonderful, when in December 1913 invitations were sent out for tenders for coal—over fifty of them—Messrs Fenwick and the Naworth Colliery did not figure therein. All the December contracts went back to South Yorkshire and Nottinghamshire.

A last note on Samuel Caudle : David L. Smith, in his *Tales of the Glasgow and South Western Railway*, remarks that after Ais Gill, Caudle was demoted to work in the shed yard at Durran Hill. From the Midland's point of view his perpetual presence on the scene may well have been engineered as an object lesson for his former colleagues, by whom it seems he was looked upon with a certain sympathy.

The last accident to occur on the Settle line before the Grouping, took place on January 19, 1918 at Little Salkeld. As the 8.50 a.m. St Pancras to Glasgow express, headed by 4-4-0 compound engine No. 1010, ran through Long Meg cutting, about ¾ mile north of Little Salkeld station, and through which a platelayer had walked but five minutes before without noticing anything unusual, the engine ran into a massive landslide brought on by a thaw which had been in progress over the past few days. The driver was on it before he could do anything and the engine, running at about a mile a minute, churned into the thick clay and came rapidly to a halt, leaning over towards the cutting slope. The two leading coaches were violently telescoped and seven passengers were killed. This time there was no fire. The engine was not badly damaged and was at work again quite soon. It had been an accident which could not have been avoided—perhaps the only one so far, bar the Giggleswick derailment of 1895. First news of the accident came from one of the passengers, Mr. A. W. Thomas, the company's assistant traffic superintendent at Carlisle, scrambled from the train and ran to Little Salkeld signal box. For Mr Thomas it was the end to a hectic 48 hours; the previous day he had accompanied one of the many explosives trains then running over the Settle line on their journey from Gretna to the south. As these frequently entailed journeying into London in the midst of Zeppelin and Gotha raids the job was anything but a picnic.

Strange to relate, No. 1010 was in another accident at Little Salkeld on July 10, 1933 when, due to a signalman having permitted a goods train to shunt without complying with block regulations, the engine, heading the 12.44 p.m. from Carlisle to St Pancras, came into sidelong collision at considerable speed, killing the goods driver. Having been in two crashes, the engine had a reputation thereafter for being unlucky.

There have been other accidents, some quite recently, but they will be dealt with in the next chapter as part of the summary of the line's further history from the Grouping to the present day. With regard to the Midland accidents, however, practically all of them easily fall into the usual categories; errors by signalmen, by drivers running through signals, or from complete disregard of working instructions. To a certain extent they served some purpose in that, together with all the other mishaps on the railways of Great Britain, they contributed to the fund of operating knowledge and safety regulations which have through the years made the railway carriage perhaps the safest form of travelling conveyance yet designed by man.

XX

From the Twenties to the Doctor's Dilemma

When the Midland became part of the London Midland & Scottish Railway by the Grouping of 1923, the Settle line began its slow and inexorable decline; the shortest route to Scotland, over Shap, naturally took first place for speed in the new company's timetables. That times had changed was apparent over the next few years; there was a progressive withdrawal from the Midland route of some of the through coaches so that passengers joining the line south of Leeds eventually found that to get to Dundee, Aberdeen, Perth, Inverness, and Fort William, they had to change *en route*.

Considering the fastest trains from London to the north, compared with the 1914 speeds, the Midland section lagged behind. 'Voyageur', writing in the *Railway Magazine* in 1923, gave a table of fastest times which is of interest. Extracting from it details of the three main lines from London to Scotland it is apparent that as regards the London–Carlisle run, the L.N.W.R. route over a distance of 299.1 miles had a fastest 1923 time on the down journey of 5 hours 50 minutes, a worsening of 2 minutes over 1914, while the Midland route over 309 miles took 6 hours 23 minutes, worse by 18 minutes over the 1914 time. On the London–Edinburgh run the 1923 East Coast timing of 7 hours 45 minutes was the same as that in 1914, as was the West Coast timing of 8 hours. The Midland 1923 fastest speed, however, of 9 hours 16 minutes compared badly with the 1914 time of 8 hours 40 minutes. This may, of course, have been due partially to the service being a joint effort with the London & North Eastern Railway north of Carlisle. On the London–Glasgow journey the situation was slightly better, though the Midland route still flagged. The L.N.E.R. did the run in 1923 in 9 hours 10 minutes, an improvement of 10 minutes on the 1914 schedule; the West Coast took 8 hours 15 minutes as opposed to 8 hours dead; while the Midland took 9 hours 5 minutes, 20 minutes longer than the 1914 timing. The two L.M.S. journeys fell together on this one.

The summer timetable for 1923, commented on in the *Railway Magazine* of that year, gives an idea of the service on the Midland section during the first season of the new regime :

'While in general, the additions to be made to these services correspond to those which usually occur to meet the special needs of the summer months, several items may be selected for reference. Thus, the 9 a.m. and 9.15 p.m. trains from St Pancras to Edinburgh are accelerated to reach Edinburgh at 6.19 p.m.

404

and 7.5 a.m. respectively. A new express runs from Leeds at 4.18 p.m. to Bradford, in connection with the 12.15 p.m. from St Pancras, and from Bradford at 3.10 p.m. to Leeds, in connection with the 3.45 p.m. train, thence to St Pancras, conveying through carriages in each direction between Bradford and London. The 3.15 p.m. Sunday train from St Pancras is now accelerated to reach Sheffield at 6.53 p.m., Leeds 8.5 p.m., and has a through portion for Bradford, due 8.38 p.m. The 12.15 p.m. Sunday train from Leeds is accelerated to reach St Pancras at 5.27 p.m.

'A new feature of the St Pancras–Harrogate service is the dining facilities provided by the running of 1st and 3rd class restaurant cars on the 11.45 a.m from St Pancras through to Harrogate. The cars return from Harrogate to St Pancras on the 12.3 train. These facilities augment the ordinary through carriages and through trains between St Pancras and Harrogate.'

The Harrogate dining cars were instituted in answer to the L.N.E.R. Pullman service to the spa from King's Cross. The L.M.S. diners were withdrawn on September 24, 1928.

Though in the matter of pro rata speed increases after the Grouping the Midland section appeared to be taking second place to the West Coast route, it was soon to have its day in the field of the locomotive building programme then being considered by the L.M.S. authorities. On the Midland side the largest engines were the compounds. They were ranged against the more powerful ex L.N.W.R. 'Claughtons', super-heated 'Precursors', 'Prince of Wales', and super-heated 'George the Fifth' classes. It had become obvious that a degree of standardisation should obtain as soon as possible and for a time it seemed as if the very small number of Midland types would not be replaced. The appointment of an ex Midland officer, John Follows, to the position of general super-intendent of the L.M.S., however, with the consequent Midland traffic control policy that came with him, meant that smaller trains would be the attempted pattern of the future. That being so, it became necessary to agree upon a locomotive class which was capable of satisfying train schedules based upon the lighter loadings. In fact, what was needed was a good class 4 locomotive. There were three such types, the Midland compound, the Midland '999' class 4-4-0, and the L.N.W.R. 4-6-0 'Prince of Wales' class. It was decided to put representatives of each' on a series of test runs over the Leeds–Settle–Carlisle route.

The locomotives selected were compound No. 1008, Deeley simple 4-4-0 No. 998, and L.N.W.R. 'Prince of Wales' class No. 388. Mr O. S. Nock has only recently recounted details of the tests—which started on December 10, 1923, and went on until January 17—in his monograph *The Midland Compounds*. Suffice it to say here that No. 1008 exceeded all expectations and was proved undeniably to be the better engine for the purpose required. It was generally better than No. 998, and though sometimes outstripped in speed on upward gradients by the 'Prince of Wales', it used less coal. It would be fair to say, however, as Mr Nock points out, that the compound was fresh out of the shops at the time of the tests whereas its rivals were not. Nevertheless, it did so well that the test load was soon increased to a point which would have seemed impossibly heavy for such an engine before the tests began. The trains used for the test runs were the 12.10 p.m. from Carlisle and the 4.7 p.m. from Leeds. Study of the results indicated beyond doubt that the compound would be a very good general engine for the L.M.S. At the time of the tests 20 compounds, Nos. 1045–1064, were under construction; a further 20 were ordered almost immediately, numbered 1065–1084.

With the Midland engine's success seemingly unbeatable it was arranged that there should be further tests over the Settle line in the autumn of 1924, the locomotives to haul the same trains as before. As the compound had been so decisively a better performer than engines of similar class, it was pitted this time against a L.N.W.R. 4-6-0 'Claughton', and a Caledonian Pickersgill 4-4-0 No. 124. The tests took place between November 18 and December 10, 1924 and the compounds were represented by No. 1065, the first in the latter batch of 20 ordered from Derby after the previous tests, No. 1023, one of the early 1906 engines, and No. 1066, sister engine to 1065. It was soon apparent that the Caledonian locomotive was not really in the running as regards anything over a 300 ton train, and that the L.N.W.R. locomotive was in poor shape. Mr Nock says that it was intended that a Carlisle engine should have taken part but that owing to the current shortage of engines the only 'Claughton' which could be prised loose from the operating people was No. 2221 *Sir Francis Dent,* out of Edge Hill shed. It was apparently about the least fit engine the shed could provide, and steamed badly. Even so, according to Mr Cecil J. Allen, writing in the *Railway Magazine* in February, 1925, it had its good moments. The older of the three Midland engines did not do too well, making very heavy weather of the gradients, but the two new engines ran excellently.

In February 1925 the Settle line was again the venue for tests, this time between compounds Nos. 1060 and 1065, each with differing modifications, and with dynamometer car attached. Again, the results of the tests, and the interesting and vital discussions which followed, have been dealt with in detail by Mr Nock. Once more they vindicated the compound design, and were followed by more tests between Preston and Carlisle during the following May. The results were deemed to justify the building of a further 100 compounds. So successful were the tests, in fact, that Sir Henry Fowler, who became chief mechanical engineer of the L.M.S. in 1925, at once prepared drawings for a 4-6-0 variety, with outside Walschaerts gear. To take this story any further would be well off the main subject. The fine test ground of the Leeds–Settle–Carlisle line, however, had been of inestimable use in deciding the engine policy of the nascent L.M.S.

Despite their success, the Midland compounds had perforce to give way eventually to something bigger. In 1927 and 28, when Sir Henry Fowler's new 'Royal Scots' released the 'Claughtons' from the West Coast route, some twenty of these engines were transferred to Holbeck and Durran Hill sheds. Though the compounds were henceforth secondary engines on the route, they continued to serve for many years.

During the late twenties there were some interesting developments concerning traffic over the northern portion of the Midland division. The first was the inauguration of two named trains over the Settle line in 1927—the 'Thames–Clyde Express', which ran between St Pancras and Glasgow St Enoch, and the 'Thames–Forth Express' which did the St Pancras–Edinburgh Waverley trip. An important addition to passenger comfort came in 1928 with the introduction of third class sleeping facilities by the L.M.S. between Euston, St Pancras, and Glasgow and Edinburgh, with through services to, amongst other places, Stranraer, Perth, Aberdeen, and Inverness. The new services, along with those of the L.N.E.R. and G.W.R. which started at the same time, commenced on September 24. The L.M.S. coaches were constructed at Derby and had seven compartments with lavatory and toilet accommodation at each end of the corridor, which had an entrance vestibule, also at either end. The compartments, which were hardly distinguishable from ordinary day coaches when not in use as sleepers, were only provided with doors at the corridor side, ensuring privacy to the occupants when the train was at a platform. Each compartment took eight passengers during the day, and four at night, when the top berths were pulled down by the attendant. Each berth was equipped with a pillow and a rug. A considerable amount of mahogany was used in the interior woodwork. The carpeting was of grey mohair and the upholstery in a light fawn velvet. The cars were 60 ft. long, weighed 29 tons, and ran on two four-wheeled bogies. The charge, which was additional to the third class fare, included the reservation and was 6s for journeys between stations in England and Wales, and between stations in Scotland, and 7s for those from England to Scotland. The trains running on the Midland division which operated the new cars included the following :

DOWN TRAINS

9.15 p.m.	St. Pancras to Edinburgh Waverley.	All week.
9.30 p.m.	St. Pancras to Glasgow St. Enoch.	Saturdays excepted.
11.45 p.m.	St. Pancras to Glasgow St. Enoch.	Saturdays only.

UP TRAINS

9.55 p.m.	Edinburgh Waverley to St. Pancras.	All week.
9.15 p.m.	Glasgow St. Enoch to St. Pancras.	Saturdays excepted.
11.15 p.m.	Glasgow St. Enoch to St. Pancras.	Saturdays only.

In 1926 the L.M.S. decided to transfer to Heysham the steamer services then operating from Fleetwood, and at the same time to rationalise the vessels then operating the Irish services by ordering three new ships to replace the more numerous and older fleet. Apart from the questionable practice of continuing to operate two ports in such close proximity, Fleetwood was becoming very congested and it was agreed that the services should be concentrated on Heysham from Monday, April 30, 1928. At the same time it was decided to drop the Isle of Man service and this was taken over—together with the vessels *Antrim* and

Duke of Cornwall—by the Isle of Man Steam Packet Company. Its new owners renamed the *Antrim* as *Ramsey Town*; the steamer was eventually broken up in 1936. Meanwhile, the *City of Belfast*, which had been returned after the First World War, was sold in 1925, and the *Londonderry* two years later. The *Duchess of Devonshire*, also back from war service, and operating on the Heysham route, was made redundant when the new vessels were delivered, and was sold. The three new twin screw ships, known as the three 'Dukes', the *Duke of Lancaster, Duke of Argyll,* and *Duke of Rothesay,* were all of about 3,600 gross tons and were capable of 21 knots. They were at the time of their delivery described in the *Railway Magazine* as 'the fastest, largest, and most luxuriously equipped on any cross-channel service, being modelled on the general principles of ocean liners. . . .' They were to operate on the Heysham Irish services for about 25 years, eventually being replaced by the present-day fleet of passenger and cargo vessels.

The summer train services for 1929, as mentioned in the *Railway Magazine* that August, showed a few alterations:

'The 9.15 a.m. restaurant-car express, Glasgow (St Enoch) to London (St Pancras), connects at Carlisle with the 12.30 p.m. restaurant-car express to Birmingham, calling at Preston, giving connections to Liverpool (Exchange) and Manchester (Victoria) . . . The 10 a.m. Sunday restaurant-car express from Glasgow (Central) conveys a portion for London (St Pancras), which connects at Carlisle with a new Sunday train leaving Carlisle at 12.55 p.m. for Bradford, Leeds, Sheffield, Nottingham, Leicester, etc. The 9.50 a.m. restaurant-car express London (St Pancras) to Glasgow (St Enoch) has a new connection to Ayr, via Mauchline. An additional restaurant-car express will leave Leicester on Sundays at 12.40 p.m. via Nottingham, Derby, Sheffield, and Leeds, for Carlisle, Glasgow (Central) and Edinburgh (Princes Street).'

On March 6, 1930 there was an accident on the Settle line. Early in the morning a ballast train was propelled into Waste Bank tunnel, near Culgaith. It was brought to a halt in the tunnel on the down line, out of sight of signals. In order that the signalman should be able to warn the flagman of the ballast if he wanted it moved, it was arranged that the former should shake the up distant signal wire. To protect the train the flagman had put detonators down at the rear, in this case 'rear' being in front of the ballast's engine, 0-6-0 No. 4009. Running on the down line was the 8.05 a.m. Hellifield–Carlisle passenger train drawn by 'Claughton' class 4-6-0 No. 5971, *Croxteth*. Several events combined to produce a collision. The arrival of another train at Culgaith apparently determined the flagman to move the ballast of his own accord and he proceeded to take up the detonators. Meanwhile, the 'Claughton' was being driven by the fireman, so as to gain experience, and after the guard had given the 'all right' signal—at a moment when he was very busy with some parcels—there was a muddled time in which the passenger train started against the signal, apparently nobody being any the wiser. Having started off, the passenger guard did not take any safeguarding action.

The result was a head-on collision of some violence in which the driver of the 'Claughton' was killed and a passenger later died in hospital. Incidentally the accident provided the excuse for the rebuilding of the passenger engine as the first of the new 'Patriot' class.

By 1931 the 'Claughtons' were responsible for most of the heavier trains on the Leeds–Settle–Carlisle line. The working at Carlisle of one of the rebuilt 'Claughton' class—or 'Baby Scots' as they were called—was noted by Mr G. J. Aston, in the *Railway Magazine* of July 1931. The engine concerned was No. 5971 again, operating in its rebuilt form daily on the 6.10 a.m. from Leeds to Carlisle. As this was a stopping train, and the engine's return working was on the 12.05 p.m. fast from Carlisle to Leeds, the turning-round time at Carlisle was reduced to a very thin 65 minutes. Apparently the procedure was for the down train to stop at Petteril Bridge, when No. 5971 beat a hasty retreat to the sheds, leaving the coaches of its train to be taken on to Citadel station by anything that could be rustled up. The use of the 'Claughtons' on the line obviated a great deal of the old piloting that had been a common feature in years past and in the main, despite a number of permanent way slacks which plagued the line at this time, they put on some good performances. The fastest speeds on the line during 1931 were over the 30.8 miles between Appleby and Carlisle, made by three down trains, the 11.06 a.m., 12.20 and 3.42 p.m., at average speeds of, for the first train 57.8 miles per hour, and for the last two 55.9 miles per hour.

The winter timetable of 1932 ushered in a number of accelerations on the Midland line which were reported in some detail by 'Mercury' in the October issue of the *Railway Magazine* :

'On the Midland Division special attention has been paid, in conjunction with the Glasgow and South Western section in Scotland, to the services between St Pancras and Glasgow, and in the improvement of these and other down trains opportunity has been taken to arrange systematic departure times as nearly as possible at even hours from St Pancras to Nottingham, Sheffield, Leeds, and the North. The 9 a.m. down 'Thames–Forth' express retains the fast timing introduced in May; the 'Thames–Clyde' express leaves at 10.0 instead of 9.50 a.m., but reaches Glasgow at 6.50 instead of 7 p.m., a gain of 20 min.; the midday train, until last July starting at 11.45 a.m., now leaves at 12 noon, but the Glasgow arrival is at 9.0 instead of 9.10 p.m.—25 min. acceleration . . .
'In the up direction the 9.20 a.m. from Glasgow leaves at 9.30 a.m., but reaches St Pancras at 6.35 p.m. as heretofore; the 12 noon, starting at 12.10 p.m., is due at 9.8 instead of 9.15 p.m.—a gain of 17 min . . . An important boon has been conferred on Leicester residents by the long-desired diversion of one of the two night Scotch expresses from St Pancras, both of which have hitherto taken the Nottingham route, via Leicester; this is the 9.30 p.m. down express, due in Leicester at 11.34 p.m., and the change will also be of benefit to travellers from Leicester northwards.
'The Glasgow and South Western accelerations have produced two runs between Carlisle and Glasgow in 2 hrs. 25 min., one in 2 hrs. 26 min., and two in 2½ hrs. In the 2 hrs. 25 min. limit, the 9.30 a.m. from St Enoch requires to make calls at Kilmarnock, Dumfries and Annan, while the 10.20 a.m. from Leeds makes the same calls in the reverse direction in the same overall time, reaching Glasgow at 3.23 p.m. . . .'

The new timings were also reflected in the freight traffic over the line, one of the fastest fitted freights being the 6.50 p.m. from Glasgow

Buchanan Street to St Pancras. This train, 'Fitted freight No. 1', ran via Carstairs, where a stop was made to join a portion from Perth, and thence went south through Carlisle and over the Midland main line. It did the distance of about 418 miles in just under 11½ hours. Another such freight was the 8.40 p.m. from Ancoats goods station, Manchester to Glasgow, via Blackburn, Hellifield, and the Settle and Carlisle line, reaching Buchanan Street at 4.50 a.m. A peculiar feature in the current train operating at this time on the Leeds and Bradford run was the continuing use of 0-4-4 tank engines to haul the heavy Bradford–London trains between the two cities. As often as not ten coach trains would be brought in to Leeds from the south, hauled by compounds with a pilot or by 'Claughtons', only to be handed over there to these much smaller engines.

The next three years saw the gradual introduction of a new locomotive class on the Leeds–Settle–Carlisle line, the 'Jubilee'. These locomotives—taper boilered 4-6-0 class 5x express passenger engines—are the first to be discussed which still work the route at the time of writing, albeit on local trains. When introduced they represented a 'New Look' on the line; gone were the L.N.W.R. lines of the 'Claughtons', and the 'Patriots', and the Midland features of the compounds which the latter had ousted; instead there was almost the appearance of a Great Western 'Castle' class about the new breed, which was, however, a development on the 'Patriots'. This was not surprising; their designer, William Stanier (later Sir William), who had taken over from Sir Henry Fowler, was an old G.W.R. man. He brought with him the taper boiler of the Great Western locomotives and proceeded to introduce it on the L.M.S. The new engines shared the duties over the Settle line with the 'Patriots'. One of them, No. 5660 *Rooke* did the 113 mile trip from Leeds to Carlisle in test conditions with a 300 ton train in October 1937 in very nearly even time. With the 'Jubilees' came the Stanier 'Black Fives'. These locomotives were built for the L.M.S. in prodigious numbers; they are maids of all work—efficient on fast passenger runs and long freight hauls. They replaced the 'Claughtons', some of which were ending their days on Settle line freights, and joined the 'Patriots' and 'Jubilees' on the fitted freights. Also working these trains were seven Fowler 2-6-0 Moguls, Nos. 13050–13056, shedded at Holbeck from 1928. With the coming of the 'Black Fives', however, their duties on the 'fitteds' lapsed somewhat. Still running on some of the freights are class 4F 0-6-0 tender engines, based on a Midland design of 1911, when two of the type, Nos. 3835 and 3836, ran on the Settle line. So successful was the class that scores more were built. Another pre-Grouping type which worked over the route in the twenties was an inside cylinder G.S.W.R. 2-6-0. The class was designed by Peter Drummond and numbered eleven engines. Built by the North British Locomotive Company in 1915, Nos. 17821 and 17827 (L.M.S. numbering) represented the series south of Carlisle on the Midland line. It was in about 1936 that

Durran Hill sheds were closed. From early February of that year the 30 locomotives which were shedded there were transferred to the Carlisle Upperby and Kingmoor sheds. December of 1936 also saw the brief appearance on the Settle line of the 'Royal Scot' train, due to a landslide blocking the West Coast main line at Dillicar, though it was not until 1941 that locomotives of the 'Royal Scot' class were permitted to work the route. In late 1938, incidentally, Carlisle Citadel, which had been of free access to the platforms, acquired its present barriers, converting it to a 'closed' station.

Following the outbreak of the Second World War, the L.M.S. put emergency timetables into operation on September 25, 1939. Once again the Midland route was severely restricted with, initially, average speeds limited to about 40 miles per hour. During the next five years the West Coast route took most of the heavy passenger traffic, while the Settle and Carlisle became progressively busier with freight. So crowded was the line in fact, with block to block working in force, that a serious engine difficulty arose. There were so many trains that pilot engines were virtually an extinct race; locomotives grinding up the 'Long Drag' on heavy freights without pilots were grossly underpowered. It was fortunate that the line was at least liberally endowed with Stanier 2-8-0 mineral engines, otherwise delays would have been chronic. The answer was, of course, to introduce on to the line a locomotive which could cope with the traffic, and 1943-44 saw the arrival of the huge 2-10-0 locomotives of the Ministry of Supply, together with the Ministry's 2-8-0 standard engines. On the passenger side, the need for heavier engines led, in 1942, to the rebuilding with larger boiler and double chimney of two of the 'Jubilees', Nos. 5735 *Comet* and 5736 *Phoenix* for use on the line, but within a year they were replaced at Holbeck by rebuilt locomotives of the 'Royal Scot' class, Nos. 6170 *British Legion* and 6103 *Royal Scots Fusilier*. Three others of the class followed, Nos. 6108 *Seaforth Highlander,* 6109 *Royal Engineer,* and 6117 *Welsh Guardsman.* Later, towards the end of the war, No. 6133 *The Green Howards* joined them at Holbeck. *British Legion,* incidentally, was a 1935 rebuild of the experimental high pressure compound locomotive *Fury* which, numbered 6399, was introduced in 1929. To cope with the heavier engines, the Snaygill Bridge at Skipton had been rebuilt in 1941.

New works during the war included the provision of a large private siding area laid in by the L.M.S. for the Air Ministry, Shell, and I.C.I., at Heysham Moss, on the east side of the Heysham branch. The L.M.S. connections and Heysham Moss Junction signal box were brought into use between October and December, 1939. During 1941 loops at Skipton, Gargrave, and Wennington came into use, and new up and down loops were put in at Blea Moor in December. 1942 saw a new loop at Bentham and an extension to siding accommodation at Kirkby Stephen. In 1943 and 1944 various minor permanent way additions were carried out at Durran Hill.

Following the war came the nationalisation of the railways of Great Britain. From January 1, 1948 the Leeds–Settle–Carlisle line passed into the London Midland Region of British Railways; at the present time, however, the part south of Skipton is in the North Eastern Region. The last year of the L.M.S. saw all traffic diverted from the main line in November when Eastburn Bridge near Steeton collapsed. For a short time the avoiding line through Ilkley was used.

Two accidents follow, both on the Settle line. The first occurred at Griseburn on November 29, 1948, when a 50 ton breakdown crane with an unsecured jib was accidentally set in motion near the ballast sidings on the falling 1 in 100 gradient towards Carlisle. The accident was due to the insufficient attention paid to securing the crane brakes, and when the job of rerailing some wagons had been completed and the crane was nudged by the locomotive prior to being coupled up and taken away the impact, though slight, was sufficient to break the scotch and send the crane running away out of control. Luckily it was on the right line so there was no likelihood of it being involved in a head on collision. In attempting to stop the vehicle one man died and two were injured. It ran for 23 miles and finally came to rest at Lazonby. For some time it was feared that it might get to Carlisle and the control staff decided to make life easy for it and cleared a path through the station. The other alternative, that of 'intercepting' it with an engine, was ruled out since the whole affair took place at night and such an attempt would have been extremely hazardous. The fatalities were caused in the first few seconds. The jib, which was in the trailing position but not fully lowered, struck the first overbridge it came to and showered stone on to the three hardy men who were attempting to stop the runaway.

The next accident concerned a passenger train. On April 18, 1952 the 9.15 a.m. 'Thames–Clyde' express from Glasgow to St Pancras became derailed at speed on the facing points on the up loop at Blea Moor. The train, which was hauled by No. 46117 *Welsh Guardsman* and piloted by compound locomotive No. 41040, consisted of ten coaches carrying about 200 passengers. From inspection of the track and the two locomotives it was found that the cause of the derailment was the coming adrift of the forward end of the right side adjustable brake rod on the tender of the compound. Examination of the track indicated that it had partly come away and dropped down on to the sleepers near the right hand rail, about a $\frac{1}{4}$ mile north of Blea Moor tunnel. A permanent way gang had noticed something was wrong as the train passed them but could do nothing. Neither of the two engine crews was aware that anything was wrong. As long as the trains stayed on uncomplicated track all was well, except for the scoring of several sleepers, but as soon as the leading engine hit the points, the rod struck the lock stretcher bar and moved the knife edges enough to derail *Welsh Guardsman* and the leading coaches. It was a case of bad maintenance; a split pin was thought to have been badly fitted. Colonel D. McMullen, the Inspecting

Officer of Railways, Ministry of Transport, thought that if the pin had been insufficiently splayed, it had probably sheared off at one leg, so permitting the other to fall out and release the brake rod. It was the third accident within a year on British Railways which was attributable to faulty engine maintenance, the others being at Weedon in September, and at Glasgow in November, of 1951. Fortunately, considering the speed at which the 'Thames–Clyde' was travelling, no passengers were killed, though 29 and several railway servants were injured. The complete absence of telescoping was undoubtedly due to the buck-eye couplings between the coaches and the latter's welded underframes, both features of modern safety design.

1953 saw a new electrified service in operation between Lancaster, Morecambe and Heysham. On February 11, 1951, the old Midland electric coaches on the line had been withdrawn. Their age was such that, but for the war, they would probably have been replaced some years back. As it was they had continued running and were by that time in an almost decrepit condition. From Monday, February 12, the service was operated by auto steam trains worked by 0-4-4 tank engines and three-coach sets. As soon as the old electric services came off, work was commenced on converting the Midland's system, working at 25 cycles, to one of 50 cycles. Towards the end of 1952 experimental runs with the new stock were made and the line was reopened as an electric system on August 17, 1953. 'New' stock is perhaps not the right description; it was nearly 40 years old when brought up to Lancaster. The coaches dated from 1914 and were originally built for the new service then instituted between Earls Court and Willesden Junction. In any event, they were fitted up with bus seats, painted green, and took over from the steam autos. In 1954 came the first of the closures of lines which have occurred in the area north of Skipton, and which have eventually left the Settle and Carlisle, and the little North Western, as the only passenger lines open between the East and the West Coast main lines. First to go was the Ingleton branch from Clapham to Low Gill. The line was closed to passengers on February 1, 1954. (Middleton-on-Lune had been closed since 1931.) Following this came the withdrawal of passenger services on the former N.E.R.'s Wensleydale line between Hawes and Northallerton. From April 26, 1954 the only service left to Hawes was of one train a day by the Midland line. This was the 3.16 p.m. from Garsdale, which left Hawes on its return journey at 4.25 p.m.

Though slightly off the area concerned, but mentionable because it has appeared in the past history of the Leeds–Settle–Carlisle line, was the withdrawal of the Bradford–Otley–Harrogate passenger service from February 25, 1957. Its demise followed a long period of neglect in favour of the far more direct route via Leeds. The year also saw the inauguration on June 17 of a new titled train the 'Waverley'—which was in fact the pre-war 'Thames–Forth Express' renamed—and the opening on June 8, of an entirely new station on the Lancaster–Morcambe line at Scale Hall.

In 1959 the Settle line became part of the route of a new and important train, the non-stop London–Glasgow 'Condor' freight. This train, which boasted of being the fastest freight in Great Britain making the longest non-stop journey and offering a competitive new form of fast and reliable goods delivery between the two cities, was started in an attempt to regain traffic which had through the years tended to go to the roads. The London traffic is handled by mobile cranes at the old Midland Railway's Hendon depot and delivery of containers on to the flat trucks can be delayed until the early evening, so that customers can load up the afternoon preceding the morning on which they require the goods to be delivered in Glasgow. The trains were hauled at the start by Metrovick 1,200 h.p. Co-Bo diesel engines. The departure time at Hendon was 7.23 p.m., and the arrival time at Gushetfaulds goods depot Glasgow was at 5.20 a.m. The new service commenced on March 16, 1959; the Settle line is no longer used for this service.

In the early hours of January 21, 1960, disaster again visited the Settle line, this time only a short distance from Settle station. On the evening of January 21, the 9.05 p.m. Glasgow St Enoch to St Pancras train was headed out of Carlisle by class '7' 4-6-2 No. 70052 *Firth of Tay*. The night was quite horrible—station master Taylor has described it as being of blizzard conditions. As the train climbed towards Ais Gill the driver heard a knocking noise from the engine and though he slowed down the noise did not stop. By the time he reached Garsdale he was worried enough to stop the train and get off to examine it. It was bitterly cold, with thick snow falling, in a heavy gale. In these conditions he was unable to do more than make a cursory examination and so failed to notice that both the right hand slide bars had fallen off. Having decided that it would be best to continue to Hellifield and there get a fitter to look at the engine, the driver set off at what the inspecting officer said was far too high a speed—some 40 miles per hour, despite the fact that the knocking was still quite severe. Eventually, the piston rod, which was under some considerable strain, fractured and drove into the ballast, misaligning the down track just at the time when the 10.40 p.m. Leeds–Carlisle goods was passing. The goods engine—a 2-6-0 No. 42881—immediately slewed across the down line and came to rest projecting far enough over the up line to foul the coaches following the engine. The accident took place at about 1.48 a.m., half a mile north of Settle station. Though the passenger driver immediately applied his brake, the momentum carried all the vehicles of the passenger train past the stationary goods locomotive, ripping their sides open. The fireman on the freight immediately ran to Settle box to warn the signalman, and the express driver arrived shortly afterwards to call out the full emergency services. The first and third coaches had their sides almost completely torn off, and the remaining five coaches of which three were sleepers, luckily with their corridors to the six-foot side, were also badly damaged. Five persons were killed and nine injured. The remarkable thing about this crash was the truly prodigious speed with which the Settle station staff were able to get help. In that bitter cold night, in darkness, the rescue services and doctors were at the crash within 27 minutes, a promptitude warmly commended by Brigadier Langley, the inspecting officer. The cause was, once more, faulty maintenance. There had apparently been four cases over the past two years of 'Britannia' class locomotives loosing their slide bars, but the known propensity of these engines to do this was not helped by what the Brigadier thought was a negligent attitude in the shops. Brigadier Langley mentioned that on one occasion, after No. 70052 had been through the Crewe shops, the right hand slide bar bolts had been reported loose nine times; he had not been able to find any record that they had been changed.

On July 4, 1960 the portion of the old South Durham & Lancashire Union line between Kirkby Stephen and Tebay was closed to all traffic and the freight trains over the route diverted to Carlisle. It was the first stage in the complete closure of all the N.E.R.'s lines which touched the Settle and Carlisle line.

When the English Electric Co-Co 'Deltic' class was under test in mid 1956, one of the lines used was the Leeds–Settle–Carlisle. No sooner had the big blue diesel's reverberations left the high parts when the line saw other newcomers—the Gresley 'A3' Pacifics which had been displaced at Gateshead shed by the introduction there of diesels. These large engines proceeded to take a major share in hauling the Scotch expresses over the line. Mr O. S. Nock details some of their runs, in the May 1961 issue of the *Railway Magazine*. Apparently they had an undoubted ability to steam freely which made them welcome on the route. Mr Nock also mentions a special run made with an excursion train from Alford in Lincolnshire to Edinburgh, hauled by the record breaking stream-liner 'A4' No. 60022 *Mallard*, in which the speed going north over Ribble-head viaduct was up to 50 miles per hour, and that with a 365 ton train. In the following December Mr Nock tells of an even greater achieve-ment when, on a trip of the 'Border Rail Tour' made on July 9, 1961, a Stanier Pacific, No. 46247 *City of Liverpool,* hauled a train of some 360 tons at an average speed of 59 miles per hour on the climb up from Settle to Blea Moor.

There were two accidents in 1961. The first occurred on August 22, when the 7.50 a.m. down freight from Leeds to Carlisle was partially derailed a short distance beyond Little Salkeld station, coming into collision with a passing up freight, the 11 a.m. from Carlisle to Warcop, on the Eden Valley line. The derailment was a peculiar one, causing the running away of part of the down train which was brought to a halt nearly 1½ miles distant. As a result of the collision the two engines and some eight wagons on the Warcop train left the rails, blocking the up and down main lines.

On September 8 the 3.5 p.m. freight from Carlisle to Leeds, hauled by a Stanier 'Black Five', No. 44757, approached Stainforth sidings signal box at what was an excessive speed. As soon as the engine had come out of Stainforth tunnel the crew noticed that the rear portion of the train had broken away, and that the rear wagons on the part still attached had become derailed. These latter vehicles completely demolished the bottom of the Stainforth signal box, giving the signalman a considerable shock. The guard of the goods was injured. The cause was probably the same as that of the previous month—faulty loading. In this case the speed of the train may well have caused oscillation and a consequent movement of the load.

From January 22, 1962, with the exception of a small length between Appleby East and Kirkby Stephen East, the remainder of the N.E.R. lines in the Settle and Carlisle's vicinity closed down. The route over Stainmore had in fact come to an end. The closure, which was to be followed by the recovery of the track, meant that one of the old avoiding routes for the Settle line was gone. The Appleby–Penrith line had sometimes been used by such trains as the 'Thames–Forth Express' on Sundays, when the Settle line north of Appleby was in the hands of the engineer, the West Coast route being used between Penrith and Carlisle. The other deviation is, of course, still provided by the Ingleton branch at the time of writing. It has been proved of use many times in the past, when snow or accidents have blocked the line. Another line to close for passenger services in 1962 was the former L.Y.R. Blackburn–Hellifield line, bringing to an end many years' association with the Settle and Carlisle line. It is still quite heavily used for through goods traffic at the present time.

As to the winter conditions on the Settle and Carlisle line, there have been two really bad spells since the end of the war. The first was that of 1947 which started in early February and held the line in a complete icy grip for eight weeks. As the snow fell its own weight turned it to ice. Some of the drifts were over 12 feet thick. Though one road was opened through for freight traffic for two days, the success was short lived in comparison with the number of days when the line was totally closed. Despite the use of snow ploughs which repeatedly charged the masses of snow, so hard that one became derailed, of the efforts of the Army, of German P.O.W.'s, and of the gangs of men from the railway service, the line remained steadfastly shut. Even a flame thrower was used for a time, but to no effect. In this freak weather period, with fuel short, and with all roads completely blocked, the railway was the only lifeline that could keep the people in the remote dales from going very hungry and cold. As soon as one line could eventually be opened, and with the road up Ribblesdale remaining impassable, a whole series of entirely new 'stations' appeared along the line where the relief trains stopped to deliver food. Bales of hay were carried for livestock. Icicles of fantastic size formed in the tunnels, engines disappeared completely under the snow, and the icy winds cut

416

through the men attempting to carve and chip through the falls. It lasted until April. The second bad time is more recent—the winter of 1962–63. By January 20 both lines were blocked by drifts. As in many other cases, the through traffic went over to the West Coast route via Ingleton. The diversion was necessary for five days in all, after which the trains on the Settle line were allowed to nudge their way carefully past cliffs of snow. The last train to attempt to run the gauntlet of snow had been the 10.5 p.m. Edinburgh to St Pancras sleeping car express. Despite the fact that snow ploughs had been out on the line since the previous afternoon the express had become stranded near Dent, at about 3 a.m. on the morning of Sunday, January 20. All the passengers were given tea and biscuits and then transferred into the rear three coaches which it was hoped could be worked back to Carlisle. The guard, working in freezing conditions and in darkness, managed the feat of uncoupling the coaches. By then the line was also blocked in the rear of the train and it was only after a snow plough had come on the scene that a locomotive could run the three rear coaches to Garsdale, there to be handed over to an engine off an abandoned Carlisle–Birmingham freight. It is a measure of the sort of spirit which animates a railwayman at times like this, that the driver and fireman volunteered to take their locomotive tender first through the teeth of the blizzard so as to get the passengers safely back to Carlisle.

The line today still carries a fair amount of traffic. The publication by H.M. Stationery Office in 1963 of the British Railways Board's report, *The Reshaping of British Railways*, appeared to number the days of life left to it. It is of interest that, according to the report, the density of passengers over the line appears to be in the region of 10,000 to 50,000 per week south of Appleby, but only between 5,000 and 10,000 north of the town. The freight traffic over the line shows a different density; an average of about 100,000 tons per week, as compared with roughly half that amount over the Shap route. The figures are very approximate as they are, of course, taken from a wide range shown on the maps accompanying the report. As to receipts, the only passenger station which appears to be in the running profit-wise is Appleby, and just possibly Settle. On the goods side Appleby, Warcop and Settle still apparently make money. But to do this necessitates the retention of over 70 miles of double tracked railway, with very heavy engineering works, not to speak of the small part of the Eden Valley line still open. As a start, therefore, the report recommended the withdrawal of all passenger train services, and at the same time a policy of goods station closures was put in hand. Though nearly all of these have now been closed, most of the passenger stations still remain open. A table of station closures to date in the area north of Leeds is given in Appendix XXIV.

At the time of writing—June, 1965—the passenger timetable shows only one named train now operating throughout the year over the Settle road north out of Leeds. Until September 1964 there were two. The first in the day was the 'Waverley' which left St Pancras at 9.15 a.m. and arrived at Leeds at 1.27. After leaving Leeds at 1.34 it called at Skipton, Hellifield, Settle, and Appleby West, and arrived at Carlisle at 3.54 p.m. It was booked to cover the Settle–Appleby stretch in 51 minutes. Leaving Appleby at 3.25 p.m. the 'Waverley' did the 30¾ miles to Carlisle at an average speed of about 64 miles per hour. The second named train was the 'Thames–Clyde Express' which left St Pancras exactly an hour after the 'Waverley', arrived at Leeds at 2.28 p.m. and leaving 7 minutes later, made a non-stop run to Carlisle in one minute over two hours, 113 miles in 121 minutes. In the opposite direction the first named train out of Carlisle for the Settle line was the 'Thames–Clyde Express' which left at 11.32 a.m. and ran non-stop to Leeds, arriving at 1.39 p.m. Following this the 'Waverley' left at 12.51 p.m. and, with stops as before, arrived at 3.08 p.m.

Now, from September 1964, the 'Waverley' no longer runs during the winter. The 'Thames–Clyde Express,' however, has had its schedule amended for the winter service so as to stop at intermediate stations previously served by the 'Waverley', and it carries through coaches for Edinburgh passengers. The current timetable—from June 1965 to April 1966—as first issued, shows the 'Thames–Clyde' leaving St Pancras at 10.15 as before. Calling at Leicester, Trent, Chesterfield, Sheffield, and Normanton, it arrives at Leeds at 2.31 p.m. It leaves Leeds 10 minutes later and calls at Skipton, Hellifield, Settle, and Appleby West, arriving at Carlisle at 4.54 p.m. The intermediate stops between Leeds and Carlisle used to be made only by the 'Waverley'. The current arrival time of the 'Thames–Clyde' in Glasgow Central station is 7.20 p.m. and the through winter Edinburgh coaches are booked to arrive at the Waverley station at 7.40 p.m. In the opposite direction the 'Thames–Clyde' leaves Carlisle at 11.31 a.m., calls at the same intermediate stations, and reaches Leeds at 1.49 p.m. and St Pancras at 6.15 p.m. The summer 'Waverley' in the up direction leaves Carlisle at 12.51 p.m., calls at the same stations as the 'Thames–Clyde' and arrives at Leeds at 3.13 p.m. and St Pancras at 7.50 p.m. Both expresses in either direction have restaurant cars attached; the 'Thames–Clyde' also has one of the popular miniature buffet cars.

Despite all the foregoing, passenger trains over the Settle and Carlisle line are already sparse. In the small hours there are two early morning arrivals at Carlisle, the first from St Pancras to Edinburgh Waverley and the second from St Pancras to Glasgow Central. They make their appearances, with sleeping cars and night-attired white peering figures at the windows, at about 4.32 and 4.59 a.m. respectively. The next arrival is some 3½ hours later—a stopping train bringing workers into Carlisle which starts from Appleby at 7.34 a.m. The next through train is a Leeds City to Glasgow express, calling at Keighley, Skipton, Hellifield, Settle, and Appleby West, and arriving at Carlisle at 12.45

p.m. After this there follows a local which leaves Hellifield at 12.08 p.m. and, calling at all stations, is due into Carlisle at 2.28 p.m. Then comes the summer 'Waverley' and the 'Thames–Clyde Express' after which there is nothing more from the Settle line into Carlisle until the final arrival of the day—due at 7.19 p.m.—an all stations (except Gargrave) train from Bradford. At the southern end of the line there is an early morning stopping train into Garsdale from Hellifield, arriving at 7 a.m.

On the up schedule the service is repeated with variations, the first train out of Carlisle being the 12.02 a.m. sleeping car train which runs non-stop to Leeds, arriving at 2.12 a.m. It leaves Leeds 11 minutes later and arrives at St Pancras at 7.05 in the morning. Next out of Carlisle is the 12.46 a.m. to St Pancras, Skipton being the first stop. There is nothing then until 8.05 a.m. when a stopping train wends a laborious way up to Hellifield, connecting there with a Morecambe to Leeds train. Incidentally, the 8.05 stops at Long Meg to drop off the guard of an up anhydrate train which leaves Long Meg sidings later in the morning. The next two passenger trains are the 'Thames–Clyde' which leaves Carlisle at 11.31, and the summer 'Waverley' at 12.51, after which there is a gap until the 4.37 p.m. all stations train to Bradford, followed by the 6.05 p.m. local train to Appleby West (timed an hour later on Saturdays). The last train is the 6.50 p.m. from Carlisle—a Glasgow Central to Leeds City semi-fast—which has dining and miniature buffet cars attached and arrives at Leeds at 9.13 p.m. There is, as on the down service, an early morning train serving the southern end of the line. This is the return working of the down arrival into Garsdale and runs to Hellifield, leaving Garsdale at 7.12 a.m. It calls at all stations and arrives at Hellifield at 7.57 p.m. to make connection with a Morecambe–Leeds train a few minutes later.

On Sundays there are only three trains each way. In the down direction there are two early morning sleeping car trains from London to Edinburgh and Glasgow, arriving at Carlisle at 4.36 and 5.06 a.m. respectively, the latter train calling at Appleby West at 4.34 a.m., as does its counterpart, 7 minutes earlier, on weekdays. In the afternoon the 'Thames–Clyde' leaves Leeds at 2.57, calls at Keighley, Skipton, and Appleby West, and arrives at Carlisle at 5.16. The first trains out of Carlisle in the up direction are the 12.02 and 12.47 a.m. sleeping car trains from Glasgow and Edinburgh, due into Leeds at 2.17 and 3 a.m. respectively, and with arrival times at St Pancras of 7.35 and 8.20 a.m. The latter train calls at Skipton at 2.22 a.m. Following these is the up 'Thames–Clyde' which leaves Carlisle at 12.37 p.m., calls at Appleby West, Hellifield, Skipton, and Keighley, and arrives at Leeds at 3.04 p.m.; it is due into St Pancras at 8.30 p.m.

Motive power on the line is in a transition stage. The main line expresses are now invariably hauled by diesels but the local stopping passenger trains are still often steam operated, either by 'Jubilees' or Stanier 'Black Fives'. Goods traffic has a motley array of motive power; B.R. stan-

419

dards, L.M.S. 4F 0-6-0s, and 'Peak' class diesels, though the latter are mostly confined to the fitted freights. So far, the ubiquitous and ever-spreading multiple unit diesel train has not succeeded in penetrating north of Settle Junction. It reigns virtually supreme south thereof, however, on all the local passenger services. Though through goods workings still use the Settle–Carlisle section, the Ingleton branch goods service was withdrawn early in 1965. For some time the traffic had been seasonable with one train only on Mondays, Wednesdays, and Fridays, quite often consisting of engine, wagon, and guards van only.

The election of a different Government in October of 1964, and the appointment of a new Minister of Transport has brought temporary reprieve to the Settle line. In a statement made in the House of Commons on Wednesday, November 4, 1964, the Minister stated that he had that day decided to refuse his consent to 'the closure of 12 stations between Carlisle and Hellifield and the withdrawal of local services from this line'. What will eventually happen, no-one knows, though the latest Railways Board report—*The Development of the Major Railway Trunk Routes*—confirms that the line is officially thought to be of secondary importance to the West Coast route.

Whatever happens in the future, nothing can take away the glory of the past, of the memories of the shriek of a Midland express in its zenith, as it tore down the Eden Valley, and of a proud if ill-paid staff turning out a service which was second not even to the 'Premier Line' in comfort, of the generations of quiet-speaking hard-working men who have spent their lives in bleak wind-battered signal boxes with the moors for company, of the drivers and firemen who have nursed and thrashed and goaded their engines up the 'Long Drag' to Blea Moor, of the hosts of passengers who have slept and laughed and loved and eaten and read or looked bored all the length of the line through all the years it has been open and in all types of carriage in all conditions of weather. To all these does the history belong.

XXI

Bad End or New Beginning?

Much has happened since 1965. Of books which have appeared four must be mentioned: aspects not developed in *North of Leeds* are given weight in David Jenkinson's *Rails in the Fells* (Peco, 1973); working memories fill Dick Fawcett's *Ganger Guard and Signalman* (Bradford Barton, 1981); W. R. Mitchell's *Men of the Settle–Carlisle* (Dalesman Publishing, 1986); and Stan Abbott's *To Kill a Railway* (Leading Edge Press & Publishing, 1986) has a detailed account of financial arguments behind attempts to close the line and of the dogged opposition which has gone a long way to keep it alive. To duplicate Mr Abbott's highly readable work would be pointless; this chapter therefore outlines the operating history of the S&C since 1965.

From January 3, 1966, Wennington–Lancaster–Morecambe closed to passengers, and the Lancaster–Morecambe–Heysham electric trains were replaced by a diesel service from Lancaster Castle via Bare Lane, though the Heysham branch remained for Irish boat trains. This left Wennington–Lancaster–Morecambe with a dozen or so freights each way daily and destined to close from June 5, 1967, though Ladies Walk ($\frac{1}{2}$ mile east of Green Ayre) to Lancaster Castle, and White Lund to Torrisholme Jct. No 1 (Morecambe) were retained as single and double sidings respectively. When Morecambe Promenade to Torrisholme No 1 closed completely on October 23, 1967, White Lund to No 1 became a single siding, while No 1 to Torrisholme No 2 was coverted to a double siding. Ladies Walk and White Lund sidings have now gone (Appendix XXIV). From May 1, 1967, main line trains ceased using Bradford Forster Square; left with the Ilkley and Keighley/Skipton trains, and a summer Saturday Morecambe service, the station was remodelled to become the city's main parcels depot until that traffic ceased in 1981 leaving only two passenger platforms in use. January 2, 1967, saw a dozen S&C stations become unstaffed halts with tickets issued and collected by train guards. The final steam-hauled up freight, the 13.10 Carlisle–Skipton, was taken south on December 30, 1967, by 70045 *Lord Rowallan*. On August 11, 1968, enthusiasts thronged stations and lineside to witness what was planned to be the last BR standard gauge steam train. Starting from Liverpool, it was taken on from Manchester via Blackburn and Settle to Carlisle by 70013 *Oliver Cromwell*. The fine, sunny day ended with the return working by 'Black Fives' 44871 and 44781. If main line steam seemed finished it was very different on the former Oxenhope branch which was acquired by the Keighley & Worth Valley Railway Preservation Society and reopened on

June 29, 1968. The K&WV has become one of the most successful of the 'preserved' lines and attracts to BR's Keighley station a not inconsiderable passenger traffic.

The May 1968 – May 1969 S&C passenger service was the last before reductions were drastically to diminish traffic. On weekdays there was one morning local each way, up from Garsdale at 07.03 and down from Appleby at 07.30, Kirkby Stephen thus waiting until the first of the through stopping trains: dep Carlisle 08.35 and 16.41 and dep Skipton 11.45 and 16.40. There was also an all stations to Appleby leaving Carlisle at 18.10. The up and down 'Thames–Clyde' passed each other at Leeds between 14.32 and 14.36. 'The Waverley' ran from June 10 to September 28, the two trains passing near Appleby at about 15.06. Both named trains called at Skipton, Settle and Appleby. There were three other weekday fast trains: a Leeds–Glasgow buffet down midday and return up early evening, and two sleeping car trains, St Pancras–Edinburgh and St Pancras–Glasgow. The down Glasgow sleeper called at Appleby at 04.26, which the slightly earlier Edinburgh had passed non-stop. On the up run, however, the Glasgow ran fast Carlisle to Leeds, while the Edinburgh called on request at Appleby to pick up for stations south of Leeds and also called at Skipton. A down Saturdays only Glasgow sleeping car train between June 29 and August 31, and three summer SO through trains completed the table: Glasgow to St Pancras, non-stop Carlisle–Leeds; Birmingham to Glasgow, calling Keighley, Skipton and Appleby; and St Pancras to Glasgow, non-stop Sheffield–Carlisle arr 16.23. Sundays saw the 'Thames–Clyde', calling Keighley, Skipton and Appleby each way, and the two sleeping car expresses. Weekend diversions of West Coast Main Line trains over the S&C was increasing, however, and would peak during electrification works. The final 'Waverley' named train ran on September 28, thenceforth through Edinburgh coaches being attached to the 'Thames–Clyde' (as in previous winters), these being withdrawn, however, sure of the old North British 'Waverley' route to passenger traffic from January 6, 1969. The through coaches joined the up 'Thames–Clyde' for the last time on Saturday January 4, the 14-coach train (10 ex Glasgow, 4 ex Edinburgh) leaving Carlisle behind D129.

Following a proposal to withdraw Skipton–Carlisle local trains and close most S&C intermediate stations from March 3, 1969, the TUCC reported that this would cause severe hardship. Nevertheless, from May 4, 1970, the local trains were taken off, just before the busy summer holiday period, and intermediate stations, except Settle and Appleby, were closed. Until service revisions seven years later it was now impossible to make a day return trip from the north. Other 1970 closures were: Colne–Skipton after January 31; and from May 4 the old Midland Heysham station, replaced by one to the east. Heysham car ferry service started on May 22.

In 1972 threatened withdrawal of the Ilkley service was rejected by the Minister but on condition that Bradford trains reversed at Apperley Junction, with closure of the Shipley–Guiseley line and withdrawal of

Bradford–Keighley trains, Keighley to be served by connections at Shipley with Leeds trains. But Bradford Corporation took on the subsidy to keep all services operating. Baildon reopened as an unstaffed station on January 5, 1973, exactly twenty years after closing. That month saw the Leeds–Skipton–Carnforth route allocated for special steam trains. From May 6, 1974, emphasising the eclipse of the old Midland Scotch service, the electrified WCML 'Royal Scot' started operating London–Glasgow in five hours. The Heysham–Belfast passenger and car ferry service ceased from April 6, 1975; from May 5 the Leeds boat train terminated at Morecambe, while on the S&C the 'Thames–Clyde' lost its name but Leeds–Glasgow services were accelerated. The May 1975 – May 1976 timetable showed three weekday trains each way. The down service started with a night-time St Pancras–Glasgow, with sleeping car/s from Nottingham, dep Leeds 02.32, calling Skipton and Appleby, arr Carlisle 05.01; the 09.01 Leeds–Glasgow buffet train, calling Keighley, Skipton, Settle and Appleby, arr Carlisle 11.24; and the former 'Thames–Clyde' St Pancras–Glasgow restaurant car and buffet train dep Leeds 12.36, calling at the same intermediate stations, arr Carlisle 15.03. In the up direction the night (Sun–Fri) Glasgow–St Pancras (sleeping car/s as far as Nottingham) dep Carlisle 01.38, calling Skipton, arr Leeds 04.01; the mid-morning former 'Thames–Clyde' Glasgow–St Pancras restaurant car and buffet train dep Carlisle 12.27, calling Appleby, Settle, Skipton, arr Leeds 14.52; and the afternoon Glasgow buffet train dep Carlisle 18.26, calling same intermediates, terminated Leeds 20.46. Sundays saw two trains each way: down overnight St Pancras–Glasgow (sleeping car/s from Nottingham), calling as weekdays but slightly later, and St Pancras–Glasgow restaurant car and buffet train, dep Leeds 15.33, calling Keighley, Skipton, Appleby, arr Carlisle 18.24; up Glasgow–Nottingham sleeper as weekdays but earlier, and Glasgow restaurant car and buffet, later, with same stops except Settle passed by in favour of Keighley. An additional midday summer Saturday train ran each way non-stop over the S&C. From the May 1976 timetable the up and down weekday morning and afternoon St Pancras–Glasgow trains were cut back to Nottingham–Glasgow as were the Sunday afternoon up and down; sleeping cars were withdrawn. On several summer weekends in 1975 an experimental 'DalesRail' service (fully described in *To Kill a Railway*), sponsored by the Yorkshire Dales National Park, operated between Leeds and Appleby, calling again at intermediate stations, where special YDNP nameboards were erected. The trains were popular with visitors to the National Park and with local people wishing to shop in town. In 1976 a Carlisle DalesRail train brought Armathwaite, Lazonby and Langwathby into the scheme. Buses took passengers on to points of interest. DalesRail Christmas shopping specials were put on, and with variations, Clitheroe joining the act from April 1978, the enterprise flourished.

Following public demand the May 1977 timetable provided more conveniently timed trains and restored full day return travel over the S&C.

The morning Leeds–Glasgow now started from Nottingham and an additional train dep Nottingham 16.05 (15.52 Sats) ran calling (after Leeds) at Keighley, Skipton, Settle and Appleby, terminating at Carlisle with Glasgow and Edinburgh connections. A corresponding up train left Carlisle 09.35, with connections from Glasgow and Edinburgh, calling at the same stations to Leeds and Nottingham. In both directions the overnight St Pancras–Glasgow trains were withdrawn, continuing as parcels only. New WCML signalling, with no catch points, meant that many unfitted and partially fitted freights were diverted to the S&C. In 1976, for instance, there were 13 weekday down freights, plus one MO, one ThO and two SO, averaging 35 mph ($25\frac{1}{2}$ up the 'Long Drag').

For the S&C's centenary many events were organised, Settle being *en fete* for May 1, 1976, with an evening marquee banquet in the station yard. A vintage train was to be steam-hauled from Blackburn by a class 5 and the restored Midland compound No 1000; and BR contributed a special train, Euston–Shap–Carlisle, returning via Settle and Blackburn. By early afternoon Settle station, under darkening skies, was an oasis of gaily coloured festive lights, platforms crowded with expectant folk, many in Victorian costume. But it rained, a real Craven soaking, and before the BR train arrived headed by a class 47 diesel, the steam special was espied in the distance, enshrouded in vapour but composed only of two locomotives: LNWR 'Jumbo' *Hardwicke* from the rival West Coast route, and LNER *Flying Scotsman* which had perhaps more business to be there as representing the A3 engines on the S&C in the early 1960s. Both scheduled engines had failed. Nevertheless, it was a hundredth birthday to remember.

In January 1978 the S&C joined the list of approved steam tour routes. The first chartered steam trains on March 25 and 27, 1978, were hauled by 4771 *Green Arrow*. On May 13 *Evening Star* worked a special, an event overshadowed by the death of the 'Railway Bishop', the Rt Rev Eric Treacy, who collapsed at Appleby station. Many people attended a memorial service there on September 30. Following a derailment at Settle Junction on May 3, 1979, the junction was remodelled; up Morecambe trains now regain the up main by the crossover east of Settle Junction box. From the May timetable a single platform on the main line down road was opened at Shipley, removing the need, since reduction of Leeds–Bradford–Keighley services in 1965, for Leeds–Keighley–Skipton trains to reverse into Shipley station. Up trains still reversed until May 12, 1980, when new crossovers, about $\frac{1}{4}$ mile north of Shipley Bingley Junction and at Shipley Guiseley Junction, permitted two-way working past the platform. September saw three HSTs on the S&C, diverted from the ECML following a derailment at Thirsk. From 1980 the Steam Locomotive Operators Association, in partnership with BR, arranged a regular steam 'Cumbrian Mountain Express' tour, based at Preston and later Crewe, with electric working between there and Carlisle and steam between Carlisle, Skipton (reverse) and Carnforth.

Early in 1981 concern over structures on the line was voiced at a meeting between BR and Cumbrian MPs and county councillors. The timing was ironic – February and April saw WCML Anglo-Scottish trains once more diverted over the S&C. An 'up market' SLOA 'Cumbrian Mountain Pullman' – seven ex BR Pullman Parlour cars with a brake composite at each end, and including the *Hadrian* bar car, 10 vehicles – had its inaugural run over the S&C on May 2. Concurrently news broke that the Nottingham–Glasgow trains were being 'restructured' via Preston and the WCML, with a connecting Leeds–Lancaster–Morecambe service. Forebodings led to the formation in June of the Friends of the Settle to Carlisle Line Association.

The last up through S&C Scotch train was the 15.15 ex Glasgow on May 16, 1982; hauled by 47 463 it was passed at Keighley by the 16.36 from Nottingham behind 45 005, this being 'the last regular Midland Scotch express of all to travel over the Settle and Carlisle road' (David Tee). Left were just two weekday S&C trains: dep Leeds 08.57 and 16.05, and dep Carlisle 10.00 and 15.37. Settle had a 07.39 commuter train to Leeds but nothing returning, city workers catching the 17.12 Leeds–Morecambe, arr Giggleswick (Settle 'old') 18.26. October saw the rerouting of the overnight parcels trains, allowing closure of the S&C between 22.00 and 06.00. To the south a new station opened at Crossflatts on May 17, 1982. By late January 1983 the S&C had only two scheduled through freights each way (Mon–Fri), with a morning ballast train to Ribblehead quarry (reactivated early 1975) returning about 10.30 and, if required, a mid-morning Carlisle–Appleby (reverse) – Warcop freight, also serving private sidings. From May 16 the remaining through freights were also diverted, the final train on May 13 being the 14.20 Carlisle–Healey Mills headed by 40 196. On November 17, 1983, BR published advance notice of withdrawal of S&C passenger services. Mr Ron Cotton was appointed project manager for closure; the Settle to Carlisle Joint Action Group began coordinating opposition; and an independent study was commissioned to assess the state of the structures and the implications of closure. All this contrasted with the seeming success of the West Yorkshire Metropolitan Network in which Saltaire station reopened on April 9, 1984 – a pleasing design echoing Midland tradition.

Having overlooked the DalesRail enterprise, BR published further notices early in 1984 for closure of Clitheroe, Horton-in-Ribblesdale, Ribblehead, Dent, Garsdale, Kirkby Stephen, Langwathby, Lazonby & Kirkoswald, and Armathwaite. From May the morning and evening Leeds–Carlisle trains started from (07.38) and terminated at (20.27) Hull. The consultants' report in July, giving future S&C maintenance forecasts, accused BR of 'wanton neglect' and claimed that huge social benefits lost on closure would almost balance the savings made. BR's riposte was that to have invested in an undertaking the future of which was uncertain would have been 'reprehensible'. The controversy, aired in national press and on television, had an unlooked-for effect: BR found themselves with an ailing asset which, with short term marketing, could produce higher than usual revenue. The emphasis swung to selling: an orange poster appeared, with an engraving of Dent Head viaduct. 'Treat yourself NOW', it exhorted, 'ENGLAND'S GREATEST HISTORICAL ROUTE, LEEDS–SETTLE–CARLISLE. New excursions from London, Liverpool & Manchester. Ask for leaflet giving details of route and all reduced fares available'. An additional daily train, York–Carlisle and return, appeared, July 14 – September 9; cheap offers brought record passenger traffic. And WCML diversions accounted for over 90 extra trains during November. The twelve successful DalesRail workings in 1984 justified WYPTE repeating its support for 1985.

In April 1985 weekday cheap fares were extended to Saturdays, and May saw introduction of a seven day 'Settle–Carlisle Rover' giving unlimited travel between Bradford and Carlisle via Settle and/or Lancaster. Between April 6 and 8, when again the WCML was closed for engineering works, the S&C carried some 80 additional trains. This was after Ribblehead viaduct had been singled, the down line running into the up which was slewed towards the centre of the viaduct in January. The first week of February 1986 saw the ballast trains withdrawn, leaving the line with no scheduled non-passenger workings in the timetable. In March, while local hearings into the closure were being held, came news that the House of Commons Select Committee on Trade and Industry had reported that tourist boards should investigate BR's marketing of its scenic routes and that government grants to loss making lines should be increased; it warned against closure of lines which have great scenic beauty for short term financial savings.

From July 14, 1986 until May 1987 two additional weekday trains (one on Saturdays) each way daily – under the name 'Dalesman', again called at S&C stations only otherwise served by seasonal weekend DalesRail trains, thus restoring eight stations to the public timetables (not Ribblehead in down direction). Trains, works, and publicity are subsidised by several local authorities and other sponsors. BR says the improvements square with marketing the line while it remains open. The trains are popular: mainly worked during August by a two-car green-liveried diesel multiple unit, loadings have frequently exceeded 200.

As this goes to press the government closure decision is imminent. But even if, before this book sees publication, there has been rejoicing in the fells, it may be for no more than a reprieve dictated by political expediency: we will only be sure that the line is safe when there are futher supportive timetable alterations and substantial capital investment to arrest deterioration of the structures. Meanwhile, unlike the unacceptably restricted, circuitous and tightly-gauged Cumbrian coast line the S&C continues to permit expeditious rerouting of frequently diverted WCML expresses – no small assistance in retaining that important traffic. A belief that in the end commonsense and longsightedness must prevail bolsters the author's hope that this uniquely grand and beautiful English railway will not be allowed to die.

APPENDIX I

STAFF APPOINTED ON THE LEEDS & BRADFORD RAILWAY BY JUNE 30, 1846

Date	Name	Address	Former Occupation	Appointment	Wage
June 4	William Baines	Pottery Fields, Leeds	Porter, Leeds Midland Railway	Guard	24s. weekly
June 8	Matthew Crabtree	Headingley, Leeds	—	Station Master, Leeds	£100 p.a.
June 15	Thomas Shoesmith	Dudley Hill	—	Porter, Bradford	17s. weekly
	George Stoney	—	Servant	Porter, Bradford	17s. weekly
	William Naylor	—	Clothier	Porter, Bradford	17s. weekly
June 19	Peter Reeves Thomas Richardson John Hopkinson John Carroll	—	—	Porters	17s. weekly
	William Sugden	—	Goods Guard, Midland Railway	Passenger Guard	24s. weekly
	Joseph Beard	—	—	Passenger Guard	24s. weekly
June 22	Luke Marshall	—	—	Porter, Bradford	17s. weekly
	Benjamin Holroyd	—	—	Pointsman, Leeds	—
	George Swaine	Shipley	—	Pointsman	—
	William Wilson	Bradford	—	Pointsman	—
	John Ward	—	—	Porter, Leeds	17s. weekly
	Alexander Hall	—	—	Booking Clerk, Leeds Under M. Crabtree	£60 p.a.
	Joseph Boothroyd	—	Employed by the Manchester & Leeds Railway	Clerk in charge at Bradford	£100 p.a.
	George Clough	—	—	Porter	17s. weekly
	John Firth	—	—	Porter	17s. weekly
	William Atha	—	Guard, Midland Railway	Guard	17s. weekly

Date	Name	Address	Former Occupation	Appointment	Wage
June 26	James Monks Abraham Bateman Thomas Smith John Hutchinson James Arthington William Lewis Thomas Mitchell Timothy Hall Robert Janson	Leeds	—	Porters	17s. weekly
	John Waddington	Leeds	Employed by Midland Railway at Leeds	Guard	24s. weekly
	Joseph Tyas James Robinson William(?)Smithies John Haigh	—	—	Policemen	17s. weekly
	Samuel Lee	—	—	Ticket Collector, Leeds	24s. weekly

APPENDIX II

FIRST PERMANENT STAFF APPOINTED ON THE NORTH WESTERN RAILWAY, JULY 12, 1849

Station Masters			Guards	
Station	Name	Weekly Wage	Name	Weekly Wage
Gargrave	Thomas Stirzaker	20s.	William Gardner	25s.
Bell Busk	Robert Ripley	20s.	Thomas Jones	25s.
Hellifield	William Ash	17s.	Alex McKie (Assistant guard)	21s.
Long Preston	Thomas Moffatt	18s.		
Settle	Thomas Parkinson	21s.		
Clapham	Richard Watson	18s.		
Ingleton	Robert Hartley	25s.		

			Porters		
			Station	Name	Weekly Wage
			Ingleton	Henry Fawcett (also appointed as an assistant guard)	20s.
			Settle	William Brennand	17s.

Other staff appointed in 1849 included:
Henry Briggs, in company's employ at Settle, sent to Gargrave 27.9.1849.
Peter Hogarth employed as a porter at Settle at 17s. a week 27.9.1849.
Richard Walker appointed pointsman at Lancaster Castle station 6.12.1849.

APPENDIX III

LOCOMOTIVES IN USE ON THE NORTH WESTERN RAILWAY,
DECEMBER 1850

Extract from Report by Thomas L. Gooch

Name of Engine	Weight Tons	Wheels Engine	Wheels Tender	Single/ Coupled	Length of Stroke Inches	Dia. of Cylinder Inches	Age in Yrs.
Hornby Castle	20	4	4	Coupled	24	15	New
Skipton Castle	20	4	4	Coupled	24	15	New
Lancaster Castle	20	4	4	Coupled	24	15	New
Whernside	15	6	—	Single	15	10	New
Pennighent (sic)	15	6	—	Single	15	10	New
Saddleback	11	4	4	Single	18	12	8
Skiddaw	11	4	4	Single	18	11½	8
Black Comb	12½	4	4	Single	18	13	9
Helvellyn	12	4	4	Single	18	13	*
Ingleborough	13	4	4	Single	18	12	4
Clougha	11	4	4	Single	18	11½	8

Note: All had 5ft. dia. driving wheels.
   Helvellyn and *Clougha* had new fireboxes.
   Helvellyn's age was uncertain.

APPENDIX IV

DATES OF OPENINGS OF THE NORTH WESTERN RAILWAY

	SINGLE LINE
12.6.1848	Lancaster Green Ayre-Poulton (Morecambe)
30.7.1849	Skipton-Clapham-Ingleton*
17.11.1849	Lancaster Green Ayre-Wennington
	(Date given at half-yearly meeting of N.W.R. board, Feb., 1850. Some other sources give 30.10.1849 or 1.11.1849)
18.12.1849	Lancaster Green Ayre-Lancaster Castle
2.5.1850	Wennington-Bentham
1.6.1850	Bentham-Clapham

	WIDENED TO DOUBLE TRACK
Autumn 1850	Hellifield-Hornby widened by this time
1.6.1852	Bell Busk-Hellifield
Summer 1853	Skipton-Bell Busk widened by this time
17.8.1861	Clapham-Ingleton*
3.4.1877	Lancaster North-Morecambe Hest Bank Junction
1880	Lancaster Green Ayre-Ladies Walk
3.3.1889	Halton-Crook o' Lune
7.4.1889	Ladies Walk-Halton
2.6.1889	Crook o' Lune-Hornby
27.10.1889	Over Crook o' Lune viaduct

Note: *On the opening of the line throughout, with the completion of the Bentham-Clapham Section, the Ingleton Branch was closed to traffic. It re-opened as a double line on Oct. 1, 1861, when through traffic to Tebay commenced.

APPENDIX V

L.N.W.R. INGLETON BRANCH SERVICE OCTOBER–DECEMBER 1866

	5.35 a.m.	11.20 a.m.	2.10 p.m.	4.00 p.m.
LEEDS ex.	5.35 a.m.	11.20 a.m.	2.10 p.m.	4.00 p.m.
Ingleton	8.25	2.00 p.m.	3.40	6.35
Kirkby Lonsdale	8.37	2.10	—	6.44
Barbon	8.47	2.20	—	6.54
Middleton	8.57	2.30	—	7.04
Sedbergh	9.05	2.37	—	7.11
Low Gill Junction	9.15	2.48	—	7.22
Tebay	9.25	2.58	4.24	7.32
Low Gill (Ingleton)	10.28*	3.15†	4.34‡	—
Tebay	10.40	3.25	—	8.18§
Shap	11.04	3.46	—	—
Clifton	11.18	4.00	—	—
Penrith	11.28	4.10	5.12	8.57
Plumpton	11.41	4.23	—	—
Calthwaite	—	—	—	—
Southwaite	11.52	4.34	—	—
Wreay	12.00	4.41	—	—
CARLISLE arr.	12.15 p.m.	4.55	6.10	9.30
Edinburgh	5.45	9.10		12.45
Glasgow	6.00	9.30		12.55

Note: *This was the 6.00 a.m. ex Liverpool stopping train.
†The 11.00 a.m. ex Liverpool semi-fast.
‡The 9.00 a.m. ex Euston express.
§The 4.25 p.m. ex Liverpool semi-fast.

Station						
Glasgow	9.10 p.m.	7.30 a.m.	9.45 a.m.			4.00 p.m.
Edinburgh	9.30	7.40	10.00			4.15
CARLISLE ex.	7.20 a.m.	12.00	1.05 p.m.	1.45 p.m.		7.50
Wreay	7.30	12.10 p.m.	———	1.58		———
Southwaite	7.37	12.17	———	2.07		———
Calthwaite	—	—	———	2.14		———
Plumpton	7.54	12.31	———	2.22		———
Penrith	8.05	12.42	1.37	2.33		8.20
Clifton	8.15	12.53	———	2.47		———
Shap	8.33	1.10	———	3.06		———
Tebay	9.25	1.27[a]	———	3.24		———
Low Gill (Ingleton)	9.35[d]		2.13[b]	3.34[e]		8.57[c]
Tebay	10.25		2.20	3.30	4.45	9.10
Low Gill Junction	10.35		———	3.40	5.00	9.28
Sedbergh	10.49		———	3.51	5.15	———
Middleton	10.56		———	3.58	5.22	———
Barbon	11.06		———	4.08	5.33	———
Kirkby Lonsdale	11.16		———	4.18	5.45	9.50
Ingleton	11.33		3.06	4.30	5.55	10.00
LEEDS arr.	3.00 p.m.		4.35	8.35		12.05

Note: (a) Arrives Liverpool Lime St. at 5.35, semi-fast. (b) Arrives London Euston at 9.50 p.m. (c) Arrives Liverpool at 12.35. (d) Arrives Liverpool at 2.25 p.m. Stopping train. (e) Arrives Manchester at 8.25 p.m.

APPENDIX VI

L.N.W.R. INGLETON BRANCH SERVICE OCTOBER 1861

UP TRAINS Stations	Week Days 1 2 3 Class	Week Days 1 & 2 Class	UP TRAINS Stations	Week Days 1 2 3 Class	Week Days 1 & 2 Class
Leave	a.m.	p.m.	Leave	a.m.	a.m.
Carlisle	8.20	2.00	Redcar		10.30
			Middlesbrough	6.00	12.10
		a.m.	Stockton	6.10	12.20
London		6.15	Darlington	7.25	1.00
Birmingham		8.45	Barnard Castle	8.05	1.40
Liverpool		11.30	Kirkby Stephen	9.10	2.45
Manchester		11.35	TEBAY	10.05	3.50
			LOW GILL JUNC. arr.	10.15	4.00
		p.m.	SEDBERGH	10.29	4.14
Preston	7.30	1.05	MIDDLETON	10.39	4.24
Lancaster	8.30	2.00	BARBON	10.50	4.35
Windermere	7.40	1.20	KIRKBY LONSDALE	11.02	4.47
Kendal	9.10	2.45	INGLETON	11.15	5.00

(Right-hand stations from Redcar to Kirkby Stephen on Stockton & Darlington Rly)

Note: The 2.00 p.m. Up Train runs in connection with 3rd Class from the North.

DOWN TRAINS Station	Week Days 1 2 3 Class	Week Days 1 & 2 Class	DOWN TRAINS Stations	Week Days 1 2 3 Class	Week Days 1 & 2 Class
Leave	a.m.	p.m.	Leave	p.m.	p.m.
INGLETON	8.30	2.00	Kendal	10.35	4.30
KIRKBY LONSDALE	8.43	2.13	Windermere	11.40	7.35
BARBON	8.55	2.25	Lancaster	11.27	5.15
MIDDLETON	9.06	2.36	Preston	12.30	6.25
SEDBERGH	9.16	2.46	Manchester	2.20	8.25
LOW GILL JUNC.	9.30	3.00	Liverpool	2.15	8.15
TEBAY arr.	9.40	3.10	Birmingham	5.40	
Kirkby Stephen	10.50	4.35	London	10.40	
Barnard Castle	12.00	5.40	Carlisle	11.00	5.00
Darlington	1.40	6.35			
Stockton	2.15	7.05			
Middlesbrough	2.23	7.15			
Redcar	3.00	7.45			

(Left-hand stations from Kirkby Stephen to Redcar on Stockton & Darlington Rly)

Note: The 2.00 p.m. Down Train runs in connection with 3rd Class to the South.

APPENDIX VII

DAY RATES PAYABLE ON VARIOUS CONTRACTS 1869–1909

CONTRACTS	1869 Settle & Carlisle Ashwell	1870 Settle & Carlisle Benton & Woodiwiss	1870 Settle & Carlisle Eckersley & Bayliss	1896 Heysham Branches Godfrey & Liddelow	1897 Heysham Harbour Price & Wills	1909 Lancaster Deviation John Butler Co.
LABOUR						
Foremen					10/–	
Fitters					10/–	10/–
Carpenters	5/–	5/6	6/–	7/6	8/6	8/2
Gangers					8/6	
Blacksmiths	4/–	5/6	6/–	6/6	8/6	12/6
Masons	5/–	6/–	6/6	7/6		10/3
Miners	4/–	6/6	8/–	6/6		
Bricklayers	5/–	6/–	6/6	7/6		10/3
Strikers	3/–	4/–	4/6	5/–	5/–	8/4
Crane Drivers					7/–	
Platelayers	3/6	4/6	4/6	5/–		
Navigators & Labourers	3/6	4/–	4/6	5/–	5/6	6/2
Boys	2/–	2/–	2/6	3/–	3/6	5/–
1 Horse, Cart, & Driver	8/–	7/6	8/–	10/6		10/–
2 Horses, Cart, & Driver	14/–	12/–	16/–	17/6		
Steam Crane, Driver & Fireman						10/–

APPENDIX VIII

SETTLE—CARLISLE

LIST OF COTTAGES ORDERED OR IN COURSE OF BUILDING, 1876

Situation	Cottages	Situation	Cottages
Carlisle	24	Ormside	2*
Scotby	6*	Crosby Garrett	6*
	(purchased)	Kirkby Stephen	6*
Cumwhinton	4*	6¼ miles north of	
High Stand Gill	4*	Hawes Junction	2
Armathwaite	6*	3 miles north of	
Samsons' Cave Plantation	2	Hawes Junction	2
Lazonby	6*	Moorcock Road	6
Salkeld	2*	Hawes Junction	22
Longwathby (sic)	6*	3½ miles south of	
New Biggin	4*	Hawes Junction	2
Long Marton	6*	Batty Green, Ingleton	
Appleby	7*	Road, near Selside	12*
	(purchased)	Horton	6*
		Settle	6*

Note: * = One station master's house to be built.

APPENDIX IX

VARIOUS CONSTRUCTION NOTES FOR THE SETTLE AND CARLISLE LINE

Ribblehead Viaduct: First stone laid by William H. Ashwell 12.10.1870.

Arten Gill Viaduct: Began 3.5.1871. Second and fifth piers to springing level by June 1874. Arches in by April 1875. Embankment approaches completed May 1875. Parapet up by July 1875. At Arten Gill the contractors took possession of the ground in March 1870.

Rise Hill Tunnel: The original line of the tunnel was to be to the west of the existing one. Contractor took possession of former site in April 1870 and latter in May 1870. The tunnel was constructed from two shafts and from both ends. Both shafts started May 1870. Southern shaft down to tunnel level by November 1870. Northern shaft nearly down to tunnel roof level by October 1870 but took further year to get to final level. Gang working south from shaft 2 met gang working north from shaft 1 on 21.3.1873. By January 1874 the gangs between the south shaft and the south end had met and the gang working north from 2 met the gang from the northern mouth in October 1874.

Moorcock Viaduct: Originally planned as embankment and later as a viaduct to have 8 arches and a heavy central pier. Commenced as a 12-arched structure on 9.5.1873. Tip head ceased on north side 31.3.1874. All piers to springing level by September 1874. Arches in by May 1875 and approach embankments 31.7.1875. Parapet completed September 1875.

Moorcock Tunnel: Masonry commenced 29.1.1874 and completed July 1874.

Lunds Viaduct: Commenced 2.4.1874. Piers to springing level by January 1875. Arches in by June 1875 and parapet during next month.

Shotlock Hill Tunnel: Masonry commenced 24.7.1874 and completed December 1874.

Ais Gill Viaduct: Commenced 24.3.1871.

Intake: There was to be a viaduct at Intake, just south of Birkett Tunnel. The viaduct was abandoned, more land on either side purchased, and the culverted embankment made instead. Work started on either side in early March 1870. Embankment joined in centre 28.2.1875.

Birkett Tunnel: Tunnel driven from north to south. Work started at north end in November 1871. Temporary shaft commenced 5.8.1873. Masonry commenced 12.10.1874. Tunnel shaft reached south end in January 1875.

Smardale Viaduct: Planned originally to have a second set of six arches at a lower level between the two heavy piers Nos. 4 and 10. Not carried out. Work commenced 14.10.1870. Piers up to springing level by January 1874. All arches in, commencing from south, between July 1874 and March 1875. Parapet completed by April 1875.

Junction lines: On the contract plans for the Settle line two short curves are shown which were not authorised. One was over ½ mile in length, at Smardale, forming a loop to the South Durham line and giving through running between the two stations at Kirkby Stephen. The other was to be at the south end of Appleby station, giving through running between Warcop and Great Ormside.

APPENDIX X

SETTLE—CARLISLE

PROPOSED L.Y.R. CONNECTING GOODS SERVICES JUNE 1875

SERVICE No. 1

7.45 p.m.	dep. Manchester		8.40 a.m.	dep. Skipton
8.20	arr. Rochdale		9.10	arr. Colne
8.40	dep. Rochdale		9.20	dep. Colne
9.10	arr. Todmorden		9.40	arr. Burnley
9.25	dep. Todmorden		9.50	dep. Burnley
9.55	arr. Burnley		10.20	arr. Todmorden
10.10	dep. Burnley		10.30	dep. Todmorden
10.30	arr. Colne		11.00	arr. Rochdale
10.40	dep. Colne		11.15	dep. Rochdale
11.15	arr. Skipton		11.50	arr. Manchester

SERVICE No. 2

7.00 p.m.	dep. Liverpool		9.00 a.m.	dep. Skipton
7.50	arr. Wigan		9.30	arr. Colne
8.05	dep. Wigan		9.40	dep. Colne
8.30	arr. Bolton		10.00	arr. Burnley
8.45	dep. Bolton		10.12	arr. Blackburn
9.25	arr. Blackburn		10.22	dep. Blackburn
9.40	dep. Blackburn		11.02	arr. Bolton
9.52	dep. Burnley		11.20	dep. Bolton
10.10	arr. Colne		11.45	arr. Wigan
10.20	dep. Colne		12.00 noon	dep. Wigan
10.55	arr. Skipton		12.50 p.m.	arr. Liverpool

SERVICE No. 3

7.00 p.m.	dep. Dewsbury		9.20 a.m.	dep. Skipton
7.15	arr. Mirfield		9.50	arr. Colne
7.30	dep. Mirfield		10.00	dep. Colne
7.42	arr. Brighouse		11.05	arr. Sowerby Bridge
7.52	dep. Brighouse		11.15	dep. Sowerby Bridge
8.03	arr. North Dean		11.25	arr. North Dean
8.13	dep. North Dean		11.35	dep. North Dean
8.23	arr. Sowerby Bridge		11.46	arr. Brighouse
8.35	dep. Sowerby Bridge		11.55	dep. Brighouse
9.50	arr. Colne		12.07 p.m.	arr. Mirfield
10.00	dep. Colne		12.20	dep. Mirfield
10.40	arr. Skipton		12.35	arr. Dewsbury

APPENDIX XI/a

MIDLAND RAILWAY STATION WORKING, PASSENGERS 1876–1883

No. of Passengers

	1876	1877	1878	1879	1880	1881	1882	1883
Carlisle	29714	36999	37398	39951	35774	33139	33584	39866
Scotby	3386	5350	5421	5442	6167	6041	5790	7785
Cumwhinton	6156	8126	7738	6521	7065	6694	6995	10297
Cotehill	3326	4307	4897	4625	4341	3807	3669	4695
Armathwaite	7232	8760	9019	8337	8806	7946	8422	10134
Lazonby	9341	8663	8344	8333	8467	7382	8058	9232
Little Salkeld	2428	3043	2898	3218	3210	2661	2702	3249
Langwathby	3418	5299	6371	5689	5507	4538	4749	5687
New Biggin	2339	3359	3719	3948	3777	3025	3096	3461
Long Marton	4016	6430	6796	6646	7145	6987	7086	7947
Appleby	11404	14916	14629	14032	17773	18487	18882	18738
Ormside	2512	2967	2987	3177	3726	3058	2755	2834
Crosby Garrett	1983	2757	2626	2171	2323	2241	2438	2336
Kirkby Stephen	4959	6370	6352	5722	6053	5293	5826	5448
Hawes			1946	6845	8056	7072	8504	7706
Hawes Junction	465	8245	9471	11837	13643	10670	11245	10904
Dent		1358	3225	3458	3100	2893	2967	2851
Ribblehead	277	3805	3335	2864	2417	2672	2388	2589
Horton	3255	4801	4535	4731	4912	4276	4209	4443
Settle	20016	16439	15784	16180	18475	17358	17748	17187
Ingleton	10188	9642	9746	10038	11006	12650	12881	11834
Skipton	167616	177476	178778	167723	172310	163973	173181	167762
Leeds	727877	712128	728424	642899	655003	652798	687135	663773
Bradford	1146644	1160883	1131928	1065749	1146857	1088070	1144023	1111497

Figures for Settle (Old), Ingleton, Skipton, Leeds, and Bradford for the two years preceding the opening of the Settle line are:

	Settle	Ingleton	Skipton	Leeds	Bradford
1874	34327	14743	156211	751380	1131560
1875	34653	13769	153151	772830	1190688

APPENDIX XI/b

MIDLAND RAILWAY STATION WORKING, LIVESTOCK, 1876-1883

No. of Trucks In and Out

	1876	1877	1878	1879	1880	1881	1882	1883
Carlisle Goods	1615	1414	1585	1162	1402	1179	1622	1300
Scotby	1	—	—	—	—	4	11	—
Cumwhinton	—	1	—	—	—	—	—	—
Cotehill	—	—	2	—	—	—	—	—
Armathwaite	98	144	196	180	256	267	302	288
Lazonby	620	777	618	635	689	640	771	812
Little Salkeld	27	4	—	—	—	—	—	—
Langwathby	325	656	615	484	539	551	552	691
New Biggin	125	180	184	169	207	169	214	198
Long Marton	32	71	72	70	78	48	84	63
Appleby	425	648	837	794	768	628	794	639
Ormside	—	—	—	—	—	3	2	—
Crosby Garrett	61	19	46	32	37	37	53	50
Kirkby Stephen	296	220	330	322	346	261	292	287
Hawes	—	—	239	452	586	378	517	388
Hawes Junction	7	441	560	317	437	326	478	445
Dent	—	14	63	45	56	65	62	57
Ribblehead	—	30	61	56	91	74	110	71
Horton	25	95	111	60	69	87	111	130
Settle	1961	1761	1966	1758	1853	1663	1848	1663
Ingleton	170	213	183	174	140	158	216	256
Long Preston	2382	2679	2915	2471	2928	2350	2530	2479
Hellifield	71	82	87	88	365	315	441	417
Skipton	4360	4633	5474	4541	4734	3642	4608	4117

Figures for Settle, Ingleton, Long Preston, Hellifield, and Skipton for the two years preceding the opening of the Settle line are:

	Settle	Ingleton	Long Preston	Hellifield	Skipton
1874	1348	250	2172	41	4065
1875	1645	194	2451	43	4244

APPENDIX XI/c

MIDLAND RAILWAY STATION WORKING, MINERALS*, 1876-1883

Tons

	1876	1877	1878	1879	1880	1881	1882	1883
Carlisle	8540	7898	9586	9909	10703	8653	10119	10035
Appleby	2054	3964	4366	3763	3160	3389	3264	3470
Ormside	—	—	—	—	49	637	650	665
Kirkby Stephen	607	1095	1076	1080	855	1071	2011	2432
Ribblehead	—	1060	561	595	325	9878	12008	18969
Horton	89	650	7971	13507	25535	20720	25058	20542
Settle	47588	38470	38691	48650	54475	43347	42131	44603
Ingleton	22554	21490	19361	21882	24228	21290	22234	24813

*These figures are for coal, coke, lime, and limestone, in and out. Figures for Settle for 1874 and 1875 were 55062 and 58310 respectively; for Ingleton—where the Settle line caused a drop, the figures for 1872, 1873, 1874, and 1875 were 44489, 43287, 27100, and 30228.

APPENDIX XII/a

WORKING TIMETABLE 1877 LOADS FOR ENGINES

EXTRACT

Leeds and North Thereof

From	To	Double Framed Engines — Loaded G	Loaded M	Empties	Single Framed Engines — Loaded G	Loaded M	Empties	Instructions
Carlisle (Mid)	Carlisle (N.B.)	25	20	33	30	24	40	Note: G = Goods
,, (N.B.)	,, (Mid)	25	20	33	30	24	40	M = Mineral
,, (Mid)	,, (Cal.)	25	20	33	30	24	40	
,, (Cal.)	,, (Mid)	25	20	33	30	24	40	
Carlisle	Lazonby	32	25	40	38	30	48	
Lazonby	Carlisle	25	20	33	30	24	40	
Lazonby	Stainforth	40	35	50	48	40	50	
Settle Junction	Lazonby	40	35	50	48	40	50	
Stainforth	Settle Junction	40	35	50	48	40	50	
Skipton	Carlisle	23*			27*			*Mixed goods and cattle, or cattle only.
Carlisle	Skipton	23*			27*			
Morecambe	Lancaster G.A.	40	35	50	48	42	50	
Lancaster G.A.	Morecambe	35	30	50	35	30	50	
,, C.S.	Green Ayre	30	24	40	30	24	40	
,, G.A.	Castle station	30	24	40	30	24	40	
,, G.A.	Clapham	40	33	50	48	40	50	When more than 15 Wagons on a Train from Oxenhope to Keighley, every fifth brake must be pinned down. In no case must more than 45 Wagons be brought down the Branch at one time.
Clapham	Lancaster	30	24	40	36	29	48	
Carnforth	Wennington	35	30	45	42	36	50	
Wennington	Carnforth	35	30	45	42	36	50	
Clapham	Ingleton	35	30	45	42	36	50	
Ingleton	Settle	35	30	45	42	36	50	

From	To	Double Framed Engines			Single Framed Engines			Instructions
		Loaded G	Loaded M	Empties	Loaded G	Loaded M	Empties	
Skipton	Clapham	30	24	40	36	29	48	† In addition to 3 Passenger Carriages
Settle & Colne	Leeds & Bradford	40	33	50	48	40	50	Total mixed load not to exceed 12.
Bradford	Shipley	35	30	50	42	36	50	
Leeds	Skipton	33	28	45	40	33	50	
Skipton	Colne							
Earby	Barnoldswick	9†						Certain Express Goods Trains convey 35 Goods when worked with double framed engines from Skipton to Clapham, as shewn in Classification.
Barnoldswick	Earby							
Keighley	Oxenhope	17†	13†	30	17†	13†	30	
Oxenhope	Keighley	30	25	40	30	25	40	
Guiseley Jcn.	Esholt	28	20	38	—	—	—	
Esholt	Guiseley Jcn.	18	14	30	18	14	30	
Ilkley Jcn. (Apperley)	Guiseley station	26	16	30	26	16	30	‡ Exclusive of two Breaks.
Esholt	Ilkley Jcn. (Apperley)							
Guiseley station	Esholt							
" "	Otley & Ilkley	30	25	40	30	25	40	
Ilkley & Otley	Guiseley	25	18	35	25	18	35	

439

Note: Three empty wagons were taken as being equivalent to two loaded wagons. No train was to exceed 50 wagons.

APPENDIX XII/b

Extract

Engines of fast passenger trains and of breakdown van trains	Two white lights—one over left hand buffer and one at foot of chimney.
Engines of slow passenger trains and light engines	A white light over left hand buffer.
Engines of special passenger and empty carriage trains	Two white lights—one over right hand buffer, and one at foot of chimney.
Engines of most important goods trains	Three white lights—one over each buffer, and one at foot of chimney.
Engines of express goods and cattle trains	Two white lights—one over each buffer.
Engines of through goods and mineral trains, and engines of ballast trains which do not have to stop on the journey for loading or unloading purposes	Two white lights—one over the other at foot of chimney.
Shunting engines, (except those employed exclusively in station yards and sidings), engines of stopping goods and mineral trains, and engines of ballast trains which have to stop on the journey for loading or unloading purposes	Two white lights—side by side, over the left hand buffer.

Note: The above applied to Midland main line working, but there were variations in the case of running powers, joint lines, etc.

APPENDIX XII/c

EXTRACT

Points at which Speed must be reduced	Max. Speed per hour
Between Petteril Junction and South Sidings, Carlisle, on up and down goods lines	10
Between Crown Street signal box (No. 5) and elevated signal box at north end of Citadel station, Carlisle	4
Over Settle Junction—Trains going to or from Clapham	20
Over Clapham Junction—Trains going to or from Wennington	20
Between North Junction and station North box, Skipton, on up goods lines	8
Over Skipton North Junction—Trains going to or from Gargrave	25
Through Skipton station	10
Between South Junction and Engine Shed box, Skipton, on down goods lines	8
Through Keighley station	30
Between Bingley Junction and Leeds Junction, and between Bradford Junction and Bingley Junction, Shipley	10
Over Guiseley Junction, Shipley—Trains going to or from Guiseley	20
Between Shipley South Sidings box and Manningham station on down goods line	15
Between Manningham station and Manningham Sidings, on up goods line	6
Over Apperley Junction—Trains going to or from Guiseley	10
Between Armley Bridge signal box and Hunslet passenger station, on up and down main lines	20
Between Hunslet South Junction and Hunslet passenger station, on up and down goods lines	6

APPENDIX XIII

N.E.R. HAWES BRANCH SERVICE JULY 1879
HAWES JUNCTION–LEYBURN–BEDALE–NORTHALLERTON

38½ Miles

	a.m.	a.m.	a.m.	p.m.	p.m.	p.m.
Hawes Junction			10.42	1.20		6.15
Hawes		7.50	10.57	1.35	4.50	
Askrigg						
Leyburn	6.05			2.20		7.15
Bedale				2.05		
Northallerton	7.05	9.40	12.45	2.30	6.45	
York	9.00	11.15	2.20	3.55	9.02	
	A	B	C	D	E	F

Notes: A. Stopping train, Leyburn–Northallerton.
      B. Stopping train, Hawes–Northallerton.
      C. Stops at all stations.
      D. Two trains. 1.20 stopping train to Leyburn from Hawes Junction, and the 2.05 stopping train from Bedale to Northallerton.
      E. 4.50 stopping train from Northallerton.
      F. 6.15 stopping train, Hawes Junction–Leyburn.

	a.m.	a.m.	p.m.	p.m.	p.m.	p.m.
York	6.00	10.00		2.45		6.25
Northallerton	7.40	10.41	1.35	3.53		8.45
Bedale			2.00			
Leyburn			3.15		7.40	9.50
Askrigg					8.15	
Hawes	10.10	12.45	4.00	5.35		
Hawes Junction	10.25	1.00		5.50		
	A	B	C	D	E	F

Notes: A. Semi-fast.*
      B. Stops at all stations, Northallerton–Hawes Junction.
      C. Two trains. 1.35 from Northallerton to Bedale, and 3.15 from Leyburn to Hawes.
      D. Stops at all stations to Hawes Junction.
      E. All stations, Leyburn to Askrigg.
      F. All stations, Northallerton to Leyburn.

*As to the 7.40 from Northallerton, this stopped when required at Scruton, Crakehall, Constable Burton, and Spennithorne.

APPENDIX XIV

N.E.R.   SOUTH DURHAM & LANCASHIRE UNION LINE SERVICE
JULY 1879

TEBAY–DARLINGTON

	a.m.	a.m.	p.m.	p.m.	p.m.
Tebay	8.10	11.15	12.55	4.00	7.25
Gaisgill	8.17	11.22	1.02	4.07	7.32
Ravenstonedale	8.25	11.30	1.10	4.15	7.40
Smardale	8.33	11.38	1.18	4.23	7.48
Penrith dep.	7.15	10.45	—	3.20	6.50
Kirkby Stephen	8.43	11.52	1.23	4.30	7.55*
Barnard Castle	9.32	12.42		5.30	8.40
Darlington	10.05	1.17		6.05	9.15

Notes: No notice has been taken of two trains which ran between Barnard Castle and
Darlington.
The train marked * ran as a semi-fast between Kirkby Stephen and Darlington,
missing Barras and Lartington. Other trains stopped at all stations.
No Sunday trains from Kirkby Stephen by this line.

DARLINGTON–TEBAY

	a.m.	a.m.	a.m.	p.m.	p.m.
Darlington		7.13	10.35	12.50	4.40
Barnard Castle		7.55	11.10	1.24	5.15
Kirkby Stephen	7.05	8.50	11.55	2.13	6.05
Penrith arr.		9.45	12.45	3.25	7.05
Smardale	7.11	8.56		2.19	6.11
Ravenstonedale	7.18	9.03		2.26	6.18
Gaisgill	7.26	9.11		2.34	6.26
Tebay	7.35	9.20	12.15	2.40	6.35

Note: The 10.35 was a semi-fast not stopping at Lartington, Barras, Smardale, Ravenstonedale, and Gaisgill. No Sunday trains from Kirkby Stephen by this line.

APPENDIX XV

N.E.R. EDEN VALLEY LINE SERVICE JULY 1879

KIRKBY STEPHEN–PENRITH

	a.m.	a.m.	p.m.	p.m.
Darlington	7.13	10.35	12.50	4.40
Kirkby Stephen	8.45	11.55	2.25	6.05
Appleby	9.10	12.17	2.50	6.30
Clifton	9.35	—	3.15	6.55
Penrith	9.45	12.45	3.25	7.05
Carlisle	12.15	1.30	5.00	8.45
	A	B	A	A

Notes: A. All stations.
B. Did not stop at Musgrave, Cliburn, or Clifton.

PENRITH–KIRKBY STEPHEN

	a.m.	a.m.	p.m.	p.m.
Carlisle	—	8.45	2.00	5.35
Penrith	7.15	10.45	3.20	6.50
Clifton	7.24	10.54	3.29	6.59
Appleby	7.51	11.21	3.56	7.26
Kirkby Stephen	8.15	11.45	4.20	7.50
Darlington	10.05	1.17	6.05	9.15

Note: All were stopping trains.

APPENDIX XVI

N.E.R. EDEN VALLEY LINE SERVICE JULY–AUGUST 1880

KIRKBY STEPHEN–PENRITH

	a.m.	a.m.	p.m.	p.m.	p.m.	p.m.	p.m.
Darlington	7.10	10.35		12.50		4.30	
Kirkby Stephen	8.42	11.55		2.25		5.55	
Musgrave	8.50	—		2.33		6.03	
Warcop	8.55	12.05		2.38		6.08	
Appleby	9.07	12.17	12.57	2.50	5.30	6.20	6.45
Kirkby Thore	9.15	12.25	—	2.58	—	6.28	—
Temple Sowerby	9.20	12.30	—	3.03	—	6.33	—
Cliburn	9.25	—	—	3.08	—	6.38	—
Clifton	9.32	—	—	3.15	—	6.45	—
Penrith	9.42	12.45	1.22	3.25	5.55	6.55	7.10
Carlisle	11.20	1.30		5.00	6.55	8.45	8.45

PENRITH–KIRKBY STEPHEN

	a.m.	a.m.	a.m.	p.m.	p.m.	p.m.	p.m.
Carlisle			8.45*		2.00	4.25	5.35
Penrith	7.15	9.25	10.45	1.00	3.20	5.35	7.00
Clifton	7.24	—	10.54	—	3.29	—	7.09
Cliburn	7.31	—	11.01	—	3.36	—	7.16
Temple Sowerby	7.36	—	11.06	—	3.41	—	7.21
Kirkby Thore	7.41	—	11.11	—	3.46	—	7.26
Appleby	7.51	9.50	11.21	1.31	3.56	6.04	7.36
Warcop	8.01		11.31		4.06		7.46
Musgrave	8.06		11.36		4.11		7.51
Kirkby Stephen	8.15		11.45		4.20		8.00
Darlington	10.05		1.17		6.05		9.20

Note: *Leaves at 9.00 a.m. on Tuesdays.

APPENDIX XVII/a

MIDLAND RAILWAY INGLETON BRANCH SERVICE JULY 1880

CLAPHAM–INGLETON

		a.m.	a.m.	p.m.	p.m.
Skipton		7.02	10.19	1.07	5.05
Clapham		7.50	11.06	1.36	6.01
Ingleton	arr.	8.05	11.30	1.55	6.40
	dep.	7.30	10.45	12.40	5.40
Carnforth		8.45	11.43		7.20
Lancaster		8.56	11.57	2.15	6.57
Morcambe		9.10	12.10	2.35	7.10
		A	B	C	D

Notes: A. All stations.
B. Semi-fast.
C. Called at Giggleswick, Bentham, and Hornby, then all stations to Lancaster.
D. All stations.
All trains went through to Morecambe. No Sunday service.

INGLETON–CLAPHAM

		a.m.	a.m.	p.m.
Morecambe		7.15		5.15
Lancaster		7.28		5.25
Carnforth		7.20		
Wennington			10.55	
Ingleton	arr.		11.30	6.40
	dep.	7.30	12.40	5.40
Clapham		8.24	1.00	6.10
Skipton		9.17	1.53	7.15
		A	B	C

Notes: A. All stations.
B. All stations but started from Wennington as a connection from the 10.11 from Lancaster Green Ayre (10.00 ex Morecambe).
C. All stations
All trains commenced at Morecambe (except B). No Sunday service.

APPENDIX XVII/b

L.N.W.R. INGLETON BRANCH SERVICE JULY 1880

TEBAY–INGLETON

	a.m.	a.m.	a.m.	p.m.	p.m.
Carlisle		7.15	8.45	1.40	5.35
Penrith		7.58	9.17	2.10	6.18
Tebay Junction		8.42	9.52	2.46	6.58
Low Gill Junction		8.58	—	—	—
Tebay	7.40	10.25	10.25	3.00	7.10
Low Gill Junction	7.50	10.35	10.35	3.13	7.20
Sedbergh	8.00	10.45	10.45	3.22	7.30
Middleton	8.08	10.52	10.52	3.29	7.38
Barbon	8.18	11.02	11.02	3.38	7.48
Kirkby Lonsdale	8.30	11.12	11.12	3.48	8.00
Ingleton (L.N.W.)	8.40	11.25	11.25	4.00	8.10
Ingleton (Midland)		12.40	12.40	5.40	
	A	B	C	D	

Notes: A. All stations.
B. All stations.
C. Alternative fast train Carlisle–Tebay.
D. Fast train Carlisle–Tebay.
No Sunday service.

INGLETON–TEBAY

	a.m.	a.m.	a.m.	p.m.
Ingleton (Midland)	8.05		11.30	
Ingleton (L.N.W.)	8.10	11.00	1.45	5.55
Kirkby Lonsdale	8.20	11.10	1.55	6.05
Barbon	8.28	11.20	2.03	6.15
Middleton	8.36	11.27	2.10	6.22
Sedbergh	8.45	11.38	2.18	6.30
Low Gill Junction	8.55	11.50	2.28	6.40
Tebay	9.10	12.00	2.38	6.50
Low Gill Junction	10.28		3.11	7.02
Tebay Junction	10.40	12.24	3.21	7.10
Penrith	11.28	1.00	4.10	8.00
Carlisle	12.15	1.30	5.00	8.45
	A	B	C	C

Notes: A. Calls all stations—Stops at Calthwaite by request.
B. Connects at 12.24 at Tebay with fast train to Carlisle.
C. Stops at all stations.
No Sunday service.

APPENDIX XVIII/a

MIDLAND RAILWAY INGLETON BRANCH SERVICE JULY 1881

CLAPHAM–INGLETON

		a.m.	a.m.	a.m.	p.m.	p.m.	p.m.
Skipton		7.02	9.35	11.32	1.04	3.30	4.43
Clapham		7.50	10.22	*	1.43	*	5.22
Ingleton	arr.	8.05	10.40	12.50		4.25	5.40
Ingleton	dep.	7.30	10.05		12.10		5.00
Carnforth		8.47	11.12			4.35	6.00
Lancaster	Green Ayre	8.53	11.22	12.50	2.22	4.48	6.18
Lancaster	Castle	9.00		1.01		4.55	6.25
Morecambe		9.10	11.40	1.05	2.35	5.05	6.28
				†	†	†	†

Notes: *Stops to set down only.
†Semi-fasts.
No Sunday service.

INGLETON–CLAPHAM

		a.m.	a.m.	a.m.	a.m.	p.m.	p.m.
Morecambe		7.15	8.00	10.20	11.20	2.15	6.05
Lancaster	Castle			10.15	11.25	1.55	6.03
Lancaster	Green Ayre	7.28	8.12	10.33	11.40	2.27	6.17
Carnforth		7.35	8.25	10.35		2.20	6.05
Ingleton	arr.			11.40	12.50	4.25	7.20
Ingleton	dep.	7.30	8.40	10.55	12.10	2.55	6.35
Clapham		8.24	9.01	11.19	12.29	3.17	6.58
Skipton		9.15	9.31	12.05	1.27	4.00	7.36
		A	B	C	A	C	C

Notes: A. All stations.
B. Belfast Boat Train. Semi-fast.
C. Semi-fasts.
No Sunday service.

APPENDIX XVIII/b

L.N.W.R. INGLETON BRANCH SERVICE JULY 1881

TEBAY–INGLETON

	a.m.	a.m.	a.m.	p.m.	p.m.	p.m.
Carlisle		7.05	8.40	12.55	1.40	5.45
Penrith		7.48	8.10	1.25	2.23	6.25
Tebay Junction		8.32	9.43	1.55	3.05	7.04
Low Gill Junction		8.45	—	—	3.18	—
Tebay	7.30	10.25	9.50	2.05	3.15	7.15
Low Gill Junction	7.45	10.35	—	—	3.28	7.25
Sedbergh	7.53	10.45	10.07	2.20	3.37	7.35
Middleton	8.01	10.52	—	—	3.44	7.43
Barbon	8.11	11.02	10.17	2.30	3.53	7.53
Kirby Lonsdale	8.23	11.12	10.26	2.38	4.03	8.05
Ingleton (L.N.W.)	8.32	11.25	10.35	2.47	4.15	8.15
Ingleton (Midland)	8.55	11.30	10.40	2.52	4.20	
	A	B	C	A	A	

Notes: A. All stations.
    B. Semi-fast.
    C. Fast.
    No Sunday service.

INGLETON–TEBAY

	a.m.	a.m.	p.m.	p.m.	p.m.	p.m.
Ingleton (Midland)	8.05	10.40	12.50	12.50	4.24	5.40
Ingleton (L.N.W.)	8.07	11.00	1.00	2.00	4.35	5.55
Kirkby Lonsdale	8.16	11.10	1.10	2.10	4.45	6.05
Barbon	8.23	11.20	1.17	2.20	4.52	6.15
Middleton	8.30	11.27	—	2.27	—	6.22
Sedbergh	8.37	11.38	1.27	2.35	5.05	6.30
Low Gill Junction	8.46	11.50	—	2.45	—	6.40
Tebay	9.00	12.00	1.45	2.55	5.25	6.50
Low Gill Junction	10.28	—	—	3.11	—	7.02
Tebay Junction	10.40	12.25	2.03	3.21	5.50	7.10
Penrith	11.28	1.00	—	4.10	6.25	8.00
Carlisle	12.15	1.30	3.05	5.00	7.00	8.45
	A	B	C	A	B	A

Notes: A. All stations.
    B. Semi-fast.
    C. Fast.
    No Sunday service.

APPENDIX XIX

MIDLAND RAILWAY HELLIFIELD LINE SERVICE JULY 1888

MANCHESTER–EDINBURGH AND GLASGOW
(Weekdays only except where stated)

		a.m.	a.m.	p.m.	p.m.	p.m.
Manchester		1.05	9.55	2.30	2.45	4.35
Bolton		1.25	10.14	2.49	3.04	*
Darwen		—		3.08	3.23	5.13
Blackburn	arr.	1.48	10.41	3.17	3.32	5.23
	dep.	1.53	10.46	3.22	3.42	5.28
Clitheroe		—	11.03	3.39	—	5.45
Hellifield		2.25	11.20	3.56	4.14	6.02
Carlisle		4.30	1.26	5.47	6.00	8.05
Edinburgh		7.25	4.20	8.24	—	—
Glasgow		7.40	4.07	—	8.35	11.27
		A				B

Notes: A. Also ran on Sundays.
B. Not shown in timetable for following October.
* Stops at Bolton on Tuesdays and Fridays when requested to set down from Manchester.

GLASGOW AND EDINBURGH–MANCHESTER

		a.m.	a.m.	p.m.	p.m.	p.m.	p.m.
Glasgow		9.15*	10.25*		2.30	5.30	9.15
Edinburgh		9.20*	10.45*		2.35	4.25	9.20
Carlisle		12.20	1.28	1.47	5.45	8.10	12.20
Hellifield		2.28	3.18	3.34	7.48	10.10	12.28
Clitheroe		—	3.35	—	8.05†	—	—
Blackburn	arr.	3.00	3.52	4.06	8.23	10.45	3.00
	dep.	3.10	3.57	4.16	8.28	10.52	3.10
Darwen		—	4.05	—	8.36	11.00	—
Bolton		3.33	4.24	4.39	8.55	11.19	3.33
Salford‡		—	4.40	4.55	9.11	11.35	—
Manchester		3.55	4.45	5.00	9.15	11.41	3.55
		A					A

Notes: A. Also ran on Sundays.
* p.m.
† Stops on Fridays when required, to set down at Gisburn and Chatburn.
‡ Ran via Prestwich.

APPENDIX XX

MIDLAND AND N.E.R. HAWES BRANCH CONNECTING SERVICES
1907

	a.m.		a.m.		p.m.	p.m.	p.m.	
Northallerton	7.14		10.50		1.35	3.30	6.33	
Hawes Junction arr.	10.25		12.36		4.12	5.47	8.25	

	a.m.	a.m.	a.m.	a.m.	p.m.	p.m.	p.m.	p.m.
Hawes Junction dep.	10.30	10.45	12.42	1.16	4.35	5.50	6.12	10.03
Skipton	11.45			2.32	5.02		8.28	11.05
Carlisle		12.25	2.30			7.40		

	a.m.	a.m.	a.m.	a.m.	a.m.	p.m.	p.m.	p.m.	p.m.
Carlisle		8.35			10.55	12.00			4.00
Skipton			9.30	11.05			1.14	4.40	
Hawes Junction arr.			10.30	10.45	12.32	12.41	1.09	3.05	5.58	6.12

	a.m.	a.m.	a.m.	p.m.	p.m.	p.m.
Hawes Junction dep.	6.42	10.54		1.05	3.15	6.25
Northallerton	8.28	12.33		2.45	5.02	8.13

APPENDIX XXI/a

MIDLAND RAILWAY STATION WORKINGS, PASSENGERS 1900–1922

No. of Passengers

	1900	1913	1914	1915	1916	1917	1918	1919	1922
Carlisle	46059	49539	48440	46148	54348	38255	40219	53861	48982
Appleby	18544	19104	17855	14470	15427	11104	11427	14465	12240
Kirkby Stephen	6681	6942	6127	6510	6651	4860	4782	5954	5979
Settle	27592	27965	27386	25355	24971	15995	19030	24323	26658
Hellifield	35971	36377	35429	33335	36899	28601	32565	40183	40210
Skipton	237421	284301	283654	313721	288030	225139	254810	329825	321591
Ingleton	15993	13660	13729	14533	15841	13211	14963	19584	16725

APPENDIX XXI/b

MIDLAND RAILWAY STATION WORKING, LIVESTOCK 1900-1922

No. of Trucks In and Out

	1900	1903	1905	1908	1910	1913	1914	1915	1920	1922
Carlisle:										
Petteril Bridge	2695	2975	2644	2620	2302	2663	2857	2450	2899	2143
Dentonholme	32	2	17	45	40	32	214	187	45	74
Scotby	60	37	67	50	45	20	31	14	15	38
Cumwhinton	—	—	—	—	—	—	—	—	—	—
Cotehill	—	—	—	—	—	—	—	—	*	—
Armathwaite	672	495	617	590	550	573	557	416	489	509
Lazonby	1196	1476	1556	1507	1681	2480	2407	2549	2429	2865
Little Salkeld	—	—	—	—	—	—	—	—	—	—
Langwathby	543	547	458	459	435	359	327	318	330	349
Culgaith	—	—	—	—	—	—	—	—	—	—
New Biggin	403	516	670	650	651	555	662	448	482	472
Long Marton	115	156	90	89	93	92	97	67	127	54
Appleby	688	820	961	1032	1100	1477	1480	1605	1210	1514
Ormside	—	—	—	—	—	—	—	—	—	—
Crosby Garrett	100	144	82	46	75	68	66	105	124	52
Kirkby Stephen	572	620	678	627	711	720	711	765	990	1103
Hawes	740	757	766	660	739	744	660	716	643	1112
Hawes Junction	412	504	391	445	393	557	508	447	631	406
Dent	121	106	83	112	104	146	129	150	190	170
Ribblehead	121	108	110	119	119	147	137	142	116	130
Horton	147	175	181	193	213	309	289	279	302	264
Settle	1256	1443	1673	1795	1522	1799	1810	1816	2148	1382
Ingleton	111	129	196	137	105	103	127	166	225	280
Long Preston	1849	1544	1138	1278	558	1405	1258	1057	1079	1044
Hellifield	1071	1137	1448	1757	1795	1995	2325	2317	2837	4796
Skipton	7430	7412	7249	7961	8429	9539	10058	10111	9404	8321

*Cotehill had one truck in 1919.

453

APPENDIX XXI/c

MIDLAND RAILWAY STATION WORKING, MINERALS 1900–1922

Coal, Coke, Lime and Limestone
Tons, In and Out

	1900	1903	1905	1908	1910	1913	1914	1915	1920	1922
Carlisle:										
Petteril Bridge	10167	14824	13616	13333	10338	7512	7986	7993	2048	4401
Dentonholme	3245	604	1714	6867	6363	5184	5869	6050	307	3993
Appleby	3231	3269	3426	3959	3625	3582	2873	3776	1680	2335
Ormside	478	504	512	502	518	532	417	493	429	547
Kirkby Stephen	1217	1046	1015	1716	2105	1940	1645	1629	68	626
Ribblehead	2680	936	355	1313	1099	425	372	353	272	366
Horton	86397	58612	45092	58753	56065	48583	39780	42638	42310	37031
Settle	53179	42753	42433	38066	47338	37424	40775	45795	51414	36132
Ingleton	2960	2365	2686	3902	2753	3901	3132	29997	80572	2675

APPENDIX XXII

CHRONOLOGY OF VARIOUS PERMANENT WAY AND OTHER ALTERATIONS FROM 1892–1923

1892 Newby Moor Crossing signal box op. February 3.
Thwaites new station op. June 1.
Bingley new station op. July 24.
New signal boxes at Long Preston and Settle Junction. The box at the latter was some 300 yards nearer Leeds than the old one.

1893 New signal boxes at Thackley Junction, Shipley, Saltaire, and Barnoldswick Junction.

1894 New signal boxes at Kirkby Stephen, Mallerstang, and Cononley.

1895 Lazonby renamed Lazonby & Kirkoswald in July, and new signal box op.
New signal box at Earby Junction. Settle Junction (track) moved some 40 yards nearer Leeds.

1896 New signal boxes at Helwith Bridge and Horton. On October 4 two additional lines op. between north end of Calverley station and Apperley Junction.

1897 Torrisholme Junction signal box op. May.
Apperley Junction to Calverley Junction down slow line extended to Apperley station. Used as down goods line.

1898 New signal boxes op. at Snaygill, Ribblehead, and on Leeds side of Thackley Tunnel, the latter being an additional block post.
At Horton additional sidings op. for Delaney's.
On November 12 the Morecambe–Heysham line opened for contractor's traffic only. Worked by Midland engines.

1899 Marley Junction, Crosby Garrett, and Esholt Junction new signal boxes opened.
Skipton South Junction to Snaygill up and down goods lines op. January 15 and February 19 respectively.
Delaney's Sidings op. at Gargrave, March 5, and signal box a week later.
In November Midland engines ceased working the Heysham line and the contractor took over.

1900 Hawes Junction renamed Hawes Junction & Garsdale.
Kirkby Stephen renamed Kirkby Stephen & Ravenstonedale.
New signal boxes op. at Gargrave station, New Biggin, Hawes East Junction, Long Marton, Low House Crossing, Bingley North, Colne No. 1, and Thackley Junction.
In May a new down goods line was op. between Marley and Thwaites. This was extended on to Bingley, and another line op. between Bingley and Thwaites, in October.

1901 New signal boxes op. at Ben Rhydding, Guiseley Junction, Calverley Junction, Apperley Bridge. During the year the Shipley & Apperley Widening was virtually completed, the new lines being to the north and south sides of the original Leeds & Bradford railway, the former being confined to the east, and the latter to the west, sides of Thackley Tunnel respectively.
In November the Craven Lime Sidings and signal box at Horton were closed.

1902 New signal boxes op. at Colne North, Embsay Junction and Newlay North.
The Grassington branch was op. for all traffic on July 29.
Thackley Tunnel signal box was closed on February 2.
At about this time the rails were removed from the Appleby South Junction.

1903   New signal boxes op. at Menston, Langwathby, Shipley Goods Sidings, Shipley Bradford Junction, and Dentonholme. A connection was made to Hellifield Gas Works in September.

1904   Up and down goods lines at Shipley extended from Bradford Junction to Leeds Junction, i.e. taken through at the rear of the down Leeds–Bradford platform, February.
Skipton to Snaygill up and down goods become slow lines and passenger lines become fast lines.
New signal box op. at Calverley.
In June on the Grassington Branch a new signal box was op. at the terminus, Delaney's Sidings were op. on the branch, and electric train tablet working began in place of train staff working.
Calverley Junction to Newlay South up and down goods lines op. in May.
On the Heysham branch: in July the block telegraph was completed to the harbour and an experimental service of motor carriages started between the harbour station and Morecambe. In August Middleton Road station was completed. The branch was opened for traffic on September 1.
Between 1904 and 1906 the Apperley & Calverley Widening was completed.
The various dates are given separately.

1905   New signal boxes op. at Kirkstall, Foulridge, and Hellifield North Junction.
Shipley Stone Sidings signal box closed.
During July an additional passenger station was op. at Kirkstall, and on July 31 Kirkstall Forge station was closed.

1906   New signal boxes at Guiseley and Skipton Station South.
Sidings op. at New Biggin.
In March the up slow line was extended from Newlay to Kirkstall Junction and the old connection at Newlay between the up slow and up main lines was dispensed with. The connection between the down slow and down main was taken up in August when the new down slow line was op. between Newlay and Kirkstall Junction. Kirkstall Forge signal box was closed at this time.

1907   New signal boxes at Giggleswick, Elslack, Shipley Bingley Junction, Low Bentham, Ormside, and Selside. At Hawes Joint Station the East Box was renamed Station Box and the old west box was done away with.
Morecambe new passenger station op. March 24.
In October Armley Canal Junction was moved to Redcote Lane Bridge and a second goods line op. from Kirkstall Junction to Redcote Lane, where a new signal box was op. This was in fact one of the first stages of the Armley & Kirkstall Widening which was not completed until 1910. Details are given separately.

1908   New signal boxes op. at Armley Cutting, Leeds Junction at Armley, Wortley Junction, Culgaith, Hellifield Old Station, Apperley Viaduct, and Lune. The viaduct box was in the nature of a block post and was closed only a fortnight later. Another temporary box, in use for permanent way alterations only was that at Lune, opened for a month early in the year.
In September a new box was opened at Whitehall Junction when an additional pair of lines came into use between there and Leeds Junction. In the following month the junction between the fast and slow lines at Whitehall Junction, on the Holbeck side of the box, came into use. The widening at this point caused a re-designation of the layout whereby the two fast and the two slow lines ran side by side, instead of the two up and two down being together.
On the Morecambe–Heysham line experimental electric trains were run

from February 1. On April 13 an electrically operated passenger service started operating between Morecambe and Heysham. From July 1 the service was extended to Lancaster Green Ayre, the trains continuing on to the Castle station from September 14.

In May a new connection was opened from the down fast to the down slow at Shipley Thackley Junction.

Newby Moor Crossing signal box was closed and dispensed with on June 14.

1909   Holbeck. New gas works sidings op. in March.

In April a new signal box was opened at Armley station to which two new lines were opened from Wortley Junction. In December the line was slewed over the new Armley Canal bridge, and new platforms were opened on Armley station.

Thwaites station closed. June 30.

Scotby signal box closed in October.

1910   Bradford Sewage Sidings op. between Apperley Bridge and Shipley.

New junction laid in between Thackley Junction and Apperley Bridge station, and new block post op. at Apperley Viaduct.

New signal box op. at Kirkstall Junction, and two additional lines between there and Armley Junction. This completed the quadrupling of the line between Shipley and Leeds. May 1910.

Hawes Junction signal boxes. On July 10 the north and south boxes were closed and a new one opened called Hawes Junction.

1911   New signal box op. at Hellifield South.

On October 15 the new viaduct over the River Lune was brought into use. At the same time the signal box at Lancaster Green Ayre station had been enlarged and the platforms lengthened.

1912   New signal box op. at Ingleton.

1913   New signal boxes op. at Otley and Ilkley.

Settle Junction. In September the connection from the down main line to the up siding, and the crossover between the up and down main lines, were removed. A new crossover line was put in, altering the site of the junction yet again, and a new signal box was opened. The new junction lines had the effect of bringing the point of the junction about 140 yards nearer Leeds. (See also under 1895.)

1914   Remileage of Midland Railway system. All old mile posts removed. Before this the Settle line, and others, had had their own mile posts. In the case of the Settle line they had commenced from the junction. By now they were inaccurate, there having been two resitings at the junction.

1915   New signal boxes opened at Clapham Junction and Skipton North Junction.

Long Meg signal box, sidings and connections removed in May.

1916   New signal boxes opened at Earby Junction, Ladies Walk, Manningham Sidings, Torrisholme Factory Sidings Morecambe, and Cumwhinton.

1917   As a wartime economy single line working was instituted in January between Embsay and Addingham, with a passing loop at Bolton Abbey. Similarly the Heysham branch was worked as a single line between Torrisholme Junction and the harbour from April 11.

1919   Skipton South signal box closed and new one opened on south side of the Skipton–Ilkley line overbridge.

New signal box opened at Keighley South, ten yards further to the north.

1920   Ingleton branch. The down main line between Clapham Junction and Barker's Siding re-opened for traffic, about April. (The line had been closed in June 1913 to provide storage accommodation for wagons.)

1921   New signal box at Keighley West opened.

Hampleton Quarry branch at Bolton Abbey closed.

From March 21 double line working restored on Skipton–Ilkley line.
From April 10 double line working restored on Heysham branch.
Torrisholme Factory platforms at Morecambe removed in December.
1923 Settle Junction South signal box closed, together with connection from the up main line to the down sidings.

APPENDIX XXIII

STRENGTHENING OF BRIDGES, SETTLE–CARLISLE LINE, 1902–3

Way and Works Committee

Minute No.	Date	Details
19267	19.6.1902	Bridges 234 and 240 at Appleby Bridge 288 at Langwathby
19898	5.6.1903*	Bridge 7 at Settle Bridges 35 and 57 at Horton Bridge 181 at Kirkby Stephen Bridge 254 at Long Marton Bridge 297 at Little Salkeld Bridge 350 at Scotby
20185	6.11.1903*	Bridges 204 and 215 at Crosby Garrett Bridges 255 and 259 at Long Marton Bridge 269 at New Biggin Bridges 279, 285 and 286 at Langwathby Bridge 295 at Little Salkeld Bridge 351 at Scotby
20247	4.12.1903*	Bridge 247 at Long Marton Bridge 287 at Langwathby Bridge 317 at Armathwaite Bridge 347 at Scotby

* Work ordered after the initial test runs of compound engines on the Settle and Carlisle line.

APPENDIX XXIV

TABLE OF VARIOUS STATION AND OTHER OPENINGS AND CLOSURES SINCE THE GROUPING

Note: This list does not pretend to be complete, though as much information as possible has been collected. To assist in placing the stations, which are all within the area covered by this book, references in brackets after the names related to the former owning pre-Grouping company i.e. (F. & M.J.) is Furness & Midland Joint.

13.4.1931	Middleton-on-Lune (L.N.W.) closed to passengers.
1.2.1942	Scotby (M.) closed to all traffic.
16.8.1943	Wreay (L.N.W.) closed to passengers.
1.6.1948	Plumpton (L.N.W.) closed to passengers.
23.5.1949	Damens (M.) closed to passengers.
27.3.1950	Burton & Holme (L.N.W.) closed.
3.3.1952	Elslack (M.) closed completely.
7.4.1952	Cotehill (M.) closed to all traffic.
7.4.1952	Calthwaite (L.N.W.) closed to passengers.
7.4.1952	Southwaite (L.N.W.) closed to passengers.
5.5.1952	Melling (F. & M.J.) closed to passengers.
2.6.1952	Ormside (M.) closed to all traffic.
7.7.1952	Crosby Garrett (M.) closed to all traffic.
3.11.1952	Musgrave (N.E.) closed completely.
1.12.1952	Kirkby Stephen East to Tebay (N.E.) closed to passengers. Intermediate stations of Smardale, Ravenstonedale, and Gaisgill.
5.1.1953	Baildon (M.) closed to passengers.
7.12.1953	Kirkby Thore (N.E.) closed to all traffic.
7.12.1953	Temple Sowerby (N.E.) closed to passengers but retained for goods traffic.
1.2.1954	Ingleton branch closed to passengers. Stations were Ingleton (M.), and Kirkby Lonsdale, Barbon, and Sedbergh, all (L.N.W.).
1.2.1954	Grayrigg (L.N.W.) closed to passengers.
26.4.1954	Hawes to Northallerton (N.E.) passenger service withdrawn.
7.5.1956	Calthwaite (L.N.W.) closed to goods.
17.9.1956	Cliburn (N.E.) closed to all traffic.
5.11.1956	Cumwhinton (M.) closed completely.
8.6.1957	Scale Hall station opened. Lancaster–Morecambe line.
–.8.1957	Garsdale. Rebuilding of waiting room and booking hall started.
6.8.1957	Newsholme (L. & Y.) closed completely.
16.9.1957	Hornby (M.) closed to passengers.
7.7.1958	Holbeck Low Level (M.) closed to passengers.
7.7.1958	Rimington (L. & Y.) closed to passengers.
5.1.1959	Foulridge (M.) closed.
16.3.1959	Hawes station closed (M. & N.E.J.) and Garsdale to Hawes line (M.) closed completely.
4.5.1959	Bell Busk (M.) closed to all traffic.
7.3.1960	Grayrigg (L.N.W.) closed completely.
7.3.1960	Low Gill (L.N.W.) closed completely.
12.9.1960	Arkholme (F. & M.J.) closed completely.
12.9.1960	Borwick (F. & M.J.) closed completely.
12.9.1960	Melling (F. & M.J.) closed completely.
1.5.1961	Caton (M.) closed completely.
12.6.1961	Apperley Bridge & Rawdon (M.) abbreviated to Apperley Bridge.
12.6.1961	Ingrow West (M.) abbreviated to Ingrow.

12.6.1961	Newlay & Horsforth abbreviated to Newlay.
1.1.1961	Keighley to Oxenhope (M.) closed to passengers. Intermediate stations closed at Ingrow, Oakworth, and Haworth. (Last passenger train ran on December 30, 1961.)
22.1.1962	Barnard Castle to Penrith (N.E.) closed to passengers. Stations at Lartington, Bowes, Barras, Kirkby Stephen East, Warcop, Appleby East, and Clifton Moor. Freight still to be dealt with at last four stations, Clifton Moor to be an unstaffed goods depot.
22.1.1962	Ravenstonedale (N.E.) goods depot closed.
22.1.1962	Temple Sowerby (N.E.) goods depot closed.
18.6.1962	Keighley & Worth Valley line (M.) scheduled date for complete closure.
18.6.1962	Oxenholme (L.N.W.) motive power depot closed.
18.6.1962	Penrith (L.N.W.) motive power depot closed.
10.9.1962	Blackburn to Hellifield (L. & Y.) closed to passengers. Stations at Gisburn, Chatburn, Clitheroe, Whalley, Langho, Wilpshire, and Daisyfield.
–.4.1963	Halton (M.) closed to goods.
1.5.1963	Bare Lane (L.N.W.) closed to goods.
17.6.1963	Carlisle Canal motive power depot closed.
17.6.1963	Hellifield (M.) motive power depot closed.
9.9.1963	Giggleswick (M.) closed to goods.
9.9.1963	Wennington (M.) closed to goods.
30.9.1963	Newlay (M.) closed to goods.
4.11.1963	Long Preston (M.) closed to goods.
2.12.1963	Armley Canal Road (M.) closed to goods.
2.3.1964	Barbon (L.N.W.) closed to goods.
2.3.1964	Plumpton (L.N.W.) closed to goods.
2.3.1964	Tebay (L.N.W.) closed to goods.
6.4.1964	Armathwaite (M.) closed to goods.
6.4.1964	Garsdale (M.) closed to goods.
6.4.1964	Long Marton (M.) closed to goods.
20.4.1964	Hellifield (M.) closed to goods.
20.4.1964	Hornby (M.) closed to goods.
27.4.1964	Cononley (M.) closed to goods.
1.6.1964	Apperley Bridge (M.) closed to goods.
6.7.1964	Clifton Moor (N.E.) closed to goods.
6.7.1964	Langwathby (M.) closed to goods.
6.7.1964	Little Salkeld (M.) closed to goods.
6.7.1964	Shap (L.N.W.) closed to goods.
6.7.1964	Southwaite (L.N.W.) closed to goods.
28.9.1964	Kirkby Stephen West (M.) closed to goods.
1.10.1964	Dent (M.) closed to goods.
1.10.1964	Kirby Lonsdale (L.N.W.) closed to goods.
1.10.1964	Sedbergh (L.N.W.) closed to goods.
5.10.1964	Culgaith (M.) closed to goods.
2.11.1964	Appleby East (N.E.) closed to goods.
2.11.1964	Lazonby & Kirkoswald (M.) closed to goods.
25.1.1965	Clapham (M.) closed to goods.
2.2.1965	Horton-in-Ribblesdale (M.) closed to goods.
1.3.1965	Ingleton (M. & L.N.W.) closed to goods. With this closure the whole of the Ingleton line became redundant.
22.3.1965	Stopping passenger services withdrawn between Leeds City and Bradford Forster Square, Bradford Forster Square and Skipton, Leeds City and Ilkley via Arthington, and Bradford Forster Square and Skipton via Ilkley. Stations closed to passenger traffic are

	Armley Canal Road, Kirkstall, Newlay, Calverley & Rodley, Apperley Bridge, Manningham, Frizinghall, Saltaire, Steeton & Silsden, Kildwick & Crosshills, Cononley, Arthington, Pool-in-Wharfedale, Otley, Embsay, Bolton Abbey, and Addingham.
13.4.1964	Lancaster Green Ayre motive power depot closed.
28.6.1965	Bingley, Kildwick & Crosshills, and Steeton & Silsden (all M.) closed to goods.
19.7.1965	Middleton Road (M.) closed to goods.
27.9.1965	Earby (M.) excl – Barnoldswick (M.) closed to passengers.
3.1.1965	On and from this date passenger services between Wennington and Morecambe and electric services between Lancaster Green Ayre, Lancaster Castle, Morecambe, and Heysham were discontinued. Halton, Lancaster Green Ayre, and Scale Hall stations were closed. The last electric train was the 23.10 from Morecambe Promenade to Lancaster Castle on Saturday January 1 (see text).
19.6.1966	Clapham Jct. (M.) – Low Gill (L.N.W.) officially closed as diversionary route.
26.7.1966	Clapham Jct. (M.) – Low Gill (L.N.W.) put out of use.
1.8.1966	Earby (M.) excl – Barnoldswick (M.) closed to goods.
2.1.1967	Horton-in-Ribblesdale, Ribblehead, Dent, Garsdale, Kirkby Stephen West, Long Marton, New Biggin, Culgaith, Langwathby, Little Salkeld, Lazonby & Kirkoswald, and Armathwaite (all M.) made unstaffed halts.
3.4.1967	Skipton motive power depot closed. S&C snow plough to Rose Grove.
5.6.1967	Wennington Jct. – Ladies Walk, and Green Ayre – White Lund (N.W.G.B.) siding ground frame closed completely.
2.10.1967	Holbeck motive power depot closed to steam.
4.1968	Bentham (M.) closed to goods.
29.6.1968	Keighley & Worth Valley Railway reopened to passengers.
11.1968	Calverley & Rodley (M.) closed to goods.
2.2.1970	Colne (M.) excl – Skipton (M.) excl, including Earby and Thornton-in-Craven (all M.) closed completely.
2.2.1970	Torrisholme Jct. – White Lund (N.W.G.B.) siding closed.
4.5.1970	Settle and Carlisle local service withdrawn. Horton-in-Ribblesdale, Ribblehead, Dent, Garsdale, Kirkby Stephen, Long Marton, New Biggin, Culgaith, Langwathby, Little Salkeld, Lazonby & Kirkoswald, and Armathwaite (all M.) closed to passengers.
4.5.1970	Heysham Harbour (M.) closed to passengers and new station opened.
10.1970	Settle (M.) closed to goods.
9.1971	Appleby (M.), Kirkby Stephen East (N.E.) and Warcop (N.E.) closed to goods. Warcop remains open for special traffic.
5.1.1973	Baildon (M.) reopened to passengers.
6.10.1975	Heysham Harbour (B.R.) closed to passengers.
17.3.1976	Lancaster Castle – Ladies Walk siding closed.
14.5.1979	Shipley new platform on down main curve opened to passengers.
12.5.1980	Shipley new platform (see above) used for reversible working.
9.1980	Shipley (M.) closed to goods.
2.1981	Dent signalbox and Ais Gill signalbox and lie-bye sidings closed.
17.5.1982	Crossflatts (W.Y.P.T.E.) opened to passengers.
9.1982	Keighley (M.) closed to goods.
27.2.1983	Guiseley – Apperley Jct. singled, followed by line to Shipley a week later. Esholt Jct. abolished, together with signalbox. New junction close to Guiseley station; new panel in Guiseley signalbox.
9.4.1984	Saltaire (M. rebuilt W.Y.P.T.E.) reopened to passengers.

LANCASTER & CARLISLE and NORTH WESTERN RAILWAYS

SKETCH MAP

Caledonian Railway Section 1, March, 1842
Caledonian Railway Act, 1845
East Lancashire Railway
Kendal & Windermere Railway Act, 1845
Lancaster & Carlisle Railway Act, 1844
Lancaster & Carlisle & Ingleton Railway Act, 1857
Ditto, line abandoned
Lancaster & Preston Junction Railway
Leeds & Bradford Railway
Morecambe Harbour & Railway Act, 1846
North Western Railway Act, 1846. Constructed
Ditto, line abandoned
North Western Railway Bill, 1846
North Western Railway Act, 1848. Abandoned
Lancaster & Carlisle Railway Bill, 1858. (This was the sharp curve objected to by the North Western Railway)

ENLARGEMENT at LOW GILL

Low Gill
Old Low Gill
Grayrigg

Sedbergh

Middleton-on-Lune

SKIPTON

COLNE

To Leeds

CARLISLE

PENRITH
Yanwath
Clifton

Lowther Park
Bampton

ORTON LINE
Sleagill
Orton

OTHER LINE

TEBAY
Low Gill

Windermere
Grayrigg
Sedbergh

Sutton

Kendal
Oxenholme
Sedgwick

Milnthorpe

KENDAL LINE

LUNE VALLEY LINE

Middleton-on-Lune

Kirkby Lonsdale
INGLETON
Clapham

LANCASTER

To Preston

Poulton
(Morecambe)

N

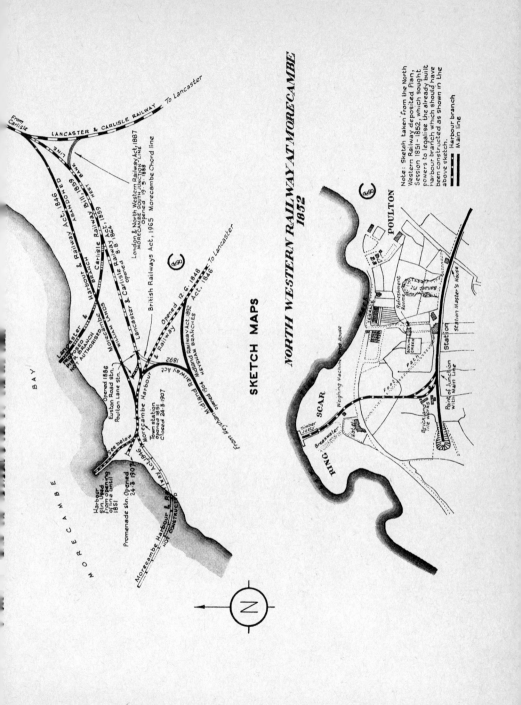

SKETCH MAPS

NORTH WESTERN RAILWAY AT MORECAMBE
1852

Note: Sketch taken from the North
Western Railway deposited Plan,
Session 1851-1852, which sought
powers to legalise the already built
harbour branch which should have
been constructed as shown in the
above sketch.

━━━━━━━ Harbour branch
━━━━━━━ Main line

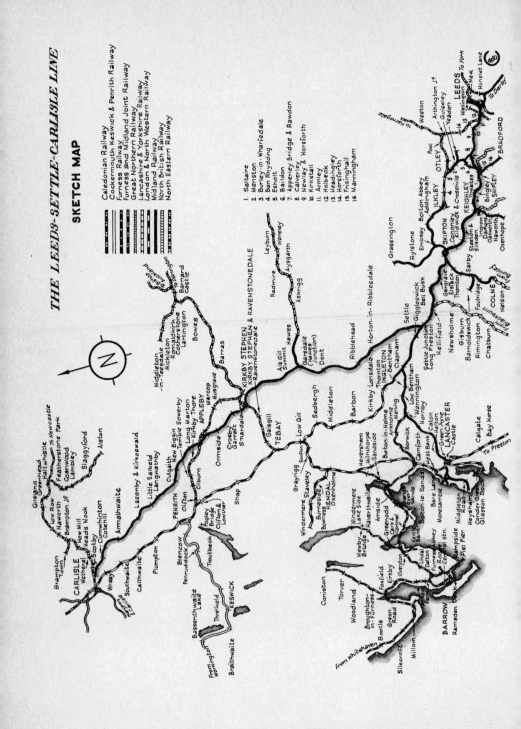

THE LEEDS-SETTLE-CARLISLE LINE

SKETCH MAP

Caledonian Railway
Cockermouth Keswick & Penrith Railway
Furness Railway
Furness and Midland Joint Railway
Great Northern Railway
Lancashire & Yorkshire Railway
London & North Western Railway
Midland Railway
North British Railway
North Eastern Railway

1. Saltaire
2. Menston
3. Burley-in-Wharfedale
4. Ben Rhydding
5. Esholt
6. Baildon
7. Apperley Bridge & Rawdon
8. Calverley
9. Newlay & Horsforth
10. Kirkstall
11. Armley
12. Holbeck
13. Headingley
14. Horsforth
15. Frizinghall
16. Manningham

PORTPATRICK & WIGTOWNSHIRE JOINT RAILWAY

SKETCH MAP

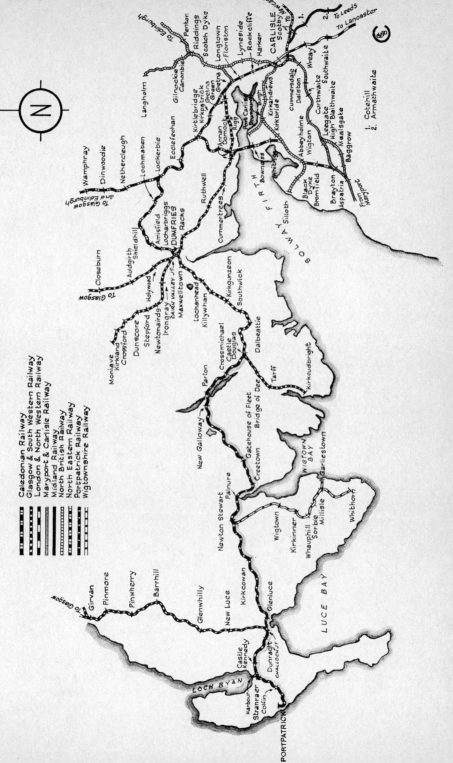

Caledonian Railway
Glasgow & South Western Railway
London & North Western Railway
Maryport & Carlisle Railway
Midland Railway
North British Railway
North Eastern Railway
Portpatrick Railway
Wigtownshire Railway

N

To Edinburgh
To Leeds
1.
2.
To Lancaster

CARLISLE
Scotby
Newcastle
Penton
Riddings
Scotch Dyke
Longtown
Floriston
Lyneside
Rockcliffe
Harker
Gilnockie
Canonbie
Kirklebridge
Kirkpatrick
Gretna
Green
Gretna
Kirkandrews
Rigg
Port Carlisle
Drumburgh
Kirkbride
Cummersdale
Dalston
Abbeyholme
Wigton
Curthwaite
Southwaite
Leegate
High Blaithwaite
Wreay
Bugh
Burgh
Mealsgate
Baggrow

1. Cotehill
2. Armathwaite

Langholm
Ecclefechan
Aman
Annock
Whitby
Bowness
SOLWAY FIRTH
Black
Dyce
Bromfield
Brayton
Aspatria
Mary
Maryport
Aspatria
Silloth

Wamphray
Dinwoodie
Nethercleugh
Lochmaben
Lockerbie
To Glasgow and Edinburgh

Closeburn
Auldgirth
Amisfield
Locharbriggs
Racks
Shieldhill
DUMFRIES
Ruthwell
Cummertrees

To Glasgow
Moniave
Kirkland
Crossford
Dunscore
Stepford
Holywood
Newtonairds
Irongray
Maxwelltown
CAIRN VALLEY JCT.
Lochanhead
Killywhan
Kirkgunzeon
Southwick

Parton
Crossmichael
Castle
Douglas
Dalbeattie
Tarff
Kirkcudbright

New Galloway
Gatehouse of Fleet
Creetown
Bridge of Dee

Nawton Stewart
Palnure
WIGTOWN
BAY
Wigtown
Kirkinner
Whauphill
Sorbie
Millisle
Garliestown
Whithorn

Glenluce
LUCE BAY

Girvan
Pinmore
Pinwherry
Barrhill
Glenwhilly
New Luce
Kirkcowan
Glenluce
To Glasgow

Castle
Kennedy
Dunragit
CHALLOCH JCT.
Harbour
Stranraer
Colfin
LOCH RYAN
PORTPATRICK

Sources and Bibliography

Archivist to the British Railways Board in London
Board and committee minutes of the various railway companies
Evidence given before Parliament on railway Bills
Railway and other Acts of Parliament
Board of Trade Reports
Bradshaw's Shareholders' Guide
Bradshaw's and other timetables
Herepath's Journal
The Engineer
The Railway Chronicle
The Railway Fly Sheet
The Railway Gazette
The Railway Magazine
The Railway News
The Railway Record
The Railway Times
Contracts, reports, maps, and other miscellania.

Books

W. M. Acworth (1900)	*The Railways of England*
E. L. Ahrons (1927)	*Locomotive and Train Working in the Latter Part of the Nineteenth Century*
E. L. Ahrons (1927)	*The British Steam Railway Locomotive 1825–1925*
George Behrend (1962)	*Pullman in Europe*
C. L. D. Duckworth and G. E. Langmuir (1948)	*Railway and Other Steamers*
Hamilton Ellis (1949)	*Nineteenth Century Railway Carriages*
Hamilton Ellis (1953)	*The Midland Railway*
Hamilton Ellis (1955)	*The North British Railway*
Richard S. Lambert (1934)	*The Railway King*
H. G. Lewin (1938)	*Early British Railways*
H. G. Lewin (1939)	*The Railway Mania and its Aftermath*
W. McAdam (1924)	*The Birth, Growth, and Eclipse of the Glasgow and South Western Railway*

Frederick McDermott (1887)	*The Life and Work of Joseph Firbank*
William M'Ilwraith (1880)	*The Glasgow & South Western Railway: Its Origin, Progress, and Present Position*
Morton & Company (1885)	*An Illustrated and Descriptive Guide to the Great Railways of England and their Connections with the Continent*
George P. Neele (1904)	*Railway Reminiscences*
O. S. Nock (1954)	*Locomotives of the North Eastern Railway*
O. S. Nock (1964)	*The Midland Compounds*
John Pendleton (1896)	*Our Railways*
Edwin A. Pratt (1921)	*British Railways and the Great War*
Railway Club (1902–1906)	*The Railway Club Journal*, Vols. 1 to 5
John Rodgers, M.P. (1951)	*British Cities: York*
L. T. C. Rolt (1964)	*A Hunslet Hundred*
David L. Smith (1939–1941)	*Tales of the Glasgow and South Western Railway*
Harry Speight (1898)	*Old Bingley*
Stephenson Locomotive Society (1950)	*The Glasgow and South Western Railway 1850–1923*
Stephenson Locomotive Society (1955)	*The Journal of the Stephenson Locomotive Society*, Vol. XXXI
J. Radford Thomson (1878)	*Guide to the District of Craven and the Settle and Carlisle Railway*
William Weaver Tomlinson (1914)	*The North Eastern Railway: Its Rise and Development*
'Veritas Vincit' (1847)	*Railway Locomotive Management in a Series of Letters*. Reprinted from the *Railway Record*
Francis Whishaw (1840)	*The Railways of Great Britain and Ireland*
Wildman of Settle (1874–1877)	*Wildman's Household Almanack and Year-Book of Useful Knowledge,* for the years 1874, 1876 and 1877. Printed and published by Wildman & Son, Booksellers, of Settle
Frederick S. Williams (1852)	*Our Iron Roads*
Frederick S. Williams (1878)	*The Midland Railway: Its Rise and Progress*

Other Periodicals and Newspapers

The Carlisle Journal
The Craven Herald
The Yorkshire Post
Modern Railways
Rail Enthusiast
Railway World
The Railway Observer
Trains Illustrated

Acknowledgements

Acknowledgements and thanks are due to the following for permission to refer to, and quote from, certain publications or to reproduce certain material.

National Railway Museum.

The Railway Magazine.

W. Heffer & Sons Ltd. (Ahrons: *Locomotive & Train Working in the Latter Part of the Nineteenth Century.*)

The Railway Club. (References and quotations from the Club Journal.)

Stephenson Locomotive Society. (References and quotations from the Society Journal.)

David & Charles Holdings Ltd. (Nock: *Midland Compounds;* Rolt: *A Hunslet Hundred.*)

Ian Allan Ltd. (*Railway World*; Ellis: *The Midland Railway.*)

The Hutchinson Publishing Group. (Pratt: *British Railways and the Great War.*)

Index

N.L.—31*

484

Traffic arrangements with Glasgow & South Western and North British Railways, *1876*, 213

Halifax Thornton & Keighley lines proposal, 244, 251

Agreement with Great Northern Railway as to Keighley station, 244

Keighley & Worth Valley Railway purchase, 244

Carlisle, trouble with owning companies, *1866–1873*, 245, 246

Carlisle Citadel Station Bill, *1882*, 246

Interest in Portpatrick & Wigtownshire Joint Railway, 256–258

Running powers to Gretna, 258

Interest in Girvan & Portpatrick Junction Railway, 259

Supports Glasgow & South Western and North British Railways' amalgamation Bill, 267, 268

Competition with London & North Western Railway, 239, 258, 264

Great fire at Leeds, *1892*, 274

Traffic policy as to 'Scotch Racing', 275

Widenings, *1898*, 277, 284

Scotch Joint Stock, *1898*, 351, 352

Proposed Colne-Manchester line, 279

Interest in Hull Barnsley & West Riding Junction Railway & Dock, 281, 282

Agreement with Lancashire & Yorkshire Railway as to West Riding Lines, 284, 285

Acquisition of Belfast & Northern Counties Railway, 292

Morecambe harbour, 87, 294–296

Agreement with Furness Railway as to steamers, 297

Interests at Barrow, 296, 297

Heysham harbour, 292, 293, 298, 300, 301, 312

Interest in Stranraer-Larne steamers, 301

Electrification, Lancaster-Morecambe-Heysham, 308, 312, 313

Company during First World War, 319–324

Questions in Parliament, First World War, 321, 324

Becomes part of London Midland & Scottish Railway, 327

Branches:

Ardwick branch, 260, 263

Ashby and Nuneaton lines, 155, 156

Barnoldswick branch, 281, 318, 362

Bradford Through Lines, 317

Carnforth and Wennington line, 130, 131, 153, 154, 196, 230, 235, 296

Guiseley Yeadon & Rawdon line, 280, 281

Halifax Connecting Lines, 285

Hawes branch, *see* Settle and Carlisle Line and Hawes Branch

Heysham branch, 278, 293, 298, 308

Huddersfield branch, 285, 308, 312

Ingleton branch, 127, 130, 138–141, 156, 157, 160, 168, 214, 243, 249, 250, 313, 314, 328, 329, 413, 420, *see also under* North Western Railway

Keighley & Worth Valley line, 17, 126, 153, 229, 244, 245, 250, 313, 314, 413, 414, 420

Lancaster-Morecambe line, 261, *see also under* North Western Railway

Leeds & Bradford Railway and Extension Line, *see separate heading*

Leicester-Hitchin line, 71, 110, 113, 118, 193

Liverpool and Cheshire lines, 155

London Extension, 125, 126, 130, 131, 148, 158

London Station, 155

Low Moor Junctions, 285

Mansfield line, 155

North Western branch, *see under* North Western Railway

Otley and Ilkley lines, 125, 138, 145, 312

Rowsley and Buxton line, 130

Settle and Carlisle line, *see separate heading*

Sheffield-Chesterfield line, 126, 132, 171

Shipley and Guiseley line, 125, 249

Skipton and Ilkley branch, 17, 253, 260, 312

Thornhill Junction line, 285, 308

West Riding Lines, 277, 283–285, 287, 303, 304, 308, 312, 313, 317

Yorkshire Dales branch (Grassington branch), 280, 281

Millburn Forest, 29

Miller, J., 84

Milnthorpe, 84, 86, 94

Milnthorpe & Furness Railway, 85

493